Creative Systems Theory

Also by Charles Johnston:

The Creative Imperative: Human Growth and Planetary Evolution

Necessary Wisdom: Meeting the Challenge of a New Cultural Maturity

Pattern and Reality: A Brief Introduction to Creative Systems Theory

The Power of Diversity: An Introduction to the Creative Systems Personality Typology

An Evolutionary History of Music: Introducing Creative Systems Theory Through the Language of Sound (DVD)

Quick and Dirty Answers to the Biggest of Questions: Creative Systems Theory Explains What It Is All About (Really)

Cultural Maturity: A Guidebook for the Future

Hope and the Future: Confronting Today's Crisis of Purpose

On the Evolution of Intimacy: A Brief Exploration into the Past, Present, and Future of Gender and Love

Rethinking How We Think: Integrative Meta-Perspective and the Cognitive "Growing Up" On Which Our Future Depends

Online:

Author/professional page: www.CharlesJohnstonMD.com

The Institute for Creative Development: www.CreativeSystems.org

Creative Systems Theory: www.CSTHome.org

Cultural Maturity: www.CulturalMaturity.org

The Creative Systems Personality Typology: www.CSPTHome.org

An Evolutionary History of Music: www.Evolmusic.org

Cultural Maturity: A Blog for the Future: www.CulturalMaturityBlog.net

Looking to the Future podcast: www.LookingtotheFuture.net

Creative Systems Theory

A COMPREHENSIVE
THEORY OF PURPOSE, CHANGE,
AND INTERRELATIONSHIP
IN HUMAN SYSTEMS

with Particular Pertinence to
understanding the Times we live in
and the Tasks Ahead for the Species

CHARLES M. JOHNSTON, MD

The Institute for Creative Development (ICD) Press
Seattle, Washington

Publisher's Cataloging-In-Publication Data
(Prepared by The Donohue Group, Inc.)

Names: Johnston, Charles M., author.

Title: Creative Systems Theory : a comprehensive theory of purpose, change, and interrelationship in human systems : (with particular pertinence to understanding the times we live in and the tasks ahead for the species) / Charles M. Johnston, MD.

Description: Seattle, Washington : The Institute for Creative Development (ICD) Press, [2021] | Include bibliographical references and index.

Identifiers: ISBN 9781732219052 (print) | ISBN 9781732219090 (ebook)

Subjects: LCSH: Social evolution. | Social systems. | Civilization, Modern—Psychological aspects. | Conduct of life. | Future, The—Psychological aspects. | Johnston, Charles M.—Philosophy.

Classification: LCC HM626 .J644 2021 (print) | LCC HM626 (ebook) | DDC 303.4—dc23

The Institute for Creative Development (ICD) Press, Seattle, Washington

Copyright © 2021 by Charles M. Johnston, MD. All rights reserved. No part of this book may be reproduced, except for reviews and brief excerpts with attribution, without the written permission of the publisher. Manufactured in the United States of America. For information, address The Institute for Creative Development (ICD) Press, 4324 Meridian Ave. N., Seattle, WA 98103, or ICDPressinfo@gmail.com.

Cover design by Mohammad Abdus Sattar
Author photo by Brad Kevelin

ISBN: 978-1-732219-0-5-2
Library of Congress Control Number: 2020915179   First printing 2021

CREATIVE SYSTEMS THEORY

Preface—Rethinking How We Think   ix

Chapter One—Setting the "Creative" Stage   1

Chapter Two—Integrative Meta-Perspective and the Power of a Creative Frame   54

Chapter Three—Patterning in Time: Change and Creative Self-Organization   99

Chapter Four—Cultural Maturity: Our Times Needed (and Now Possible) "New Common Sense"   164

Chapter Five—Whole-Person/Whole-System Patterning Concepts: Truth, Identity, and the Future of Human Purpose   211

Chapter Six—Patterning in Space: Diversity, Multiplicity, and Human Possibility   260

Chapter Seven—A Creative Lens and the Power of Comparison: Separating the Wheat from the Chaff as We Look to the Future   308

Chapter Eight—Hands-On Methods   360

Chapter Nine—Applying Creative Systems Theory Patterning Concepts #1: Front-Page News Concerns — 404

Chapter Ten—Applying Creative Systems Theory Patterning Concepts #2: Broader Questions (Love, Gender, and Relationships Between the Sexes) — 455

Chapter Eleven—Applying Creative Systems Theory Patterning Concepts #3: Academic Disciplines and Cultural Domains — 503

Chapter Twelve—Applying Creative Systems Theory Patterning Concepts #4: Ultimate Human Quandaries (New Insights for Timeless Questions) — 555

Afterword—Contribution, Evidence, and the Legitimacy of Hope — 595

Appendix—A Glossary of Selected Creative Systems Theory Terms — 601

Index — 615

PREFACE

Rethinking How We Think

I am a psychiatrist and also a futurist. People often refer to me as a "cultural psychiatrist." My interest lies with humanity's long-term well-being and just what it will require of us. Much of my life's work has been hands-on, working with others to address the important questions of our time. And much that is most important has been more conceptual.

This book presents the thinking of Creative Systems Theory (CST), the body of conceptual work that has most defined and guided my efforts. Its pages provide the most complete examination of the theory's ideas. They also engage the theory's history: the story of how the theory came into being, how its ideas have evolved over the course of my life, and how the theory has come to make the contribution that it does today. The ideas the book presents are the product of over fifty years of committed inquiry and in-the-trenches application.

A striking recognition that has been central in my efforts to address the future makes an appropriate jumping-off point for these reflections. It has become increasingly clear to me that advancing successfully as a species will require that we think and act in some fundamentally new ways. Critical questions before us are demanding that we bring a maturity to our decision-making that before now would not have made sense to us, nor would it have really been an option. Without this needed leap in how we make choices, our future as a species will not be bright.

Creative Systems Theory provides support for this conclusion and also essential guidance for going forward. It makes understandable why a new kind of human maturity is required and just how that might be possible. It clarifies what necessary changes in how we think and act entail. And it provides a multifaceted set of tools for making the more nuanced and sophisticated kind of decisions on which our future depends.

The theory didn't begin with such overarching concerns. It had its origins early in my life in a fascination with innovation, and with creativity more generally. And for many years, the theory's primary focus was better understanding human development—how human systems of all sorts grow and change. But we can think of CST as always coming back to the central recognition that new ways of thinking and acting will be necessary. All of the theory's more specific concepts reflect what that needed leap in understanding requires of us and where it necessarily takes us.

Over time, CST has had an extremely wide reach. It has provided original insights in multiple fields—psychology, history, philosophy, international relations, and more. It has also served as the basis for the training of leaders for the complex tasks ahead. And it has contributed in important ways to the larger history of ideas.

This book engages the whole of CST's contribution. You can think of it as part guidebook, part memoir, part compilation, and part an effort on my part to extend my thinking as far into the future as I am able. To a degree I would not have imagined with the theory's original insights, CST has continued to challenge me and provide me with new understanding over the course of my life. Today it very much continues to do so. I invite you to join me in that continuing inquiry.

Radical Claims

A friend and colleague has given me a hard time through the years for too often "burying the headline" in my writing. She accurately points out that I tend to wait until the end of a piece to clearly state its most consequential implications. In my defense, I've done this for what has seemed a good reason. Given that the points I am trying to make often require that people think in new ways, it has seemed only fair to my reader—and indeed, necessary to understanding—that I first fully establish the groundwork and argument for my assertions. Otherwise I would seem only to be making claims—and often what could seem rather audacious claims.

With this book, I will take my friend's advice and start right out by making some assertions that risk seeming overly dramatic. CST adds to understanding not just by providing new detail, or even by providing new topics for examination. It challenges the foundations of how we think. A quick look at how this is the case provides a provocative way in that my friend and colleague would likely appreciate.

Right off, the theory confronts us with two radical claims. Each relates directly to my observation that today's challenges are requiring us to think and act in new ways. With each claim, CST goes beyond just affirming the claim and provides an original answer to the challenge that the claim presents. Neither claim is wholly original. But the way the theory addresses each claim is new, and powerful in its implications.

The first claim both follows from the theory and provides essential argument for the importance of what the theory provides. We tend to think of today's Modern Age beliefs and institutions as ideals and end points, needing at best some final polishing. CST describes how Modern Age assumptions instead reflect but one chapter in culture's developmental story. And it argues that without a willingness to take on a needed further chapter—what the theory calls Cultural Maturity—humanity's future will not be positive. The theory describes how addressing—or even just effectively understanding—the most important challenges ahead for the species will require abilities and ways of understanding that only become possible with Cultural Maturity's changes. I will argue that if the concept of Cultural Maturity is not basically correct, it is hard to imagine a future we would want to live in.

The second claim is more conceptual. The theory challenges the fundamental underlying assumption of Modern Age understanding, the idea introduced some 300 years back that the sort of thinking commonly used to describe machines captures truth at its most complete and precise. CST affirms that our Modern Age "universe as a great machine" worldview has served us powerfully. But the theory also clarifies how it can't be enough going forward, particularly if the universe in question includes life, and more specifically, if it includes human life.

CST notes that what ultimately most defines us as humans is our striking toolmaking, meaning-making natures—our capacity for innovation. The theory then makes a key observation consistent with this recognition: A deep look at human intelligence suggests a more dynamic, indeed generative, picture of understanding and its workings. It goes on to propose a new Fundamental Organizing Concept[1] to replace the Modern Age machine metaphor. The theory offers that we can better think of human experience as organizing "creatively."

Given that the term "creative" can easily be misinterpreted, we must be careful in using the word. As applied in the theory, it concerns art no more than science, nor the beginning of things any more than completions. But, at the least, the word provides a provocative place to start. And when grasped deeply, the new step in how we understand truth at its most basic that it reflects has dramatic and powerful consequences.

Most immediately, it fundamentally alters how we understand ourselves. The whole of CST's comprehensive framework for understanding purpose, change, and interrelationship in human systems follows from this important further step in our thinking—including the concept of Cultural Maturity. Ultimately, because the only kind of understanding we can know is the kind that human intelligence produces, it alters understanding as a whole, whatever our concern.

Deeply understanding CST concepts necessarily presents challenges. Both of these claims are indeed radical—and CST's answers to them even more so. If nothing else, engaging these ideas will require that the reader begin to make the leap in how we understand that the concept of Cultural Maturity describes. That means entertaining conclusions that are only beginning to make sense from where we currently reside. It also means thinking in ways that are more nuanced than we are used to. CST is very specifically about getting beyond the simplified, ideology-based assumptions of times past and better appreciating life's very real complexities.

But people who spend time with the theory tend in fact to find its conclusions surprisingly accessible. Indeed, with familiarity, CST's conclusions can seem not just straightforward, but simple, like common sense. To start there is an essential recognition that we will examine extensively. Culturally mature perspective is in fact only about observing and understanding more accurately. There is also the particular kind of systemic perspective that CST draws on. It not only offers that we might better appreciate complexities that before now would have overwhelmed and confused us, often it allows us to capture great

---

[1] Throughout the book, I will capitalize formal CST notions.

complexity with single-brushstroke observations. The kind of simplicity and common sense that CST offers has not before been available to us. But I will argue that it reflects a kind of thinking that is becoming necessary—a kind of thinking that, to use Victor Hugo's evocative phrase, "whose time has come."

A "Snapshot" Introduction

A few words of more formal introduction are warranted in getting started. Since the kind of thinking that the theory represents really makes sense—and really only becomes useful—once we have begun to step into Cultural Maturity's new territory of experience, let's start with a closer look at the concept of Cultural Maturity.

You can think of Cultural Maturity's essential new chapter in culture's developmental story as a kind of "growing up" as a species. Most immediately it manifests in changes to our relationship as individuals to our cultural contexts. Culture in times past has functioned like a symbolic parent in the lives of individuals, providing clear rules to live by. Today this is becoming less and less the case. Truths that in times past were tied to strict cultural dictates—about right and wrong behavior; about what it means to be a man or a woman; about our identities as Americans, Russians, or Chinese; about spiritual experience—are becoming less absolute. The most basic of truths are more and more often becoming ours to determine.

Creative Systems Theory provides explanation for why we might see this lessening of our past tendency to view culture as a mythic parent. The theory describes how this result is what we would expect if we are beginning to engage the more mature stages in culture's development. CST also clarifies how these changes are not just products of fresh insights, but reflect specific cognitive changes.

This added recognition is key to understanding the implications of Cultural Maturity. If changes were to stop with a simple loss of past "parental" absolutes, we would be left in a most tenuous state, one that in today's transitional times we all too often encounter. We would appropriately celebrate new freedoms, but at the same time, we would too often find ourselves wandering aimlessly in an anything-goes world, and all too easily overwhelmed by uncertainty.

The cognitive changes that accompany Cultural Maturity are what make "something more" possible. Creative Systems Theory calls the result of this cognitive reordering Integrative Meta-perspective. While the term is a mouthful, it captures quite succinctly what is involved. Integrative Meta-perspective offers that we might at once step back from, and more deeply engage, the whole of our human complexity, or at least the whole of understanding's complexity. In the process, Integrative Meta-perspective provides a more mature and complete vantage for seeing our world.

Fully grasping all that Integrative Meta-perspective involves will require the topics of later chapters in the book. For now, we can note a couple of essential consequences. Most immediately, Integrative Meta-perspective invites an engagement with purpose and direction in our lives that is not dependent on past absolutes. Leaving behind culture's parental status can be deeply disturbing. Recognizing that doing so is happening in conjunction with changes that provide a fuller kind of connection in who we are is no small thing.

Integrative Meta-perspective also invites new, more encompassing kinds of values and more complete ways of understanding. One result is the more mature skills and capacities that we will more and more often need if we are to effectively address essential questions before us as a species. Another is the possibility of new kinds of conceptual frameworks such as those we see with Creative Systems Theory, ways of thinking able to take us beyond the mechanistic assumptions of times past.

The importance of leaving behind polarized and polarizing beliefs begins to get at what is necessarily different. Getting beyond the either/or assumptions that have relegated ally and enemy to wholly separate worlds, for example, will be essential to a healthy—and perhaps even survivable—future. Later, we will look at how thinking in the ways needed if we are to effectively advance will require that we get our minds around all manner of juxtapositions that we have before thought of in either/or terms—such as political left and political right, male and female, mind and body, and even life and death. The needed new, more systemic kind of thinking must help us engage truths that before now we have assumed to be incompatible.

A further essential way that the resulting new kind of understanding is different more explicitly distinguishes what is needed from the kind of systemic thinking used historically by good engineers to build bridges and design buildings. It is implied by these examples, but not so obvious.

Later, I will address it in depth. The needed new kind of understanding requires that we learn to think systemically in ways that honor the fact that we are alive, and more than this, alive in the particular ways that make us human.

Creative Systems Theory makes the needed leap in understanding through the application of a creative frame. The theory describes how human intelligence, when understood in its full complexity, is structured to support and drive our audacious creative capacities. And it delineates how thinking in creative terms makes it possible to understand both ourselves and the world around us in more complete and dynamic ways. CST delineates how we can effectively think of the reality of human experience (the only kind we can know) as "creative." And it describes how the leap in understanding that this recognition reflects allows us to develop new kinds of concepts better able to address the challenges we now face. It then takes a creative frame and translates it into a detailed and comprehensive set of creative "pattern language" tools for thinking with the needed new systemic sophistication.

There is an important way in which human understanding has always been creative in this sense, even Modern Age mechanistic understanding. CST describes how the "clockworks" assumptions of Newton or Descartes reflect a predicted stage within culture as a creative process. What becomes different with culturally mature perspective is that we become newly capable of consciously recognizing this more dynamic and systemic kind of picture. We also become newly capable of conceiving in ways that explicitly reflect its workings.

CST is structured around three basic kinds of creative "patterning concepts," what it calls Patterning in Time, Whole-Person/Whole-System Patterning Concepts, and Patterning in Space. Patterning in Time concepts are developmental. They help us better understand how systems of all sorts—individuals, relationships, organizations, and larger social systems—grow and change. Whole-Person/Whole-System Patterning Concepts address systemically encompassing concerns such as purpose, morality, and identity. Patterning in Space concepts address more here-and-now distinctions. They help address diversity of all sorts in more sophisticated ways.

This book addresses each of these patterning concepts with greater depth and detail than I have in previous writings. We will examine what makes each of these notions new and significant. And I will apply them individually and together to a wide array of questions—from front-page-news concerns to ultimate philosophical quandaries. All the while, I will attempt to bring overarching perspective to understanding the new kind of thinking that our future will require of us more generally and CST's specific contribution in meeting this larger challenge.

What CST Accomplishes

A brief outline of ways CST adds to understanding provides a good "preview-of-coming-attractions" introduction for the chapters ahead. Some of CST's contributions have obvious here-and-now pertinence. Other contributions are of a more encompassing, big-picture sort. Each of these claims could in its own way seem audacious. But I am fine making the assertion that, by the book's conclusion, each of them will have been substantiated.

- CST helps us make sense of the easily confusing and overwhelming times in which we live and provides essential guidance for times ahead. With the concept of Cultural Maturity, CST articulates a new defining story, a way of thinking about human purpose and human progress consistent with a healthy and vital future. And by offering that we might address concerns of all sorts more systemically, the theory helps make understandable what good decision-making in all parts of our personal and collective lives will require of us.

- CST clarifies how the future will require not just that we think new things, but that we learn to think in fundamentally new ways. With the idea of a needed, and developmentally predicted, cognitive reordering (what I have described with the phrase "Integrative Meta-perspective"), the theory delineates how more dynamic and systemic approaches to understanding will be essential and also how they might become possible. And with the application of a creative frame, the theory offers an encompassing systemic approach that succeeds as culturally mature conception.

- CST helps us get beyond the simple-answer, ideological conclusions of times past. (The theory defines ideology as any belief

that takes one part of a larger systemic complexity and makes it the whole of truth.) Integrative Meta-perspective directly challenges ideological beliefs of all sorts—political, religious, philosophical, scientific. It also helps make visible the more demanding questions that ideological beliefs have protected us from recognizing.
- CST deepens our understanding of human intelligence. In the process, it brings us closer to fully understanding what it means to be human. The theory makes clear that intelligence has multiple aspects, each of which has specific and special functions. And it goes on to describe how the various aspects of human intelligence work together to make our amazing innovative capacities possible. The whole of CST can be understood to follow from this creative framing of intelligence's mechanisms.
- The theory provides a dynamic and integrated picture of human developmental processes of all sorts, from individual psychological development, to the growth of relationships, to the evolution of social systems at the largest of scales. It highlights essential parallels between what might seem to be very different kinds of growth processes. And it goes further to delineate how, in each case, we can see in developmental stages an underlying "creative" organization and patterning.
- CST helps us better understand history—and not just the facts of history, but the evolution of beliefs, institutional forms, and our felt experience of meaning. It helps us better understand the human story as a story, and as a story with chapters, one that changes, and continues to change. CST not only effectively maps history, arguably its predicts it. If the theory had been around 5,000 years ago (which it obviously could not have been), its creative framing of development would have allowed us to anticipate the general contours of what we have witnessed since that time.
- CST helps us recognize how new human capacities will be increasingly necessary in times ahead. Some examples: Going forward will require a greater ability to tolerate uncertainty and complexity (necessary if we are to get beyond the

ideological easy answers of times past). Equally significant, it will require the ability to better appreciate the fact of real limits (of all sorts—environmental limits, limits to what we can afford, limits to what we can know and be for one another). I've mentioned the importance of getting beyond the us-versus-them thinking of times past (necessary if "chosen-people/evil-other" assumptions of times past are not to be the end of us). Over the course of the book, we will look at additional needed new skills and abilities. We will also look at how we can think of each of these new capacities as "creative," part of what becomes possible when we are able to consciously hold the whole of our generative complexity.

- CST helps us bring big-picture perspective to a wide array of truth-related concerns where the thinking of times past becomes inadequate today. As illustration, it helps us address moral quandaries more systemically, recognize how, in the end. most such quandaries are less about good and evil than about competing goods (and how all questions are in the end moral—questions of value, of human significance). CST also challenges us to rethink human identity. It helps us appreciate, for example, how the Modern Age picture of individuality that we find reflected in everything from Romeo of Juliet–style romantic love to heroic notions of leadership not only fails us going forward, it was never really about what we thought it was. (We will look in detail at what CST calls The Myth of the Individual.) CST helps us understand truth, relationships of all sorts, and the dynamics of identity in more complete—dynamic and systemic—ways.

- CST highlights how understanding always happens in a context. This includes change-related contexts, what we find with an appreciation for developmental dynamics, and also more here-and-now contextual relativities. The theory helps us more deeply understand ideological differences, differences associated with gender or ethnic diversity, and differences that are products of temperament/personality style. All of CST's "patterning concepts" are in some way about bringing greater nuance to our appreciation of context.

- CST helps us separate the wheat from the chaff in our thinking. It includes a nuanced set of tools for identifying traps in our understanding, both in our personal understandings and more collectively when it comes to thinking about the future. Besides helping us appreciate how the more obvious of ideological beliefs fail us, it also helps us grasp how postmodern thinking or ideas that view the future only in terms of new technologies are also ideological, and how today they often put us in particular danger.
- CST also helps address many eternal quandaries—from the nature of conscious awareness to how the relationship between the spiritual and material might best be understood—ultimate questions that have always before left us baffled. The theory proposes that the reason the answers to such questions have often eluded us is that culturally mature perspective is needed to ask them in ultimately useful ways. And a creative frame often makes answers not just possible, but—with reflection—almost obvious.
- CST provides not just ideas, but also methodologies. It includes an array of specific "hands-on" methods that actively support the kind of understanding on which our future depends.

The Book's Approach

This book engages the whole of CST's contribution. Chapter One helps further set the stage for the book's inquiry by reflecting more deeply on CST's origins and the kind of leap the theory's thinking entails. Chapter Two more specifically links Integrative Meta-perspective and a creative frame by coming at the idea of creative organization from multiple directions that help bring it alive. Chapter Three provides a detailed look at creative Patterning in Time, the developmental notions that give CST its conception of history and provide the basis for its conclusions about the times in which we live. And Chapter Four fills out the concept of Cultural Maturity, both by more clearly establishing its basic rationale and by providing examples of the concept's implications for major questions before us as a species.

Chapter Five examines Whole-Person/Whole-System Patterning Concepts and how they provide fresh perspective for addressing encompassing concerns such as purpose, identity, morality, love, progress, and truth more generally. Chapter Six turns to CST Patterning in Space concepts and how they help us think about human differences—such as ideological differences, gender diversity, and differences in temperament/personality style—in more overarching and ultimately creative ways. Chapter Seven brings a more finely focused lens to understanding how CST differs from other conceptual approaches and also to how we can best separate the wheat from the chaff more generally in our thinking about the future. And Chapter Eight examines "hands-on" approaches that can be used to catalyze the cognitive changes necessary for culturally mature understanding.

The book's remaining chapters turn more specifically to application. Chapter Nine applies CST Patterning Concepts to major front-page-news concerns such as climate change, immigration, and gun violence. Chapter Ten turns to one broad change topic that affects multiple parts of our lives—the future of love and gender. Chapter Eleven addresses implications for specific domains of understanding, from government, to education, to art, to economics. And Chapter Twelve addresses more "ultimate questions," in keeping with my claim that culturally mature perspective—and a creative frame more specifically—makes it possible to address big-picture quandaries that before now we could not fully get our minds around.

The book concludes with an Afterword section that offers a few summary reflections and an Appendix with a glossary of key CST terms.

Throughout this extended effort, I will often reach back for content to past writings. I will do this for a couple of reasons. With certain topics I touch on, I will have given them greatest attention at particular times in CST's development—and with some topics that may have been very early on. Where I have not since said things better, I may quote such material directly. I may also draw on such earlier material simply to highlight how much these ideas have themselves been part of a creative process. When topics relate to specific socio-cultural issues, for example, I will often draw on books, articles, blog posts, and podcasts from the time when I first attempted to bring attention to the issue's importance. My struggles with the task of making the implications of culturally mature perspective understandable can often be as illuminating as particular conclusions.

Throughout this effort, I will also extend my thinking further than I have in previous writings. I often use the metaphor of a threshold when addressing the degree ideas succeed as culturally mature understanding. When writing articles for a general audience—where even the general idea that new ways of thinking may be needed can be a stretch—I will tend to shoot at most for one or two steps over Cultural Maturity's threshold. When working with think tank groups convened to address key future concerns, I know we will need to progress a solid three or four steps if we are to make a major contribution. When I'm brainstorming at the edge of my understanding with close colleagues, we may venture a few further steps—of many more that the future will require.

When I shared my sense of this book with a close friend recently, he asked me a great question: So how many steps into culturally mature territory will you be reaching with this book? Without hesitation, to my surprise I said ten. I will do my best to make basic notions accessible, to succeed with that one- or two-step contribution. I will also engage specific issues, as I would in think tank efforts, in ways that extend reflections necessary further steps. And, in addition, I will not hesitate to take thinking as far as I am able. I feel blessed to be engaging in an effort that so fully demands all of which I am capable.

CHAPTER ONE

Setting the "Creative" Stage

Reflecting on a small handful of big-picture topics helps more solidly set the stage for the book's many more detailed observations. I'll start by sharing more about Creative Systems Theory's (CST's) origins and the effort over time that has brought the theory into being. Next, to bring us up to current circumstances and further clarify the conceptual task that CST takes on, I'll reflect some on the history of narrative, on the evolution of the stories we've told about who we are and how things work. I will also touch some on the larger evolution of understanding, on how our ideas about what makes something true have changed over time.

I'll then turn to the two words that give the theory its name: "system" and "creative." Each term in different ways helps fill out the conceptual leap that underlies the theory's significance. Then I'll more specifically tie needed new ways of understanding to challenges ahead for us as a species. I'll more formally introduce CST's various patterning concepts. And finally, I'll more directly address some of the challenges that necessarily accompany articulating the ideas of CST, both to further delineate the needed leap in understanding, and also to introduce some of the representational tools that I find most useful in communicating about them.

How Creative Systems Theory Came to Be

If nothing else, reflecting on CST's origins makes for a fascinating detective story. It sheds light on how a set of simple observations could result in an original body of work that is this encompassing. But more importantly, it provides valuable further perspective for understanding what makes the theory's ideas significant, and just why they stretch us in the ways that they necessarily do.

Understanding the theory's beginnings also helps address a possible source of confusion, even suspicion. Particularly when I speak in academic settings, people's first questions often concern whose thinking my ideas build on. While academic discovery can make leaps, even when it does it tends to continue generally recognizable traditions of thought. This is not so much the case with Creative Systems Theory. Certainly these notions have antecedents (as I will describe). The insights that produced them are not of some magical, rabbit-out-of-a-hat sort. But the degree to which these ideas have their origins in discovery of a "whole cloth" sort can, for some people, be startling. Reflecting on the process of discovery that produced them provides needed perspective.

Such reflection also helps clarify some of my own relationship to that process and to the ideas themselves. Given all that Creative Systems Theory accomplishes, a person could assume that the development of these notions was motivated by some dramatic intent—to have major influence on social/political events, to address grand philosophical questions, or, at the least, to make a significant original contribution. In fact, these notions have much more humble roots. And the process that has brought them into being has rarely been one of design.

I can't even claim that these notions reflect exceptional intelligence on my part. I'm intelligent enough, but a couple of characteristics of my makeup—of my particular personality style[1]—have been more important in CST's origins. One is simply curiosity. I've been blessed/cursed with abundant curiosity and of an unusually persistent sort. The other is the fact that the way my mind naturally works provides more than usual access to different aspects of intelligence—not just the more rational and emotional ways of knowing that are most acknowledged in our time, but also more germinal sensibilities that are key in how creative mechanisms work. An important result is that my curiosity has found equal comfort and fascination through the years in worlds that for many people would seem disparate—the arts equally with the sciences, the most personal alongside the social and political, both the distant past and future possibilities.

---

[1] Chapter Six's examination of the Creative Systems Personality Typology will make both of these characteristics more understandable.

The theory had its origins in a series of insights over the early decades of my life that built one upon the next. Each insight came from simply following where my curiosity led me. Sometimes these were directions that generated excitement from the outset. Other times, at least initially, I was less than happy to recognize all that they would ask of me.

The first insight had its seeds in my teen years. At that time, I found special fulfillment in the creative arts—in particular, sculpture and music. In my early twenties, I became increasingly fascinated with creative process itself—with how it is that things that matter (of any sort, not just artistic) come into being. I started teaching classes designed to help facilitate creative process in others. I found this very rewarding.

Wanting to understand all I could about how creative process worked, I turned to psychology to research what had been written about it. I assumed that the topic had been extensively studied. To my great surprise, very little had been written, and almost all that had been written was superficial at best. As I will describe shortly, I now better understand why I found this absence and appreciate its implications. But at that time, all I knew was that I was going to be more on my own in this inquiry than I had imagined.

That initial insight actually had a couple of parts. The first was not original but was certainly important: Creative processes progress through a generally consistent sequence of stages. In my earliest writings, I documented these stages and some of the unique demands that come with each of them. The second observation was more fully original and proved of particular significance: Understanding creative process requires an appreciation for how intelligence has multiple aspects. I saw how each formative stage draws preferentially on different aspects of intelligence and different relationships between intelligences.

The following is a simplified outline.[2] Creativity's initial "incubation stage" draws in particular on the more primordial, bodily aspects of intelligence. With creativity's next stage—we could call it the "inspiration stage"—we more directly engage intelligence's imaginal and mythic aspects. With creativity's "perspiration stage" and the task of bringing first possibility into more manifest form, the more emotional aspects of intelligence necessarily come to the fore. And with creative

---

2 See Chapter Two for a more detailed look.

process's "finishing and polishing" stages and the need of more detailed discernment, intelligence's more rational dimensions come to play the larger role.

Besides being pivotal in helping make sense of creative process, this second observation also helped me better understand why academic psychology had provided so little help. Academia is only beginning to question its Age of Reason–based assumption that truth—certainly truth of a theoretical sort—can always ultimately be described in rational terms. Restricted to the rational, what we can say about creative process is limited at best.

Being happy to have made a useful contribution to understanding creativity, I assumed then that my process of investigation was complete. But, in fact, it was just getting started. Further insights would alter not just my thinking, but also the trajectory of my life.

One in particular was instrumental with regard to my life choices. Teaching those classes on creativity confronted me with how creative process—at least at the depth we were engaging it—was ultimately just life process. I saw that in an important sense I had been doing psychotherapy. Recognizing that I needed to learn more about what others before me had contributed if I was to continue on with my life's work responsibly. I decided to enter medical school and to become a psychiatrist.

A second further insight was more specifically conceptual, but it also played a major role in my life direction, at least the direction of my understanding. With my psychological training, I found special fascination with developmental psychology, and in particular, with the work of developmental thinkers, such as Jean Piaget, who recognized that different stages in development altered not just how people acted, but also the ways in which they interpreted their worlds. I was struck by an observation that very much took me by surprise. It appeared that stages in individual psychological development followed a progression very similar to what I had previously identified for invention and artistic creativity.

I found myself wondering if it might be accurate to think of individual development as itself a creative process. I recognized important evidence for this conclusion in an observation similar to that which had been key in my earlier studies of creativity—the essential role of multiple intelligences. It turns out that not only do we go through a related sequence of stages in creating our personal identities as we do in creating an idea or a work of art, we can understand how we experience each stage in individual development in terms of the aspects of our complex cognitive nature that we most make use of at that stage—from body intelligence in our "sensori-motor" beginnings (to use Piaget's terminology), to the imaginal with the "let's-pretend" world of childhood, to the emotional with the charged intensities of adolescence, to rationality's new prominence with adult perspective.

This was a striking, and again clearly significant observation. And once more I felt satisfied to have contributed something useful, in this case to developmental thought. But there would again be more to come—and much that would prove of particular importance.

During my psychiatry residency, I studied closely with Joseph Campbell, one of our time's most articulate chroniclers of myth and its history.[3] During this time, I became fascinated increasingly with our larger human story, with the diverse ways through history we humans have made sense of ourselves and the world around us. These learnings—and conversations that followed—brought further, especially startling and consequential recognitions. They tied directly to my earlier observations.

I saw that the different ways that the human species has made sense of experience through time also appeared to follow a developmental progression. I also recognized that this progression had clear parallels with what I had previously observed for creative process and for individual development. The basic sequence of stages was similar. And of particular significance, the underlying sensibilities/intelligences needed to engage each stage were also similar—from tribal culture's reality of ritual dance and connectedness in nature; to the mythic vibrancy of Ancient Egypt or classical Greece; to the emotional/moral intensities of the European Middle Ages; to Modern Age culture's world of rationality, individuality, and dramatic technological prowess.

I recognized that thinking in this way would easily be controversial. We are more used to describing history in terms of leaders, wars, and inventions. Understanding the human story in terms of underlying

---

3 See Joseph Campbell, *The Hero With a Thousand Faces*, New World Library, 1949, or *Masks of God*, Penguin Books, 1959 to 1968.

sensibilities and patterns of cognitive organization is a very different kind of approach. But I also appreciated that the implications of this kind of perspective could be great.

These additional insights prompted an essential time of stepping back. The idea that underlying parallels link a simple creative process, personal development, and chapters in culture's story, if accurate, was radical and obviously of major importance. And I kept coming back to the fact that in each case, observing what I did had been possible because I had been consciously drawing on more of myself—including more of intelligence's rich complexity—than we are accustomed to applying. My fascination turned increasingly to the question of what this larger picture said about what ultimately makes us who we are.

I reflected on the fact that what seems ultimately to define us as a species is our toolmaking, idea-making prowess. And I noted that what these various observations seemed to suggest—that human intelligence is structured to support our creative/innovative capacities—is what we might expect if this were the case. And I saw, too, that it similarly should not surprise us to find creative patterns in how human change processes more generally work.

These insights gradually began to come together in a coherent picture. I wrote my first book, *The Creative Imperative*, as an attempt to articulate how a creative frame can help us more deeply understand the human experience. Over time, these reflections would form the foundations of Creative Systems Theory.

I was then quite sure that my job was complete. *The Creative Imperative* did a remarkably good job of laying out these insights.[4] And writing it was a seven-year marathon. I was more than ready to set it all aside. But this would not be so. I would later quip that I had failed to recognize that having birthed a child, I now had no choice but to raise it. Over succeeding years, the further growth of these ideas would both continue to surprise me and be a continuing teacher in my own understanding.

---

4 *The Creative Imperative* remains a definitive source for many people. Of all my writings, it is the place where I've addressed intelligence's multiplicity in greatest depth and where I most explicitly established the link between formative process and developmental dynamics of various sorts.

With *The Creative Imperative*'s initial articulation of Creative Systems ideas, I didn't give much attention to current times in culture. While I went into considerable depth with regard to how a creative frame helps us make sense of the growth of cultural systems, I had found greatest interest in the past, with how and why our human story to this point has progressed in the ways that it has. Only with the book's last chapter did I turn to how CST's thinking might contribute to understanding our times and challenges that might lie ahead for the species.

That changed following *The Creative Imperative*'s release. Increasingly, I came to see that the most important applications of these ideas might be more immediate and practical. The developmental notions that I had articulated made clear that the stage in culture's story that had given us Modern Age institutions and beliefs is not some culminating ideal, that a necessary further chapter in the human endeavor potentially lies ahead. In doing so, they offered essential perspective for understanding today's often-confusing new tasks and new possibilities. I realized I needed to give greater attention to the concept of Cultural Maturity.

I also found myself expanding how I thought about my psychiatrist's role. More and more I was struck by how the core "mental health" crisis in our time was really a cultural crisis. I also came to better appreciate how the way the concept of Cultural Maturity frames today's challenges—in terms of a time of transition, and with this a cultural Crisis of Purpose[5]—provides a way to understand and address what I was sensing. It was at this time that I began often to refer to myself as a "cultural psychiatrist." I saw that a major portion of my life's work needed to focus more directly on today's challenges. And it needed to focus specifically on Cultural Maturity and the changes in how we think and act that culturally mature perspective makes possible.

In response to these recognitions, I joined together with colleagues and started the Institute for Creative Development, a small, Seattle-based, non-profit think tank and center for advanced leadership training. The Institute trained people in the new, more sophisticated leadership capacities that the future's new questions will increasingly

---

5 The phrase "Crisis of Purpose" is a formal notion within CST. We will return to the concept throughout the book.

demand. It also brought together exceptional people from around the world to confront many of our times' most important questions. In addition, the Institute deeply explored Cultural Maturity's implications and further developed the ideas of Creative Systems Theory.[6]

It was a time of rich inquiry and deeply fulfilling collaboration. I knew that the Institute's work would not be easy. Our interest lay with human abilities and ways of thinking that, at best, we were only beginning to understand. But it was obvious that what we were endeavoring to do together could not be more important.

Important aspects of Creative Systems Theory were filled out and refined during that time. I think in particular of aspects that focus on leadership—and leadership's future. Deeper attention was also given to ideas that focused less on change and more on here-and-now systemic relationships, such as the theory's framework for understanding temperament diversity—the Creative Systems Personality Typology. This is also when many of the theory's specific tools for separating ideas that can help us from those that cannot as we look to the future were developed.

During this time, I wrote *Necessary Wisdom: Meeting the Challenge of a New Cultural Maturity* to more specifically introduce the concept of Cultural Maturity and its implications. I also wrote two shorter CST-related works adapted from Institute teaching resources, *Pattern and Reality: A Brief Introduction to Creative Systems Theory* and *The Power of Diversity: An Introduction to the Creative Systems Personality Typology*.

But this, again, would not be the end of Creative Systems Theory's development story. After formally leading the Institute's efforts for over two decades, I saw that a further phase in my own life and work would be required. If the ideas and approaches we had drawn on had a significant place in the history and evolution of understanding—as they must have if they effectively reflect a needed new chapter in our human narrative—they warranted further research to substantiate that significance. And given their great practical value, it was important that they be made available to a wider audience.

Fifteen years of research and writing followed, with three further books the result. I wrote *Hope and the Future: An Introduction to the*

---

6   The Institute existed as a bricks-and-mortar institution for twenty-five years. Its work continues today online and internationally.

Concept of Cultural Maturity as an attempt to write a short volume on Cultural Maturity for a general audience. Next came *Cultural Maturity: A Guidebook for the Future*, a much lengthier work intended for those wanting to develop culturally mature leadership skills. I also wrote *Quick and Dirty Answers to the Biggest of Questions: Creative Systems Theory Explains What It Is All About (Really)* as a bit of a teaser for those who have interest in some of the theory's more big-picture implications. In addition, at this time, I set up a series of teaching websites that focused on different aspects of Creative Systems Theory (see www.creativesystems.org). And I developed a blog (www.culturalmaturityblog.net) and a podcast (www.lookingtothefuture.net) that in various ways focused on culturally mature leadership and its implications.

I then took a couple of years off from being an author to speak and teach. It was a time of further surprises. Much in these efforts was deeply enjoyable, but other aspects proved less rewarding. My timing coincided with the start of a time of backsliding in culture, a period of regression that today continues. As a result, these efforts came gradually to not seem the best use of my time.[7] I decided to once again turn to writing, a form of expression that can better weather changing circumstances.

The first thing I did was write an updated version of *Hope and the Future* that put the book's observations in the context of these regressive dynamics. (To highlight the immediacy of the book's importance, I changed the subtitle to *Confronting Today's Crisis of Purpose*.) I then wrote a couple of books that applied CST in somewhat different ways than I had previously. With *On the Evolution of Intimacy: A Brief Exploration of the Past, Present, and Future of Gender and Love*, I used the theory to address one particularly timely topic in depth. With *Rethinking How We Think: Integrative Meta-perspective and the Cognitive "Growing Up" on Which Our Future Depends*, I brought a more cognitive science lens both to understanding CST and to addressing today's essential tasks.

---

7 We see this backsliding in growing polarization with regard to political and social issues of most every sort and also in the rise of more authoritarian thinking around the globe. It made my efforts to engage people around major cultural challenges often less successful, and thus less satisfying, than it had been previously. Chapter Three addresses what CST can tell us about this apparent regression, both its likely causes and what we might expect going forward.

This takes us up to today and my intent with this volume to more thoroughly articulate the ideas of Creative Systems Theory. As I dive in, I'm struck by how much these years of writing and reflection have provided important perspective with regard to CST and its contribution. That perspective has been powerfully affirming both in terms of the accuracy of CST's formulations and the importance of what the theory has to offer. And I am happy that I have been able to put enough about the theory into writing that I need not be personally present for people to learn about the larger portion of the theory and make good use of it. In all of these ways, I couldn't be more pleased with what CST has taught me and where this journey has come.

That said, these efforts have also left me wishing at times that things could be easier. More than I like to admit, I've been humbled by the stretch that needed new ways of understanding can require. While it is true that when people are ready for them, culturally mature perspective and ideas like those of CST can seem simple, like common sense, developing these notions has repeatedly confronted me with just how demanding they can be—and how demanding they remain for most people in our time. The simple fact that culturally mature notions are as multidisciplinary as they are can make them difficult for many people. We also aren't accustomed to drawing on intelligence's multiple aspects. And the way CST's conclusions challenge familiar ideologies—and in the end, ideologies of every sort—increases the stretch considerably.

And it is not just other people who can find culturally mature understanding unexpectedly demanding. I remember feeling a bit embarrassed in first attempting to write in depth about the concept of Cultural Maturity. I had discovered what I assumed would be an easily accessible approach. I would simply describe the new skills and capacities that culturally mature perspective makes possible and needed insights would follow naturally. But often it would take me many more pages to write about a capacity than I had anticipated. And frequently even then I would not be satisfied. The process of writing was confronting me with an obstacle that should have been obvious given my years of familiarity with Cultural Maturity and its implications. Like it or not, it takes culturally mature capacities to fully make sense of culturally mature capacities. I had to face that no matter how cleaver I might be in my formulations or how skilled I might be in my use of words, writing about culturally mature understanding would never be as straightforward as I might prefer.

Attempting to address particular cultural challenges in my teaching and speaking—such as health care reform, climate change, or issues related to changing gender realities—would further confront me with the magnitude of the challenge that culturally mature understanding presents to most people. Repeatedly, I've had to face the fact that broad understanding with regard to recognitions that become obvious with culturally mature perspective can remain a long way off—how they may very often require twenty, thirty, or even fifty years to manifest in any widely recognized sense. The basic fact that change processes can happen only as fast as they can is compounded by how we often reside in an awkward, in-between, easily confusing place with regard to essential aspects of these changes.

It is hard to know what the decades immediately ahead will bring. I can imagine scenarios in which culturally mature capacities increasingly gain influence. But I can also imagine the years before us being at best very rough going.

As I approach the later decades of my life, I confront the fact that many of the conversations about culturally mature policy and leadership that I would love to be a part of may not happen in my lifetime. And while Creative Systems Theory is appreciated and respected—deeply by a good number of people—it is also very possible that it may take some significant time before the larger number of people who will eventually find it of value are able to discover it and put it to work. I very much look forward to the exchanges and collaborations this book will help support in my remaining years. But I will also make the effort with this book to write so that it can be a resource for those engaged in related processes of inquiry well into the future.

The Evolution of Narrative and the Necessary Future of Understanding

I've made the claim that CST maps how human values and ways of understanding have evolved over the course of human history. I've also described how the theory proposes that there is no reason to assume that this evolution is complete. A couple of cultural evolution–related topics help us begin to engage this creative picture and where we reside in it. First is how the stories we humans have told have changed over time. Second is how the ways we think about truth are today becoming different from how we have understood truth in times past. Each helps further put content in the pages ahead in perspective.

It is important with either topic to acknowledge that the whole notion that culture evolves can be controversial in some circles—and often for good reasons. In times past, the idea that culture goes through evolutionary stages has been used to justify some of the least savory of human sentiments.[8] But dismissing evolutionary perspective throws the baby out with the bath and shortchanges us of essential understanding. It leaves us without the depth of engagement needed to fully appreciate the unique richnesses of different cultural times and places. And today it shortchanges us in a more immediate and critical way. It makes it very hard to make sense of the times that we live in and the particular challenges and possibilities life in today's world presents.

How Creative Systems Theory chronicles and explains this evolutionary picture will be a major focus of this book. But we don't need the theory's detailed notions to appreciate that culture evolves, and continues to evolve. One simple way to think about how culture has changed over time turns to the evolution of narrative, to the stories we have told throughout history about who we are and how things work.

It turns out that cultural narratives have evolved in related ways wherever in the world we might look. In tribal times, our stories were animistic. We described existence in terms of interplays between nature's great forces. Later, with the rise of early civilizations, our stories became more magical and mystical. Our great tales described the exploits of pantheons of gods and the efforts of mere mortals to reconcile their whims. Later still, as with the European Middle Ages, stories became either more specifically religious or told us of kingly might and struggles for dominion.

The evolution of narrative over the last 500 years provides a good jumping off point for making sense of our time. Belief with Modern Age culture has juxtaposed two kinds of narratives: heroic and romantic. Heroic narratives describe the overcoming of obstacles to realize

---

8 Racism and slavery, for example. Chapter Three looks more closely at this kind of objection and also at how a creative frame effectively gets beyond it.

some ultimate achievement. Romantic narratives describe some meeting—either personal or more encompassing—that results in emotional or spiritual oneness. Both heroic and romantic narratives are ideological in the sense that they promise final fulfillment and last-word truth.

Heroic and romantic narratives can work alone or together. The most familiar social narratives—the American Dream, opposing political worldviews, the traditional beliefs of our various religions, progress' promise of ever onward-and-upward scientific discovery and technological advancement—are all of this heroic/romantic sort.

More recently, we find stories of a transitional sort, stories that straddle the threshold into Cultural Maturity's new territory of experience. I will use the word "postmodern" as a catchall term to describe this kind of story. Postmodern narrative first appeared with existentialism in the nineteenth century. In the later years of the last century, it came to have an increasingly prominent role in academia with social constructivist thinking. Today, it is a major influence in the popular arts.

Postmodern thought and culturally mature thought share certain similarities. The postmodernist appreciates that the cultural absolutes of times past are ceasing to serve us as they have before. And in a related way to what we see with culturally mature perspective, postmodern perspective recognizes a newly multifaceted and often uncertain reality in which meaning is increasingly ours to determine.

But as we might expect with such "straddling" belief, postmodern perspective only gets us part of the way. And it fails with what is ultimately the most consequential part of the task. It recognizes the limitations of ideological belief, but it is capable of only a beginning grasp of what—if anything—may lie beyond such belief. Thus it easily reduces to a different-strokes-for-different-folks arbitrariness and a confusion of irony and contradiction with significance. If we are not careful, postmodern thinking becomes, in effect, but another kind of ideology (and a kind of ideology that is particularly tedious and difficult to counter).[9]

We can think of culturally mature narrative as "post-postmodern." It affirms the best of postmodern insight, then moves decisively beyond it. It describes the possibility of engaging experience more consciously

---

[9] See Chapter Seven for a more detailed look at the strengths and inherent limitations of postmodern perspective.

and fully from the complex whole of who we are. In the process, it more fully confronts the complexities of the world around us and provides new, more detailed formulations and essential guidance as we look to the future. It also invites a new and deeper sense of purpose in our experience of being human.

Fig. 1-1. The Modern Evolution of Narrative

Briefly shifting our attention from narrative to the evolution of understanding helps fill out just where this new kind of picture take us. I've described how culturally mature perspective involves a fundamental leap in how we understand. Cultural Maturity's cognitive changes make it possible to think in fundamentally new, more dynamic and encompassing—and ultimately more complete—ways.

The last time we saw a leap in understanding's basic assumptions was with the end of the Middle Ages. The European Renaissance brought insights that were fundamentally disruptive. We saw first intimations in the arts. The visual arts of the Italian Renaissance, for example—best known in the works of Leonardo DaVinci and Michelangelo—embodied a whole new kind of vantage, one in which we could step back and see more literally and directly, with a new "objectivity." Art also in a new way highlighted our humanness and individuality. Where figures depicted in art had before been flat and more symbolic than human, increasingly they were three-dimensional and mortal. And for the first time, artists began signing their work.

It is in the nature of the best of art that it presages more explicit conceptual innovation.[10] In the succeeding centuries, Rene` Descartes brought a related new explicitness to the philosophical world. Where mysticism reigned supreme in the Middle Ages, his formulations made conscious awareness and individual reason the new arbiters of identity and understanding. "I think, therefore I am." Descartes went on to

---

10 Later we will see how CST provides explanation for why this is the case.

propose that the world as a whole functions like a great machine. This includes not just the physical, but also the creaturely, and of particular importance, ourselves.[11]

This new picture was fundamentally transforming. Isaac Newton's later application of this new kind of perspective gave us the foundations of modern science. Newton proposed that we can understand everything—including ourselves—in terms of actions and reactions, simple laws of cause and effect. Most everything that we identify with accomplishment over the last 300 years follows directly from the resulting new approach to understanding: the industrial revolution, modern medicine, our familiar concept of the individual, representative government, widely available higher education. In its time, this new way of thinking could not have been more significant.

I've emphasized that there is no reason to assume that such thinking reflects some culminating achievement—and every reason to hope that it does not. Why should we need more? Over the course of this book, we will examine multiple reasons why further steps have become essential, but a couple that come back to the mechanistic assumptions that underlie such thinking are sufficient for now. Each in different ways highlights how the most important questions of our time remain impossible to effectively frame, much less answer, limited to Modern Age belief.

One relates to the greater complexity of thought needed to address essential questions. The Cartesian/Newtonian worldview can be reduced to a few basic characteristics. It is mechanistic (based on simple laws of cause and effect), dualistic (structured as polar juxtapositions—objective versus subjective, mind versus body, or humankind versus nature, to name just a few), and reductionistic (based on the assumption that reducing a phenomenon to its smallest constituent parts provides complete understanding). We will see

---

11 Descartes's familiar words from his *Discourse on the Method* give voice to the far-reaching extent of Enlightenment thought's machine model assumptions: "I wish you to consider, finally, that all the functions which I attribute to this machine, such as ... waking and sleeping; the reception of light, sounds, odors ..., the impressions of ideas in the memory; the inferior movements of the appetites and passions ...; I desire, I say that you consider that these functions occur naturally in this machine solely by the dispositions of its organs, not less than the movements of a clock."

how the most important social/cultural challenges before us require that we successfully step beyond such assumptions.

The second relates to the kinds of questions we need to address. Rational intelligence alone is very limited in what it can tell us when it comes to many of the concerns that are most important to us in daily life—such as purpose, love, creativity, integrity, or what it means to make wise choices. Arguably such concerns will only become more important in the centuries ahead. Today's new questions require us to think in ways that are more complete in what they draw on in ourselves.

New ways of understanding first began to make their appearance early in the last century. The most common popular reference is to new thinking in the sciences.[12] Albert Einstein did not consider his most well-known ideas a threat to fundamental assumptions, and rightly so, but they are appropriately seen as having radical significance. (Special and general relativity included dramatic reformulations, but they left mechanistic/deterministic thinking intact.) The early ideas of quantum mechanics (in which Einstein also played a role—sometimes ambivalently) presented a more direct challenge. With the later work of Niels Bohr and an international group of collaborators, quantum mechanics threw understanding into a shape-shifting, often contradictory-seeming world that directly confronted deterministic assumptions. Werner Heisenberg's demonstration that at a subatomic level it was not possible to simultaneously measure position and momentum (his famous "uncertainty principle") proved initially at least as disruptive—and controversial. (Einstein famously countered in response that "God does not play dice with the universe.")

At the same time, art continued to carry out its anticipatory function. The cubism of Pablo Picasso and Georges Braque required us to replace three-dimensional objectivity with a view that affirmed the validity of multiple perspectives. And a bit later, the abstract expressionism of Jackson Pollock and the surrealism of Salvador Dali challenged us to entertain irrational aspects of understanding and the possibility that they might have a valid place in knowing.

---

12 In times of change, innovations in the sciences will often first be broadly acknowledged for the simple reason that scientific claims can be most explicitly verified.

In my book *Cultural Maturity: A Guidebook for the Future*, I chronicle how we can recognize similar first intimations in numerous culture domains around this time. The book also describes how initial culturally mature insights have continued to evolve in decades since, frequently beneath the surface without people being aware that anything fundamental was becoming different, and often in a two-steps-forward-one-step-back fashion. Over the course of this book, I will highlight how a major portion of the twentieth century's most essential advances would not have been possible without culturally mature sensibility at least beginning to influence our values and our choices.

New cultural narratives and new chapters in understanding do not follow in a simple progression, one after another. Rather their relationships are more like tectonic plates, with the endings of one story significantly overlapping with the beginnings of the next. Consistent with this, over the course of the last century we saw a mix of stories and belief systems: culminating expressions of Modern Age belief, more postmodern sensibility gradually becoming prominent, and first acknowledgements—and articulations—of more culturally mature understanding.

Rethinking Systems

To understand how Creative Systems Theory achieves what it does, and also the particular importance of its contribution, we can take a look at the two terms—"systems" and "creative"—that give it its name. Neither term is perfect. Indeed, as we shall see, each can lead to conclusions that have nothing to do with what the theory is about. But nudge each of the terms a bit and we find that they at least provide good beginning insights. In the end, more than just a nudge is required, but the history of how each of these terms has been used offers a good vantage for understanding what this "more" entails.

It is reasonable to ask why we would want to give significant attention to systems approaches and their history even though the word "systems" is right there in Creative Systems Theory's name. Formal systems thinking had its beginnings with the biological sciences, while the primary concern of CST is ourselves. And I had in fact not even heard of systems thinking when I first articulated the basic ideas that later became Creative Systems Theory. A close colleague who taught systems ideas at a college level made the connection on reading an early draft of *The Creative Imperative*. He proposed that not only was what I described systems thinking, it represented an important and particularly encompassing addition to systems understanding. Previous systems notions contributed in any significant way to my thinking only after the development of CST was well underway.

Reflecting briefly on systems thinking's history is worth our time for a couple of reasons. By filling out the observation I made in the Preface about the importance of thinking systemically in ways that better reflect that we are alive (and human), it provides additional perspective for understanding the conceptual leap that gives CST its paradigmatic significance. It also further highlights how insights from early in the last century presaged needed new ways of thinking that we are only now beginning to fully grasp.

We should start with the basic question of just what it is that makes an idea "systemic." Systems thinking emphasizes the need to consider all the pieces. It also brings attention to how connections can be as important as differences. Such thinking, at least at its most basic, is not wholly new to modern times. The familiar story of the blind men and the elephant described the application of systemic perspective at least at a personal level. But our times are particular in the sense that the critical challenges we face today almost all require systemic understanding if they are to be addressed at all effectively. More than this, they require thinking systemically in ways that are in fact quite new.

Formal systems understanding had its beginnings in the initial years of the twentieth century. Important thinkers in multiple fields, each at around the same time and in similar ways, began to see fundamental limitations in the simple cause-and-effect assumptions that had given us the scientific revolution. The earliest voices taking on the systems challenge were biologists attempting to grapple with the basic fact of life.

While it is hard to escape that living beings are different in some fundamental ways from machines, the question of just how has remained a quandary even for those who observe living things most closely. Biology is the study of life. But ask a biologist about the nature of life, about what makes one thing alive and another not, and you will get ultimately unsatisfying answers. The honest biologist will throw up his hands, or refer you to a philosopher (who in the end can do no better).

Historically, the life question has been answered in a couple of basic ways. Extending Descartes' clockworks picture, people have thought of life as just a very complex kind of machine. We also find more dualistic explanations that locate life's source in some separate animating force—from Aristotle's "unmoved mover;" to, in medieval times, a soul, distinct from the body, that determines action; to more recently with nineteenth-century vitalism, a life-giving energy such as Henri Bergson's *élan vital*.

Systems theorists early in the last century recognized that for something to be alive, it must be more than just a machine. They also recognized that dualistic explanations just as fundamentally failed as explanation. They proposed that somehow we must understand living systems as systems, integrated "self-organizing" wholes.

Biologist Ludwig von Bertalanffy presented the first formal explication of this kind of understanding with his 1940 book *General Systems Theory*.[13] His thinking emphasized the need for new kinds of concepts if we are to understand life and introduced the essential notion of "open systems." Open systems depend on a continued flow-through of matter and energy and maintain themselves in highly dynamic states far from equilibrium. (Living things eat and expel the remains, with the energy difference fueling the organism's ongoing self-maintenance and self-organization). Von Bertalanffy failed in his dream to develop a formal mathematics of living systems, but the fresh attention he brought to the "what is life" question and his emphasis on the role of open systems each made critical contributions.

Later systems thinkers continued this search for ways of thinking that might better address life. Cybernetics, the invention of Norbert Weiner and a circle of colleagues, gave particular attention to feedback loops and other mechanisms of self-regulation. Weiner once wrote: "We are not stuff that abides but patterns that perpetuate themselves."[14] The

---

13 Ludwig von Bertalanffy, *General Systems Theory*, George Braziller, 1968.

14 Norbert Wiener, *The Human Use of Human Beings: Cybernetics and Society*,

formal concepts of cybernetics remain mechanistic, but they provide important insights that we still draw on to understand how important systemic dynamics in living systems work.

The ideas of two later systems theorists, Gregory Bateson[15] and Humberto Maturana,[16] are notable in this context not just for the particular attention they gave to the "what is life" conundrum, but also because of how each interpreted the role of cognition. In different ways, each arrived at the same recognition: The question of life and the question of cognition (when we think in terms of cognition at its most fundamental—the capacity to in some way make sense of and act in one's world) are in the end the same question. Understand understanding deeply, both agreed, and in the process we will have understood life.

CST is different from all of these contributions in that its primary focus is the human sphere. It is concerned with how we as conscious beings understand and with the very different ways we understand at different times and places. But we find a direct parallel in the question biologists recognized and the foundational question of CST. In a related way to how early systems efforts were stimulated by a desire on the part of biologists to think in ways that better address the fact of life, CST takes on the challenge of more effectively depicting the particular kind of life we are by virtue of being human.

We saw efforts that at least began to address human concerns more systemically throughout the last century. The use of formal systems language was rare, and it was unusual for efforts to fundamentally confront mechanistic assumptions, but we can think of some of the most important

---

Houghton Mifflin, 1955. Weiner also brought together remarkable people from diverse backgrounds in an attempt to push the edges of systems understanding more broadly.

15 Gregory Bateson, *Steps to an Ecology of Mind*, University of Chicago Press, 2000 (First published in 1972). Bateson was fond of placing a live crab before his students and challenging them to tell him how they knew it was alive. Inevitably they would fail. Do we know because it moves? Tractors move. Do we know because it responds to stimuli? So does your garage door opener. Do we know because it reproduces? Crystals reproduce.

16 Humberto Maturana and Francisco J. Varela, *The Tree of Knowledge*, Shambhala, 1987.

twentieth century advances in the human sphere as attempts to bring more encompassing perspective to how we understand ourselves.

The simple observation that a major portion of human functioning takes place unconsciously had particular significance. In the old picture, conscious awareness and rationality together served as captain of the cellular ship. Freud's formulation of the unconscious only partly challenged this picture. He viewed the task as making unconscious dynamics conscious, and his formulations were ultimately mechanistic—with id, ego, and superego existing in what is essentially a hydraulic relationship. But the basic idea that much of who we are lay out of sight and out of mind was not just radical, but heretical. It also pointed toward the need for a more complete kind of understanding.

More was to follow. The early German Gestalt psychologists directly challenged the classical science assumption that even complex systems could be understood in terms of the properties of their constituent parts, proposing that instead we needed to think in terms of organizational wholes. And other innovators are appropriately noted here for how they gave particular attention to aspects of intelligence beyond just the rational, aspects that in modern times had functioned largely unconsciously or had, at the least, been given secondary status. I think in particular in this regard of Carl Jung for the mythic and imaginal dimensions of cognition, Wilhelm Reich for the psychology of the body, and later humanistic thinkers such as Carl Rogers and Abraham Maslow for more emotional and even spiritual aspects of our natures.

Later in the century, the advent of family therapy brought systems thinking more formally into the psychotherapeutic realm. We also saw human sphere–related systemic insights that extended beyond the personal. Modern sociology and anthropology, for example, explicitly emphasized the need to think about the larger human experience more systemically. These advances at best anticipated the conceptual leap that is our interest here, but certainly they brought attention to the limitations of previous individualistic assumptions.

CST is unique in that it brings systemic perspective to the whole of human functioning, how it is pertinent equally to the lives of individuals, the workings of human relationships, and the evolving story of culture. It is also unique in how, with the application of a creative frame, it successfully engages the task of thinking about human systems of all sorts in ways that affirm that we are living beings, and more than this, human beings. Its conclusions have less immediate relevance to the physical and the biological, but the theory at least helps us better understand why we have thought about the world around us—including the physical and the biological—in the various ways that we have at different times in the human story.

For these reflections on systems, CST makes the additional important contribution of helping us separate the wheat from the chaff in our thinking. In just how it does, it provides further important insight into what makes the kind of systems thinking our times are requiring different from understanding of times past.

While we find systems language used today with growing frequency, most often what people refer to in using such language stops well short of the fully integrative kind of thinking that CST argues is today's systemic task. The most common way the use of systems language falls short simply extends the Modern Age mechanistic/rationalist worldview. The system of interest may be a human body or an ecosystem teeming with organisms, but the language remains machine language—pumps and hydraulics, pulleys and opposing forces.

Such use of systems language often reflects thinking that today serves us, for example, with how "systems science" helps us address many complex phenomena. The advent of high-speed computers combined with an appreciation for feedback mechanisms and nonlinear mathematics means that we can model and inquire into all manner of phenomena that before now would have eluded us—such as complex weather patterns, biological processes that help us devise new medications, machine learning, and the general management of "big data." But it is also the case that this kind of thinking is fundamentally different from our concern here. With rare exception, the assumptions of such systems science remain of those of an engineer—albeit one with more powerful engineering tools at his disposal. Such ideas necessarily leave us short if our concern is living systems, and, as we shall see, even for making sense of inanimate systems at the level that cutting-edge understanding today often requires.

We can also find systems language used today to argue for an almost opposite worldview. Systems thinking can become in effect a synonym for spiritual thinking. The recognition that systemic understanding of the sort I have described affirms the essential role of connectedness is interpreted in a way that makes connectedness what it is all about. We can find this use of systems language with thinking that identities with being "holistic" or that is given special status as "new paradigm" thought (drawing on historian Thomas Kuhn's descriptions of how scientific understanding makes leaps). But as with the mechanistic thinking of systems science, there is in fact nothing new in thinking that identifies with connectedness. Later we will explore how this kind of identification manifests in various forms with eighteenth century romanticism, medieval mysticism, the larger part of classical Eastern thought, the idealism of Plato, and the animistic beliefs of tribal times.

In contrast, the kind of systemic understanding needed for times ahead is fundamentally new. A specific CST concept—the Dilemma of Differentiation—helps tie together the different ways that systems language can leave us short with previous reflections about the importance of learning to think about living systems in living terms. In the process, it both helps us further appreciate what CST achieves and helps distinguish what the theory accomplishes from ideas we might confuse it with. The Dilemma of Differentiation brings attention to a quandary that confronts us with any effort to develop practical culturally mature concepts. It alerts us to how the simple fact that culturally mature truth requires that we make distinctions immediately puts us in a life-related pickle. Differentiation, the ability to say "this as opposed to that," is ultimately what makes thinking work. But usual ways of addressing difference have us falling off of one side or the other of the conceptual roadway. And we won't find our "living" quarry on either side.

We can depict difference in traditional parts terms—that is, in an atomistic, mechanistic manner with parts being separately analyzable entities in causal relationship. But if we do this, no matter how subtle and sensitive our delineations, when we put the parts together, we end up back in a machine world. We can also come at things using an opposite strategy, ignoring parts altogether and talking only in terms of relationship. But in the end, this approach gets us no closer. It leaves us with notions that, however sophisticated their language, become nothing but elaborate ways of saying "all is one." Recognizing ultimate unity can be comforting—and it identifies a truth just as important and accurate as the "all is many" claims of atomistic or mechanistic belief. But begging the question of parts makes for impoverished conception at best. Worse, it makes for misleading conception. Real relationships (unity in the systemic sense we have interest in)—whether personal or conceptual—require difference. Certainly life does.

CST provides language for making the needed wheat-from-chaff distinctions. In Chapter Two, we will examine how polar opposites, wherever we find them, manifest an underlying symmetry. They juxtapose some more difference-affirming quality with a quality of a more connectedness-affirming sort. For simplicity's sake, the theory often speaks of polarity as juxtaposing more right-hand and more left-hand, or more archetypally masculine and feminine characteristics.[17]

CST calls conclusions that identity only with right-hand sensibilities Separation Fallacies and conclusions that identify with left-hand sensibilities Unity Fallacies. It calls conclusions that split the difference—which CST argues gets us no closer at least when it comes to human systems—Compromise Fallacies. Thinking that does not ultimately fall for one or the other of these traps is as yet rare.[18]

A creative frame provides a way of thinking that reconciles the Dilemma of Differentiation and propels us beyond polar fallacies of each of these sorts. It turns out that creative processes are by their natures equally about difference and interconnectedness. Later we will see how we can understand all polar juxtaposition as creatively predicted—time-and-place-specific—expressions of more difference/distinction–related and more connectedness/oneness–related characteristics.[19]

---

[17] Such gender-linked language can initially cause confusion, but as we will see, when applied with appropriate care, it can prove particularly useful. It helps clarify why we experience the results with particular polar juxtapositions as we do. And it will help both Patterning in Time and Patterning in Space discernments come most fully alive. Chapter Ten provides a detailed look at just what gives experience the qualities I'm describing with the terms "archetypally masculine" and "archetypally feminine." There we will also examine how the evolution of these aspects of experience provides important insights for understanding the past, present, and future of gender and love.

[18] Chapter Seven includes a closer look at polar fallacies and the dynamics that create them.

[19] For example, in Chapter Twelve, I will describe how the various ways we have thought about science and religion throughout history can be under-

CREATIVE SYSTEMS THEORY 25

When we apply a creative frame to understanding as a whole, we get language we can use to develop comprehensive and detailed culturally mature conceptual approaches.

I often draw on a familiar image that depicts the kind of systemic thinking that Creative Systems Theory involves remarkably well: a simple box of crayons. The crayons represent creative aspects. The box represents culturally mature systemic perspective, the ability to at once consciously hold and apply all the pertinent aspects. The fact that the crayons are not just different, but different in hue—red, yellow, blue, green—helps get at the deep diversity of elements we are always dealing with when our interest is not just mechanical systems, but creative systems.

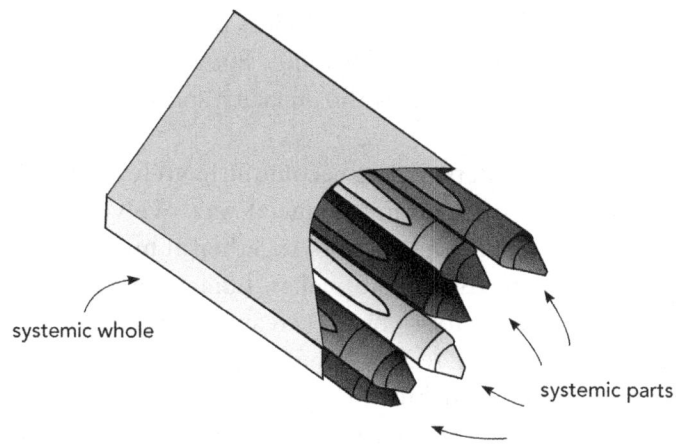

Fig. 1-2. Whole-Box-of-Crayons Systemic Understanding

Creative Systems Theory views understanding throughout history as an evolving sequence of creatively appropriate, but systemically partial, approaches to seeing the world. It also helps clarify just what will be needed if our thinking going forward is to be systemic in the full and encompassing, whole-box-of-crayons sense that challenges of the future will increasingly require of us.

---

stood in this way—an observation that hints at how CST might help us address many questions of an "ultimate" sort.

Creativity and Human Cognition

While the word "creative" is directly pertinent to here-and-now systemic relationships—what the box-of-crayons image most explicitly depicts—the term most immediately highlights the central significance of change in the thinking of Creative Systems Theory. The theory never lets us forget that what is true at one time may not be true at another. And just as it requires that we get beyond thinking of interrelationship only in mechanistic terms, similarly it challenges us to understand change in ways that are more dynamic than in times past.

We've made a good start with the basic relationship of understanding and change in CST. I've described how CST takes as its starting point the question of what most defines us as humans. Is it that we stand upright, or that we use language? CST's answer: We are "toolmakers," and makers not just of things but also of ideas and social structures. And ultimately we are makers of meaning. Put most simply, what makes us unusual, if not unique, is the audacity and richness of our creative capacities.

In CST, change and understanding become ultimately inseparable, and in a particularly powerful and nuanced way. We've glimpsed how intelligence's multiple aspects work together in human change process. CST proposes that what makes human understanding different is the sophistication of its creative structuring. The more dynamic picture that results is pertinent most immediately to understanding change in human systems. But because human understanding is the lens through which we make sense of things more generally, the outcome is a more change-permeated picture, whatever our concern.

To fully appreciate the radical implications of a creative framing of change, it helps to again step back historically—to put changes in our thinking about change, like we did for understanding as a whole and for systemic understanding in particular, in temporal perspective. In the old picture, change was the product of some separate external force, either an action producing an equal and opposite reaction, or divine influence. The picture that has begun to emerge over the last century is more inherently generative.

The first major contribution to such thinking predates the turn of the century. Charles Darwin's 1859 publication of *On the Origin of*

Species and Gregor Mendel's 1866 publication of his work with pea plants presented a picture in which creation, rather than being something that happens to life, is understood as following in an ongoing way from the nature of life. Later contributions at the biggest of cosmic scales would prove just as revolutionary. Edwin Hubble's demonstration that the universe is expanding required that science abandon its previous picture of a stable, eternally constant universe. (Here, again, Einstein had to set aside assumptions. In later writings, he described his inclusion of a constant in his early calculations designed to keep the appearance of a stable universe his greatest mistake.) The Big Bang Theory—the idea that the universe in fact had a beginning, and a dramatic one—followed from these essential observations. In the new picture, creation, rather than being either created or timeless and ever-present, became inherent to the larger story of existence.[20]

The recognition of change's intrinsic role came to have an increasingly important place, too, with thinking that focused more on ourselves. In psychology, we saw the appearance of "developmental" thinking, and of particular pertinence to these reflections, ideas that focused not just on the acquisition of new abilities, but on developmental stages that involved new ways of organizing experience and seeing the world.[21] Attention also began to be given not just to the developmental processes though which we become adults, but also to the developmental significance of later life changes.[22]

---

20 A further contribution to change's emerging picture has particular historical significance because it creatively links life and the simply physical. It also has more personal significance to me because its author and I corresponded during the early development of Creative Systems Theory. Thermodynamic chemist and complexity theorist Ilya Prigogine won the 1977 Nobel Prize for adding a critical missing piece to the recognition that living systems are open systems. He demonstrated how certain non-living open systems could also self-maintain and self-organize. Prigogine's work contributed to an increasing consensus among scientists that the emergent property we call life, rather than being a rare, perhaps one-off chance occurrence, may be, if not almost inevitable, certainly more readily achieved than we have before assumed.

21 I've mentioned the influence that the ideas of Jean Piaget had on my early thinking.

22 I think in particular of the contributions of Erik Erikson and Carl Jung in

CST expands on the best of such developmental thinking. It also extends such thinking beyond the personal, being as concerned ultimately with questions of how relationships, organizations, and larger social systems evolve. And it engages specifically in questions of why human developmental processes—of all sorts—happen in the particular ways that they do.

The theory's application of a creative frame is what makes all of this possible. I've noted that the word "creative" can be a source of misunderstanding. The theory uses the term in a way that is more expansive than is our custom. Creative in this sense is not about people with special abilities or just about moments of particular insight. It is also not just about particular activities. It is about science as much as art, and just as much it is about education, government, and religion. It might be better for us to use a more neutral term like "formative process." Often I will use combination terms such as "creative/formative" or "creative/developmental." Whatever language we choose to use, the implications of a creative frame are dramatic and encompassing.[23]

In the end, the word "creative" in CST refers to how human cognition is structured, and in particular, how it is structured to support our toolmaking, meaning-making natures. With regard to change, it is about how an appreciation for how we think helps us understand

---

this regard. Later we will see how this addition has direct pertinence to the specific kind of maturity needed more collectively in our time.

23 Given that we tend to associate the word "creative" with things artistic, misunderstandings most often have their roots in an assumed bias toward more archetypally feminine sensibilities. I've frequently had people initially attracted to CST ideas because they assumed the theory would support their creatively "left-hand" inclinations. In fact it does, but no more than it does inclinations of a more "right-hand" sort. For a similar reason, I've also had people of more academic and scientific bent dismiss CST's thinking without taking time to really examine it. The theory in fact directly affirms the great importance of rational inquiry (in the process expanding our relationship to it so that we can use rationality most effectively going forward). And it specifically applauds the profound advances of the scientific revolution. In the end, it not only celebrates more "right-hand" contribution, it invites the possibility of such contribution being realized in new, more ultimately consequential ways.

change in human systems in more dynamic, life-acknowledging ways. And it is about how the ability to hold the various aspects of cognition's complexity in more conscious and embracing ways results in a more dynamic picture of change more generally.

From Creative Systems Theory's vantage, not only are we toolmaking creatures infinitely creative, how we think, act, and relate reflects our creative natures. The theory describes how even the structures we give our worlds (governmental forms, architecture, particular inventions we are capable of and willing to accept) reflect underlying creative organization. Alfred North Whitehead spoke of creativity as the "universal of universals."[24] CST observes something similar, then goes on to use this observation to develop a general approach for making sense of how we understand—both understanding's mechanisms and why we understand in the diverse and often contradictory ways that we do.

A couple of characteristics of human creative dynamics wherever we find them make the term "creative" particularly powerful when it comes to the challenge of mature systemic thought. Together they will provide the foundation for the next chapter's introduction to Patterning in Time. Each helps us appreciate how understanding of a more fully creative and systemic sort is a possibility while also helping us avoid traps in our thinking.

I pointed toward the first characteristic with this chapter's biographical reflections. It concerns intelligence's multiplicity. We reasonably ask why human intelligence should have the diverse aspects that I've noted—along with the rational, also the body, the imagination, and emotions (to use the particular way that CST cuts up the pie of intelligence). I've observed that these multiple aspects of intelligence manifest in predictable ways with each stage in any human creative/formative process. The picture that results provides an evocative answer to the question of why we should find such dramatically different ways of processing information. CST argues that our multiple ways of knowing are essential to our toolmaking natures. In chapters ahead, we will examine how they work together to support and drive creative/formative process.

---

24 Alfred North Whitehead, *Process and Reality* (Gifford Lectures Delivered in the University of Edinburgh During the Session 1927-28), Free Press, 1979.

The second characteristic turns to the topic of polarity. I've suggested that a defining attribute of culturally mature perspective is that it helps us think in ways that get beyond defining truth in polar terms. In the next chapter, we will look at how the generation of polarity is similarly intrinsic to how creative processes work. The short version: Creative processes begin with an original unity—an initial, prevailing common sense—then bud off new possibility. They then progress as an evolving play of sometimes obviously complementary, at other times directly antagonistic polar relationships.

Of particular significance for this inquiry is what happens to polarity with the mature stages of any creative/formative process. We become newly able both to appreciate the larger process through which polarity is generated and to think in ways that leave behind past polarized and polarizing assumptions. The result is a new, now more nuanced and systemic kind of understanding.

I've described how Cultural Maturity's cognitive changes let us at once step back from and more deeply engage the whole of who we are. More specifically, it lets us more consciously recognize and draw on the whole of our richly creative cognitive complexity. That includes our multiple intelligences. It also includes the polar juxtapositions that in times past have defined understanding. In doing so, we become better able to think about living systems in living terms, and about ourselves in ways that honor the unique kind of life we are by virtue of being human.

Chapter Three examines in depth how we find a similar kind of creative patterning—sequences of defining intelligences, underlying polarities, and resulting ways of seeing reality—with human formative processes of all sorts, from a simple creative act, to the growth of a relationship, to the stages of psychological development, to the big-picture workings of history. We will also see how the result with Cultural Maturity's cognitive changes is a more dynamic—and "creative"—picture of existence more generally.

Just as we did previously for understanding here-and-now systemic dynamics, we can draw on the Dilemma of Differentiation and the notion of polar fallacies to help separate the wheat from the chaff in our thinking about change. Particularly important are essential differences when it comes to thinking about the changes that will define our human future— differences in how people conceive of advancement and just what real advancement will require.

Most more familiar change-related notions continue Modern Age assumptions and describe change in simple cause-and-effect terms. When extended into the future, they suggest that advancement should take the form of continued onward-and-upward material progress. We find their ultimate expression in contemporary techno-utopian notions. Many change-related beliefs—and many of the most dangerous as we look to the future—are best thought of as Separation Fallacies.

We also see ideas about change that reduce to Unity Fallacies. Ultimately they are just as partial and in their own ways can be just as dangerous. More populist political views are of this sort. Such views suggest that progress lies ultimately with taking down established social structures. We also find change-related notions that are more specifically philosophical or spiritual. I think of philosophical idealism in this way. Similar to what I described earlier for vitalism in the biological sphere, philosophical idealism postulates some separate determining entity—for example, with more philosophical formulations, Plato's Ideas or Forms, or with more spiritual conceptions, some essence or divine spark. Because such notions can frame change in quasi-evolutionary terms, they can initially be confused with culturally mature thought. But in the end, being ultimately dualistic, they fail the Dilemma of Differentiation's test. And when we find ideas about the future, they tend, like their more materialist twins, to reduce to utopian images with idealized end points.[25] New Age[26] thinking can take philosophical idealism to an absurd extreme.

In contrast, change from the perspective of Creative Systems Theory draws on both more right-hand and more left-hand creative sensibilities equally. And it does so in the more conscious and explicitly integrative sense that becomes newly possible with Cultural Maturity's cognitive reordering. With regard to the future, it asks that we leave behind simple-answer beliefs that before have protected us from life's complexities and uncertainties. That includes systemically partial,

---

[25] We find a good example of this kind of "creative" misconception with the thinking of French idealist philosopher and Jesuit priest Pierre Teilhard de Chardin and his notion of an ultimate "Omega Point."

[26] I will use the term "New Age" in the book as a shorthand for the more simplistic of modern spiritual interpretations.

and thus ultimately ideological, beliefs of all sorts—whether political, religious, moral, scientific, or partial by virtue of cultural stage or individual personality style.

The result, while more demanding of us, is also in important ways more "ordinary." I've described Cultural Maturity as a new common sense, proposing that what it asks is simply that we better see what has always been the case. From the vantage of culturally mature perspective, utopian conclusions of any sort (and ultimately, too, dystopian assumptions) become red flags warning us that our thinking remains yet well short of the more complete and encompassing—maturely creative—understanding on which our future depends. The kind of thought that CST proposes is needed for the future, thought that draws on Integrative Meta-perspective's more encompassing embrace, is simply thought that better acknowledges and applies all the crayons in the systemic box.

Creative Systems Theory's application of a creative frame helps us appreciate how this newly mature kind of common sense is not just necessary going forward, but predicted if we can effectively respond to all it asks of us. The theory also provides language and a set of conceptual tools that help us make our way in a change-permeated world that when fully grasped is appropriately experienced at once as really nothing special—just what is—and really quite profound.

Needed New Capacities and Challenges That Could Be Our Undoing

A good way to get a feel for how needed new ways of understanding, while more demanding, are also common sense (and essential) is to take time with what some of the challenges that necessarily confront us as we look to the future ask of us. I've proposed that effectively addressing the most important tasks ahead will require skills and capacities new to us as a species. A quick look at some of those needed new human skills and capacities helps make the importance of the kind of thinking that becomes possible with culturally mature perspective more understandable—even inescapable.

The reflections in this section are adapted from my most recent book, *Rethinking How We Think: Integrative Meta-perspective and the Cognitive "Growing Up" on Which Our Future Depends*. They bring particular attention to the need for three such new capacities: the ability to get beyond past us-versus-them assumptions, a new maturity in our relationship to limits, and learning to think about advancement—and what most matters to us more generally—in more complete ways. In Chapter Four I will expand this list and also be more specific about how we can think of each of these new capacities as a "creative" capacity. But we benefit at this point from some introductory reflections.

Each of these needed new capacities in different ways supports the essential recognition that the most important challenges before us are not just technical challenges, but human challenges. Each also brings emphasis to the importance of new ways of understanding and how such understanding must be more systemic. And each at least begins to point toward how the needed more systemic understanding is necessarily of the whole-box-of-crayons, change-permeated sort that Integrative Meta-perspective makes possible.

These descriptions will focus on challenges of a particularly consequential sort—indeed, challenges that could be our undoing. With the examples I will touch on, failing to bring the needed maturity of perspective to bear will at least bring significant pain. The result could also be catastrophe. Together, they highlight the inescapable fact that unless a significant portion of the population can begin to manifest the new values and ways of understanding that culturally mature perspective makes possible, life in times ahead will at best be decidedly unpleasant.

How Us-Versus-Them Beliefs Could Be the End of Us

Our human tendency to see the world in polar, us-versus-them terms plays a central role in a great many of today's most pressing human concerns. Certainly we recognize it in conflict between nations. But we see it too in political gridlock, and in racism, sexism, class divisions, and ethnic hatreds. CST helps us understand both why we have before thought about differences in the language of polarity and why we have done so in specific ways at different times and places. It also helps us understand the possibility of getting beyond this kind of thinking that has always before been a defining aspect of the human experience.

Importantly, CST doesn't view us-versus-them thinking as simply some reflection of human failing. In times past, polarized assumptions have served us. They have protected us from life's multihued complexities by reducing options to a more manageable black and white. And the absoluteness of this way of thinking has similarly protected us from needing to confront uncertainties that before now would have been more than we could tolerate. But just as important today is the recognition that such protection no longer provides benefit. As we look to the future, if we hold to this historically essential way of keeping experience manageable, the result can easily be calamity.

The dangers are easiest to appreciate with relationships between nations. Throughout history, collective identity has depended on dividing the world into "chosen people" and "evil others." Having clear enemies has served to solidify social bonds and protect us from truths that we have not yet been ready to accept. But we can't escape that projecting our less savory aspects onto others now threatens to have an opposite result. In our increasingly globalized world with readily available weapons of mass destruction, chosen-people/evil-other thinking on the global stage becomes inconsistent with survival. War at any major scale has stopped being an option.

And like it or not, neither technological solutions nor simple changes in policy can save us from such consequences. Depending on our political persuasion, we will tend to miss how this is the case in different, even opposite ways. We may assume that we can be safe if only we have the largest stockpile of arms. Or we can conclude with equal certainty that disarmament will provide the necessary answer. But while good defenses and reducing armaments each have a place, in the end, neither can protect us. Our only hope lies ultimately with getting beyond the projective dynamics that have traditionally led to conflict.

Given human behavior to this point, this result might seem beyond anything we might hope to achieve. And the fact that many of the world's people today occupy cultural realities far from where needed more mature sensibilities could even be considered magnifies the task's difficulty. But leaving behind chosen-people/evil-other mechanisms can't be beyond us if any kind of optimism as we look to the future is to be warranted.

In fact, there are good reasons to think that needed changes are possible. We can derive at least limited encouragement from accomplishments already realized. I think, most immediately, of the fall of the Berlin Wall. In the end, the Berlin Wall fell not because one side had prevailed, but because people had grown tired of what the wall represented. And that is not the only example. In *Cultural Maturity: A Guidebook for the Future*, I argue that the modern West would likely have responded much more dangerously and reactively to the threat of terrorism if we were not seeing at least the beginnings of more mature sensibilities.

More specifically there is how Cultural Maturity's cognitive reordering directly supports the needed changes. The box-of-crayons metaphor helps clarify just how this is so. With mythologized thinking, we elevate certain "crayons" and demonize others. In relationships between nations, we've identified with the elevated crayons and projected the demonized crayons, making them attributes of peoples we perceived to be different from ourselves. With Integrative Meta-perspective, we become newly able to own the whole box. We better appreciate the various crayons as aspects of ourselves. We also recognize that other systems similarly manifest such multifaceted complexity.

In keeping with an observation I made earlier about Integrative Meta-perspective, in what might at first seem a paradox, the needed new ways of thinking at once require that we think more complexly than we have in times past and produce understanding that is in important ways simpler. The picture that results is more complex in that it requires us to give up the idealizations and projections that before have protected us from the fact of real differences[27] and how complicated relationships can be. But at the same time, instead of seeing the world through the distorting lens of mythologized truths, we come a critical step closer to seeing things for just how they are. In essential ways it is more straightforward—in the end, more common sense.

Us-versus-them ideological beliefs that manifest at smaller scales, such as in the political arena, might seem to present less immediate concern, but the dangers may ultimately be just as great. In times past, such thinking again has served us. At the least, in a related way it has protected us from complexity and uncertainty. And CST suggests

---

27 While we tend to assume that polarized conflict is about difference—indeed, extreme difference—in fact, because projection involves attributing aspects of ourselves to another system, polarization functions to protect us from the experience of real difference.

deeper kinds of benefit. In *Cultural Maturity*, I describe how the alternating of liberal and conservative tendencies has in times past worked to drive creative change.

But more local us-versus-them thinking, too, is ceasing to provide benefit. I find the degree of partisan pettiness and polarization we so often witness today seriously worrisome. Polarization has reached such an extreme that often very little of substance can get accomplished. It is reasonable to fear that if we can't get beyond it, not only will we fail to advance further beyond Modern Age assumptions, we might regress and lose the essential progress we have made in recent centuries. In the worst-case scenario, functional government may become impossible and we could see the end of the democratic experiment.

Here again the possibility of getting beyond us-versus-them reactiveness might initially seem only to be wishful thinking. But just as the polarizations that lead to war are based on projection rather than on accurate perceptions of difference, so too are the polarizations that produce partisan gridlock. Ultimately, they are more about the clashing of opposite-hued crayons than reasoned reflection, or even the kind of impassioned debate we may find with real differences of opinion.

The notion that political polarization has more to do with our cognitive mechanisms than the real complexities of policy can for many people seem radical. At the least it comes as a surprise. We find some of the best evidence in the way issues that later become highly polarized are often not thought of in partisan terms at all when they first come to the public's attention.[28] Indeed, it is frequently not clear what the "sides" would be, much less who would take them, if the issue did become politicized. Only later do battle lines get drawn.

---

28 This was the case, for example, with both climate change and health care reform. There were no obvious sides to the climate change debate when the evidence first came to light. And The Affordable Care Act (commonly known as "ObamaCare") was initially modeled on Republican Mitt Romney's plan in Massachusetts. We often encounter related surprises with us-versus-them antagonisms on the world stage. It turns out that wars are less often the result of major differences than we tend to assume. Think of how World War I began with the assassination of Austro-Hungarian heir Archduke Franz Ferdinand. While it was a significant event, few people had any idea it could have such world-altering consequences.

The common closeness of elections provides another kind of evidence. If voting were based on the perceived intelligence of the candidates' ideas, much more often than we do we would see general agreement as to which candidate is the most qualified. Instead, elections are most often won by a few percentage points, or less. This is what we would predict if we are dealing not just with differences of opinion, but polar opposite cognitive patterns.

Culturally mature perspective makes clear that Right, Left, and somewhere (more moderate) in between are not the only options—and can't be if we are to get where we need to go. On my blog and podcast, I put on my cultural psychiatrist's hat and attempt to bring culturally mature perspective to contemporary issues.[29] When a social concern becomes highly polarized—as we've see in recent years, for example, with health care reform, abortion, climate change, immigration, or issues of gender and appropriate sexual behavior—I attempt to step back and engage the concern from the needed more systemic vantage.

A series of recognitions that follow from the whole-box-of-crayons nature of needed answers inevitably comes into play. First, while each polar position holds at least a small a piece of the truth, neither can provide ultimately useful solutions (each reflects a crayon). Second, each position in the end stops short of recognizing the hard question that needs to be addressed (the question being systemic in nature, it can only be grasped from a larger vantage). And third, compromise between polarized positions ultimately gets us no closer to where we need to go (splitting the difference between crayons is fundamentally different from holding the whole box).

With any issue, I start by attempting to identify the hard question that neither position effectively recognizes. This in itself does not supply needed solutions, but it does mean that our inquiry will at least be in the right territory. As solutions do begin to become apparent, we generally find that each of the opposing positions has at least something useful to contribute. But we also find that any kind of useful contribution requires the holder of the original position to surrender basic assumptions.[30]

---

29 See www.culturalmaturityblog.net and www.lookingtothefuture.net.

30 Over the course of this book, I will apply this kind of systemic teasing apart

I've noted how partisan pettiness today threatens to take us backwards and put the Modern Age democratic experiment at risk. Certainly, it will get in the way of further progress in how we think about government and governance. Functional government in the long term will depend on the kind of whole-box-of-crayons systemic understanding that Cultural Maturity's cognitive changes make possible. It will require leaders who are able to hold issues more systemically and voters who are interested in supporting leaders capable of doing so. It may also require new, more systemically conceived governmental structures. What we can know is that without more whole-box-of-crayons ways of understanding, we will simply not be able to make the kinds of more mature and systemic decisions on which effective governance going forward depends.[31]

We can sum up this first theme with a simple lesson. In times past, when we encountered polarized positions and partisan advocacy, our task was obvious and unquestioned. We assumed that there were only two options and that our task was to fight for the side that was right. With Integrative Meta-perspective, the fact of polarity has very different implications. It alerts us to how we need to expand our vantage, see a bigger picture. When we do, we recognize that neither side is yet asking the hard question that ultimately needs to be answered. We also recognize that while each side may hold a piece of the truth, neither side by itself, nor some simple compromise between sides, can get us where we need to go.

The Fact of Real Limits and the Possibility of Ecological Catastrophe

It is the threat of ecological catastrophe that for many people most conjures up images of our undoing. Take your pick—climate change,

---

to a variety of contemporary front-page-news concerns, including many of those just noted. I will also touch on a handful of more philosophical topics that traditionally get framed in polar terms—for example, the traditional assumptions of morality, the often conflicting worldviews of science and religion, the apparent contradiction between free will and determinism, and how we best understand the relationship between humankind and the natural world.

31 See Chapter Eleven of this book, *Cultural Maturity: A Guidebook for the Future*, or "Governance" in the ICD blog library for reflections on the future of government and governance.

the growing rate of species extinctions, the loss of needed resources such as adequate food supplies or clean air and water. Any of these circumstances by themselves could result in immense harm. And any one could readily combine with other challenges to create even more ultimately dangerous realities. One of the greatest risks with climate change, for example, is that the disruptions that come with warming temperatures will increase conflict on the planet and with this the likelihood of the use of weapons of mass destruction.

To effectively address the possibility of ecological catastrophe, we must first recognize that once again we are dealing not just with a technological challenge, but with what is ultimately a human challenge. Further development of renewable energy sources and the achievement of greater energy efficiency will have clear roles in responding to these dangers. But in the end, whether we succeed at avoiding environmental devastation will be determined by our human choices.

We also need again to recognize that choosing and acting effectively will depend on capacities new to us as a species. Most immediately, doing so will require greater capacity for foresight and concern for the long term.[32] Put simply, it will demand a new, more grown-up kind of responsibility. This same greater responsibility is ultimately needed if we are to effectively get beyond the us-versus-them beliefs of times past, but the fact that the consequences with environmental questions so directly concern not just our human well-being, but the well-being of life as a whole, brings particular emphasis to its newness and importance.

Making needed choices will also depend on a further, more specific new capacity. We must learn to better appreciate the fact of real limits. We can effectively address environmental dangers only if we can accept that there are real limits to resources. We also have to accept that there are certain things that we simply can't continue to do. And we have to face that there are also real limits to what we as humans can understand and control.[33]

Besides highlighting the need to acknowledge limits in especially stark ways, the possibility of environmental catastrophe also brings particularly

---

32 Note that we have all before taken classes on the past, but very few people have had classes on the future.

33 Again this is a new capacity that I have written about extensively. *Cultural Maturity: A Guidebook for the Future* provides the most detailed analysis.

direct attention to the importance of thinking more systemically. Words like "ecological" and "environmental" refer specifically to the importance of considering contexts and interconnections. Environmental limits also help further fill out our understanding of the particular sort of systemic thinking the future depends on. They directly confront us with the importance of having systems ideas that can effectively address living systems.

Mechanical systems may break if they are pushed too far, but they can usually be fixed, and designs can always be refined and improved. With living systems, real limits are inherent to how things work. Bears can't fly, and the result if a bear believes otherwise is not going to be pretty. Make a creature too hot or too cold and it will not long survive. With living systems, inviolable limits come with the territory. Ignore them and life ceases to exist.

Our relationship to limits changes fundamentally with Integrative Meta-perspective. How it does follows directly from the way Cultural Maturity's changes require that we draw on the entirety of who we are as systems. From the more whole-box-of-crayons, life-acknowledging and human-life-acknowledging vantage that results, that fact of limits becomes obvious, and obviously important to always take into account.

Given that the fact of real limits might seem self-evident, it is reasonable to ask why the ability to acknowledge them has thus far been so difficult for us. Again we come back to how we think—or rather, how we have thought in times past. I've described how Modern Age narratives have most often been of one of two sorts—either heroic or romantic. Heroic and romantic narratives each celebrate limitlessness. Heroic narratives proclaim that if only we sufficiently persevere, any obstacle can be transcended. Romantic narratives promise that if we find the right kind of connectedness—with another person, with nature, with some particular poetic or spiritual belief—anything can be possible.

Like beliefs that divide humanity into chosen people and evil others, myths of limitlessness, in their time, have served us. They've supported the Modern Age emphasis on individual achievement and helped get us beyond the constraining prohibitions of the Middle Ages. They've also protected us from recognitions—about what is possible and what is not—that before now we would have found too much to tolerate. But these once-inspiring stories today invite calamity. If we can't come to grips with the fact of real limits, we will fail to address not just environmental challenges, but most any of the really important questions of our time.

Over the course of this book, I will touch on how a new maturity in our relationship to limits will be central to success with all manner of future challenges, from leading and loving in ways that can work, to designing effective health care systems, to effectively managing emerging technologies. Integrative Meta-perspective makes clear that recognizing where real limits may exist is one of the necessary first steps if we wish to engage a question in a culturally mature way. Historically, acknowledging limits would be interpreted as failure or weakness. From Integrative Meta-perspective's more systemic vantage, the recognition of inviolable limits becomes key to success and the making of wise—and thus ultimately powerful—choices.

We can sum up this second theme again with a simple lesson. Prior to now, when we encountered limits, we have assumed that our task was to heroically (or romantically) break through them. With Integrative Meta-perspective, we first pause and take time to discern just what kind of limit we face. If it is a limit that warrants a more traditional response, we proceed as before—and with added conviction. But we are also open to the possibility that the limit is inviolable. In a culturally mature reality, making this kind of distinction becomes a central task of leadership in all parts of our personal and collective lives.

Defining Advancement More Systemically and Today's Crisis of Narrative

The last of our examples in important ways encompasses the others. If we are to effectively advance, we need to rethink what advancement should entail. A simple way to put it is that we need new, more systemic, more whole-box-of-crayons measures for wealth and progress.

Our Modern Age definitions are so familiar that we tend not to question them. Wealth is the accumulation of material assets. And progress is new inventions and economic growth. Today, if we don't question these definitions—and question them fundamentally—the consequences will be dire.

As with us-versus-them beliefs and the heroic and romantic myths of times past, thinking about advancement as we have in modern times has benefitted us. Our familiar definition of wealth has been closely tied to our modern concept of the individual. And defining progress as we have has been central to the wondrous achievements of the Industrial Age and the great power of modern economies. But as with these other aspects of the Modern Age worldview, while our familiar definitions of wealth and progress might seem logical, they are products primarily of how we have thought in times past. And in a similar way, they cannot continue to provide benefit going forward.

When I want to help a person get at what more is needed, I will often first engage them at a personal level. I will ask them to talk to me about what creates meaning—"wealth" in the largest sense—in their individual lives. Most people mention money, but most recognize too that beyond a certain point money is less tied to meaning than one might think. Invention, too, most always has a place—people like their gadgets. But most people recognize that other things are ultimately as important, or often much more important: one's family, one's friends, one's community, one's felt relationship with nature, one's health, one's creative and intellectual pursuits.

People doing this exercise are often surprised to find that a significant mismatch exists between what they have described as most important for a meaningful life and many of their day-to-day choices. I may joke with the person as they confront this recognition, pointing out—only partly tongue in cheek—that this kind of discrepancy would seem to be almost the definition of insanity. When working in therapy, this kind of recognition can result in people making major life changes.

Later, I may engage the person in the same kind of inquiry with regard to how collectively we tend to define wealth and progress today. The degree to which our current world circumstances reflect a related kind of mismatch becomes hard to escape. Too often, today, we hold to an outmoded definition of advancement that excludes much that is in fact most important to us. And just as we appropriately think of an individual who makes choices that are not in keeping with what the person finds most important as deranged, the implications are huge. Later in this book, I will describe how taking the Modern Age narrative beyond its timeliness threatens to distance us from much that most matters to us in quite fundamental ways.[34]

Earlier I made reference to a specific result that follows from this kind of disconnect, what CST calls our time's Crisis of Purpose. I introduced my recent book, *Hope and the Future: Confronting Today's Crisis of Purpose*, by describing therapy work with a young man who had attempted to hang himself. It became strikingly clear in our conversations that the hopelessness he felt was only in limited ways personal.

---

34 See the discussion of the Dilemma of Trajectory in Chapters Two and Three.

CREATIVE SYSTEMS THEORY

It was more about the state of the world. He described having a hard time thinking of a future he would want to be a part of. The aspects of therapy that most helped him involved asking together what a meaningful human future might look like, exploring how we would need to rethink the human story to get there, and him asking how he in his life might contribute to that new story.

In our time, we find marked increases in rates of depression and suicide. We also witness increasing rates of addiction, and not just substance addiction as with the opioid crisis, but addiction to consumption as we see with the obesity epidemic,[35] and I suspect of greatest long-term concern, addiction to distraction and artificial stimulation as we see with how addiction to electronic devices has today come to be in effect a social norm.[36]

How do we best think about needed new measures for wealth and progress? For our task here, the central recognition is that they must be of our more whole-box-of-crayons systemic sort. Whole-box-of-crayons measures will be required if we are to successfully assess the benefits and risks of new technologies. (We need such measures if we are to effectively determine what we are to call benefit.) Such measures will similarly be critical to making good environmental decisions. (It is only through them that we can appreciate how impoverished further environmental destruction would leave us.) And, certainly, more mature and systemic measures for wealth and progress will be necessary if we are to effectively address the ever-widening gap between the world's haves and have-nots. (Ask about benefit more consciously and we begin to better recognize not just how such disparities are ethically troubling, but how they risk destabilizing societies and putting everyone's well-being in peril.)

We can think of the task of redefining wealth and progress as a particularly encompassing example of a more basic kind of challenge that confronts us with culturally mature questions of every sort. In the end, the task is about learning to think about what matters in more complete

---

35 It is estimated that 50 percent of Americans will be medically obese by 2030.

36 Chapters Four and Five examine today's Crisis of Purpose in greater depth. And in Chapter Nine, I will address device addiction specifically, in particular how both understanding it and confronting it successfully relates to holding intelligence in the more systemic and complete way that Integrative Meta-perspective makes possible.

ways. Confronting any kind of important concern necessarily starts with asking what most matters to us in doing so, addressing what CST calls the pertinent Question of Referent.[37] Once we are over Cultural Maturity's threshold, referents that work are necessarily of a more integrative, whole-box-of-crayons, systemic sort. Redefining wealth and progress engages the task of addressing today's Question of Referent for humanity as a whole.

We can think of the concept of Cultural Maturity as an attempt to answer humanity's now-defining Question of Referent. At the concept's heart is a more complete appreciation of all that matters to us in being human. Integrative Meta-perspective offers that we might learn to live consciously from such more complete understanding and thus have the greatest chance of effectively advancing as a species.

We can sum up this third theme, like the others, with a simple lesson. Historically, when making decisions, we would look to culturally prescribed truths. With modern times, we've also looked specifically to prescribed truths of a materialist/individualist/objectivist sort. With Cultural Maturity, truths become ours to determine and necessarily if a more encompassing sort. At the largest of scales, today's truth task challenges us to define advancement in more complete and ultimately life-affirming ways. Our future well-being as a species depends on it.

Creative Systems Patterning Concepts

I recently had a conversation with that same professor who forty years ago pointed out that the approach to understanding that I'd begun to develop with *The Creative Imperative* might best be called systemic. I asked him what he saw as the most important advances when it came to systems thinking. He paused, and then responded that he recognized increasingly that as yet we don't really have systems theories, at least of any comprehensive sort, only attempts to think in ways that are more systemic.

Creative Systems Theory's various patterning concepts don't achieve that goal with regard to understanding as a whole. Their concern, most specifically, is human experience. That includes spheres of inquiry that turn understanding's lens specifically on ourselves. (In Chapter Eleven, I will describe how we can think of CST as rewriting the social sciences

---

37 Addressing pertinent Questions of Referent is a Whole-Person/Whole-System discernment task. See Chapter Five.

and humanities, at least many of their most important underlying assumptions.) It also includes helping us better understand the uniquely human ways we give expression to life, as with the arts. It is reasonable to ask why we make art and music or why we dance, and why we do these things in the particular ways we do at different times and places (again, see Chapter Eleven). And with philosophy, CST lets us map how, over time, we humans have addressed the most basic of questions (see Chapter Three) and, as a bonus, lets us answer quandaries that always before have left us puzzled (see Chapter Twelve).

As I've suggested, CST also contributes to better understanding things we tend to think of as wholly separate from ourselves, such as the conclusions of science or religion—though in more limited ways. This is what we should expect if CST is most fundamentally about how we understand, rather than what we understand. It is just as reasonable to ask why, historically, our ways of describing the biological and physical worlds have been different in the particular ways that they have (see Chapter Twelve). And in times such as ours when conflict seems so often rooted in religious belief, it becomes ever more important to understand how such belief can serve and how, too, it can lead us astray (again, see Chapter Twelve).

The chapters ahead turn most specifically to the theory's various patterning notions and how they make these diverse kinds of discernment possible. These patterning notions warrant a bit more introduction before we get into their particulars. I've observed how CST employs three kinds of such creatively framed discernment tools, what it calls Patterning in Time concepts, Whole-Person/Whole-System patterning concepts, and Patterning in Space concepts. Each helps us make the kinds of distinctions essential to good future decision-making. And each helps us think in more living, indeed human, terms.

Patterning in Time and Patterning in Space notions represent Concepts of Creative Differentiation. They make what the theory calls culturally mature "multiplicity" distinctions, address difference in dynamic systems terms. Patterning in Time and Patterning in Space concepts share that their concern is parts, distinctions not just between the "how much" of systems, but between the "whats, the whys, and the how manys." Using our box-of-crayons analogy, they address the available crayons (or to be more precise, the crayons plus when and where colors are most usefully applied). Whole-Person/Whole-System Patterning Concepts make what

CST calls culturally mature "crux" distinctions. Using the box-of-crayons analogy, their perspective is that of the encompassing box. In various ways, they are concerned with a system's overall vitality and well-being, systemic truth at its most basic.[38]

Patterning in Time is just what it sounds like—though time in this sense refers not just to clock time, but to developmental time.[39] Patterning in Time concepts address change in human systems. They help make sense of underlying processes in human growth (including not just individual growth but also the growth of relationships), predict change dynamics in organizations, and clarify how various realms of human inquiry—science, government, education, religion—have evolved over time.

Patterning in Time concepts address the fact that what makes a system creatively vital very much has its seasons. Whether our concern is the span of a creative project, the duration of a relationship, a personal lifetime, or the story of culture, different stages not only give voice to very different truths, they reflect very different notions about what makes something true. Patterning in Time concepts describe how various scales of formative process layer one atop the other and together define the context of any creative moment. Of particular significance for today, they provide perspective for making sense of the changes that define our time.

The book's next two chapters turn specifically to creative Patterning in Time. Chapter Two delves into the particulars of Integrative Meta-perspective and looks specifically at how the way such perspective alters our relationship to both intelligence and polarity produces a creative picture of the workings of change. Chapter Three looks in more detail at how Patterning

---

38 Note that this description of Whole-Person/Whole-System Patterning Concepts presents an apparent paradox. I've described such notions simultaneously as if they are about the "crux" of truth, something we would more conventionally associate with some kind of abstract essence, and about understanding in its entirety. Chapter Five examines how we must think of them in both of these seemingly contradictory ways at the same time. Either more familiar way of thinking leaves us fundamentally short of what Whole-Person/Whole-System patterning discernments necessarily accomplish.

39 Chapter Three addresses how our perceptions of time are themselves relative in time (developmental time).

in Time concepts map experience and examines the kinds of questions that the recognition of such temporal relationships helps us address.

Chapter Five shifts our attention to Whole-Person/Whole-System Patterning Concepts. Whole-Person/Whole-System patterning concepts address what truth at its most basic becomes when cultural guideposts no longer provide reliable direction. Their interest lies with the foundational concern of the degree to which an act or idea is "life-giving"—in the language of formative process, how fully it supports and enhances our creative growth and well-being. They address questions like purpose, morality, capacity, and violence. While Whole-Person/Whole-System Patterning Concepts can initially seem less consequential than creative truth's two more differentiated sorts of notions, many people find them the most transforming in their implications. In introducing Questions of Referent and the importance of new, more systemic referents when addressing wealth and progress, I was emphasizing the need for a particularly critical kind of Whole-Person/Whole-System patterning discernment.

Chapter Six turns to Patterning in Space concepts. Patterning in Space notions address here-and-now systemic interrelationships. We can use them to make sense of our own internal workings, to better understand relationships of every sort (from intimate bonds to the bonds of communities, institutions, and nations), and of particular pertinence for today, to tease apart the complexly interrelated implications of our present human condition. Patterning in Space discriminations address creative relativity in the here and now, one's place in a system's diversity. They describe how our inner and outer worlds are each profoundly plural.

CST also includes numerous more particular concepts such as the Dilemma of Differentiation. Some are conceptually very specific. For example, what CST calls the Dilemma of Trajectory helps us make sense of many of the most confusing, and often disturbing phenomena of our time.[40] Others are more broadly philosophical. For example, here I've made reference to the "crux" and "multiplicity" aspects of truth and hinted at how the terms come to have fundamentally different implications

---

40 This is particularly so when combined with a further notion, what CST calls Transitional Absurdity. (See Chapter Three.)

with Cultural Maturity's cognitive changes. I've also described how recognizing Separation Fallacies, Unity Fallacies, and Compromise Fallacies can help us appreciate when our thinking may fall short of what is needed.

It is important in getting started to recognize what Creative Systems Theory concepts are good for and what they are not. Their contribution lies with questions of underlying pattern. Much in the particulars that we observe may have different origins. For example, personality style differences explain only part of why a person may act the way he or she does. As important are personal idiosyncrasies and life events that have nothing to do with temperament—or anything else a creative perspective has much to say about. And while aspects of what we see in a culture's artistic forms, religious beliefs, and governmental structures reflect cultural stage, as much is a result of more particular historical events and, again, numerous effects for which creative mechanisms at any level play little if any significant role.

But, limitations acknowledged, Creative Systems Theory concepts represent a powerfully useful set of tools. The recognition of underlying patterns is often what is most missing in modern thought. When our concern is purpose—as it must more and more be today as traditional guideposts fail us—questions of how experience organizes necessarily move to the forefront. Recognition of organizing patterns provides the big picture that allows us to make our choices about particulars in ultimately useful ways.

What Makes Culturally Mature Conception a Challenge— Including One More Specific "Dilemma"

I've suggested multiple factors that make culturally mature concepts such as the ideas of Creative Systems Theory more challenging to understand than we might anticipate. One is the simple fact that we are dealing with ideas that are necessarily at least a bit ahead of their time. I've described how the degree to which this can be the case has often surprised (and sometimes frustrated) me over the course of the theory's development. While it is very much true that culturally mature perspective ultimately represents common sense, we can't escape that this is a maturity of common sense that before now has neither been needed nor been possible—and that today remains unusual.

Related is how whole-box-of-crayons systemic conception necessarily asks more of us than familiar ways of understanding. Right off, it requires that we step beyond the single-crayon conclusions of ideology—and this includes ideology of all sorts. More beneath the surface, there is the way in which conclusions require that we draw on all of intelligence's multiplicity. This alone means culturally mature understanding challenges the basic assumptions of the larger part of academic thought. In chapters ahead, we will see how every Creative Systems notion necessarily draws on the entirety of our whole-box-of-crayons systemic complexity.

An additional CST conceptual "dilemma," what the theory calls the Dilemma of Representation, is important to note in getting started both because it adds to understanding's challenge and because of the further insight it provides into how that challenge can be effectively met. The Dilemma of Representation describes how neither language as we conventionally use it nor traditional pictorial representation can wholly capture any culturally mature concept. It's a result that follows from the fully encompassing nature of whole-box-of-crayons systemic perspective.

It is easy to miss how this might be the case with language, but the conundrum follows directly from this chapter's introductory reflections. Conventional usage tends to be mechanistic. When we speak, the underlying causalities are most often of the basic heroic, cause-and-effect sort. Nouns act as subjects to objects and verbs describe the actions and reactions. More poetic language might seem to address this deficiency, but by itself it gets us no closer. It draws most often on the complementary romantic causality of connectedness and oneness—"a rose is a rose."

I often use language in somewhat unconventional ways in response to these limitations. At the least, I am more likely to use metaphors (drawing on imaginal intelligence) and figures of speech (an aspect of language that taps into body experience) than do most writers of more conceptual work. Often my writing can seem at once poetry and prose. I do my best to have my use of language reflect causality of a more systemic—and specifically creative—sort.

Pictorial depiction ultimately presents the same kind of quandary. Visual images are limited to two or at best three dimensions of representation. It is possible to suggest more, but only that, and without some added understanding ahead of time, it can be hard to grasp just what is being implied. CST uses the term "three-plus" representation to describe depiction that makes at least a start. In some way, such depiction uses three dimensions of expression to communicate something for which simple pictorial representation is not sufficient.

I'm always delighted when I hit upon an image that does at least a "good enough" job of representing culturally mature understanding. I will draw on a handful in this book. Each of these "three-plus" representations incorporates some "sleight of hand," some trick that helps make the needed leap.

Fig. 1-3. Cultural Maturity's Threshold

One is the image I implied in my speaking of a threshold marking the transition from modern age belief into culturally mature territory. Note how the image of a threshold communicates a result that might at first seem a contradiction. Stepping over that threshold is about nothing more than continuing on as before. And at once it results in a wholly new world of experience. We find this kind of result with major breakpoints in any developmental process. But we aren't used to thinking in developmental terms.

Another such image is the box-of-crayons depiction I introduced in this chapter. Again we find a result that might at first seem contradictory.

CREATIVE SYSTEMS THEORY 51

The box-of-crayons image at once highlights real difference—the separate crayons—and how differences, when used together consciously, can result in a more integrative kind of understanding. The image also highlights how a picture that might initially seem static produces a result that is inherently dynamic. The fact that the crayons' various hues are not just different, but different in ways that are creatively related, is what produces the needed more dynamic result.

In pages ahead, I will make use of a couple of additional representations that more specifically address the changes that produce culturally mature perspective. A diagram I will introduce in Chapter Two contrasts Modern Age from-a-balcony objectivity with Integrative Meta-perspective. Directly depicting Cultural Maturity's new kind of cognitive organization in this way necessarily confronts the Dilemma of Representation—at multiple levels—but the addition of comparison and explanation will work to help fill out our understanding of just what Integrative Meta-perspective involves.

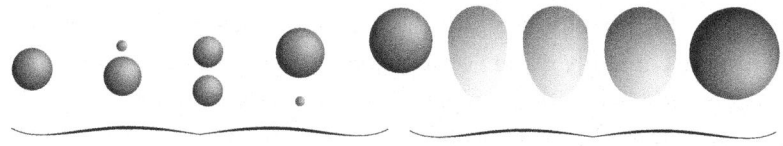

Fig. 1-4. The Creative Function

Also in Chapter Two, I will introduce an image that has particularly central significance in the thinking of CST, what the theory calls The Creative Function. The Creative Function maps formative process at its most fundamental. We will see how there are ways in which the whole of CST, with all of its various kinds of patterning concepts, is mirrored in this single representation.

I will present one further image in Chapter Eight. It has its roots in a technique. CST describes methodologies that support culturally mature perspective. One such methodology, what CST calls Parts Work, provides the most direct and effective way I know to facilitate Cultural Maturity's cognitive reordering. Parts Work engages various systemic aspects like characters in a play. If Parts Work is done well and a person is ready, the approach provides almost no option but to entertain more culturally mature ways of thinking and acting. We can think of the result with Parts Work as a kind of "cognitive rewiring." Chapter Eight provides "before" and "after" "wiring diagrams" for just what happens when Parts Work is done successfully.

More Simplicity and Complexity

Several times I've noted how results with culturally mature conception can at first seem contradictory or paradoxical. I'm very specifically not suggesting that outcomes are obscure or mysterious. Rather, I'm making reference to a characteristic of any understanding that is systemic in the whole-box-of-crayons, life-acknowledging, change-permeated sense that is our interest. The fact that the results might seem contradictory follows from the simple fact that Integrative Meta-perspective juxtaposes opposite truths neither of which themselves can capture the whole of understanding. Every culturally mature concept is at some level paradoxical/contradictory in this sense.

Returning to a key apparent paradox that I observed early on provides a good conclusion for this chapter's introductory reflections. We can think of culturally mature conception as at once more complex than the modern age beliefs that it replaces, and also simpler. This recognition helps put Cultural Maturity's challenge as a whole in perspective. It also provides added insight into how addressing that challenge effectively may be more in the cards than we might imagine, given all that it asks of us.

The complexity part of the apparent paradox is easiest to grasp. Certainly such thinking pushes into new territories of understanding. In addition, with particular questions it requires us to take much more into account than is generally our practice—both more in the world around us and more aspects of ourselves. And the fact that culturally mature perspective is as encompassing as it is—there is pretty much no sphere of understanding that it doesn't in potential at least touch on—further adds to the complexity. Add CST patterning concepts, and the complexity side of things becomes even more explicit. Arguably the theory is quite specifically about understanding and representing complexity.

But we can learn just as much from better appreciating the simplicity side of things. I've previously noted a handful of results that can make culturally mature understanding at least more accessible than we might imagine. One is just that such ideas are timely. If CST is accurate, it reflects the kind of thinking that should more and more seem like common sense in times ahead. There is also how, in being more complete, culturally mature perspective better captures what is simply true. And CST pattern concepts provide an important exclamation point. CST's more systemic notions often make it possible to capture complex interrelationships with single-brushstroke observations.

When it comes specifically to Creative Systems Theory, one recognition highlights the simplicity side of the apparent paradox in a particularly provocative way. It turns out that we can understand the whole of the theory as a response to a single question: How does our understanding of the human experience change when we recognize that human intelligence organizes creatively? Every one of CST's concepts follows directly from attempting to answer this simple question. Note that this fact, by creating separation between the theory's ideas and the beliefs of its author, also invites others to contribute to the theory's evolution. Anyone can take that core question and argue for particular implications.

The fact that all of CST's distinctions follow from the nature of formative process also results in an important practical kind of simplicity. Learning how to make one kind of discernment takes us a long way toward understanding how to make them all. And, if CST is right, that single fundamental patterning dynamic organizes how we think. At some level—though less consciously—we've been making these kinds of distinctions since our species' beginnings.

CST goes on to argue that such patterning is not only familiar, in a sense it is almost inevitable. It follows directly from the fact of conscious awareness and its purpose, that we might be "toolmakers," creative at a new depth and constancy. Such patterning is not some invention of conscious awareness, a handy choreography designed for that task. Rather, it comes with the creative territory. Any formative process follows a predictable progression. There really aren't other ways to go about it. Be toolmakers and this is pretty much how it has to work.

CHAPTER TWO

Integrative Meta-Perspective and the Power of a Creative Frame

I've introduced how Creative Systems Theory views culture's story as having chapters, identifiable "developmental" stages. Cultural chapters are distinguished ultimately not just by differing beliefs and values, but by the kinds of cognitive organization that underlie their assumptions. As I've described, CST claims that a specific kind of cognitive organization—what it calls Integrative Meta-perspective—defines our time's particular developmental challenge.

The theory calls the sort of thinking on which each of these conclusions is based creative Patterning in Time. Here, to more solidly establish the foundation for the theory's Patterning in Time observations, I will more directly address Integrative Meta-perspective and how it alters the ways we think and act. We will examine how Integrative Meta-perspective contrasts with the kind of cognitive organization that has produced Modern Age belief. We will also look at how one outcome is the kind of systemic understanding that CST draws on and that will be required if we are to effectively address challenges ahead. And, in particular, we will reflect on how a key result is the ability to understand change in human systems in more dynamic and encompassing ways.

We've already made a start with understanding Integrative Meta-perspective and where it takes us. I've described how Cultural Maturity's cognitive reordering offers that we might draw more consciously on the whole of who we are. I've also observed how one consequence is the possibility of understanding that is systemic in the sense needed to address the fact that we are living beings, and in particular human beings. And I've at least introduced Integrative Meta-perspective's relationship to a creative frame, how in drawing on the diverse aspects of cognition's complexity we are also drawing on the source of our audacious toolmaking, meaning-making capacities.

We aren't used to thinking of social/cultural change in cognitive terms. That I might I'm sure comes in part from the fact that I am a psychiatrist as well as a futurist. In work with individuals, I'm used to thinking about change not just in terms of behavior, but in relationship to psychological development. I am also used to thinking about critical points in psychological development in terms of underlying cognitive changes. It was not a major leap for me to start thinking about large-scale societal changes in developmental/cognitive terms.

The two ways of thinking about cognition's complexity that I used to introduce the idea of a creative frame in the previous chapter—the fact that intelligence has multiple aspects and the role of polarity in how we think—will have central roles with this chapter's inquiry. We will look at how better understanding intelligence and polarity each helps us make sense of Integrative Meta-perspective and what about it is new. We will also examine how bringing culturally mature perspective to these two aspects of our cognitive complexity provides important insight into creative organization—just how it works, and how an appreciation for how it works can serve as the basis for new ways of understanding.

The Patterning in Time reflections in this chapter and the next will help us in essential ways. When combined with the previous chapter's descriptions of essential challenges and needed new skills and capacities, they make the argument for Cultural Maturity's necessary "growing up" as a species particularly hard to refute. They also more clearly cement the relationship between the concept of Cultural Maturity and the power of a creative frame. We will see how the concept of Cultural Maturity makes little sense if culture's story is not ordered developmentally, and ordered in some way at least similar to what CST Patterning in Time notions predict. We will also see how the idea that human experience is creatively ordered becomes almost self-evident with a close look at the cognitive mechanisms that make us who we are.

The fact that we can understand Cultural Maturity and the possibility of ideas like those of CST in terms of developmentally predicted cognitive changes also has important, more general kinds of implications as far as the future. It supports being legitimately hopeful about what may lie ahead. I've argued that without Cultural Maturity's changes it is hard to imagine an ultimately positive—or even simply survivable—human future. If Cultural Maturity's necessary "growing up" as a species was something we needed to invent, I would not be optimistic. But if it is a product of cognitive changes that as potential are built into who we are, then the likelihood that we can thrive and prosper in times ahead increases significantly.

Integrative Meta-Perspective and Intelligence's Multiplicity

The more complex picture of intelligence that comes with Cultural Maturity's changes is sufficiently central to these reflections that I will take the time here for some extended reflection. I've described the key role that the recognition of intelligence's multiplicity played in Creative Systems Theory's original insights. The observation that human intelligence has multiple aspects provides one of the best ways to make sense of Integrative Meta-perspective and where it takes us. It also provides some of the best evidence for the power of a creative frame.

We've made a good start with the topic. I've described how intelligence has other dimensions besides the rational, some more emotional or symbolic, others more sensory. And I've tied the needed new relationship to intelligence's multiplicity to Cultural Maturity's cognitive reordering. I've described how Integrative Meta-perspective alerts us to the fact that more is involved in how we think than we may have assumed. And I've pointed toward how it makes it possible to apply our multiple intelligences in newly conscious and integrated ways. The kind of thinking this book is about is one result.

Appreciating just how this works begins with the recognition noted earlier that Integrative Meta-perspective involves two almost opposite processes. We see both of these processes, simply at different scales of significance, with personal maturity and Cultural Maturity. The first produces greater awareness, a more complete kind of stepping back. The second produces the new depth of engagement needed if the result is to be not just further abstraction, but the deeply embodied kind of understanding that is necessary for mature—wise—decision-making. Each of these processes is new, the first certainly in its implications, the second more fundamentally. And each can be usefully understood in terms of intelligence's multiplicity.

The first kind of process, that more complete stepping back, differs from what we have seen in times past, at least in all it involves. With Cultural Maturity we become newly able to step back from ourselves as cultural beings—leave behind the parental assumptions and mythologized truths of times past. We also step back from aspects of ourselves, including past ways of knowing, that in times past did not allow such perspective.

Modern Age thought similarly had its origins in a new kind of cognitive orientation, and stepping back from previous ways of knowing was similarly a big part of it. We became newly able to step back from the more mystical sensibilities that had given us the beliefs of the Middle Ages. At the same time, rationality assumed a newly central significance. With Enlightenment/Age of Reason belief, the rational came to stand clearly separate from the other aspects of intelligence. It also became specifically allied with conscious awareness. The resulting as-if-from-a-balcony sense of clarity and objectivity, along with the new belief in the individual as logical choice-maker that came as a consequence, can be thought of as producing all of the great advances of modern times.

While Enlightenment perspective was a grand achievement, Integrative Meta-perspective represents a wholly different kind of accomplishment. To start, it involves a more complete kind of stepping back. With Cultural Maturity's cognitive reordering, awareness comes to stand more fully separate from the whole of our intelligence's systemic complexity—including the rational. Integrative Meta-perspective offers that we might step back equally from aspects of ourselves that before we might have treated as objective and those that we before thought of as subjective. In the process, it offers that we might better step back from the whole systemic box of crayons, whatever our concern.

Importantly, Cultural Maturity's cognitive reordering doesn't stop with such stepping back. The further changes that come with Integrative Meta-perspective's second kind of process are not just different from what we have known, they find no parallel at all in earlier developmental stages. Along with that more complete stepping back, Integrative Meta-perspective engages all of who we are with a new depth. It involves a newly possible connectedness with the full complexity of human experience. The result is Integrative Meta-perspective's both more encompassing and more fully embodied relationship with ourselves and our worlds.

Just what exactly do we newly engage with? We will see how what we engage with ultimately is the whole of ourselves as systems. But for now it works to keep things simple and continue to focus on intelligence's multiplicity. We more deeply draw on the whole of intelligence—all the diverse aspects of how we make sense of things.

Integrative Meta-perspective involves the conscious involvement of more aspects of intelligence—more of our diverse ways of knowing—than before we've applied in one place. It involves thinking in a rational sense—indeed, it expands rationality's role. But just as much it requires that we more directly plumb the more feeling, imagining, and sensing aspects of who we are. And this is so just as much for the most rigorous of hard theory as when our concerns are more personal. The image in Fig. 2-1 contrasts the cognitive structures that give us Enlightenment objectivity and from-a-balcony perspective with culturally mature awareness and Integrative Meta-perspective.

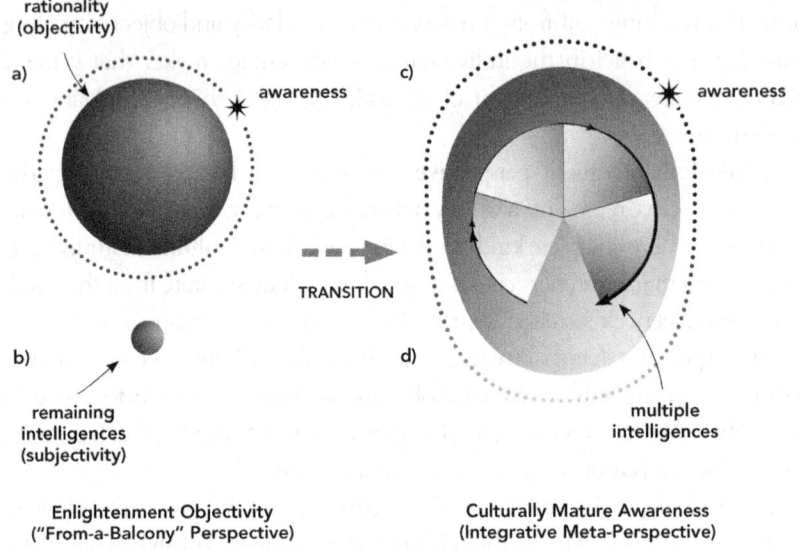

a) Rational intelligence (allied with awareness to produce from-a-balcony objectivity)
b) The subjective (all remaining intelligences as experienced in Modern Age reality)
c) < ------ * --------- >   Culturally mature awareness in its various more and less conscious permutations[1]
d) Multiple intelligences (made newly explicit with culturally mature perspective)

Fig. 2-1. Cultural Maturity's Cognitive Reordering[2]

In a more limited sense, we have always drawn on multiple aspects of intelligence. In doing a math problem, talking with a friend, or painting a

---

1 Being maturely conscious is not the same as being conscious of everything. Different intelligences require different degrees of conscious involvement.

2 As we will see later in this chapter, the relationship of poles on the left side of the diagram reflects what we find with Modern Age dynamics.

picture, we tap very different parts of our neurology. But Integrative Meta-perspective involves more than just this. Culturally mature understanding consciously links facts with feelings, the workings of the imagination with more practical considerations, and observations of the mind with things that only our bodies can know. It explicitly draws on the whole of ourselves as cognitive systems. It is this that produces the possibility of thinking with the needed new kind of systemic sophistication.

Making analogy with personal psychological development helps clarify the relationship between Integrative Meta-perspective's more complete picture of intelligence and the demands of our time in culture. The fact that our thinking in life's later years can become more nuanced is similarly a product not just of how we think, but of what we think with. Knowledge can be articulated quite well by the intellect alone. But wisdom requires a more fully embodied kind of intelligence, one that better draws on the whole of our cognitive complexity. Wisdom results not just because we better include all the aspects of our questions, but also because, when seeking answers, we don't leave out essential parts of ourselves. If the concept of Cultural Maturity is correct, we should expect an analogous result at a species level.

It is a result that will be more and more critical in times ahead. Culturally mature perspective makes clear that If we limit ourselves to the rational, the life-acknowledging kinds of understanding needed for good future decision-making will elude us—in isolation, our intellect knows only an engineering world. And this expanded picture of intelligence raises intriguing questions about more than just thought. Our intelligences represent not only the ways in which we think, but the various lenses and filters through which we discern and make sense of our worlds (and ultimately ourselves). A more differentiated picture of intelligence asks that we revisit all manner of assumptions that before we have left unquestioned. Our perceptions must suddenly always be understood in relation to the sensibilities through which they are organized and interpreted.

Rethinking Intelligence

Shortly we will turn more specifically to the creative implications of intelligence's new picture. But before we go there, we should first reflect more generally on just what is becoming different in our understanding of intelligence. The recognition that rational discourse is not by itself sufficient for culturally mature understanding can at first be disorienting—we like to believe that being smart and thinking hard enough will get us to the truth. And we tend to believe that when we are not wholly rational, we are less exact. But success is a great motivator. We find that when we apply the whole of our cognitive complexity in the needed more conscious and integrative fashion, new, even more precise ways of thinking become available to us. We also become able to grasp answers to questions that before have eluded us.

At the time of the initial insights that led to the development of CST, changes in how people thought about intelligence were just beginning. I recognized then not just that thinking about intelligence in more encompassing ways was going to be increasingly important, but that I would need to give special attention to intelligence's more creatively germinal dimensions. People are rarely very conscious of intelligence's more body- and imagination-related aspects at our time in culture, and if they are, they tend not to really think of them as intelligence.

It was this second recognition that drew me to Joseph Campbell, with his keen understanding of symbol and myth. It also motivated me to study with practitioners who were attempting to bring the body more directly into the psychotherapeutic process.[3] I wanted to understand as deeply as possible just what each intelligence brings to understanding—including those we have tended most to keep at arm's length—and how our various intelligences work together to make us who we are.

Over the last century, we've made significant steps toward acknowledging the need for a larger picture of intelligence. We hear educators debating whether IQ adequately measures the whole of intelligence. Medicine is beginning to recognize how mind and body, far from being separate worlds, interlink through a complex array of communications molecules. And we find intelligence's traditional picture challenged even in the hardest of the hard sciences. I think of physicist Niels Bohr's famous assertion that, "when it comes to atoms, language can be used only as in poetry."

---

[3] Most notably Stanley Keleman, an earlier innovator in the "bioenergetic" approach to body psychology. See Stanley Keleman, *Your Body Speaks Its Mind*, Center Press, 1981.

We've also seen important efforts toward delineating today's needed more differentiated (and integrated) picture of intelligence's workings. The neurosciences have replaced old images of a single managerial, rational brain with a view that recognizes multiple quasi-independent "brains"—in one familiar interpretation, a reptilian brain and a mammalian brain, capped with that thin outer cerebral layer in which we humans take special and appropriate pride. Educational theorists offer an array of interpretations, the most well known being Howard Gardner's eight-part smorgasbord of intelligences—linguistic, musical, mathematical, spatial, kinesthetic, interpersonal, intra-personal, and naturalistic.[4] The popular assertion that we need to think with "both sides of the brain," while neurologically simplistic, draws our attention to how the task is not just to have lots of intelligences at our disposal, but to find ways in which various aspects of how we make sense of things might more consciously work together.

The relationship between Integrative Meta-perspective and intelligence's multiplicity provides a further way to distinguish culturally mature thought from other approaches to understanding. This difference is most obvious when contrasting Integrative Meta-perspective with the rationality-based assumptions of engineering models. But we can also contrast more imagination- and emotion-based Modern Age belief systems such as those we find with romanticism and with more humanistic inclinations. And intelligence's role also helps us distinguish culturally mature perspective from more recent approaches to understanding.

I've made reference to how postmodern thought by itself fails to provide what is needed going forward. Postmodern thinking successfully takes on the first half of Integrative Meta-perspective's two-part process—the stepping back part. Where it fails is that it stops short of engaging intelligence in the deeper, more integrative way that new, more complex and complete ways of understanding require. The fact that postmodern conclusions too often leave us wandering with only vague relativities to guide us is what we would expect. If we are to make the discernments necessary to effectively make our way, we need, in addition, Integrative Meta-perspective's new and deeper engagement with intelligence's multiplicity.

---

4 Howard Gardner, *Frames of Mind: The Theory of Multiple Intelligences*, Basic Books, 2011.

Creativity and Ways of Knowing

Creative Systems Theory's approach to thinking about intelligence's multiplicity represents only one strategy, but it proves especially useful for our purposes. I've proposed that our toolmaking nature means that human intelligence must, at the least, effectively support creative/formative process. CST goes on to describe how our various intelligences—or we might say "sensibilities," to better reflect all they encompass—relate in specifically creative ways. It delineates how particular ways of knowing, and particular relationships between ways of knowing, predominate at specific times in any human developmental process. It also ties the underlying structures of intelligence to patterns we see in how human systems change—thereby both helping us better understand change and hinting at the possibility of being more intelligent, and even wise, in the face of change.[5]

We should start by briefly examining creative organization most generally and adding some further, more specific language. In Chapter One, I made reference to how we see two different kinds of processes over the course of any creative dynamic. CST speaks of any formative process as having a Differentiation Phase and an Integration Phase. During the Differentiation Phase, newly created form is generated, splits off from its original context, develops, and with time takes fully realized form. With creative process's Integration Phase, the newly created entity reengages with its original context, becoming in the process "second nature," now part of a newly expanded whole.

CST identifies specific stages during the Differentiation Phase—a time of incubation, a time of first inspiration, a time when new form is made manifest, and a time of completion, of finishing and polishing. With formative process's Integration Phase, the stages are more variable in how they manifest, but it is with this second half of the creative cycle that we gradually become capable of fully seeing what we have been up to and to engaging the task from the whole of who we are (including the whole of intelligence).

The theory identifies four basic types of intelligence, what for ease of understanding I've referred to simply as body intelligence, the imaginal,

---

5 Creative Systems Theory's picture of multiple intelligences is unusual both for its emphasis on change and for the attention it gives to how various cognitive aspects work together.

the emotional, and the rational. Shortly, I will introduce more formal language and also expand on how we think about each kind of intelligence. But at this point, familiar terms and associations will suffice.

CST proposes that these different ways of knowing represent not just diverse approaches to processing information, but also the windows through which we make sense of our worlds and the formative tendencies that lead us to shape our worlds in the ways that we do. The theory also describes how these various intelligences work together in ways that are not just collaborative,[6] but that directly support creative change.

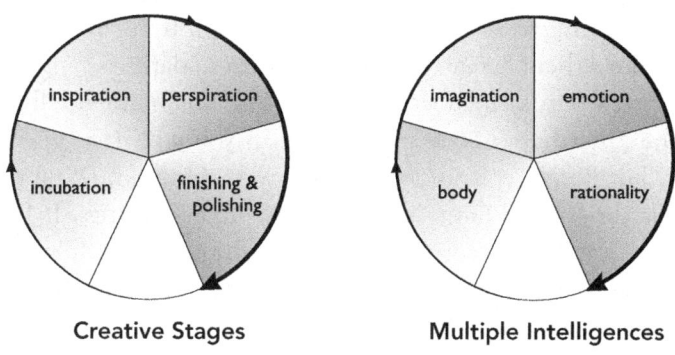

Fig. 2-2. Formative Process and Intelligence's Multiplicity

Our various modes of intelligence, juxtaposed like colors on a color wheel, function together as creativity's mechanism. That wheel, like the wheel of a car or a Ferris wheel, is continually turning, continually in motion. The way the various facets of intelligence are juxtaposed makes change, and specifically purposeful change, inherent to

---

6 To say that our diverse intelligences work in ways that are collaborative is not to say that they don't at times work at cross purposes to one another. Often they arrive at conflicting conclusions—sometimes because they simply do, but also often because conflict is a natural and necessary part of an underlying developmental dynamic. For example, internal wars between thoughts and emotions play an essential role in the developmental tasks of adolescence.

our natures. The diagram in Figure 2-2 depicts these links between intelligence's multiplicity and the stages of formative process.

A brief look at a single creative process—let's take as an example the writing of a book such as this—helps clarify this result. In subtly overlapping and multilayered ways, the process by which a book comes to be takes me through a progression of creative stages and associated sensibilities. Creative processes unfold in varied ways, but the following outline is generally representative:

Creativity's "Incubation" Stage (and Body Intelligence)

Before I begin to write, my sense of a book may be murky at best. I can be aware that I have ideas I want to communicate but have only the most beginning sense of just what ideas I want to include or how I want to address them. Creative processes begin in darkness.

This is creativity's "incubation" stage. The dominant intelligence here is the kinesthetic, body intelligence, if you will. It is like I am pregnant, but don't yet know with what. What I do know takes the form of "inklings" and faint "glimmerings," inner sensings. If I want to feed this part of the creative process, I do things that help me to be reflective and to connect in my body. I take a long walk in the woods, draw a warm bath, build a fire in the fireplace.

Creativity's "Inspiration" Stage (and Imaginal Intelligence)

Creativity's second stage propels the new thing created out of darkness into first light. I begin to have "ahas"—my mind floods with notions about what I might express in the book and possible approaches for expression. Some of these first insights take the form of thoughts. Others manifest more as images or metaphors. In this "inspiration" stage, the dominant intelligence is the imaginal—that which most defines art, myth, and the let's-pretend world of young children. The products of this period in the creative process may appear suddenly— like Archimedes's "eureka"—or they may come more subtly and gradually. It is this stage, and this part of our larger sensibility, that we tend to most traditionally associate with things creative.[7]

---

7 Earlier I observed that contributions from the arts often anticipate later cultural innovations. Because the imaginal indirectly anticipates final form, there is a sense in which it presages fact. I am reminded of Rainer Maria Rilke's assertion that "The future enters into us in order to transform

Creativity's "Perspiration" Stage (and Emotional Intelligence)

The next stage leaves behind the realm of first possibilities and takes us into the world of manifest form. With the book, I may try out specific structural approaches. And I get down to the hard work of writing and revising—and writing and revising some more. This is creation's "perspiration" stage. The dominant intelligence is different still, more emotional and visceral—the intelligence of heart and guts. It is here that we confront the hard work of finding the right approach and the most satisfying means of expression. We also confront limits to our skills and are challenged to push beyond them. The perspiration stage tends to bring a new moral commitment and emotional edginess. We must compassionately but unswervingly confront what we have created if it is to stand the test of time.

Creativity's "Finishing and Polishing" Stage (and Rational Intelligence)

Generativity's fourth stage is more concerned with detail and refinement. Although the book's basic form is established, much yet remains to do. Both the book's ideas and how they are expressed need a more fine-toothed examination. Rational intelligence orders this "finishing and polishing" stage. This period is more conscious and more concerned with aesthetic precision than the periods previous. It is also more concerned with audience and outcome. It brings final focus to the creative work, and offers the clarity of thought and nuances of style needed for effective communication.

Creative Integration (and Integrative/Systemic Intelligence)

Formative process's further stages get us a bit ahead of ourselves. But their existence has been implied with previous reflections on culturally mature perspective. Creative expression is often placed in the world at this point. But a further stage—or more accurately, an additional series of stages—remains. These stages are as important as any of the others—and of particular significance to our understanding of culturally mature perspective. Creative Systems Theory calls this further generative sequence *Creative Integration*.

---

us long before it happens"—an observation about both creative process and understanding's broader generativity.

With the process of refinement complete, we can now step back from the work and appreciate it with new perspective. We become better able to recognize the relationship of one part to another. And we become more able to appreciate the relationship of the work to its creative contexts, to ourselves and to the time and place in which it was created. We might call creativity's integrative stages the time of seasoning or ripening.[8]

With Creative Integration we engage the second half of formative process. Creative Integration forms a complement to the more differentiation-defined tasks of earlier stages. With regard to our multiple intelligences, Creative Integration is about learning to use our diverse ways of knowing more consciously together. It is about applying our intelligences in various combinations and balances as time and situation warrant, and about a growing ability not just to engage the work as a whole, but to draw on ourselves as a whole in relationship to it. Because wholeness is where we started—before the disruptive birth of new creation—in a certain sense Creative Integration returns us to where we began. But just as much, this new place could not be more different. The fact of new creation changes everything.[9]

---

8 Sometimes this set of stages takes place well after a work has taken expression. When this is the case, its underlying emphasis tends to be more on maturity in the creator's life than on the process of the specific work, or about finding mature expression in a body of work. At other times, especially when the work represents mature stages in the creator's efforts, it may manifest fully as a part of the creative process that brings a work into being. This is particularly likely when the needed maturity is cultural as well as personal. In either case, these stages draw on intelligence as a (now more creatively integrated) whole.

9 In Chapter Nine I will draw on a consequence of this specifically creative picture of intelligence that has important implications for the future. Two facts—that it is inherently generative and that it includes aspects that are as concerned with how we are connected as how we are separate—means that just by how our cognitive processes work we are moral/ethical beings. We are concerned with betterment, and also with things larger than ourselves along with individual well-being. I will make reference to this consequence in distinguishing human intelligence from artificial intelligence, and also in reflecting further on whether we should be hopeful as we look to the future.

CST proposes that these intelligence-related observations pertain ultimately to the relationship between intelligence and human experience as a whole. It describes how the same general progression of sensibilities that we see with a creative project orders the creative growth of all human systems. The theory describes how we see similar patterns at all levels—from the growth of an individual, to the development of an organization, to culture and its evolution. A few snapshots:

The same bodily intelligence that orders creative "incubation" plays a particularly prominent role in the infant's rhythmic world of movement, touch, and taste. The realities of early tribal cultures also draw deeply on body sensibilities. Truth in tribal societies is synonymous with the rhythms of nature and, through dance, song, story, and drumbeat, with the body of the tribe.

The same imaginal intelligence that we saw ordering creative "inspiration" takes prominence in the play-centered world of the young child. We also hear its voice with particular strength in early civilizations—such as in ancient Greece or Egypt, with the Incas and Aztecs in the Americas, or in the classical East—with their mythic pantheons and great symbolic tales.

The same emotional and moral intelligence that orders creative "perspiration" comes to occupy center stage in adolescence, with its deepening passions and pivotal struggles for identity. It can be felt with particular strength also in the beliefs and values of the European Middle Ages, times marked by feudal struggle and ardent moral conviction (and, today, in places where struggle and conflict seem to be forever recurring).

The same rational intelligence that comes forward for the finishing-and-polishing tasks of creativity takes new prominence in young adulthood, as we strive to create our unique place in the world of adult expectations. This more refined and refining aspect of intelligence stepped to the fore culturally with the Renaissance and the Age of Reason and, in the West, has held sway into modern times.

Of particular pertinence to the concept of Cultural Maturity, the same more consciously integrative intelligence that we see in the "seasoning" stage of a creative act orders the unique developmental capacities—the wisdom—of a lifetime's second half. And we can see this same more integrative relationship with intelligence just beneath the surface in our current cultural stage in the West in the advances that have most transformed understanding through the last century.

We associate the Age of Reason with Descartes's assertion that "I think, therefore I am." We could make a parallel assertion for each of these other cultural stages: "I am embodied, therefore I am"; "I imagine, therefore I am"; "I am a moral being, therefore I am"; and, if the concept of Cultural Maturity is accurate, "I understand maturely and systemically—with the whole of myself—therefore I am." The concept of Cultural Maturity also proposes that these observations about intelligence's creative workings have been possible because such consciously integrative dynamics are beginning to reorder how today we think and perceive.

The importance of bringing the whole of intelligence to bear applies not just to thinking about change, but equally to each of the kinds of patterning discernments that Creative Systems Theory highlights. Certainly we see this with what CST calls Whole-Person/Whole-System distinctions. We can get our minds around the larger whole of any systemic truth only to the degree to which we can engage experience with the whole of who we are as systems. And the same conclusion applies to more detailed pattern-language distinctions—with the addition that now we draw on the whole of who we are in more differentiated ways. With more here-and-now, Patterning in Space distinctions, the world looks very different depending on which intelligence holds the larger sway. And this way it applies to more temporal, Patterning in Time distinctions is particularly consequential for our inquiry. Developmental/evolutionary perspective makes little sense without an appreciation for multiple intelligences and how they shape who we are.

A Closer Look at Intelligence's Multiplicity

Since the whole notion that intelligence has multiple aspects can be foreign to usual understanding—and the implications are so pivotal—it is worth taking the time to look at each of the four kinds of intelligence I've made reference to more closely. I first attempted to articulate what makes each aspect of intelligence particular and the

CREATIVE SYSTEMS THEORY

role each plays in the workings of formative process in The Creative Imperative. Since I've not since done a better job—particularly with those nonrational aspects (where language most easily escapes us)—I will excerpt directly from it.

I've noted that CST uses more formal language when describing body, imaginal, emotional, and rational ways of knowing. I will apply the more formal terms here: Somatic/Kinesthetic Intelligence, Symbolic/Imaginal Intelligence, Emotional/Moral Intelligence, and Rational/Material Intelligence. This more filled-out language helps point toward the complexity of experience that each different kind of intelligence ultimately reflects.

Somatic/kinesthetic Intelligence:

> *God guard me from those thoughts men think*
> *In the mind alone:*
> *He that sings a lasting song*
> *Thinks in a marrow-bone.*
>
> William Butler Yeats

The earliest knowing in any life process is bodily knowing. Body in this most germinal stage in creation is very different from the body as we conceive of it through the isolated and isolating eye of Modern Age understanding. It is much more than simply sensation; also much more than simply anatomy and physiology; and more than one side of an either/or: body versus mind, body versus spirit. In this first stage of formativeness, the body is not something we have, but who we are. It is our intelligence. It is how we organize our experience of both ourselves and our world.

While we don't usually give the knowing of bodily reality much status in formal thought, it has a central place in the concrete experience of our lives. For example, if you say you love someone and you are asked how you know, eventually you will begin to talk in the language of the body. You know you feel love because when you are with that person your "heart" opens, there is a warm expanding in the area of the chest. This experienced "heart" cannot be found by dissection, but it is undeniably very real, very close to what is most essential in us.

This kinesthetic aspect of experience, while often unconscious, can take colorful expression in our figures of speech.[10] We speak of feeling "moved" or "touched," of being "beside ourselves" or feeling that something is "over our heads." And if we take the time, a lot of this sort of experience is available to us consciously. As a simple example, if I pay attention, I recognize that I feel my bodily connection to different people at different times in quite different ways. With one person I may feel it most as a sense of fullness and solidity in my belly or shoulders. With another, I may know it most as a sense of animation in my eyes and face, or erotic arousal in my genitals. With some people, our meeting touches very close to the core of my body; with others, the bodily experience of meeting may feel much more peripheral, more "superficial."[11]

Symbolic/Imaginal Intelligence:

> *Dreams are the true interpreter of our inclinations.*
>
> Michel de Montaigne

---

[10] Note that the phrase "figure of speech' could be thought of as a reference to bodily knowing.

[11] We might commonly think of the word "superficial" as disparaging. Here I use it only to refer to the more surface layers of body experience. See "Creative Evolution and the Body" in Chapter Three for an examination of how, with each creative stage, experience organizes closer to the surface of the body. This kind of recognition will prove particularly important when we turn to kinds of discernments made by the Creative Systems Personality Typology (see Chapter Six).

Symbol—the vehicle of myth, dream, metaphor, and much in artistic expression—also speaks from close to the beginnings of things, but not quite so close. When a storyteller utters the words, "Once upon a time...," it is more than simple convention. The words are a bidding to remember an ancient fecundity and magic.

The symbolic is both the organizing truth and the chief mode of expression in the second major stage of formative process. As myth, it serves as truth's most direct expression in early cultural times. As imagination, it defines the reality of childhood. The symbolic is present in a similar way with the beginnings of any creative task. It organizes reality in the stage of inspiration, that critical time when bubblings from the dream work of the unconscious give us our first visible sense of what is asking to become.

Joseph Campbell described the mythic aspect of the imaginal this way in his book *Myths to Live By*: "It would not be too much to say that myth is the secret opening through which the inexhaustible energies of the cosmos pour into human cultural manifestation. Religion, philosophies, social forms of primitive and historic man, prime discoveries in science and technology, the very dreams that blister sleep boil up from the basic magic ring of myth."[12]

Emotional/Moral intelligence:

> *The perception of beauty is a moral test.*
>
> Henry David Thoreau

The next intelligence, the language of emotions, is more familiar to us than the first two. It is one step closer to the rational sensibilities that today we are most likely to identify with truth. When emotional intelligence is preeminent, life is imbued with a visceral immediacy, and strong ethical and moral responses. We can feel

---

12 Joseph Campbell, *Myths To Live By*, Penguin, 1993.

its presence in the fervencies and allegiances of adolescence. It is there in a similar way in the crusading ardency and codes of honor and chivalry of the Middle Ages. And we see it in the courage to struggle and the devoted commitment necessary to take any personal experience of creative inspiration into manifest form.

While we may tend to be more conscious of emotional/moral intelligence, beginning to think of the affective realm as intelligence also stretches usual understanding. To start, emotional intelligence becomes an integral part not just of our feeling lives, but also of our conceptual understanding. With Modern Age thought, we specifically cleansed the emotions from our theoretical formulations so that our ideas would have the rigor needed for arm's-length understanding.

In addition, we engage the emotional in a deeper sense than we have been accustomed to. The emotional as we have known it in our current stage in culture has been only a faint vestige of the feeling dimension at its full grandeur as a primary organizing reality.

The fact that somehow we must more deeply engage this aspect of ourselves and do so as an integral part of how we understand truth becomes obvious if we examine the issues that now confront us as a species. Solving the dilemmas of our future will require a keen sensitivity to the fact of human relationship and deep levels of personal integrity and ethical responsibility. It is our emotional selves that most appreciate and understand these sorts of concerns.

Rational/Material Intelligence

> *Cogito ergo sum—I think, therefore I am.*
>
> René Descartes

The rational (rational/material intelligence) is what we measure with IQ tests and most engage and reward with formal education.

CREATIVE SYSTEMS THEORY

It is the intelligence of syllogistic logic—if A, then B, then C. In creative work, it comes most strongly to the fore with formative process's time of finishing and polishing. With individual psychological development, it orders adult understanding. In modern times, it represents the kind of cognitive processing that we equate almost exclusively with intelligence.

That we specifically elevate the rational in modern culture doesn't mean that rational processing doesn't have an important place in the cognitive processes of earlier cultural times. But depending on the cultural stage, the underlying premises of our "logic" will have their roots in the pertinent (often decidedly nonrational) organizing sensibilities. In earliest times, for example, it will reflect underlying animistic (body intelligence) assumptions. Imagine two cave dwellers discussing the various creatures depicted on a cave wall.

With Modern Age culture, the underlying premises of our logical assertions come to have their roots as well in rational/material assumptions. Rationality is allied with awareness, and together with it becomes, in effect, final truth. With Modern Age from-a-balcony perspective, the rational sits in polar juxtaposition to the irrational, a catchall category for all the previously reigning intelligences. This supremacy for rational intelligence is regarded as culminating and alters how we understand everything about our worlds. We come to view causality increasingly in terms of actions and their concomitant reactions, identity in terms of what we think, and wealth and progress almost exclusively in terms of material acquisition and technological innovation.

Beyond One Intelligence/One Stage

This expanded picture of intelligence needs one further recognition if it is to adequately capture intelligence's role in formative process. For the most part thus far, to keep things simple, I've spoken as if we can identify each intelligence with a particular creative stage. In fact, each intelligence plays a role at each creative stage. Specific intelligences do most define understanding with each creative stage. But in a manner similar to what I just suggested for the rational, each intelligence also has a part in the workings of each stage, manifesting in a particular and predictable way as an aspect of the larger sensibility that orders that stage's generative task.

We need this further recognition if our thinking is to have any degree of nuance. It will become particularly important in Chapter Three when we begin teasing apart the details of culture's evolution. For now, we can briefly parse the remaining intelligences.

While the intelligence of the body is primary in tribal times, body experience remains distinctly present with the mythic intensities of the early high cultures. And certainly too we find it with the deep moral convictions and emotional allegiances of medieval sensibilities. And while body intelligence's role is least explicit in modern times, where we tend to think of the body primarily in physical terms, certainly it manifests in our sensory worlds, with erotic impulses, and in limited ways with the arts (as a sculptor, I thought of what I did to be primarily an expression of bodily knowing).

We find a related progression with imaginal/symbolic intelligence. The imaginal takes most dominant expression in "inspiration stage" cultural realities, with their pantheons of gods, elaborate mythic tales, and great richnesses of artistic expression. But while imaginal/symbolic intelligence takes a back seat to bodily knowing in tribal times, it nonetheless has an important role then, too, manifesting as animistic imagery, with its clear message of inseparability from nature (think of the evocative power of those cave paintings). With "perspiration stage" times in culture, imaginal/symbolic intelligence takes a secondary role to emotional/moral intelligence's now defining presence, but it continues to contribute. Myth's numinosity gives way to the more explicitly moral sensibilities of legend—think of the medieval tales of the Knights of the Round Table—and while art ceases to be itself a definer of truth, it continues to serve powerfully as a language for religious sensibility. With "finishing and polishing" stage realities, while we still appreciate imaginal/symbolic intelligence—indeed, with the arts, it can have an elevated presence—increasingly its role becomes more decorative. With more popular expression, it takes the form of fantasy.

CREATIVE SYSTEMS THEORY

The same kind of progression also manifests with emotional/moral intelligence. Emotional/moral intelligence plays the most defining role in "perspiration stage" times. But the bond a tribesperson feels with nature or with other members of the tribe clearly has emotional aspects. And certainly the inspired mythic tales of the early high cultures are emotionally evocative. In Modern Age times, anything we would attribute to the humanities as opposed to the sciences or business reflects the emotional as much as the rational. The humanities have less direct influence than their more right-hand complements, and in our time that influence has markedly diminished, but they nonetheless garner respect. The word "sentiment" perhaps best captures this aspect of emotional intelligence.

The chart in Figure 2-3 outlines these relationships. I've indicated the primary intelligences at each stage with an asterisk (*).

Creative Stages:

incubation	inspiration	perspiration	finishing/polishing

Intelligences:

The Body *(Somatic/Kinesthetic Intelligence)*

*creature body	body as mystery	visceral/muscular body	sensory/physical body

The Imaginal *(Imaginal/Symbolic Intelligence)*

animistic imagery	*myth	legend	fantasy

The Emotional *(Emotional/Moral Intelligence)*

felt connectedness	inspired feelings	*visceral emotion	sentiment

The Rational *(Rational/Material Intelligence)*

naturalistic logic	magical logic	moral logic	*material logic

Fig. 2-3. Multiple Intelligences' Multilayered Manifestations[13]

---

13 Finding useful language for these more detailed distinctions presents a challenge, but it is a different kind of challenge than what I've described with the Dilemma of Differentiation—where the basic sort of organization necessarily escapes conventional depiction. The challenge here is a product of two factors

An important outcome when we frame Integrative Meta-perspective in terms of intelligence's multilayered multiplicity again might seem to present a paradox. On one hand, because culturally mature understanding draws on diverse, often conflicting aspects of who we are, its conclusions are going to be less absolute and once-and-for-all than those we are used to. But at the same time, one could argue that the result is more objective than what it replaces. Certainly it is more complete. Enlightenment thought might have claimed ultimate objectivity, but this was in fact objectivity of a most limited sort. Besides leaving culture's parental status untouched, it left experience as a whole divided—objective (in the old sense) set opposed to subjective, mind set opposed to body, thoughts set opposed to feelings (and anything else that does not conform to modernity's rationalist/materialist worldview). We cannot ultimately claim to be objective if we have left out half of the evidence. Culturally mature "objectivity" is of a more specifically whole-box-of-crayons sort.

Integrative Meta-Perspective and Polarity

While drawing on intelligence's multiplicity to fill out the relationship between Integrative Meta-perspective and creative self-organization provides a solid beginning sense of why we experience each creative stage in the particular ways that we do, we could just as well have focused on the workings of polarity. Indeed, more often in my writings I've made polarity the place to start. An understanding

---

in combination: the simple fact that many of these intelligences by their nature tend not to function at the level of language, and the way that modern times can leave us far-distanced from their underlying realities. Language is particularly tricky with body intelligence given that it lies furthest from the more verbal parts of our cognitive functioning. We could also call what here I've called the "creature body" the body of nature or the organic body. We can think of the "body as mystery" alternatively as the inspired body or the energy body. I often call what I have here labeled the "visceral/muscular body" the body of heart and guts. The "sensory/physical body" is both the body of anatomy and physiology and the body of sensation and of appearances. Conventional language tends to work better for the remaining intelligences, but we still often need to stretch conventional usage to get at all that is involved.

of polar dynamics supports the creative nature of change in human systems in a way that is especially concise and clear. It also provides the basis for a particularly accessible way to map the details of creative self-organization.

Here, we've also made a start. In the Preface, I emphasized the importance of leaving behind polarized and polarizing beliefs and tied doing so to the general task of transcending ideology. In Chapter One, I described how our Modern Age story has juxtaposed heroic and romantic narrative and also how Modern Age belief, whatever the sphere, has been dualistic. I also tied polar dynamics both to the challenge of thinking systemically in new ways and to the implications of a creative frame. I described how polarities of all sorts reflect an underlying symmetry and also how the generation of polarity is intrinsic to how creative processes work.

Filling out our understanding of polar dynamics adds to previous more intelligence-related observations at both the largest and smallest of scales. In the big picture, thinking in terms of the evolution of polarity offers an elegantly simple way to make overarching Patterning in Time observations. It helps us tie together different kinds of creative/formative processes. It also helps refine our understanding of just how creative/formative mechanisms work.

Thinking in terms of the evolution of polarity also proves valuable with more specific discernments. For example, thinking in terms of polar relationships brings nuance to our understanding of dynamics that involve projection, as with the reactive, chosen-people/evil-other mechanisms that I referenced in Chapter One. In Chapter Four, I will describe how a similar kind of reincorporating of past polar projections that I proposed would be necessary for the future of international relations will be key to the future of leadership and love.

For this chapter, an understanding of polar dynamics provide an accessible way to appreciate how and why Integrative Meta-perspective alters experience in the ways that I have begun to describe. It will also help more concretely link Cultural Maturity's cognitive changes to creative organization. Creative Systems Theory delineates how, with each stage in culture to this point, we've thought in terms of qualities set in polar juxtaposition. With Cultural Maturity's cognitive reordering, we both step back from and more deeply engage such juxtaposed elements. In the process, we become able to appreciate them as aspects of larger systemic realities. The diagram shown earlier in Figure 2-1 depicts a newly integrative relationship not just to intelligence, but also to polarity.

But we don't need CST's detailed formulations to appreciate the basic relationship between polarity and Integrative Metaperspective—or its pertinence to the future. I structured the whole of my 1991 book *Necessary Wisdom* around the importance of getting our minds around the polar assumptions of times past. There I described a more basic way to think about polarity's changing significance:

> Scott Fitzgerald proposed that the sign of a first-rate intelligence (we might say a mature intelligence) is the ability to hold two contradictory truths simultaneously in mind without going mad. His reference was to personal maturity. But this capacity is such an inescapable part of culturally mature perspective that we could almost say it defines it. One of the most useful ways to think about how Cultural Maturity changes how we understand draws on a basic observation: Needed new understandings of every sort require that our thinking create links, "bridges"—and not just between phenomena we've regarded as different, but often between things that before now we've treated as complete opposites—as polarities.

Note that I put the word "bridging" in quotes. I did so to avoid confusing this result with a couple of more readily understandable outcomes that I described earlier in introducing polar fallacies. "Bridging" as I am using the term is wholly different from an identification with oneness, what we commonly see with more spiritual interpretations. And just as much it is wholly different from averaging or compromise. "Bridging" in this sense is about consciously engaging the larger whole-box-of-crayons picture.

Expanding on the "three-plus" image I used in Chapter One to depict

Cultural Maturity's threshold helps establish this essential difference. Think of the columns on each side of the doorway as polar opposites. The task with "bridging" in this sense is not to join the poles, nor to find some halfway point, but rather to walk through the doorway and into the new territory beyond.

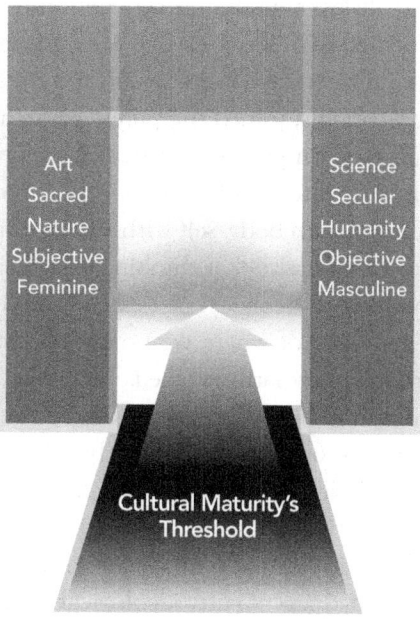

Fig. 2-4. "Bridging" and Cultural Maturity's Threshold

We can think of Cultural Maturity's point of departure as itself a "bridging" dynamic. We step back and see the relationship of culture and the individual in newly encompassing terms. Cultural Maturity bridges ourselves and our societal contexts (or, put another way, ourselves and final truth). It is through this most fundamental bridging that we leave behind society's past parental function.

Such "bridging" is not about culture's role disappearing, as a more postmodern interpretation might suggest. Rather, it is about a new and deeper recognition of how the individual and culture relate—about how, through our thoughts and actions, we create culture, and how personal and cultural realities each inform the other. It is also about making our understanding of both being an individual and being an individual who lives in an interpersonal context more dynamic and complete.

This most encompassing linkage holds within it a multitude of more local "bridgings." Nothing more characterized the last century's defining conceptual advances than how their thinking linked previously unquestioned polar truths. I've noted how physics' new picture provocatively circumscribed the realities of matter and energy, and space and time. (it also bridges the observed with its observer). New understandings in biology linked humankind with the natural world, and by reopening timeless questions about life's origins, joined the purely physical with the organic. And the ideas of modern psychology, neurology, and sociology have provided an increasingly integrated picture of the workings of conscious with unconscious, mind with body, self with society, and more.

It is important to reemphasize that thinking in the language of polarity is not by itself a problem. The fact that today it has very much become a problem is an expression of where we now reside in the story of understanding. In times past, polarity worked. The polar tensions between church and crown in the Middle Ages, for example, were tied intimately to that time's experience of meaning. With the Modern Age—and just as right and timely in their contributions—we saw Descartes's cleaving of truth into separate objective and subjective realities, along with the competing arguments of positivist and romantic worldviews. And while I've highlighted the outmodedness of petty ideological squabbles between political left and political right, I am just as comfortable proposing that such squabbles, in their time, were creative and essential. They then drove the important conversations. The problem is not with polarity itself, but with its inability in our current time to effectively generate truth and meaning.

"Bridging" in the sense that comes with Cultural Maturity's cognitive reordering expands understanding in ways central to this book's argument. Integrative Meta-perspective takes an either/or world and replaces it with a picture that is more multihued and rich in its implications than we could have understood in times past. Thinking that is systemic in the needed more complete sense is an inherent result. We find understanding of just the idea-whose-time-has-come, whole-box-of-crayons sort needed for a vital and healthy future.

A good place to recognize such bridging—and also to appreciate its fundamental newness—is my earlier observation that culturally mature concepts often at first seem contradictory. Polarity-related paradoxes are most obvious with ideas that are not so much about us—for example, with how cutting-edge notions in physics are perfectly comfortable with something being at once a particle and a wave. But as I have suggested, they are just as inescapably present with explicitly human concerns. In Chapter Four, I will describe the important sense in which culturally mature love makes us at once more separate and more deeply connected, and also how culturally mature leadership is both more powerful and more humble than what it replaces.

I've emphasized that such apparent paradox has to do with how we think rather than some mysterious outcome. Polarity's necessary role in cognition's mechanism helps clarify this assertion. When polar dynamics define cognition's primary relationships, we find one of two circumstances. We may recognize the fact of polarity, but fail to appreciate that opposites in any way contradict—as with dualistic thinking. Or we may miss the fact of polarity entirely. We find the latter outcome when we identify with (and idealize) certain polar aspects while projecting (and denigrating) others—as with chosen-people/evil-other dynamics on the global stage.

Stepping over Cultural Maturity's threshold highlights the existence of polarity. It also confronts us with the fact that a polar picture is inadequate. And it alerts us to the fact that the important (more systemic) questions have yet to be asked. As we ask the hard questions and begin to progress into Cultural Maturity's new territory of experience, bit by bit things become more of a whole. Importantly, this is a more dynamic and multifaceted kind of whole than we are used to, one where the seeming contradictions of paradox are not ultimately at odds.[14]

Polarity's "Procreative" Symmetry

To fully appreciate polarity's relationship to creative self-organization,

---

14 With *Necessary Wisdom* and other early writings, I gave particular emphasis to the concept of "bridging" as a way of representing Cultural Maturity's changes. I would often refer to the result as "third space" understanding. But over time, I have found that even with careful clarification, people too easily confuse the concept of bridging with averaging or joining. Thus I am now more apt to use the box-of-crayons metaphor to describe where Integrative Meta-perspective takes us or turn to the language of Parts Work that we will explore in Chapter Eight.

we should first return to the previous chapter's observation that polar relationships reflect a specific kind of symmetry. Put most conceptually, they juxtapose qualities that are defined most by separateness and qualities defined more by connectedness. We tend to think of polarities as contrasting opposite kinds of difference. More fundamentally, they contrast elements that identify most with difference with elements that identify more with oneness.[15]

I've introduced a couple of simpler ways of speaking about this underlying symmetry. We can think of conceptual polarities as having complementary right and left hands. With polarity's right hand, we find harder, commonly more rational, and more clearly delineated qualities. With polarity's left hand, we find qualities of a softer, more poetic, and often more spiritual sort. Facts juxtapose with feelings, mind with body,[16] matter with energy, and so on.

We can also use more psychological language drawn from the study of myth noted earlier and think of polarities as juxtaposing more "archetypally masculine" and more "archetypally feminine" qualities. The gender-linked language can sometimes get in the way, particularly today as women and men each seek to make both poles their own, but the sexual connotations are evocative and in a way particularly pertinent to our inquiry. The relationship between polar extremes becomes explicitly "procreative."

An appreciation for such underlying symmetry assists us most immediately by more explicitly establishing the relationship between polarity and formative process. We can think of more right-hand, archetypally masculine sensibilities and more left-hand, archetypally feminine sensibilities as reflecting the more creatively manifest and creatively germinal aspects of polar relationship. The progression of stages in any creative/formative process can

---

15 This recognition has major implications and can be difficult for many people, at least initially, to get their minds around. It is worth taking a moment to let it sink in.

16 We must be attentive to language when we make such distinctions. For example, with mind and body, what is "left" and what is "right" may differ depending on how we use words. If "mind" refers to the intellect and "body" to our more sensory life, the order in which I listed the terms—mind and body—is consistent with the other polarities mentioned in the sentence. But if we make "mind" that which produces human sentience and "body" simply anatomy, the order is reversed: body and mind.

CREATIVE SYSTEMS THEORY

be understood as an evolving sequence of right-hand/left-hand, archetypally masculine/archetypally feminine polar relationships.

But this recognition of underlying symmetry also has practical applications. Easiest to appreciate is how it helps us flesh out systemic relationships of the here-and-now sort. For example, we can understand a lot about opposing conservative and liberal tendencies in the political arena by thinking of them in terms of juxtaposed archetypally masculine and archetypally feminine tendencies. On the Right we find harder, more difference-biased values—competition in the marketplace, a strong military, the integrity of national borders, and rugged individualism. On the Left we find values of a softer, more relationship-biased sort—identification with the disadvantaged, government as advocate for the common good, environmentalism, and equal rights. It is a simplistic approach that leaves out a lot, but it also provides useful insight. (MSNBC commentator Chris Mathews jokingly referred to the Republican and Democratic parties in the U.S. as the "daddy party" and the "mommy party." This turns out to be a fairly apt shorthand.)[17]

An appreciation of this underlying generative symmetry also helps us with systemic discernments of the more temporal sort. I will draw on one such temporal application extensively in chapters to come. It has critical implications for future well-being. Over the course of any creative/formative process, polar tendencies and their relationships with one another evolve in predictable ways. Early on, left-hand, archetypally feminine sensibilities are most determining. Then, over the course of creative differentiation right-hand/archetypally masculine sensibilities gradually gain the larger influence.

Recognizing that cultural change unfolds in this way provides one of the best ways to understand why we witness what we do with each stage in history, including what we observe today. Through time, we've see a gradual progression from tribal times in which left-hand/archetypally feminine values—connection with nature, tribe, and spirit (values that emphasize oneness)—almost wholly order experience, to a reality in our time in which

---

17 Chapter Six provides a more detailed way of making this kind of distinction by tying this basic observation to personality style differences and the specific ways archetypal qualities manifest with particular personality patterns.

right-hand/archetypally masculine values—individualism, materialism, competition, or the logic of science (values that emphasize separateness)—have come to play the much larger role. Shortly we will see how the place this progression takes us provides one of the most powerful arguments for Cultural Maturity's changes (at least their necessity). We will see, too, how it alerts us to some of the greatest dangers ahead for the species.

Polarity and Creative Self-Organization

When I use polarity to introduce formative process's creative workings, I often start with a provocatively compact observation. We can get most of the way toward understanding Creative Systems Theory as a whole by answering three polarity-related questions: Why do we humans think in the language of polarity in the first place? Why have we now begun to see understanding that "bridges" familiar polar assumptions? And how do we best think about what happens when polarities are "bridged"?

CST's answer to the first question is now familiar. I've proposed that the reason we think in polar terms in the first place is that polarity is essential to the workings of formative process. Creative processes begin in a womb world—in original unity. The newly created thing then buds off from that initial wholeness, creating polarity in the process. Over time, the newly created thing, and polarity with it, evolves and matures, with polarity manifesting in predictable forms with each creative stage. The diagram in Figure 2-5 depicts how polarity evolves over the Differentiation Phase of any formative process.

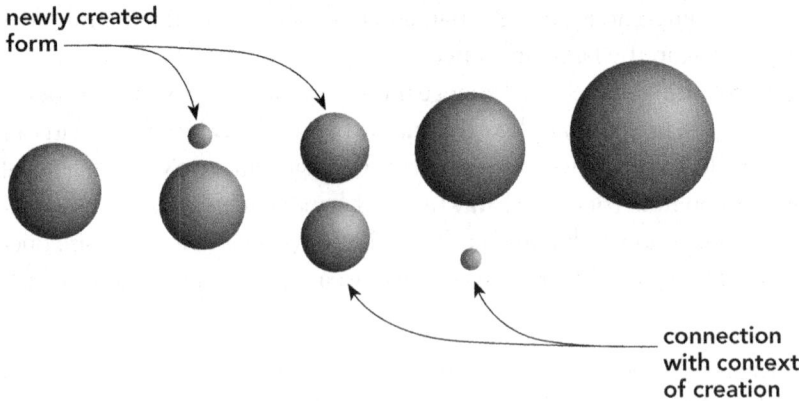

Fig. 2-5. Polarity's Evolution Over the First Half of Formative Process

CREATIVE SYSTEMS THEORY

The recognition that creative poles juxtapose complementary systemic aspects helps fill out this depiction. The more manifest half of any polar pair (the "newly created form," Upper Pole with each creative stage) gives expression to more archetypally masculine qualities. The more germinal half of any polar pair (the "creative context," Lower Pole with each creative stage) gives expression to more archetypally feminine qualities.

A creative frame's answer to why now we might see the "bridging" of past polar assumptions comes with the recognition that the creative stages that bring new creation into being aren't the end of things. Once new possibility has become established, that possibility reengages with the context from which it was born, becoming part of a newly expanded whole. We then experience this now-expanded whole as "second nature"—as the new common sense. The diagram in Figure 2-6 depicts formative process's two halves most simply.

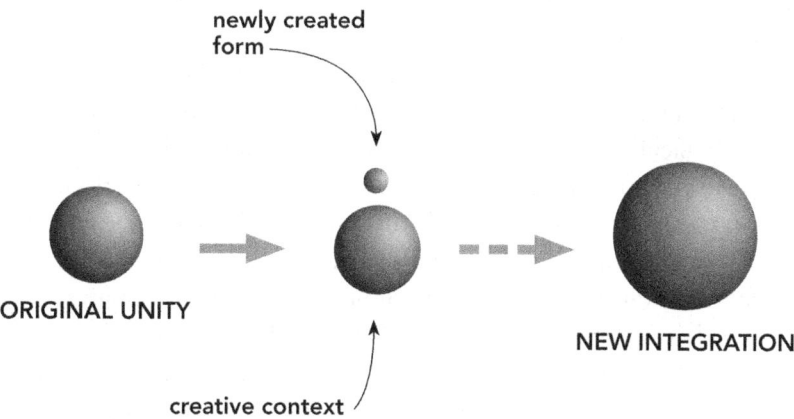

Fig. 2-6. Differentiation and New Integration in Creative/Formative Process

For the answer to the third question, we can turn to any of this book's observations about the changes that come with Cultural Maturity's cognitive reordering. I've proposed that the new ways of thinking and acting needed for the future follow naturally from the more whole-box-of-crayons, polarity-transcending view of the world that comes with Integrative Meta-perspective.

We can witness the same basic progression of polar relationships over the course of any creative/formative process. Formative dynamics begin in oneness, become manifest through polarity, and then reconcile into a larger, more inclusive entirety. With simple creative acts of a personal sort, for example, at first there is only the known. Next comes excitement with a fresh insight's newness. Gradually that insight becomes more distinct and grows and evolves in the process. Then, with time, we begin to experience it differently. We relate to it now as simply one part of a new, expanded me. Similarly, when an innovative idea first arises in a culture, it creates excitement and controversy. It is something new and unique. Then, gradually, having been challenged and having matured, the idea can become an accepted part of a now-expanded cultural reality.

We see a related sequence of creatively related polar dynamics with personal psychological development. With the developmental tasks that define the first half of an individual's life, the underlying impetus with each is toward distinction and the establishing of identity. With childhood we begin discovering who we are, with adolescence we make our first forays into the social world, and during adulthood we establish our unique place in that world. Second-half-of-life maturation involves more specifically integrative tasks. It is about learning how to live in the world with the greatest perspective, integrity, and proportion.

And particularly important for this book's reflections, we find this progression of creatively related polar dynamics manifesting as predictably at a cultural scale as we do with more circumscribed formative processes such as the creation of a work of art or individual human development. This observation strongly supports both the power of a creative frame and the concept of Cultural Maturity's essential conclusions.

Previously, I briefly introduced what CST calls the Creative Function and highlighted its central place in Creative Systems Theory. We can use the Creative Function to summarize this basic relationship between polarity and creative/formative process. The Creative Function expands the image in Figure 2-6 like the bellows of an accordion. Just as we can map creative/formative processes according to the aspects of intelligence each stage draws on, so too can we map any kind of developmental dynamic in terms of a predictable sequence of creatively ordered polar juxtapositions. The Creative Function presents a simplified picture. Stages can vary in length and emphasis depending on the kind of system and surrounding circumstances, and formative processes can be aborted at any stage. But the general sequence holds with remarkable consistency. The Creative Function provides a concise, information-filled way to depict how polar relationships evolve over the course of any human formative process.

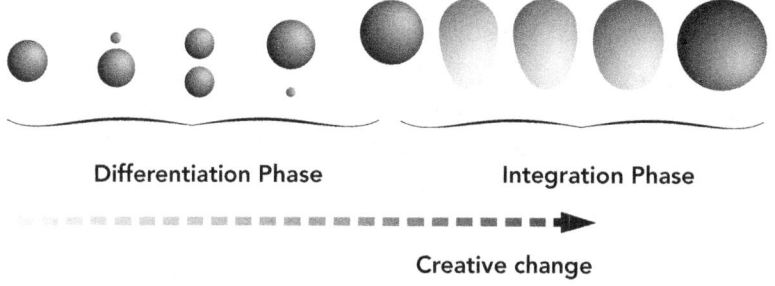

Fig. 2-7. The Creative Function

In anticipation of Chapter Three's more extended Patterning in Time observations, the chart in Figure 2-8 summarizes how the Creative Function and the evolution of polarity tie to the various kinds of creative/formative processes that I've touched on in this chapter. You will note that the chart also includes an additional such process, one that I will address with Chapter Three's reflections: the generative process through which a love relationship comes into being.

The chart also introduces further language for creative stages. CST has more formal terms for what I have called the incubation, inspiration, perspiration, and finishing and polishing stages: Pre-Axis, Early- Axis, Middle-Axis, and Late-Axis, respectively.[18] This more formal language helps clarify parallels between different scales of creative/formative process (what CST calls "creative periodicities"). It also helps us recognize important relationships between different kinds of patterning distinctions. In Chapter Six, we will see how Patterning in Time and Patterning in Space each use this same language. The fact that they do reflects

---

[18] The use of the term "Axis" had its origins in early observations about how each stage as bodily experience organizes in a different way in relationship to the body's axis (see "The Creative Evolution of the Body" in Chapter Three).

essential connections between kinds of systemic observations that more conventionally we would think of as wholly distinct.[19]

---

19 The chart also includes an additional stage—or, more precisely, a time between stages—that I will address with Chapter Three's more detailed reflections, what CST calls Transition.

20 In Chapter One, I noted that the Creative Function is an example of what I have called "three-plus" depiction. It necessarily confronts the Dilemma of Representation, and does so in multiple ways. The various ways that it does help further refine our understanding of the underlying dynamics of creative Patterning in Time.

During creation's first half, for the most part the Dilemma of Differentiation intrudes only in the limited sense it always does with polarity. We can adequately depict creative differentiation as discrete circles—at least as adequately as with any paired-circle representation. In fact, opposing poles creatively interlink, and each stage links to the next, but within any stage-specific slice, none of this is visible. Colluding polar pairs can seem like the most extreme of opposites, and each polar juxtaposition will be experienced as complete and final truth. The representation thus comes close if our interest is reality as perceived through the eyes of each stage.

Beyond formative process's first half, representation works much less well. The Creative Function's midpoint gives us the disorienting dynamics that produce midlife's fundamental questionings in our individual lives and result in postmodern sensibilities with the evolution of culture. Visual representation here provides some information, but as much through the Lower Pole's absence as what can be more concretely depicted.

As we proceed into formative process's second half, visual depiction fails us fundamentally. The complexities of maturity appear as an inadequate, and really misleading, dissolving of one pole into the next. We've seen how a defining characteristic of culturally mature systemic conception is that it expands our appreciation not just for connections, but also for the intricacies and dynamic interplays of real difference. Again, this failure is not a product of inexactness or because what the Creative Function depicts is ultimately mysterious. Rather, it is because the Creative Function reflects systemic conception of the needed new, more complete sort.

CREATIVE SYSTEMS THEORY

CREATIVE STAGES

	Pre-Axis	Early-Axis	Middle-Axis	Late-Axis	Transition	Integrative Stages
MAJOR PERIODICITIES						
A CREATIVE EVENT	Incubation	Inspiration	Perspiration	Finishing & Polishing	Presentation	Becoming "Second Nature" (Integration of the newly created form into self and culture)
A LIFETIME	Prenatal Period & Infancy	Childhood	Adolescence	Early Adulthood	Midlife Transition	Mature Adulthood (From knowledge to wisdom—integration of self as formed identity with the ground of being)
A RELATIONSHIP	Pre-relationship	Falling in Love	Time of Struggle	Established Relationship	Time of Questioning	Mature Intimacy (Relationship as two whole people—marriage of the "loved" and the "lover" within each person)
THE HISTORY OF CULTURE	Pre-History	Golden Ages	Middle Ages	Age of Reason	Transitional Culture	Cultural Maturity (Larger meeting of the form and context of culture)

Fig. 2-8. The Creative Function with Major Formative Periodicities[20]

Additional Polarity-Related Recognitions

A couple of further polarity-related recognitions are important to note before we turn to the next chapter's closer look at Patterning in Time. Each observes ways that we need to fill out the Creative Function's basic representation if we are to effectively depict what we experience with creative stages.

The first concerns how poles at each stage relate one to the other. The Creative Function's basic representation depicts how poles get further apart and change in relative size over the course of creative differentiation. We need to add that the relationship between poles manifests very differently—and is felt very differently—at each stage. Those differences determine much of how we then experience ourselves and the world around us.

The short version: With Pre-Axis, it works adequately to think as if there is as yet only one pole—original unity. In fact, particularly as we begin to progress through Pre-Axial reality, our worlds can reflect considerable detail, but differences always remain secondary to this defining connectedness. With Early-Axis there is now clear difference, but poles are still experienced as ultimately complementary. Depending on what pole gets our attention, the relationship may feel more inspired and magical (when experienced from an Upper Pole perspective) or more mystical and organic (when viewed from the Lower Pole). With Middle-Axis, for the first time there is clear tension, even felt conflict between poles. For new form to take expression, it must actively push away from its context. Pushing away results in a new sense of solidity, but as when doing an isometric exercise, this solidity is achieved through poles functioning in apparent opposition. With Late-Axis, the newly created entity has become sufficiently established that this tension can subside. The Lower Pole again more overtly complements, but now in a very different, explicitly secondary role. These different creative relationships deeply color what we find with different stages in each of the kinds of creative/formative process we will examine.

The second recognition notes that depicting creative/formative process as an evolving set of vertical (Upper Pole/Lower Pole) relationships misses important aspects of polarity's workings. In fact, creative polarity also manifests more horizontally—as Inner and Outer Aspects. The polarity of leader and follower is adequately represented vertically, but if we want to juxtapose the personal and the social, for example, horizontal representation more accurately represents what we feel. In the next chapter, I will turn to the essential recognition needed to fully appreciate this distinction. The Creative Function is not just an abstract depiction; it represents how polarity organizes in the human body. We will examine how creative/developmental dynamics of all sorts, when experienced bodily, have vertical and horizontal aspects. We will also look at how horizontal dynamics, like their vertical counterparts, evolve in characteristic ways over the course of creative/formative processes, with a gradual progression from Inner toward Outer over the course of the first half of any creative process, and more integrative dynamics coming to the fore with second-half formative mechanisms.

Horizontal dynamics will become most obviously important to consider when we turn to more here-and-now—Patterning in Space—distinctions in Chapter Six. For example, we experience the difference between people who are more "introverted" or more "extroverted" as horizontal—in terms of more Inner versus more Outer ways of being in the world.[21] In the next chapter's more elaborated Patterning in Time descriptions, I will draw in limited ways on horizontal dynamics. The way any creative stage manifests in a particular context will depend on the balance that exists between poles—including Upper and Lower Poles and Inner and Outer Aspects.

On the Nature of Conscious Awareness

I've suggested that Integrative Meta-perspective makes it possible to address many "ultimate" questions, concerns that before now have left us baffled. I will devote the whole of Chapter Twelve to this provocative consequence of Cultural Maturity's cognitive reordering. But one example that I will address there in more detail—the nature of conscious awareness—is appropriately introduced at this point. It helps further clarify just what Integrative Meta-perspective involves and also provides additional support for a creative picture of cognitive functioning.

---

21 CST uses the terms Inner and Outer rather than introvert and extrovert because doing so allows it to make more detailed discernments. Inner and Outer versions of various basic temperaments can manifest in ways that are quite different.

Trying to make sense of conscious awareness—its nature and purpose—has been a source of debate since our human beginnings. Integrative Meta-perspective, particularly with the additional insights provided by a creative frame, offers a new kind of answer to the question of awareness. I addressed just what becomes different in my book *Cultural Maturity: A Guidebook for the Future*. The following is adapted from those reflections, as they describe the basic quandary and its resolution particularly well:

> Pulitzer prize–winning author John Noble Wilford summed up awareness' contribution thusly: "Alone among all creatures, the species that styles itself wise, *Homo Sapiens*, has an abiding interest in its distant origins, knows that its allotted time is short, worries about the future and wonders about the past." A person could well describe humanity's defining future task as that of being more conscious than in times past. Depending on what we mean, that would be right.
>
> But this observation is of limited use—indeed it can easily lead us astray—if we don't begin by revisiting what conscious awareness is and how it works. The last century has provided fascinating new insight. In the traditional picture, awareness has been who we are, director of the show—a point of clear and final perspective. The Enlightenment's stated grand task was to bring all of truth into the light of such awareness. This picture is changing.
>
> Few truths become more obvious when practicing the craft of the psychotherapist than how different the reality of conscious awareness is from how the conscious mind tends to view itself. (Comic Emo Philips once quipped: "I used to think the brain was the most important organ in the body, until I realized who was telling me that.") In fact, that conscious awareness is limited in what it can grasp is exactly as it should be. The larger part of our functioning works best without volition's interference. (Recall Kipling's centipede who walks gracefully with its hundred legs until praised for her exquisite memory.)

Increasingly our picture of the functioning of awareness is coming to better match this reality. A central achievement of modern psychology and psychiatry has been the elucidation of more complex and multihued pictures of our inner workings. The oft-used psychological metaphor that compares the psyche to an iceberg, part visible, part submerged, gets us started in the right direction. Awareness's task becomes that of recognizing as much of this multihued complexity as we are able and making the most life-enhancing choices from within the options it reveals.

Such a broader view has a price. It requires humility to all that necessarily lies forever beyond awareness' reach. But we gain in return a greater maturity and fullness of perspective and an important new step in our potential generative potency. Today, we see a growing capacity to step back from all parts of our cognitive functioning—including the more rational parts of ourselves that in the past we tended to identify with awareness (and ourselves). We also see a new ability to appreciate all the various parts of our cognitive complexity, both those before shielded from awareness and those we may have identified with—to more deeply embody intelligence as a whole.

And there is a further important piece. We are better recognizing how the various pieces of our cognitive complexity may work together (and to have them work together in more conscious and obviously complementary ways). CST views these shifts as key to the new picture we get with the best of emergent thinking. What we see is necessarily a product of how we see, and we would predict this new way of seeing to change what we see in ultimately radical ways.

Certainly this is so with regard to awareness itself. A creative metaphor helps paint the new picture. Imagine being a composer writing a symphony. Ask yourself what the right role for conscious awareness should be in the symphony's creation if the piece is to be most powerful and beautiful. Clearly that role is not to write the piece, for conscious awareness can write only what it knows—nothing new would be created. But just as much, the task of conscious awareness is not simply to get out of the way.

Conscious awareness in this context has multiple functions. We use it to affirm the importance of creating, to commit the time and attention that the symphony requires. We use it to consider where we are going and to bring together needed resources. We use it to create the safe places needed for deep creative work. And we utilize conscious awareness to refine our sensibilities, to better appreciate the uniquely sonorous voice of the bassoon, or the subtle and critical differences in the emotional tone of a flute or a piccolo, to better understand the geography of musical creation, the hills and valleys of crescendos and arpeggios, how one movement intricately plays into the next like a lush forest transitioning into a broad plain. Each of these functions is more humble than its historically conceived role, but each in its own ways is explicitly creative.

This more filled-out picture of awareness' function is directly pertinent to today's needed new skills and abilities. One of the most important such new abilities is a greater capacity for responsibility. Importantly, this is not just responsibility in the sense of doing the right thing. The needed new responsibility is more explicitly creative. It is different from more familiar notions of responsibility in the same way the function of awareness in musical composition is different from awareness' more familiar Enlightenment interpretation.

The composer's reflective responsibility is not to craft (no matter how elegantly) a predefined product—that would not be composition. Rather, it is to help bring forth the commitment, sensitivity, and perspective needed for the artistic effort. It is the same if we are creating relationships, communities, organizations, or societies when reliable handholds are absent. Mature responsibility becomes a measure of the imagination, courage, and integrity we bring to our personal and collective choices. We may not get to know what the ultimate outcome of our efforts will be. But we can know that anything that helps us bring these qualities to bear increases the likelihood that what results will enhance life. In the end, responsibility has always been creative. But now, as culture's assisting guideposts become less reliable, it becomes more explicitly so.

A Couple of Concluding Patterning in Time Observations —and Three Additional CST Terms

Before we engage the next chapter's more detailed look at CST's developmental concepts, we need just a bit more preparation.

A couple of further Patterning in Time–related observations are necessary if the relationship between Integrative Meta-perspective and a creative frame is to make full sense. Each provides important further support for Integrative Meta-perspective's necessity and important further insight into all that its changes involve. Each also provides additional language that we will draw on in chapters ahead.

The first observation adds essential detail to our understanding of how developmental processes of all sorts work. We've seen how development involves stages and also how the process that takes us from one stage to the next is not just additive—it involves leaps in organization. The first observation adds that such developmental breakpoints, along with offering new possibilities, also involve necessary "forgettings"—amnesias for realities we've moved beyond. We leave previous realities behind us, certainly. But more than just this is involved. With each organizational leap, doors close to past experience.

A look to individual development provides a ready reference. Adolescents, we find, have a difficult time making sense of the reality of young children even though this is a world that they have only recently left behind. And while we might expect young adults to be our great experts on the attitudes and needs of adolescence, it is often they who find adolescent assumptions most baffling.

Such forgetting serves a critical developmental purpose: It keeps us from falling back into familiar, but no longer timely worlds of experience. Growing up requires not just separation from family as home, but also separation from the ways of organizing experience that at different, earlier times have served as our cognitive/experiential homes.

With such developmental amnesias, we forget more than just memories. We disconnect from the organizing intelligences of the realities we have left behind—the primacy of body intelligence during infancy, of imagination during childhood, of special emotional and affiliative sensibilities during adolescence. We also disconnect from the values and ways of seeing the world that accompany each intelligence. With each stage, we distance ourselves from fundamental dimensions of our being.

Importantly, we find a similar kind of "forgetting" at a cultural scale. Without culturally mature perspective, it becomes very difficult to appreciate earlier-stage cultural realities. Either we fail to acknowledge them at all, or we see them only through the eyes of our projections. At the very least, this observation helps us recognize ways our thinking can go astray. When we put the realities of whole cultures at arm's length, we become vulnerable to ignoring or denigrating people who are different from ourselves.

The observation also provides further insight into the essential role played by Cultural Maturity's cognitive changes and the workings of their underlying mechanisms. We can again draw on personal development for reference. With an individual life's second half, we witness an almost opposite mechanism. Once the basic structures of identity and belief have been established, the protective doors provided by these developmental amnesias can begin to reopen. We no longer need to fear the past. Memories from earlier times in life often become newly available. And of ultimately greater significance, maturity bit by bit reconnects us with those earlier ordering principles—the intelligences, values, aesthetics, and creative juxtapositions that have given each developmental stage its unique character and power. We reengage forgotten dimensions of who we are.

Reengagement in this sense of dissolving developmental amnesias is a formal concept within CST. We know it in our later years personally with the possibility of becoming more wise in our discernments. Wisdom is a product not just of experience, but also what we experience with. We also find it in our individual lives with more everyday observations, such as how grandparents often have an easier time connecting with the realities of their grandchildren than do the children's parents and with how dreams often become more vivid in our later years.

Integrative Meta-perspective provides the related needed reengagement at a cultural scale. We find an everyday sort of support for such cultural Reengagement in the way that most people who spend time in settings we would call not yet modern quickly recognize that much—and much of real significance—has been lost as well as gained in the phenomenon we call progress. There are clearly qualities and affinities present in these earlier realities that are not only important, but somehow essential to recapture if our future world is to be a healthy place. Few people remain happy for long if plunked down in a cultural reality earlier than their own. But going backwards is specifically not what we are talking about. The point is that sensibilities before forgotten—and forgotten for good reasons—are somehow now becoming newly pertinent. We can add the dissolving of developmental amnesias to the list of key changes that define Integrative Meta-perspective.

I will address the second further observation in detail in Chapter Three, but being that it relates directly to ideas in this chapter and is of major importance, it should at least be introduced. What CST calls the Dilemma of Trajectory follows from earlier observations about what happens to polar opposites over the first half of any formative process. I've described a progression from realities where the archetypally feminine holds the greatest influence in culture's beginnings to today in which archetypally masculine values hold much the larger sway. Earlier I observed that where this progression takes us provides one of the best arguments for the necessity of the kind of change that Integrative Meta-perspective makes possible and also alerts us to real dangers ahead.

Notice that this trajectory necessarily reaches a dead end. Going further in this direction stops giving us anything of value. Indeed, there is an important sense in which it really stops being possible at all. The Dilemma of Trajectory describes a critical quandary that might seem a show-stopper. It is significant not just because ignoring it will result in misguided actions. It presents real dangers. In the next chapter, we will look at how the past's story of growing distinction, taken far enough, threatens to sever us from much that is most important in being human.

Chapter Three will also introduce a related CST concept, what the theory calls Transitional Absurdity. The concept captures the roots of much that today we can find most disturbing. We find Transitional Absurdities when we "overshoot the mark" developmentally,[22] when we try to apply truths of times past to today's new questions. Inevitably in doing so we fail—and do so in predictable, and easily cataclysmic ways.

Integrative Meta-perspective's cognitive reordering is what makes it possible that the Dilemma of Trajectory need not be the end of the road. It also provides the necessary antidote to the considerable dangers presented by Transitional Absurdity. Cultural Maturity—or at least something that can produce related cognitive changes—becomes the only real option.

---

22 Actually, this is just one of several mechanisms that we will examine.

CHAPTER THREE

Patterning in Time: Change and Creative Self-Organization

With the foundations for Creative Systems Theory's developmental/evolutionary approach now established, we can take a more filled-out and extended look at how the theory maps change in human systems. I will again here draw on creative organization as a whole, but I will also give particular attention to culture's evolution. The application of Patterning in Time notions at this largest of formative scales provides the context for all of this book's observations. And the implication of this creative picture of change for today represents one of the most important reasons to take these notions seriously.

For this mapping project, I will start with some further general observations about addressing cultural change in this way. I will then offer a more elaborated description of the parallel organizational patterns that we find with human developmental processes at all scales—from an act of innovation, to personal development, to the growth of a relationship, to the rise of civilizations—drawing on CST's creative/developmental framework. I will make some basic observations about the implications and applications of this temporal mapping. And finally, I will address how this mapping, applied at a societal scale, manifests across widely diverse aspects of culture's creative landscape—from philosophy, to architecture, to our experience of time, to our relationship with nature, to how we understand the human body.

Needed Distinctions

We should first reflect a bit further on the whole endeavor of thinking about human systems in evolutionary terms—particularly cultural systems. I've observed that people might take issue with this effort from the start. And even among people who have no problem with thinking about cultural change in this way, CST's Patterning in Time approach may run counter to favorite assumptions.

I've previously noted a couple of ways in which thinking of culture's story as having chapters—developmental stages—can be controversial. With the first, thinkers may dismiss such ideas out of hand for what, at least on the surface, might seem a good reason. Ideas that make one culture more "advanced" than another have been used in times past to justify some of the worst of human behavior.

The important recognition with regard to this first kind of objection is that the conclusions it finds problematical are products of a wholly different kind of thinking than that which CST represents. Critics who make this argument often reference Georg Hegel's philosophically idealist formulations. Philosophical idealism views history as progressing toward some point of cultural perfection. One result is that such thinking can be readily used to justify the elevation of one's own "ideal" kind and the denigration of others. Hegel's thinking cast a mythically elevated Prussian state as culture's culminating expression and purportedly later influenced the thinking of Adolf Hitler.

People who voice this first kind of objection often then turn instead to postmodern interpretation, with its common aversion to judgement. Such views avoid any risk of denigration by making differences simply different. But again, here we see conclusions based on a fundamentally different kind of thinking than is our focus here. And with it much gets lost—and much that is of great importance. CST proposes that such different-strokes-for-different-folks conclusions become acceptable today only because the ways in which we commonly think reflect only the most surface layers of intelligence's complexity.

Creative Systems Theory's approach takes us solidly beyond this first kind of objection. It avoids the traps that we've seen with the past use of evolutionary views by challenging our historical tendency to base our perceptions of difference on idealization and demonization. And by cutting through the amnesias that before have distanced us from the realities of stages we have progressed beyond, it deepens our appreciation for what has been uniques in the worldviews of times past. CST's developmental/evolutionary approach, being a product of Integrative Meta-perspective, makes possible a more dynamic and affirming picture, one that both celebrates the creative significance of previous developmental chapters and is comfortable with the idea that history's story involves advancement.

The second kind of objection, while also understandable, tends to be less conscious. Evolutionary thinking, at least of the deep sort we have interest in, can also meet with suspicion because of the way it requires that we draw on the whole of our cognitive complexity. If the previous chapter's conclusions about intelligence's multiplicity hold, it requires that we draw on all of intelligence's multiple aspects. I've observed how modern academic thought has its roots in Age-of-Reason belief and for the most part still equates truth with rationality. While the first kind of objection to evolutionary perspective is most often cited in academic circles, I suspect that the larger reason that at least the particular kind of evolutionary perspective that a creative frame represents tends not to be readily acknowledged is that the needed depth of understanding requires stepping beyond the intellectual assumptions of academia's consensus worldview.

The best response to this second kind of objection is simply the power and utility of the kind of understanding that thinking in developmental/evolutionary terms makes possible. Given that cultural groups can reside in wholly different developmental stages, effective policy in today's global world becomes very difficult without such perspective. And if what I've described thus far is accurate, such perspective is necessary if we are to effectively understand the times in which we live. I've gone so far as to argue that being optimistic about the future is justified only if the picture CST proposes for times ahead is basically correct.

It is also important to distinguish the particular kind of evolutionary perspective that CST represents from other ways of thinking about how cultures change. Teasing apart what is different starts with the obvious but necessary recognition that our concern is evolution of a cultural sort. I've heard people use evolutionary language to argue that needed new capacities are really not humanly possible. They may claim, for example, that "we've evolved to be warlike, and that will never change." In reaching this conclusion, people miss the fact that evolution has two meanings. There is biological evolution, and on that front we are unlikely to see much that will help us, certainly not anytime soon. But there is also cultural evolution—the ways in which social systems grow and evolve over time. Cultural evolution—certainly as framed here—supports some very different kinds of conclusions.

Creative Systems Theory's approach also represents a very particular way of thinking about how cultures change. Most immediately different is that its focus is on how we understand—on worldviews and the evolution of cognition and perspective. If people in modern times have thought of culture as evolving at all, they've tended to assume that cultural change is driven by invention (as CST would predict, given the assumptions of Modern Age perspective). In response, they've mapped human progress in terms of the effects of invention—a time of hunter-gatherers, an age of agriculture, a modern industrial age. CST's developmental/evolutionary approach gives primary attention to changes in how we humans make sense of our worlds. While invention often plays an important role in such change, here the causality always goes both ways. New invention may alter how we think, but at the same time, changes in how we understand—many of them products of developmental processes—make new kinds of invention conceivable.[1]

Creative Systems Theory's developmental/evolutionary approach is also distinctive even among views that give primary attention to changes at the level of understanding. It is unusual in consciously drawing on the whole of our cognitive complexity. And it is unique in bringing a specifically creative lens to understanding change's mechanisms over time. It is also unique in how it frames current changes and the tasks before us.

In Chapter Seven I will describe five "Scenarios for the Future"—the most common ways of thinking about what may lie ahead. At this point, we can put these various scenarios into two broad categories—

---

1 And often, just as important, it makes them acceptable. For example, China had all the requisite ingredients for something like Europe's Industrial Revolution two thousand years ago. Why did we not then see something similar? I suspect the reason is that China did not then have the materialist values and individualist motivations that came with Modern Age sensibilities. The situation today has changed considerably.

those that are generally optimistic about the future and those of a more dystopian sort. Distinguishing them from how CST views today's challenges helps further tease apart what makes CST's developmental/evolutionary interpretation particular—and important.

Most views of the more optimistic sort in some way assume the continued viability of the trajectory that has gotten us here. Some such "onward-and-upward" interpretations hold that our institutions and our ways of understanding are basically sound. They see the task ahead as primarily one of refinement. Others acknowledge that there will be bumps in the road ahead, at times big ones, but assume that we can count on our amazing capacities for insight and invention to pull us through whatever difficulties we might face. Onward-and-upward views find their most extreme expression in techno-utopian beliefs.

Contrasting such generally optimistic conclusions, we find an array of views that see our present condition to be in some basic way broken. Extreme examples regard it as irretrievably so, perceiving if not a looming Armageddon, at least a world in which we have erred so fundamentally that there is little reason for hope. Milder cynical interpretations warn of things "going to hell in a handbasket" and may call, either explicitly or by implication, for radical transformation, either of a more political or more spiritual sort. We can think of views that call for radical transformation as at once dystopian and utopian.

CST proposes that both more optimistic interpretations and their dystopian complements have major problems—certainly in their extremes, but also in more tempered interpretations. With regard to onward-and-upward views, it argues that there is no reason to assume that new cultural forms—educational, economic, governmental, scientific, and more—do not lie ahead, and every reason to hope that they do. And it makes clear that while minor tweaks may provide benefit, in the end, few of the major challenges ahead can be solved by policy means alone. As far as technology being our savior, it emphasizes that only very rarely will technological fixes suffice. It delineates how going forward will also require changes in how we think, and more deeply, in who we are.

With regard to the second, more dystopian set of views, CST observes that most of the conundrums we face today are less the result of going astray than of the need to confront challenges that are products of our success. This is the case whether the challenge is more external, as with climate change, or more obviously about ourselves, as with the need to address moral questions without past one-size-fits-all cultural guideposts. CST acknowledges that it is possible that this great success may ultimately be our undoing. But it proposes that at least the more extreme of dystopian views have less to do with accurately perceived conditions in the world than with the psychologies of those who hold them. And it clarifies how views that argue for radical transformation similarly tend to miss critical pieces of the puzzle. Later we will look at how most such interpretations advocate for idealized outcomes that we could not achieve, and more importantly, would not want to achieve.[2]

Creative Systems Theory's notion of a needed and newly possible collective "growing up" offers a way of thinking about the future that is different from each of these more familiar kinds of interpretation, both in the sort of idea it represents and in its conclusions about the tasks before us. CST argues that change—indeed, fundamental change—is required. But Cultural Maturity is not about the correcting of past error (which is not to say that the human enterprise has been without error). It is also not about idealized or magical solutions. Cultural Maturity is about engaging a next natural step in the human endeavor, a step that is predicted, but only now within our capabilities to realize, or even to fully understand.

I've described how Cultural Maturity's picture of the future confronts us with an apparent paradox. While it is ultimately more radical in what it asks of us than more familiar ways of thinking about what may lie ahead (both to make manifest and to fully understand), at the same time it is in an important way more "ordinary". In the end, it is only about seeing things a bit more clearly and fully than has been an options in times past. I've proposed that we can think of it as a "new common sense."

We are left with the question of whether we should think of Cultural Maturity's framing of the future as hopeful. It does not guarantee our

---

2 See "Transformational/New Paradigm Scenarios" in Chapter Seven.

safety or even our survival. And it makes demands that we may well not be up to. But it is at least consistent with hope. I've proposed that legitimate hope for the future depends on the new skills and capacities that Cultural Maturity's changes make possible. For this book's reflections, there is also the more particular recognition that the kind of thinking CST represents requires Cultural Maturity's cognitive changes. I don't propose CST's developmental/evolutionary interpretation as some last word. But as I see things, the kind of thinking it represents adds to understanding in ways that will become increasingly critical in times ahead.

Mapping Patterning in Time

But we are getting ahead of ourselves. For CST's developmental/evolutionary picture to inform our understanding of the future in ways that are truly persuasive, we need first to bring greater nuance to the patterning notions that inform these conclusions. The more elaborated Patterning in Time picture that follows covers much that should now feel familiar. Think of it both as a summary and as a bringing together of observations where connections may not before have been sufficiently established.

These descriptions will draw on each of the ways of depicting change in human systems that I've touched on in previous chapters: the predictable sequence of polar relationships we see over the course of any human formative process, intelligence's role in creative self-organization, the evolution of narrative, and the fact that through time we find creative leaps in our understanding of truth. They will also apply, and provide context for, more specific change-related concepts that I've introduced previously, such as conscious awareness's evolving significance, the effects of developmental amnesias, the Dilemma of Trajectory, Transitional worldviews like those we find with postmodern belief, and the concept of Transitional Absurdity.

While here I will give special attention to culture's developmental story (and with this particularly to its later stages), all of the other creative periodicities that I've previously referenced will continue to provide context. And to help further fill out the creative picture, I will also include the generative process through which a new love relationship begins, grows, and evolves. (I could as easily have chosen the generative story of a friendship, an organization, a community, or a social movement.) Figure 2-5 in the previous chapter gave us a bird's eye overview for the observations that follow.

Creative "Incubation" (Pre-Axis)

I've described how formative process starts before the appearance of creation as form—in the unbroken whole of established context. Pre-Axis extends from original formlessness into realized form's first intimations and as-yet barely differentiated earliest manifestations. Particularly early on, creation works beneath the surface, outside of conscious awareness. Later we may feel it as first impressions, or perhaps as a subtle first sense of direction.

Over the course of Pre-Axis, we experience the beginnings of distinction, but connectedness always remains primary. Parts, if felt, are experienced as aspects of an organic entirety. The primary intelligence throughout this stage is body intelligence, the intelligence of the kinesthetic, of knowing as a felt sense of things.

A Simple Creative Act: In a simple creative act—the generation of an idea or invention, the writing of a song, the shaping of a piece of sculpture—this is the incubation stage. The new creation must first have its time of gestation. In this stage the role of polarity is minimal; we begin before its appearance. The primary intelligence is bodily knowing. The thing created must first be born out of its original womb-like world. We may have a vague sense that something is preparing to happen, but nothing is yet visible. Later on, we may recognize the fact of new creation, but we experience it only as a felt sense of possibility. We may feel attraction to a certain aesthetic quality or to a certain kind of shape or movement. Or we may find ourselves surprised to be thinking about some topic that we had not before given concern. In writing or playing music, we may find significance in a certain phrase or theme. In doing sculpture, we may feel ourselves moved by a particular quality of shape or texture.

The most important role for conscious awareness at this stage is often to simply get out of the way. But conscious awareness in fact does make contributions, simply ones that have less to do with the creative act itself than what it takes to support it. Sometimes new possibility can only come with significant preparation, doing one's homework. And while we tend to focus most on the content of creation, at this stage attention's significance often pertains more to context. I commonly counsel clients that if they get the creative "containers" right, the creative content will often take care of itself.[3] "Container" in this sense may be a physical space—a "room of one's own." For me it is often a favorite rocking chair or the bathtub. "Container" may also be the larger context of one's life—having good friends, getting exercise, making a good night's sleep a priority. Or it may be a particular activity. I do some of my best thinking on road trips—with the rhythm of the road my "container." When a phrase or theme comes to me, I pull over and jot down what I am able—then I'm back on the road.

A Lifetime: In a lifetime, Pre-Axis conforms to the prenatal period, infancy, and the first year or so of life. Again we reside largely in an unbroken whole. The unbroken whole manifests here in the infant's relationship both to the mother and to itself. Following well past birth, the bond to the mother remains primary. And the light of conscious awareness, that evidence of first distinction more internally, is only beginning to awaken. The unbroken whole is also felt in the very young child's relationship to time. In the early months of our lives, to feel is to act; there is no separation. Only late in this period do we see the beginnings of obvious volition.

Again, body intelligence is primary. The reality of the prenatal period is an unselfconscious creature world. And even with infancy and childhood's beginnings, we engage our worlds primarily through our senses and through movement. If you want to engage a young infant, you do so through holding, rocking, and the making of sounds. And as the beginning parent quickly learns, everything must be touched—and much also must go into the mouth for more direct perusal. A bit later, if you are relating to a young child rather than an infant, you might expand your language of connection to include more elaborate gestures and a few words, though words are used then as much for

---

[3] Chapter Eight's examination of "hands-on" tools looks in detail at the power of attention to creative "containers" in all parts of our personal and collective lives.

their music or poetry as for their content (observe how hard it is to use words with a very young child without making them sound like a song). Further on in this stage, you might add more interactive bodily "language" to your connections, perhaps together crawling around on the floor and sharing delight in finding a bug or noting a beam of light coming in through the window.

A Relationship: In a new relationship, this is the time before there is visible connection—again the unbroken whole. We may have a sense of being open to possibility. We may even have met the person that we will later engage deeply and we may have felt a certain inner response in his/her presence. But the spark of conscious recognition has yet to ignite. Again body intelligence is primary. Being ready is about inner preparation, and knowing is very much a felt sense. A bit later, when the first inklings of initial recognition do happen, we may use a word like "chemistry" to describe what we feel.

The Story of Culture: In the history of civilization, the incubation stage begins with Stone Age times. For the most part, this is a reality of our far distant past, though there are still a few places on our planet—in the New Guinea highlands, the upper Amazon basin, and certain places in Africa and the Australian outback—where such primordial sensibilities continue to prevail. Wherever basic social structures are tribal,[4] we know that Pre-Axial truths continue to play a role.

The unbroken whole at a cultural scale has multiple layers—manifesting at once as the tribe, nature, and time. In early tribal realities, it is the tribe rather than the individual members that is primary. If a person breaks a taboo important enough to cause him to be expelled from the tribe, it is common for the person to simply go off and die. He doesn't have to kill himself—to be excluded from the womb of tribal existence is tantamount to nonexistence. In a similar way, there is no perceived separation between truth and nature. Tribal deities are simply the faces of nature set animate: the wind, the mountain, bear, eagle, coyote. Health is one's degree of

---

4 We need to temper this assertion with the recognition that the word "tribal" can get used informally today to refer to all manner of premodern societal structures.

CREATIVE SYSTEMS THEORY

harmony with this living nature. Knowing is one's bodily connection in and as this wholeness. And time further affirms this unbroken entirety. Existence takes place in an eternally cycling present. Each generation and each turning of the seasons is seen as reenacting a timeless story.

The primary intelligence in tribal times is again body intelligence. It is not possible to be part of a tribe without knowing its songs and dances. Other intelligences besides that of the body contribute during this cultural stage, but their roles are more limited and specifically reflect Pre-Axial sensibility. The imaginal's contribution manifests in the centrality of ritual, the artistry of bodily adornment, and how decoration is brought to everyday life in this stage. We find the emotional in the deep affective connection with tribe and with nature. And while underlying beliefs are animistic, the rational plays out in the verbal expression of those beliefs. In my experience, words tend to be used more sparingly in tribal cultures, but when they are used, they are often given special significance.

Creative "Inspiration" (Early-Axis)

With Early-Axis, newly created form steps forth from the primordial into the light. This legitimately creates excitement—new possibility has been born. It is with this stage that the magic and numinosity of the creative becomes most explicit.

How we then perceive the order of things changes fundamentally. While connectedness retains a key, indeed often determining role, truth for the first time becomes overtly polar—there is now something separate to see and engage. And as far as intelligence, the primary mode shifts from the kinesthetic to the symbolic, to the language of myth and metaphor. Conscious awareness now comes to have a more acknowledged place, but causality remains only to a limited extent a product of intent. Rather, it is felt as magical or mysterious (more magical if viewed from an upper pole perspective, more mysterious if experienced from below).

A Simple Creative Act: In the generation of an idea or invention, the writing of a song, or the shaping of a piece of sculpture, this is the time of first insight. What was before only a faint quickening now becomes visibly present. Sometimes visibility is sudden, a moment of "Eureka." But even if it is more gradual, it is felt as having special significance.

With regard to polarity, while creator and created are still closely tied, and creative context continues to hold the greater influence, new creation now has clear and separate existence. With intelligence, the imagination has become primary. The task over the course of Early-Axis is to play with images and possibilities, to feel where in them the deepest power lies, and to risk giving that power first form. Conscious awareness now has a more obvious relationship to the creative act. And at the same time, it is often the person's comfort with surprises that is most important in that relationship.

A Lifetime: In a lifetime, this is the magical world of childhood. Here, too, Early-Axis tends to come with special feelings of excitement. And this is sonot just for the child. Given the presence of new possibilities, it is appropriate that everyone tends to feel joy in the presence of young children.

It is at this time in development that we see the first establishment of clear distinctions. Distinction manifests most obviously in initial separation from the mother. But just as important, we see the beginnings of individual consciousness, and with it, first clear separation from the infant's more creature-like reality. We also find more solidly established distinctions in the world around us. This stage begins at about the time that we see what Jean Piaget spoke of as "object permanence." Young children find delight in peekaboo because they need to grasp how objects continue to exist even if they momentarily disappear. With childhood, the ability to separate "this from that" has ever greater significance.

Again, imaginal intelligence is primary, manifesting both in the activities that most create interest and in how children make sense of their reality. Every child is an artist at heart. And truth in a child world works ultimately according to the laws of magical causality. The critical work of the child is play, trying out images of possibility on the stage of let's pretend.

A Relationship: The Early-Axis stage in intimacy begins with the first blush of real attraction. This tends to be a magical time, filled with tentative first touchings and fantasies of the possible. There is now polarity, but it tends to play out in largely invisible ways. We are very much distinct—the amount we really know about each other is as yet small, and what we do know, we often know most at unconscious levels. But we can feel remarkably close—our connection, having just been born, is appropriately experienced as amazing and numinous. Again, imaginal intelligence is central, both to what we see and to how we make choices. Our connecting at this point is often more as symbols than as mortals—a fair princess, a handsome prince. And our images of the future tend to be most based on imagined possibilities.

The Story of Culture: With culture, Early-Axis marks the time of the early civilizations. It finds first manifestation in the coming together of tribes into broader alliances. And it reaches its full splendor with the classical high cultures of both the West and the East. This is the time of culture's initial flowerings.

We recognize Early-Axis sensibility in the West with civilization's rise in ancient Mesopotamia, with the mystical monumentality of ancient Egypt, and with the great mythic tales and philosophical inventiveness of Olympian Greece. We recognize Early-Axis dynamics in the East in ancient India's complex arrays of colorful gods and goddesses, in the rich artistry and striking inventive capacities of classical China, and in the mythic intensity of early temples in Southeast Asia such as Angkor Wat. In the Americas, we find Early-Axis cultural expression in the vibrant artistry of the early Mesoamerican cultures—the Incas, the Aztecs, the Toltecs, and more. There also exist examples in current times where largely Early-Axis beliefs and practices continue to prevail—in places like Tibet (though Chinese occupation has tempered the inspiration) or Bali (though more so prior to modern tourism).

First clear separation between poles manifests most obviously in the simple fact of civilization's ascent. Humanity and nature have now become distinct. We see it too in the elevated splendor that so commonly marks cultural expression at this time. But in spite of this realization of clear distinction, poles at this point remain close, and only rarely do we find them significantly at odds. The intertwined serpents of the Greek caduceus and the balanced yin and yang of Chinese Taoist philosophy give symbolic expression to this ultimately complementary relationship.

As far as ways of knowing, again imaginal intelligence now prevails. Something more than just nature (spirit, essence, magic, beauty—no single word quite describes it) emerges as the new cultural referent in these times. Meaning speaks with particular directness through the language of myth, manifesting as epic tales and complex pantheons of major and minor gods. This is also a time of rich artistic potency. Art during this stage becomes not just expression, but in and of itself a primary form of truth.

As we see with the defining intelligences of other cultural stages, other intelligences besides just the imaginal play more limited roles with Early-Axis. We experience body intelligence's now more background presence in how magic and mystery can be felt directly in our tissues. Emotional intelligence takes expression as mythic passion. And we encounter rational intelligence in the growing role for more philosophical inclinations. Modern philosophy had its birth in Early-Axis times.

Creative "Perspiration" (Middle-Axis)

Creation's perspiration stage takes new possibility into solid form. It galvanizes the conviction, focus, and endurance that concrete manifestation requires. The language of truth now shifts from the mythic to the moral and the emotional. The work progresses by virtue of heart and guts.

As we begin to engage this stage, we can easily feel that something is being lost. The preceding stage was magical and numinous. The predominant feelings now are often hard work and struggle. But while Middle-Axis can initially feel less inspired, it is in no way less significant, and in the end, no less creative. The moment of first inspiration is indeed wondrous. But it is only a first step on the road to fully realized manifestation.

The underlying polar dynamics explain why the experience of struggle might be common. By the middle of this stage, the power of the newly created and the power of the context of creation have become equivalent. Reality exists as a polar isometric between at once opposite and conspiring forces. The newly formed needs to distance itself strongly from its origins if it is not to fall back into the more comfortable and safe realities of times past.

A Simple Creative Act: Whether the creative task is the generation of an idea, the writing of a song, or the crafting of an invention, it is here that we most directly confront the hard demands of our calling. With regard to polarity, the newly created object now becomes clearly separate, something we can more directly grapple with. With regard to what we draw on in ourselves, emotional intelligence now becomes primary. Creation becomes increasingly a visceral act.

Feelings with Middle-Axis can be mixed, and over its course, the creator's relationship to the work can change in marked ways. We are easily at first most aware of the work's demands. The process of creation can seem almost to be conspiring against us. In my days as a sculptor, it was at this stage that I would necessarily confront both the brute fact that stone is a difficult medium and my own limitations. I remember not always responding well to these circumstances. Sometimes the work proceeded with the patient rhythms and quiet satisfactions of the craftsman. But other times I would rage. Later on, feelings would change further. I would find the work's demands bringing forth in me a new vigor and confidence. Eventually with Middle-Axis, we come to experience identity and power in the fact of expression.

A Lifetime: In a lifetime, Middle-Axis marks entry into adolescence. Adolescence is a dramatic time, but also often an awkward and troubled time. The innocence of childhood must be left behind. With regard to polarity, it is a time for more fully standing separate. The adolescent appropriately questions—and often directly defies—parental rules and expectations. From the outside, the effort can often seem contradictory—adolescents not uncommonly pledge loyalty to social groups that are rigidly conformist in their expectations. But in the end, the result is more established identity. Increasingly, emotional intelligence dominates. Feelings can be strong and often take the person in conflicting directions. This is a time for trying out moral principles and establishing moral beliefs. The reward for perseverance in Middle-Axis's easily confusing vicissitudes is successful preparation for entry into the adult world.

A Relationship: In a developing love relationship, Middle-Axis confronts us with the tasks of relationship building. This process can be immensely satisfying—coming to better know the other person's gifts and peculiarities, beginning to build a life together. It can also bring strong—and mixed—feelings. The glow of the honeymoon period—when we view the other as a dream image—necessarily fades somewhat. Polarity is felt more explicitly in the simple fact that we now more clearly recognize our separateness. It also again manifests in ways that can feel ambivalent and contradictory. This is the stage at which we most directly deal with questions of control and territory. But the reward for taking on these more "heart and guts" kinds of tasks is considerable. We discover the possibility of a solidity and practicality in how we relate to one another that otherwise we could not have known.

The Story of Culture: The Middle-Axis stage in culture brings the consolidation of disparate populations and rule by kings and emperors. In the West, this chapter in culture's narrative predominated from the time of the Roman Empire through the Middle Ages. I associate its beginnings in the East with the rule of Qin Shi Huang, the first Emperor of China (which we know in the West from the Terracotta Warriors). Middle-Axis dynamics continue to define experience today in much of the Middle East, as well as in parts of Eastern Europe, Asia, and Central and South America.

A newly equal, and frequently ambivalent, balance between polar forces orders Middle-Axis in cultural development. With the European Middle Ages, we see this polar tension in social structures that grew increasingly feudal: landed lords above, serfs and the otherwise impoverished below. Likewise, church and state (here in the form of kingly rule) became newly separate, newly equal in power, and ever more frequently at odds. And the ancients' many gods, with their differing proclivities, began to surrender their power to the notion of a single deity—or, more accurately, a dual deity: a monotheistic godhead on one side in eternal battle with the forces of evil on the other. Whether we look to history or to present day cultures where Middle-Axis dynamics predominate, polarity becomes more explicitly about opposites. Truth manifests as an isometric—though still ultimately co-generative—relationship between explicitly contrasting forces.[5]

In keeping with what we would expect with the motive power of "perspiration stage" dynamics, this stage in culture is marked by dramatic accomplishments. In the West, we find major architectural achievements, from Rome's aqueducts and the Pantheon early on in this period

---

5 These changes have taken somewhat different expression in the West and the East. For example, in the East, instead of monotheism, we tend to see Middle-Axis sensibilities manifesting in clearly delineated codes of social conduct such as those we find with Confucianism in China. In general, the West tends to manifest the realities of each cultural stage in ways that are somewhat more Outer, while the East tends to manifest these same changes in ways that are more Inner.

to Europe's Gothic cathedrals near its conclusion. In the East, further along in this period we find the building of the Great Wall. But consistent with the inherently struggled nature of Middle-Axis dynamics, we commonly also find discord—and not infrequently pain and inhumanity. Middle-Axis cultural dynamics in the West brought us the Crusades and the Spanish Inquisition, the European Dark Ages, and, in more modern times, often the tyranny of brutal dictatorships. In the modern world, one of the easiest ways to find Middle-Axis cultural sensibilities is to note where conflict is common and particularly intractable.

Here again, a person could feel regret that a certain magic has been lost, but once more this is not at all regression. The reward for this loss is increasingly established social structure. The Middle Ages gave the West a new solidification of social organization with kingly rule, establishment of an institutional church, radical validation of rights with the Magna Carta, and increasingly formal structures of communication and commerce. We find related advances—and related contradictions—wherever perspiration stage developmental realities dominate in contemporary times.

As far as the aspects of intelligence we most draw on, with Middle-Axis in culture the emotional and the moral again assume new prominence. In the Middle Ages, Europe saw values like honor and chivalry newly revered, along with the first intimations of romantic love (though at this point it was unrequited love that was idealized—love held at a safe moral distance). Cultural beliefs at this stage commonly have an emotional—indeed fervently fundamentalist—ardency.

As we witness with the primary intelligences of previous cultural stages, other intelligences besides the emotional/moral also have significant, if more limited, roles with Middle-Axis. The body is where moral intensities are felt. The imaginal finds dramatic expression in religious symbolism. And while the underlying assumptions of belief have their roots in emotional/moral absolutes, utterances that follow from those assumptions can be detailed and precise in their logic (and, particularly when driven by dogmatism, highly elaborated and eloquent).[6]

---

6 I have given greatest emphasis to the West in describing this stage and will continue to do so with stages that follow. I do this for the simple reason that further development preceeded more rapidly in the West than in the East.

Creative "Finishing and Polishing" (Late-Axis)

Patterning in Time's progression has thus far taken us from the mystery of the formless, through magical possibility and first form, and further into a time of solidification of form. Late-Axis gives new form its finishing touches. Attention shifts increasingly to refinement and detail. With these further changes, the tension between poles found with Middle-Axis subsides significantly. The distance between poles is sufficient that they come close to inhabiting separate worlds. And the Upper Pole has now become clearly dominant. Lower Pole sensibilities are treated increasingly as secondary, often celebrated as adornment and sources of pleasure, but in the end, seen as having their significance after the fact.

With Late-Axis, reality comes to have two nearly distinct faces ordered by two very different-feeling kinds of sensibility. From formative process's Upper Pole, truth becomes increasingly rational and material, defined in terms of logic and in terms of phenomena that can be seen and measured. From formative process's Lower Pole, truth becomes newly personal and subjective—the truth of aesthetics and even whim.

While every stage has both vertical and horizontal aspects, with Late-Axis, the horizontal gains more obvious significance. With Late-Axis, Outer priorities assume a new primacy of importance and draw our attention increasingly into the world. Late-Axis shifts attention to the more surface—finishing and polishing—aspects of creation. And audience-related concerns become increasingly pertinent. Delineation and refinement of voice is needed if the newly created contribution to be communicated clearly.

A Simple Creative Act: With the generation of an idea or invention, the writing of a song, or the shaping of a piece of sculpture, in the Late-Axis stage we become newly able to objectively step back. The work now sits before us as a "piece," something separate and ready for completion. Our focus can shift to issues of detail, to making sure

---

Just why this might have been the case presents an intriguing question. I suspect the answer has something to do with my previous observation that the West tends to manifest the realities of each cultural stage in ways that are somewhat more Outer, the East in ways that are more Inner. Greater Outer focus might be expected to produce more drive toward manifest expression. But I don't have an answer to the question of why we might see these Outer/Inner differences.

all the elements are there and fit correctly together—to questions of aesthetic refinement and final nuance.

Our felt relationship to the piece can change significantly at this stage. In a way it becomes more rational, more objective. And at the same time the relationship can feel more personal. The thing created now becomes more overtly one's own generative creation, less something of mystery. Needed attention to issues of finish and audience—those more Outer concerns—highlights both of these changes. At this stage it becomes more important to see what one is creating as others might see it. To do so requires a greater ability to step back. It also requires a different, now more refined, emotional and aesthetic sensitivity.

A Lifetime: Late-Axis in personal development confronts us with the tasks of adulthood. Adulthood is a time for bringing clarity and detail—and our personal stamp—to our lives. It is a time for making essential decisions—for example, regarding career and family. It is also a time for refining our sense of identity and where we want our lives to go.

With adulthood, we again see greater separation between poles, and with this, a shift in the intelligences we most draw on. We become better able to step back and to be rational about ourselves. This change is reflected not just in how we think but in what we think about. More than at any other time in our lives, at this stage we are likely to describe who we are in terms of things we can objectively see and measure—our jobs, how many children we have, our economic status. And at the same time, there are important ways in which our lives become more subjective. At least they become more our own. We are better able to say, "these are my beliefs and feelings" and appreciate that other people may have beliefs and feelings that are different. As adults, we become at once more rational and more sophisticated as feeling/aesthetic beings. These changes easily create their own contradictory realities. For example, while we might better know ourselves as individuals, we can also be particularly prone to comparing ourselves with others and to be concerned with appearances, with what others might think.

A Relationship: With love's Late-Axis stage, relationship becomes established and defined. The major issues of being together have been sorted out, and general agreement on the roles and boundaries of the relationship—who does what, how, and when—have been reached. Partners have largely stopped asking what their relationship will be, because it now is. Attention can shift to details and fine-tuning. If the people have chosen to continue together, love's connection at this point frequently has a feeling of acceptance and accomplishment not present with earlier stages.

As far as polarity, while love at this stage is closer in the sense of being more developed, it also involves clearer separation between the people involved—it is felt more as love between individuals.[7] Love also reflects clearer separation between parts of ourselves—the intelligences it draws on. It can seem more rational—communication tends at least to feel more direct. And at the same time, it can feel more romantic. As we become better able to leave control-related struggles behind us, we are better able to acknowledge appreciation and affection.

The Story of Culture: In the story of civilization, this is the Modern Age, the last 500 years in the West. In much of the world this stage has come only more recently. For example, with the East it made its first appearance with the early decades of the twentieth century.[8] Late-Axis sensibilities today have an important role in most all cultural systems.

If classical times marked Europe's childhood, and the medieval period its adolescence, modernity marked the West's coming of age. Oral and kingly truths gradually gave way to more materially ordered realities—a personal reality of individuality, achievement, and intellect; a social reality of law, industry, and economics; and a physical reality of actions and their concomitant reactions. Institutions came to reflect a new appreciation for individual freedom and personal initiative. Governmental forms became representative; religion entertained newly personal and direct relationships with the divine; and economic competition became its own ethic, freeing business from moral constraint.

Polarity in Late-Axis culture reflects greater separation, and for just

---

7 Though it is in fact not fully this. In Chapter Four, we will look at how love between individuals in any Whole-Person sense requires Cultural Maturity's changes.

8 I think of Sun Yat-sen's establishment of democratic rule in China as marking Late-Axis's first formal expression in Asia. Rule by emperors did not end in Japan until after World War Two.

CREATIVE SYSTEMS THEORY

this reason loses much of the tension that defined polarity in times past. Conceptually, key juxtapositions—such as objective and subjective, mind and body, material and spiritual—are experienced as inhabiting wholly separate worlds. More personally, the Modern Age worldview celebrates individual freedom and thinks of it as now fully realized.[9]

Again, rational intelligence prevails. With the Modern Age in Europe we witnessed the Age of Reason, the growing prominence of science with its emphasis on the empirical, and ever greater focus on technological achievement. We also experienced reason's polar counterbalance in romantic sensibilities. The Romantic Age put new emphasis on nature, on the artistic, and on a more personal kind of bond between the sexes. And the medieval practice of having marriages determined by families was gradually replaced by Romeo-and-Juliet images of romantic love.

Creative Transition

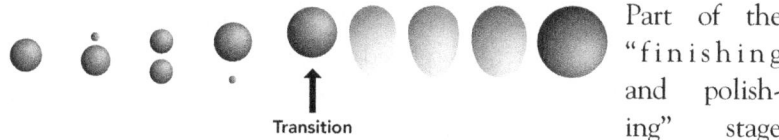

Part of the "finishing and polishing" stage story is the belief that we are done. In a creative act, the object is completed; in individual development, identity is established; with love, the hard work of relationship is over; and with the evolution of culture, in bringing understanding fully into the light of reason we assume that we have understood once and for all. But, in fact, creation has told at best but half of its story. Much that is most important in the "respiration" of creative life has yet to take place. It is the additional creative stages in the Creative Function that give us Cultural Maturity and the kind of perspective this book draws upon.

But before we turn to such specifically integrative mechanisms, we need first to include an additional stage—or more precisely, a time between stages. I only hinted at it with Chapter Two's introductory Patterning in Time reflections. But appreciating this dynamic—what CST

---

9 Later we will see how the belief that individuality is then fully realized is an illusion. CST delineates how further steps are needed for individuality in any complete sense. See "The Myth of the Individual" in Chapter Five.

calls simply Transition—has particular pertinence to understanding our current time in culture and much that we now see around us.

Transition marks the line separating the creative journey's two halves. With it we reside at a doorway joining two related but also fundamentally different worlds. It can be a profound time. In its confrontations lie the seeds of a new kind of maturity within that particular periodicity's world of experience. But it can also be a time of major disorientation. Inescapably, it is a time of uncertainty. We stand at a precipice. Do we leap and trust that we will find solid ground? Do we go back? Proceeding depends on the gradual discovery of a new completeness in how we relate to both ourselves and our world. Transition is creation's "continental divide."

A Simple Creative Act: With a simple creative act, the work is now essentially complete—a crowning achievement. But what now? During the process of its creation, we have come to be almost more it than ourselves. And now, suddenly, we must let it go. We could be tempted out of fear to cling to the object, refuse its surrender. But if we do that, it becomes increasingly tired and purposeless, and we ourselves become increasingly absurd. We could just blindly walk away. But where do we go—indeed, is there any place to go?[10]

A Lifetime: With individual development, just as we thought we were done growing up, we confront the uniquely perplexing challenges of midlife. The most fundamental of questions reappear and block our way. In time, this necessary questioning touches every part of our lives—our work, our love, ultimately our most basic ideas about who we are and how the world works. The sense of purpose we once took for granted can suddenly feel elusive. We ask, "So who am I, really? And what really matters to me?" At this point we have no way of knowing whether anything that lies ahead will ever again excite us as before. We can fear that being simply "over the hill" may be our necessary

---

10 Transition in a simple creative act may coincide with a creative manifestation's release into the world, or the needed severance may instead be more internal, a necessary letting go if the work is to proceed. Especially with greater maturity in the creative person's personal development (either in his life as a whole, or more specifically, in the development of his craft), the piece's completion may wait until further seasoning has taken place. Whichever is the case, the underlying experience is similar.

fate. Some people respond to this uncertainty by abandoning what has been—by leaving their jobs, getting a divorce. Others cling to old beliefs or try to return to their youth. But we have no real choice but to live with the uncertainty. When we attempt to hide from it, perversely, we only feel more empty and confused.[11]

A Relationship: We see something similar with the midpoint in intimacy as a creative process. Suddenly, just as we thought love's work was complete, the passions that have driven love can seem to elude us. The same sense of completion that before gave us pride can start to feel like habit, and the comfort of familiarity can begin to feel like taking one another for granted. We have become for each other all-too-familiar objects. Where to go from here? Stepping forward requires that we surrender that familiarity, and with it our dreams of perfection and completion. But is there anything beyond these things? We have no way to be sure. In fear, we often cling to what we have known from before. But when we do, relationship becomes increasingly empty and stale.

The Story of Culture: CST proposes that much of what we see in the world in our time is a product of Transitional dynamics. I've described how humanity today confronts a Crisis of Purpose. Old answers are ceasing to work. And by all evidence they will not be replaced by new ones, at least not of the same sort. What lies ahead? Anything? From the position of the apex of Transition we cannot know. We can try to cling to familiar truths—from the onward-and-upward story of material progress to religious predictions of final salvation or damnation. But when we do, beneath the surface, we only feel more desperate.

Recognizing this Transitional predicament in the evolution of culture helps clarify previous reflections on the postmodern contribution. I've described how postmodern thought emphasizes the diminishing usefulness of culturally-specific truths, and, in the end, final truths more generally. And I've proposed that while postmodern formulations shed light on our times, in that they provide us with little to replace what they insightfully take away, in the end they stop short. We can understand both how such views help us and where they fail in terms of the dynamics of Transition. Postmodern views eloquently describe

---

11 Forty-seven is the age at which people are most likely to feel depressed and unhappy in their lives.

the Transitional quandary. But by themselves they give us no way to understand what may lie beyond it—indeed, whether anything of real significance could possibly lie ahead.

It is important in engaging Transition in culture to appreciate that it represents something fundamentally different than what we have encountered with previous societal developmental leaps. It involves more than just letting go of one stage and moving on to another. It brings into question the entire developmental orientation (toward ever greater ascendancy, separation, and solidification of form) that to this point has defined growth and truth. We can think of what I've referred to with the phrase Transitional Absurdity as a response to this legitimately disturbing circumstance. If the way that CST describes Transitional dynamics is accurate, it should not surprise us that we might react to them in less than sane ways.

Creative Integration

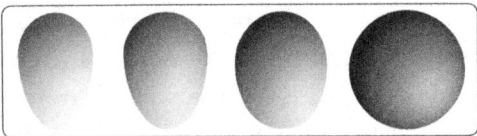

As we begin to step over maturity's threshold—whatever the creative scale—we leave Transition's precarious reality behind us. We are necessarily surprised by what we encounter—surprised that so much of creation's journey remains, surprised at the immense demands that steps yet to come present, and surprised too by the depth and richness of potential rewards.

While Transition in one sense marks a completion, in another sense it marks a beginning—the start of a systemically mature creative life. We may have thought creation finished, or nearly so, but in fact we have barely approached its midpoint. Yes, the new object of creation (that new invention or artwork, now-solidified personal identity, relationship as an entity, or culture as structure) stands shining before us. But it has yet to be significantly tested, either in the world or in ourselves. Creative Integration is about that testing and about the creative changes that result—change not just in the newly created object, but also in the systems that have done the creating.

The second half of any creative/formative process, in reconnecting the new creation with the personal and social contexts from which it was born, begins to take us beyond the disturbing reality presented by Transition.

It brings at once a further stepping back and a new and deeper kind of engagement. We become newly able to step back from what we have created, from who we have been in the creating, and also from the creative process as a process, from formative process as a progression. And at the same time, we engage both ourselves and what we have created with new depth and clarity. In the process, we come to better appreciate both where the process of creation has taken us, and what ultimately it has been about. We also begin to step forward into a more complete kind of reality.

While the word "integration" begins to get at what takes place, as I've emphasized, this is not integration in any simple additive or averaging sense. The changes that we encounter in these integrative stages are as fully creative as any that have come before. Indeed they are so in a particularly fundamental sense. Like previous changes, they involve not just what we think, but how we think. But in this case, the result is not just a next step in a familiar kind of creative progression, but a whole new kind of cognitive orientation and organization.

The dual changes that produce it change everything. With any creative periodicity, we find the possibility of a less mythologized and absolutist, no longer "parental" picture of how things work—the mythic "parent" in question being variously ourselves with any individual process of creation,[12] a person who gave birth to us, cut-and-dried notions about how relationships work, or culture as a system. We also see a new and deeper engagement with our human complexity—with pertinent polarities, with our multiple intelligences, and in the specific context of that particular formative process, with our larger whole-box-of-crayons natures.

With Creative Integration's cognitive reordering, our interest comes to lie increasingly not just with the newly created object, but with that object in living relationship with all that surrounds it. Within the limits of any formative process's particular creative scale, Integrative Stage mechanisms propel us into a more conscious and explicitly complex and

---

12 With any creative act of the more conventional sort, we must surrender equally beliefs we might have that make ourselves as individuals the sole parent/source of the creation and opposite sorts of beliefs that place that source of creation solely in some mythologized, and thus equally parental, notion of mystery. In the process, creativity becomes more "ordinary," and at the same time, more ultimately worthy of our wonder.

systemic world of experience. Previous to this point in development, this result would have seemed disorienting and overwhelming. As Integrative Stage dynamics become timely, we experience these changes as positive. They make possible a sophistication of understanding—and of life—that we could not have known before.

A Simple Creative Act: With a new idea, invention, or work of art, we begin to recognize how the journey of its creation is in fact far from over. The piece may need further seasoning. And, even if it does not, it has yet to be placed in the world. And in an important sense, it also has yet to be placed in ourselves. Much remains to happen and to be learned. I remember being struck in my years sculpting how often on "completing" a piece of real significance it was years before I understood with any clarity what the piece was really about, what it had to teach. The conscious object of creation before has been the piece. Creative maturity reveals that my engagement with it had always been as much about creating myself, and, if it was truly functioning as art, about new possibilities in the creation of culture.

A Lifetime: In our individual lives, the primary achievements of the first half of development—self-definition, the acquisition of skills and knowledge, perhaps creating a family—all in some way involve establishing ourselves as form. The developmental challenges of life's second half make real, in ever more subtle ways, the fact that creative Transition first made inescapable—that such forms in themselves stop shot of fully addressing truth and identity. Questions of a newly contextual sort—questions of perspective and meaning—increasingly come to the fore. We reexamine our professions, looking to see if they still provide challenge and fulfillment in our lives—and, as important, if they contribute in satisfying ways. We do the same with our relationships and our beliefs. In the process, who we are in each of these spheres deepens. Frequently our choices remain largely as before—it is primarily our relationship to our choices that changes. But sometimes, too, we make new choices, venture off in wholly new directions. When we say someone is mature, seasoned, or wise, we are appreciating that that person has engaged and weathered at least the most important of life's Integration Stage developmental tasks.

A Relationship: With intimate relationships, again we become newly capable of more fully stepping back. We also become more capable of appreciating what love of a deep sort is ultimately about. Love's second-half tasks give emphasis increasingly to the uniqueness of each person and to the unique needs of the relationship. As we become more fully ourselves, our connection can also become more full. This can happen only with the acceptance of limits to what one person can be for another, but in the end this is not loss. Being together with integrity, caring, and honesty—however that might look—increasingly defines affection and commitment. Within the encompassing assumptions of our particular cultural place and time, we more deeply appreciate self and other as particular and complex beings.

The Story of Culture: The "growing up" I've described with the concept of Cultural Maturity refers specifically to this "second-half" kind of developmental process. With Integrative Meta-perspective, we become better able to at once step back from and more deeply engage the larger experience of being human. One result is the kind of whole-box-of-crayons systemic understanding of ourselves and our worlds that future human choices will increasingly depend on. Another is new, more mature kinds of skills and capacities. We find ourselves better recognizing how truths that before seemed separate or even adversarial—many of which are essential to our sense of identity and meaning—may in fact work as colluding partners. We also better appreciate the fact of real limits in all part of our personal and collective lives. And we are able to better grasp how the way we perceive always affects what we perceive, including our conclusions about what ultimately has importance.

The Dilemma of Trajectory and Transitional Absurdity

I've briefly introduced a concept that provides some of the most solid evidence for the concept of Cultural Maturity—what CST calls the Dilemma of Trajectory. It deserves a closer look. This chapter's observations help fill out the Dilemma of Trajectory and also make more understandable some of people's common reactions in confronting it. I've suggested that the concept sheds important light on much that we can find most disturbing in our time.

Earlier, I framed the Dilemma of Trajectory in terms of polarity's underlying "procreative" symmetry. I described how, over the first half of any creative/formative process we see a progression from more archetypally feminine dominance to realities in which the archetypally masculine has the much greater influence. I observed that this trajectory of change ultimately leaves us at a dead end.

Framing the Dilemma of Trajectory in terms of the evolution of difference helps make its implications more concrete. The Creative Function describes how each stage in any developmental process's first half produces greater emphasis on difference—distance between polar extremes and difference more generally. At Transition, this defining impetus reaches an extreme. The Dilemma of Trajectory brings attention to how going further in this direction really stops being an option.

We can again draw on the analogy with personal development. The first half of personal psychological development is marked by processes that produce ever-greater independence, individuality, and authority over the world around us—each expressions of increasing separation and emphasis on difference. This general direction of change in effect defines growth in the first half of our lives. But in an individual life's second half, it stops serving us in the same way. Indeed, if we continue on as we have, the second half of life becomes increasingly absurd, at best a thin caricature of youth.

In a similar way, history to this point has produced ever greater emphasis on distinction. Each cultural stage has brought a growing impetus toward independence and individual authority, from the early rise of civilization's first clear separation from nature, to later, the Magna Carta's affirmation of basic human privilege and the Declaration of Independence's proclamation of the right of the individual to the pursuit of happiness. It has also brought ever greater perceived control over the world around us culminating with how the Industrial Age promised an ultimate kind of human dominion and how today's Information Age gives that promise an all-encompassing kind of expression.

While such achievement could not have been more significant, as with Transition in individual development, today, this developmental trajectory has stopped serving us. While much of what we have reaped, and will continue to reap, from our ability to stand separate in the sense of individuality and autonomy of choice is profound, the future cries out as much for a new appreciation of how we are related, a fresh understanding of caring, community, and the common good. And while culture's evolution has also brought with it increasing human control—over nature, over our own bodies, over life's deep mysteries—today almost the opposite is equally a part of what is needed, a new humility to what we cannot control, a new sensitivity to when we should be listening as opposed to directing (whether the voice needing attention is the natural world, our tissues, or the unfathomable).

We can usefully frame the Dilemma of Trajectory in terms of leadership, what Cultural Maturity is most ultimately about. Today, we confront profound questions, indeed questions with God-like implications. But the authority needed to address them is not some ascension to a chair of final dominion (ourselves somehow becoming God). It is also different from some further iteration of the Enlightenment's grand goal of bringing all of understanding into the pure light of awareness and realizing final control over the untamed. Indeed, many of the problems we face in today's world derive from just such hubristic notions of what right action is about. We are left in a pickle that cannot be resolved by continuing on the course we have known. If more systemic understanding is in fact what today's new questions require, then culturally mature perspective—or at least something that provides a similar more aware and integrative outcome—becomes the only real option.

Framing the Dilemma of Trajectory more specifically in creative terms brings attention to the fundamental nature of these consequences and depths of their implications. At Transition we stand in a world of all content and no context, of all right hand and no left, of life as ultimate abstraction stretched ever more distant from experience's roots. Taken far enough, proceeding further in this direction of distinction and separation leads to circumstances that are not just ludicrous, but ultimately self-destructive. It threatens to sever us from much that is most important in being human—such as the body, the child's world of imagination, our human connectedness with one another, and our felt relationship with the spiritual and with nature.

With Chapter Seven's look at commonly expressed "scenarios for the future," I will describe how each of our more familiar ways of thinking about the tasks ahead ultimately fails to address the Dilemma of Trajectory. I will also describe how the Dilemma of Trajectory alerts us to particular ways our thinking can go astray. I've touched briefly on the CST concept of Transitional Absurdity. In Chapter Seven, I will address specific Transitional Absurdities. For now, the important recognition is their relationship to the Dilemma of Trajectory.

Some Transitional Absurdities protect us by simply helping us ignore what is being asked of us. Denial in the face of critical environmental challenges such as climate change provides the most obvious example. Others more specifically "overshoot the mark," apply outmoded, onward-and-upward ways of thinking to questions that now demand much more of us. Earlier I contrasted utopian beliefs with Cultural Maturity's new-common-sense outcome. Techno-utopian beliefs at the least ignore that the ability to invent and the capacity to use invention wisely are not at all the same. Utopian beliefs of a more spiritual/religious sort, whether of a fundamentalist inclination that promises final salvation for a few, or of the more New Age sort that sees humanity's future as a whole in terms of some ultimate realization, reflect a more Inner Aspect kind of overshooting the mark.

We also encounter Transitional Absurdities that are better thought of as regressive reactions to feeling overwhelmed by the magnitude of current challenges. Some of today's extreme polarization in the social and political spheres may reflect little more than the two-steps-forward-one-step-back nature of change or reactive responses to particular events, but I suspect a major part of it reflects this specifically regressive sort of Transitional Absurdity.

The important recognition at this point is that Cultural Maturity's cognitive reordering, besides reconciling the Dilemma of Trajectory, also provides the needed antidote to Transitional Absurdities, whatever their roots. Cultural Maturity's cognitive changes don't diminish challenges or eliminate overwhelm—indeed, they specifically contribute to our time's demands.[13] But they do provide the perspective needed to deal with current circumstances and what may lie ahead in the most healthy and creative ways.

Conceptual Implications and Practical Applications

Patterning in Time's developmental/evolutionary picture is significant at multiple levels. Certainly it has important conceptual implications. Most immediately significant conceptually is the support it provides for the concept of Cultural Maturity. It explicitly predicts Cultural Maturity's changes. If in fact it is accurate to frame cultural change in developmental terms, then it should only be a matter of time before we confront the possibilities—and new responsibilities—that the concept of Cultural Maturity describes.

---

13 In Chapter Five, we will examine the CST concept of Capacitance. CST describes how, when systems are challenged to more than they can handle—in ways that exceed their available Capacitance—they respond with symptoms.

Patterning in Time's picture also provides conceptual support for my claim that Creative Systems Theory reflects the new kind of thinking that our future will depend on. The fact that CST Patterning in Time notions engage the whole of intelligence and "bridge" pertinent polarities means that they succeed at the critical conceptual task of taking us beyond the mechanistic assumptions of Modern Age thought—in particular with regard to change, but also more broadly. Patterning in Time notions illustrate how the use of a creative frame allows us to leave behind engineering-model beliefs and think in ways that more directly reflect what it means to be alive, and human.

And more specifically, CST Patterning in Time notions are significant conceptually for how directly they support the observation that serves as the foundation for CST. We come back to CST's assertion that what makes us unique is our audacious toolmaking, meaning-making—"creative"— natures. The whole of the developmental/evolutionary picture we have looked at follows predictably from what we would expect if human cognition organizes creatively. We can think of all the remaining topics in this book—more filled-out reflections on Cultural Maturity's needed new skills and capacities, further patterning notions, and applications from front-page-news questions to ultimate human concerns—as following from where these creatively framed Patterning in Time observations take us.

But the average person will find greatest significance in the more everyday implications of various Patterning in Time observations. At the level of specific creative acts, anyone whose life involves creative work of any depth will appreciate more fully understanding the demands and rewards that come at different points in a creative endeavor. And CST's picture of individual development will be of particular help for parents, teachers, hospice workers, and anyone else engaged in age-related endeavors, particularly people who are committed to the future of such endeavors. In addition, people will find benefit in how this kind of perspective helps clarify relationship's tasks. When I do psychotherapy with couples, making the simple observation that certain kinds of struggle or misperception pretty much come with the territory at particular points in a relationship can be remarkably freeing.

The most provocative of such more practical implications for most people will lie at a cultural scale. Beyond how CST Patterning in Time observations make today's challenges and the capacities needed to address them more understandable, there is also, for example, the particular guidance such recognitions provide for engaging with cultures that inhabit different developmental realities. This century's conflicts in Iraq and Afghanistan provide illustration. With both Iraq and Afghanistan, applying a Patterning in Time lens would have resulted in decidedly better policy.

The belief among American leaders at the beginning of the second Iraq War that the Iraqi people would celebrate the presence of U.S. soldiers—certainly for any length of time—would be naïve enough were Iraq a modern nation. But the larger portion of modern Iraq's population in fact resides in the equivalent of a late medieval (late Middle-Axis) reality. (There is significant diversity—some people embody more modern sensibilities, and some reflect sensibilities of an earlier sort—but drawing analogy to the 14th or 15th centuries in the West makes a useful analogy for policy.) Appreciation of this fact, and its implications, would have produced some very different choices. Given the cultural stage, polar intolerance for occupying forces was totally predictable, as were protracted antagonisms and struggles for power between ethnic factions following the end of Saddam Hussein's rule.

U.S. military action in Afghanistan was arguably more justified, but seen from a developmental perspective, we would predict the task to be even more daunting. In his book *The Wrong War*, Bing West (who spent ten years fighting in Afghanistan) describes how he reluctantly came to the conclusion that modern Afghanistan resides in the equivalent of about 9th century Europe.[14] (We also find more Early-Axis cultural stage dynamics in Afghanistan, but early medieval makes a good general approximation.) Note that this observation not only affects the prognosis for success, it also means that lessons learned in Iraq were not going to be as applicable as leaders assumed. We can debate whether U.S. involvement in Afghanistan ultimately provided value. With regard to disrupting the training of international terrorists, it may have been of benefit. But it is also the case that at the time of this book's writing, the Taliban has a stronger presence in the country than it did at the time of first U.S. involvement in the country.

With both Iraq and Afghanistan, applying a Patterning in Time lens would have at the least alerted the modern world to the fact that efforts at regime change and nation building—and, in particular, efforts that

---

14 Bing West, *The Wrong War*, Random House, 2011.

might consider the establishment of Western-style democratic systems an appropriate goal—were very unlikely to be successful, and would easily lead only to further destabilization.

These examples highlight an essential kind of responsibility that modern societies confront in today's global world. More advanced nations will increasingly need to make leadership decisions in the face of developmentally asymmetrical relationships. The demands of such leadership can often seem unfair (for example, rarely with developmentally asymmetrical relationships are proportional responses to conflict appropriate). But they are not wholly unfamiliar. When grown-ups interact with adolescents, they don't expect the adolescent to meet them as equals. They assume that at times they will have to deal with adolescent reactiveness and respond by "being the adult in the room." When dealing with asymmetrical relationships on the world stage, in a similar way modern societies must stand ready to meet circumstances with a degree of perspective—and wisdom—that they will only rarely get in return.[15]

A further way that bringing evolutionary perspective to cultural stage differences provides benefit is by helping us make sense of easily confusing historical circumstances. One example concerns colonialism and just what made it possible. We tend to assume that European nations were able to establish their colonial empires because of military and technological superiority, and certainly these factors played major roles.[16] More advanced weaponry was essential to what we saw. But I don't think military might alone fully explains the ease and rapidity with which even small European nations were often able to gain the submission of large populations. I suspect the fact that people historically have tended to mythologize groups from more advanced cultural stages also played a role.[17] In our time, this dynamic less and less comes into play, in part because of the greater knowledge that comes with globalization, in part

---

15 This description might immediately lead to accusations of elitism. But note that if this kind of responsibility is denied, future consequences could easily be catastrophic.

16 This is essentially the argument made in Jared Diamond's popular work, *Guns, Germs, and Steel*.

17 Indeed, in some instances, colonial invaders, at least initially, have been seen as having special, almost magical powers.

likely also because mythologizing everywhere is at least beginning to lose its historical power. Thus we find occupiers from more developed culture stages less often tolerated. Indeed, as is increasingly the case with the Middle East, more often they are viewed simply as invaders.

Appreciation for cultural stage differences also adds important detail to our understanding of the kind of mythologizing that in times past has produced chosen-people/evil-other dynamics on the world stage. For simplicity's sake, I've previously spoken as if such reactive mythologizing was happening in interactions between developmentally parallel cultural systems. But such dynamics have historically often been compounded by projective mechanisms particular to relationships between different cultural stages. Along with simple demonization, we often then see further, even more severe kinds of distancing. Like with the pushing away that produces developmental amnesias, such additional distancing serves the purpose of protecting a system from aspects of reality it finds unconsciously threatening. Stage-specific polarizations commonly come into play with severe oppression and genocide. It was demonic projections of this sort, for example, that allowed white settlers in the Americas to think of native populations not as people, but as ignorant savages, and to act accordingly.

Understanding cultural stage dynamics can also add important nuance to our grasp of more particular events in global affairs. What transpired in the former Soviet Union with the presidency of Mikhail Gorbachev provides a good example. It highlights how stage-related dynamics can influence the internal workings of countries. It also highlights an important leadership recognition. Effective nation-state leaders tend to be just a bit more evolved than the populace they govern—not behind the populace, but also not too far ahead.

The former Soviet Union resided primarily in the middle substages of Late-Axis—analogous to Europe's Age of Empire. Mikhail Gorbachev was celebrated by the West for instituting more late substage Late-Axis policies such as glasnost ("openness") and perestroika ("restructuring"). But the result was not wholly positive. Arguably the collapse of the Soviet Union was a consequence. And today Gorbachev tends not to be well thought of in Russia. In contrast, Vladimir Putin, while not as evolved in his sensibilities, has demonstrated impressive staying power and in Russia is generally respected. I suspect a major reason is that the creative substage in cultural development that he embodies is a better match for where the larger portion of the Russian population currently resides.

We may very well be witnessing a related tension currently in the United States, but one where the implications are almost the opposite. When Barack Obama first became president, I observed that his election was significant not just because he was a black man, but also because he embodied beginning culturally mature leadership capacities. (I warned my more liberal colleagues that because of this they might not be as happy with him as they imagined.) I've described how we find ourselves today in a period of socio-political regression. This regression is global. But I suspect that here in the U.S. at least some of it is also a backlash to leadership that was a bit ahead of its time. The difference in this case is that it was ahead of its time in just the way needed if the U.S. is to advance in the ways that our times require.

These more specific Patterning in Time observations, when combined with earlier reflections about asymmetrical relationships, highlight a key challenge—we could say an essential obligation—for people in the modern West as we look to the future. I've proposed that humanity's long-term well-being will depend on culturally mature leadership. Given that the greatest potential for culturally mature leadership, at least in the short term, resides in the West, arguably the task of making needed further steps—and sooner rather than later—takes on added significance in Western nations. It is impossible to predict how long the current time of regression will continue. But the modern West doesn't have the option of letting it continue for long.

Finer Distinctions

These more applied recognitions provide a good segue into an important additional kind of Patterning in Time observation. While thus far I've given attention primarily to the big-picture contours of Patterning in Time mappings, here I've at least hinted at the possibility of making finer distinctions (for example, with the description of modern day Russia). More fine-grained discernments often prove particularly valuable when it comes to the practical tasks of application.

Such more detailed Patterning in Time distinctions have their basis in the recognition that creative stages are themselves creative processes and organize creatively. Thus we can identify creatively ordered substages within larger change processes. The diagram in Fig. 3-1 from *The Creative Imperative* depicts creative substages within our most recent cultural stage.

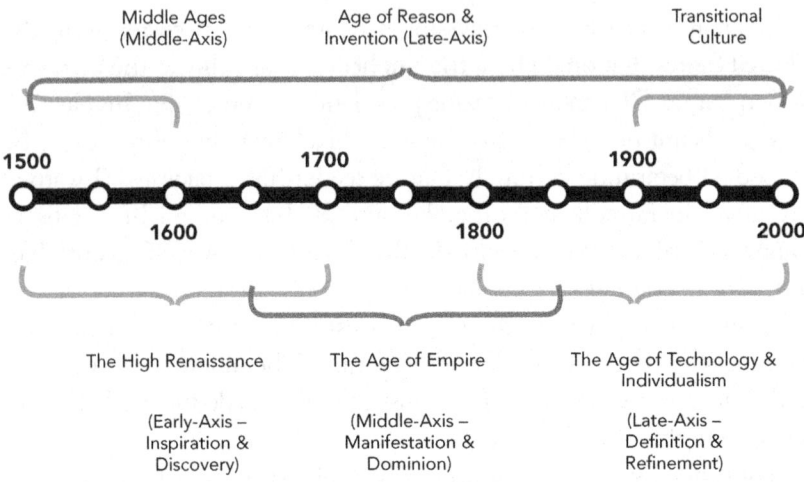

Fig. 3-1. Major Substages in Late-Axis Culture

A close look back through Late-Axis cultural times reveals periods with distinct Early-, Middle-, and Late-Axis coloration. First came a period of initial inspiration and discovery. This was the time of Columbus, Cortez, and Magellan, and the birth of a new Age of Exploration; of Michelangelo, da Vinci, and Raphael, and the beginnings of Europe's artistic renaissance; of Galileo, Newton, and Descartes, and the emergence of the scientific paradigm; and of Martin Luther and the first suggestions of a new, more personal kind of relationship with the divine. After this came a period with a decidedly more Middle-Axis flavor, the Age of Empire. We then saw struggles between the great European powers for dominance in the new world, open conflict between social classes, and the first establishment of the structures of industrialization. The last 200 years, what we might call the Age of Technology and Individualism, has been most definitively Late-Axis, with the final establishment of democratic institutions, a new elevation of the individual in the writings of people like Thomas Paine and Jean-Jacques Rousseau, the realization of universal education, and the full flowering of scientific preeminence.

Within any substage, we can also identify even smaller creative fluctuations. As a rough rule of thumb, such subcycles tend to span thirty to forty years.[18] For

---

[18] This kind of pattern manifests within the thinking of particular domains as well as with broad cultural tendencies. For example, Arthur Schlesinger,

example, when we look to the later part of the twentieth century and the early parts of the current century, we find fluctuations that imbue early Transitional aesthetics with qualities we know from our now-familiar creative stages.

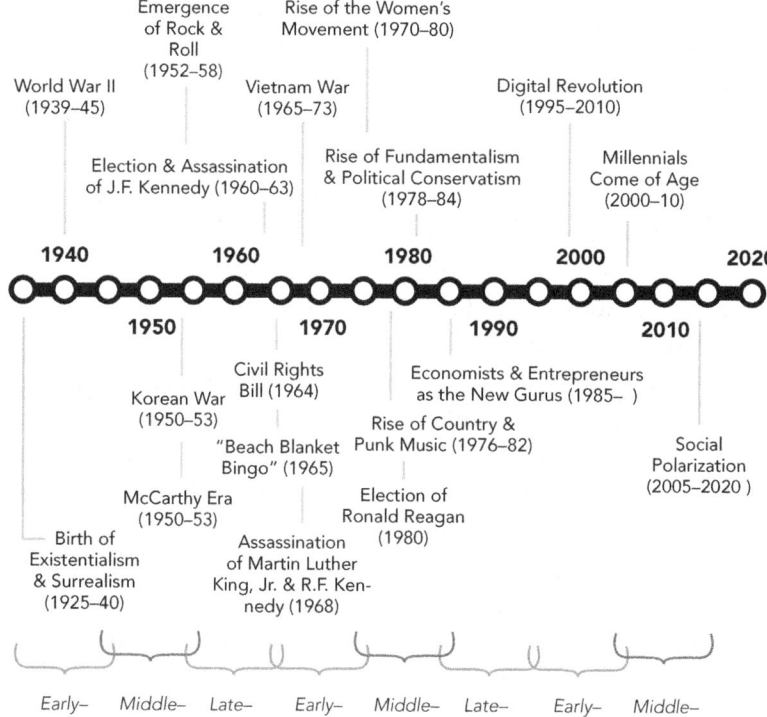

Fig. 3-2. Rhythmic Fluctuations Over the Last Eighty Years

In the 60s and early 70s, Early-Axis sensibilities flavored the emerging Transitional picture: the magical youth of the "flower child," strong advocacy of matriarchal values such as peace and reverence for nature, neopagan sexual norms, and fascination spiritually with both Eastern and Western mystical thought. The mid-70s and early 80s were marked by values of an increasingly Middle-Axis sort: renewed fundamentalism and moralism in religion, mounting

---

Jr., in his book *The Cycles of American History*, describes how liberal and conservative dominance in the political sphere have alternated predictably over the course of American politics, moving in roughly thirty-year cycles.

conservatism in politics, and in music the emergence of punk and rap and the sudden popularity of Middle-Axis forms such as country music that had been largely ignored by the broader culture. With the mid-80s and 90s we witnessed a growing emphasis on more Late-Axis, individualistic and materialistic values. Increasingly the "best and the brightest" went to Wall Street.

The early years of the twenty-first century reflected a further turning of this thirty- to forty-year cycle. Radical innovation again prevailed—in this case, that of the digital revolution. While in the 60s and early 70s people who wanted answers looked to gurus, antiwar leaders, and hip psychologists, with the beginnings of the twenty-first century, they looked instead to the wizards of high tech. More recently, we have seen evidence of Middle-Axis tendencies with increasing tension between social and political extremes.

Today as we move ever further into Transitional dynamics, this level of detail tends not to provide the same precision as before. Partly this is because such rhythmic fluctuations take place in the context of a growing complexity of other factors that affect what we see (for example, globalization). But it is just as much because of how Transitional dynamics "flatten out" creative fluctuations. Such rhythmic dynamics require the involvement of both left-hand and right-hand sensibilities if they are to manifest in any deep way. With left-hand sensibilities largely eclipsed, creative substages are going to manifest less visibly and more often be overshadowed by other factors.

Rewriting History

Oscar Wilde wrote, "The one duty we owe to history is to rewrite it." Patterning in Time concepts applied at a cultural scale help clarify a claim I made at the book's beginning. Culturally mature perspective invites—indeed, demands—that we rewrite history. Patterning in Time concepts challenge us to revisit not just certain of history's facts, but also modern notions of what constitutes history. In the end, they rewrite both what we mean by history and our understanding of ourselves as participants in history.

Most immediately, Patterning in Time concepts help us see the past more accurately. They help us get beyond projective distortions—both those that demonize and those that romantically idealize[19]—and better

---

19 Romantic idealization can make association with any cultural stage. Academics tend to idealize the Age of Reason (or sometimes the ancient

appreciate what has been particular about various cultural times. The dissolving of cultural amnesias that comes with Integrative Meta-perspective provides a clearer and more nuanced, if not always so self-affirming, picture of what has brought us to where we are.

Patterning in Time's picture also brings important greater depth to our understanding of history. Even when projection has not distorted our perceptions, the sensibilities that have defined Modern Age thought have caused us to miss much that is most important. Because the lens provided by a rational/material worldview is able to describe only the most surface layers of experience's full richness and complexity, history has often become little more than a chronicling of leaders, wars, and inventions. And what we have missed has often been exactly that which is most essential not to miss if we wish to make sense of values, motivations, and worldviews—particularly those of premodern peoples (including ourselves prior to the Industrial Age). Our modern conception of history is, in the end, limited when it tries to describe the past, to the same degree—and for the same reasons—that Modern Age definitions of intelligence are limited if we wish to capture cognition's full complexity.

Patterning in Time concepts also make possible a more richly dynamic understanding of history. This comes naturally from what we newly bring to the process of understanding. At the least, culturally mature developmental/evolutionary perspective helps us better put past events in context and grasp how one moment of history ties to another—insights that can radically alter how we interpret events. It also helps us better recognize how aspects of history to which we may

---

> Greeks). Adamant conservative and fundamentalist religious views can by inference idealize almost medieval sensibilities (drawing on belief from a time previous to modern secular humanism and after the rise of monotheism). And New Age ideologies, along with the beliefs of environmentalists and certain feminists, may draw on idealized references to cultural times and places where archetypally feminine sensibilities held clear influence—for example, to tribal cultures, earlier agrarian societies, and classical Eastern belief. Later, with our examination of ways that personality style differences affect how we see the future, we will look at how different temperaments are prone to particular kinds of romantic idealizations. (See Chapters Six and Seven.)

have ascribed secondary importance at best—such as art, music, religion, moral belief, or the life of the body—in fact have considerable pertinence to making sense of cultural change. Good teachers of history have always drawn on certain such less obvious contributors to help make history come alive, and the best of historians have gone further, noting patterns and relationships. But with Cultural Maturity's cognitive reordering, these added ingredients stop being condiments and become explicit parts of the main meal.

Of particular importance, culturally mature perspective provides a more purpose-centered appreciation of the human endeavor. It transforms history from a chronicling of events and beliefs to a multifaceted study of human significance and our relationship to it. While purpose too has always been a part of well-told history, when we consciously bring more of ourselves to the task of understanding, history becomes more specifically an inquiry into who we are as storytellers and makers of meaning. Also, by implication, history becomes as much about the possible nature of meaning in the future as it is about the stories that have brought us to where we are today.

CST Patterning in Time notions also suggest an important "historical" reward beyond history itself. They make the study of history a "hands-on" tool for acquiring culturally mature capacities. Just as more deeply engaging the complexities of intelligence or appreciating the consequences of "bridging" polarities can bring us closer to culturally mature understanding, so too can a sufficiently deep engagement with where we have come from. Grasping history more deeply can provide a particularly powerful way to realize the more complete kind of understanding that future tasks of all sorts will increasingly require of us.

An approach I've applied in my teaching makes use of developmental/evolutionary perspective in this way. It is notable for making music the creative vehicle—not a topic an academic treatment of history would be likely to emphasize. The inspiration for this approach came from an exceptional series of classes on world music that I took while in college.[20] What I heard in those classes greatly

---

20 Robert Garfias, founder of one of the country's first ethnomusicology

moved me and provided many insights that were important to the later development of CST.[21]

Once each year during the Institute for Creative Development's brick-and-mortar years, I did a presentation that I called "An Evolutionary History of Music." Over the course of a day, I would play music from each of culture's creative stages and engaged people—through story, dance, and conversation—in the underlying sensibilities of each stage. My intent in doing this elaborate and lengthy presentation was in part to fill out history, to involve people in the past in a way that would help dissolve the developmental amnesias that before have distanced us from history's full depth and richness. But as much it was to provide a direct experience of the larger—whole-box-of-crayons—complexity on which future human understanding and choice must be based. Participants have described the experience as bringing history—and history's larger significance—alive in ways they had not felt before. It became a much-anticipated event.[22]

More Patterning in Time—The History of Philosophy

One of Patterning in Time's particularly provocative contributions is the way it helps us put not just truth more generally, but specific kinds of truth, in historical perspective. We can apply the Creative Function to help delineate how truths tied to particular sorts of understanding have evolved through time—scientific truth, religious truth, artistic truth, our ideas about government or education, or truth conclusions about the human body. The

---

departments (at the University of Washington), taught these classes. While today it is not uncommon to hear music from far-flung parts of the planet, back then this was a rare and special experience. Each morning we would listen to sounds that we'd never heard before, but that were nonetheless deeply rooted in time and culture.

21 Recognizing commonalities tied to cultural stages not only helped refine my thinking about how culture has evolved, it also provided initial insights for CST's framework for understanding temperament (see Chapter Six). During the classes, I noticed that people with different personality styles tended to be attracted to music from different times in culture. The recognition—central (and unique) to CST—that related patterning principles underlie temporal and here-and-now systemic differences had its origins in these observations.

22 This presentation can be viewed at www.Evolmusic.org.

way the Creative Function provides a big-picture vantage for thinking about philosophical truth provides a particularly significant example.

Creative Systems Theory starts out by alerting us to limits inherent in philosophy's approach. Philosophy, even when interpreted very broadly as here, means ideas that can be verbally articulated and put into some rational form (even if their focus is the nonrational[23]). Thus, while philosophy claims to be about truth itself, the perspective from which it views truth often limits what it is capable of grasping.[24] John Keats voiced the limitation as a rhetorical question, "Do not all charms fly at the mere touch of cold philosophy?"[25]

But once we recognize philosophy's limitations, philosophical truth provides a valuable window. At the least it is representative of broader understanding. And because it tends toward verbal descriptions and logical analysis, philosophy is more amenable to brief synopsis (ignoring for the moment the fact that philosophers are rarely brief) than, say, the historical "beliefs" of art, government, or religion.

The Creative Function provides a crude but provocative way to "map" the history of philosophy. Besides applying the Creative Function's general evolutionary picture, such mapping draws on a key recognition. We can think of philosophical tradition as having left and right hands (or at least traditions that lean variously to the right or left). Philosophy refers to these two fundamental currents in different ways—the transcendental as opposed

---

23 With both modern and postmodern thinking, the rational bias then often manifests in a way that ironically relies even more on the rational. We can see lengthy, highly rational treatises on the limits of rationality. The length of such treatises and the fact that we would refer to them as treatises makes the rational's continued preeminence clear.

24 Because rationality represents the most creatively manifest of intelligences, we could conclude that philosophy is a solely right-hand activity. But our picture needs to be more nuanced. Creative Systems Theory affirms that philosophy is largely an Upper-Pole activity (in the Creative Function and in ourselves, an activity of the head more than the body or emotions). But it also delineates how each pole has more reflective (Inner) and expressive (Outer) aspects. Philosophy most draws on the Inner aspect of Upper-Pole sensibilities. This additional recognition is essential to appreciating what philosophy observes in general, and, in particular, to what happens to philosophy at Transition's threshold.

25 From his poem Lamia.

to the empirical, the approach of the idealist or the romantic as opposed to the positivist or the materialist. Each at times flows into the other, but the simplification supports understanding. Jean Gebser described the situation this way: "Idealists and materialists are like two children on a seesaw who have been teetering back and forth for two thousand years."[26]

The more left-hand current includes thinkers such as Plato and philosophers of more religious bent who believe that what we can ultimately most rely on is inner experience, whether mental or spiritual. The more right-hand current includes thinkers who in one way or another believe we rely ultimately (or at least most usefully) on our senses, such as the early natural philosophers, Aristotle, and most of modern science. CST expands on this recognition by applying the observation that polarities organize creatively. The history of ideas becomes a chronicling of the diverse ways in which this two-handed interplay has been perceived through time, and from different perspectives at particular points in time. If nothing else, this approach offers the possibility of synopsis and an antidote to that common lack of brevity in philosophical writings.

Two basic change processes shape this philosophical trek through time, both now familiar. The first is that gradual shift from more left-hand (archetypally feminine) to right-hand (archetypally masculine) emphasis over the course of creative differentiation. Left-handed cosmologies predominate in earliest cultural periods, while more right-handed worldviews come to the fore as we move toward the present. The second is how creative stages—Pre-Axis, Early-Axis, Middle-Axis, Late-Axis—give each hand identifiable characteristics depending on when it manifests.

The descriptions that follow are highly (even absurdly) abridged. I will mention thinkers and belief systems without great elaboration. Readers may find some familiarity with philosophical thought's key figures and traditions to be helpful, but the most important recognitions concern the suggested underlying patterns.

Many people would not consider where we must start philosophy, given that tribal (Pre-Axis) beliefs precede written language. But the animistic assumptions of Pre-Axis times do produce a consistent kind of worldview. I've described how left-hand sensibilities almost wholly define experience in tribal societies. It is not that right-hand elements

---

26 Jean Gebser, *The Ever-Present Origin*, Ohio University Press, 1986

are denied; rather, simply, they are not yet strongly present. All is seen as connected—tribe, nature, spirit, time—and these connections define truth. People may assume more right-hand and left-hand roles—a tribal chief's duties are more "secular" than those of a shaman. But differences manifest within an almost entirely unitary holding of experience.

While the cosmologies of civilization's early rise (Early-Axis) more overtly acknowledge both hands of truth, the left hand, as I've observed, retains dominance. The magical and mythic beliefs of ancient Egypt, the Incas and Aztecs, classical India,[27] or Olympian Greece each gave primary emphasis to the archetypally feminine. Plato's philosophy belongs in this left-hand tradition, though he conceived of truth's left hand more in terms of mind than spirit. In Plato's cave, external reality is a play of shadows cast by internal essences—the "forms" or "ideas." Aristotle, along with the earlier Greek natural philosophers, focused more outwardly, on phenomena that could be understood with the senses: the natural world, speech, behavior. Their thinking laid the foundation for modern scientific thought. But even Aristotle's ideas made but a start to the right. Aristotle saw divine action as what began it all—the "unmoved mover"—and invisible causal forces behind motion of every sort.

The strength of truth's two hands became more balanced with culture's perspiration stage (Middle-Axis), but because philosophy tends to take expression from the more Inner, reflective side of our rationality (in contrast to politics or economics), medieval philosophical writings tend still to lean toward the archetypally feminine. This continued left-handed emphasis is particularly evident in expressly theistic formulations such as the fourth-century ideas of St. Augustine of Hippo or those of medieval mystics such as Meister Eckhart or Hildegard of Bingen. But the Middle Ages saw also a manifesting of expressly secular philosophy. While St. Thomas Aquinas's ideas were deeply grounded in religious principle, they followed on and extended the tradition of Aristotle. William of Ockham went even further in pressing against the constraints of orthodox religious cosmology.

With the Modern Age (Late-Axis), archetypally masculine philosophical sensibilities moved to the forefront. In the empiricism of Bacon, Locke, and Hume, right-hand truths were assumed to shape the left. Positivist formulations, such those of Saint-Simon and Comte, relied almost exclusively on truth's right hand, as did the more extreme of materialist

---

27 The major portion of Eastern philosophy has its roots in this stage.

and early scientific views (Hobbes and Laplace).[28] Dualism became explicit in the seventeenth-century thinking of Descartes[29] (and in a less absolutely cleaved form in the ideas of Leibniz). We see the greatest right-hand preeminence in current times with the claims of extreme behaviorism and scientism that material explanation is all we need.

Modern Age left-hand cosmologies arose either as a counterbalance to or a reaction against this new right-hand supremacy. The most important include modern forms of idealism (Berkeley, Kant, or Hegel) along with eighteenth- and nineteenth-century romanticism (Rousseau, Schelling, or Goethe). Idealist cosmologies acknowledge the validity of both of truth's hands and assume that they interact, but with them truth's left hand in the end drives the right and determines truth. Spinoza's equating of God with nature set the stage for romanticism's polar response to the growing dominance of right-hand sensibilities.

Note that this progression brings us eventually to the Dilemma of Trajectory, the critical impasse that is central to CST's argument for Cultural Maturity. As left-hand sensibilities surrender their dominance to right-hand beliefs, eventually their influence becomes largely eclipsed. Thought's history describes a step-by-step replacing of mysticism by "hard truth." Contemporary thought proclaims final victory for arm's-length objectivity (and assumes that future thought will simply reap the rewards of that victory). We are left with the question of whether there is anywhere left to go.

At the least, we are left with the question of whether philosophy has anywhere left to go. If extreme advocates of right-hand truth are correct and right-hand truth is all there ever really was (the left hand was just a pleasant illusion), then in effect we've arrived. Philosophy has appropriately reached the end of its usefulness—it is now a historical artifact, its functions replaced by economics, science, and technology. (It is understandable that today we might find so few job openings for philosophers.)

---

28 I say "extreme" because most early scientists, and most we associate with the birth of the Scientific Age, were religious people.

29 We might assume dualism to give equal weight to each hand. However, which hand ultimately predominates is a function of dualism's larger context. The separate-worlds ideas of Descartes, while expressly affirming of religion's place, represented an important victory for distinction over connectedness.

The postmodern current in contemporary thought has at once called for the end of philosophy and vainly attempted to rescue it. Most people who mention philosophers from the last century will describe contributors of existentialist or social constructivist bent.[30] But as I've emphasized, the postmodern contribution can only be a start. While it accurately describes much in current circumstances, it gives us little to help us with the task of proceeding forward.

Realities that confront us as we begin to make our way beyond Transition's precipice help fill out the challenge that philosophy now faces—and also hint at further possibilities. The difficulty faced by the transcendental thread in philosophy is most stark. An extreme subjectivity that leaves out the subject—at least in any embodied sense—is ultimately empty. But the empirical thread—even if we extend it beyond the explicitly philosophical to include more isolatedly right-hand forms of inquiry—in the end confronts its own kind of Transitional Absurdity. I've described how an extreme objectivity that leaves out key parts of the data can hardly be considered objective.

The way in which the concept of Cultural Maturity resolves philosophy's Transitional predicaments is now familiar. Cultural Maturity's cognitive changes do three things with regard to philosophy's right- and left-hand traditions. First, it challenges either hand's claim to be the last word. Second, it steps back and affirms a more dynamic and encompassing picture. (It proposes that even just making right- and left-hand truths separate but equal—as with Cartesian dualism—is not enough.) And finally, it emphasizes the importance of not just systemically reframing here-and-now differences, but also finding fresh ways to understand how differences have taken expression through time.

One result of how Integrative Meta-perspective makes possible pattern language concepts that give expression to human experience's full whole-box-of-crayons complexity is more complete ways of framing the philosophical endeavor. Within this newly integrative picture, neither hand gets away unscathed. But at the same time, the truth of each hand becomes more robust, more multihued in conception, and more extensive in its appropriate concerns. In some small way, we see this with any sphere of understanding. But it is true in especially striking and consequential ways for the particularly defining systemic relationships that through history have been the concern of philosophy. The diagram in Figure 3-3 provides an outline:

---

30 See "Postmodern/Constructivist Scenarios" in Chapter Seven.

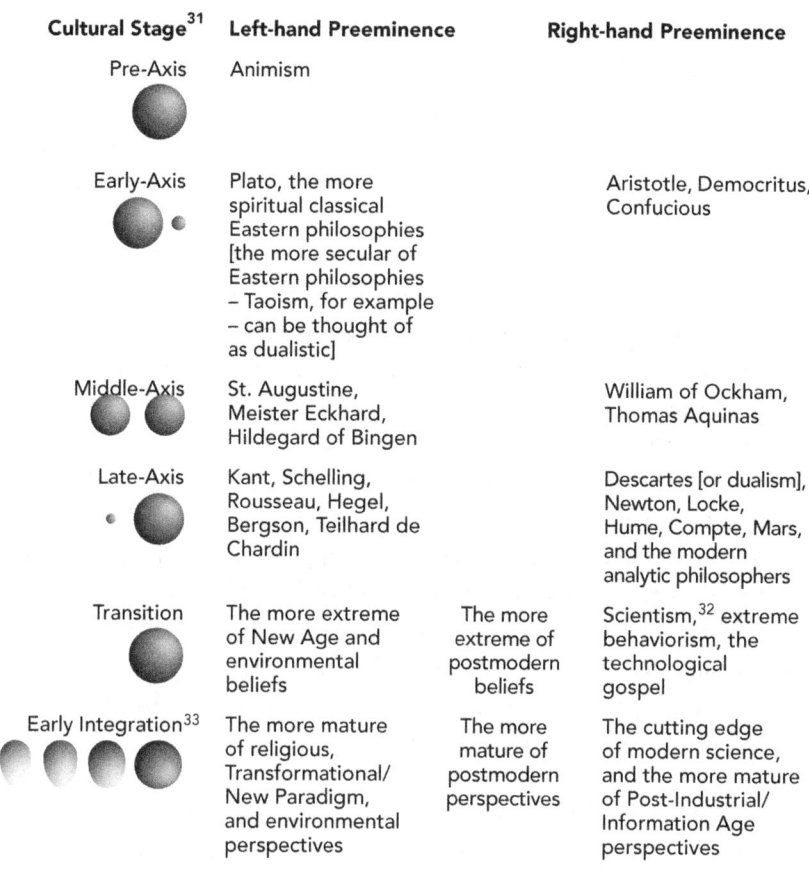

Cultural Stage[31]	Left-hand Preeminence		Right-hand Preeminence
Pre-Axis	Animism		
Early-Axis	Plato, the more spiritual classical Eastern philosophies [the more secular of Eastern philosophies – Taoism, for example – can be thought of as dualistic]		Aristotle, Democritus, Confucious
Middle-Axis	St. Augustine, Meister Eckhard, Hildegard of Bingen		William of Ockham, Thomas Aquinas
Late-Axis	Kant, Schelling, Rousseau, Hegel, Bergson, Teilhard de Chardin		Descartes [or dualism], Newton, Locke, Hume, Compte, Mars, and the modern analytic philosophers
Transition	The more extreme of New Age and environmental beliefs	The more extreme of postmodern beliefs	Scientism,[32] extreme behaviorism, the technological gospel
Early Integration[33]	The more mature of religious, Transformational/ New Paradigm, and environmental perspectives	The more mature of postmodern perspectives	The cutting edge of modern science, and the more mature of Post-Industrial/ Information Age perspectives

Fig. 3-10. Philosophy and Patterning in Time

Reflecting on this big-picture interpretation, a person might appropriately ask whether culturally mature perspective is itself accurately

---

31 When the more "horizontal," left-hand versus right-hand aspect of polarity is most pertinent, it helps to turn the Creative Function on its side. Philosophy, because of its conscious rational formulation, is uniformly an Upper-Pole activity. Philosophical differences thus reflect more Inner versus Outer dynamics.

32 While scientism is not limited to Transitional times, it gains wider acceptance with Transitional dynamics (where the archetypally-feminine pole is so diminished that it exerts little influence).

33 See "Scenarios for the Future" in Chapter Seven.

thought of as philosophy. The postmodern argument for the end of philosophy—at least as a pursuit of final abstracted truths—is legitimate. And culturally mature truth is never just philosophical. It is always as much about politics, science, sociology, religion, or art. But with regard to the question of what makes truth true, its concerns certainly parallel those of philosophical inquiry.

Wherever we end up with our answer, culturally mature perspective succeeds in bringing fresh life to the philosophical enterprise. We find a result similar to what we encountered for the broad study of history. Culturally mature systemic perspective offers that philosophical inquiry might be newly vital and substantive. At the least, Cultural Maturity makes the "big picture" newly relevant—indeed, essential. What culturally mature truth gives us is necessarily more humble than the ultimate answers to which classical philosophy aspired. But it succeeds in providing new appreciation for the wonders (along with the wondrous absurdities) of being human. And it offers a kind of practical applicability that philosophy has rarely been able to achieve. Perhaps a time will come when parents no longer cringe—appropriately—when they hear that their children have chosen philosophy as a college major.

More Patterning in Time—Particularly Intriguing Expressions

Let's now turn to a small handful of additional Patterning in Time-related topics. Each is fascinating in its own right. Each, too, because it focuses on a concern for which more creatively germinal aspects of intelligence are key to understanding, provides a good counterbalance to philosophy as an example. I've noted that in our time the sensibilities that order formative process's earliest stages can be particularly difficult for us to understand and consciously access. These additional Patterning in Time topics help deepen our understanding of these more germinal contributions. And because each topic spans the entirety of cultural time, in a further way it can function as a lens for more deeply appreciating developmental/evolutionary perspective as a whole. These topics also, each in its own way, provide a further useful glimpse into the future's needed more dynamic and complete ways of holding experience.

The Relativity of Time in Time

Just what is time? We can't ask about time without being confronted with contradiction. A watched pot never boils, yet time flies when you are having fun. Time is the "best medicine" (Ovid) and also "all-devouring, all-destroying" (Jonathan Swift). Time in the ecstasy of sexual passion can seem to disappear entirely; while with waiting in line it can feel like an eternity. Saint Augustine's words in his *Confessions* most famously express the conceptual frustration: "What then is time? If no one asks me, I know; if I want to explain it to someone who does ask me, I do not know." Luis Borges put time's endless paradoxes more poetically: "Time is a river which carries me along, but I am the river; it is a tiger that devours me, but I am the tiger; it is a fire that consumes me, but I am the fire."

Time today is entering the human conversation in a way that might seem only to confuse the situation further. Modern physics presents a newly fluid picture of time—with relativity, time expands and contracts and gets equal billing with the three dimensions of space. Certainly time has become a "timely" topic as our rush-rush world leaves us with never enough of it.

Cultural Maturity's cognitive reordering offers that we might engage time in deeper and more complete ways than were possible in the past. Just how it does can at first seem to make time even more difficult to grasp. But particularly when we add a creative frame, the result is a fuller and more dynamic understanding of time. CST brings together our often very different relationships to time and makes them part of a larger, at once more detailed and more integrated picture.

Integrative Meta-perspective "bridges" common polar experiences of time. It links the time of "being" with the time of "doing," the sacred time of the priest with the time of Galileo's desire "to measure everything measurable and to make everything measurable that is not yet measurable." It also alerts us to the fact that time is not always the same thing. Patterning in Time takes the additional step of stretching our understanding of time out over time. It helps us appreciate time's developmental dimension. Time as experience becomes itself "relative in time."

Time's relativity in time is a kind of contextual relativity that we all at some level recognize. The time of the young child fascinated with the odd amblings of a caterpillar goes on forever. The time of the adult who needs to be on time and not waste time is much more linear and lockstep. And the time of life's last years is different still, more tempered and better able to respond to circumstances. CST's creative frame offers a way to map this relativity of time in time. I will focus here on how this progression manifests with cultural change.

Time in Pre-Axis cultures is circular (or even more immediately, timeless—as with the almost psychedelic "dream time" of the Australian Aborigines). Time is measured by the repetitive turning of seasons and the enactment of ritual. In an important sense, past, present, and future exist simultaneously (ancestors are commonly seen to reside in a parallel here-and-now). The durational is clearly secondary to the eternal—to time as timelessness, to what we might call "deep time."

Time in Early-Axis cultures begins to acquire a more overt sense of progression, though the timeless retains its strong influence. We witness the advent of more formal "timepieces"—ritual observatories like Stonehenge, the stone calendar wheels of the Aztecs. Such structures marked duration, but with them, it was time's cycles that most commanded our attention. And the mystical awe with which these structures were regarded makes clear the continued power of left-hand sensibility. Still, time as experience has distinctly evolved, becoming now a spiral more than a circle. The perceived relationship of the living and the dead again sheds useful light (our perceptions of death and of time are intimately linked). Death in Early-Axis times is thought to be followed not by life in a parallel world, but by reincarnation (or something similar). We return to where we started, but now in altered form.

In Middle-Axis cultural times, time as timelessness and time as progression juxtapose more as equals. With the advent of monotheism, death no longer means returning to where we started, but going to some distinct afterlife. The world of time stands increasingly on its own, with the timeless now inhabiting a separate heavenly world. Timepieces become more precise (and less overtly sacred)—from the sundial and the hourglass to, in the thirteenth century, the first mechanical clocks. Time has not become totally divorced from the sacred—the impetus for the creation of mechanical clocks was the need for medieval monks to know the time for prayer (an ironic beginning for the device that would become the lord of secular time). But time has become something we can separately consider.

Time in Late-Axis culture becomes our familiar linear time, the time of being on time, of not wasting time, time as duration. It is time as division, the time of parts, each second equal and adding to the next. It is the time of classical science—measuring an object's speed from here to there. It is also the time of commerce (as Francis Bacon said, "time is the measure of business as money is of wares"). With their needs for reliable minute-to-minute, and even second-to-second accuracy, science and commerce were the primary drivers for the development of modern timepieces. While primordial time connects, linking all in the timeless, linear time separates, cleanly cleaving one moment from the next. It is secular time. And still in essential ways we deify it. We organize our days around it, make it "of the essence." Ironically, while we tend today to assume that linear time represents the real meaning of time—time finally stripped of its mysticism—a person could argue equally well that its inception marks time's extinction as a part of truth. (In a Newtonian world, the three dimensions of space define truth, and time, like art or spirit, becomes something separate, and secondary.)

Can this developmental/evolutionary picture of time help us with the future? If the concept of Cultural Maturity is accurate, in times ahead we should at least become better able to recognize time's elasticity of meaning. The temporal wars between the eternal and the durational should increasingly find resolution in more encompassing ways of thinking about time. We should also become better able to appreciate the particular values and states of experience that accompany different relationships to time.

An appreciation of time's relativity in cultural time is directly pertinent ultimately to how we think about some of the most important tasks ahead for the species. I think most immediately of how closely rethinking progress relates to rethinking time. Our modern onward-and-upward image of progress requires the more goal-oriented sensibilities that arrived on culture's stage with time's Modern Age definition. Advancing effectively will require that we recognize the price we pay, and will increasingly pay, for making time (with money) our secular deity.

Our various definitions of time come together in the importance of addressing questions of timeliness. Note that all Creative Systems patterning concepts are in one way or another about what makes a thought or action "right and timely." Prior to now, culture as parent gave us one-size-fits-all rules that made the great majority of time-related determinations for us. We encountered such predetermination, for example, with common assumptions related to age. More recently we've seen it with the expectations of the nine-to-five workweek. With Cultural Maturity, our temporal options expand and come to lie increasingly in our own hands. They also come to exist in the context of a deepening appreciation for how diverse aspects of experience live in time in very different ways.

In Chapter Six, we will look at how we can map out a similar creatively contextual picture of time's significance for Patterning in Space differences. People with different temperaments do not experience time in exactly the same way. The time of the artist differs from that of the businessman as fundamentally as that of the child and the adult (and, as CST predicts, in a related way).

On the Nature of Nature

The question of how we best understand and relate to nature offers further insight into how Patterning in Time perspective can help us. We could think of it too as an eternal quandary. It has always fascinated us, and has often, too, presented answers that contradict. How we answer it today has critical implications as we move into the future.

Our times challenge us to an essential "growing up" in our relationship to nature. Most obviously, we must relate to nature differently for the sake of human survival and the health of the planet. Nature is our home, and the level of damage we are doing to it cannot long continue. But just as much we need a shift in our relationship with nature for more personal/psychological reasons. We need it for the sake of our souls. John Muir once observed, "I only went out for a walk and finally concluded to stay till sundown. For going out, I found I was really going in." We too are nature. In forgetting nature, we, in a very important sense, forget ourselves as well. The task is not only to better protect nature, but to develop a new and deeper kind of relationship with and understanding of nature.

Developmental/evolutionary perspective can help us with this essential task. At the least, it helps clarify how our understandings of our biological and physical worlds have never been as objective and final as we have thought them to be. Our beliefs have always been as much about polar projection as actuality, or at least as much about the lenses through which we have been able to see as what we have endeavored to see. Is the creature world a "peaceable kingdom" (and thus to be emulated), or "red in tooth and claw" (something to fear and, if possible, to tame)? Is the physical world animate and spiritful (and thus best treated as an expression of the divine), or is it dead and inert (and thus regarded at best as a resource for fulfilling human needs)?

Developmental/evolutionary perspective also helps us more clearly grasp what we need to leave behind—and, just a bit, where we need to go. The common conclusion in modern times that nature is in effect a machine would have seemed ludicrous within any other cultural period. But it makes perfect sense in the context of the kind of cognitive organization that has given us our Modern Age worldview. With the recognition that the way we see nature is time-specific, it also makes sense that further ways of understanding and relating to nature likely lie ahead. Integrative Meta-perspective's larger picture helps us begin to understand what we need to get in touch with in ourselves if we are to think about nature and our relationship to it in the needed new ways.

What is nature—at least to us? CST maps how our perceptions of nature differ as a function of any Patterning in Time (or Patterning in Space) variable. It also helps answer the question of just what needs to change in our time. In sketching this progression, I will give special emphasis not just to how poles become more separate with each stage in creative differentiation, but also to how markedly the felt relationship between poles becomes different. Of particular importance here is how the newly created content (the archetypally masculine pole) actively distances itself from its creative context (the archetypally feminine pole). At certain points, because the attraction of creation's origin can be so powerful that it threatens to undermine needed separation, that pushing away can be extreme. This active distancing manifests most strongly with the later parts of Middle-Axis and the early parts of Late-Axis. Then it can translate into direct condemnation. We find this active distancing with any formative juxtaposition, but it is particularly easy to recognize in our historical relationship with nature.

The basic contours of the evolving sequence of relationships with nature that CST describes should now feel familiar. Nature in early tribal (Pre-Axis) times—mountain, river, forest, and soil—was cherished as the divine source of all life. Mortals stood small in relationship to her mysterious immensity. Truth and nature were one and the same.

With the rise of early civilizations (Early-Axis times in culture), we saw the first real separation from nature. Animism gave way to ascendant pantheons of gods, and man came to inhabit a realm now distinct from the creaturely—nature and humanity were no longer seen as one. And, at the same time, the perceived relationship with nature remained strong. The early Greek gods were viewed as ascendant above nature, but it was never forgotten that they were born from Gaia, the earth. The Eleusinian Mysteries, while beyond animism, embodied a deep awe of nature and expressed a message of shared consciousness between matter and humanity.

Humanity's relationship with nature first grew overtly contentious with the beginnings of Middle-Axis and the rise of monotheism. These changes took expression in at once a more forceful ascendancy of the divine and a new ascendancy of man. The divine now stood as a singular lord on high. And mortals, while still respectful of nature's power, saw themselves now as sovereign over her. From the book of Genesis come these words: "Be fruitful and multiply, and replenish the earth and subdue it; and have dominion over the fish of the sea and over the fowl of the air and over every living thing that moveth upon the earth."

This voice of dominion would continue to rise in volume, calling out with ever-greater force for the taming of nature. Nature's wildness became increasingly something to control and conquer. By the early Renaissance, we heard statements such as this from French theologian and poet Jacques-Benigne Bossuet: "May the earth be cursed, may the earth be cursed, a thousand times be cursed because from it that heavy fog and those black vapors continually rise that ascend from the dark passions and hide heaven and its light from us and draw down the lightning of God's justice against the corruption of the human race."

Progress into Late-Axis brought a significant further distancing from nature. Much of the moral condemnation subsided, but this occurred less because humanity had come to terms with nature's power than because we had put nature's power sufficiently at arm's length that it no longer threatened. We had risen far enough above our creaturely origins that nature could be seen, for all intents and purposes, as inert. With the scientific revolution and the Industrial Age we came to view animal behavior in terms of instinct and reflex, the earth became an assortment of material resources to be exploited for the practical tasks of human achievement, and our bodies increasingly became things we had rather than were. This mechanistic picture of nature was tempered by the Romantic Age's idealization of nature, and in important ways still is. But what we saw with the Romantic Age was more reactive and compensatory than anything that really helped us understand nature more deeply.

The task ahead? Clearly, we need a next step in how we think about our relationship with nature. The question today becomes less whether we will achieve a more culturally mature relationship with nature than how much we will make ourselves and the other inhabitants of our planet suffer on the road to achieving it. As the Roman poet Horace wrote, "You may chase Nature out with a pitchfork, but she will ever hurry back to triumph in stealth over your foolish contempt."

With barely our toes over Cultural Maturity's threshold, we can only begin to grasp what a needed "growing up" in our relationship with nature looks like. Certainly we can know that our relationship with nature must emphasize sustainability—nature must remain vital into the future, and responsibility for keeping it so lies in our hands. We can also know a few things as far as our more psychological relationship with nature. We can know that in some way we must remember our connection with nature. We can also know that we must do so in a way that fills out rather than diminishes our appreciation of the uniqueness of our human natures.

The reality of each previous cultural stage points toward something important in the new picture. As was unquestioned in Pre-Axis and Early-Axis times, we must better appreciate how we are always part of nature, and it of us. Middle-Axis emotional and moral sensibilities similarly have an important role, though now the moral conviction must come from a commitment to making the future's hard choices (in relation to both ourselves and nature), not from fears of chaos and regression. We also need the more Late-Axis kind of stepping back that can address nature "objectively" as a resource, but now not simply in the sense of something to exploit. A sustainable use of resources requires sophisticated scientific understanding of resource relationships along with a keen appreciation of the ways in which economic factors influence how resource sustainability can best be achieved. All of these ingredients are essential to the maturity of systemic perspective needed if we are to be effective planetary stewards going forward.

Architecture and the Developmental "Anatomy" of History

As a sculptor, I've often found myself intrigued by how architecture's monumental physical expressions, like the best of sculpture, reflect the way we hold reality at the time and place of their creation. In modern times, people often assume that architecture's changes through history are products largely of invention, of what we had become capable of building. More accurately, particular shapes move us when they speak from how we are coming to experience and shape reality as a whole.

Appreciating pattern in this sense requires engaging experience from the kind of body intelligence a sculptor draws on. But the evolution of architecture, particularly architecture that is regarded by the people of its time as in some way sacred or special, makes a particularly fascinating lens through which to observe culture's creative metamorphosis. The picture that results provides striking further confirmation of Patterning in Time principles.

The following observations are adapted from *The Creative Imperative*. Similarities noted not only cut across cultural traditions, they reflect patterns found everywhere at parallel stages in culture.

In earliest prehistory (early Pre-Axis), the most common ritual dwelling was the earth itself. The "medicine" of early Stone Age people—drawings and ritual objects—has been found most often in the deep recesses of caves. It was apparently these caves, and such sites as sacred wells and burial mounds, that were the most common places for the shaman's "discourses" with the primordial powers of nature. Sculpturally, the sacred forms in this most archetypally feminine of periods were spherical containers and gentle mounds.

With the beginnings of Early-Axis sensibility, attention began to shift upward. Ritual spaces increasingly became ritual structures, and these structures specifically places for conferring with the heavens. The Neolithic stone circles of Europe provide some of the earliest examples, while the pyramids of Egypt and Mesoamerica are somewhat later, and the temples of early Greece and the ritual dwellings of the classical East—Buddhist stupas, Hindu temples—somewhat later still. The architectural mass remains in secure juxtaposition to the earth's belly, but now there is a clear verticality. Worshippers stand below and gaze upward.

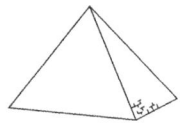

Approaching Middle-Axis times, places of worship increasingly reflect an equal structural affinity with Above and Below. The domes of the Byzantine period very nearly balance in their upward might the weight of the foundation and sanctuary beneath. In the uplifted towers and high rounded arches of Romanesque architecture, we see the first gestures toward real ascendant preeminence, a statement made fully manifest by the last centuries of Middle-Axis culture in Europe in the Gothic cathedral's surging buttresses and poetic spires.

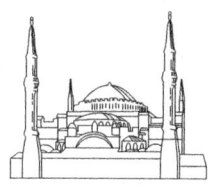

With the beginnings of Late-Axis culture, we find two important architectural themes. The first is the continuation of upward movement. The second is the secularization of the ascendant. The most powerful gods of industrial high culture reside in the material realm, not the church. The culminating form of this period is the skyscraper. With its glass and steel purity, it is a perfect monument to objectivity and rational abstraction.

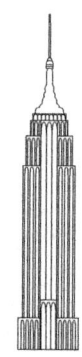

With Transitional times, we have taken one further step. The skyscraper continues to have an important place, but it is joined by an even more ascendant image: the spaceship. The spaceship is a ritual dwelling in which humans not only contemplate the heavens, they inhabit them.

Looking ahead? We see beginnings of further steps. The postmodern sensibility in architecture directly questions Late-Axis orthodoxies. And in keeping with the idea that earlier stages might have lessons to teach, it makes at least a start at entertaining aesthetics from earlier times. The worst of postmodern architecture presents little more than a hodgepodge of influences. But the best can bring together diverse aesthetics in truly striking and inspiring ways. I think most immediately of Jørn Utzon's Sydney Opera House and Frank Gehry's Guggenheim Museum in Bilbao. I look forward to what more the future may bring.

Creative Evolution and the Body

These additional developmental/evolutionary reflections have brought us close to some of life's most intriguing questions—and up against some of today's most important concerns. With the last further topic, we turn to one of the most basic and primal questions we could ask: What is a body?

On the surface, the question "What is a body?" might seem simple to answer. We need only look down; there it is. In fact, the question is not at all simple. Certainly it is perplexing philosophically. The body is at once something we have and something we are—not an easy fact to reconcile. And the question increasingly confronts us as we consider the body scientifically and medically. We are used to inquiring about how neurons work, about the biochemistry of digestion, or about the role of genes in disease. But more and more we are recognizing that we have only begun to understand the body's rich systemic complexity.

Part of the reason we have more to learn is simply that there is research yet to be done. But the reason has as much to do, ultimately, with how we think. I've observed our Modern Age tendency to view a machine model of understanding as sufficient and culminating. At Transition, with its near absence of lower-pole sensibility, we would expect to find ourselves even more distanced from anything more than the most rudimentary action/reaction notions of bodily functioning. The extreme level of disconnection from bodily experience that we find in our time plays a role in many of the most consequential Transitional Absurdities.

The importance of thinking of the body in more complete ways brings us back to earlier key themes. Previous reflections on the importance of understanding living systems in ways that better reflect the fact that they are alive are certainly pertinent to how we think about the body. In particular, they are pertinent to how we conceive of bodily well-being. Health and healing must ultimately be about enhancing life. We've always known at some level that healing was more complex than fixing broken anatomy. I am reminded of Benjamin Franklin's quip, "God heals and the doctor takes the fees." Bit by bit, a more dynamic picture of health and healing is being acknowledged, and often even embraced.

The notion that we can speak of the body as "intelligence" is similarly pertinent. And similarly, it stretches us in fundamental ways. I've commented on the trickiness of talking about the body as a way of knowing given that we have so little connection with the body as experience in our time. But I've also emphasized the essential role that body intelligence comes to play with culturally mature understanding. In particular, I've emphasized its pivotal significance in a creative picture of cognitive functioning.

When we "bridge" mind and body—as culturally mature perspective always does—the question of just what it means to have a body becomes a new sort of question. It also, in a whole new way, becomes a question of deep significance. Creative Systems Theory not only invites us to consider a larger picture, it provides us with a way to map body realities and body dynamics.

Here, very briefly, I will draw on CST's framing of bodily experience in a couple of ways. First, I will expand on earlier observations about the different ways we experience bodily intelligence at different stages in any creative/formative process. I will then turn to how, with each stage in creative/formative process—including culture as a developmental process—we not only experience what it means to have a body in particular ways, we live in our bodies in particular ways.

In Chapter Two I outlined how each intelligence—bodily intelligence included—along with being primary at a particular creative stage, makes a more limited contribution with other stages. Here, along with summarizing some of these more detailed body-related distinctions, I've added some further "flesh" to where they take us by including some observations about ways health and healing are experienced at each creative stage. I will limit my observations to the body as it is experienced in culture as a creative process.

I've called the Pre-Axis body the "creature body." With culture, this is the body that knows the tribal dances and that moves in harmony with the beings of the forest, the skies, and the oceans. With the Pre-Axis body, healing happens primarily through ritual and through the application of remedies found in nature. Tribal ritual reestablishes primal connectedness.

The Early-Axis "body as mystery" tends to be described culturally more in the language of energies and essences, as with the acupuncture meridians of traditional Chinese medicine and the chakras of India's yogic traditions. Healing comes then through the balancing of these energies.

The Middle-Axis "visceral/muscular body" took expression in the West in interplays of emotion-laden fluids—blood, phlegm, yellow bile, black bile. (Here lie the roots of words like "bilious" and "phlegmatic.") Healing then came through removing blockages to the movements of fluids and eliminating fluids of a harmful sort.

The final body in this sequence—or at least the one we know from most recent times—is our familiar Late-Axis body of anatomy and physiology, the Modern Age's body as great machine. Modern medicine views disease as damage to that machine—the cause being variously trauma, microbes, genetic defect, or wear and tear. The purpose of healing, whether through surgery or the prescribing of drugs, has been to repair broken tissues and restore its functioning.

Which of these is the real body? Were early conceptions simply naïve? In major ways, certainly they were—especially when it comes to implications for health and healing. The greater portion of the knowledge we draw on today, including discoveries as basic as the role of pathogens in disease or the importance of sterile technique, is remarkably recent. But Creative Systems Theory suggests that differences in how we've understood the body may also reflect our complexity as much as our past ignorance.

It is important to appreciate that we've never really just studied the body—objectively stood back from it—even the modern scientific body. We've always studied mind/bodies, albeit of different sorts (and being mind/bodies ourselves, never from a purely objective perspective). Creative Systems Theory proposes that the way we experience our bodies today reflects a particular time-relative and space-relative relationship between mind and body. It also proposes that this felt relationship is changing.

One place to see the beginnings of this changing relationship is with how medicine is starting to appreciate a more systemic picture of bodily functioning. Increasingly we recognize, for example, that other aspects of the body than just the nervous system are "intelligent"—this in the sense that they learn and also direct complex evolving processes. I think in particular of the immune system (which among other functions constantly creates new antibodies to fight disease), the digestive system (which manages an intricate ecosystem of supportive microorganisms), and the endocrine system (which organizes complex hormonal responses). We are also better recognizing the importance of taking into account human differences—such as gender, race, and genetic variability—how the body we consider must be the body as *somebody*. While we are just beginning to grasp the full implications of this more dynamic—indeed, "creative"—picture of bodily response, we can be sure that those implications are significant. I suspect that in the twenty-first century, the body will provide many of humanity's most dramatic and important new learnings.

The second way of approaching who we are as bodies turns to how we can use the way bodily experience organizes creatively to help us more deeply understand creative Patterning in Time. In describing how polarities have both vertical and horizontal aspects, I introduced a critical recognition: Rather than being just some abstract representation, the Creative Function depicts how polarity organizes in the human body. (The use of the words vertical and horizontal to describe polar aspects refers to different ways experience is embodied.[34]) We can think of CST patterning concepts as

---

[34] When I first used the words "vertical" and "horizontal" in this way, people often responded with confusion. I responded by being confused that they

describing different ways of being in our tissues. The Creative Function maps this dynamically systemic picture. It describes how what it means to be embodied evolves in a characteristic manner over the course of any formative process.

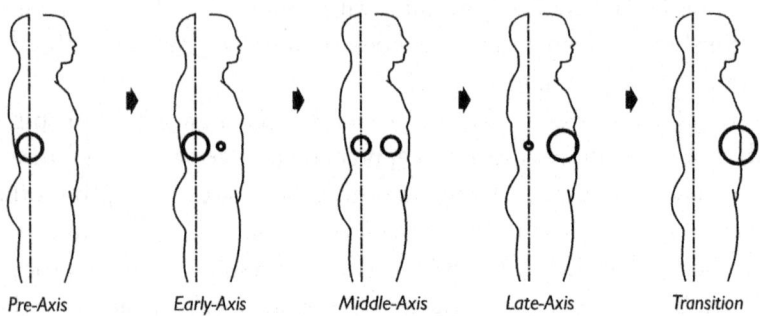

Pre-Axis   Early-Axis   Middle-Axis   Late-Axis   Transition

Fig. 3-4. The Evolution of Horizontal Polarity

The diagram in Figure 3-4—from *The Creative Imperative*—depicts how horizontal polarity manifests differently depending on when and where we find it. I've described how Inner aspects of experience get greater emphasis early on while Outer sensibilities have the greater influence later. This is consistent with what we see bodily. As we move from Pre-Axis, to Early-Axis, to Middle-Axis, to Late-Axis, embodied experience moves gradually from closer to the body's core toward the

---

might be confused. I couldn't think of any way to be more concrete, being that I was directly describing bodily experience. Since then, I have come to appreciate how my personality style means body intelligence observations are going to be easier for me than they are for most people. Inner and Outer seem easiest for most people to grasp. Sometimes we experience more at the core of ourselves, at other time more from the body's surface. In a related way, we encounter more vertical polar dynamics bodily with how one person's temperament may seem more Upper, more in his head, while another person acts in ways that are more Lower, more from the gut. To illustrate vertical dynamics when working with a group, I will often line people up from those whose temperaments are most Lower to those whose temperaments are most Upper and then just walk down the line, pointing my finger at the center of balance of each person's body.

body's more surface layers. This mapping can be applied equally well to Patterning in Time and Patterning in Space observations.[35]

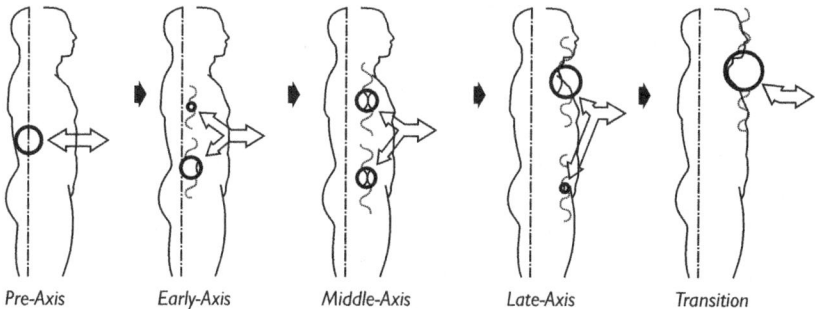

Pre-Axis   Early-Axis   Middle-Axis   Late-Axis   Transition

Fig. 3-5. The Evolution of Horizontal and Vertical Polarity

The diagram in Figure 3-5—also from *The Creative Imperative*—adds vertical polarity to the representation. Note how it makes the Creative Function specifically a mapping of embodied experience. It illustrates how horizontal and vertical polarity together generate our felt experience of ourselves and how we perceive our worlds. It similarly can be applied to both Patterning in Time and Patterning in Space observations.

How does our experience of being embodied change with Integrative Meta-perspective? We become more in touch with bodily experience, certainly, better able to read our body's cues and derive fulfillment from the life of the body. There are also deeper rewards. A client described the changes this way. He observed that early in his life he had felt rooted in his beliefs. Then those beliefs were challenged, and he went through a period where he felt that he had no roots. Later, as he connected with

---

35 I've noted how CST uses the terms Inner and Outer rather than the more familiar words "introvert" and "extrovert" when addressing personality style differences to avoid lumping together temperaments that are in fact fundamentally different. The diagram in Figure 3-4 points toward why more differentiated language is important. It follows from the creative organization of temperament that even the most Outer of Earlies will often be more Inner than most Lates, and conversely. See Chapter Six for more detailed reflections on Inner and Out Patterning in Space distinctions.

more culturally mature sensibilities, he described in a new way feeling "rooted in the fact of rootedness." He could have said simply, rooted in his body. The way Reengagement gives us a new, more complete relationship to bodily experience is key to how Cultural Maturity provides an answer to today's Crisis of Purpose.[36]

More to Come

Chapters ahead will draw extensively on these various Patterning in Time observations. In Chapters Four and Five I will draw on developmental perspective to address the history of moral/ethical understanding, including our human relationship with death. In Chapter Seven, I will use observations about how major ideological themes through history today get extended into the future to help identify common traps in our thinking about the tasks ahead. Chapter Ten addresses gender and love from a developmental/evolutionary perspective. In Chapter Eleven, I will turn to the history of specific cultural domains—from government to art—both to further support CST's developmental picture and to make some additional, more specific predictions about the future. And in Chapter Twelve, I will use big-picture developmental perspective to address a couple of further "ultimate" questions: how the often conflicting conclusions of science and religion ultimately relate, and our place as humans in the larger scheme of things.

In addition, throughout the book, I will come back repeatedly to a more encompassing kind of pertinence. Arguably the whole of CST can be thought of as following from these Patterning in Time observations. For me, these Patterning in Time notions also have a more personal kind of significance because they provided the theory's initial insights.

Patterning in Time Summary Exercise

> At what creative stage do you currently reside in the important creative endeavors in your life? In your personal psychological development? In your main life relationships? How would you

---

36 *The Creative Imperative* describes this evolution of body sensibility in greater detail. Further detail can also be found on the Creative Systems Theory website (www.CSTHome.org.)

estimate the developmental stages of groups and organizations that you are a part of? And how do you think about your personal worldview in relation to culture's evolving story—Late-Axis, Transition, early Cultural Maturity? In each case, how might this recognition help in meeting the challenges that that particular aspect of your life presents?

CHAPTER FOUR

Cultural Maturity: Our Time's Needed (and Now Possible) "New Common Sense"

Creative Systems Patterning in Time notions provide direct support for the concept of Cultural Maturity. We've seen how Cultural Maturity's changes follow directly from what we would expect if culture's evolution conforms to the general progression we find with change in other human systems. And we've examined how the Dilemma of Trajectory makes the necessity for something at least similar to what the concept of Cultural Maturity describes inescapable.

With this chapter, we turn more specifically to the concept of Cultural Maturity and its implications. The focus of my Creative Systems Theory–related work through the years has alternated between developing CST's more conceptual aspects and more explicitly wearing my "cultural psychiatrist's" hat. The latter role has included helping people make sense of the times we live in—through writing and speaking—and also actively training people in the leadership capacities that challenges ahead will increasingly require of us. The concept of Cultural Maturity has been central to these further contributions.

We've previously examined most of the concept's theoretical foundations. I've described Cultural Maturity as a developmentally predicted "growing up" as a species. I've also described how we can understand it in terms of a new ability to step beyond what always before has been a parent-and-child relationship between culture and the individual, combined with a cognitive reordering that produces a more encompassing—systemic—picture of both ourselves and the world around us.

We've also touched on multiple ways that the concept of Cultural Maturity helps us. Most immediately it provides a new cultural narrative. I've argued that without something like it, we are at best left with postmodern aimlessness, at worst with outmoded ideological stories and increasingly dangerous regressive responses. I've introduced how Cultural Maturity's cognitive changes make possible essential new skills and capacities. And I've observed how Integrative Meta-perspective invites new, more dynamic and complete ways of understanding. Creative Systems Theory's encompassing framework can be thought of as following directly from how Cultural Maturity's cognitive reordering alters our experience of truth, identity, and the world around us.

With this chapter, we focus our attention more specifically on ways the concept of Cultural Maturity provides practical guidance as we look to the future. We will look more closely at the new skills and capacities that come with Cultural Maturity's changes and how they are essential if we are to make effective choices going forward. We will also examine some of the questions and challenges that those capabilities can help us address. Such practical guidance could not be more important. And it could be enough for many people. Much that is implied by the concept of Cultural Maturity doesn't require extensive theoretical understanding. And because Cultural Maturity's changes as potential are developmentally built into us, engaging them can happen more naturally than we might expect. The important thing is that we succeed at them, not necessarily how we think about them.

That said, conceptual observations will continue to have a place with this chapter's inquiry. I've argued that one of the things that most defines culturally mature perspective is the way it increases our ability to bring big-picture understanding to our circumstances. The questions and challenges that we will examine will each in different ways bring detail to this recognition. I've also emphasized how needed new skills and capacities can be more difficult to fully grasp than we might at first imagine, how they are easily confused with things they are not about. The likelihood of Cultural Maturity's changes being realized—at least any time soon—increases dramatically if we have a solid sense of how they expand understanding and just what they make possible.

In Chapter One, I introduced three needed new skills and capacities—getting beyond the polarized and polarizing ideological assumptions of times past, realizing a new maturity in our relationship to limits, and learning to think about what matters (and advancement in particular) in more encompassing and complete ways. Since then, I've implied a handful of other new abilities. With this chapter, I'll start by filling out the list, adding those skills and capacities I have only suggested, and for each of them, further addressing their implications. I will also more specifically tie the demands each presents to a "creative" picture of understanding.

I will then offer four short articles that address topics that cut across challenges new to our time. I've chosen the topics that I have—morality, love, leadership, and the need for a new maturity in our relationship to death—both because they are each of obvious importance and because they illustrate Cultural Maturity's changes particularly well. Each article highlights how culturally mature perspective alters both the questions we ask and where our answers take us. And together, by illustrating how needed skills and abilities are remarkably similar even when the topics come from widely different parts of our lives, they support the concept of Cultural Maturity's broader interpretation.

During the years that I led extended trainings at the Institute, I would often start workshops by having participants list future concerns that they found especially important—challenges where they would feel particular pain if somehow we failed at what is being asked of us. While people were involved in this task, I would list some of the new skills and capacities that Cultural Maturity's cognitive changes make possible on a board at the front of the room. Eventually, I would have people one by one share concerns that they had identified. With each concern, I would engage the group in examining how culturally mature abilities would be needed to effectively address it—and more often than not, simply to get to the place where the important questions could be asked in useful ways. People quickly saw that without culturally mature understanding and culturally mature capacities, it would be very hard to move forward effectively—that indeed, moving forward effectively might be impossible.

In addressing specific change topics and the new capacities needed to address them, this chapter applies a similar approach. By its end, in a related way, the reader should come away with a good beginning sense of just what realizing and applying Cultural Maturity's more "grown-up" ways of thinking and acting entail. And as with the trainings, the importance of culturally mature thought and action should seem obvious.

I will conclude the chapter by summarizing where these reflections have taken us and also by looking at the evidence that we have thus far that the concept of Cultural Maturity is in fact correct. And I will note one further, particularly provocative implication.

Needed New Skills and Capacities

Below I've briefly described eight needed new skills and capacities, drawing on the three I noted earlier with five more added that in the end are just as pivotal. These new capabilities will each be essential if we are to effectively address future concerns. Indeed, arguably, each will be required if we are to have a human future at all.

Three essential characteristics shared by these new skills and capacities should be noted before we dive in for this closer look. One is just how fundamentally they are new. I've described how I have often missed this fact—for example, how in first writing about the concept of Cultural Maturity, I failed to recognize that culturally mature perspective is needed to understand new capacities at all fully. Here I will give particular attention to just what is new and also highlight where some of the most ready confusions lie.

The second characteristic is the way each of these new capabilities follows directly from Cultural Maturity's cognitive reordering. Practicing them is important. But we don't have to invent them. They are direct products of the way Integrative Meta-perspective alters how we understand ourselves and our worlds. Indeed, with Integrative Meta-perspective, we can often find needed new skills and capacities manifesting without any awareness of their necessity. One of the most important kinds of evidence for Cultural Maturity's needed "growing up" as a species is how Cultural Maturity's cognitive reordering supports the development of those new capabilities.

The third characteristic ties more specifically to this book's broader conceptual argument. We can think of each of these new skills and capacities as a "creative" capability. Each can be understood to follow from how experience changes when we step back and better appreciate what it means to be living beings, and in particular, human beings. And, more specifically, each follows from the recognition that human intelligence, when understood systemically, organizes creatively.

Because these new skills and capacities are interrelated, I could divide them up and describe them in multiple ways, and often will. And the fact that fully grasping any of them makes new kinds of demands means that understanding will at times require some committed reflection. But in the end, when viewed from the vantage of Integrative Meta-perspective, each is common sense. I organized my books *Hope and the Future* and *Cultural Maturity* around these needed, and newly possible, new skills and capacities.

Accepting fundamental responsibility: Cultural Maturity's changes challenge us to accept a new, more fundamental kind of responsibility. They also make it possible for us to do so. When we leave behind relating to culture as a mythic parent, our decisions necessarily come to lie more directly in our human hands. We become more ultimately responsible for our actions, certainly. We also become more ultimately responsible for the beliefs on which we base our actions. This is the case for the choices we make in every part of our personal lives. It is also the case for more collective choices of every sort.

In a more rudimentary sense, we have always been responsible for the truths we apply. Responsibility is implied by the fact that we are conscious beings, capable of choice. And because each new chapter in culture's story has conferred greater freedom of choice—the age of kings more than that of god-kings, and our modern age of the individual more than that of royal rule and decree—each stage in culture's evolution has increased such responsibility. But what our times ask of us is different. Cultural Maturity's changes make a new, more demanding kind of responsibility possible—and newly necessary. Every kind of responsibility has today become a double responsibility. Along with being responsible for our choices, we have become newly responsible for determining just what it means for a choice to be responsible. Ultimately, we become responsible for making choices with the new kind of systemic sophistication that Integrative Meta-perspective makes possible.

It is important to appreciate that responsibility in this twice-over sense is necessarily a "creative" kind of responsibility. It requires that we draw on the whole of intelligence with its multiple aspects. It also demands that we step forward into a world of experience that as yet we can only begin to know at all deeply. When we find the courage to do so, the result is a new, more mature kind of leadership not just in our personal lives, but also in the realization of the full creative potential of humanity.[1]

---

[1] I will address the creative nature of the needed double responsibility more specifically in Chapter Five.

Learning to better tolerate uncertainty and complexity: Like it or not, the world we are being thrown into, even if we can make general sense of it, is less certain and more multifaceted than anything we have known in times past. A look at the postmodern loss of traditional guideposts provides useful first-cut insights into why this might be so. Without clear cultural rules, there is much less we can claim to know for sure, and options multiply dramatically. But if we stop there, we are left with anything-goes decision-making, and as far as complexity, only more of it to deal with.

Culturally Maturity's changes make it possible to more directly address uncertainty and complexity. Integrative Meta-perspective, along with leaving behind the past's parent/child relationship with culture, also gives us the ability to better get our minds around the whole of who we are. With regard to uncertainty, the more whole-box-of-crayons understanding that results, in taking us beyond past ideological beliefs, both confronts us with the fact of uncertainty and helps make us more comfortable in the face of uncertainty. We also become better able to engage not just our own complexity, but also systemic complexity in the world around us—including the particular kind of systemic complexity that makes us alive, and human.

CST's claim that human cognition functions ultimately to support our audaciously creative natures both supports these conclusions and fills them out in essential ways. It means that we may be better designed for tolerating uncertainty and complexity than we might imagine. Understood deeply, it also expands how we think about both uncertainty and complexity. Uncertainty becomes not just an absence, but an attribute of a dynamic and systemic—"creative"—world. And complexity stops being only about the complicated, and becomes instead inherent to how order in a maturely conceived systemic reality works.

Better appreciating the fact of real limits: I introduced this capacity in Chapter One. Real limits here include inviolable constraints of every sort—limits to what we can do, limits to what we can be, limits to what we can know and predict. Most immediately this new capacity is pertinent to addressing environmental limits, as with climate change. But the importance of better appreciating the fact of real limits encompasses questions of every sort. One of the articles that follows addresses how a defining capacity of a needed new chapter in love's evolution is a greater willingness to accept limits to what one person can be for another. In another article, I will describe how a new maturity in our relationship to death will be critical to health care's future. Death confronts us with life's ultimate limit—certainly to what we can control.

Chapter One included a summary description of just what becomes different with regard to limits: "Prior to now, when we encountered limits, we have assumed that our task was to heroically (or romantically) break through them. With Integrative Meta-perspective, we first pause and take time to discern just what kind of limit we face. If it is a limit that warrants a more traditional response, we proceed as before—and with added conviction. But we are also open to the possibility that the limit is inviolable. In a culturally mature reality, making this kind of distinction becomes a central task of leadership in all parts of our personal and collective lives."

Restricted to historical ways of thinking about limits, the only understandable result when we confronted inviolable limits (beyond denial) was failure. With Integrative Meta-perspective, we come to experience inviolable limits in a very different way, as an inherent property of any systemic reality. Exactly what before might have seemed the most insurmountable of adversaries becomes instead one of Cultural Maturity's most reliable teachers. The single word that best captures the more sophisticated kind of understanding that comes with Cultural Maturity's cognitive reordering is "wisdom." Nothing more directly teaches us about wisdom than the need to confront inviolable limits. We could also frame the result using the perspective of creative/formative process. Nothing more defines the second-half development task—whatever the creative/developmental process—than the need to acknowledge the fact of real limits.

Getting beyond the either/or assumptions of times past: This is another capacity introduced in Chapter One. Our later look at the workings of polarity added further conceptual detail. Integrative Meta-perspective helps us leave behind the polarized beliefs of times past and think in more encompassing ways. This new capability is critical to the possibility of getting along in the future. It is also central to the more systemic kind of understanding needed in every sphere.

As far as getting along, leaving behind past either/or assumptions is most obviously pertinent to the chosen-people/evil-other polarizations that have traditionally led to war. But I've described how this new capacity is just as pertinent to confronting knee-jerk differences that keep us from addressing policy questions with the needed systemic sophistication. In Chapter One, I summarized just what changes in this regard with culturally mature perspective: "In times past, when we encountered polarized positions and partisan advocacy, our task was obvious and unquestioned. We assumed that there were only two options and that our task was to fight for the side that was right. With Integrative Meta-perspective, the fact of polarity has very different implications. It alerts us to how we need to expand our vantage, see a big enough picture. When we do, we recognize that neither side is yet asking the hard question that ultimately needs to be answered. We also recognize that while each side may hold a piece of the truth, neither side by itself, nor some simple compromise between sides, can get us where we need to go."

I've pointed toward how getting beyond the either/or assumptions of times past is an essential part of the new kind of understanding needed, and newly possible, in every sphere. In working with groups from particular cultural domains, I will often have them start by listing the polarities that have before most defined understanding in that domain (for example, if they are physicians—doctor and patient, mind and body, or public and private; if they are educators—teacher and student, facts and feelings, or young and old). I then have them explore how "bridging" these various juxtapositions invites a more complete and timely picture of what is needed.

Realizing Whole-Person/Whole-System relationship: Relationships of all sorts in times past have been based as much on projection as on actual connection. This is the case not just with the polarized perceptions of us-versus-them relationships, but also, as we shall see, with more personal and everyday bonds of all sorts, from those between intimate partners to those that have defined connections between leaders and followers. Integrative Meta-perspective makes possible relationships in which the bonds are products of the whole of our own complexity and that more fully engage the complexity of the entity we are relating with. Such more Whole-Person/Whole-System bonds demand more of us, but they also offer much more in return. Creative possibilities increase dramatically.

Learning to think about what matters in more inclusive and complete ways: Again, Chapter One got us started. There I introduced the importance of more consciously asking pertinent Questions of Referent and of addressing them systemically—I could also say "in ways that get beyond ideology." I've described how CST defines ideology as any way of thinking that associates truth with one aspect of a larger systemic reality. Truths of times past have always been ideological, either because they originated from a specific cultural stage or because they identified with a particular polar truth within a cultural stage. In every part of our lives, we are being challenged to think about what matters in more encompassing ways, to draw on more systemic, more whole-box-of-crayons measures. Cultural Maturity makes it possible for us to do so. Learning to think about significance more systemically comes part and parcel with Cultural Maturity's cognitive reordering. In better drawing on the whole of our own complexity, we better take into account all that matters to us.

I've emphasized how this new capacity is particularly pertinent to the task of rethinking advancement. Our time's familiar way of defining wealth and progress can't continue to work for the simple reason that it fails to address more than a narrow slice of all that is ultimately important to us. Moving forward effectively will require that we define benefit in more complete ways, ways that better address the full complexity of our human needs, and ultimately also those of the planet as a whole. Rethinking wealth and progress represents our ultimate new human responsibility, and our ultimately most defining new-truth challenge. Our future well-being as a species depends on it.

Whatever the concern, effective decision-making in a culturally mature reality requires that we think about what matters in more complete ways. In the articles that follow, we will see how this new capacity has become critical with questions of every sort. Not only is addressing what matters more systemically essential if we are to arrive at answers that can ultimately serve us, it is where we necessarily start. If we don't begin there, we fail to ask the right questions and end up going off into ultimately unhelpful directions.

Better understanding how events always happen in a context—particularly in the context of their time in culture's story: The previous chapter addressed how what makes something true is always relative in time. It also described how this recognition requires culturally mature perspective. Over the course of this book, we will examine closely how understanding truth's contextual relativity in time is just one kind of more contextual understanding that culturally mature perspective makes possible.

Integrative Meta-perspective makes clear that we can understand effectively only to the degree to which we are attentive to all the various ways the question at hand interconnects with understanding as a whole. CST is about contextual relativity, about the very particular ways right choice becomes different depending on who we are and when and where we are choosing. When we appreciate systemic context, not only do we make different choices, our understanding of what it means to make a choice becomes fundamentally different.

A new capacity for foresight: Culturally mature perspective dramatically increases our ability to engage events yet to come. It makes us more able to entertain the future. It also makes it possible to consider the future in ways that ultimately work, not as an extension of ideology, but in terms of purpose, possibility, assessment of risk, and pattern. This is the case with every kind of choice we make in every part of our lives.

This needed new capacity for foresight is particularly pertinent to our larger human task. We can miss how the basic ability to take the future seriously is new. We have all had classes on history, but very few people have had classes on what may lie ahead. Cultural Maturity's cognitive changes make us more capable of foresight. More specifically, they make it newly possible to think about the future, as we have here, in ways that place who we are and how we think at the center of the equation. They also invite us to entertain how a next chapter in the human story might require that we think and act in the kind of fundamentally new more dynamic and complete ways that the concept of Cultural Maturity describes.

Chapter Five brings a creative frame more explicitly into the task by highlighting the importance and power of more consciously "exploratory" approaches to decision-making. The kind of foresight I'm referring to is most always more about direction and potential than about knowing for sure. While such foresight requires being more comfortable with uncertainty, the result is a more solid and reliable, ultimately common-sense way of relating to what may lie ahead.

This more creative kind of foresight is what we necessarily draw on in our personal lives when we lack the reliable guideposts of times past. And it is just as pertinent to the most encompassing of questions. In

Chapter Nine, I will propose that the climate change debate has always been about assessing risk rather than knowing for sure (and that on that basis, it was resolved twenty years ago). I will also address how confronting a pandemic effectively is similarly a question of risk assessment, and one in which risk is invariably a moving target (we never know as much as we would like).

Integrative Meta-perspective's more creative picture not only makes the future something we can more readily consider, it invites us to consider it in ways that are most likely to result in effective choices going forward.

Each of our eight new skills and capacities come together—and come together with Creative Systems Theory's broader thesis—in the new picture that results. Each capacity reflects a different aspect of what it means to take a newly conscious responsibility in life as a creative process, and in human life as a whole as a creative process.

Application—Some General Topics

We could—and will—apply these new skills and capacities to addressing challenges of every sort and scale. In later chapters, I will apply them to front-page-news issues like climate change, immigration, and gun violence, and to whole domains of understanding, from art to business. They will also help us engage even more overarching and ultimate concerns. Here I will apply them to a handful of more specific topics that nonetheless have implications across a wide range of issues and realms of experience: morality (including the recognition that all concerns in a culturally mature reality are ultimately moral concerns), love (along with relationships of all sorts, including our relationship with ourselves), leadership (acknowledging that leadership is what Integrative Meta-perspective is ultimately about), and the need for a new maturity in our relationship to the fact of our mortality (with reflections on the surprising implications that engaging death differently has across spheres of understanding).

The articles that follow are adapted from a series that I published in a variety of settings early in the century to introduce the concept of Cultural Maturity. The people reading them often had no previous contact with me or the concept of Cultural Maturity, and I wrote them with this in mind. Sometimes the articles were modified so they could stand on their own. But when I could, I would include the whole series.

I would then usually start with a short piece that offered the kind of general stage-setting reflections that I provided with this book in the Preface and in Chapter One.

In introducing the concept of Cultural Maturity in this way, I would note a couple of key recognitions that should now be familiar. First is how there is nothing esoteric or ultimately complicated in what I will describe, how culturally mature perspective is in the end only about seeing more fully what is in fact the case. I would also give attention to how, while we see the beginnings of all these specific changes in our time, it is likely that we will not see much of what I propose broadly accepted for decades into the future.

At times, content in these pieces will overlap with ideas I've presented previously in this book. This will happen most frequently with regard to observations used to introduce the broader concept of Cultural Maturity. I've chosen for the most part to leave content from the articles intact. I see this chapter as having a dual purpose. Along with filling out the concept of Cultural Maturity, the pieces together illustrate ways I've attempted to communicate about it, particularly when the concept might be new to my audience.

Article One: The Future of Morality—Why Moral Decisions in Times Ahead Will Require Skills New to Us as a Species

[The topic of morality provides one of the most accessible ways to introduce the concept of Cultural Maturity, and also one of the topics with most universal application. I begin with it because it so immediately confronts us with how today's challenges require that we think and act in new ways. It is a topic that readily ties to needed new skills and capacities.]

The moral dimension today presents a startling—and easily unsettling— circumstance. Effectively addressing moral questions is requiring abilities that before now we could not have fully understood, much less applied. In part this is because we confront new kinds of moral concerns—for example, those that follow from the need to manage the often two-edged implications of new technologies and the frequently confusing and overwhelming complexities of our increasingly globalized world. But the reason is ultimately deeper. Changes are taking place in what it means to make good decisions—including moral decisions. And these changes permeate every part of our lives.

Today people think about many morally charged concerns—such as gender roles and gender identity, racism, capital punishment, or abortion—quite differently than they did just a few decades ago. Not everyone finds these changes positive. And even people who see them as ultimately good can find them confusing and overwhelming. It is essential that we understand just what is changing and why.

I've introduced the CST concept of Cultural Maturity, the notion that our times are demanding—and also making possible—an essential "growing up" as a species. The concept describes how changes we are seeing in what it means to think and act morally are predicted. It also proposes that what we witness today represents only a beginning. It goes on to argue that understanding needed new ethical capacities and learning to put them into practice will be key to a healthy human future.

It is helpful to think about what is becoming different in a couple of steps. These two steps are not ultimately separate—in the end, they are products of the same change process. But because each requires careful consideration to fully grasp, I will take them one at a time. Following these big-picture reflections, I will describe four specific new human capacities that addressing moral questions effectively will increasingly require.

Cultural Maturity and Morality: Big-Picture Reflections

The first step turns our attention to today's marked weakening of traditional moral guideposts. Prior to now in history, culture has provided us with reliable moral absolutes. Today, the sources of such clear guidance, from unquestioned national and ethnic allegiances to once-and-for-all religious beliefs, are losing their historical power.

This loss is of immense consequence. Moral absolutes have provided our rules to live by and, in the process, a sense of identity and connectedness with others. Cultural absolutes have also protected us from truths that would have been beyond us to tolerate—the depths of life's uncertainties, limits to what may actually be possible, and in general how complex things can be.

Contrasting interpretations for why we see this weakening of absolutes can become highly charged. People of more conservative bent tend to view these changes negatively, as a loss of social order—or worse, as a sign of impending moral chaos. More liberal types are most apt to think of them positively, as expressions of new freedom, evidence of liberation from past constraining rules.

Academics often view today's loss of past cultural guideposts more neutrally, as a reflection of a new "postmodern" cultural narrative. This interpretation at least helps us get beyond moralizing about moralizing. It also helps us begin to frame the new task. It highlights how today's changes are putting responsibility for making moral choices more directly in our individual human hands.

But the postmodern interpretation can only get us part of the way. It tells us little about why we see these changes. And as far as possible positive consequences, it gives us nothing of substance to replace what it takes away. Indeed, it can undermine needed understanding. Too easily, it translates into an empty moral relativism that leaves us wandering aimlessly in an increasingly complex moral landscape. This circumstance reaches an absurd extreme today as "likes" and "clicks" increasingly become our modern measures of significance.

The concept of Cultural Maturity paints a larger picture that helps explain this loss of absolutes and begins to clarify why interpreting it positively may be warranted. The concept describes how culture has functioned historically like a parent to the lives of individuals. Providing clear moral rules was central to this past parental function. The concept also describes how our times are requiring—and making possible—a next, more "grown-up" chapter in our human story.

With Cultural Maturity, our past need for moral absolutes gradually falls away. We begin to be able to hold the realities of cultural authority and individual identity more systemically, recognize how they represent elements of a larger picture. One result is the need to take greater moral responsibility that is emphasized in the postmodern interpretation. Another is that this greater responsibility can be understood as an expression of appropriate and timely development.

The second step turns more specifically to needed new capacities. If we are to assume that greater responsibility and do so in a way that gets beyond the postmodern conundrum, we need to think and act in new ways.

The key to this second step is how Cultural Maturity alters not just what we think, but how we think—how it involves specific cognitive changes that allow us to understand in more integrative and encompassing ways. With this cognitive reordering, we are better able to step back from our human complexities. We also become able to confront those complexities in ways that are deeper and more complete. Cultural Maturity's changes help us engage ourselves more deeply when making moral choices, get more directly at what for us makes a choice moral. They also make possible new kinds of conceptual tools that can help us find our way in this more demanding and dynamic moral landscape. With time, we come to experience them as common sense.

Below I've described four themes that today redefine what it means to make moral choices. Each involves beginning to address ethical questions in more encompassing ways. That means better including all the important pieces. It also means learning to think in ways that get more directly at what makes any act or thought moral.

Getting Beyond Moral Polarization—the Fact of "Competing Goods." We tend to assume that moral quandaries require us to distinguish right from wrong. But in fact, this is rarely the case. Rather, they challenge us to choose in the face of competing goods. When a decision can be reduced to right versus wrong, we are unlikely to experience it as a quandary. The best choice will seem self-evident (most people won't recognize that anything needs deciding).

A couple of contemporary issues provide illustration: The abortion debate tends to reduce quickly to shrill advocacy. But it is very much about competing goods—the sanctity of life on one hand and the choice of the mother on the other. Immigration—a more collective moral quandary that commonly generates extreme positions—similarly juxtaposes ultimately commendable values. Immigration responds to needs that should move any compassionate person, and has historically supported vibrant societies. But it is also correct that people who have worked—perhaps for generations—to create institutions and economies should not be forced to make the rewards of those efforts freely available to anyone who might desire them. Boundaries have a legitimate function.

We are left with an essential question: If it is true that moral quandaries juxtapose competing goods, why do moral questions commonly get reduced to polarized, good-versus-evil arguments? In fact, we commonly turn all sorts of questions into moral debates that might initially seem not to be about morality at all—witness partisan pettiness in the political arena. Creative Systems Theory describes how our minds are wired to respond in this way. It also clarifies how this kind of response has served us. Reducing systemic challenges to simple either/ors has dramatically lessened the uncertainty and complexity that we have had to deal with.

But if the concept of Cultural Maturity is correct, this kind of simplification will prove less and less helpful—and necessary—going forward. Cultural Maturity's cognitive changes help us address a more systemically complete picture. Culturally mature perspective lets us better step back from the full complexity of what we encounter. It also helps us more deeply appreciate each dimension of that complexity. It becomes newly possible both to tolerate the fact that multiple elements interplay within moral quandaries and to make sense of just how they do.

In suggesting that we need to get beyond framing moral distinctions in polarized, good-versus-evil terms, I am not at all arguing against taking strong moral stands. In fact, Cultural Maturity specifically encourages us to take such stands. It also supports us in doing so. Engaging moral questions systemically provides the perspective needed to take moral stands confidently and to do so in ways that will support the greatest good going forward.

Recognizing How Questions of All Sorts Are Ultimately Moral Concerns. The second theme in a different way reflects the importance of a more encompassing perspective. In times past, only certain kinds of concerns were thought of as moral. Culturally mature perspective's more systemic vantage helps us appreciate how questions of all sorts are questions of value, and thus moral in their implications.

This change affects not just personal moral choices, but also moral concerns we must address together. We better recognize, for example, how domains we've before thought of as "value-free"—such as business and science—reflect values just as much as domains such as religion or politics, where choices are more obviously value-laden. With Wall Street's role in the 2008 financial collapse, we were confronted by how critical it is to recognize—and question when necessary—values that have been common in business. We appreciate something related for science and technology with the growing recognition that future human well-being will depend as much on the maturity needed to use invention wisely as it will on the particulars of what we might invent.

Learning to Think Directly In Terms of Whether a Thought or Act is "Life-Enhancing." The third theme is implied in each of the first two. We could frame it in terms of a question: If the moral task is not just to choose right over wrong (as I suggested earlier in emphasizing the fact of competing goods), just what is it? What is the distinction we need to make? Culturally mature perspective suggests that what we ultimately want to determine is the degree to which an act enhances life.

This conclusion requires that we expand how we customarily use language (for example, how we relate to life's opposite—death—is a pertinent consideration). But, in the end, the degree to which an act is life-enhancing is what moral truth has always been about. Culturally specific moral dictates have provided shared, one-size-fits-all shorthands for this kind of determination. With Cultural Maturity's changes it becomes increasingly possible to set shorthands aside. Culturally mature perspective lets us think more directly in terms of what makes an act moral. We become better able to take into account all that is involved and to articulate where our considerations take us in more whole-box-of-crayons terms.

The ability to do so is becoming increasingly essential. For example, while a rewarding life as a man or a woman today requires a willingness to question past gender dictates, necessarily this is just a first step. Each of us also needs to more deeply engage the whole of who we are—our full complexity as gendered beings. Similarly, success in love has come to require more than just confronting past assumptions and allowing the possibility of new options. It also demands a new and deeper appreciation for the needs that love fulfills—companionship, intimate bonds, parental cooperation, and so on (see the next article). In a related way, a fulfilling sense of identity requires that we go beyond just questioning past cultural expectations. In addition, we must draw on a more personal and complete relationship to the question of what for us creates worth.

With each of these examples, the task is the same. We need, first, to be attentive to all the factors that may be pertinent. Then, from this more encompassing vantage, we need to take our best shot at choosing the most life-enhancing way forward. Cultural Maturity's cognitive changes make it newly possible to engage in this at once more personal and more sophisticated kind of determination.

Recognizing that Moral Choice Always Happens in a Context. The fourth theme even more explicitly takes us beyond postmodern arbitrariness. While moral relativity of the postmodern, "anything goes" sort is a dangerous trap, the recognition that good moral choices are always relative in the sense of being context-dependent could not be more important. It is also a new kind of recognition, one that requires culturally mature perspective to fully appreciate and put into practice.

Moral dictates of times past were thought of as eternal—once-and-for-all. They were also thought to apply in exactly the same way to everyone—they were one-size-fits-all rules. Culturally mature perspective helps us appreciate that what makes an act life-affirming may be very different depending on its time and place. It also makes possible specific tools for making needed, more context-specific discernments.

The Golden Rule—"Do unto others as you would have them do unto you"—is a remarkably reliable guide for making moral choices. But stepping into Cultural Maturity's new territory of understanding quickly confronts us with how the Golden Rule's usefulness ultimately depends on context. It is simply true that different people want different things "done unto them"—as a function of cultural stage, upbringing, personality style, and more.

Some of morality's relativities are temporal. They relate to the fact that what is going to be most life-enhancing is relative in time. Of particular importance, morality is relative in developmental time. For example, we don't have the same expectations of a child that we do of an adolescent, or of an adolescent that we do of an adult. If we miss how this is so, we can easily act in ways that violate those we most care about. This same kind of temporal relativity plays out culturally. It takes an understanding of cultural stage differences, for example, if we are to fully appreciate why a Muslim woman might prefer to wear the hijab.[2]

Other aspects of morality's relativity are of a more here-and-now sort. I'm particularly aware of how this kind of contextual relativity plays out with temperament—with personality style differences. The Creative Systems Personality Typology describes the profoundly

---

2 See Chapter Ten or *On the Evolution of Intimacy*.

different ways the world looks through the eyes of people with contrasting personality styles.

In Summary—A New Moral Imperative

The future is demanding—and making possible—a new kind of moral maturity. This greater maturity requires taking greater personal and collective responsibility in our choices. It also requires engaging what makes a choice moral more directly and applying new kinds of conceptual tools that can help us make needed, more nuanced distinctions. All these things become newly possible with Cultural Maturity's cognitive changes and the more systemic view of the world that results.

This new moral reality presents what might at first seem a paradox. Unquestionably, it makes new demands. It requires that we think in ways that are more multifaceted and complete. And the distinctions that Cultural Maturity's cognitive reordering make possible require a level of sophistication that before now would not have made sense to us. Yet at the same time, Cultural Maturity's changes make moral choices, if not simpler, at the least more straightforward. The detailed knowledge of culture-specific social mores needed in times past becomes not so necessary. Engaging moral questions effectively starts with discerning just what a question asks and tolerating the implications. From there, as best we are able, we attempt to discern what choices will produce the outcomes that are most aligned with life and meaning.[3]

Article Two: How Changes Reshaping Love Are More Fundamental Than We Realize—and More Fundamental Than We Could Before Have Realized

[The topic of love provides some of the best evidence for the foundational nature of Cultural Maturity's changes. While this piece's claim can initially take people by surprise, with reflection, its accuracy becomes obvious. Ultimately, the new picture it points toward is pertinent not just to love, but also to how we understand relationship, identity, and truth more generally.]

The title I've used for this piece might seem overly dramatic. But I will argue that it is not. I will also argue that changes happening in the

---

3 Chapter Five expands on these morality-related observations.

world of love can help us understand equally dramatic changes taking place in human relationships of all sorts. They can help us too to more fully understand the broader "growing up" as a species—what I call Cultural Maturity—that will be more and more essential if we are to have a healthy and vital human future.

Thirty years ago, I wrote an article I titled "Beyond Romeo and Juliet: A New Meaning for Love." It described how love in our time is changing— fundamentally. While I've written numerous books and articles since, no piece has been more often cited. The changes I then described have only become more pronounced. We see love-related changes most readily in today's rapidly evolving assumptions about gender roles and expectations. But ultimately they go deeper. They concern just how love works—what makes love love.

For love's new picture to make sense, we need first to recognize that love does indeed change. Commonly we regard love to be timeless—we assume that love is love. But in fact, love has evolved over the course of history, with Romeo and Juliet-style romantic love only one chapter in this evolution. Indeed, it is a relatively recent cultural "invention"—a product of Modern Age understanding. People in the European Middle Ages often idealized romantic love, but it was unrequited love they put on a pedestal.

Even if we do recognize that changes, even fundamental changes, have taken place over time, we still tend to assume that love as we have most recently known it represents a kind of culmination. But this assumption, too, fails to hold up. If indeed love evolves, then there is no reason to believe that it should now stand still. And there is a deeper reason to question this assumption. It turns out that the Modern Age ideal is not only not some final manifestation of love, in fact it represents something quite different from what we have thought it to be about.

We tend to think of—and idealize—modern romantic love as love based on individual choice. In the sense that romantic love has taken us beyond the historical practice of having partners chosen by families or matchmakers, it does reflect greater freedom of choice. But this is not yet individual choice in any fully realized sense—in the sense of choosing as whole people. The Modern Age romantic ideal reflects what we could call "two-halves-make-a-whole" love. My grandparents make a wonderful example. They met when they were five and were inseparable throughout their lives. When my grandfather died, my grandmother died soon thereafter. We speak of spouses being our "better half" to reflect the beauty of this kind of connecting.

But relationships that work today are beginning to require more of us. Two-halves-make-a-whole connecting depends on the mechanism that psychologists speak of as projection. With romantic love, we put the other on a pedestal—make them our white knight or fair maiden. What we see on that pedestal is, in fact, as much a part of ourselves as the person we care about—a masculine or feminine aspect that we have yet to fully incorporate into our own identities. In its time, this mechanism provided a very reliable sort of bond. We related like two opposite poles of a magnet. But our times are asking more. Two-halves-make-a-whole love is not yet about loving another just for who they are—fully as a person.

Whole-Person love—love that sets aside the ready magnetisms of projection—represents a fundamentally different kind of connecting. It requires that we better recognize how, as Lily Tomlin put it, "we are all in this alone." And, simultaneously, it requires that we recognize the possibility of fuller ways of being together. These changes are only beginning, and certainly only beginning to be recognized. But when I work as a psychiatrist with couples, it is rare that the challenges and rewards of loving more fully as whole people does not become a point of discussion.

The fact that love as we have witnessed it to this point has been love of a two-halves-make-a-whole sort becomes obvious with reflection. Projection is what makes it possible to fall quickly in love with no real knowledge of the other person. It is also what makes it possible for the sound of wedding bells at a movie's conclusion to assure us that the protagonists will live "happily ever after" when, in fact, love's journey has barely begun.

The common result when we fall out of love provides even more inescapable evidence for this two-halves-make-a-whole mechanism. People tend to assume that we will then have distaste, even antipathy for the other person—which with high frequency proves to be what we in fact feel. Notice that this outcome makes no sense if love had been between two whole people, when we have loved each other simply for who we are. The ending of such a relationship can bring sadness that something special has run its course. It can also bring regret that mistakes were made. But only in very unusual circumstances would antipathy be warranted. Why do we assume antipathy? When love involves projection, antipathy is needed in order to extract the projected part and regain our full sense of ourselves. The more common sentiment when the feelings of Whole-Person love begin to fade is gratitude for what the other person has added to our lives.

I need to emphasize that I am not at all being critical of love as we have known it. It was right for its time. We would not have had love that worked without the reliable magnetisms that these mechanisms provided. My point is simply that our times are challenging us to turn first pages in an important further chapter in love's story.

While what that new chapter in love ultimately brings is exciting, we may not at first celebrate these changes. Leaving behind the romantic dream's promise that there is another person who can be our completion and answer may look only like loss. And as yet we have little to guide us in engaging the changes this more mature kind of love requires of us. Imagery in the media, today, rarely gets much beyond the old romantic ideal—indeed, it rarely goes beyond absurd caricatures of it.

But when we begin to engage love's new picture, the power of what it represents becomes obvious. We see that that which has been taken away was ultimately illusion—an illusion that, while once necessary for love to work, today has become an obstacle. We also see how, because love of the more Whole-Person sort better reflects two people's unique lives, it can be much more significant—and thus more romantic in the deepest sense. And because the two people are no longer two halves of a predictable story, possible ways of being together increase dramatically.

Cultural Maturity's Cognitive Changes

We don't need to invent this new capacity for Whole-Person love—at least not in any whole-cloth sense—thankfully. Otherwise it would certainly be too much of a stretch. Whole-Person relating follows directly from the cognitive changes that produce Cultural Maturity's more encompassing new chapter in our human story. These are the same changes that I've described as making it newly possible to get beyond the chosen-people/evil-other beliefs that before have been the basis for war, and reshaping the moral landscape.

With Cultural Maturity's cognitive reordering, we more consciously hold all the diverse parts that make us who we are. In the process, we come to engage experiences of all sorts in more encompassing—more systemic—ways. I've described how the idealized imagery of two-halves-make-a-whole relationships (or demonized imagery if things are not going well) involves projecting parts of ourselves onto the other. When such relationship is historically right, we experience finding an appropriate home for our projections as completing us. With Cultural Maturity's cognitive changes, we gradually come to experience such projective dynamics as diminishing us—making us less rather than more.

While Whole-Person love requires holding reality more generously than before, when we are ready for it, rather than anything exotic, it feels like "common sense." This is a sophistication of common sense that we are only just now beginning to appreciate. But when it is timely, it feels like what love that matters is obviously about.

As should be clear from this description, Whole-Person love is as much about a new kind of relationship with ourselves as it is about being able to relate more fully with another person. I've observed that describing Romeo and Juliet–style romantic love as love based on individual choice refers at best to individuality of a limited sort. Whole-Person love reflects a wholly new, more complete understanding of—and way of embodying—what it means to be an individual. Arguably, we are only just learning what being an individual—in any full sense—is about. CST refers to this Modern Age misconception about the nature of identity as The Myth of the Individual.[4]

Needed New Capacities

We can think of what Whole-Person love demands in terms of a handful of new capacities. Each requires holding reality in the fuller way that Cultural Maturity's cognitive changes make possible.

A New and Greater Ability to Tolerate Limits, Uncertainty, and the Fact That Relationship Is a Process. With romantic love, the other is experienced as an answer—our completion. Whole-Person love requires that we accept limits to what another person can be for us and, in turn, what we can be for them. It also requires that we accept fundamental limits to what we can know. (In therapy, I will often respond to a person's implied expectation that their partner should somehow understand them

---

4 See "The Myth of the Individual" in Chapter Five.

completely with the observation that they are lucky if they understand five percent of themselves.) In addition, it requires that we recognize that getting to know another person deeply takes time. Relationship done well becomes experienced as a creative process—with all the necessary uncertainties and unexpected twists and turns.

Learning to Re-Own Projections and to "Measure" Love in More Encompassing Ways. With two-halves-make-a-whole love, love as experience is an expression of the degree to which we find completion in another person. We know it is love because we feel the requisite "chemistry" and by the experience of "falling in love." With Whole-Person love, the connection can be ultimately much deeper, but our "measure" is more basic—more ordinary, if you will. Our attention turns to the depth of connection and complementarity we feel with one another. We know love is love not by one part of us being excited at being made complete, but by the whole of ourselves appreciating the ways life becomes more in the presence of this other person.

Comfort with Making More Nuanced Distinctions. It is important to appreciate that success in love today has to do not just with what we bring to love—the whole of ourselves—but also with how we understand it. Love that surrenders traditional projections requires more subtle understandings of love's workings. We aren't used to thinking this much about love. Indeed, thinking and love have often been viewed almost as opposites. But as cultural dictates stop doing much of our thinking for us, we need to bring new levels of awareness and discernment to our experience of love.

Our times invite—indeed demand (and also begin to make possible)—a new maturity not just in our experience of love, but also in the sophistication with which we make sense of it. For example, successful love in the future will require a deeper appreciation of how love can be different for different people. It will also require a fuller recognition of how love changes and evolves, both through the course of a relationship and more broadly. In addition, it will require a more encompassing grasp of how love creatively interplays with other parts of our lives.

I find one example of this need to make more nuanced distinctions particularly intriguing. I write a lot about personality differences—how profoundly differently various people can see the world, as a product of temperament. Fifty years ago, it was rare for people with different personality styles to form romantic bonds (when we said "opposites attract," that was opposites within the same general slice in temperament). Today, relationships between people with very different temperaments are increasingly common (as we see with other kinds of diversity such as racial differences). Because such relationships bring together this richness of difference, they can be particularly fulfilling. But they can work only to the degree to which people appreciate how deep differences can be and approach relationship with the needed perspective and understanding.[5]

Love's Complexity/Love's Simplicity

There are ways in which bringing greater maturity to love makes love more complex. Certainly, it makes love more challenging. Whole-Person love requires that we know both ourselves and the person we are with more deeply. There is also how needed new capacities require bringing greater sophistication to our choices and greater nuance to how we connect. And while getting beyond two-halves-make-a-whole assumptions can open the door to a greater variety of options in the forms love can take, the fact that we have more options doesn't necessarily make love easier.

But there are important ways too in which Whole-Person connecting can make love simpler. Love becomes more about just being oneself and loving another person for who they are—it is about love simply as love. With this recognition, we can leave much of love's past trappings and expectations behind us if we so wish, shape love in the ways that best fit who we are together. It also becomes much easier to recognize and step beyond soap opera and drama that in the end only get in the way of real relationship.

Whichever most stands out—the complexity or the simplicity—it is these changes that will allow love to remain something powerful in the future. Whole-Person connecting is not some luxury. In the long term, this next chapter in love's story will be essential to love that works—and essential also to ways of understanding identity and purpose that work. The future of intimacy depends increasingly on this ability to realize a fuller kind of relationship with ourselves and with those we care about.

---

[5] I will address this topic in more detail in Chapter Six.

We gain additional insight into the changes reshaping love with the recognition that related changes are taking place in relationships of all sorts—from those between friends; to new, more mature approaches to leadership; and ultimately to how we think about and structure our institutions. Each new sort of relating is a product of the same kind of cognitive reordering. And with each, we see the need for related new capacities. We also see the possibility of relationship that is at once more ordinary and more profound.

But love provides an especially striking and useful example of this evolution and one of the most ready places to recognize it. Just where are we in these changes? Love's next more mature chapter remains a stretch for most people. Popular depictions of love still rarely get beyond fairy tale romance. It may be many decades before this is how a major portion of people begin to think about love. But love's changes are well under way. In just how they are, they help us appreciate how these are changes "whose time has come" and support the hope that Cultural Maturity's broader changes are more in the cards then we might assume."[6]

Article Three: How Changes in What It Means to Lead Are Redefining Our Human Task

[The topic of this article—leadership—makes an especially powerful lens for understanding our time's larger challenge. In the end, Cultural Maturity is about leadership, about right authority in all parts of our personal and collective lives. Ultimately, it is about right authority in ourselves.]

It is important to appreciate how much leadership today is changing. The picture is not all reassuring. Trust in leadership of all sorts today is less than it was at the height of anti-authoritarian rhetoric in the 1960s. Respected thinkers have argued that this modern lack of confidence in leadership reflects something gone terribly wrong—broad failure on the part of leaders, a loss of moral integrity on the part of those being led, or even an impending collapse of society. But there is a more optimistic explanation, one that ties what we see to broader changes reshaping

---

6 *On the Evolution of Intimacy: A Brief Exploration into the Past, Present, and Future of Gender and Love* addresses this article's observations with additional depth and detail.

culture in our time. The crisis of confidence in leadership we see today may have less to do with leaders themselves failing than how old forms of leadership are failing.

Nothing more defines Cultural Maturity than a "growing up" in how we understand, relate to, and embody authority. That includes authority of every sort—from that exercised in leading nations; to the expertise of teachers, doctors, or ministers; to that we apply in making the most intimate of personal life choices. If the needed "growing up" in relationship to leadership the concept describes is not a major factor in the disruptions we now see, it will certainly be a major factor in changes in the long term. Arguably it will be needed if leadership is to work at all going forward.

Many of the leadership-related changes that the concept of Cultural Maturity points toward have been described by thinkers other than myself. But the concept of Cultural Maturity provides a unique depth of understanding with regard to both why we should see these changes and what they entail.

It helps in getting started to put leadership and how we think about it in historical perspective. We can miss how dramatically what we call leadership has changed through time. We witnessed the last major change point in leadership's evolution some three hundred years ago with the rise of democratic principles and the emergence of individual determination as a rallying cry. Leadership with the previous stage in culture's story had been heredity-based and authoritarian in approach. Now, at least in theory, anyone could be a leader. And good leadership came increasingly to be seen as leadership based on making sound—rational—choices. These new steps in leadership's evolution were critical to the advances of the Modern Age.

It is reasonable to ask why anything more should be necessary. The mechanism I've called "projection" provides the essential insight. Projecting our power onto leaders has always before been central to the workings of leadership. When we project our power, we make leaders mythic figures. This is most obvious with leaders of times well past, such as pharaohs and kings, who were seen, if not as gods, then certainly as god-like. But in a similar if not quite so absolute way, we have continued to make leaders heroic symbols in modern times. We described John Kennedy using the imagery of Camelot. We depicted Ronald Reagan as a mythic father figure. In a related way, we've symbolically elevated not just political leaders, but authorities of all sorts—religious leaders, professors, doctors, and leaders in business.

The mythologizing of leadership becomes a problem going forward for a couple of critical reasons. First, the tasks before us require a more empowered relationship to leadership—and ultimately a more powerful kind of leadership. While turning authority over to symbolic figures can make circumstances appear more secure, increasingly today it undermines real possibility. Second is how projection distorts reality at a time when it is becoming increasingly essential that leadership choices reflect what is actually the case. Such distortion gets in the way both of clarity and of the more nuanced discernments that good leadership will increasingly require.

The concept of Cultural Maturity describes how the possibility of a healthy and vital human future hinges on new, more mature and sophisticated ways of understanding—and embodying—leadership. Needed changes are deeper than just new leadership skills. They have to do with authority itself—how we conceive of it and how we manifest it.

The Rewards—and Limitations—of Mythologized Leadership

If we are to move beyond projecting our power onto leaders, we need to appreciate how mythologizing has served us. In times past, the idealizing of authority has been essential not just to effective leadership, but to the effective working of social systems. Mythologizing has provided a sense of order in a world that would otherwise be too complex and deeply uncertain to tolerate. It has protected us from life's easily overwhelming bigness.

In *Cultural Maturity: A Guidebook for the Future*, I describe an experience that helped me as a physician appreciate our past mythologizing of leadership: "I'm drawn back to my training in medical school. Much that we did—from the wearing of white coats to thirty-six-hour ritual stints in the emergency room—in the end had more to do with the assumption of a ceremonial role than the learning of medicine. I was initially critical of this. But experience helped me recognize its historical purpose. I remember once wondering, as I watched a surgeon cut into the Jello-fragile tissue of a young woman's brain, whether he could still have carried out this task—there with life or death balanced on the tip of his scalpel—if he had not had medicine's mythic trappings to protect him from the full responsibility and uncertainty of his craft."

But while it is important that we don't dismiss the important role that the mythologizing of leadership has played, it is becoming increasingly clear that protective idealizations can't continue to serve us in the same way. Leadership going forward will require more of us. It must be of a more expressly human sort in the sense of taking responsibility in a world in which uncertainties and complexities are inescapable. It must also be capable of a subtlety of understanding possible only when we surrender past protective distortions.

Drawing again briefly on my surgeon example helps make the point. Acknowledging the depth of responsibility and necessary uncertainty that comes with being a physician will be key to good health care going forward at multiple levels. At the least it will help to minimize medical errors. Maintaining a mythologized status is not compatible with expressing doubt and the ready acknowledgment of mistakes. And new understandings of leadership are integrally related to broader changes necessary to health care's future. In the next article, I will describe how affordable, compassionate, and effective health care in times ahead will require getting beyond modern medicine's heroic "defeat death and disease at any cost" mindset. That heroic mindset and the mythologizing of the physician's role go hand in hand.

Given today's crisis of confidence in leadership, it would be easy to argue that the more mature kind of leadership I'm describing is at least a long way off. And in many spheres, this is certainly the case. But it is also true that we see changes consistent with the needed, more sophisticated leadership with authority relationships of many sorts. Some of the most significant social innovations of our time link the opposite halves of authority-related polarities—teacher and student, doctor and patient, minister and churchgoer. They reflect a more mature and systemic leadership picture. Authority relationships of all sorts are becoming more two-way, with more listening and flexibility on the part of leaders and more engaged and empowered roles for those who draw on a leader's expertise and guidance.

In most spheres today we reside in an awkward in-between time in the realization of leadership's new picture. We tend to be much better at demanding the gift of culturally mature leadership than at knowing what to do with it. We may want leaders to get off their pedestals; but frequently when they attempt to do so, we respect them less, not more. We want leaders to be more transparent, to reveal more of themselves and to make fewer decisions behind closed doors; however, when they do, our first response is often to attack them for their human frailties. It is important to appreciate how much of a stretch this further chapter in leadership's story represents.

Culturally Mature Leadership

How do we best understand what is becoming different? And how do we best make sense of just what these changes ask of us? Four themes I've touched on in previous articles help fill out leadership's new picture.

Culture as Parent. I've described how in times past culture has functioned as a mythic parent to the lives of individuals. I've also described how Cultural Maturity is about stepping beyond this parent/child kind of relationship. With the idealized leadership of times past, leaders in effect served as emissaries for culture as mythic parent. In the new picture, leadership becomes a more mortal enterprise, about ordinary people taking on tough and important jobs.

Cognitive Changes. Cultural Maturity is not just about new ideas. It is a product of specific cognitive changes. Leadership's new picture follows directly from these changes. We get a glimpse in the observation that culturally mature perspective makes it possible to more consciously hold the diverse aspects of who we are—to step back and in a more integrated way recognize and apply the whole of our human complexity. In previous articles, I've described how these changes help us think about moral questions in more encompassing ways and entertain more sophisticated understandings of love. The ability to think about questions of all sorts in more encompassing—more systemic—ways that comes with Cultural Maturity's cognitive changes in effect defines culturally mature leadership.

Whole-Person/Whole-System Relationship. One of the most striking and significant results of Cultural Maturity's cognitive changes is that they make it newly possible to engage relationships of all sorts—whether those are between countries or between lovers—as relationships between whole systems. The leader/follower relationship is another place we see this result. In no way does this change dismiss the importance of good leadership—make leader and follower suddenly the same. In fact, it brings new attention to the importance of exceptional leadership. But it does make the leader/follower relationship more explicitly a human relationship, and often more specifically a collaborative relationship. It also highlights how culturally mature followership can often be as important as culturally mature leadership. We can get away with deeply flawed leaders if others stand ready to call them to task.

New Capacities. I've described Cultural Maturity in terms of new human capacities. Each new capacity that I've noted applies directly to leadership. Indeed, we usefully think of them specifically as "leadership capacities." The topic of leadership makes a great place to bring our skills and capacities together: *"Accepting fundamental responsibility"* comes hand in hand with setting aside mythologized concepts of leadership. When we no longer project our authority, we become ultimately responsible, not just for our actions, but also for our beliefs. *"Learning to better tolerate uncertainty and complexity"* becomes essential in a world where traditional guideposts and cut-and-dried leader/follower dictates less and less serve us. *"Better appreciating the fact of real limits"* comes into play with inviolable limits of every sort, from limits to what a leader can know and control, to limits to what leaders and followers can be for one another. And the importance of *"Getting beyond the either/or assumptions of times past"* takes essential expression in how culturally mature leadership requires leaving behind both projection and ideology.

We've just looked at how *"Realizing Whole-Person/Whole-System relationship"* is key to being either a culturally mature leader or a culturally mature follower. *"Learning to think about what matters in more inclusive and complete ways"* is what replaces our past reliance on cultural absolutes. *"Better understanding how events always happen in a context"* provides needed big-picture perspective and the nuance necessary to make good choices in a diverse and ever-changing world. In particular, it helps us understand our time and the particular challenges and possibilities that make our time unique. And if culturally mature leadership is about anything, it is about *"A new capacity for foresight,"* a greater ability to anticipate and to manage systems in the face of changing circumstances.

An additional observation that follows from Cultural Maturity's cognitive changes is key to fully grasping Cultural Maturity's implications for leadership. It concerns how leadership's new picture has as much to do with how we relate to authority in ourselves as it does with how we relate to outside authority. Culturally mature perspective reveals how parts of ourselves that we have identified with authority and truth reflect only aspects of how understanding and determination ultimately work—and only aspects of what we must draw on in the future if we are to make effective personal decisions.

Key to what made modernity's new step significant was how it replaced medieval superstition with a picture that elevated—and mythologized—conscious awareness. It also elevated one particular aspect of intelligence's ultimately multifaceted workings—the rational. With the Age of Reason, we came to see these two aspects of our cognitive complexity working together as captain of the cellular ship—what defined identity and truth, and determined action. This change was more than philosophical. It described a new way of being in ourselves—and ultimately of being a "self."

With Cultural Maturity's cognitive changes, we see an essential further step. We come to engage both identity and truth in fuller and more dynamic ways. At the least, these changes make personal choice a more rich and multifaceted enterprise. And again, too, we see a more fundamental kind of significance. Not just what we choose, but where in ourselves we choose from—and who ultimately we are—comes to reflect a more complete, more systemic picture.

Political Leadership

It is important to remember that Cultural Maturity is about changes over the long term. Just how much this is the case can be frustrating. I've written extensively about how important aspects of Cultural Maturity's needed "growing up" are not happening as quickly as we might wish. With some of the leadership changes I've described, we've made significant progress; with others, we have barely made a start.

Political leadership is one of the places where we obviously have a long way to go. And partisan pettiness is only one manifestation of the immaturity that too often pervades the halls of government. But, obstacles acknowledged, the challenges of governmental leadership provide powerful big-picture insights, ones we can draw on to even more deeply understand the needed new stage in leadership's evolution.

As we face critical, awkward in-between realities in the political sphere, we need to be wary of three kinds of unhelpful reactions. First, as old formulas cease to work, we can become cynical and despairing. Feeling powerless, we can, in effect, opt out of the leader/follower relationship. Second, as old forms of leadership prove no longer reliable, we can become advocates for traditional leadership's opposite. This can take the form of replacing top-down assumptions with bottom-up ideals of determination—more populist from the Left or more libertarian or simply anti-government from the Right. At worst, we see anarchism and violence. Or third, we can find ourselves attracted to authoritarian leaders who in promising the return of old securities in fact make our world only more dangerous.

What do our times demand when it comes to governmental leadership? On the leadership side of the leader/follower equation, our times require people able to articulate and manifest all the new capacities I've noted. On the follower side of the equation, they ask us all to be leaders in the sense of being actively involved in the choices that need to be made. They also ask us not to cop out, to become self-righteously anti-authoritarian, or to in any other way undermine effective leadership. We need to deeply respect and cherish culturally mature leadership wherever it can be found—because it is so vitally important, and also because it is as yet rare.

One further observation with regard to governmental leadership is pertinent. If the concept of Cultural Maturity is accurate, there is no reason to assume that our current chapter in government's evolution is some ideal and end point. These reflections on leadership provide an added way to appreciate why something more might be expected. They also provide essential additional insights into what would make a next stage in government's evolution new—and important.

It turns out that representative government as we have known it—like love—represents something quite different from what we have assumed it to be about. We like to think of modern institutional democracy as "government by the people." But in fact we remain yet short of that ideal. This is most obvious with the simple recognition that election results tend to more closely reflect "one dollar, one vote" than "one person, one vote." But these observations on the evolution of authority provide important further perspective for understanding this conclusion.

In the previous article, I briefly made reference to what CST calls The Myth of the Individual. I described how, while we like to think of modern romantic love as love based on individual choice, it is not yet this in the sense of choosing as whole people. Given that the leader/follower relationship, too, has been a two-halves-make-a-whole relationship, in a related way modern institutional democracy stops short of our stated democratic ideal.[7]

This recognition helps support the conclusion that a next chapter in government's developmental story is both needed and possible. It also helps us appreciate important aspects of what such a new chapter must accomplish. I know no more intriguing leadership question than what a next stage in government's evolution might look like. The concept of Cultural Maturity offers multiple ways to approach the question. One is to ponder what government that comes closer to being real "government by the people" might look like. Cultural Maturity's changes should more and more push this essential question to the fore as we come to experience both what matters and ourselves in more complete ways.[8]

Article Four: The Radical Implications of a New Maturity in Our Relationship with Death

[The topic of the next piece does not so obviously cut across diverse spheres of understanding. But in fact, it has some of the broadest implications. And it gets at the depths of what is being asked of us in ways that are particularly inescapable.]

The ability to better engage limits represents one of the most significant of Cultural Maturity's new capacities. Of particular importance, we become better able to recognize that some limits are inviolable. Nothing more defined the Modern Age narrative than the fact

---

7 Again, see "The Myth of the Individual" in Chapter Five.

8 See "Government and Governance" in Chapter Eleven for a closer look at what the evolution of government may hold for the future.

that it was heroic—our task on confronting limits was to defeat them. With Cultural Maturity, we better appreciate that certain limits, no matter how hard we try, cannot be defeated. We also recognize that when we ignore this fact, we make ultimately unwise, and often dangerous, decisions.

I've given special attention in my books to one particular inviolable limit: the fact of our mortality. Death represents life's ultimate limit to what we can know and control. Always before in our history, cultural belief has served to keep death's full significance at arm's length. Later I will address how religious belief in particular has served this protective function. Such protection has been essential. Looking as directly at death as I will argue our times require would have stretched us beyond what we could have tolerated.

Appreciating how this picture is changing sheds valuable light on a handful of critical cultural challenges. It also offers insight into the more general significance of our times and provides important evidence for the concept of Cultural Maturity. I've described Cultural Maturity as a new—and newly demanding—common sense. A new, more mature relationship to death is an essential aspect of that needed new common sense.

With some of the specific death-related challenges I will describe, we see important beginnings of the needed greater maturity. With others, consistent with how Cultural Maturity is ultimately about the long term, possible consequences I will touch on may remain well in the future. But even where it may be many decades before changes are broadly appreciated, we can learn a lot from reflecting on just where these changes might ultimately take us.

Death and the Future of Health Care

I've written most extensively about the importance of a new, more mature relationship to death as it pertains to the future of health care. Viewing death as an enemy to be conquered has been central to many of modern medicine's grand achievements. Today this picture is changing—and in fundamental ways. Leaving behind modern medicine's heroic mindset that has made defeating death and disease, essentially at any cost, its bottom-line task will be critical going forward. I've argued that good health care policy in the future will require a maturity in our relationship with death not before necessary, nor within our human capacity to handle.

This necessity confronts us most immediately with the importance of containing costs. As medical interventions become ever more expensive, continuing to see death as an enemy to defeat results inevitably in medicine that is simply not affordable. But in the end, whether we are to have ultimately compassionate and effective care similarly hinges on a new maturity in our relationship to death. When we view death as an enemy, too often we confuse the prolongation of life with supporting life. The common result is extreme interventions that violate the Hippocratic Oath to "do no harm"—well-intended measures that are, in the end, simply not moral.

A closer look at the task of cost containment highlights how deeply challenging and fundamentally disruptive the needed changes will be. People tend to think of the health care delivery crisis in terms of opposing economic strategies: free market on one hand versus more centralized approaches. They assume that their preferred approach, by eliminating inefficiencies, will provide a solution. But health care expenditures are spiraling uncontrollably—for everyone, whatever kind of system they employ—and there is no natural end in sight.

While inefficiencies and excesses play some role in what we see, the most important factor is more basic—and no one's fault. Spiraling costs are primarily a product of modern medicine's great success. Early innovations—like sterile technique and penicillin—were relatively cheap. More recent advances—sophisticated diagnostic procedures, exotic new medications, transplant surgeries, and more—are increasingly expensive and promise only to get more so.

This recognition might suggest that escalating costs can't be stopped. But they must be. Increasingly they threaten not just medical care, but the health of economies. We face a stark reality. Unless we are willing to use an ever-expanding percentage of national resources for health care, we have no choice but to restrict health care spending.

This new circumstance puts before us a whole new order of ethical challenge. We need only look to extreme reactions that follow the suggestion that we might have to "ration" care to appreciate the newness of what is being asked of us. We've always rationed care, at least in the sense of often withholding care from those not able to pay for it. And often there has simply not been effective care available. But restricting care consciously in the way that our times demand is different.

Not providing care when we have effective care to offer fundamentally calls into question the heroic mythology that has defined modern medicine. More deeply, restricting care demands a new relationship to that most taboo of topics: the fact that we die. Medicine has always been about life-and-death decisions. But limiting care in the sense I'm suggesting involves consciously withholding care that might at least delay death's arrival.

An exercise I've done with groups puts the unsettling reality of what is being asked of us in high relief. I start by handing participants a list of ten patient profiles—including information about both patient's lives and their illnesses—along with a budget. Then I send the group off to a room for two hours with instructions to decide how the money should be spent. The choices that the exercise requires of participants can be so emotionally and morally wrenching that people refuse to make them. But the exercise is not an abstraction. It presents the task we inescapably face if we are to effectively address health care limits.

It is important to appreciate that we already see important changes in how the health care world relates to death. These changes represent only first steps, but they are significant. We witness growing recognition of the importance of end-of-life conversations between patients and doctors. The role of quality hospice care is increasingly appreciated. And states are beginning to pass legislation that supports doctor-assisted suicide.

It is hard to predict just how long realizing the degree of maturity needed to effectively address spiraling costs will take. It is possible that we are talking about changes that are yet far in the future. As yet, people rarely appreciate what will ultimately be required. (I find it fascinating how often politicians have assumed that making changes in health care delivery policy is low-hanging fruit, only to be blindsided by controversy and the task's complexity.) But there is also an important reason that changes could happen faster than we might imagine. Very soon, escalating costs will stop us in our tracks. However quickly changes do happen, continuing to move beyond the Modern Age's heroic narrative when it comes to death should be more and more central to health care being a life-affirming enterprise in the decades and centuries ahead.

Putting Our Relationship with Death in Historical Perspective

A person could argue that looking more squarely at death is nothing new—just new for medicine. For example, one might claim that religion is a sphere that long ago made its peace with death. Funerals most commonly take place in churches. And religious settings are where we are most likely to encounter conversations about our mortality and find solace in the face of death. Indeed, if we go back far enough, we often find death-related imagery intimately tied to spiritual experience. Burial mounds were places of worship for the ancient Celts, and writings such as The Tibetan Book of the Dead have served as guides to spiritual realization.

But this argument misses an essential recognition. I've proposed that cultural belief has served to keep death's full significance at arm's length. Religion has played a key role in this necessary obfuscation. By providing unquestioned explanation for what happens after death, religion has served to protect us from death as experience.

Putting how religion has conceived of death in historical perspective supports this conclusion. It also helps us appreciate how our relationship to death has changed before. Each stage in the evolution of spiritual/religious understanding has provided us with a somewhat different picture of what happens after we die. In tribal times, death was thought of as allowing us to rejoin nature and our ancestors in a parallel world. Later, with the early rise of civilizations and more polytheistic sensibilities, we commonly encounter belief in reincarnation, with death bringing a return to the present in some new form. With the emergence of monotheism, we came to think of death as providing entry into a now separate world—depending on our life choices, of either a heavenly or hellish sort. With the more liberal monotheism of Modern Age times, we tend most often to think of that separate world as simply a better and happier place. Each of these pictures, in a way consistent with the realities of that cultural stage, offered a sense of order and gave us a way to reconcile with death. But each also, in the end, protected us from the fact of death.

We can easily miss that religion, today, continues to protect us from death's easily overwhelming implications. While different modern religions vary in the degree to which they emphasize this protective function, it is never totally absent. I remember at my mother's funeral how the minister seemed ultimately more concerned with reassuring everyone that my mother was now with God (and that everything was thus right and as it should be) than with my mother as a person. It became quickly clear to me that this was really not the place to be if I wished to grieve my mother's passing with the depth that had come to feel important to me.

Death and the Future of Religion—and Science, Too

Drawing on religion's history in this way leaves us with a fascinating question: How might religion change if it underwent similar changes to those I've described for medicine? The question helps us further appreciate the radical newness of the needed new human relationship to death. It also provides important insights as we ponder the future of religion. It is possible that the needed "growing up" in our human relationship with death could here be even more fundamentally transforming.

People of more secular bent have argued that religion doesn't really have a future. While the concept of Cultural Maturity challenges religion at the level of fundamental assumptions, it reaches a different kind of conclusion as far as religion's future. Two recognitions related to religion's past relationship to death get us started.

First is how religion has always had a particularly close relationship with death, and not just because it has provided protective explanation. Religion has served to bring us close to the more mysterious aspects of experience. We've always experienced death and mystery as closely linked.

The second recognition concerns the particular way this relationship has evolved. Even if we get that religion's protective function with regard to death extends into modern times, we tend to assume that contemporary beliefs are more enlightened in the sense of reflecting greater understanding of death. While there are ways that this is the case, there are also important ways in which the truth is almost the opposite. Creative Systems Theory describes how each stage in culture's evolution has involved greater separation between the darker, more mysterious dimensions of ourselves and the more conscious aspects of experience. Arguably we are more distanced from death as experience today than at any time in our history.

These two recognitions by themselves don't do much to support a positive future for religion. If religion's old protective function no longer serves us in the same way and religion today offers only the most limited engagement with death as experience, it would seem appropriate to conclude that religion in the future won't have a great deal to offer—at least when it comes to death.

But there is a third essential recognition that points toward a different conclusion. Cultural Maturity's cognitive reordering challenges the Age of Reason's assumption that rationality is truth's last word. It helps us again appreciate how less rational aspects of intelligence—aspects of intelligence that Modern Age thought might have dismissed as simply subjective—have essential roles to play. This includes the sensibilities that in times past have linked us with experiences we call spiritual or religious.

Cultural Maturity's cognitive changes don't in any way make these aspects of intelligence now the last word. Culturally mature perspective doesn't side with mystery over the manifest as religion traditionally has. But its more encompassing picture does make at least the cognitive roots of religion more relevant. If religion could also help us meet death from the needed new, more mature place, this achievement could go a long way toward revitalizing—might we say resurrecting—religion's contribution.

In asking how a new, more mature relationship with death might alter religion, it is only fair that we ask the same question of science. A person might imagine that in challenging religion's protective role I am instead siding with science's conclusion—that death is just death, the end of us. But death's challenge to science is ultimately just as basic. At the very least we have to acknowledge that science's conclusion is ultimately just as much an "article of faith." Scientists share with theologians the fact that neither can describe death from personal experience.

And the same cognitive reordering that invites us to reflect anew on the future of religion takes death's challenge to science an important step further. Culturally mature perspective makes clear that while modern science's view of the world has contributed powerfully, the kind of "objectivity" that science relies on remains partial. The aspects of experience that the traditional scientific worldview leaves out would be expected to make scientific interpretation especially unhelpful when it comes to making sense of death. In the end, the death question confronts science (at least science of the narrow scientism sort) as fundamentally as it does religion, and the implications could be just as profound.

CST's more detailed formulations support death's challenge to the traditional thinking of both religion and science in a further, more conceptual way. The theory describes how any time we find beliefs that we commonly frame as polar opposites—such as the positions of Left and Right in the political sphere, or here, with the conclusions of religion and science—something important is likely missing in each belief. And it is not just that each half of the polarity captures only part of a larger, more systemic picture—though there is that. We also discover that all along neither side has been asking quite the right question. We appropriately expect this to be the case with religion, science, and the question of death.[9]

Further Implications

There are other spheres where the needed greater maturity in our relationship to death is pertinent. With some the connection is obvious and changes are already underway. For example, I don't think we would see today's questioning of capital punishment—and willingness to entertain more nuanced decisions about where it might be appropriate—without these changes. There are also domains where these changes are pertinent but where death's role is not so obviously significant. I think most immediately of the media, both serious media—such as news media—and media of a more entertainment sort. Many of the most important media-related changes may be a long way off. But given time, they could be of particular consequence.

Our ambivalent feelings toward death—at once attraction and repulsion—are key to much of modern media's success. News of an "if it bleeds, it leads" sort commonly garners the greater portion of airtime. It is rare to find television intended for adults that doesn't involve at least one shooting (often it involves many more). And killing—and the possibility of being killed—is pretty much what "action" movies and most popular video games are about. Modern media draw us in by creating a narrative tension between life and death.

---

9 See "Science and Religion: Toward a Larger Picture (and How Creative Systems Theory Gets Us Very Close)" in Chapter Twelve for additional science- and religion-related reflections.

But if what I have described for other spheres is accurate, this narrative tension is born of an increasingly outmoded and unhelpful relationship with death. It is based on a polarized and mythologized picture that makes death, if not evil, certainly our adversary. I find it fascinating to reflect on how the kind of "growing up" in how we view death that the concept of Cultural Maturity describes might, in the long term, alter media—of all sorts. Because media have the potential to provide major leadership with regard to broader cultural changes, we should demand it.

The place where a new, more mature relationship with death may have its most significant effect is even less immediately obvious. The need for a new maturity in our human relationship with death pertains directly to today's ultimate cultural challenge. I've proposed that the core crisis of our time is a Crisis of Purpose. As understandings of significance tied to culture's past parental role fail us (whether it be the American Dream or our favorite religious or political ideology), we are being called on to address what matters in more conscious and encompassing ways. Coming face to face with mortality in our individual lives teaches us about what most matters to us as individuals—death is a personal life's most pointed teacher of meaning, and ultimately of wisdom. As we learn to engage death collectively with a new maturity, it is reasonable to think that this engagement should help us in a similar way to more deeply confront what most ultimately matters to us more broadly—as humans.

An Essential Paradox

Why is looking directly at death so difficult that historically it has been essentially impossible? Certainly, death confronts us with the fact that life as we know it ends—not a comfortable recognition. But as I noted in introducing these reflections, death also confronts us with what is an even more final and disturbing limit. It confronts us in an ultimate way with limits to what is possible to control, and also, in the end, to understand. Before now, facing this most absolute kind of limit would not have been compatible with sanity.

To fully grasp why we would want to do so even with Cultural Maturity's changes, we need to appreciate an essential paradox. We encounter it any time we address limits more systemically—as with personal maturity in our individual development and in a more encompassing sense with Cultural Maturity. Lacking mature perspective, we experience real limits as problems, at best as adversaries to be defeated, at worst as evil. With Cultural Maturity's cognitive changes, we better see how inviolable limits are nothing exceptional. They are just part of how reality works—an essential aspect of what is.

This recognition could not be more important. As far as finding reason to engage the needed new relationship with death, at the least it helps us see how acknowledging limits lets us perceive more clearly. And there is more. Perceiving more clearly in this sense helps us better take in life's complexities and nuances. Because of this, acknowledging real limits, rather than limiting us, ultimately does the opposite. It frees us to better see options, to recognize what in fact is possible.

Nothing is more inescapable and obvious than the fact that we die. And at the same time, directly confronting this simple fact—both within specific domains and more broadly—should prove to be one of our most important teachers going forward. The humility required to do so deeply should play an essential role in generating the complexity of perspective—and wisdom—that effective future decision-making in all parts of our personal and collective lives will increasingly require.

Some Additional Stepping Back: Where Cultural Maturity Takes Us, Summarizing the Evidence, and Additional Implications

As important as understanding what Cultural Maturity's changes accomplish is appreciating what they don't. They don't provide new absolutes or new images of final realization to replace those that are being lost. And they don't offer immediate solutions to today's problems—much in Cultural Maturity's new picture may be a long time in coming. But limitations noted, what Cultural Maturity's cognitive changes do accomplish could not be more significant. A quick overview is appropriate in concluding this chapter's reflections.

Most fundamentally, Integrative Meta-perspective makes it possible to more fully engage and apply the systemic whole of ourselves in all that we do. In the process, it invites new options, provides greater ultimate freedom of choice. It also makes all manner of challenges newly understandable and newly addressable. And it makes available all the new skills and capacities that this chapter has described. Of particular importance for this book's reflections, it helps us get beyond the protective ideological simplifications of times past and understand our worlds in ways that are more encompassing and complete.

Another overarching topic pertinent in concluding is the question of evidence. It is important if we are to draw on the concept of Cultural Maturity that we have confidence in the correctness of its conclusions. Most people will not find the notion immediately obvious, and we've seen how making real sense of it requires us to think in unfamiliar ways. Reflections to this point in the book have provided multiple layers of evidence. No one kind of evidence by itself is wholly conclusive, but together they comprise an argument that I find hard to refute.

Observations I've made with this chapter offer a basic kind of evidence. Much of what I have described—such as the possibility of rethinking love and leadership—is itself a direct product of Cultural Maturity's changes. And while other new challenges—such as the need to limit spiraling health care costs—have different origins, the fact that related new skills and capacities are needed to address them at least provides support for the importance of what Cultural Maturity's changes accomplish.

We find further evidence in the developmental parallels that I outlined in Chapter Three. Argument by analogy is legitimately suspect, particularly when the argument is this far-reaching. But most people will concur that the parallels are at least intriguing, and most find the simple reference to a needed "growing up" in our time consistent with their experience. The fact that we can understand Cultural Maturity in terms of cognitive changes predicted by these parallels makes the developmental argument more concrete and robust.

Other observations from previous chapters that draw specifically on Creative Systems Theory further add to the evidence. Right off, there is the theory itself. The fact that Cultural Maturity's vantage supports the crafting of detailed frameworks able to provide the needed new, more dynamic and systemic—post-postmodern, if you will—kind of understanding represents important evidence. More specifically, the way culturally mature perspective reconciles the Dilemma of Differentiation makes the concept persuasive philosophically. And the Dilemma of Trajectory provides particularly solid evidence for the importance of Cultural Maturity's changes. In observing that neither going forward as we have nor going back can ultimately work, it makes Cultural Maturity—or at least something that could provide a similarly integrative result—the only real option.

Some of the more immediate accomplishments that come with Cultural Maturity's changes can also be thought of as evidence. I think in particular of how Cultural Maturity offers an answer to today's Crisis of Purpose. I've described how contemporary realities frequently leave people feeling at best confused, at worst cynical and hopeless. And I've observed how Cultural Maturity's changes, in offering a new guiding story, provide an antidote. Importantly, while the resulting new kind of story is ultimately hopeful, this is not hope in some idealized or utopian sense, but rather a down-to-earth kind of hope rooted in what it means to be human. The concept of Cultural Maturity doesn't provide final answers, but it does provide reliable direction for making our way in the uncertainties and complexities ahead.

There are also all the more specific challenges that Integrative Meta-perspective allows us to better understand and that culturally mature capacities help us address. Those I've engaged with this chapter are only a beginning. With the wide-ranging array of concerns we will take on in chapters to come, it should become increasingly clear that Cultural Maturity's changes are essential to future understanding pretty much wherever we look. Given the critical importance of so many of the challenges we will touch on, Cultural Maturity becomes, arguably, the only way forward.

There are also further overarching topics that are important to at least touch on in concluding that are pertinent specifically to the question of hope. While Cultural Maturity's changes make significant demands, they also hold surprises that make success in engaging those demands more in the cards than we might imagine.

One is how, at least as potential, Cultural Maturity's changes are built into our natures as developmental beings. We don't have to invent them from whole cloth. There is also how Cultural Maturity works as a single solution to a wide multiplicity of concerns. Aspects of how this result benefits us can at first seem paradoxical. I've described how Cultural Maturity's changes at once offer that we might more effectively address our time's great complexity and provide ways of thinking that are ultimately simpler and more straightforward than what we have known. But when we grasp deeply what Integrative Meta-perspective entails, we appreciate how it makes successfully addressing a diverse array of challenges more within our reach. And there is an additional recognition that at least supports finding the courage needed to engage Cultural Maturity's considerable demands. We've seen how the rewards for doing so could very well be not just exciting, but profound.

These various observations don't guarantee a hopeful future. Even if the concept of Cultural Maturity is correct, we can't know for sure whether we can pull off all that Cultural Maturity's changes ask of us. But together they make a strong argument for the conclusion that ultimately we may very well be up to the task.

I will note one additional, particularly provocative implication of Cultural Maturity's cognitive changes in wrapping up. It concerns the concept's long-term significance. I've put primary emphasis in these pages on the concept of Cultural Maturity's importance for today, on what it tells us about the challenges we now face and the capacities required to meet them effectively. But the Patterning in Time picture we have looked at supports the conclusion that we can also think of Cultural Maturity's changes as having more extended significance. If what I have outlined is correct, Cultural Maturity's threshold marks not just the beginning of a next chapter in the human story, but the turning of first pages in a new, second kind of story that in the end should define our ultimate human task. It may be that culturally mature understanding represents not just the only game in town for today, but in its full manifestation, what must ultimately guide right action for the whole of humanity's future.

Cultural Maturity Summary Exercise:

What would be on your list of the most important questions and challenges ahead for the species? Which of them could be at least adequately addressed with ways of thinking currently available to us? Which of them will be require new capabilities like those I've described becoming newly possible with Cultural Maturity's changes.

How would you estimate your ability to manifest the various needed new skills and capacities that I've described: taking ultimate responsibility, better tolerating uncertainty and complexity, better appreciating the fact of real limits, getting beyond the us-versus-them assumptions of times past, realizing Whole-Person/Whole-System relationship, learning to think about what matters in more inclusive and complete ways, better understanding how events always happen in a context, and becoming more capable of foresight? And how does where you are in relation to each of these abilities affect the various aspects of your life—your felt sense of identity, your work, the important relationships in your life, and your sense of connection with things larger than yourself?

CHAPTER FIVE

Whole-Person/Whole-System Patterning Concepts: Truth, Identity, and the Future of Human Purpose

I've described how Creative Systems Theory applies two kinds of patterning notions. Patterning in Time is an example of the first, Concepts of Creative Differentiation. We now turn to the second kind of patterning notion, Whole-Person/Whole-System Patterning Concepts.

Whole-Person/Whole-System distinctions address what truth at its most basic—truth as a single encompassing observation—becomes when understood from the entirety of our whole-box-of-crayons systemic complexity. They are where we find needed first guidance when we step beyond the simplified answers provided in times past by culture's parental dictates, or at any time by ideological assumptions.

It is not so obvious that Whole-Person/Whole-System Patterning Concepts represent anything new. But ultimately they are just as radical in their newness as their more explicitly differentiated complements. Indeed, because they necessarily come into play with every kind of decision we make in a culturally mature reality, they are arguably of greater ultimate significance.

Previous big-picture reflections have pointed toward the need for Whole-Person/Whole-System discernments. In listing needed new skills and capacities, for example, I described how culturally mature decision-making implies a double responsibility—we become responsible not just for our actions but also for determining the truths on which we base our actions. Whole-Person/Whole-System discernments are where culturally mature perspective's responsibility-twice-over task necessarily begins. In the end, they are also what we come back to when we wish to confirm the substance of our decisions.

I've also implied Whole-Person/Whole-System Patterning discernments when addressing specific issues. They are where we go to find solutions when moral choices confront us with competing goods. They are also what we necessarily turn to when mythologized answers with love or leadership fail us. And of particular importance, they are where we ultimately look when seeking more complete measures for human advancement.

As with Concepts of Creative Differentiation, Whole-Person/Whole-System Patterning Concepts draw on Integrative Meta-perspective's encompassing vantage. That means that even the most basic such truths apply the whole of intelligence and "bridge" polar assumptions. It also means that any Whole-Person/Whole-System Patterning discernment is by its nature systemic—and in today's needed more dynamic, life-acknowledging and human life–acknowledging sense.

CST identifies two primary kinds of Whole-Person/Whole-System Patterning Concepts. I introduced the first in Chapter One in describing how any important concern necessarily starts by addressing what CST calls the pertinent Question of Referent. Our answers to culturally mature Questions of Referent bring new, more overarching attention to what most matters—in any moment and also more generally. They address whether a choice we are contemplating is ultimately aligned with meaning—put another way, whether a direction we are contemplating is ultimately creative (in our encompassing definition of the word "creative").[1]

CST uses the word "referent" rather than a term like "truth" to emphasize all that we need to draw on—refer to—in making such bottom-line distinctions. Whole-Person/Whole-System discernments require that we access the whole of ourselves, all that we are capable of "referring to," all the diverse "feedbacks"—emotional feedback,

---

1 We could think of any truth as a response to a pertinent Question of Referent. But I tend to reserve the use of the phrase for culturally mature understanding. Culturally mature truths answer questions of a specifically integrative, systemic sort. I've described how, when I encounter polarized beliefs, I assume that there is a larger question that neither side has addressed or even recognized. The term "Question of Referent," when applied to culturally mature understanding, refers to this more encompassing kind of question, whether it relates to broad cultural issues or concerns of the most personal sort.

CREATIVE SYSTEMS THEORY

intellectual feedback, spiritual feedback, bodily feedback, interpersonal feedback, cultural feedback—that we humans rely on to make our way in the world. And they require that we do so in ways that are more conscious and complete than has been an option in times past.

I often use the more informal term Aliveness as a shorthand to get at what this kind of distinction measures. With any issue, from the most personal to the most far-reaching, our bottom-line concern must be what makes experience most ultimately alive. The term Aliveness can be vulnerable to misinterpretation,[2] but we will see how it describes what our first kind of Whole-Person/Whole-System Patterning Concept is about in a concise, and ultimately quite precise, way.

CST calls the second kind of Whole-Person/Whole-System Patterning Concept Capacitance. Capacitance measures generic capacity—the amount of creation/life a system can handle before being overwhelmed. Capacitance describes possibility. It also describes one of the most important kinds of limits we need to be attentive to if we are to make intelligent decisions and live healthy and effective lives. With any choice, we want to know not just where the most vital options lie, but also whether we are up to what various options might ask of us.

We will start here by looking closely at just how Whole-Person/Whole-System Patterning Concepts are different from truth notions from times past. We will also examine just why it is that such concepts are now needed. We will then take some extended time with each of the two kinds of Whole-Person/Whole-System Patterning Concepts that I've noted. Throughout, I will give attention to how a creative frame helps us understand what Whole-Person/Whole-System Patterning Concepts involve and provides guidance in making the kinds of discriminations they ask of us.

Later, I will turn to a small handful of CST notions that we can think of as lying partway between more formal Whole-Person/Whole-System Patterning Concepts and Concepts of Creative Differentiation. These further notions more explicitly separate this from that than concepts like

---

2 If we are attracted to ideology, we are likely to find ideological belief seeming most compelling—most "alive." We need to be responding to a systemic Question of Referent for the shorthand term to be directly useful.

Aliveness and Capacitance, but they do so in a more general way than we see with Patterning in Time and Pattering in Space distinctions.

We will look first at how CST expands how we think about psychological symptoms. The theory proposes that what we commonly describe with symptom language reflects ways that systems react when overwhelmed—when they lack the Capacitance that responding more directly requires. We will also examine how Integrative Meta-perspective offers that we might think about violence in ways that are more encompassing and systemically conceived. We can understand violent acts most broadly as acts that do damage to Capacitance. In each instance, Integrative Meta-perspective, particularly when combined with a creative frame, helps us both more deeply grasp underlying mechanisms and better appreciate the different—and often not obvious—ways that these phenomena can manifest.

I will conclude by touching on some distinctions that get a bit closer to where more fully differentiated Concepts of Creative Differentiation take us but that are still of a more general sort. We will look at how culturally mature truth's various contextual relativities reflect the "rhythm, boundary, and container" choices that determine a creative life.

What Exactly Is New

It is important in getting started to have a solid grasp of how Whole-Person/Whole-System Patterning Concepts are different from ways of thinking with which we are more familiar. In that they are products of Cultural Maturity's cognitive reordering, we would expect them to be new in all the ways we have looked at previously. But while such newness can be what most stands out with Concepts of Creative Differentiation, with Whole-Person/Whole-System Patterning Concepts, it can be missed. Certainly Whole-Person/Whole-System Patterning notions are more easily confused with things they are not at all about.

The conceptual quandary I've called the Dilemma of Differentiation helps clarify the added challenge to understanding. The Dilemma of Differentiation notes that whenever we take a perfectly good way of thinking about interconnectedness and try to make distinctions—divide the whole into parts—we end up back in a machine world. With Concepts of Creative Differentiation like the Patterning in Time notions that we've examined, it is obvious that we are dividing into parts.

And the fact that we are doing so in a newly dynamic and integrative way becomes clear if we look at all closely. Whole-Person/Whole-System Patterning Concepts similarly involve both appreciating interconnectedness and making distinctions, but because their focus is on truth at its most basic, we can fail to recognize the equal significance of the difference aspect of the contribution. If we do, we become vulnerable to confusing what Whole-Person/Whole-System Patterning Concepts accomplish with postmodern, anything-goes conclusions or with views that identify with the opposite of difference, whether more humanistic/emotional or more spiritual. In the name of new thought, we end up falling for Compromise Fallacies or Unity Fallacies.

In fact, the distinctions made by Whole-Person/Whole-System Patterning Concepts are as fundamentally different from what we have known in times past as CST's more obviously differentiated kin. Stepping back for some historical and philosophical perspective on understanding as a whole helps further clarify the fundamental newness. An essential recognition provides the basic insight. Besides altering the particular truths we might draw on, Cultural Maturity's cognitive reordering also alters the basic categories we use to define truth. Truth comes to reside in two wholly new conceptual groupings.

There is a sense in which each grouping reflects a kind of distinction that we humans have always made. To keep historical reflections simple, we can refer to these perennial truth categories as the "crux" and "multiplicity" aspects of truth. The important recognition here is that with Cultural Maturity's changes, we come to engage each kind of discernment in a manner that is fundamentally different from what we have seen in times past. Whole-Person/Whole-System Patterning Concepts and Concepts of Creative Differentiation reflect these two new kinds of truth categories.

Since the beginnings of human understanding, we have placed our truths in two worlds. People have spoken of this two-part picture in a variety of ways—truth's essence as opposed to truth's particulars, inner truth as opposed to worldly truth, spiritual truths as opposed to material truth. I've made reference to it in another way in describing how polarities have an underlying symmetry. Plato, in contrasting eternal "forms" with their projected shadows on the cave's wall, gave ultimate credence to the more inner dimensions of truth. Descartes, in contrasting objective and subjective worlds, made an almost opposite claim. The important point is that whenever and wherever we look, up to this point in culture's story we encounter a related two-part basic division of truth.[3]

But I strongly emphasize that phrase, "up to this point." Culturally mature crux and multiplicity discernments represent wholly new kinds of concepts, new not just in the sense of next chapters in a continuing story, but new fundamentally. Two things change in what before has been a consistent picture. First, each kind of truth loses its parental trappings. In a new sense, each must be engaged unadorned. Second, because each now reflects Integrative Meta-perspective's more encompassing picture, each becomes expressly systemic, and systemic in today's needed new, more dynamic and complete sense.

Certainly this is the case with culturally mature crux distinctions, our interest with this chapter. Integrative Meta-perspective fundamentally reframes the crux truth task. Philosophers, theologians, and poets have always sought to get at truth's crux in the earlier definition I've referred to—in the sense of some "essence" or "core" of truth. But culturally mature crux distinctions are not just about essences. And certainly they are not about timeless essences (which in the past has been the implication). They are what we get when we succeed at taking everything that needs to be considered into account—supposed core, supposed periphery, and everything else.

Drawing on the box-of-crayons metaphor, "crux" in the old sense referred to a single crayon of a more Inner—aesthetic or spiritual—sort. Culturally mature crux distinctions consider all that we encounter in the concrete world of particulars to be equally essential. Culturally mature crux distinctions challenge us to hold and appreciate the whole box. Once we step over Cultural Maturity's threshold, effective decision-making necessarily starts with taking into account everything that might make our choices vital and meaningful—in ourselves and in the

---

3 With Chapter Three's reflections on philosophical understanding, we saw how we have given one half or the other of this basic juxtaposition greater emphasis at various times and places in culture's story. When the archetypally feminine has had strongest influence, truth as "essence" has similarly prevailed. When the archetypally masculine has had strongest influence, truth's particulars have gotten the greater attention.

world around us. Whole-Person/Whole-System Patterning Concepts are Creative Systems Theory's language for making needed culturally mature "crux" discernments.

Why We Need Whole-Person/Whole-System Patterning Concepts

Such notions are now becoming essential at all systemic scales, from the most personal to the global. Observations made in previous chapters help clarify how this is the case. At a personal scale, I've described how moral decision-making in a culturally mature world requires taking into account all the competing goods that go into an act's significance. I've also described how, in doing so, we engage more directly what makes a choice affirming of life. I've also introduced the Myth of the Individual and how it challenges us to think about identity more systemically (a topic we will return to for a closer look later in this chapter). Notice that a key result is that as individuals we necessarily also think about truth more systemically, leave behind the systemically partial—mythologized and ideological—truths of times past and address what matters in at once more direct and encompassing ways.

We've seen too how this kind of discernment has become essential for success in relationships. When we move beyond love based on projection, making good choices requires getting more directly at how love adds to who we are. I've described how successful love in the future will demand a deeper and more direct appreciation for all the various needs that love fulfills. The challenge is similar with simple friendships. More than we tend to recognize, friendship too has before been based on projection and on us-versus-them allegiances. Whole-Person friendship requires a more direct appreciation for how a particular relationship is life-enhancing.

The importance of more encompassing measures applies similarly to whole domains of understanding. With any new cultural chapter, primary realms of activity acquire new defining truths. But today, with the diminishing of culture's past parental influence and the need for more multifaceted understanding, it is essential that we engage what matters in ways that are more direct and more systemically complete.

Previously I've given greatest attention to how this more complex (and in the end also simpler, more stripped-down) task pertains to the field of medicine. I've described how modern medicine's heroic bottom-line measure has become not just unsustainable, but by itself limited and limiting. Measures that can work for the future must be of a more encompassing sort, able somehow to acknowledge quality of life along with the fact of life; psychological, social, and spiritual aspects of health and healing in addition to the purely physical; and not just individual health but also larger societal well-being. Health care's new yardstick must address health itself—in the fullest, most complete sense.[4]

The sphere of education provides a good place to expand in this kind of observation. Education's future depends not just on us rethinking educational policy, but also on reexamining what education is ultimately about. We tend to take education's purpose for granted—assume it to be obvious and unchanging. In a sense, it is unchanging—as T.H. White put it in *The Once and Future King*, the purpose of education has been to "learn why the world wags and what wags it." But education's purpose has taken expression in very different ways at various times in culture's story. In the future, education must manifest that purpose in ways that are both more conscious and more encompassing than at any time previous.

Modern "classroom" education had its origins in providing the universal literacy necessary for democratic governance and the Industrial Revolution. Toward this end, it has served us well. But education able to support and teach culturally mature capacities requires a more complete definition and new, more embracing measures. The essential tasks ahead for our species will necessarily involve learnings that are not just different from what we have known, but also often learnings incompatible with education's purpose as we have most recently thought of it.

Moral decision-making's new demands help illustrate. With modern public education, we've taken great care to keep moral concerns out of the classroom—carefully preserving the separation of church and state. But we can't escape the fact that any kind of healthy future will require the confronting of increasingly complex ethical questions. The fact that essential concerns of every sort today have moral/ethical implications dramatically compounds the challenge. For future education to serve us, it must make learning to engage complex moral/ethical questions "core curriculum."

---

4 Chapter Eleven reflects further on this critical topic.

This essential recognition expands education's task dramatically. Learning becomes necessarily more interdisciplinary and more acknowledging of understanding's complexity. And along with teaching more traditional curriculum, education must somehow serve to increase students' ability to realize each of the new skills and capacities needed for culturally mature understanding and action. That means both a more complete picture of learning and more complete bottom-line measures for educational success.[5]

Such rethinking of truth at its more basic in the end applies to every sphere of understanding and action. In the previous chapter, I gave particular emphasis to how it applies to the broadest of collective concerns. As old ways of thinking about wealth and progress cease to serve us, we rightly ask just what is to replace them. The concept of Cultural Maturity is an attempt to answer this most encompassing of crux-truth questions. I've described how we can think of needed new measures for advancement as simply what we get when we better take into account all that ultimately matters to us. Any act or idea consistent with Cultural Maturity's changes becomes "true" in this now most essential sense.

Whatever the concern, whether intimately personal or broadly collective, our times require increasingly that we engage it with the whole-box-of-crayons sorts of discernments that Whole-Person/Whole-System Patterning Concepts represent. Increasingly, we really have no choice but to make such measures our point of reference. Any "pattern language" framework that is at all complete must have concepts that address questions at this most basic level of significance.

Aliveness and the Question of Referent

The two primary kinds of Whole-Person/Whole-System Patterning Concepts that I have noted can never be wholly separated. Follow one concept far enough and inevitably we find the other. Later we will look more specifically at their relationship. But at least for the task of practical application—and also ultimately more conceptually—it helps to think about them one at a time.

Let's start with what I've referred to with that phrase "Question of Referent." I've previously noted its relationship to today's Crisis of Purpose.

---

5 Chapter Eleven reflects further on the future of education.

I've described how the answer to today's Crisis of Purpose at a personal level lies in asking each day what most matters to us and making our life choices accordingly. And I've emphasized how as citizens and members of the human species our future well-being depends ultimately on asking that most basic of truth questions more collectively. Doing so requires a fundamental leap in how we understand and hold experience. In times past we have thought of truths that get at where significance most lies in terms of culturally prescribed goals or objectives, either the prescriptions of culturally explicit belief or, more recently, the implied prescriptions of mass culture. In a culturally mature reality, goals and objectives still matter, but guidance that works is necessarily more ours to determine, and necessarily of a more systemic sort.

Addressing truth in such a bare-boned and at once encompassing manner would before now have seemed, if not nonsensical, certainly dangerous. But as we move beyond strict cultural dictates, it becomes suddenly not just relevant but essential. Such discrimination would also have seemed impossible to achieve—an all-too-slippery enterprise at best. From a culturally mature perspective, it becomes truth at its most immediate and straightforward. When we bring the whole of ourselves to engaging the pertinent Questions of Referent, our answer gives us our North Star, our directing arrow, our compass point for making decisions.

I've described how I often use the term Aliveness as a shorthand language for the kind of answer that Questions of Referent require. Joseph Campbell once observed: "People say what they are seeking is the meaning of life. I don't think that is what we are really seeking. I think what we are seeking is an experience of being alive." The concept of Aliveness refers to what at any moment a system finds most significant and purposeful—and thus most enlivening.

Aliveness might seem like a terribly informal term for something this fundamental, but in fact, if understood systemically, the word captures the kind of truth we have interest in remarkably well. I find it helpful to get there in a series of steps. The first step observes that once we traverse Cultural Maturity's threshold, the measures we use for determining where significance lies become at once most spare and most inclusive. Our bottom line becomes not the isolated rightness or wrongness of particular thoughts or behaviors, but the degree to which a thought or action in the end provides benefit.

That's a good basic answer, but the idea that meaningful acts serve well-being is too general to provide ultimately useful guidance. To be a bit more precise, we can make our answer quantitative: An act derives significance when it makes things (pertinent systems) "more"—a more encompassing, and by implication generative—way of describing meaning.

But a further essential question remains if this more specific response is to help us—"more what?" The word "more" needs something to refer to. From Integrative Meta-perspective's overarching vantage, conclusions become true in any functional sense (the only sense that ultimately matters) to the degree which they enhance life—or, more specifically, to the degree which they enhance the particular kind of life we are by virtue of being human.

This answer might still seem vague, but in fact it could not be more precise. And it is precise in just the dynamic and systemic sense that needed new thought requires. The Dilemma of Differentiation helps clarify how this is so. The concept of Aliveness gets around the trap of falling back into mechanistic thinking by making the basis for distinction a measure that is already integrative—life itself. In purely biological systems, truth—in the sense of what works—concerns the degree to which an act is enhancing of life. Aliveness measures the degree to which a particular thought, feeling, or action enhances who we are as conscious life. Another CST "dilemma" further clarifies the confusion. What might appear to be vagueness is instead the Dilemma of Representation playing its now predictable role in depiction that reflects the needed completeness.

While the fact that Aliveness is a deep systemic concept means that it is necessarily beyond definition as we commonly think of it, we can in fact define Aliveness quite directly using CST's language of creative/formative process. Aliveness measures what at a specific time and place is most creative (most systemically generative). It asks about both the questions that might best occupy a system's creative attention and the responses to those questions most likely to increase that system's vitality and potential. An act or idea is true in the sense of Aliveness to the degree to which it serves to support or increase systemic (creative) health and vitality. Aliveness is what we experience at the growing— "creative"—edge of understanding and action.

I noted earlier that the shorthand term "Aliveness" can be vulnerable to misinterpretation. This can be the case even if we aren't confusing it with attraction we might feel toward a particular kind of ideological conclusion. The most frequent confusion is similar to what I've described for the word "creative." Common associations to the word Aliveness—associations with excitement or enthusiasm—are not sufficiently inclusive. At a particular moment, the courage to grieve, doubt, or struggle might be as enhancing of life as joyfulness. No thought, act, or feeling exists that might not, given appropriate circumstances, represent the most Alive—most creative in a systemic sense—response. The term can also be misconstrued by making it some opposite to rationality. As is always the case when attempting to make culturally mature choices, determining what thoughts or actions are most life-enhancing necessarily draws on all aspects of intelligence. There are many situations where the "cold and logical" is the best, most Alive, route to an effective decision.

Possible confusions acknowledged, the term Aliveness has ready references. Its meaning is perhaps closest to what we point toward when we say a piece of writing "comes alive." The concept also captures not just truth as experienced in the moment, but truth in its contextual complexity. We experience truth as life-enhancing when it is "right and timely." Attention to Aliveness involves both the discernment of where creative edges lie and the feedback that tells us we have successfully engaged those edges. Aliveness is about interactions, ideas, and ways of being whose time has come.

In an important sense, what I'm referring to with the term Aliveness is the kind of feedback we've always used to make our way. Isaac Newton's laws of motion were a right and timely response to right and timely cultural questions, as were the words of Moses, Jesus, or Mohammed with the rise of monotheism; the words of Churchill in England's "darkest hour;" or the art of Kandinsky, Picasso, Klee, or Pollack to the existential contradictions of a postmodern world. But today's challenges require us to be newly conscious of this fact. And when questions specifically demand culturally mature answers, they require that we be newly complete, more fully systemic, in what we measure.

Importantly, Aliveness can manifest in diverse forms—we again confront the essential role of context. The precise "more" depends on what is being creatively called for. With regard to personal choices, for example, it could translate to more assertive, more sensitive, more irreverent, more intelligent, more sexy, more playful, more skilled—whatever. But we could also say more Alive, or more systemically creative—or simply more true. This recognition applies to every part of our personal and collective lives.

The concept of Aliveness again brings together the complexity and simplicity aspects of culturally mature truth. What exactly makes love love? The answer is in one sense complicated and certainly different for different kinds of love. But we can also answer the question very simply—we experience love, or certainly relationship, when somehow "one plus one equals more than two." On a more collective level, when we ask what determines health beyond the mere absence of disease, or what, in a culturally mature world, makes education successful, it is truth in this at once most direct and complete sense that becomes ultimately our measure. And this is the question we necessarily start with at a species level if we wish to effectively redefine wealth and progress.

Aliveness and Reengagement

Fully grasping the implications of this first Whole-Person/Whole-System patterning notion requires touching briefly on an easily unexpected characteristic. It turns out that addressing any question in terms of Aliveness in our time requires too that, at least a bit, we engage it in relation to how its implications have been addressed through history. This need not be conscious, but if we look closely, we see this result reflected in any effectively conceived Question of Referent discernment.

This result follows from the dynamic that I have called Reengagement. As the dissolving of amnesias that comes with culturally mature perspective helps us draw on intelligence's full complexity, we also become newly able to step back and appreciate the larger story that underlies any specific kind of truth. Today's needed new truths incorporate that larger story in a way that truths of times past could not. In an important new sense, culturally mature truth at its most basic addresses what "mattering" in relation to any particular kind of question has always been about.

Comparing Cultural Maturity with maturity in an individual lifetime again sheds useful light. Maturity in individual development in a more limited way similarly involves engaging truth at its most basic in both a here-and-now systemic sense and in this more encompassing temporal meaning. The more nuanced kind of understanding we refer to when we use a word like "wisdom" involves better getting our minds around not just significance in the moment, but also significance as it pertains to the whole of our lives. The more encompassing kind of truth that results asks more of us. But it also lets us engage our personal lives with a new and greater fullness and elegance, and with a more embracing and reliable kind of potency.

Concerns that I've touched on previously highlight how this more wholly embracing picture—embracing not just in the immediate moment but also temporally—applies to culturally mature decision-making. While getting more directly at what makes a choice moral today very much means what is moral specifically in our time, at least a bit, too, determining what is moral now also means better appreciating what at any time has made a choice moral. I've described the important sense in which moral decision-making has always been about determining what acts are most life-enhancing. In a related way, the more direct recognition of the needs that love fulfills refers to more than just how we think about love in our time. At least to some degree, it also means better appreciating the needs that love has fulfilled all along, throughout our human history.

More domain-focused changes that I've described further highlight how this more temporal kind of systemic engagement comes into play. With Chapter Three's look at the history of the body, I described how understanding what it means to be embodied, and in particular what it means to be embodied in a healthy way, benefits from a more encompassing picture over time. With this chapter's reflections on education we saw something similar. I described how the complex challenges before us require that we draw on more embracing measures for educational success. Most immediately, "more embracing" refers to the demands of education in our time. But at least a bit, too, it refers to a more temporal kind of completeness. Giving the moral dimension of learning a central place in education, for example, lay at the heart of medieval monastic education. I cannot emphasize too strongly that what I'm suggesting with this observation is fundamentally different from going back to the education methods of an earlier time. But we very much need to learn how to ask our questions and make our deliberations from a vantage that better appreciates all that goes into making us human.

The importance of engaging the Whole-Person/Whole-System truth task in a way that incorporates both more here-and-now and more temporal aspects of our complexity applies also to the future more generally. Rethinking wealth and progress in a way that works for our time is not just about better addressing what most matters right here and right now, but also, too, about stepping back and more fully appreciating what most ultimately matters as a function of being human.

Notice that this more multidimensional picture of Aliveness presents us with a particularly striking and inclusive version of a now familiar kind of paradox. Because discerning where Aliveness lies requires addressing truth in all its aspects—including its multiple forms over time—it is very much about affirming truth's multifaceted complexity. And at the same time, because it involves getting at what matters in the most direct, bare-boned fashion, at once it is about truth at its simplest. In fact, we must think about Aliveness in both of these ways and, in effect, simultaneously, if our discernments are to reflect the kind of systemic thinking required once we step over Cultural Maturity's threshold.

Aliveness and Pseudo-Significance

Our first kind of Whole-Person/Whole-System Patterning discernment would be challenging enough if it were just that it was new and demands more of us. But there is a further factor that today adds to the difficulty of what it asks of us. With growing frequency we encounter imposters—influences that work to distance us from our ability to discern and act from our experience of Aliveness.

We find in our time all manner of pseudo-significance masquerading as meaning. Sometimes this takes the form simply of misrepresentation, as with fake news. Often it manifests in more sophisticated forms of "bait and switch," as with how advertising promises fulfillment if we only buy this or that product, with reality TV's supposed "emotionally significant" encounters, and "if it bleeds, it leads" journalism. More recently, we find even more extreme examples of pseudo-significance masquerading as meaning with video games and action movies, where what substitutes for meaning is often little more than artificial stimulation, and with the less helpful—and often intentionally addictive—manifestations of social media.

This added kind of challenge is important to recognize not just because it makes what is required more difficult. The selling of pseudo-significance represents Transitional Absurdity and has critical consequences. I see it being a major contributor to today's Crisis of Purpose. We can also recognize more specific effects. For example, I see it as a significant factor in today's addiction epidemic. The underlying mechanism with addiction—of any sort—is the substitution of pseudo-significance for real meaning. The pseudo-significance can be provided by specific entities—by drugs as with the opioid epidemic, by food as with the obesity epidemic, or by electronic stimulation with device addiction. I suspect our time's more general climate of pseudo-significance is increasing our vulnerability to addictions of all of these sorts.

The importance of Whole-Person/Whole-System discernments when I work with addiction in therapy both helps confirm this interpretation and further supports such discernments' importance. Therapeutic efforts that work always in the end come back to assisting the person in getting better in touch with what for them creates real meaning. Addiction can lose its hold only to the degree to which the feedback loops through which that person knows real Aliveness—real significance—can be reestablished. Succeed with this essential step and the rest of the work follows naturally. Most people become less and less patient with imposters (and with being exploited by those who would peddle addiction) and decide that their life needs to be about the real thing.

This kind of recognition is most obviously pertinent to distractions and addictions as they confront us as individuals. But its implications for our health as societies and as a species should now be obvious. Our future depends ultimately on our ability to distinguish pseudo-significance from what is in fact life-affirming and ally our choices with the real thing. It also depends on confronting the selling of pseudo-significance in all its manifestations, on demanding real leadership—actions that authentically make us more—from every part of society.

An Aliveness Exercise:

> Rate the current Aliveness of different aspects of your life on a scale of 1 to 100 (your job, your family and friendships, your leisure, your spirituality, your social/political involvement). What did you draw on to arrive at your numbers? Now turn to your profession—teacher, plumber, doctor, police officer, lawyer. Rate the current Aliveness of that profession as a whole (not just your experience in it), the degree to which people in it are asking the important—Alive—questions and effectively contributing. Do the same for your community, your country, and for civilization as a whole. For each example, what one single act do you think would most contribute to Aliveness becoming greater?

"Exploratory" Truth

I've given greatest attention thus far in the book to how a creative frame applies to truth at the level of content. This has been the case with Aliveness. I've described Aliveness in terms of what thought or action at a particular moment will be most creative. But a creative frame is pertinent equally to the more process-related aspects of culturally mature truth. I pointed toward this further recognition in the previous chapter in suggesting that the needed double responsibility was necessarily a creative kind of responsibility.

We aren't used to thinking of truth in process terms. We are more apt to think of truth as almost the opposite of a process—if not fixed and absolute, at least the end product of our inquiries. But culturally mature perspective makes it inescapable that what constitutes right choice is ultimately a moving target. As I've noted, it also makes clear that what is most important to know is often permeated by change and uncertainty in ways that the more cut-and-dried truths of times past were not. Cultural Maturity's most basic truth task has as much to do with how we make choices as just what we might choose—even if we choose wisely. This is not at all to simply reduce truth to process.[6] But

---

6 If we are to avoid traps in our thinking, we need to recognize that while most often we make the content side of experience what ultimately defines truth, we can fall off of the roadway of culturally mature understanding just

it is true that in a whole new sense, content and process cease being wholly separate concerns.

A good place to see the process side of this more dynamic picture is with how culturally mature decision-making is often more exploratory and experimental than what it replaces. I often use exploratory metaphors in my therapy practice—to help people confront questions of basic life direction and also to address specific life choices (with regard to profession, relationships, where to live, values to hold). Such metaphors help people shape their lives in ways that best honor their unique identity and contribution. In a sense, such concerns have always been exploratory. But in the past, cultural dictates—for both good and ill—have dramatically restricted options.

For people of more rational bent, I might talk about such inquiry as akin to the best of scientific experiments. Well-done experiments engage the experimenter in a sequence of creative responsibilities. The first is responsibility for asking a good question, one worthy of the experimenter's time and focus. Next comes responsibility for crafting experiments and developing hypotheses that might shed new light on that question. Finally comes responsibility for obtaining the most accurate and useful results.

Making good choices in a well-lived life tends to be messier than this. But when external guideposts are limited, we necessarily engage in a similar kind of progression. We start by selecting a worthy creative starting point (if the question concerns work, selecting an endeavor that excites and could prove fulfilling; if it concerns love, choosing someone for whom we feel caring and who could be good for us). And we experiment. We observe and we try things out. And we listen for what brings fulfillment. In the process, we learn about ourselves (and, with love, the other person). And we learn about the shapes that choices might take (how we might approach work, or how to engage love in ways that best reflect two people's unique natures and their growing connection).

When approaching life experimentally, we need to be exceedingly honest with regard to what works and what does not. Like good science,

---

as readily by making truth primarily about process. We often see this kind of trap with more humanistic psychological and organizational approaches.

a creatively lived life is only in a limited way about getting the answers we want. With both, the most irresponsible thing one can do is alter data so as to better fit our hopes. The task is to seek out what is creatively true. It is through this that we make choices that are right, and choices that matter.

Science metaphors are likely to get blank stares—or worse—from people of more emotional or intuitive bent. But the metaphor of the artist's creative process works equally well. I might talk about how a composer writes a piece of music or how a painter applies his or her craft. The artist's first responsibility is to discover a worthy creative impulse—a possibility to which one is deeply drawn. Next comes trying out different ways to give that impulse expression. Lastly, there is the task of discerning what works and what does not. Artistic expression is about listening for what is beautiful and exploring different ways to make that beauty manifest. As with good science, eloquent artistry requires incorruptible self-honesty—fudging the results gets us nowhere. And in a similar sense, we cannot know ahead of time exactly where that honesty will lead.

People can object to such use of experimental/exploratory metaphors. For example, some can find them initially too analytical. This is particularly common if the topic is something like love. My response is that consciously engaging love (or life more generally) as a process does in fact require careful discernment—though something ultimately more than analytical discernment. Culturally mature decision-making requires bringing nuanced perspective to all kinds of questions for which simple being, faith, or subjective passion have been the more appropriate kind of engagement in times past.

In an opposite sort of objection, a person might claim that experimental imagery is just too imprecise—too "loosey-goosey." Again, using love as an example, a person might argue that it leaves out the most important ingredient in relationship—commitment. But, in fact, approaching love as a creative process in the end implies greater attention to commitment. Certainly, commitment can be one of the most powerful tools we have for making relationship's creative life possible and sustainable. More, the absence of clear guidelines in a culturally mature reality gives the articulation of commitment and the determination of its forms ever greater importance. Even if the commitment choices we make are very traditional, they need a deeper level of personal commitment to sustain them. What the exploratory metaphor adds to traditional notions of commitment is a better appreciation for how the rules for success in love—and the meaning of commitment—change when we no longer have the luxury of established goals and procedures.[7]

Exploratory language can be applied just as usefully to decision-making of a more collective sort. I've noted that with both climate change and confronting a pandemic, we have to think not in terms of what we can know for sure, but in terms of how best to assess risk and make choices accordingly. And with pandemic in particular, the kind of risk we are trying to assess is necessarily a moving target.

We find another good example in the question of how we should best manage the often-contradictory potentials of modern invention. Because many of our most important advances, along with promising good, also present significant danger, responsible management will be critical. But responsibility in the sense of just doing the right thing can be only of limited help when much that is most important to know can't be known in advance. Evaluation may involve complexly interwoven, ever-changing causal factors—and there is always the possibility of wildcard events. There is no way to be certain—except to those of dogmatic persuasion—just what doing the right thing means.

Faced with such uncertainty, how do we best proceed? Some people reflexively call for extreme caution. Others may assert that free and open discovery is the only hope we have. And looming over choices is the question of whether responsibly managing human invention and its consequences is really even possible. The drive to be toolmakers may be simply unstoppable, impervious to self-reflection.

The perspective offered by an experimental/creative frame provides at least the beginnings of a way beyond what might seem an impasse.

---

7 Exploratory metaphors do run the risk of biasing understanding toward the more unformed and uncertain aspects of formativeness (we tend to associate exploration and experimentation with beginnings). They thus must be used carefully. But because it is the beginning aspects of formative process that in our time often feel most foreign to us, such metaphors, if used skillfully, can be provocative and powerful.

It suggests that "management" as we customarily think of it may not be the right word. In the end, we can't really manage invention any more than we can once and for all manage the outcome of love, the creation of a work of art, or the results of scientific experimentation—and we would not want to. This lack of final control does not save us from responsibility. Indeed, it can quite specifically demand that we take charge and make hard choices. When outcomes defy prediction, acting responsibly requires assessing risk as we are able, and if choice becomes necessary, acting decisively. In any such effort, keeping in mind that what we are engaged in is necessarily an experiment helps assure the right balance of humility and courage.

Where are we in our ability to carry out such difficult shared decision-making? At best we are taking first baby steps. But we can be sure our well-being will more and more depend on it. When we look back at ourselves in a hundred years, if we are at all successful at devising social structures and mechanisms for making such choices, we will surely regard these as some of our times' greatest achievements.

An exploratory framing of choice and truth translates readily to the more encompassing task of addressing our human future as a whole. Facing the future responsibly requires that we accept that what lies ahead necessarily defies final prediction. Notions like Cultural Maturity and the ideas of CST can serve as crude maps, but such maps provide only general direction. Today, nothing more defines the tasks of our time—and the excitement of our time—than the need to take ownership in the exploratory creation of a human future beyond what we can yet imagine.

While this more creative kind of responsibility demands more of us, with Cultural Maturity's changes it becomes something we can be capable of. And increasingly we are seeing that it is the only kind that can work. We also increasingly recognize that when we consciously move beyond absolutist beliefs and think in more exploratory ways, not only do we make better headway, very often we find wholly unexpected solutions.

Here I've used two terms—"experimental" and "creative"—with subtly but significantly different implications (with the term "exploratory" reflecting a bit of the meaning of each). The difference is important. The word "experimental" adequately describes the basic postmodern task of making our way without familiar guideposts. The word "creative" implies underlying generativity and pattern in a sense that the term "experimental" does not. Creative Systems Theory proposes that "creative" is the more precise term. The theory argues that if the truths we draw on are not ultimately creative, it would be impossible to effectively make our way—at any time, but certainly now. We've seen how the concept of Cultural Maturity makes sense only within an explicitly creative understanding of human nature and the human endeavor.

A further formal creative systems term captures this more creative picture of change and truth. CST calls human change processes Meta-determinant. The notion "bridges" usual notions of predictability and unpredictability. Creative outcomes are not predetermined—nothing more marks creative processes than the fact that we cannot know ahead of time exactly what they will produce. But they are also not simply uncertain. Creative processes are highly patterned, and the results they produce are always in some way linked to their creative contexts.

Capacitance

Let's turn now to the second of our Whole-Person/Whole-System Patterning Concepts. Capacitance concerns how much of life, how much of creation's intensity, a system can handle. It refers to a system's overall ability to tolerate and engage experience. The concept could not be more important—both for its practical usefulness and for its more theoretical implications. T.S. Eliot observed that "man cannot handle very much reality." In fact, it is amazing that we humans can handle as much reality as we do. But there are limits. And a critical piece of Cultural Maturity is learning to be newly conscious of those limits and the way they play out in our personal and collective lives. A system's Capacitance marks where those limits lie.

Capacitance is not about particular capacities—even general ones. It systemically circumscribes measures such as intelligence, skill, emotional maturity, power, adaptability, and sensitivity. It is also about more than simple awareness. Capacitance is about what at any point in time we are systemically capable of. I often use the metaphor of a balloon to introduce the concept of Capacitance. Capacitance describes the size of the balloon, the "volume" of life a system can handle before things become too much. In the movie *A Few Good Men*, when Jack

Nicholson's character was asked at trial to tell the whole truth and nothing but the truth, he responded, "You want the truth? You can't handle the truth." Nicholson's character was making an observation about Capacitance. The volumes within the circles in the Creative Function represent evolving Capacitance.

It helps in getting started to contrast Capacitance with our first Whole-Person/Whole-System Patterning Concept. Aliveness has to do with truth at its most bare-boned, Capacitance with how much truth we can manage.

Aliveness refers to significance, Capacitance to the possible magnitude of that significance. Aliveness is about sensing where we need to walk, Capacitance about how much we can carry in walking without losing our balance. A creative frame helps further fill out the difference and also highlights how deeply the two concepts are related. I've described how we can think of Aliveness as truth's "creative edge." It is this as far as the direction in which that edge points us. But we can just as accurately describe that edge in terms of Capacitance. Pull back too far from available Capacitance and experience goes dead. But push past Capacitance limits and the system risks being overwhelmed and damaged.

As with all Creative Systems concepts, Capacitance escapes wholly logical definition and concrete pictorial representation (again that Dilemma of Representation). But our first Whole-Person/Whole-System Patterning Concept in combination with the language of formative process provides a good start. CST defines Capacitance as the amount of Aliveness—the amount of formative intensity—a system is capable of embracing and tolerating. At any moment, individuals, relationships, communities, organizations, or states possess a certain capacity for experience. As a function of where each is in its development and how each has uniquely evolved, there is a specific "volume" of creation that the "vessel" that each has become can hold. Capacitance, like the space in a jar or bowl, defines both possibilities and limits. Step beyond those limits and the container may break.

As with Aliveness, Capacitance as a phenomenon is not new. It is new only in our ability to use it consciously as a measure and to apply it with the needed systemic completeness. At some level, a recognition of Capacitance is what we have always used to discern potential. And the mature stages of any formative process reveal the fact of real constraints—a sense of proportion is a key ingredient of wisdom. Common phrases and figures of speech reflect that at some level we know this is how things work. We recognize that things can become "too much." In sports we refer to "playing within one's game." There is the modern notion of "information overload."

But while the phenomenon of Capacitance of not new, the need for a formal concept like Capacitance and the cognitive maturity needed to put it into practice are new. They are products of our time in culture's developmental story. Measuring Capacitance more consciously and directly is not necessary if culturally mature understanding and action are not required. Split mind and body and we can measure intelligence well enough with an IQ test, and we can adequately evaluate the body with a physical exam. But with increasing frequency, today's circumstances demand that we address questions of possibility and capacity more systemically. If I wish to hire someone to fill a leadership position for which the job description could change dramatically—as is so often the case today—I don't want to base my decision purely on present skills. I am interested as much, if not more, in the person's ability to learn new skills, or even more generally, how successfully the person handles complex and changing circumstances. I am interested in how much of the "stuff of life" the person can effectively hold and manage—their overall capacity to learn, act, relate, and grow.

With almost all of today's new tasks, from the most personal to the global, we need to discern not just attributes, but what circumscribes them—how, and how generously and robustly, they are held. Our personal capacity for Whole-Person relationships—between friends, lovers, parents and children, leaders and followers—is ultimately a function of Capacitance. So is our ability as larger systems—communities, organizations, ethnicities, and countries—to relate with the new maturity our world increasingly demands. When I choose participants for think-tank groups designed to address major social issues, I think carefully about what level of Capacitance will be needed to effectively take on the particular issue. It doesn't matter how skilled or clever I may be as a facilitator; if the group can't manage the needed level of engagement, we will fail at our task.

The new skills and capacities that I've previously described as accompanying Cultural Maturity's changes help fill out Capacitance as a concept. We can use several to in effect define Capacitance, at least as that can be done. Capacitance can be thought of as a system's capacity for responsibility (with a specific level of Capacitance needed for responsibility in our responsibility-twice-over sense). Capacitance can also be thought of as the amount of uncertainty a system can tolerate (noting that wallowing in uncertainty is a great way to diminish uncertainty). Equally we can think of Capacitance as a measure of the amount of complexity a system can effectively embody (not forgetting the difference between systemic complexity and the merely complicated). Other new capacities that I touched on in the previous chapter—for example, getting beyond the either/or assumptions of times past, thinking more contextually, or a greater capacity for foresight—don't so directly describe Capacitance, but they are certainly Capacitance-dependent.

The concept of Capacitance has easily unwelcome aspects. The most immediate is how inescapably it confronts us with the fact of inviolable limits. We like to believe that options are infinite and that people—and larger social systems—have unlimited potential. The concept of Capacitance reminds us that neither is the case. Our options are limited by how much our systemic vessel can hold before breaking. I've made reference to how we don't have the same expectations of people at different ages. A caring parent does not inflict responsibilities on a five-year-old that require a ten-year-old's maturity. And a good teacher recognizes that while yes, "any child can learn," not all children can learn as well or at the same speed. It is the same with larger systems. Sometimes the growth a challenge might demand is beyond what a system is currently capable of engaging.

Capacitance, like Aliveness, also confronts us more specifically with limits to what we can objectively measure. No litmus test exists for Capacitance. While higher-Capacitance systems tend to share certain general characteristics, in the end, the only "device" capable of directly measuring the Capacitance of a human system is another human system. Further complicating the task of discerning Capacitance is that we are all highly vulnerable to bias in our determinations. Depending on our professions, ethnic backgrounds, personality styles, and more, we carry inherent prejudices with regard to what comprises "real" Capacitance. (Most people tend to over-estimate the Capacitances of individuals and groups similar to themselve and underestimate Capacitance when there is marked difference.) All this means that our measurements will never be cleanly objective nor totally precise in the sense that parts of ourselves might prefer.

Given the inherent uncertainty involved in discerning Capacitance and this vulnerability to bias, a person might rightly ask why we should make the effort. The answer, of course, is that with increasing frequency Capacitance is what we need to measure—and all we have available to measure. Fortunately, the situation with regard to measuring Capacitance is not as dire as these observations might suggest. If what makes measurement uncertain is understanding's ultimately creative nature and we are creative systems, then we arrive in the world with the necessary equipment for measuring. While we may not be conscious of the fact, we are all already pretty good discerners of Capacitance. Such has always been an essential ingredient in how we choose friends, mates, mentors, livelihoods, and beliefs.

Capacitance comes in many colors and flavors—reflecting how it situates contextually in creative time and space. Like Aliveness, it is a single gesture concept that reaches over a broad terrain. Some aspects of personal Capacitance are more intellectual, others more interpersonal, practical and applied, athletic, or artistic. Different kinds of Capacitance are needed for different professions and different kinds of Capacitance manifest most at different times in a system's lifetime. We can usefully apply the concept in both more specific and more encompassing ways. Keeping different kinds of Capacitance distinct in our thinking can sometimes best serve us. But, with increasing frequency, we face challenges that require us also to address Capacitance more broadly—with regard to more general human capacity, or indeed our Capacitance as a species.

It is rare in my work as a therapist that I don't at some point talk with clients about the importance of effectively managing Capacitance. As traditional cultural guideposts less and less define the structures of our daily lives, attention to Capacitance—both how much we have available and the Capacitance demands our lives make of us—becomes key to crafting our lives in ultimately healthy ways. The importance of a concept like Capacitance comes into particularly high relief with the recognition of how, with today's ever more rush-rush existence, living over one's Capacitance has for many people become the norm. Attention to Capacitance gives us the feedback we need to live our personal lives in healthy and sustainable ways.

I often advocate for what I call the "80 percent rule"—approaching one's day with a 20 percent buffer. This might seem like a conservative approach. But there are always surprises. And when we honor the 80 percent rule, we soon realize that most of life's great joys happen within that extra 20 percent. We can only have fresh experience if we have Capacitance to spare. Henry David Thoreau observed that we should leave "wider margins for life." As with inviolable limits more generally, the result when we acknowledge Capacitance limits might seem paradoxical. Doing so makes us not just safer, but more vital. We become able to act in ways that are maximally creative.

Given the important relationship between Capacitance and potential, it is reasonable to ask whether it is possible to increase a system's Capacitance. The answer is "yes," but not as readily as a person might hope. The natural developmental course of any creative system involves gradually increasing Capacitance. And any new learning or self-awareness expands Capacitance. But while new capabilities can be acquired rapidly, such is not the case with new Capacitance. Capacitance walks one step at a time and is not easily rushed. The greatest predictor of increasing Capacitance is current Capacitance—unfair, but true. Capacitance begets Capacitance.

This observation might seem to run counter to my earlier assertion that creative systems make leaps in organization. But leaps have less to do with Capacitance than with underlying cognitive organization and the worldviews that result. In thinking about Capacitance and its relationship to change, I often draw on the image of a snake shedding its skin. The skin shedding represents such leaps in organization. The gradually expanding girth of the snake represents increasing Capacitance.

While the concept of Capacitance is most obviously important with personal systems, just as much it provides essential insight when making more collective decisions. As ideological beliefs and traditional institutional structures begin to break down, effective social policy hinges increasingly on our ability to understand what is possible and what is not. Capacitance is often what most determines possibility. Crafting approaches that are most likely to be helpful requires a keen sensitivity to Capacitance limits and to differences that may exist in the Capacitance available to different systems.

High Capacitance today becomes an increasingly essential leadership characteristic. The future depends on having leaders who can leave behind ideological easy answers and make wise choices in the face of often overwhelming uncertainty and complexity. Notice that one implication is that the ability to accurately discern Capacitance becomes one of the most important skills required of the culturally mature citizen. Given that elections today tend to be torn by conflicting ideologies, arguably the best way to ensure good leadership is to cast one's vote based not so much on political allegiances as on a candidate's Capacitance.

Capacitance-related observations are also pertinent at the most encompassing of scales. I've noted that while it is possible that the regressive dynamics that we currently witness globally may reflect simply the two-steps-forward/one-step-back nature of change, such backsliding may very well be a product of something more basic—humanity becoming overwhelmed as factors such as globalization, rapid change, challenges with potentially catastrophic consequences, and today's loss of cultural guideposts gives us more and more to deal with. With this additional possibility, I was making an observation about Capacitance—and what happens when we exceed its limits.

Capacitance Exercises:

> Identify four or five systems important to you in your life (individual people, interpersonal relationships, and at least one larger system). For each, how would you describe its Capacitance: as high, about average, low? Try discerning more precisely—on a scale from 1 to 100. (Most people find this easier than they might expect.) For each, also, say what you can about the kind of Capacitance it most manifests.
>
> Now take a moment to identify at least one challenge that each system will likely confront at some time in the future. For each challenge, ask yourself whether it can be met within the system's existing Capacitance. If it cannot, ask whether the stretching of

Capacitance (growth) that addressing the challenge would demand seems possible and, if so, what it would require. If it seems not possible, ask yourself the implications of this for your relationship with the system.

Whole-Person/Whole-System Patterning Concepts Applied Together

While often we are best served by applying the concepts of Aliveness and Capacitance separately, we also often benefit from using them together. I did this in first introducing the idea of Whole-Person/Whole-System Patterning Concepts earlier in this chapter to keep things simple. But doing so in more nuanced ways also further fills out understanding and helps us more effectively frame some important big-picture challenges.

In one sense we always use the two concepts together. I've observed that we can never wholly separate Aliveness and Capacitance. I've spoken of Aliveness in terms of how right choices make us "more." "More" is ultimately a statement about Capacitance. And similarly, Capacitance makes no real sense without a notion like Aliveness. In introducing the concept of Capacitance, I defined it as the quantity of Aliveness a system can hold and tolerate. The reason being attentive to Capacitance is important is that doing so supports engaging experience in the most Alive way.

But we also benefit from using Aliveness and Capacitance together more formally. At the least, appreciating how they relate helps us most effectively apply each kind of concept. We can see this with the now familiar challenge of bringing culturally mature perspective to moral/ethical concerns. Combine the two concepts and they provide a quite precise way to think about moral/ethical decision-making. Acts that support a system's ability to discern Aliveness and the Capacitance needed to make the most Alive choices manifest are moral. Acts that undermine these outcomes become immoral.

We can think of these shared roles for Aliveness and Capacitance as a template for truth discernments of all sorts. I've described how one result of Cultural Maturity's cognitive changes is that all questions become moral/ethical questions. Certainly this general relationship works for thinking about the future of specific domains. We can think of the tasks of government, education, science, health care, or religion going forward each in terms of needed, newly Alive narratives. We can also think of them in terms of structures and ways of thinking that support greater human Capacitance.

At the most encompassing of human systemic scales, the concepts of Aliveness and Capacitance together provide a good general definition of Cultural Maturity—or at least a good basic description of what Cultural Maturity ultimately asks of us. Put in the language of systems, Cultural Maturity is about thinking in ways that, uniquely in our time, become most affirming of human life. It is also about the substance and fortitude needed to do so and to transform such thought into action.

I've described how the concept of Cultural Maturity describes right-and-timely emergent possibility—the most Alive option for today, and really the only option going forward. Including the concept of Capacitance adds an essential recognition: Cultural Maturity is Capacitance-dependent. Any developmentally related change process is tied to Capacitance. But the connection to Capacitance manifests with Cultural Maturity in ways that are particularly consequential if we are to effectively move forward.

The topic of limits helps clarify what is different. I've described the way Cultural Maturity's cognitive changes help us recognize the fact that ultimate limits are consistent with—indeed inherent to—life. Culturally mature perspective is needed if we are to understand inviolable limits in ways that are at all positive. I've also described one particularly fundamental limit, how the Dilemma of Trajectory confronts us with the fact that none of the options that follow from usual ways of thinking—going forward as before, collapsing, or going back—can get us where we need to go. Advancement depends on sufficient Capacitance that the Dilemma of Trajectory, rather than a dead end, is experienced as an invitation to proceed onward in a new way.

The new Capacitance-dependent picture that results includes both "bad news" and a very important kind of "good news." On the bad news side, we have to accept that without sufficient Capacitance, culturally mature perspective is simply not possible. If this is the case, calamity may be inescapable. Cultural Maturity's changes require that we be able to engage a certain magnitude, or "volume," of experience. If there is not adequate Capacitance, the challenge presented by the need to rethink progress can only overwhelm.

The good news comes with the recognition that the reverse is also the case when it comes to Capacitance and Cultural Maturity. It is a result we saw earlier in a different way with the recognition that needed new skills and capacities follow directly from Cultural Maturity's cognitive changes. At a certain Capacitance, Cultural Maturity's conclusions become almost self-evident, a recognition with provocative implications for culturally mature advocacy. We find that we often don't have to advocate for different culturally mature policies separately. Specific-issue interventions may prove valuable, but it can often be enough to simply support the needed growth in a system's Capacitance.

The concepts of Aliveness and Capacitance together also assist us by letting us think more specifically about how the Dilemma of Trajectory need not be the end of the road. Capacitance is the one thing that increases in a consistent way over the entire course of formative process. (I've described how Capacitance is represented by the volume within the circles in the Creative Function.) This steady increase occurs irrespective of the leaps that mark transitions between creative stages. Critical to looking forward culturally, it also continues with Cultural Maturity's more integrative kind of trajectory.

We can sum up the Dilemma of Trajectory with the recognition that our old "onward-and-upward" definition of progress has lost its connection with Capacitance, and through this with Aliveness. Cultural Maturity's new trajectory, by making possible a continued increase in Capacitance, quite specifically carries on progress's tradition. The task we face in redefining advancement involves finding ways to think about growth that successfully reflect what, in our time, makes us personally and collectively more, that are Alive in ways that produce actual and necessary growth in Capacitance. If we frame progress in terms of Aliveness and Capacitance, we are no longer limited to images of heroic achievement or collapse when looking to the future.

The Myth of the Individual

In Chapter Four, I briefly introduced what CST calls the Myth of the Individual and promised to address it later in more detail. The Myth of the Individual has essential implications for how we understand ourselves. It also has critical implications for our understanding of what makes truth true. A somewhat closer examination helps us further appreciate why Whole-Person/Whole-System truth discernments today are needed and what makes them possible. It also helps us better recognize ways our thinking can miss the mark in attempting to make such discernments.

We tend to take our modern concept of the individual for granted—see little reason to question it or to think we might need anything more. But CST makes clear that in fact it is a developmental notion, specific to our Modern Age. CST also makes clear that there is no reason to think of it as an end point and every reason to be fascinated by what may come next. The previous chapter's reflections on love and leadership help us understand just what has been missing.

In looking at love, I described how we've thought of romantic love as love based on individual choice. I also described how perceptions with romantic love are in fact based as much on projection and mythologizing as on seeing clearly what is before us. Success with love in times ahead will require not just a more complete picture of love, but also a more complete idea of what it means to be an individual.

With leadership we encountered something very similar. Modern representative government is based on the belief that it is a product of individual choice—we speak of "government by the people." I've described how in fact leadership with modern governance remains idealized and mythologized. I also described the importance of leadership (or followership) that has its foundations in Whole-Person identity.

My field of psychology provides a particularly good example of what can happen when our thinking about identity stops short of being fully systemic. The example concerns opposite ways in which psychotherapeutic schools have framed what is most important to consider—in the end where "real" truth lies, and ultimately where real identity lies. Psychologists and psychiatrists prefer not to acknowledge that what they do is often based more on ideology than on well-thought-out and demonstrated conclusions. Historically, practitioners have often held to opposite interpretations and have frequently been at odds (behaving more like members of competing fundamentalist sects than the objective professionals they claim to be). Psychotherapists who apply either of these contrasting formulations pay the price of predictable blindnesses and severe constraints to how deeply they can be helpful. We can think of

CREATIVE SYSTEMS THEORY

the contrasting views of identity held by these often warring camps as heroic and romantic versions of the Myth of the Individual.

Let's start with the more romantic side of things, as that is where we most often find confusion with traditional ideas about truth's crux. Certain schools of psychology elevate an "inner self" and equate it with a "true self" or "authentic self." This is common with certain analytic, and almost all humanistic, existential, and transpersonal psychological approaches. The formulations of people who think this way commonly identify the feeling side of experience (or sometimes spiritual sensibilities) with truth, and ultimately with identity as a whole. It should now make sense that this is an ultimately partial—systemically incomplete—way of seeing things.

On the other side of the fence, we find behaviorists who see significance only with in-the-world particulars. They identify with a scientific worldview and consider more Inner concerns to be of secondary significance at best. Just as much, the picture they draw on is limited, and limiting. And just as much, these polar opposite conclusions about truth and identity can get practitioners into trouble.

The more appropriate truth/identity task—at least if our interest is "self" in a culturally mature, Whole-Person sense—should now be clear. It involves getting our minds around the entirety of our complexity—Inner and Outer aspects equally—and appreciating them as parts of a larger entirety. Self becomes what results with Integrative Meta-perspective. It is who we are when we consciously hold the whole box of crayons.

Deeper engagement with Inner aspects can provide useful guidance in cases where a person has tended to identify with more Outer, worldly concerns. But it is just as much the case that a person who has identified with more internal sensibilities benefits from developing their more in-the-world capacities. Fail to recognize this larger picture and we end up with ultimately unhelpful conclusions and dangerous errors in our thinking.

In the next chapter, we will examine a related observation that makes the importance of more systemic ways of thinking about truth, identity, and psychotherapeutic practice particularly inescapable. More Inner sensibilities or more Outer sensibilities appropriately play the larger role in people with different personality styles. To make Inner truth or Outer truth the "real truth" is also to make people of certain temperaments not just superior, but in an important sense "chosen."

Pragmatism

One of the best ways to refine our understanding of CST concepts is to compare them with notions with which they might be confused. With Whole-Person/Whole-System Patterning Concepts, pragmatism makes a particularly good point of comparison. The pragmatist proposes that truths that work are helpful not because they are true in some absolute sense, but because they get us where we need to go. Pragmatism has formal philosophical roots,[8] but its basic meaning has become part of common usage.

I think of pragmatism as one of the most useful contributions of postmodern thought. And much in its conclusions closely parallel observations in this chapter. But while pragmatism makes a good start toward describing the kind of truth we find from Integrative Meta-perspective's more systemically embracing vantage, CST calls into question many of traditional pragmatism's common associations and stretches and challenges much in pragmatism's more philosophical formulations.

Whole-Person/Whole-System truth and pragmatic truth in the more familiar sense are similar in that the interest of each is truth stripped of ideology. Mythologized truth is dramatic—heroic, romantic, claiming of the absolute. With both culturally mature perspective and pragmatism, beliefs become tools, ways of thinking that if used well move us toward "what works." But Whole-Person/Whole-System truth is wholly different from pragmatic truth as commonly conceived in that its concern is "what works" in a particular temporal circumstance. It is about what gets us where we need to go specifically within a culturally mature reality.

This recognition alerts us to what can be a dangerous flaw when pragmatism is simplistically conceived. Unless we step back and put its conclusions in context, pragmatism can be used to support almost any conclusion. It is a solid step forward to say that truth is "what works." But we gain little—indeed, make ourselves open to harmful consequences—if we fail to answer the question, "works toward what end?"

If we make our referent undiluted power, pragmatism becomes justification for a narrowly Machiavellian ethos. If we make our referent

---

8 In fact, pragmatism has uniquely American roots—in the late nineteenth- and early twentieth-century ideas of Charles Sanders Pierce, William James, Oliver Wendell Holmes, and John Dewey.

CREATIVE SYSTEMS THEORY

wealth alone, then both generosity and truthfulness become threats to success. If we make our referent always being agreeable so that we will not offend, then we have a kind of pragmatism that may make us momentarily safe, but which also makes us pushovers. Any ideology can serve as pragmatic truth's yardstick. A person can be a liberal pragmatist, a conservative pragmatist, a scientific pragmatist, or a fundamentalist pragmatist. It all depends on where we believe last-word truth to lie.

More formal explications of pragmatism tend to avoid the worst excesses of this trap. But they share with postmodern philosophical views more generally that while they may help us surrender past cultural absolutes, they offer very little to replace them. Richard Rorty put it this way in *Consequences of Pragmatism:* "[Pragmatists] see certain acts as good ones to perform under the circumstances, but doubt that there is anything general and useful to say about what makes them all good."[9]

Culturally mature pragmatism requires us to consciously examine the feedback we use to determine if something does, in fact, work. It also requires that we make whether our choices serve culturally mature ends our measure of "what works." It is right that we should strive to succeed and to avoid failure. Culturally mature pragmatism simply adds, "but what is success, and what does it mean to fail?" And most important for the challenges of today, it asks whether we are measuring the kind of success and failure pertinent to a healthy and sustainable future. Only truths that in the end support culturally mature possibilities remain pragmatic.

We can usefully think of what a culturally mature pragmatism involves in terms of truth's complementary "crux" and "multiplicity" tasks. To start, it necessarily involves both kinds of Whole-Person/Whole-System Patterning distinctions. Making culturally mature pragmatic decisions requires consciously asking Aliveness's bare-boned, crux truth question—inquiring about the direction in which "what works" takes us, answering the pertinent Question of Referent. And we need to ask about the Capacitance available for understanding what works and for getting the needed work done.

---

9 Richard Rorty, *Consequences of Pragmatism*, University of Minnesota Press, 1982.

With regard to Concepts of Creative Differentiation, culturally mature pragmatism is also necessarily a highly context-specific, multiplicity-sensitive pragmatism. It is deeply attentive to how what is most life-affirming—and thus ultimately pragmatic—will be different at different times and places. That includes at different times both in our personal development and in culture's evolving story. It also includes more here-and-now, one-crayon-as-opposed-to-another distinctions such as we see with temperament differences. Culturally mature pragmatism is alert to all the various kinds of multiplicity distinctions that might be pertinent.

The observation that culturally mature leadership is pragmatic adds an important recognition to the previous chapter's leadership observations. It alerts us to a confusion that can get in the way of appreciating culturally mature leadership when we find it. Culturally mature leadership can seem less "sexy" than leadership based on ideology. Indeed, it can seem rather ordinary. If we are to advance effectively, we must know how to distinguish the ordinariness of mature pragmatic leadership—which demands exceptional Capacitance—from the ordinariness of leadership that is in fact just—well—ordinary. Fail to understand the difference and we may not recognize culturally mature leadership when it is right in front of us—or, at the least, badly misconstrue its significance.

Rethinking "Symptoms"

I've promised to include a third group of distinctions with this chapter in addition to the previous two more formal Whole-Person/Whole-System Patterning Concepts. These notions are a bit more delineated than what we find with Aliveness and Capacitance but are still more general than we encounter with Patterning in Time and Patterning in Space distinctions. Each draws on both Aliveness and Capacitance observations.

The first is a specifically systemic approach to thinking about what a psychologist or psychiatrist might call "symptoms." This application will be most obviously important to people working with individuals in the helping professions, but as I use the word "Symptom," it applies to systems of every sort. (I will capitalize Symptom when using it as a specific CST notion.)

The concept of Capacitance raises the obvious—and illuminating—question of what systems do when they lack needed Capacitance. Without protective mechanisms, the consequences of exceeding Capacitance limits can be severe. The way CST reframes symptomology addresses this question of protection. It also helps us make sense of easily confusing behaviors and better understand how to assist systems when Symptoms manifest.

CST observes that human systems perceive challenging experiences as meaningful—Alive, true in a creative sense—up to the limits of their Capacitance. At that point they become unsettled—perturbation ensues. We have common language for more symptomatic ways individuals may respond when they lack the Capacitance a situation requires. We talk of people "losing it," getting "bent out of shape."

At Capacitance's limit, a system does one of three things. It expands itself and grows. It acts consciously to protect itself (so the creative vessel will not be extended too far). Or in some way it protects itself covertly—hopefully with enough effectiveness that major damage is avoided.

We tend to think of the first response as most ideal, and in a sense it is. But growing in response works only if we have close to the needed Capacitance in the first place. The second approach—the conscious making of boundaries—offers safety while also leaving options available. However, this approach too can require significant Capacitance—and often at just the time when Capacitance may be lacking. And while conscious boundaries let us be more nuanced in our responses, they can also put us further at risk. They make a system more visible and thus a more obvious target.

Symptom, as CST uses the term, refers to the third option. Because this kind of response tends not to be conscious, it provides a particularly impenetrable kind of boundary and an effective last line of defense. But we also pay a considerable price for the added safety. Symptoms diminish flexibility—they are "reactive," and often habitual. They also block "good" experience along with "bad," not just experience that threatens to harm but also that needed to learn and adapt. When chronic, Symptoms can slow or even arrest development.

"Symptom" is not an ideal term. The word as CST uses it does not necessarily imply pathology. The price I've described can be very much worth it if significant harm would result with the breaching of boundaries. Boundaries, however they are made, are critical components of health.

But the link between Symptoms in this specifically systemic sense and other dynamics with which we associate the word is strong enough that I've chosen to use the term. Better understanding mechanisms that may underlie symptoms in the word's more conventional usage is one of the most important applications of the way that CST reframes the concept.

While Symptoms take a great multiplicity of forms, CST proposes that the underlying strategy with all of them is the same. We retreat into identification with isolated aspects of our complexity. We could say "with a single crayon in the systemic box," but it is usually more complicated than just this. At the least, crayons tend to exist in polar relationships. Symptoms commonly amplify polarity. Polarization protects the system either by getting it out of the line of fire or by neutralizing the challenge to Capacitance (or sometimes both).

We could look to any scale or type of system for examples, but drawing on parallels with how a psychotherapist might use the word "symptom" offers the most ready illustration. Unconscious psychological protective mechanisms can be thought of as exaggerated manifestations of common vertical and horizontal psychological polarities. Some polar diversions shield us by lifting us above the perceived threat (e.g., intellectualization or grandiosity). Others drop us below the potential insult (e.g., depression or the victim posture of passive aggression). Some shift our attention internal to the threat (e.g., withdrawal or denial). Others direct our focus external to the threat (e.g., combativeness or obsessively busying ourselves).

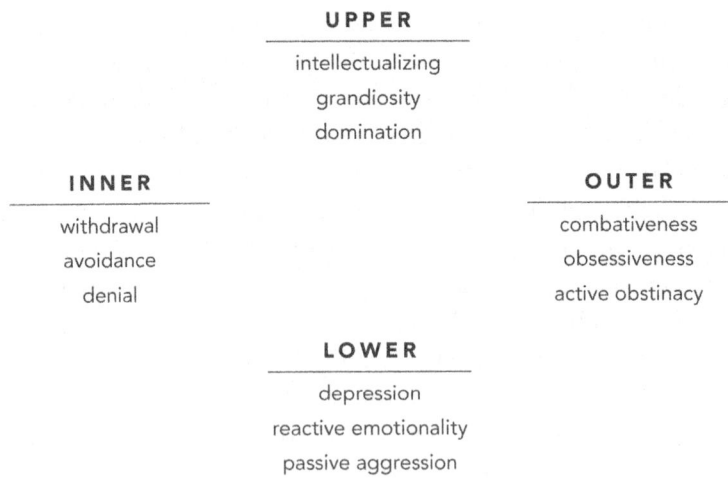

Fig. 5-1. A Sampling of Vertical and Horizontal Psychological Symptoms

CREATIVE SYSTEMS THEORY

Note that each kind of Symptom exists on a continuum with everyday responses. Each reflects an exaggerated expression of a polar tendency. At one extreme, rigor becomes rigor mortis. At the opposite extreme, flexibility becomes a lifeless puddle.

Further distinctions can help clarify how particular Symptoms work. For example, some of these responses shield us from contact (e.g., obsessiveness or withdrawal), while others function by engaging the perceived threat in ways designed to diminish its effect (e.g., combative or reactively undermining behavior). Strategies can be applied alone, but just as often we apply two or more of them simultaneously. And such strategies can be ongoing ways of relating to the bigness of life or time-specific responses to particular kinds or intensities of challenge.

In Chapter Eight, I will present the experiential approach that CST calls Parts Work. Parts Work engages the various aspects of a person's psychology as if they were characters in a play. The approach provides a way to frame Symptoms that takes us beyond thinking just in terms of polarity. When a system confronts too great a challenge to Capacitance, parts—alone or working together—take over. They do this to protect the system. The kind of Symptom we encounter will depend on the specific part or parts that take charge.

We tend to use different language when addressing Symptoms at different systemic scales, but families and organizations too can become depressed, grandiose, or oblivious. And as I've suggested in talking about possible regressive dynamics in our time, countries and whole cultures are similarly vulnerable—and just as creatively clever. Thus the CST concept of Symptom provides a common language for describing protective responses at all systemic scales and also provides an integrated framework for addressing responses that may involve multiple, interplaying systems.

How do we best think of the significance of Symptoms—wherever they occur? We can frame them just as appropriately as good, as bad, or in a more general way simply as information. Symptoms represent important ways systems protect themselves (good). They are evidence of a discrepancy between the Capacitance a system has available and the Capacitance a situation requires (if not bad, then certainly an indication of deficiency). And just as much they point toward where growth in a system may be possible and timely (information, and perhaps information of value).

Framing symptomatic responses systemically has important implications when it comes to intervention. For example, it predicts that attention to boundaries—which help protect systems from overwhelm—should provide a good general antidote. Sometimes the needed boundaries are more external—to another person, to unnecessary life demands. Sometimes they are more internal—in Parts Work terms, to a part that is being less than helpful (an overzealous inner critic, a melodramatic part that is making a mountain of a molehill). Note that the need to make boundaries consciously and skillfully has specific pertinence for our time. In the past, the major portion of external and internal boundaries (both for individuals and social systems) were culturally determined. Learning to make boundaries more consciously is an essential part of culturally mature decision-making. Think of it as the flip side of the needed new appreciation of limits.

A more systemic understanding of Symptoms helps us when it comes to intervention in another (also limits-related) way by alerting us to the care and humility needed to successfully effect change. It reminds the psychotherapist, for example, that efforts to promote growth and alleviate Symptoms, if not carefully crafted and timely in execution, may push the person even further beyond available Capacitance. And it similarly helps the cultural change agent act most wisely. In Chapter Three, I proposed that one of the most important skills we can bring to international relations is a sensitivity to the necessary stages of economic and political development. Helping nations progress is important. But just as important is avoiding developmentally inappropriate changes or attempts to change too much too fast. One of the great dangers of globalization is how dramatically it can stretch the Capacitance of social groups who may not be ready for the demands of a globalized world—with resulting symptomatic responses.

Given the diversity of forms Symptoms can take, a person could be tempted to categorize them with Patterning in Time and Patterning in Space as Concepts of Creative Differentiation. In the end, they represent a more general sort of notion, but it is worth appreciating how differentiated the distinctions they make can be. We see significant detail with any Whole-System Patterning Concept. By referring to Aliveness and Capacitance as having diverse colors and flavors, I've already implied creative multiplicity. But the concept of Symptom, framed creatively, makes such multiplicity even more explicit. The concept makes no sense without an appreciation for the fact of polarity. And the specific forms Symptoms take follow directly from the way Patterning in Time and Patterning in Space mechanisms shape polar dynamics. People at different periods in their lives are most prone to certain kinds of Symptomatic responses (for example, the same individual who as a child may tend to become withdrawn may, as an adult, become combative). And while an academic may rise above a perceived threat by intellectualizing, a corporate executive is more likely to do so by "lording over," or an artist by keeping his or her "head in the clouds." Symptoms amplify and caricature underlying time- and space-relative creative mechanisms.[10]

As we saw with Aliveness and Capacitance, bringing systemic perspective to how we think about Symptoms in this way stretches how we usually think. Before now, this kind of interpretation would have demanded greater systemic awareness and greater comfort with uncertainty and complexity than our available Capacitance would have allowed. The concept would itself only have created Symptoms. But going forward, we should find related, more systemic notions of health and disease increasingly common. We recognize an example currently in the growing acceptance by physicians that "stress" can contribute not just to psychological discomfort but also to physical illness. The term "stress" as used today tends to be applied simplistically (a topic I will return to shortly), but it points toward something important. What is "stress"? It is what we feel when a system is chronically challenged to more than it can effectively handle.

An important illustration of applying the concept of Symptom at a cultural scale brings attention to a unique danger we face as we look to the future. I've described how polarizing helps keep challenges to a system's Capacitance at a safe arm's length. In times past when such polarizing happened in a major way at a societal level, it didn't radically change circumstances, it only increased polarization that was already

---

10 Chapter Six expands on these reflections by addressing the forms that Symptoms are most likely to take with people of different personality styles.

part of consensus reality. The result could be a war, but it was likely a familiar kind of war. Today, as polarization directly undermines the needed maturity of perspective, the implications of this sort of response are very different. I've described how one of the greatest dangers we face in our time is that today's array of newly god-like challenges—along with the more encompassing task of Cultural Maturity—will stretch Capacitance beyond what we can tolerate. The resulting polarization and projection could distance us from the needed maturity of perspective just as such maturity has become imperative.

A Symptom Exercise:

> What kinds of day-to-day situations are most apt to stretch you beyond what you can comfortably handle? With each kind of situation, what protective mechanisms have you been most likely to utilize? If you have drawn on Symptoms, what might now be a more creative and healthful response? Ask the same questions with regard to a larger system you are a part of—your family, your community, a business or other organization, an ethnic group, your profession. Do this also for the country you live in and for the planet as a whole.

Rethinking Violence

Integrative Meta-perspective's more encompassing vantage offers a related more systemic way to think about violence. As with Symptoms, we can use the concepts of Aliveness and Capacitance to help us more deeply grasp how violence works. And in a similar way, we can use creative patterning concepts more generally to bring important detail to how we think about violence. I will similarly capitalize the word "Violence" when applying a CST lens.

The way CST reframes Violence parallels reflections from earlier in this chapter on morality. The difference is primarily one of emphasis. In reflecting on morality, while I drew on both Aliveness and Capacitance observations, I focused most on Aliveness. I've described how moral acts are those that are life-enhancing, while immoral acts diminish Aliveness. In addressing Violence, CST focuses more on Capacitance. Violent acts are those that result in damage to a system's capacity for life. Morally inappropriate acts, while harmful, are more likely to be transitory in their effects. With Violence, damage is often long-term or even permanent.

We can apply observations just made with regard to the underlying dynamics of Symptoms with this reframing of Violence. Mechanisms are often similar, and the distinctions I've made with regard to different kinds of Symptoms help add detail—differentiate kinds of Violence. For example, "combativeness," "domination," or "reactive emotionality" can each function more simply as Symptoms or actively do damage to another system's Capacitance. And each, if it does result in harm, does so in specifically different ways.

Previous reflections about polarity at its most basic alert to how we can think of Violence in this sense as taking place through two opposite kinds of mechanisms. Put simply, we can divide Violence when understood systemically into archetypally masculine and archetypally feminine forms (keeping in mind that both men and women perpetrate each kind of Violence). While this observation requires culturally mature perspective to understand deeply and apply in ways that avoid conceptual traps, it makes possible increasingly important kinds of discernments.

Archetypally masculine Violence damages Capacitance through direct insult. It may take the form of physical assault, damaging words, or the explicit thwarting of possibility. Archetypally feminine Violence does its damage more covertly. It may take the form of undermining, passive aggression, emotional entanglement, or seductiveness. Either kind of Violence can prove the more damaging depending on the context.

We can break this recognition down a bit further by speaking of Violence that is of a more Upper or Outer sort (where we find more archetypally masculine sensibilities) and Violence that is of a more Lower or Inner sort (where we find more archetypally feminine sensibilities). Most of what we commonly think of as violence is archetypally masculine Violence of the horizontal sort. Here the life-giving impulse to penetration becomes violation. Physical abuse or sexual abuse reflects this kind of Violence. So does gun violence. In some way a boundary necessary to life—physical or psychological—is not honored, and harm results. With archetypally masculine Violence of the more vertical sort, the generative power of ascent becomes "power over" in a way that specifically does harm. The offending force may be physical control, an institutional structure that limits and constrains, or words that are critical in ways that damage more than they benefit.

Archetypally feminine Violence of the horizontal sort invites us in on false pretenses. While it may appear to be receptive, it has the intent ultimately to seduce and manipulate. The implied receptivity may be emotional or sexual. At the extreme, the intent may be not just dishonest gain, but destruction. Archetypally feminine Violence of the vertical sort does harm from below. In some way it undermines, keeps life from effectively standing. We best recognize it in everyday life with passive-aggressive behavior. The passive-aggressive person presents themselves as powerless, but in fact exerts an ultimate kind of control and often does great harm. While archetypally feminine Violence of the vertical sort may play out in any kind of relationship, as with the positive aspects of this kind of power, it has its greatest effect with parenting and the family. Carl Jung used the images of the "suffocating mother," and the "tooth mother" to symbolize two particularly destructive forms.

There is an important Cultural Maturity–related reason to expand our thinking about Violence to include contrasting aspects in this way. I've described how Integrative Meta-perspective helps us more deeply engage the archetypally feminine (or alternatively, the Inner and Lower aspects of culturally mature truth). We most comfortably think about this in terms of the more positive aspects of the feminine. But in fact we can have the courage to engage the positive aspects of the feminine deeply only to the degree to which we are also willing to confront the feminine's less savory manifestations.

Wherever more archetypally masculine or feminine characteristics predominate, we are more likely to encounter not just the related more positive aspects of ultimate polarity, but also archetypally masculine or archetypally feminine Violence. Culturally Mature identity and relationship require that we be more conscious of the multiple forms that Violence can take. They also require that we commit ourselves to not perpetrating Violence, whatever the sort. In relationship, these various kinds of Violence often play one off the other. If we fail to appreciate how Violence takes these multiple forms, we can totally miss what is actually going on.[11]

---

11 Chapter Ten expands on these observations by examining the forms that

Rhythms, Boundaries, and Containers

CST also includes notions that come even closer to fully differentiated Concepts of Creative Differentiation but that still address distinctions in more general ways. People find one set of observations of this sort particularly helpful. CST describes how we can get much of the way towards the needed sophistication of thought by being attentive in making choices to pertinent "rhythms, boundaries, and containers."

The word "rhythm" refers to context in the temporal sense. At a personal scale, many daily determinations concern a right relationship to rhythms—for example, sensing when to go to sleep and to awaken, or the best times to eat throughout the day. Other rhythm variables extend over time, but generally repeat—for example, the right rhythmic relationship between time alone and time spent with others, or the best balance between more structured and less structured activities. All Patterning in Time discernment determinations are about attention to rhythms. We are happiest and healthiest when we honor what is timely in the various formative processes that make up our lives.

I've just highlighted the importance of attention to boundaries. Boundary choices have to do with our relational yeses and nos. A key characteristic of Cultural Maturity is that it makes us more personally responsible for our boundaries. It also makes us more conscious of boundary relationships and more able to craft our boundaries in subtle and dynamic ways. We become skilled at making our boundaries "hard and fast" when necessary and also at surrendering and dissolving boundaries when appropriate. One result is that we are able to be both closer and more fully separate in relationships of all sorts.

Attention to boundaries most obviously relates to needed yeses and nos in our relationships with others. But intrapersonal boundaries—those that relate to needed yeses and nos in our internal relationships—are, in the end, just as important. A good place to see the importance of both Inner and Outer boundary skills brings us back to that word "stress." While we commonly speak as if the healthy thing is to "reduce" stress, stress in itself is not bad. We can think of stress being of two kinds: the positive stress of creative challenge and the negative stress

---

archetypally masculine and archetypally feminine Violence are most likely to take with people of different personality styles.

that produces chronically elevated stress hormones. If we can make both good outer boundaries and good inner boundaries, the greater portion of stress we experience will be of the positive sort.

When we encounter something that might produce stress in the negative sense—for example, a person saying something we could interpret as an insult—we have two options available short of succumbing to Symptoms. We can establish an Outer boundary. This could be either by confronting the person or by just getting out of the line of fire. We might also decide that there is really no great concern, that the "problem" is a part within ourselves unnecessarily feeling threatened. (If the person making an insulting comment was a schizophrenic standing at a street corner, taking his comments personally would misperceive the situation.) Then the needed boundary is an internal one, with the part that is reacting in an ultimately unhelpful way.

The formula with regard to negative stress is simple (though not always easy to execute). Our parts need to know that we will make external boundaries when such boundaries are needed. And we need to be ready to make internal boundaries when parts react in unhelpful ways. Do these two things, and the stress that remains in our lives will be of the creative sort.

The notion of containers refers to the structures that define a system's relationships and activities. Containers include physical structures such as where we choose to live (our house, our neighborhood, even our country). They also include relationship structures (a marriage, what for us constitutes community, the relationships of our workplaces). In addition, they include beliefs, our ideational containers—how we think about experience to a very large degree determines the experience it is possible for us to have.

Most rhythm, boundary, and container questions were not so much personal concerns in times past. Cultural dictates took care of such choices for us—through assumed moral dictates, gender and class roles, and broadly shared assumptions about the workings of daily life. The more experimental world of culturally mature choice makes being attentive to such context concerns increasingly essential. Very often, these are the things we can control. When we get them right, what we can't control has the highest likelihood of working to our creative benefit.

As a therapist, I keep rhythm, boundary, and container questions always forefront in my mind. For example, when I work with a couple,

I will very early on inquire about the rhythms that define their relationship—in particular, how much time they spend together and how much apart, but also how much time they spend doing different kinds of things when they are together. People tend to want to first focus on the content of their relationship—who said this, who said that, who did what to whom. But very often the result of such focus is further entanglement rather than communication. When couples get rhythms right (and right rhythm can be very different for different couples), conflict often "magically" disappears.

Much of conflict in relationship has its roots in fears of the simple rhythms that good relationships require. Conflict protects us not just from the vulnerability of getting too close, but also from the risk of real separateness (it is hard to stop thinking about someone when you are in conflict with them). Getting the rhythms right makes us face our vulnerabilities—which may not be easy. But it also gives relationship a new simplicity—the ease of being together in ways that simply honor who we are.

Along with asking about rhythms, I may also inquire into whether boundaries are honest and honored. People often assume that being a loving person and being "open" means not having boundaries. In fact, the most loving thing we can do is be knowledgeable about and respectful of boundary needs (in ourselves and others). We always make boundaries— the only question is whether we do so consciously and caringly or covertly, and often unpleasantly. Relationships are much more likely to be healthy when boundaries are made in straightforward ways, and when boundaries are respected.

And I am interested, too, in the integrity and appropriateness of the relationship containers. I want to know whether the structures in which relationship takes place acknowledge each person's unique makeup. I also want to know whether these structures honor who these two unique people are together. Too often the containers we end up with are more a reflection of parental or societal expectations than what would produce the most loving and creative life. In a culturally mature reality, container questions must be asked consciously. No two culturally mature relationships look exactly the same.

Just as greater sophistication in our understanding of rhythms, boundaries, and containers supports—indeed, is essential to—Whole-Person relationships between individuals, it is important too when it comes to relationships between systems at larger scales—communities, organizations, or nations. Certainly this is so when dealing with global conflict. Too easily, we get caught up in the content of differences and beliefs—and with less-than-helpful consequences. Focusing our attention instead on contextual variables often produces much better outcomes. This is particularly the case if our interest lies with long-term benefit.

This includes attentiveness to rhythms—certainly those of cultural stage differences, but also those of shifting allegiances and economic and social cycles. It also includes sensitivity to boundary relationships, which with globalization must be understood with ever-greater sophistication. In addition, it requires that we be always aware of the containers available to us and which ones may provide the highest likelihood of effective communication. More and more often we will be called on to craft new sorts of cultural containers, ones better able to address the complexities and challenges of a new kind of world. Such new cultural containers can, in potential, take a variety of forms—such as new governmental mechanisms, nongovernmental organizations that can bring multinational cooperation to addressing larger social concerns, globally integrated information systems to help head off disasters, or conferences and think tank processes that bring together the best hearts and minds to address difficult issues.

The best of diplomacy pays attention to all these variables. But having language that explicitly combines context and content variables helps us do so more consciously and creatively, whether that language is informal as with this section, or that provided by CST's various, more detailed patterning notions.

Rhythm, Boundary, and Container Exercises
(for yourself as an individual system):

> Rhythms: Think of the most important rhythms in your life—waking and sleeping, activity and recuperation, social time and alone time. How good are you currently at honoring them?
>
> Boundaries: How effective are the boundaries in your life? Where might more attention to right boundary relationships provide

greatest benefit: with boundaries at home, boundaries in the workplace, boundaries to social expectations, boundaries to parts of yourself that can take over?

Containers: Examine all the important containers in your life: your own body, your home, your important relationships, your community, organizations you are a part of, larger social systems of which you are a member. Can you think of ways attention to any of these containers could increase potency, meaning, and generativity in your life?

In Summary

Whole-Person/Whole-System distinctions provide both encompassing guidance for making right choices and essential feedback we can use to know if our choices have proven successful. Personally, in the end, they ask a single question: How do we make our lives the greatest gift to ourselves and to others (meaning is always at some level relational)? The ultimate future of our collective human story will be defined by the courage that together we bring to civilization's analogous question. Aliveness and Capacitance in combination describe the courage we bring to discerning and acting on what ultimately matters. More differentiated systemic notions, even those of an informal sort, can bring valuable additional nuance to our discernments.

CHAPTER SIX

Patterning in Space: Diversity, Multiplicity, and Human Possibility

CST describes how human systems pattern creatively not just over time but also in the here and now. Patterning in Space concepts address diversity within human systems of all scales—domains in a society, professions, departments in a university, functions in a business, roles in a family, personality styles, or parts within ourselves. Biological systems inhabit ecological niches. CST proposes that human systems similarly differentiate into a predictable array of creatively ordered psychological/social niches. Over the years, Patterning in Space distinctions have provided many of Creative Systems Theory's most fascinating insights. They've also offered some of the most rewarding—and fun—interactions with colleagues and students.

Basic Patterning in Space observations have been embedded in previous reflections. The simple recognition that human understanding organizes as polar juxtapositions reflects a basic Patterning in Space relationship (with the additional observation that poles reflect generative complementarities making it a specifically creative kind of relationship). And our box-of-crayons image provides a way to think about here-and-now differences that alerts us both to complementarities and to the role that Integrative Meta-perspective plays in making Patterning in Space distinctions understandable. CST Patterning in Space concepts are pertinent any time our interest lies with human here-and-now systemic differences, but with this chapter's observations, I will give primary attention to personality style differences. It is here that this aspect of the theory had its beginnings and also where it has been most developed.

I've observed that CST Patterning in Space concepts apply the same creative language I've used to delineate Patterning in Time notions. Later I will describe how this recognition provides important further confirmation of the radical newness of culturally mature conception more generally. The way that the recognition of a relationship between periods in culture and personality style first opened the door to the development of CST Patterning in Space notions helps make the connection. In Chapter Three I described a college class on world music and how deeply it would influence my thinking. Patterning in Time observations—appreciation for how aesthetic sensibilities organize differently at various stages in culture—were part of it, but as important ultimately were surprising observations that linked personality styles with cultural stage.

Each day the class introduced us to music that we had never before heard, from far-flung places in the world. As I listened, I was struck by how differently various people in the room reacted to what they heard. Certain people, on experiencing a particular kind of music, would respond with immediate identification. It was like the music was saying "come home to mama." For other people, the reaction might be almost the opposite. At the extreme, they would respond with aversion, as if the music was fingernails on a blackboard. A few days later, with a different kind of music, the reactions might be just the opposite. The "come home to mama" group might now respond as if what they were hearing was fingernails on a blackboard, and the reverse.

Over time, I began to recognize patterns in these responses. People with similar personalities were reacting in related ways to music from specific cultural stages. With further reflection I made the additional connection that specific personality styles, like cultural stages, drew preferentially on particular intelligences. The development of the Creative Systems Personality Typology (CSPT) grew out of these observations.

The typology frames temperament differences in terms of locales on the Creative Function—creative niches if you will—the polar dynamics and aspects of intelligence a person most draws on. The basic outline should make sense from earlier reflections: A person who derives deepest meaning from things imaginative—such as a visual artist or someone who finds particular satisfaction working with children—will tend to preferentially inhabit the more germinal (Early-Axis) parts of intelligence's creative workings. A person who strongly identifies with moral conviction, helping others, and hard work will likely live most from the middle parts (Middle-Axis) of the creative cycle. And a person who finds greatest satisfaction in the world of finance or the media is more apt to derive their Aliveness from the most manifest and material (Late-Axis) creative sensibilities.

The Creative Systems Personality Typology also differentiates according to more vertical and horizontal observations. Within any temperament axis we find people who are more Upper in their sensibilities, more "lofty" (whether spiritually or intellectually), and others who are more Lower, more "down to earth." And similarly, we find some people who are more Inner, more introverted or reflective, and others who are more Outer, more expressive or outgoing.

CST applies this same general kind of Patterning in Space thinking to here-and-now systemic relationships more generally. It describes how, in a related way, we can talk of positions in an organization in terms of niches in the Creative Function. Roles in a business provide a good example. Put in Creative Systems language, the research arm reflects a more Early-Axis role, the manufacturing and hands-on management arms more Middle-Axis roles, and the finance and marketing arms more Late-Axis roles. We can think of cultural systems in a related way. With regard to cultural domains, art and the spiritual most engage the more symbolic and inspirational sensibilities we find with Early-Axis dynamics. Education, medicine, and government draw most on the applied, heart-and-guts emotional-intelligence sensibilities we find with Middle-Axis dynamics. And science and business tend to reflect the more rational and material sensibilities that we find with Late-Axis dynamics.

As with personality style differences, we can further fill out any scale of Patterning in Space observation by including vertical and horizontal polar aspects. In Figure 6-1, I've crudely mapped culture as a creative system in this way, drawing on skills, tendencies, and realms/domains of understanding—niches in the societal psyche.

		Inner/Outer			Upper
art, philosophy, spiritual practice	invention, scientific and artistic innovation	religion, education, moral leadership	government, medicine, management, engineering	science, literature, academic leadership	finance, business, media leadership
					Lower
work with animals, small children and the dying	improvisational and "alternative" arts, work with young children	family, community, social services	labor, military, athletics, sales	humanism; visual, poetic, & performing arts	entertainment, fashion, marketing, media talent
Early-Axis		**Middle-Axis**		**Late-Axis**	

Fig. 6-1. Patterning in Space in Culture as a Creative System

There are further ways we can expand Patterning in Space observations. For example, if we wish, we can map ways the contributions from different realms of understanding manifest more broadly. While we can usefully identify cultural domains with particular locales on the Creative Function, it is also the case that any domain's contribution can be seen manifesting in particular ways across the Creative Function as a whole. Figure 6-2 applies this approach to the world of art by mapping more Upper Pole and Lower Pole manifestations of Early, Middle, and Late artistic contributions—those that draw most on the ascendant and descendent aspects of the inspiration, perspiration, and finishing and polishing dimensions of creative process as they take expression in Late-Axis culture:

Fig. 6-2. Patterning in Space and the World of Art

We can also often derive valuable insights by overlaying Patterning in Space observations at different systemic scales. For example, we can associate cultural roles people commonly assume with temperament dynamics. I'll use Middle-Axis to illustrate: Priests, ministers, and rabbis fulfill predominantly Middle-Axis, Upper Pole, Inner Aspect (Middle/Upper/Inner) cultural functions. Their roles express the softer (more Inner) and more lofty (more Upper) aspects of the axis most concerned with moral order and community. Not surprisingly, the larger portion of priests, ministers, and rabbis have Middle/Upper/Inner personalities. Politicians tend toward the same axis and pole (their role is similarly concerned with social order, and just as lofty). But their temperaments need to be considerably more Outer. The hardball realities of institutional leadership require them to be more "in the world." Later in this chapter I will expand on this kind of layered analysis to help tease apart the origins of contrasting ideological beliefs. We will look in particular at religious and political ideologies.

We also often benefit from overlaying Patterning in Space and Patterning in Time observations. I drew on this kind of overlapping of Patterning in Time and Patterning in Space observations at a cultural scale in Chapter Three when I observed that the sensibilities of Eastern cultures tended to be more Inner in contrast with the West's more Outer proclivities. We can differentiate experience at any point in any creative/developmental process in terms of Upper, Lower, Inner, and Outer aspects and in terms of the more general Patterning in Space gifts and partialities of the individuals, belief systems, and organizational systems that comprise it.

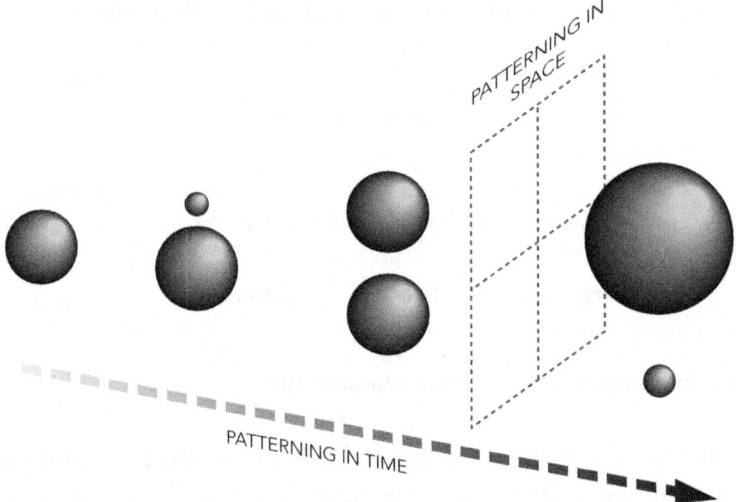

Fig. 6-3. Patterning in Time and Space

Creative Systems "Multiplicity" Distinctions

Before we more directly address temperament and the Creative Systems Personality Typology, it is important to again affirm how we are dealing with a new kind of endeavor. These are notions that make no real sense without Cultural Maturity's cognitive reordering. Patterning in Space notions of the sort we have interest in represent a kind of distinction that as a species we have not really before made—of before been capable of making. We encounter some aspects of this newness with every kind of CST concept, and much of what is new should be familiar from the book's introductory chapters. As with Patterning in Time concepts and Whole-Person/Whole-System concepts, applying multiple intelligences and "bridging" conventional polarities in our thinking are needed to grasp Patterning in Space notions at all deeply. But Patterning in Space notions are also new in ways that they share in particular with Patterning in Time notions.

In the previous chapter, I touched on how culturally mature "crux" and "multiplicity" distinctions are fundamentally different from what they replace. There I gave particular attention to how this is the case with culturally mature crux concepts. It is worth taking time for a similar, more detailed look at what makes culturally mature multiplicity concepts different from what we have known. These observations apply equally to earlier Patterning in Time distinctions and to the Patterning in Space concepts that are our more particular focus with this chapter.

Culturally mature multiplicity notions are concerned with the difference aspect of complexity. We've seen how culturally mature crux discernments can also involve nuanced distinctions, but culturally mature multiplicity observations address difference more specifically. Returning to the box-of-crayons image, with culturally mature multiplicity concepts our attention shifts from the box (representing truth's crux—with the more encompassing aspects of its two-part, core and periphery, definition emphasized) to the multiple hues of the crayons within.

Again, historical perspective helps fill out our understanding. In a similar way to what we saw with truth's crux, multiplicity distinctions are represented historically by a grand lineage. Certainly we have before made observations that differentiate this from that. But in times past, such distinctions have taken the form either of mythologized opposites (various manifestations of "us" versus "them") or more detailed but still cut-and-dried, this-versus-that lists and categories. Effectively addressing the new challenges before us again requires more dynamic and complete ways of thinking—here about complexity's aspects.

The same two basic differences that we encountered with crux distinctions apply to what is new when it comes to culturally mature multiplicity distinctions. First, they are necessarily made without the benefit of past cultural guideposts. In times past, culturally specific dictates—whether moral codes, assumptions about appropriate institutional forms, or a people's concept of the divine—provided one-size-fits-all answers. Second, they become necessarily of a more consciously systemic sort, and systemic in the now-familiar, newly dynamic and encompassing sense. The result is the possibility of discernments that are more nuanced than in times past, and in ways that more directly reflect that we are alive in the unique way that makes us human. Culturally mature multiplicity discernments also offer a compactness of expression we have not seen previously.

I've noted a simple, but in fact quite precise, way to think about multiplicity in this sense. Culturally mature multiplicity distinctions describe how truth, in the end, always exists in a context. Time and place—when an act occurs and the locale or system where it occurs—become ultimately as important to what makes something true as the content of the act. We could say that culturally mature perspective makes truth relative, but as I have emphasized, this is explicitly not relativity of the casual different-strokes-for-different-folks sort. This sort of relativity is about recognizing that if we want to be precise in our thinking, observations about context become as critical as more obvious sorts of particulars.

I've observed how such contextual subtlety really didn't need to be our concern historically, how cultural dictates have before provided needed answers. In point of fact, answers in times past were also time- and place-specific (specific to their particular time and place in humanity's story), but our limited capacity to see outside our own time and place, and especially to see importance outside of it, meant that this relativity was not something we could recognize or needed to recognize. In contrast, truth beyond Cultural Maturity's threshold makes no real sense separate from contextual considerations.

We need to appreciate just how deeply contextual variables shape experience and how important recognizing their roles is to effective understanding. While historically we've tended to miss such relativity, even at the level of the biological our truths have always been dramatically contextual. We evolve not to see, hear, and taste what is true in some absolute sense, but to perceive in the specific ways that will most support our unique approach to survival. The perceptual world of a dog, a bee, a bear, or an amoeba is much different from our own. And while we reflexively assume that our reality is the most sophisticated, if I were lost in the woods with only the scent of my previous steps to guide me home, the perceptual reality of the dog or the bear would provide much more sensitive and useful truth.

We can think of our human contextual relativities as layered. Because we are creatures, such biological relativities always come into play, and not just when our concern is the ways in which we are different from other creatures on the planet. This first layer plays a role, for example, when we ask what factors make men and women similar and different. The "nature" side of the common nature-versus-nurture debate is concerned with this first layer.

Beyond the wholly biological, we find aspects of perceptual and conceptual relativity that are products of learning—the complementary "nurture" side of things. Our immense capacity to adapt, learn, and grow means that to a degree not present with other creatures, what I see and what you see may not be the same. The sources of such conditioning-related differences are endless: differing ethnic or religious backgrounds, gender expectations, birth order, or simple happenstance—a particular teacher who influenced you, or an odd event that is not part of most other people's experience.

The third, more uniquely human layer[1] in truth's relativity is more particularly pertinent to our inquiry. We can be different for reasons that are more nuanced and specific than biology as we customarily think of it, and also deeper than just conditioning. We often make reference to this further kind of difference colloquially. When we talk about "where a person is coming from," it is often this third sort of contextual difference that we are most observing. The first two kinds of contextual relativity require Cultural Maturity's changes if they are to be understood deeply, but the third requires Integrative Meta-perspective to be recognized at all. Culturally mature patterning discernments of the multiplicity sort draw on this further layer of contextual relativity.

Some of these further differences are more temporal—about context in the sense of *when* things happen. The Creative Systems Patterning in Time concepts we examined in Chapter Three address such temporal relativities. Other such contextual differences are of a more here-and-now sort, concerned with place as opposed to time. The Creative

---

1 It might be better to say, "more expressly human." Animals also manifest such differences, but they tend not to be so marked (at least not so far as we can recognize).

Systems Patterning in Space concepts we will examine in this chapter address such in-the-moment differences. Here-and-now relativities become significant whenever present-time differences with origins deeper than just conditioning come into play.

Cultural Maturity's cognitive changes make truth's relativities at all three levels I've described newly tolerable and understandable (even fascinating). Sometimes the answers to our questions require that we take multiple relativities into account. How we experience gender, for example, includes biological differences, simple conditioning, variation that is a product of the predictably different ways various cultural stages view men and women, and how we may respond differently to any of these variables depending on personality style. Cultural differences can in a similar way involve all these levels—ethnicity at the level of the biological, tradition and mores at the level of conditioning (learning), and both cultural stage and locale at the level of our more specifically human relativities.

Effectively addressing the complex questions before us will require increasingly that we be conscious of contextual relativities. We must never forget how what is true in one situation may not be true in another. And we can't stop there. The needed sophistication of inquiry must be able to tell us something about the specifics of difference, why we see the differences that we do, and how an appreciation of such difference brings new clarity and creativity to our considerations. CST Concepts of Creative Differentiation take on this essential "multiplicity" task. The fact that they succeed in doing so in a further way confirms the fundamental newness of the theory's contribution.

I've promised to return to the curious fact that we can apply the same language to Patterning in Time and Patterning in Space contextual observations. I say "curious" because there is no obvious reason to think we should find such an association. And CST is the only conceptual framework I am aware of that observes this kind of relationship. The fact that Patterning in Time and Patterning in Space contextual observations are related in the sense that they are further highlights the fundamental newness of CST's approach and supports the conclusions on which the theory is based.

I've described how my recognition of this relationship came from the unusual opportunity provided by my college music class rather than from theoretical reflection. But in fact, if my thinking had then been further developed, I could have gotten to the same place more conceptually. The way Patterning in Time and Patterning in Space contextual observations relate follows from how Integrative Meta-perspective draws on the whole of cognition's complexity. More specifically, it follows from the CST recognition that intelligence, when understood systemically, is ordered creatively. We can think of the way Patterning in Time and Patterning in Space observations reflect a similar creative architecture as evidence for the ultimately creative nature of human intelligence—and ultimately of human identity and purpose.[2]

The Creative Systems Personality Typology

As Lucretius said many centuries ago, "What is food for one man is to the other poison." To a sometimes almost frightening degree, people with different personality styles live in distinct worlds. It is becoming possible today to appreciate such differences with a depth that has not before been an option. And as with the importance of recognizing how remarkably different reality can look through the eyes of people at different stages in culture, appreciating differences that are products of personality style is becoming newly critical.

Before we turn to specifics, we should note a couple of particular dilemmas that confront us with temperament differences. The first follows from how each of us, by virtue of being human, most embodies one of the personality constellations that I will be describing. Avoiding bias can therefore be a challenge. We need to have made solid progress in learning to step back from and engage our internal complexities if we are to effectively make sense of this more in-the-world kind of complexity.

The second dilemma, one shared with Patterning in Time distinctions, is more basic. To even get started with understanding, we need to recognize that there are differences to understand. Even psychologists and teachers commonly acknowledge only the most superficial of differences. This might seem hard to believe given that these are people

---

2 The greatest contribution of the Creative Systems Personality Typology may lie ultimately less with its specific temperament insights than with how it affirms the notion that not just human change, but human difference—and human experience as a whole—is creatively ordered.

for whom an appreciation of temperament difference would seem essential. We reasonably ask why this kind of recognition is difficult for us. The reason is the same as what we encountered with our look at Patterning in Time. We need Cultural Maturity's cognitive changes to grasp such differences deeply. Without Integrative Meta-perspective, we at best recognize superficial differences. And we are likely to attribute what we do observe to other people's ignorance or inadequacy. Where Capacitance is even more limited, the experience of difference may reactively translate into polarized projection—most often of a denigrating, but also sometimes of an idealizing, sort.

Consistent with what the concept of Cultural Maturity predicts, we've seen beginning acknowledgement of personality style differences in recent decades. Frameworks like the Myers-Briggs typology[3] are now routinely utilized in organizational settings. And "learning styles" has become a common curriculum focus in schools of education. But approaches to this point rarely address much beyond the most surface layers of such observations. The Creative Systems Personality Typology goes significantly deeper. Because it draws on the whole of intelligence's complexity, we can think of it equally well as a framework for understanding difference in how people think, feel, imagine, and live in their bodies. It is also particularly powerful in its ability to look beneath behaviors and beliefs and get more directly at underlying values and worldviews.

The CSPT proposes that people of different temperaments are different because they preferentially inhabit—and derive their gifts from—different parts of our toolmaking, meaning-making complexity. If this is accurate, Integrative Meta-perspective should make this fact newly visible. And the application of a creative frame should help us bring nuance to our distinctions. Creatively defined temperament concepts should also help us better understand not just how people are different, but why, just what makes each of us "tick" in the particular ways that we do.

While any approach to understanding human differences can assist us in understanding ourselves and learning to better get along with others, CST's particular framework also assists us in ways particular to the tasks of Cultural Maturity. Reflections from my years leading yearlong

---

3 Based on the work of Carl Jung.

CREATIVE SYSTEMS THEORY

trainings at the Institute provide a glimpse. I would select participants for programs according to a couple of criteria. I mentioned Capacitance in Chapter Five. People needed to be "up to the task." But just as important, ultimately, was personality style. I chose participants so that temperament diversity was fully represented. (One of the things that most struck people on the first day of the yearlong training was how different many of the people in the room were from the people they were most used to spending time with.) Each "crayon" in the creative box thus had its advocates.

Most immediately, having that diversity—and that particular kind of diversity—in the room was powerful at a personal level. It helped catalyze the internal integration needed for culturally mature thought. One may never be a jazz musician, a professional football player, or an advertising executive, but if one can begin to understand what might make such people who they are—and better, even slightly embody their felt realities—these people's presence can help one more deeply engage creation's full systemic complexity in oneself. Partway through the year, I would engage the group in a deep immersion into the Creative Systems Personality Typology to help make these learnings more conscious.

Having that particular kind of diversity in the room also became essential for our shared work together. The mosaic of realities that personality style differences represent supported the collaborative efforts needed to address the deeply systemic questions these emerging culturally mature leaders were there to engage. Near the end of the training, I had participants divide up into small think tank teams to work on future issues in specific domains—education, government, business, and so on. By that time, it had become clear to participants that choosing like-minded team members was not the right approach if they wanted culturally mature results. They recognized that if their teams were going to be most powerfully creative, they would need the contributions of each basic temperament axis.

A couple of further observations help avoid common confusions before we dive in. One concerns the relationship between Patterning in Time and temperament distinctions. I've described how the Creative Systems Personality Typology applies the same language of creative differentiation that we saw with Patterning in Time. Temperament differences reflect embodying more germinal or more manifest aspects of creative organization.

A common beginner's mistake is to assume that "later" personality styles are somehow more evolved than "earlier" ones. We must always keep in mind that development and temperament are wholly different concerns. Each of us over the course of personal development (and within any endeavor we undertake) goes through the same sequence of organizing realities. And, at the same time, each of us, whatever our developmental stage, has special affinity for certain creative sensibilities.

We also need to appreciate the fact that we are dealing ultimately with locales along a continuum. I will describe discrete categories—Early-, Middle-, and Late-Axis personalities, and within these, people for whom Upper or Lower, Inner or Outer qualities most predominate. But only rarely do we find pure types. It is similar to what we see with color. We may say a color is green. But at once we know that there exist many different greens, indeed that there is no absolute line that makes one color blue-green and another greenish-blue.

For each temperament axis, I will make a series of observations. I will address its underlying creative mechanisms, discuss general personality characteristics, mention some familiar people as examples, list professions that people with that temperament often assume, and address that temperament's particular strengths and common blindnesses. Reflecting my background as a therapist, I will also go into some detail as far as how that temperament might be expected to respond if the Capacitance challenge is too great. With each axis and each aspect within each axis, certain Symptoms are most common.

I'll also include a particular kind of observation that follows from my assertion that CSPT can be thought of in relation to any intelligence. I will describe each temperament using the lens of body intelligence. The fact that we can draw on body intelligence in this way is particularly affirming of the framework's depth and significance. I can sit in a cafe, watch people come through the door, and guess their personality style with pretty high accuracy. What I'm observing has most to do with how a person lives in their body—how they move, whether they inhabit more the inner or surface layers of bodily experience. But body structure is much easier to talk about, and here too there are observations that generally hold.[4]

---

4 This kind of observation might again seem controversial, at least initially.

It is important to emphasize that these are necessarily simplified notions. For example, while I will make reference to commonly seen professions or beliefs, major exceptions exist to every such behavioral generality. Indeed, the exceptions are often where the most interesting and useful discoveries lie. I walk into a room of CEOs and expect those present to be Lates, but many are not. I assume that a firefighter who comes to see me as a client is a Middle, but instead he is an Early. In each case, the equation changes dramatically.

Pre-Axial Patterns

Pre-Axial patterns differ from other temperament constellations in that they rarely manifest in modern times as primary dynamics in healthy individuals (the one exception being people with a strongly Pre-Axial cultural background). We encounter Pre-Axial dynamics most frequently in people who have significant psychological or neurological limitations. Because they are principally of interest to those in the therapeutic professions, they are beyond the scope of this discussion of normal variation. (I've included some further reflections on Pre-Axial dynamics at the end of this chapter.)

Early-Axis Patterns

Early-Axis temperaments reflect a special affinity with the inspiration stage in formative process—that period when the buds of new creation first find their way into the world of the manifest. The reality of Early-Axis individuals is born from the organizing sensibilities of possibility and imagination.

Following are a few quotes that capture Early-Axis sensibilities and values: From Albert Einstein, "He who can no longer wonder, no longer feel amazement, is as good as dead." From Miles Davis, "I'll play it first and tell you what it is later." From Henry David Thoreau, "It is life near the bone where it is sweetest." From Orson Welles, "I don't say we all ought to misbehave, but we ought to look as if we could." From

---

It could seem to harken back to discredited (and dangerous) notions of difference from times past. But spend time with these observations and they clearly prove sound. And they are often particularly informative.

Tom Robbins, "In the haunted house of life, art is the only stair that doesn't creak." And from Pablo Picasso, "Everything is miraculous. It is miraculous that one does not melt in one's bath."

Where do we find Earlies? Often they work with young children (a grade school teacher, a day-care worker). Frequently they become artists—visual artists (particularly those of more abstract inclination), dancers (particularly those whose aesthetic tends toward the improvisational), musicians (most jazz musicians, some classical and many rock and roll musicians), or writers (particularly poets and most writers of science fiction). Earlies also make important contributions in the sciences. (Many of science's major innovators have been Earlies—though the larger number of scientists are Lates.) Recently, Earlies have starred in the high-tech revolution. (Steve Jobs, Bill Gates, and Elon Musk are all Earlies.) Most people who teach reflective techniques such as meditation and yoga are Earlies. (It is Earlies who are most attracted to things spiritual, particularly practices with roots in Early-Axis cultures.)

A few famous Earlies: Leonardo da Vinci, Georgia O'Keeffe, Rainer Maria Rilke, Stephen Hawking, Carl Jung, Isadora Duncan, Albert Einstein, Mary Cassatt, Jonathan Winters, Antoine de Saint-Exupéry, May Sarton, Groucho Marx, Pablo Neruda, Anaïs Nin, Howard Hughes, Alan Watts, Robin Williams, John Coltrane, Boris Karloff, Emmett Kelly, Gary Larson, Pablo Picasso, Buckminster Fuller, Frank Zappa, Nikola Tesla, Jack Nicholson, and Mrs. Saunders (my kindergarten teacher). More notorious Earlies include Charles Manson, David Kaczynski, and Rasputin.

This listing skews toward the more manifest Early-Axis types. This is in no way to imply that they have greatest importance. As is the case with every axis, Uppers and Outers are most in the world and thus tend to be most visible. It is only with the more universally manifest world of Late-Axis personality structures that we see Lower/Inner personalities acknowledged historically, and even then they are underrepresented. Mrs. Saunders is the only Early/Lower/Inner in this list.

The Early's defining intelligence speaks the language of symbol, myth, and metaphor (for the modern Early, as experienced within the rational/material context of today's Late-Axis culture). Edgar Allan Poe captured the inner world of the Early when he wrote: "All that we see or seem is a dream within a dream." The magical and imaginative dimensions of this intelligence predominate with Early/Uppers and Early/Outers. The mythical and mystery-centered dimensions hold sway in the psyches of Early/Lowers and Early/Inners. In keeping with their relationship to the earliest parts of formative process, Earlies tend to have an affinity for the beginnings of things. Of all axes, they are most comfortable with situations where the unknown outweighs the known. Often their contributions are quite visionary. (Jonathan Swift reminds us that "vision is the art of seeing things invisible.") And as we would expect with archetypally feminine sensibilities dominant, Earlies tend to be drawn more to interconnections than differences, and to things fluid more than things fixed. Their greatest contributions often derive from their fascination with underlying principle and pattern. (I am reminded of Albert Einstein's famous assertion, "I am interested in God's thoughts; the rest are details.") Earlies can take great joy in the nonsensical and contradictory. (From Lewis Carroll in *Through the Looking Glass:* "'Contrariwise,' continued Tweedledee, 'if it was so, it might be; and if this were so, it would be: but it isn't, it ain't. That is logic.'") Earlies, particularly Early/Lowers tend to be more comfortable in their bodies than other temperaments and derive particular fulfillment through bodily experience. (Indeed, for many Earlies, body and spirit can be hard to distinguish.) Earlies generally feel a more immediate connection with nature than other temperaments, and greater comfort with solitude (whether alone in nature or just with themselves). I am reminded of the familiar words of Yeats:

> "I will arise and go now, and go to Innisfree,
> And a small cabin build there, of clay and wattles made:
> Nine bean-rows will I have there, a hive for the honeybee.
> And live alone in the bee-loud glade."

Of all temperaments, Earlies have the most permeable boundary structures (which we would expect given that Early sensibilities are the least manifest). One result is that the Early-Axis person can seem fragile or frail and encounter difficulties in situations where strong boundary structure is needed. But this boundary permeability is also the source of many of the Early's great gifts and strengths—such as intuitiveness, sensitivity to interconnections, and an ability to "go with the flow." On meeting an Early, one is often first stuck by a childlike quality. Again in keeping with their relationship to creative development's beginnings, Early-Axis people tend to have a special appreciation for childhood sensibilities both in themselves and in the world around them. A certain non-conformism is a common Early Axis trait, but its origin is less rebellion than a mistrust of—and even ignorance of—established convention.

These characteristics take expression in particular ways with various Early-Axis patterns. With Early/Uppers, qualities such as imaginativeness, intuitiveness, charisma, and spiritual and artistic sensitivity predominate. Early/Uppers make manifest the sensibilities of the "magical child."

Where Inner aspects predominate, the Early/Upper's "artistry" is most internal. We often see Early/Upper/Inner sensibilities in poets, painters, and people drawn to the more ascendant and ascetic of spiritual practices. I think of the words of Pablo Neruda—"My obligation is this: to be transparent." Where Early/Upper/Outer aspects are strongest, the Early/Upper's imaginativeness manifests with greatest visibility—through more dramatic forms of artistic expression or through scientific or technical invention. It is here we find the notorious "mad professor." Note this description of colleague and Nobel physicist Theodore B. Taylor: "She found him attractive—tall, gangling with a broad forehead, a somewhat parted chin, and great thoughtful brown eyes, which often seemed to be focusing on something no one else could see."[5]

With Early/Lowers, attributes like connection to nature and mystery, a deep capacity to nurture, and spontaneity are most prominent. We see embodied simultaneously the playful aspects of the child (as opposed to the numinous and magical) and the child's connection with the primordial. Early/Lowers find a comfort with darkness not seen with other temperaments. I think of Antoine de Saint-Exupéry's description of night as "when words fade and things come alive." With Early/Lower/Outers we are often most struck by their capacity for abandon. Spontaneity and the ability to improvise come easily. Here, mythically, we find the wild man and wild woman. Early/Lower/Outers often manifest the artistic in particularly dramatic ways. Salvador Dali once exclaimed, "I do not take drugs—I am drugs." With Early/Lower/Inners, qualities like the ability to nurture and a delight in the mysterious predominate. Such people

---

5 From John McPhee, *The Curve of Binding Energy: A Journey into the Awesome and Alarming World of Theodore B. Taylor,* 1994, Farrar, Straus and Giroux.

CREATIVE SYSTEMS THEORY

also often manifest through artistic expression, but most frequently of a more personal sort. And many contribute through work with children—attracted either to selflessly serving the children's "magic" or to the possibility of living immersed in the unformed. They also often find fulfillment in work with animals. Early/Lower/Inners in particular would appreciate these words of poet Izumi Shikibu: "As I dig for wild orchids in the autumn fields, it is the deeply bedded root that I desire, not the flower."

Figure 6-4 uses some common qualities to map the four Early-Axis quadrants:

Upper/Inner	Upper/Outer
reflective, spiritual, philosophical	artisically creative, scientifically innovative, charismatic
nuturing, loving of nature and mystery	spontaneous, improvisational, love of the "wild"
Lower/Inner	Lower/Outer

Fig. 6-4. Early-Axis Qualities

Common shortcomings of Earlies parallel their strengths. Earlies often have a difficult time finding satisfaction in the traditional work world—tending to like more freedom than most jobs provide and often being a bit too eccentric or original in their thinking to fit in well. They also often lack the facility with detail and comfort with repetitive tasks that the workplace often demands. Whatever the setting, Earlies can also have problems distinguishing between dreams and dreams made manifest. (Or they recognize the difference, but are simply not good at carrying tasks to completion. A recent newspaper column jokingly referred to an obviously Early-Axis person as "planning impaired.") Weaknesses of Earlies are frequently direct products of that permeability of boundary structure. Earlies can do poorly in situations that involve significant struggle or conflict. Often they lack the "thick skin" needed for extended combat or, more generally, for the often "hardball" realities of modern life.

Earlies are much more likely than Middles or Lates to feel awkward in social situations. Even more expressive Earlies can seem quite introverted and a bit "nerdy." Earlies also frequently find societally expected forms of commitment either challenging or not of real interest. Relationship can be very important, but it must somehow complement the Early's creative, primordial, and spiritual sensitivities to be long lasting.

When Symptoms manifest in an ongoing way with Early/Upper dynamics (when the available Capacitance is chronically insufficient for the challenges of daily life), the Early/Upper's charisma can transform into grandiosity, often with a touch of paranoia. The Early's reality becomes like that of the mythic god-king. If his charisma brings him followers (people to be one with him within a reality he defines), he can be quite magical and charming. But where this is lacking, and certainly most often as an adult it will be, he can feel frightened and alone. Where the dynamic is more inward, the grandiosity tends to be spiritual rather than personality-focused.

Where Symptoms manifest in an ongoing way with Early/Lower dynamics, we often find a strong tendency toward depression. The spark of inspiration is simply swallowed before it can appear. Particularly with more Early/Lower/Inner patterns, dependency is also common. Where in Early/Upper we saw the grandiosely self-centered child, here we see the needy child. A magical causality again operates, but rather than emanating from the self, it is centered on an external agent such as a charismatic individual or a group (like a religious cult). With more Early/Lower/Outer patterns, the Early's rudimentary boundary capacity is apt to be expressed less through such dependent merging than through avoidance of social contact or antisocial behavior. Related kinds of Symptoms can take expression more interpersonally. Just as Early/Lower personalities can find it difficult to manifest in any visible way in the world, they can also have a hard time dealing with such manifestation in others. The other side of the unique sensitivity to children often seen here is a common difficulty as parents in dealing with their children's maturation. If such people are not careful, they become suffocating or undermining, acting out their fear of letting new Aliveness rise and separate.

Bodily, Early-Axis people often look young for their age. The bodies of Early/Uppers tend to be thin and unusually flexible. Appearance can range from the awkward child look of a Lyle Lovett to the Adonis-like beautiful child look of an Andre Agassi. The major parts of Aliveness are carried in the inner, "magical" layers of the upper chest, face, and eyes. Tissues tend to be on the soft side. When the dynamics of Early/Upper personalities are particularly ascendant, tissues and movements can take on a brittle quality. As a person moves beyond an age where childlike narcissism is appropriate, this brittleness can become the dominant body characteristic. Early/Upper people tend to be taller than the norm. This is likely a function of their later-than-usual onset of puberty and, with this, a delay in closing of the skeletal growth plates.

We see several body patterns with Early/Lower dynamics. These patterns have in common a tendency toward unboundedness and the carrying of Aliveness primarily in the belly and pelvis. With more Early/Lower/Outer dynamics, the body tends again to be unusually flexible and often quite animated, not unlike what we see with more ascendant patterns, but with a lower center of balance and most often with greater body mass. With Early/Lower/Inner dynamics, we see two patterns. In one, the person tends toward being thin and gaunt, a "hungry child." In the second, there is more pudginess, like a child yet to lose its baby fat. Here there may be significant obesity. The bulk serves as a covert boundary, both keeping distance and obscuring clarity of interface.

When I do personality style workshops, I often ask people to write down words and phrases that capture the experience of their particular temperament. These are some statements from the mouths of Earlies: "It can help if I have others around who can take my wild brainstormings and put them into reality"— "I've often named the cars I've owned. The ones I remember most fondly are not the ones that ran best, but those with special or quirky personalities."—"I am most happy when things have a sense of almost sacred balance."—"I can feel least alone when I am by myself."—"My hair has a mind of its own."—"People sometimes think I am sad or depressed when actually I am just deep inside myself, and in fact most happy."—"In having children, I particularly love the almost vegetative state of pregnancy and very early mothering."—"I love things primordial: the roar of the ocean, the musky smell that lingers after sex."

Middle-Axis Patterns

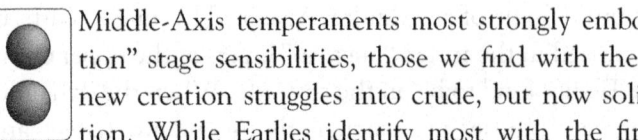

Middle-Axis temperaments most strongly embody "perspiration" stage sensibilities, those we find with the period when new creation struggles into crude, but now solid, manifestation. While Earlies identify most with the first improvisational sparks of creation, Middles find greatest meaning turning sparks into usable fire. This requires the ability to provoke and nurture the flames—blow air on them so they will heighten—and, simultaneously, to contain the flames, so that the fire burns usefully and safely. The Middle-Axis fire both does work and warms the hearth of community.

Here are a few words of familiar Middles: From Albert Schweitzer, "A man can only do what he can do. But if he does that each day, he can sleep at night and do it again the next day." From Margaret Mead, "One of the oldest human needs is having someone wonder where you are when you don't come home at night." From Douglas MacArthur, "In war there is no substitute for victory." From Abraham Lincoln, "The better part of a man's life consists of his friendships." From Winston Churchill, "This is a lesson: Never give in—never, never, never, never." From Samuel Johnson, "Great works are performed not by strength, but by perseverance." And from Jesse James, "Everybody loves an outlaw. At least they never forget 'em."[6]

Where are we likely to find people with Middle-Axis temperaments? Middles often become teachers, managers in business, military officers, social workers, athletes and coaches, union bosses, ministers or priests, physicians (about an equal balance of Middle/Upper and Late/Upper), politicians (a similar balance), police officers and firefighters, bankers, loggers, owners of family businesses, machinists, miners, and carpenters. In addition, Middles make up the greater portion of stay-at-home parents. (It is with Middle-Axis that we find the strongest identification with home, family, and community.) Women who think of themselves first as wives and mothers are commonly Middles, as are the most

---

6 Note that we find very similar sentiments with the Middle-Axis stage in cultural development (from the Koran, "God helps those who persevere"; from Proverbs 24:16, "For a just man falleth seven times and riseth up again") and with Middle-Axis functions within a cultural stage (from Aesop—and the moral voice of fable—"Slow and steady wins the race.").

devoted husbands and fathers. Middle-Axis individuals of both sexes frequently play strong roles in their neighborhoods and churches, and in social service organizations. Most of the "real work" in society is done by Middles.

Some better known Middles include Teddy Roosevelt, Mother Teresa, Margaret Thatcher, Joe Louis, Billy Graham, George Washington, Babe Ruth, Eleanor Roosevelt, Chris Evert, Thurgood Marshall, Florence Nightingale, Colin Powell, Roy Rogers and Dale Evans, Aretha Franklin, Clint Eastwood, Bella Abzug, Julia Child, Queen Victoria, Tugboat Annie, Johnny Cash, Jimmy Carter, J. Edgar Hoover, Frederick Douglass, Hulk Hogan, Cesar Chavez, Golda Meir, Mary Lou Retton, Rush Limbaugh, Boris Yeltsin, Betty Friedan, Norman Schwarzkopf, Willie Nelson, Bear Bryant, Jimmy Hoffa, Barbara Bush, and Fred and Ethel Mertz. More notorious Middles include Joseph Stalin, Adolf Hitler, Ma Barker, and, as above, Jesse James.

Again, Lower Pole figures—particularly Lower/Inners—are not well represented in this list. But Middle/Lower is where we find many of the most important, if unheralded, figures in our lives: the neighborhood police officer or firefighter, the friend who is there no matter what, the parent who puts a special note in a child's lunchbox.

Emotional-moral intelligence, the intelligence of heart and guts (as it manifests within Late-Axis culture) orders the Middle's world. The stuff of the heart holds sway in Middle/Inner and Middle/Lower temperaments—where the archetypally feminine is strongest. Harder sensibilities—the stuff of guts and fortitude—dominate with Middle/Upper and Middle/Outer temperaments.

Middle-Axis dynamics move us firmly into the human dimension. Early-Axis and Late-Axis realities are each in their own ways abstracted from the personal. Early-Axis deals with the pre-personal reality of creative buddings; Late-Axis deals with the post-personal world of the intellectual, the social, and the material. Middle-Axis puts us right in the middle, engaged directly in the tasks of mortal existence.

Throughout Middle-Axis we see a strong capacity for hard work, deep emotional and moral convictions, and the ability to persevere and to sacrifice when necessary. (Napoleon Bonaparte once said, "The first virtue in a soldier is endurance of fatigue, courage is only the second virtue.") Middles are attracted to the basic. ("Home is where the heart is.") Loyalty is an especially valued trait. The phrase "salt of the earth" would rarely be used except to refer to a Middle-Axis person. Middle-Axis creativity tends to be less that of glaring originality than of the application of new possibility to what exists. The most skilled craftspeople are Middles. With some notable exceptions, Middle-Axis people tend to be incrementalists rather than leapers. "A bird in the hand is worth two in the bush" is a Middle-Axis sentiment." Here we find the best day-to-day, hands-on problem solvers, whether in the halls of Congress, in the office, in the home, or on the factory floor.

Middles tend to respect strong moral fiber and often speak with a bluntness not found with other temperaments. (Charles de Gaulle admonished that, "People get the history they deserve.") Middle-Axis personalities tend toward the traditional in their leanings (though this does not necessarily translate to conservative). Humility and unpretentiousness are often strong values (though bravado can prevail with Outer aspects). It is not uncommon for Middle-Axis parents to warn of the dangers of getting "too big for your britches." Teddy Roosevelt said it well for the political sphere: "Speak softly and carry a big stick." (Note the tendency toward sayings and homilies in these descriptions. Homilies are a peculiarly Middle-Axis art form—"a stitch in time saves nine," "people who live in glass houses shouldn't throw stones," "haste makes waste," etc.) Middles tend to love a good story and are often adept at telling them.

Middle-Axis dynamics juxtapose opposites in near equal balance. Like two ends of a teeter-totter, opposites simultaneously battle and collude. In the Middle-Axis psyche, strength struggles with weakness, thoughts with feelings, good with evil, domination with submission, control with abandon, honor with dishonor. Meaning for a Middle is a reflection of timely balance (though often of a conflicted sort) between such isometrically interplaying forces. The reward for this creative push-pull is the realization of substance and the satisfaction of a job well done.

Words we might associate with Middle/Upper personalities include fortitude, courage, uprightness, fairness, and moral conviction. Middle/Uppers are often strong leaders. With Middle/Upper/Outers this is frequently formal organizational leadership—the leadership of politicians, captains of industry, coaches, military officers. We hear both the fortitude and the generosity of spirit often found with Middle/Upper/Outer sentiments in these words of George Patton: "Wars may be fought with weapons, but they are won by men. It is the spirit of the men who follow and the man who leads that gives the victory."

Middle/Upper/Inner leadership tends to manifest in ways that are more personal and interactional. Upper/Inner sensibilities are common in teachers, managers, and religious leaders. Middle/Upper/Inner leadership commonly has a strong moral component. It is compassionate, but also resolute. Benjamin Franklin observed that, "Sin is not hurtful because it is forbidden, but it is forbidden because it is hurtful."

People of Middle/Lower temperament tend to be most known for their perseverance, loyalty, capacity to support or nurture, and sometimes for their often-irreverent sense of humor.[7] Middle/Lowers place great importance on relationship.[8] For Middle/Lower/Inners, the most defining relationships tend to be with friends, family, and immediate community. Besides being good parents, Middle/Lower/Inners often contribute through working as teachers (particularly with children and adolescents), as social workers, as behind-the-counter salespeople, in nursing, or in the food industry. These words of Goethe capture the dedication common to Middle/Lower/Inner temperaments: "It is not doing the things we like to do, but liking the things we have to do that makes life blessed."

For Middle/Lower/Outers, the key relationships tend to be with community in a broader sense, with team members, or even more broadly, with one's ethnic group or nation. Middle/Lower/Outers are capable of strong bonds of allegiance. They are the loyal fans yelling at a football game.[9] Middle/Lower/Outers become farmers, soldiers,

---

7   Middle/Lower/Outers in particular enjoy the jostling camaraderie of a good joke, story, or put-down. Jack Dempsey once offered the following piece of practical wisdom: "Some night you'll catch a punch and all of a sudden you'll see three guys in the ring around you. Pick out the one in the middle and hit him, because he is the one who hit you."

8   But they are not known for being romantics. A Czech proverb (here Middle both in Patterning in Time and Patterning in Space) counsels, "Do not pick your wife at a dance, but in the field among the harvesters."

9   The explanation for why football coaches pat their players on the butt? The gesture engages the Lower Pole of heart-and-guts Middle-Axis sensibility. (Businesspeople tend more often to be Lates. A handshake expresses the needed greater distance.)

police officers, carpenters, and professional athletes. It is they who do the hands-on protecting and heavy lifting of society. They like to get things done. Henry Wadsworth Longfellow's familiar poem "The Village Blacksmith" reflects Middle/Lower values:

> Under the spreading chest-nut tree
> The village smithy stands;
> The smith a mighty man is he,
> With large and sinewy hands,
> And the muscles of his brawny arms
> Are strong as iron bands.
> His hair is crisp, and black, and long;
> His face is like the tan;
> His brow is wet with honest sweat,
> He earns whate'er he can,
> And looks the whole world in the face,
> For he owes not any man.

Some descriptive words and common qualities for the Middle-Axis quadrants are shown in Figure 6-5.

Upper/Inner	Upper/Outer
moral stature, aptitude for mentoring and teaching	natural leadership ability, organizational adeptness, action orientation
unpretentiousness, commitment to home and community	toughness, loyalty, capacity for hard work
Lower/Inner	Lower/Outer

Fig. 6-5. Middle-Axis Attributes

Shortcomings again tend to express the flip side of common strengths. For example, because we see less of both the intuitive sensitivity common in Early-Axis patterns and the refinement and differentiation found in more Late-Axis sensibilities, the attitudes and beliefs of some Middles can seem to others coarse or simplistic, a conclusion reinforced by the common Middle-Axis tendency toward concreteness. (Middles are notorious for retelling all the details of an event rather than summarizing and abstracting.)

The Middle's great capacity for control can also be an impediment—indeed, sometimes his or her undoing. The Middle/Upper's need to be on top (both of others and his or her own impulses) can make it hard either to surrender authority or to let go of oneself sufficiently to find fulfillment. The Middle/Lower's tendency to feel most safe (and in control) if someone else is in charge can also be limiting. If Middle/Lowers are not careful they can become passive or undermining of authority. (As Montaigne said, "Obstinacy is the sister of constancy.") The need for occasional release of control can make alcohol attractive for both Uppers and Lowers, with the potential for abuse.

Where Symptoms prevail in Middle-Axis, control dynamics become amplified. In Middle/Upper/Inner patterns, this can take expression as ardent moralism or more personally in harsh self-criticism or compulsiveness. With Middle/Upper/Outer patterns, it can manifest interpersonally in abusive patterns or socially in racist and dictatorial attitudes and actions. With Middle/Lower/Inner patterns, we can see passivity, undermining behavior, and not infrequently, through undermining oneself, depression. With Middle/Lower/Outer patterns, the struggle from below usually gets acted out more directly in oppositional tendencies and aggression—or sometimes criminal behavior. (The great majority of people in prison are either Middle/Lower/Outers or Early/Lower/Outers.)

As far as the body, Middles tend to carry their Aliveness predominantly in the muscles and viscera. The muscle mass in Middle-Axis patterns characteristically exceeds what one would expect just from exercise (the isometric posture keeps the musculature in a constant state of exertion). Where the Middle/Upper/Outer predominates, this manifests in the classical "machismo" body, with major mass concentrated in the chest, shoulders and neck. Where Middle/Upper/Inner predominates, we tend to see a more symmetrical, wiry, or block-like body.

In Middle/Lower personalities, the visceral and muscular layers of the body are again most engaged, though here, especially with Middle/Lower/Inner, the focus shifts more to the viscera. Structurally, we find the complement to what we saw with more Upper Pole patterns. Again there is isometric tension and, with this, structural hypertrophy, but here the primary engagement is from below. Where there is a preponderance of more Outer aspect dynamics, we see again a block-like body, relatively symmetrical but strongly bound. Where the Inner Aspect predominates, the mass shifts into the belly, hips, and thighs.

Identifying words and phrases given to me by Middles include: "A good education is the key to a productive life. Teachers are our real heroes."—"Politics has to do with power, who has it and who doesn't."—"Never say die."—"The caterpillar does all the work and the butterfly gets all the publicity."—"Children, family, and God. In these lie life's true riches."—"I like people who are plainspoken, people who are unpretentious and forthright."—"Shit or get off the pot."—"There is nothing more precious than a good friend."—"A good leader has to be willing to make tough, often uncomfortable decisions. You will not always be loved, but in the end you will be respected."—"A penny saved is a penny earned."—"I know how to be there for others."—"You play the cards you're dealt."—"Few things give me more pleasure than working in my garden."

Late-Axis Patterns

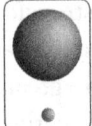

Late-Axis patterns correspond to the finishing and polishing stage in formative process—the developmental period that turns our attention to questions of detail. Rational/material intelligence orders experience, bringing emphasis to the intellect and to the more refined (manifest) aspects of the emotional and the aesthetic. Because Late-Axis is the most natively Outer of patterns, Lates tend to function most easily and efficiently in the external world.

Following are a few words from well-known Lates: From Francis Bacon, "Reading maketh a full man, conference a ready man, and writing an exact man." From Elizabeth Cady Stanton, "In a word, I am always busy, which is perhaps the chief reason I am always well." From Alfred, Lord Tennyson, "'Tis better to have loved and lost, than never to have loved at all." From John F. Kennedy, "In times of turbulence and change, it is more true than ever that knowledge is power." From Bill Blass, "When in doubt, wear red." From Ted Koppel, "Look...ours is a business of appearances, and it's terribly important to appear to be self-confident...the minute you give evidence of doubt, people are going to eat you alive." From Alexander Dumas, "Nothing succeeds like success." From T.H. Huxley, "Science is nothing but trained and organized common sense." From Sophie Tucker, "I have seen poor and I have seen rich. Rich is better." And from Bertrand Russell, "To be able to fill leisure intelligently is the last product of civilization."

Lates often become professors, writers, lawyers, CEOs, scientists, fashion models, ballet or modern dancers, Wall Street financiers, marketers, or actors. More than with any other axis, various individuals can differ widely in their inclinations.[10] Within Late-Axis we find the people who are most rational in their perspective, and also those who tend most toward the romantic. We find the people who are most materialistically driven, and at once many of those most committed to artistic and intellectual pursuits where monetary remuneration is often slight. We find the people most aggressively in the world, and also many of those most internal and reflective in their proclivities.

Some familiar Lates include: Walter Cronkite, Marie Curie, Carl Sagan, Julia Roberts, Sammy Davis, Jr., Elizabeth Taylor, Jonas Salk, Alistair Cooke, Frank Sinatra, Bertrand Russell, Mikhail Gorbachev (really more Middle than Late, but notable because he embodies significantly more Late than any previous Soviet leader), Ted Turner, Harry Belafonte, Gloria Steinem, Woodrow Wilson, Johnny Carson, Steve Martin, Peter Lynch, Clark Gable, Kenneth Clark, Mikhail Baryshnikov, Peggy Fleming, William F. Buckley, Norman Rockwell, and Robert Redford.[11] Less savory sorts tend to engage in white collar crime, so are less visible and less often prosecuted than Early and Late lawbreakers—Michael Milkin comes to mind, along with those involved in the Enron debacle and the investment bank excesses of the 2008 financial collapse.

Of all temperaments, Lates tend to move most effectively in the world of form and structure—whether the sphere is ideas or professional accomplishment. When we say someone is scholarly or intellectual, most often we are making reference to a Late. Lates tend to

---

10 A look to the patterning diagram helps explain. It is here that we see the greatest natural separation between poles.

11 The word "celebrity" more often than not refers to a Late.

be socially comfortable and speak persuasively. And more than other temperaments, they tend to be materially successful. They are the most natively competitive and the most likely to value external reward.

Lates can be quite creative, but their creativity tends to be of a different sort than the whole-cloth originality of Earlies. Late-Axis scientists are more likely to be recognized for the precision and detail of their experimental work and for their ability to bring together existing work to reach new conclusions. Late-Axis visual artists, dancers, and musicians tend to work from established traditions or written scores and make their primary creative contributions through refinement and subtlety of aesthetic expression.

Lates tend to value and manifest the skills of social discourse more than other temperaments. This can take highly formal expression—etiquette and the fine art of diplomacy come naturally to many Lates. (From Lord Chesterfield, "Politeness and good breeding is absolutely necessary to adorn any, or all, other good qualities or talents.") As often, it manifests in a simple ease and comfort in the social sphere. Lates commonly have an unusual degree of interpersonal adeptness and flair. When we say someone has "personality" or "style," when we say someone is sophisticated or looks "sharp," we are usually referring to a Late. More than other temperaments, Lates attend to physical appearance, and generally pull off looking good. (Ralph Waldo Emerson reflected on having "heard with admiring submission the experience of the lady who declared that the sense of being perfectly well-dressed gives a feeling of inward tranquility which religion is powerless to bestow." Estee Lauder offered this advice: "Never just 'run out for a few minutes' without looking your best. This is not vanity—it is self-liking.")

The qualities that most stand out with Upper Pole, Late-Axis personalities are clarity of thought, verbal facility, and the ability to deal easily and effectively with the material world. With Late/Upper/Inners, the more intellectual of these qualities stand out. University professors, scientific researchers, and nonfiction writers commonly have Late/Upper/Inner personalities. Late/Upper/Inner is also where we find the greatest appreciation for the formal. Refinement and etiquette are Late/Upper/Inner notions. (In the words of Lady Montague, "Civility costs nothing and buys everything.")

With Late/Upper/Outers, more external and material concerns take center stage. It is here that we commonly find the people who are most facile with money and the complexities of the business world—corporate executives, economists, media moguls, and stockbrokers. We also find "serious" media personalities such as television commentators. While for Late/Upper/Inners the intellect resides most comfortably in the ivory tower, Late/Upper/Outers apply it to the most worldly concerns.

With Late/Lower patterns, qualities such as gregariousness, talent, sensuality, and emotional presence often most stand out. Of all personality groups, Late/Lowers are most likely to enjoy being "on stage." People in the performing arts most always have at least some Late/Lower in their makeup, as do the great majority of fashion models and television entertainers. Late/Lowers often have a rich sense of the dramatic, as well as the smoothness and presence needed to pull it off. Sophia Loren once observed that "sex appeal is fifty percent what you've got, and fifty percent what people think you've got."

Where the balance is toward Inner, the dramatic focus highlights emotional and aesthetic nuance. Late/Lower/Inner is the most common personality style of people involved in artistic performance—dancers, actors. Novelists and visual artists of a more realist bent also often find their creative source in Late/Lower/Inner sensibilities, as do interior and fashion designers.[12]

With Late/Lower/Outers we find the people with the greatest capacity to project and be visible. Late/Lower/Outers are those most successful at marketing and promotion (both of things and themselves). They define the entertainment industry—glamour and celebrity are Late/Lower/Outer words. The more glittery and flamboyant of actors and actresses have Late/Lower/Outer personalities, as often do the more packaged and promoted of popular musicians. More day-to-day, Late/Lower/Outers may work for advertising agencies or sell high-end clothing or real estate.

---

12 Note that even the most Inner of Late-Axis personalities may pursue what might seem Outer pursuits. Because Late dynamics are the most manifest, even sensibilities that are particularly internal may take expression in the world of forms.

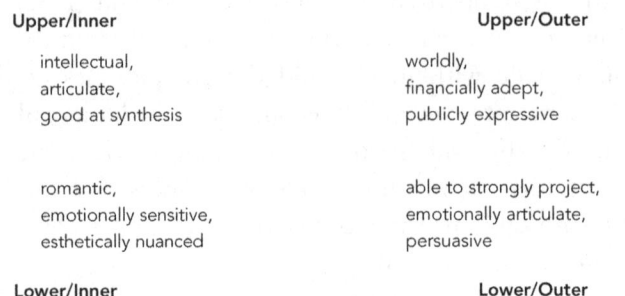

Fig. 6-6. Late-Axis Attributes

Weaknesses again reflect the flip side of common strengths. Lates who are especially intellectual, competitive, or materialistic can have a difficult time with emotional closeness or anything that requires creative depth. It is not so much that they fear these things (as can be the case with Early/Uppers and Middle/Uppers) than that they often live a long way from where these things reside. Also, Late/Uppers can lose perspective in their obsession with detail and the ideal. The other side of the Late/Uppers' valuing of objectivity and excellence is a common tendency to be overly perfectionistic and often critical. Achievement is the Late/Upper's great two-edged sword. While Late/Uppers tend to do very well at climbing the ladder of success, often they have a difficult time stepping away from it.

Late/Lower failings are related, but more personal. Excessive outgoingness can translate into feeling distant from oneself—and paradoxically also from others. Breezy can become only superficial; smooth only slick; romantic seductively manipulative. (Oscar Wilde, a Late/Lower who often played humorously with the gifts and blindnesses of Late-Axis life, quipped, "In matters of sincerity, style, not sincerity, is the vital thing.") Competitive spirit can become cattiness and backbiting. (Bette Davis once remarked of a fellow actress, "There goes the good time that was had by all.") Isolation can be compounded by the Late/Lower's reluctance to "look bad" by admitting aloneness or confusion. Late/Lowers are often tormented by self-doubt—particularly in relation to physical appearance (ironic in that it is they who most easily succeed at accepted standards of beauty).

Where we see Symptoms, the most common Late/Upper pattern is the "workaholic," one who uses activity as a way to stay high. When life situations challenge the ascendant posture, we can see marked anxiety and often suicidal degrees of despair. The increasing use of the term "burnout" points toward a growing willingness to examine the partialities of these patterns.

Symptoms with Late/Lower personalities often find the person feeling estranged, both from themselves and from others. Because the Late/Lower's connection with feelings is from the more surface layers of the emotional, it can easily be disrupted. Late/Lower/Inners especially can become frightened and withdrawn. One of the great traps for people with this temperament is that their identity is often so tied to being visible and on stage, that they can't take off their smile and admit their aloneness and confusion. Not surprisingly, eating disorders are especially common in Early/Lower young people. For related reasons, Late/Lowers often have a difficult time with the changes of life's later years.

As far as body dynamics, the person with a Late/Upper personality tends to carry their Aliveness predominantly at the body surface, and vertically in the regions of the face, head, and hands. The musculature tends to be taut and the body lean. Where Symptom effects are pronounced, both movements and tissue quality tend toward the rigid. With Late/Lower personalities, Aliveness tends similarly to be carried primarily at the body surface, but here it is distributed fairly evenly. Where there is concentration, it tends to be in the regions of the face and genitals.

Some words from the diverse world of Late-Axis sensibility: "I like to relax by listening to classical music or reading a good book."—"I was usually quite popular in school. I am still the person who can take a dull party and bring it to life."—"I don't like to admit it, but I can be pretty competitive. I like to win."—"I feel very at home in the world of ideas."—"I make lists. Sometimes I even make lists of lists."—"I like to feel classy and put-together. Presentation can make all the difference."—"I would make a good television news person."—"In the end, most of the world's problems are economic."—"I like performing. I love the feeling that comes from connecting deeply with an audience."—"Diamonds are a girl's best friend."—"I can be a bit excitable. People say they like this in me. They think I'm a fun person.

But sometimes it gets in the way. I get scattered and people think I am less intelligent than I really am."—"I love the feel of silk pajamas."

CSPT's Role in the Early Development of CST

Beginning to recognize how personality differences might relate to creative patterning more generally had a major impact on the very early stages of CST's development. In an important way, it was with these recognitions that it first became fully clear to me that what I was attempting to accomplish would require not just new ideas, but a major leap in understanding.

My native temperament is largely Early. In keeping with this fact, when I started to write *The Creative Imperative*, the lens with which I saw the world had a strong Early-Axis bias. But as I wrote, I could not escape that where the ideas were taking me was more and more often challenging my Early-Axis assumptions. I was confronted initially with the simple fact that Middle-Axis and Late-Axis sensibilities were each also creative. But ultimately I was confronted more deeply. I had to face that what I was trying to do would require not just some expansion of the lens I was applying—being somehow more inclusive in my considerations—but a fundamentally new kind of perspective.

A year into work on the book, I gathered the pages I had written and placed them in the fireplace. It would not be enough to simply revise and edit what I had written—the old story was somehow embedded in every sentence. I had been very happy with much I had written. Indeed, it had seemed quite inspiring. But if I was to honor what gave the book a reason to be written in the first place, I would need to again start from scratch. It has been said that good writing and thinking requires that one be willing to kill one's "children"—and particularly those one finds most beautiful. In the development of CST, this was one of the most important "killing one's favorite child" moments.

The Power of CSPT Perspective—Two Stories

I'll share a couple of temperament-related stories. Each illustrates ways in which the CSPT can be applied and also the power of the kind of perspective the framework provides. The first concerns the person who for many years worked most closely with me on this aspect of the theory and how she first came to appreciate its contribution.

She had previously taught university courses on conflict resolution and communication. These courses included some basic ideas about personality differences. She now was taking part in one of my extended trainings.

My colleague had two daughters. One daughter had a Late-Axis personality style not too different from her own (my colleague's temperament spanned Middle/Upper/Inner and Late/Upper/Inner). The second daughter was decidedly Early and also quite Inner. She frequently left my colleague baffled, and often they bumped heads.

After one particularly unsettling interaction, my colleague asked if she could explore her confusion in the training. She and the Early-Axis daughter had had an argument, and my colleague had tried to apply the tools that she had so often taught others for dealing with such circumstances. She made direct eye contact with her daughter, asked her to describe her feelings, and then fed back what she had heard. The daughter responded by breaking into tears, running upstairs to her bedroom, and slamming the door. My colleague started to go upstairs and try again, but then somehow sensed that this would be a mistake.

When she shared this story in the training, I proposed that while her approach would likely have worked well with a Late and adequately with a Middle, it wasn't likely to work with an Early/Inner. Asking her daughter to describe her feelings and then repeating back her words would imply that words could capture what she felt (which for an Early will rarely be the case). And direct eye contact could easily feel like intimidation. Predictably, instead of my colleague's daughter feeling seen and heard with her well-intentioned strategy, the daughter had felt the opposite.

I suggested to my colleague that she try a very different approach if her daughter again retreated upstairs in response to conflict. First she should let some time go by. Then she should walk quietly up the stairs and knock gently on the daughter's door. Then after a pause she should walk quietly into the room without making eye contact and sit on the floor with her back to the bed. She should sit there for a couple minutes without saying anything. Then she should simply whisper "I love you" and return downstairs.

My colleague promised to try this approach and report back. The result: The daughter came back downstairs after about a half hour and said nothing. Indeed, the topic of concern never came up again. Somehow it had been resolved. This experience convinced my colleague that she needed ways of thinking that could address personality differences at a deeper level than those she had learned and had been teaching.

The second story comes from my own childhood. It combines Patterning in Space with Patterning in Time observations. And of particular pertinence to a creative frame, it draws specifically on the creative parallels between Patterning in Time and Patterning in Space observations.

My mother was an Early (primarily a visual artist). In contrast, my father was dead-on Middle. When I was a young child (in my Early-Axis developmental stage), my mother was an exceptional parent. We would create songs, make and act puppets, take long walks in nature. Together we immersed ourselves in the imaginal.

While I appreciated my father during this time, the connection was not nearly as strong. But an odd thing happened as I reached age seven or eight. My mother turned back to her studio. It was almost as if she was saying, "OK, I've done what I know how to do." And suddenly I felt less interest and significance in what we had done together. What had been a rich connection almost disappeared.

I might have felt loss and loneliness if it weren't for my dad. Just in time, there he was with fishing pole and hiking boots ready to accompany me on a whole different kind of creative adventure. I was beginning to move into Middle-Axis developmentally and I had a good Middle right there and ready to support and teach in just the ways I was needing. I had never really seen him before. And he had not really had a way to connect with me (particularly given that temperament-wise I have much more Early in me than Middle).

Because of their contrasting personality styles, my parents made a great developmental tag team. It is fun now to look back having CST temperament concepts to draw on. I am able to more deeply appreciate each of my parents (both their particular gifts and each of their limitations and absurdities).

Further Observations

This chapter's presentation of the Creative Systems Personality Typology has necessarily been only an overview. A few further observations help highlight key recognitions and clarify possible confusions.

First, a bit more attention to nuance is warranted. I've noted that while it can help for initial understanding to think of CST personality groupings as discrete categories, in fact pure types are rare. More often we see Earlies with some Middle or Middles with some Late. And we never find just Upper or just Inner. However extreme the temperament, Upper and Lower, Inner and Outer tendencies are each always present. To appreciate differences with any subtlety, we need to think not in terms of boxes, but balances and interplays.

This kind of additional nuance can provide valuable insights. A look to the temperaments we most commonly find with political leadership illustrates. Middle/Upper/Outer dynamics tend to predominate in the personalities of politicians. To be effective, a political leader needs to project strength and also have the ability to connect personally with the voters. But to be successful, politicians also need at least a touch of the Late's greater aptitude for detail, abstraction, and marketing. We could imagine a continuum with John F. Kennedy, Woodrow Wilson, Barack Obama, and Franklin Roosevelt on the Late-Axis end; Abraham Lincoln, Harry Truman, and Angela Merkel more toward Middle; and more narrowly conservative figures such as Richard Nixon, George W. Bush, and Margaret Thatcher almost pure Middle.

We should also note important observations about the relationship of Cultural Maturity and temperament. Right off, there is the essential recognition that each major temperament group, given necessary Capacitance, is equally capable of culturally mature perspective. No temperament has a leg up when it comes to Cultural Maturity.

It is also the case that all temperaments in potential have equally significant roles to play in a culturally mature world. And those roles are complementary. High-Capacitance Earlies are the most likely to provide us with needed fresh ideas. And while Middles frequently question innovation and are often the last to get on board, when a new idea passes the scrutiny of a high-Capacitance Middle, it is likely a good one. Middles are also some of the best at putting good new ideas into practice. High-Capacitance Lates contribute a keen analytical eye. In addition, they are especially adept at popularizing, which is essential when the time arrives for important new ideas to reach a broad audience. If you want potent culturally mature decision-making, put a team together that includes solid representatives from each axis.

With the growing need for culturally mature leadership, such understanding of temperament characteristics gains ever greater importance. Using the box-of-crayons metaphor, effective culturally mature leadership requires an appreciation for one's own specific "crayon," both one's particular temperament's significance in diversity as a whole and the blindnesses it can produce. And especially when collaboration is required, sensitivity to other people's specific gifts and vulnerabilities becomes similarly essential. We need a solid sense of how we can use crayons together and also how we can best draw on such interrelationship when confronting different sorts of creative challenges.

A further important recognition concerns how applying temperament distinctions most precisely and powerfully requires that we draw on all of the various kinds of patterning distinctions we have touched on. Certainly this is the case for Capacitance. Temperament conclusions can be highly misleading unless they are accompanied by attention to Capacitance. A person who has the requisite sensibility for a certain kind of contribution may nonetheless lack the Capacitance needed to effectively carry out that contribution's tasks or to function effectively in the relationships it requires.

We also benefit from making connections with other Patterning in Space distinctions. For example, I've made reference to how we can use Patterning in Space language to map out ideological differences. We find that people with different temperaments are most drawn to particular kinds of beliefs. This recognition can help us better understand not just why people reach certain conclusions, but also the particular contributions—and particular blindnesses—that accompany different conclusions. Here are some quick reflections pertinent to applying this kind of patterning observation—first to religious belief and then to political ideology.

When it comes to religion, Earlies tend to prefer the word "spirituality." We commonly see attraction to meditation, simply being in nature, and also to Eastern forms of thought and practice. Middles are the most apt to identify with religion in a traditional institutional sense. While the more conservative sectors of religious tradition often have particular appeal—fundamentalist Christian, more orthodox Jewish, more conservative Catholic or traditionalist Islamic views—the greater portion of attendance in all but the most liberal of congregations tends to be preponderantly Middle. While Late-Axis people tend to be more secular in their sensibilities, they are also often church or synagogue attendees. Commonly they opt for a religious persuasion that is more philosophical than ritualistic or moralistic.

I made a start with regard to political belief in Chapter Two in noting the general association of more archetypally feminine sensibilities with liberal advocacy and more archetypally masculine sensibilities with advocacy of a more conservative sort. Temperament provides more detail. If Earlies choose to engage the political world (politics can feel too Middle/Upper-Late/Upper for Earlies to get actively involved), they tend to be liberal or progressive/populist in their beliefs. They also tend to be more drawn to issues than partisan advocacy (and here to particular kinds of issues—for example, peace, the environment, or social justice). It is Middles who are most likely to identify with the political. Of all temperaments, they feel most at home with the struggles of conventional partisanship. Middle/Upper/Outers tend toward the conservative—that strong identification with control. Middle/Upper/Inners, with their additional touch of the archetypally feminine, can be either liberal or conservative. Middle/Lower/Outers are often the most ardently conservative, with beliefs of an extreme right-wing sort common. Middle/Lower/Inners can also be conservative (traditional values remain strong), but many associate more with liberal beliefs (we can find strong identification with worker's rights or the underprivileged). Late/Upper/Outers tend to be conservative out of identification with social and economic advantage. Late/Upper/Inners and Late/Lowers tend to be liberal, Late/Upper/Inners out of their humanistic values and Late/Lowers out of their identification with the feeling side of experience.

One application of this sort of observation proves particularly helpful for those interested in bringing more systemic perspective to understanding within a specific cultural domain or academic discipline. A close look reveals that the contrasting beliefs of differing schools of thought in any sphere tend to mirror the personality style biases of the school's originator. As illustration, in my field of psychology/psychiatry, B.F. Skinner was a Late/Upper/Inner, Sigmund Freud a Middle/Upper, and Carl Jung an Early/Upper/Inner. These men's contributions to modern psychology each directly reflect what we would expect from their temperaments' place within a larger systemic picture.

Certain commonly found temperament dynamics can initially cause confusion and warrant a closer look. In one—what CST calls "cross-polar" patterns—the pole a person identifies with and the pole they most speak from are not the same. We encounter a common cross-polar dynamic in the self-righteous victim who identifies with being oppressed while at the same time criticizing from a position of "on-high" superiority. This pattern is most common with Middles and Earlies. With Lates, we often encounter cross-polar dynamics when there is strong identification with the archetypally feminine in the context of Late-Axis sensibility's strong archetypally masculine leanings. One place we see this is with how Late-Axis academic thought that derives from left-hand sensibilities can manifest as a highly intellectual anti-intellectualism. (The worst of postmodern thought gets caught in this sort of contradiction.) Late-Axis cross-polar patterns are also common with political beliefs of the more progressive or liberal/populist sort. A common result is advocacy in which anti-authoritarian dynamics work to undermine the advocate's authority (thus the often startling ability of Democrats in the United States to shoot themselves in the foot in their attempts to win elections or get policy enacted).

Relationships between certain specific personality types can also cause confusion. One example involves two personality types commonly found in academia. The majority of professors have Late/Upper/Inner personalities. But we also see a fair number of Early/Upper/Outers. If an Early-Axis person's temperament is highly Upper Pole, he or she can be just as comfortable with the intellect and just as fascinated by objective inquiry. Useful clues for teasing them apart: The Earlies have a harder time keeping their hair combed and are frequently difficult to find beneath the "ecological complexity" of their offices. They are also less naturally comfortable with the structure of academic life. But we must go beyond behavior to the underlying temperament dynamic to really make the distinction.

We find a second easily confusing distinction with people of more artistic inclination. Artistic interests manifest most strongly with two temperaments that on the surface could hardly be more different: Earlies (more Early/Outers with the expressive arts) and Late/Lower/Inners. Dancers and visual artists come from both. We get a few temperament clues from looking at the form of the person's art. In dance, the

Earlies often most enjoy improvisation, while the Lates are going to prefer dance that is more choreographed. In painting, the Early artist is more apt to work abstractly, the Late artist more representationally. An essential insight makes the connection we see more understandable. While in a sense Early/Outer and Late/Inner reflects dynamics that are far apart, within each, the balance between more creatively manifest (more archetypically masculine) and more creatively germinal (archetypically feminine) is very similar. Early/Outer represents the most form-defined dynamic within the least form-defined axis. Late/Inner represents the least form-defined dynamic within the most form-defined axis. It is not surprising, then, that at least at first blush, these styles can appear quite similar.

Some of the most intriguing implications of the link between temperament and Cultural Maturity concern new ways in which temperament diversity is adding to our lives. In Chapter Four's examination of changes reshaping love, I observed how it has become increasingly common for people to feel attracted to potential partners from temperament groups different from their own. Such cross-type attraction is most common when individuals are beginning to live their lives as a whole in culturally mature ways. This change is predicted by Cultural Maturity's cognitive reordering. If love's attraction comes ultimately from our ability to make each other's lives more, and "more" today increasingly means the ability to hold the whole of systemic complexity, then we would expect differences that before might have produced only confusion and conflict to now become newly attractive.

Adding temperament diversity to love's equation doesn't at all make love easier. Whole-Person love by itself is demanding enough. The Whole-Person love task becomes even more demanding when the other person, along with inhabiting his or her own particular uniqueness, also lives in a territory of experience that even with the best of efforts we can never understand as directly as our own. But this added ingredient, in a further, timely and significant sense, is what makes partners in love potential "teachers" to one another.

In *On the Evolution of Intimacy*, I include a handful of stories that illustrate how relationships can go astray (and often also provide particular rewards) when people with different personality styles decide to share their lives. I'll mention one. It comes from early on in the relationship of two friends and colleagues of mine who would later get married. He is very much the Middle—a solid, down-to-earth engineer. She is an Early-Axis teacher—more creative, less predictable. They met and married fairly late in life. She had two sons from a previous marriage.

As a present, he bought her a four-slice toaster to replace her old two-slice version. To him, the toaster symbolized how deeply he was there not just for her, but also for the boys. He felt that he had purchased the perfect gift. Unfortunately, her response was to feel confused and a bit insulted. As an Early, the present made no sense to her. It said nothing about her as a creative person. And while being romantic was not a great priority for her, it seemed not romantic at all. On seeing her hurt feelings, his feelings ended up just as hurt.

They had an advantage in dealing with the situation because they were each familiar with personality style differences. Indeed, they had met in one of my classes. They now laugh together about how completely what was meant as a caring gesture failed. I often share the story in personality style workshops as an example of how fundamentally communication can go astray even with the best of intentions.

In today's world, a sophisticated understanding of temperament—both the gifts and limitations that come with particular ways of being in the world—becomes increasingly essential. And it does so with almost every kind of creative challenge we face, from finding identity without familiar cultural handholds, to seeking what is needed for healthy and fulfilling love, to addressing the newly systemic demands of the contemporary workplace, to the broader tasks of collective decision-making.

Common Questions

Answers to common questions people ask about the Creative Systems Personality Typology add further perspective:

How does the CSPT understand the etiology of temperament?

CST addresses the "what" of personality difference, and also the "why" in the sense of why the result is the kinds of differences we observe. But "why" in the sense of why a particular person ends up with a particular temperament remains a fascinating open question. I can say with confidence that something more than just learning is involved. While children frequently have personality styles similar to their parents, as often there are major differences—something we would not see if conditioning were the only factor. Some genetic mechanism is most likely, but other possibilities exist. Some kind of ecological niche dynamic, for example, certainly plays at least a minor role. Multiple children in a family tend to distribute within the personality spectrum—most likely as a way to provide distinct territory for each child's identity.

For Patterning in Space observations at other scales, questions of etiology similarly remain unanswered. For example, different countries can seem to have quite distinct "personality styles." In Europe, the stiff-upper-lip British can seem like caricatures of Late/Upper/Inner. The traditionally stolid posture of the German would seem most to reflect Middle/Upper. And it is difficult not to associate the romantic and aesthetic sensibilities of the French with Late/Lower. I have no idea why we see these patterns. Similarly, while I have made the empirical observation that sensibility in the East tends to be generally more Inner in relationship to the West's more Outer leanings, I don't have an answer for why this might be so.

How does the CSPT understand the relationship of temperament and gender?

The question of gender differences today produces rich—and often contentious—debate, and not just with regard to the nature of differences and why we might see them, but over whether differences exist at all. One group argues that men and women can't communicate because, innately, we think differently—men (in popular parlance, being from Mars) more linearly, women (being from Venus) more relationally. Another group claims that there are no innate psychological differences between men and women—arguing that any differences we find are products only of conditioning.

CST proposes that while there are more similarities than differences—and marked exceptions to the patterns we do see—certain generalities do hold up and are of value. (CST suggests that denying differences of any kind has more to do with ideology—a kind of postmodern Compromise Fallacy—than actual experience.) Two empirical temperament-related observations help capture CST's contribution in this regard. First, within any axis we see about equal numbers of men and women. Second, within this, we find on average about a 60/40 balance relative to gender between the more archetypally masculine and archetypally feminine poles—men with a greater leaning toward Upper Pole and Outer aspects, women toward Lower Pole and Inner Aspects.

Cultural Maturity's cognitive changes are needed if addressing gender differences in this way is to make full sense. In *On the Evolution of Intimacy*, I put traditional views of gender differences in historical perspective. I argue that just as traditional understandings of love have been based on projection, so too have past understandings of gender. I will address this topic in greater depth in Chapter Ten. For now it is enough to note that when we've viewed men and women as "opposite sexes," rather than seeing what is before us, we've been observing polar caricatures of gender attributes—projected gender archetypes. *On the Evolution of Intimacy* describes how perceptions of gender differences through history have taken the specific forms they have because of particular ways in which polarized perceptions manifest with each cultural stage. With Integrative Meta-perspective—and its more Whole-Person understanding of identity—we are able to more accurately see what is actually the case (that general 60/40 balance, with great diversity in style and role options, being the result).

Again, the question of etiology for the differences we do see is left unanswered. But an observation that comes from applying the lens of body intelligence supports the conclusion that something beyond just conditioning is most certainly at work. Women's bodies remain on average softer to the touch than men's, even with the same amount of exercise (consistent with a greater natural tendency toward Inner aspects). With this, men carry their center of balance on average about two inches higher than women (consistent with a greater natural tendency toward Upper Pole dynamics).[13]

---

13 A fascinating consequence of how a creative frame draws on the whole of intelligence is the way it helps us bridge the nature/nurture dichotomy. This is easiest to grasp with Patterning in Time distinctions. Culture (what we

How does the CSPT understand the relationships between temperament and ethnicity?

This topic, too, can be controversial, and at the same time it contributes useful insights. Again, we can start with some empirical observations. People of various ethnic backgrounds tend to differ not just in cultural mores and assumptions, but as well in the balance of personality styles within their populations. Sometimes differences we see are specifically a product of Patterning in Time (cultural stage). But we see the same general personality tendencies even if we remove the cultural stage variable.

The differences are rarely large, but they are significant. Among people of similar Capacitance, we find a somewhat higher percentage than average of Early/Lower and Middle/Lower personalities in Native American, South Sea Islander, Hispanic, and African American populations, a somewhat higher percentage than average of Early/Upper/Inner and Middle/Upper/Inner personalities in Americans of Asian background, a somewhat higher percentage than average of Middle-Axis personalities (both Upper and Lower) in Americans of Eastern European, Scandinavian, and Irish extraction, and a somewhat higher percentage than average of Late-Axis personalities in Americans of predominantly Northern European heritage.

That such claims can be controversial is legitimate given that they could be used to support prejudice. But at the least they help free us to make observations that we may otherwise tend to keep at arm's

---

would traditionally associate with the nurture side of the equation) comes to be viewed as an evolutionary story and part of our creative natures rather than as an essentially arbitrary set of taught behaviors. But the observation also applies with Patterning in Space concerns. At intelligence's extremes, we tend to think of the body more in terms of nature, the intellect more in terms of conditioning. In fact, each has more complex roots, but the simple recognition that all intelligences ultimately come into play takes us a long way toward thinking about the relationship of nature and nurture more systemically. This doesn't in any way make nature versus nurture questions less significant. Which most prevails in a particular situation continues to have essential implications. But it does help us get beyond our historical tendency to think in either/or terms.

length. It is fascinating how often modern conventions of thought and behavior can leave us blind to, or at least hesitant to voice, the obvious. For example, while African Americans are much more apt to excel at being athletes or musicians than people of Caucasian background, we tend either to hide from this fact or ascribe what we see to a lack of opportunity in other spheres rather than real differences. But it is hard to deny that deeper tendencies must also be at work (having played a little basketball, I have to accept that there is basis for the stereotype that "white men can't jump"—or at least not jump as well). The observation that people with Early/Lower and Middle/Lower temperaments, whatever their backgrounds, tend to be natively better at athletics or music, is not a complete explanation. But it does help us get beyond denial and begin to acknowledge real differences.

This kind of recognition can also benefit us in more specific ways. For example, it can help us be more creative when it comes to policy. An illustration: Traditional public education does very poorly at addressing the needs of Early/Lower and Middle/Lower kids—whatever their background. The aspects of intelligence where these personality styles on average most excel are largely ignored. Not surprisingly, youth from cultural groups where these personality styles occur with higher than average frequency tend more often than others to feel estranged in public education and to thrive there less well than one might hope and expect. This observation suggests that while ensuring that educational opportunities are equal and increasing the amount of educational content that specifically addresses the experiences of people with different backgrounds will be important to educational reform, just as important in the long run may be making education more responsive to our multiple intelligences and to the unique realities of different temperaments.

Can you say more about Pre-Axial dynamics?

I've described how, with rare exceptions, we don't find predominantly Pre-Axial patterns in healthy individuals. Such patterns are primarily of interest to people in the helping professions. But the perspective provided by using a temperament frame has significant implications both theoretically and for the tasks of intervention. It helps get us beyond some of the nature/nurture controversies that have marked much of modern psychiatry's history. It also helps make some of the Symptoms we see with severe mental illness more understandable. I'll make some quick observations for those who might have interest.

Pre-Axial patterns, having a special affinity with the most unformed parts of the creative, inherently confront a difficult circumstance. It is extremely hard to carry the major part of one's Aliveness in the earliest parts of the creative cycle and function effectively in the context of the highly form-defined reality of contemporary times. Because of this, we see Pre-Axial dynamics most often in situations where there has been some kind of major disturbance, either an extremely unhealthy childhood environment or a significant biochemical defect. These disturbances act at the most germinal substages to inhibit the person's capacity to move toward form.

This observation proves particularly helpful when thinking about psychotic processes. For example, it helps link what may seem like very different dynamics. With organic psychoses—where what we see is a result of direct tissue damage, internal toxicity, or an external pharmacologic agent—the effect appears to happen earliest in the creative cycle. Here we see a particularly fundamental kind of disorganization. In schizophrenic patterns, the effect seems to be somewhat later. Here, while we find a fragmenting of experience, we can also usually recognize a kind of underlying order. In the affective psychoses—severe manias and depressions—the dynamic intercedes later still, when there is beginning establishment of structure. Here we encounter the even more organized response of severe polarization. The fact that schizophrenic and affective patterns often blend and overlap is easily understandable within this framework.

This way of framing psychosis can also help us bring more nuance to how we think about symptomology.[14] For example, schizophrenic symptoms can be thought of in terms of two counterpoised dynamics. First, they reflect the Pre-Axial unformedness of the system. We commonly see such symptoms as hallucinations (the taking of inner reality for external fact), loose associations (a lack of organization in thought), delusions (commonly reflecting a loss of boundary distinction—for example, the belief that a person on TV is talking directly to you), and withdrawal (from the world of things). At the same time, such symptoms give expres-

---

14 I use the word "symptom" in its small "s" sense here, as the etiologies for what we see are most often far from clear.

sion to a particular kind of structure, a making of form from what is available within that particular reality. In an important sense, the psychotic response is not so much a disintegration of the psyche, as an attempt to salvage it. Those loose associations make very effective boundaries. Delusions function to create unique identity and, along with hallucinations, provide a safe sense of connection and communication with others. The common bodily disorganization in chronic patterns—in which the different body parts seem fragmented—reflects each of these complementary mechanisms, being a kind of disruption and, yet, a very effective way to keep the whole from merging into unity.

I've proposed that this conceptual vantage helps address historical nature-versus-nurture controversies. While it doesn't once and for all reconcile disagreements over whether particular psychotic patterns result from biochemical defects or aberrant childhood experiences, it does help us think about options more systemically. Many kinds of factors can interrupt the germinal substages of the creative cycle. Biochemically the cause could be a genetic defect, one that affects either the general capacity for rhythmic progression or the child's specific ability to establish early life bonds. Environmentally, it could be a family matrix in which primary bonding is disrupted or, alternatively, where little if any individual identity is tolerated within the system. I think of the various psychotic patterns as "final common pathways" for a multiplicity of often interwoven etiological processes. The connecting link is that symptoms serve creative/protective functions expressive of the unique reality and the unique needs of the Pre-Axial part of creative experience. (At present, with the advent of modern genetics, the biological or "nature" side of the argument tends to be winning most of the battles. And with new brain imaging techniques, we are seeing clear anatomical changes in certain cases. But these kinds of beliefs tend to go in cycles. The more "nurture" side of the argument could well flex its muscles once again.)

Personality Style Exercise:

How would you describe your temperament within the Creative Systems Personality Typology? How does this observation fit with your personal strengths and weaknesses? Also how would you describe the various people who are most important in your life within the typology? Are there ways these similarities and differences between you and these various people influence communication with them. And how do you experience these similarities and differences in how you add to each other's lives?

CHAPTER SEVEN

A Creative Lens and the Power of Comparison: Separating the Wheat From the Chaff as We Look to the Future

The book's overview of Creative Systems Theory patterning concepts now complete, let's turn more specifically to comparison. Distinguishing CST's ideas from notions with which they might be confused provides one of the best ways to clarify and refine understanding. Better appreciating what CST doesn't say helps give us a more solid grasp of what it does. And by letting us test if CST's conclusions best fit the evidence, comparison also helps substantiate a notion's accuracy. Comparison also helps us confirm the importance of ideas. If a CST notion is not just different, but different in ways that take us a solid step forward in our thinking, we have major evidence for its significance.

Comparison can help us at any time, but it has particular importance with the essential beginning task of taking first steps into culturally mature territory. The common tendency when we encounter a new idea is to assume it will work within assumptions we are familiar with. If we somehow confront problems, we are likely to try to force-fit the idea. Careful comparison helps us to appreciate when familiar assumptions fail us—and to perhaps even find excitement in discovering that more than what we have known before is being asked of us. Given that Integrative Meta-perspective results not just in fresh ideas, but in a whole new kind of idea, such first-step recognition takes on added importance. And given the audacity of my claim that the application of a creative frame makes it possible to apply that new kind of idea in all parts of our lives, it takes on further importance still.

I've observed four essential ways that CST redefines understanding. It reframes human cognition, and with this, our understanding of how we experience truth. It provides a more dynamic, specifically developmental picture of history (and of human change processes more generally). It offers a way to understand our time's particular tasks and opportunities. And it gives us the basis for a detailed pattern language that meets understanding's new requirements. Over the course of the book, I've made more limited comparison observations with regard to each of these major contributions.

With this chapter's comparison observations, I will focus on big-picture distinctions rather than patterning detail such as differences in how we interpret the specifics of history or temperament. These more overarching comparisons will be of two general sorts. Some will focus most on how CST views our time in culture's story and the challenges ahead for the species—on the concept of Cultural Maturity and its implications. Others will focus most on the general kind of concept that CST represents and how the theory goes about making needed distinctions. Often these kinds of comparison will interweave. As should now be clear, the concept of Cultural Maturity really only makes sense with CST's developmental/evolutionary picture of history. And for a creative frame to be fully understandable, we need an appreciation of Cultural Maturity's cognitive reordering.

I'll begin this comparison effort by reminding the reader of observations with important comparison-related implications from earlier in the book, such as how the kind of narrative CST Patterning in Time represents contrasts with more familiar notions of history, the way CST's systemic vantage takes us beyond more familiar kinds of systemic understanding, and how it is that culturally mature "crux" and multiplicity" distinctions offer a deeper and more complete kind understanding than we have seen before .

I will then expand on the concept of "scenarios for the future" that I introduced in Chapter Three. I will go into detail with regard to the five most common ways people conceive of times ahead and clarify how each differs fundamentally from CST's conclusions. I will also tie each of these pictures of the future to ways people think more generally and use these observations to further fill out the very particular kind of understanding Integrative Meta-perspective represents.

Next we will turn to a few more specific comparison tools. We'll reflect further on the notion of "steps" into culturally mature territory.

We'll take a closer look at how being alert to polar fallacies helps us recognize when ideas fail as culturally mature conception. And we'll more closely examine how an appreciation for personality style dynamics can alert us to biases in our assumptions.

We will conclude with some less obvious comparison topics that nonetheless have important this-from-that implications. We will look at some of the particular challenges that culturally mature leadership confronts when the leadership task involves not just right action, but being an advocate for culturally mature understanding. We will also take a closer look at the concept of Transitional Absurdity, how Transitional dynamics can result in beliefs that are not just distorted, but crazy. And we will return to the fact of paradox and look at how the specific kind that accompanies Integrative Meta-perspective provides particularly good evidence that its thinking makes the needed leap in understanding.

Previous Comparison Observations

I made reference to some of the most important comparison-related observations early on in the book. And in chapters since, I've further fleshed out these basic recognitions. We benefit from bringing some of these previous recognitions together. Each observation in some way relates both to Cultural Maturity as a way of understanding our time and to the power of CST's application of a creative frame.

In Chapter One, I described how an appreciation for narrative and the forms it has taken over time provides a ready way to recognize when ideas fall short. We examined how Modern Age heroic and romantic narratives each in different ways are based on myths of limitlessness, and also how postmodern narrative, in making options essentially endless, adds much less to understanding than we might hope. I observed how culturally mature narrative engages understanding's multiplicity in ways these previous stories could not and, in doing so, provides concrete guidance for the tasks ahead.

Also in Chapter One, I introduced the concept of systems and contrasted culturally mature systems understanding with two other kinds of thinking where the word "systemic" is often applied: mechanistic, engineering models on one hand and all-is-one, everything-is-connected beliefs on the other. I also described how a creative frame, by successfully addressing the Dilemma of Differentiation, makes possible a new kind of systemic thinking better able to address the fact that we are alive—and alive in the particular way that makes us human.

In Chapters Two and Three, I compared developmental/evolutionary perspective and other ways of thinking about change in human systems—and in particular about history. I emphasized how CST's claim that history is developmental distinguishes it at the level of fundamental assumption from historical accounts that view cultural change primarily in terms of inventions, leaders, and wars. And I used the Dilemma of Trajectory and the need for a more encompassing view of progress to distinguish where Cultural Maturity's changes take us from both utopian and dystopian conclusions.

A key comparison distinction I have made throughout these pages highlights the essential difference between ideology and culturally mature understanding. I've described how ideological beliefs take one part of a systemic complexity and make it the whole of truth. Most commonly "part" in this sense refers to contrasting here-and-now—Patterning in Space—aspects. But we've seen, too, how ideology is also a Pattering in Time notion. The differing narratives of various cultural stages can be thought of as ideological, with more here-and-now ideological differences manifesting as aspects of such time-specific stories.

The two observations that I first used to clarify the workings of Integrative Meta-perspective and then to support the use of a creative frame—the fact of multiple intelligences and the role of polarity in how we think—can also each be used for comparison. The recognition that a viewpoint associates a particular aspect of intelligence with truth helps us better appreciate both the fact that it falls short and the particular ways that it does. This applies to identification with any kind of intelligence—from the rational absolutism we find with a narrow scientism, to the emotion-based beliefs we see with romantic belief, to the mythologizing of the symbolic common with New Age thought, to views that equate body intelligence with final truth (Martha Graham famously asserted that "the body never lies," when in fact the body lies with high frequency, as we see with obesity and addiction). In a similar way, the recognition that a viewpoint is polar alerts us to the fact that its conclusions are ideological. And the particular kind of polar identification a viewpoint reflects alerts us to the specific kind of ideology it represents.

Chapter Four's deeper look at the concept of Cultural Maturity added the essential recognition that confronting the important challenges ahead will require skills and capacities new to us as a species—a wholly new kind of human responsibility, a new maturity in our relationships with limits, the ability to get beyond the polarized us-versus-them assumptions of times past, and more. The fact that these skills and capacities are new—and essential—provides important comparison insights. In addition, the way each ultimately makes sense only with culturally mature understanding helps us further distinguish the needed leap from thinking of times past. And the fact that each can be understood as a specifically "creative" capacity helps further support the particular pertinence of a creative frame.

In Chapters Five and Six I introduced a key comparison concept with the notion that we could think of difference in human systems in terms of "crux" and "multiplicity" distinctions. I observed that while we humans have always made related kinds of delineations, culturally mature "crux" and "multiplicity" notions reflect a fundamentally different, deeper, and more complete kind of distinction than we have been capable of making in times past. Appreciating these differences provides a ready way to understand how each of the three kinds of Creative Systems patterning concepts we have looked at are of a wholly new sort.

We can think of additional observations in Chapter Six as comparative in the sense that they highlight particular ways that CST Patterning in Space distinctions add to understanding. We saw in a further way how Integrative Meta-perspective helps us leave behind the projective dynamics that before have been the basis of bigotry (adding nuances that apply more specifically to temperament, gender, and ethnicity to earlier more general us-versus-them dynamics). We also examined how the fact that the Creative Systems Personality Typology draws on the whole of intelligence means that it engages difference in deeper ways than more familiar personality frameworks. And we saw how the way that it draws on the dynamics of creative organization helps us better appreciate how temperaments can work creatively together.

I've also described more specific CST concepts that effectively function as comparison tools. For example, we've seen how the Dilemma of Differentiation and the Dilemma of Representation each in different ways help us distinguish needed new kinds of understanding both from past more mechanistic ideas and ideas that identify instead with oneness, mystery, or the impossibility of knowing. We've also seen how the Myth of the Individual clarifies how both what it means to be a person and what it means to have a relationship changes fundamentally with Cultural Maturity's cognitive changes.

Scenarios for the Future

I spend a lot of time with people interested in what lies ahead—from self-identified futurists, to groups struggling to chart the paths of their professions, to individuals just generally concerned about what to expect going forward. Among all the diverse opinions, I hear a small handful of general conclusions about where as a species we are at and where we might be headed. Sometimes these conclusions are overt and eloquently articulated; other times they are only implied (though often dogmatically, particularly in groups of the like-minded). As frequently they exist more as unconscious assumptions, shaping beliefs from beneath the surface.

In my book *Cultural Maturity: A Guidebook for the Future* I contrast where Cultural Maturity's changes take us with the five most common ways of thinking about what may lie ahead. Here I will expand on these reflections, filling them out with observations from previous chapters in this book where doing so adds useful detail. This endeavor will serve our comparison task most explicitly by helping us refine our understanding of the concept of Cultural Maturity and its implications. But as important will be the insights it provides into how various kinds of ideological perspectives produce different understandings of truth and of the human endeavor as a whole.

The first two futures scenarios I will address—We've Arrived and We've Gone Astray scenarios—in opposite ways stop short of Cultural Maturity's threshold. I will touch on them just briefly. We will look more closely at the remaining three—what I will call Post-industrial/Information Age, Postmodern/Constructivist, and Transformational/New Paradigm scenarios. Each of these at its best approaches Cultural Maturity's threshold. But, as we shall examine, each is also vulnerable to conceptual traps that can lead our thinking far astray.

Importantly, these contrasting ways of thinking about the future represent much more than just alternative interpretations of the facts. They reflect overarching worldviews, distinct ways of understanding not just the future but also the past and the present, different stories about who we are and our human significance. More deeply, they reflect alternative kinds of cognitive organization, ways of thinking that draw on contrasting aspects of intelligence and different ways of structuring experience. Recognizing this depth of significance adds greatly to understanding. Certainly it helps us make sense of why we might reach such varied conclusions. It also helps us recognize when particular conclusions may include useful pieces of the truth and where limiting blindnesses will inevitably be found. It also helps us see how these diverse stories relate to one another and appreciate the possibility of a larger, more embracing picture.

Because certain of these worldviews can on the surface seem to reach similar conclusions, it helps in getting started to make a more basic kind of distinction. In Chapter Three, I described how we can divide common futures scenarios into two categories: those that are generally optimistic about what may lie ahead and those that are less than positive. We've Arrived and Post-industrial/Information Age scenarios fall into the first camp. Each in different ways interprets history's journey to this point as advancement and views the future as its logical consequence—either because we've reached that journey's triumphant culmination or because the future extends out along the same general path. We've Gone Astray scenarios most obviously fall into the second camp. They consider something to be fundamentally wrong or broken in our current human narrative. Transformational/New Paradigm views tend to fall a bit into both camps, seeing both positive future possibility and fundamental failing, though the best of such views may regard modern-day truths as simply outdated rather than misguided. Postmodern/Constructivist scenarios, depending on whose views we are talking about, can produce a grab bag of results—they may hide mildly optimistic predictions, suggest ultimately "gone astray" sorts of conclusions, or simply be noncommittal.

CST directly and equally challenges each of these opposite basic interpretations (and in the process helps us begin to tease apart the diverse ways in which such conclusions might result). With regard to the first, more history-affirming kind of conclusion, the theory makes clear that continuing on as we have cannot work for times ahead.

Indeed, the Dilemma of Trajectory suggests that the consequences would be catastrophic. With regard to the second, more condemning conclusion, CST emphasizes that each past cultural stage—including our most recent—while it has had its particular partialities and blindnesses, in its time has also taken us generally forward. CST also argues that further productive stages, at least as potential, lie ahead. CST's interpretation contrasts with Postmodern/Constructivist formulations in providing overarching explanation for why we see what we do today, and also by helping us more effectively formulate ways of thinking that can take us forward.

We've Arrived Scenarios

Advocates of We've Arrived conclusions regard the present as a cultural end point, as most people through history have done with regard to their particular present. They assume that current institutions and ways of thinking—political, religious, scientific, or economic—at most need a bit of further polishing.

Modern Western We've Arrived scenarios elevate (alone or in combination) the structures and assumptions of established democratic forms, free-market capitalism, contemporary monotheistic religion, material progress, scientific objectivity, individualism, and modern aesthetics. Such belief defines much of modern consensus reality. It may be ardently held or just assumed. A We've Arrived scenario's prescription for the future? We should keep doing what we are doing—and see if we can get others to follow our example.

While CST strongly affirms the achievements of the Modern Age, it makes clear that there is no more reason to assume that we've arrived at some culminating truth in our time than in any age previous—and every reason to hope that we have not. Culturally mature perspective regards neither modern institutional structures nor modern social values and aesthetics as last chapters. It argues that carrying modern Western culture's great successes unmodified into the future—in particular its onward-and-upward conception of progress and its extreme materialist, individualist values, but also its specific institutional structures—would, in fact, have most unfortunate consequences. It also counsels against assuming that modern Western cultural forms represent ideals to which people everywhere, irrespective of their cultural context, should ascribe.

We've Gone Astray Scenarios

Advocates of We've Gone Astray conclusions believe almost the opposite—that in some significant way humanity has failed. Often the implication is not just that we have made mistakes in judgment or policy, but that we have erred fundamentally.

We've Gone Astray scenarios take their most radical form in the predictions of impending Armageddon put forward by certain extreme religious groups and in popular culture portrayals of dystopian cataclysm. But other more restrained We've Gone Astray interpretations—such as those we see with environmentalist positions of a reactively pessimistic sort, with romantic and idealist philosophical beliefs,[1] and with certain historical views of both the political left and the political right[2]—can translate into an "it's all going to hell in a hand basket" cynicism that, while not as terminal in its predictions, can be just as severe in its criticism (and often just as limiting when it comes to useful action).

We've Gone Astray scenarios produce different advice depending on who is offering it. For some, the task is simply to fix what we've broken. For many, the answer lies in going back to the values and assumptions of some earlier time. For others, as with We've Arrived adherents, it means there is really nothing to do—in this case, because the damage has already been done. We have gone so far astray that we are beyond redemption.

CST views We've Gone Astray scenarios as inappropriately condemning and, in the end, diversions from the true magnitude of what the future asks of us. It affirms that modern times often find us in denial about much that desperately needs attention. And it agrees that we have made plenty of mistakes. But it also argues that most of the dilemmas we confront are the result not of our failings, but of our successes.

---

1 While philosophically idealist views are most characterized by their claims for a yet-to-be-realized ideal cultural end point, they often also include the assumption that getting there will be preceded by a time of destruction.

2 We tend to think that it is political conservatives who are most likely to identify with the past. But as I've noted, people of liberal/progressive bent can similarly be vulnerable to self-righteous negativity accompanied by its own kind of romantic idealization of previous historical times.

CST also makes clear that going back is not an answer. This is the case even if we wish to retrieve things we appropriately perceive to be lost. CST supports the claim that important truths—for example, about nature, about the sacred, about community, and more—have been "forgotten." But it emphasizes that if we are to give these truths the needed value going forward, this must happen not through returning to the past, but through coming to think in more mature and complete ways. It describes how the natural trajectory of cultural systems, like that of individuals, is growth—and proposes that that is what we have seen.

CST also warns of a particular danger that accompanies We've Gone Astray conclusions—how they can work as self-fulfilling prophecies. We see this danger most explicitly with views that make endgame scenarios inevitable expressions of God's will. But we can encounter something just as incapacitating and self-fulfilling with reactive cynicism. The cynic gets to feel right and superior while taking no real action that might make things different.

Post-industrial/Information Age Scenarios

Post-industrial/Information Age interpretations treat invention as the fundamental driver of cultural change and emphasize the transforming effects that inventions of the future will have on every aspect of our lives. In the end, they make technology the solution. Such views are common in popular culture and academic thought and find special favor in futurist circles. The digital revolution has given such beliefs a new generation of adherents.

CST affirms technology's essential role in future possibilities and applauds many Post-industrial/Information Age ideas. But at the same time, it directly challenges much that is most basic in Post-industrial/Information Age thinking. Most obviously, it does so in cautioning against the assumption that the consequences of invention will necessarily be positive.[3] It reminds us that inventing is not the same thing as using invention wisely. It also emphasizes that technological solutions will rarely in themselves be sufficient for addressing the tasks ahead.

---

3   The best of Post-industrial/Information Age formulations do not make this assumption.

The most limited of Post-industrial/Information Age thinking contributes little to this inquiry. It simply extends the Industrial Age's onward-and-upward story. But Post-industrial/Information Age thinking can also alert us to many of the questions culturally mature perspective highlights. Indeed, the best of Post-industrial/Information Age thought can put forward ideas that are nearly as far-reaching in their implications as those we have examined here.[4]

We see this result for two very different reasons. First, emerging technologies often serve to support Cultural Maturity–related changes. Global access to technologies that make possible greater resource efficiency, for example, will be critical to long-term environmental sustainability. And emerging technologies can support needed changes not just in what we do, but also in how we think. For example, decentralized information technologies thrust us into a systemically networked reality that just by its structure transcends conventional expertise and authority.

The second reason we may see related predictions has to do with unwarranted conclusions. Post-industrial/Information Age thinkers can predict outcomes that, while accurate and helpful, don't really follow from Post-industrial/Information Age interpretation. One example: Theorists who observe some of the more positive effects of decentralized information technologies that I just noted can then talk as if the needed kinds of psychological and social changes will follow naturally from them. This conclusion is not justified, certainly not if we are talking about the depth of psychological and social changes required if we are to bring needed wisdom to future decision-making. Indeed, often the effect is quite the opposite. For example, new information technologies can work to fuel the addiction to artificial stimulation and pseudo-significance that presents one of our greatest dangers going forward. Certainly, by themselves, they do nothing to counter it.

Culturally mature perspective applauds the contributions made by the more sophisticated of Post-industrial/Information Age thinkers.

---

4 Alvin Toffler and John Naisbitt, who provided some of the best early futures-oriented thinking for a popular audience, addressed broad social concerns. And some of the more insightful commentators on the information revolution reflect on specific social dilemmas.

And, at the same time, it warns even those who make an effort to think in more complete ways that they may need to reexamine their explanations if their ideas are to hold up—and, more importantly, if their ideas are to ultimately serve advancement. Put more conceptually, both explanations and solutions must be of more than just a right-hand sort if they are to help us effectively make our way.

Post-industrial/Information Age interpretation and CST more explicitly part company regarding the common Post-industrial/Information Age assumption that technological innovation is what ultimately drives cultural change. Integrative Meta-perspective affirms the importance of technology as a major contributor to change, but it also emphasizes that this explanation in isolation leaves out much of what is most significant—for understanding change, and more importantly, for usefully addressing the future. It argues that, more accurately, the causality goes both ways. Invention catalyzes change. But what we are capable of inventing is also always a function of who we are and how we are able to understand and perceive. In particular, innovation reflects our time in culture's story.[5] With regard to today's needed changes, while invention helps drive and support Cultural Maturity, it is just as true that invention sufficiently innovative to push us toward needed changes could not happen—and certainly would not be supported—without the new sensibilities and perspectives that Cultural Maturity begins to make possible.

Another way in which CST takes issue with Post-industrial/Information Age assumptions concerns just what needed changes in how we understand, if recognized, entail. I've described how the best of Post-industrial/Information Age thinking affirms the importance not just of technical advancement, but also of new ways of thinking, and how there can be similarities in the kinds of conceptual changes proposed. We often see emphasis, for example, on the importance of systemic understanding. But a strong mechanistic bias most often gets in the way of the needed sophistication of conceptual perspective. With regard to systemic understanding, what we encounter is rarely more than systemic conception of the engineering sort.

---

5 I've proposed cultural stage as an explanation for why we did not see something analogous to Europe's industrial revolution in China two thousand years ago.

We can miss the strong ideological component that commonly permeates Post-industrial/Information Age conclusions—for a now familiar reason: Technology includes much that we most mythologize in our time. Post-industrial/Information Age assertions can simply appear smart and logical. The hidden ideological thread becomes most apparent when such interpretation takes a utopian turn—think of science fiction–like prognostications from the middle of the previous century that claimed that we should all by now be living in glass-enclosed cities and flying around in personal transporters. With the computer revolution, techno-utopian beliefs too often become the norm.

A good place to see this common ideological component in Post-industrial/Information Age belief is with knee-jerk conclusions that with close examination become questionable at best. Consider the common assumption that going to Mars is a good idea. It very well might be, and even if the effort were not an ideal use of resources, it could be a lot of fun. But the notion that going to other planets is somehow a solution to problems here on earth is really quite crazy. If we can't get along with each other and act sustainably in a world that we've specifically evolved to live in, there is certainly no reason to think we could do so in a wholly inhospitable environment such as that on Mars.

We also encounter this ideological thread in the generally unquestioned belief in artificial intelligence circles that computers will soon become more intelligent than we are. In a purely computational sense, they already are—indeed much more intelligent. But belief that they might become more intelligent than we are in the ways that are most important to us—and certainly when it comes to the wisdom-related cognitive capacities that will be increasingly important to us in the future—reflects decidedly limited, and ultimately ideological ideas about the nature of intelligence.[6]

---

6 In an article in Chapter Nine, I propose that it would be best if we replaced the phrase "artificial intelligence" with the more accurate term "machine learning." I've emphasized how Integrative Meta-perspective draws on the whole of human intelligence's rich multiplicity. Recent advances in machine learning have added complexity and, through greater application of divergent processing, introduced additional "creativity." But the "intelligence" of even the most sophisticated of computers is very different from human cognition. I will argue that understanding these

This ideological distortion manifests in a particularly revealing way with recent claims that artificial intelligence will make eternal life finally possible (this by offering the option of wholly disembodied existence). Besides being a conclusion that again depends on a naïvely simplistic picture of intelligence, we see a kind of ultimate limits-denying ambition that is a giveaway for ideology. Having everyone live indefinitely would produce a world that no one would want to live in. Such extreme expressions of a technological gospel can titillate, but they are best thought of as Transitional Absurdity.

In summary: Post-industrial/Information Age interpretations, while often helpful, most often stop well short of providing the completeness of perspective our times demand. Indeed, because such interpretations tend to leave out so much that needs to be considered as we go forward—in particular, just how fundamental and personal that change must be—they often work to hide from us the depths of what our times require. In the end, too, they stop short at the level of "story"—they fail to provide ultimately compelling images for the future. Technological advancement is wonderful, but it is only part of what we need for a future that is worth living.

Postmodern/Constructivist Scenarios

Because of its important relationship to questions that culturally mature understanding begins to address, I've previously given the postmodern thesis significant attention. I've observed how the best of formal postmodern thought takes us right up to Cultural Maturity's threshold. But I've also emphasized that postmodern ideas vary greatly in their success at stepping over it, or even usefully recognizing its implications. Postmodern/Constructivist perspective today gives us at once some of the best and some of the weakest of future-related thought.

Postmodern belief had its start in the philosophical ponderings of existentialism. With the growing influence of social constructivism in the later part of the twentieth century, it came to be a central influence in academic circles. Today, postmodern sensibility has come to define much of popular culture, helping take us beyond the heroic/romantic

---

differences will be key to what is being called artificial intelligence not being the end of us.

narrative that until recently defined the larger portion of shared cultural expression. But while on both fronts—more formal thought and popular expression—postmodern perspective has made important contributions, in each case, it stops well short of where we need to go.

Formal Postmodern/Constructivist ideas share with the concept of Cultural Maturity that they question the absoluteness of past ways of understanding. They bring attention to our time's loss of familiar cultural guideposts and challenge final, "essentialist" truths in general. And they point out accurately that beliefs vary widely between cultures, evolve over time, and are subject to human manipulation. In all of these ways, they alert us to the Transitional predicament. But Postmodern/Constructivist ideas fail to help us understand at all deeply why today we see such fundamental questioning of past belief. And of particular importance, rarely do they offer much of real substance that can help us continue forward.

The best of formal Postmodern/Constructivist thought does make a start. Existentialism brings attention to how we are ultimately responsible—and, consistent with the concept of Cultural Maturity, responsible not just for our actions but also for the truths on which we base our actions. And with its emphasis on "meaning," it begins to articulate the kind of questioning such responsibility requires. I've described contemporary pragmatism as a postmodern contribution and proposed that it gives us a good general reference for understanding where needed answers take us. And social constructivism's thesis that we "construct" the realities we live in at least implies the possibility of crafting our world in more effective ways.

Postmodern/Constructivist thinkers also often make predictions that are at least generally consistent with a more systemically conceived picture—for example, how institutions and assumptions of our Modern Age will give way to more fluid and pluralistic cultural structures, and how understanding in the future will be more and more often characterized by multiple perspectives and often by contradiction.

But fears of falling back into old absolutes severely limit Postmodern/Constructivist thinking. Even the most fully developed ideas stop short of the critical next step. They fail to help us think with the needed complexity and new sophistication—to "construct" our personal and collective realities in the needed "post-essentialist" ways. The result is a precarious circumstance. We are easily left wandering aimlessly with only empty relativism to guide us. An anything-goes world offers new freedoms but, in the end, very little more.

Indeed, Postmodern/Constructivist beliefs often directly interfere with efforts to go further. Postmodern/Constructivist thinkers tend to assume that there are no universal truths, only truths specific to particular times and places. Formal Postmodern/Constructivist thinking can get stuck in an immediate skepticism toward anything that might look like an overarching idea.

I remember some thirty years ago introducing the basic ideas of Creative Systems Theory on a panel composed mostly of people with strong postmodernist leanings. At that time I had had little contact with such thinking. I was surprised to find what I presented met with knee-jerk dismissal—a response summed up by one person's assertion that CST was "just a construct." After a brief moment to collect myself, I offered that this criticism was nonsensical, that every kind of truth claim is ultimately a construct (including postmodernist claims). The essential question is not whether CST is a construct, but rather whether it represents a good and useful construct, a way of thinking that can provide effective guidance.

In fact, postmodern belief's common skepticism toward big-picture conception has admirable roots. Overarching ideas in times past have frequently had their origins in narrow and often self-serving belief. But Postmodern/Constructivist thought's common distaste for encompassing conception—indeed, conception of any substantive sort—undercuts its ability to contribute creatively to the larger conversation. Postmodern theorists tend to be better at critique than they are at providing anything constructive. And often theirs is a most limited—indeed, limiting and deadening—kind of critique. Identification with the inability to know for sure and with everything-is-equally-valid notions of difference ultimately undermines efforts to move forward.

Over the last couple of decades, Postmodern/Constructivist sensibility has come simultaneously to have less of a hold in academic circles and a growing influence in spheres of popular expression. With contemporary art, music, humor, and popular cultural more generally, we see increased use of irony and a mixing of influences often from far-flung sources. As with the earlier, more formal postmodern contribution, this popular influence has at once invited the beginnings of more multifaceted sensibility and resulted in efforts that often contribute much less than they claim. Too often we find popular expression that confuses the glib, ironic, and often simply random with substance.

Postmodern sensibilities find their most questionable contemporary manifestations in social media. Social media provides potential benefit in making it possible for everyone to have a voice and offering new ways to connect. But often what results is so superficial that it becomes the antithesis of significance. As everyone's voice becomes equal, content can reduce to little more than random expression. And apparent connectedness easily ends up in fact undermining real connection. Too often, we get distraction masquerading as meaning and relationship.

In summary: The Postmodern/Constructivist contribution, whether of a more formal or more popular sort, effectively voices the situation at Transition. When timely, it helps us get beyond traditional cultural assumptions, challenge ideology, and engage worlds that may seem only contradictory from the perspective of what we have known. But in the end, Postmodern/Constructivist beliefs fail to grasp at all clearly what, if anything, may lie beyond Transition's threshold. When this failure is extreme, we find sensibility that becomes, in effect, but another kind of Transitional Absurdity.[7]

Transformational/New Paradigm Scenarios

The last grouping is composed of people who frame our future task in terms of "changes in consciousness" or new scientific and spiritual "paradigms." With it we find both efforts that make a serious and concerted attempt to understand cultural change and a wide array of highly simplistic and ultimately unhelpful popular interpretations. Transformational/New Paradigm ideas at their best encourage us to think radically about what the future will require of us. At their worst, they present intractably ideological conclusions that are not in the end new at all.

---

7 There are thinkers of Postmodern/Constructivist bent whose contributions I very much respect—for example, Richard Rorty in the philosophical sphere and the many important contributors to constructivist perspective in education. But Postmodern/Constructivist views, even at their best, can provide but a start toward understanding either the present or the future.

Transformational/New Paradigm thinking can share important characteristics with culturally mature perspective. It highlights the need for change that makes a fundamental leap. It tends to emphasize that changes need to be as much about ourselves as about what we might do or invent. And almost always, too, it acknowledges the importance of seeing interconnections that before we have ignored and better including more archetypally feminine, left-hand values and sensibilities, along with those of a more right-hand sort.

Transformational/New Paradigm thinkers have sometimes brought these recognitions together in ways that at least knock on Cultural Maturity's door. Such perspective at its best is represented by historically significant contributors to big-picture understanding such as Carl Jung and Jean Gebser. Leadership theorists with Transformational/New Paradigm inclinations have also made useful contributions.[8]

At the same time, Transformational/New Paradigm ideas—certainly those commonly found with popular, New Age sorts of beliefs—frequently have nothing at all to do with Cultural Maturity. Indeed, they commonly have nothing to do with the future. More accurately they represent modern explications of timeless romantic, philosophically idealist,[9] or mystical beliefs. Transformational/New Paradigm ideas tend to reflect polarized identification with left-hand, archetypally feminine sensibilities and fail to recognize that truth claims that result get us no closer to culturally mature perspective than do ideological beliefs of a solely mechanistic sort. It is common for thinkers to conclude that real truth lies with classical Eastern belief or perhaps the more nature-centered beliefs of tribal

---

8 I think, for example, of Margaret Wheatley and Peter Senge.

9 I've described how philosophical idealism views history as progressing toward some social or spiritual ideal. Hegel's views illustrate philosophical idealism that posits a social ideal. With simplistic Transformational/New Paradigm thought, the ideal is more spiritual. I've described how we find a good example of philosophical idealism of the more spiritual sort in the early twentieth-century thinking of French philosopher and Jesuit priest Teilhard de Chardin, who postulated that history would end at a spiritual enlightenment–like "Omega Point." Both left-hand and right-hand sensibilities are acknowledged with philosophical idealism, but the left hand (essence or spirit) is seen as the ultimately determining force, driving and shaping the right-hand world of manifest forms (see Figure 7-3).

societies. Even Transformational/New Paradigm views that succeed at being helpful are commonly limited by their strong left-hand biases.

We can miss this left-hand bias with certain Transformational/New Paradigm theorists because they make science their primary focus. But at least with the more simplistic of Transformational/New Paradigm scientific writing, science ends up reduced to interpretation that makes interconnectedness, if not what it is all about, certainly primary. Notions from physics such as entanglement and the participatory role of the observer are often interpreted simplistically in this way.[10] Transformational/New Paradigm interpretations of science can then be as limited and ultimately unhelpful as the narrowest kinds of scientism—just limited and unhelpful in an opposite way. I've described how we find a similar kind of simplistic interpretation with popular systems writing that reduces to little more than an elaborate way of arguing for ultimate unity.

Transformational/New Paradigm ideas often find significant overlap with We've Gone Astray interpretations—more so than Transformational/New Paradigm supporters, with their commonly upbeat identification with things inspirational, might wish to admit. People of more romantic or philosophically idealist inclination can fall into either camp or vacillate back and forth. When people who make left-hand sensibilities primary look to the future, they are often drawn to images of collapse and resurrection. People who ascribe to Transformational/New Paradigm views can be some of the quickest to see the future in cataclysmic terms—whether physical cataclysm such as environmental catastrophe or fundamental failure of past worldviews.[11]

---

10 The mathematics of complexity (chaos theory the most familiar example) can suffer a related kind of misinterpretation with the pivotal role of uncertainty offering the attraction. Transformational/New Paradigm scientific interpretations also often give particular attention to "paranormal" kinds of phenomena. Sometimes with Transformational/New Paradigm thinkers we find good and interesting science. But more often a left-hand agenda means that data must be taken with a considerable grain of salt.

11 I remember being surprised at a conference I attended in the late 1990s on the Y2K millennium computer bug to find that the people who seemed most sure that the Y2K bug would have devastating consequences were not the Information Age types, but rather those of a more Transformational bent.

Sometimes Transformational/New Paradigm thinkers interpret history in ways that are at least superficially similar to what I've described with developmental/evolutionary perspective. Often, in particular, they depict early cultural stages in ways that can be quite helpful.[12] But at least with more simplistic interpretations, when they turn to making sense of our times and the challenges ahead, we tend to find descriptions that have more to do with utopian wishful thinking—some hoped-for new Golden Age—than anything that is really possible. And because, more often than not, what gets put forward as radically new is in fact idealized projection from a reality of times well past, the result is a picture of the future that, even if it were realizable, we would not want.

The conclusion that we would not ultimately desire the outcomes that Transformational/New Paradigm thinking tends to suggest should be obvious from earlier big-picture reflections on the kind of thinking that the future will require. But we find a particularly concrete kind of support in a characteristic we commonly find even with the most well-meant of Transformational/New Paradigm belief. Like ideology more generally, it tends to attract people with specific personality styles. Drawing distinction between culturally mature perspective and a version of Transformational/New Paradigm perspective that has gained popularity in recent decades—what is commonly referred to as "integral" thought—highlights this result. The language might seem to suggest conclusions similar to what we see with Cultural Maturity.[13] But while we find people who identify with such perspective sincerely attempting to address the future, such thinking most often has its roots in a spiritual form of philosophical idealism. At best the result is ideas with a strong left-hand bias. At

---

12 I've described how a deep appreciation for archetypally feminine sensibilities is necessary for any at all complete understanding of history's early stages (and today is generally lacking). Given the left-hand bias of Transformational/New Paradigm views, however, even where we find helpful observations, we must stay alert to where romantic projection may masquerade as accurate description.

13 In my earliest writings, I sometimes used the word "integral" to refer to systemic understanding that bridges polarities. I've since stopped using the term—replacing it with terms like "integrative" and "systemic" to avoid confusion with this fundamentally different kind of worldview.

worst, we find all-too-familiar New Age ideology, just dressed in fancier clothing. We also find that such views predictably attract specific kinds of people (in this case, people who have personality styles that are highly vulnerable to left-leaning conceptual traps).

Later in this chapter, I will further address how people with different personality styles tend to be attracted to specific kinds of ideological views. At this point, the important recognition is that the greater portion of Transformational/New Paradigm thinking—including that of the "integral" sort—misses the mark not just because it fails to be complete, but also because in characterizing the native sensibilities of certain temperaments as more enlightened, it is ultimately self-serving in the "chosen-people," ideological sense. With regard to the future, we do not benefit from further chosen-people worldviews, even if they are advocated with the best of intentions.

In summary: The best of Transformational/New Paradigm ideas, like culturally mature perspective, encourage us to look to the future and also to incorporate aspects of ourselves that through history we have forgotten. But only rarely do such ideas take us forward in ultimately useful ways. More often they reduce to spiritual wishful thinking—idealized images of the future that are not attainable, and, more importantly, that we would not want even if they were. Commonly they in fact have nothing to do with the future at all—being more accurately timeworn spiritual beliefs clothed in contemporary attire.

Further Comparison Concepts

CST includes other comparison concepts that relate specifically to the tasks of Cultural Maturity. Here I will fill out three of them that I have briefly referenced previously in the book: the idea of steps into culturally mature territory, the concept of polar fallacies, and the different ways that people with various personality styles commonly react to Cultural Maturity's challenge.

Steps into Culturally Mature Territory

We can draw on the fact that Cultural Maturity is a developmental concept in a couple of different ways that are each pertinent to the comparison task. We can treat Cultural Maturity as a threshold notion, a way to demarcate the fundamental newness of needed changes. But we can also think of Cultural Maturity as a territory of experience. This second approach lets us speak more quantitatively, in terms of the number of "steps" into culturally mature understanding a particular idea or action reflects. I used this kind of language in the Preface to introduce my strategy with this book.

Fig. 7-1. Steps into Culturally Mature Territory

There is no exact way to measure what comprises a "step," but we can make some crude generalities. With a first step beyond Cultural Maturity's threshold, we recognize the fact of new questions and avoid the most egregious of conceptual fallacies. A step further finds us able to frame major questions in more integrative ways and begin to grasp the importance of Whole-Person/Whole-System notions of identity and relationship. And a third step brings more conceptual insight into what makes culturally mature understanding particular (for example, an appreciation for how the various formal "Dilemmas"—of Trajectory, of Differentiation, of Representation—point toward something fundamentally new) and a solid capacity to distinguish ideas that succeed at being culturally mature from those that do not.

In the Preface, I made reference to how the number of steps I draw on in my efforts depends on the task and the audience. With introductory articles, I may limit my focus to Cultural Maturity's threshold. But when addressing specific contemporary issues, I will most often need to communicate from a solid step or two into culturally mature territory. With think tank groups convened to address major cultural challenges or whole domains of understanding, taking three or four steps together will often be required. And inquiry with my closest colleagues and expression at the edge of my own understanding frequently pushes out considerably further. I've observed that for this book, I've needed my thinking to at times venture at least ten steps into culturally mature territory. Content in these pages may engage understanding at any of these levels depending on the demands of the topic, and with articles, the particular audience that the content was originally designed to reach.

Polarity-Based Comparison Tools

In Chapter Two, I made the essential observation that needed new ways of understanding "bridge" the common polar assumptions of times past. I tied this result to Integrative Meta-perspective's larger whole-box-of-crayons picture and was careful to distinguish it from other outcomes we might confuse it with, such as averaging, compromise, or simple oneness. This basic observation provides a simple, yet powerful, comparison tool. If ideas succeed at bridging polarities in this sense, they likely make a solid start toward the needed maturity of perspective. Ideas that fail to do so necessarily stop short.

We can apply this basic comparison observation to the futures scenarios I've just described. Each scenario, at least in its more simplistic manifestations, reduces to polar argument. We've Arrived and Postindustrial/Information Age scenarios juxtapose with We've Gone Astray views to form the polarity reflected in the Dilemma of Trajectory—all is well juxtaposed with destruction and collapse. The more extreme of Postindustrial/Information Age and Transformational/New Paradigm interpretations reduce to opposing right-hand and left-hand ideologies. And while with Postmodern/Constructivist belief cross-polar dynamics often hide polarity's role, such belief can be in its own way the most intractably polar. (I've described how Postmodern/Constructivist thinkers can at once identify with the impossibility of knowing and assume a stance that produces a particularly intractable sort of absolutism.)

CREATIVE SYSTEMS THEORY

Previously I introduced how CST includes specific polar fallacy language. The terms Separation Fallacy, Unity Fallacy, and Compromise Fallacy refer to the three basic ways we can fail when attempting to engage polar juxtapositions systemically. This basic fallacy framework served as the foundation for my 1991 book *Necessary Wisdom*. There I used it to tease apart common conceptual blindnesses found with concerns as diverse as leadership, love, morality, medicine, science, religion, and global relations. Sometimes falling for a polar fallacy is a consequence only of momentary misunderstanding, but more often, it reflects underlying psychological/cognitive pattern. If we are vulnerable to polar fallacies, we are likely to fall for the same general sort of trap whatever the question we consider.

Adding some further detail to the earlier doorway image helps clarify how each of these kinds of polar fallacies misses the mark and also how they relate one to the other.

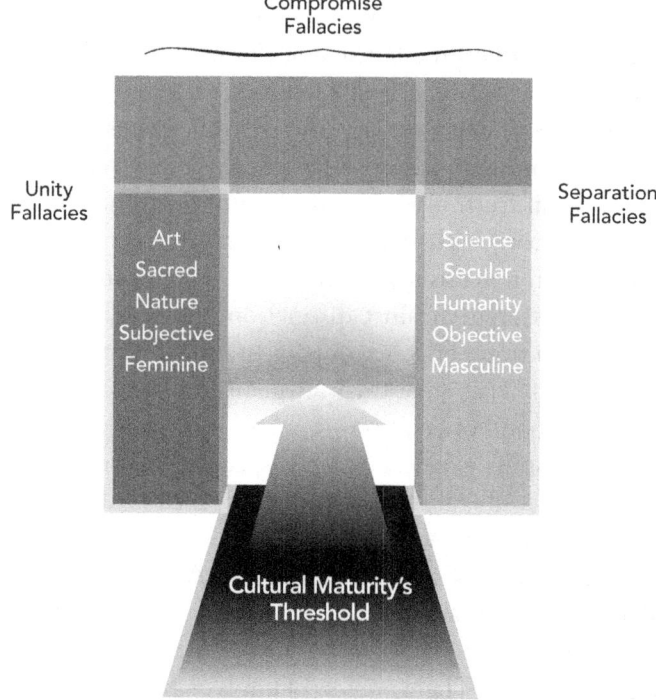

Fig. 7-2. Polar Fallacies

Separation Fallacies fall off the right side of Cultural Maturity's threshold. They identify with the archetypally masculine. In doing so they equate truth with difference—with perceived fundamental distinctions such as between men and women, the material and the spiritual, or the intellect and the emotions. They also give greatest value to the more creatively manifest side of the pertinent polarity (here men, the material, and the intellect).

Some common Separation Fallacies: We are each wholly unique, individual. Experts have the answers. Final truth is what can be rationally articulated and objectively demonstrated. Humanity is wholly separate from nature and has rightful dominion over it. Change is a simple product of cause and effect.

We see Separation Fallacies suggested with positivist and behaviorist views, and also with ideas that reduce to a narrow scientism. We also encounter Separation Fallacies with technological gospel beliefs that make invention the assumed answer to future problems, and with extreme materialist economic models that idealize unfettered free markets.

Unity Fallacies fall off the left side of Cultural Maturity's threshold. They identify with the archetypally feminine. Related Unity Fallacies might include: In the end, we are all one (differences are ultimately irrelevant). The ordinary person knows best (better than leaders and institutions). Final truth is what we know from within. The task is to always live in accord with nature. Everything happens for a reason, even if that reason remains mysterious (it is all connected).

Unity Fallacies argue against distinction and emphasize oneness. They may claim a transcendence of polarity, but in fact they very specifically take sides. They give their allegiance to the softer, more creatively germinal hand of creation—to the spiritual over the material, feelings over facts, the timeless over the specific. We find Unity Fallacies with romantic, liberal/humanist, philosophically idealist, extreme environmentalist, and New Age views.

Compromise Fallacies split the difference. A few related Compromise Fallacies are: We are all different in our own ways ("different strokes for different folks"). Good decisions come from everybody having their particular say. There are lots of kinds of truth, and each has its merits. Nature can be different things to different people. In the end, life is what we make of it.

Some Compromise Fallacies advocate a safe, additive middle ground. Others argue correctly for multiple options, but give us nothing to help us beyond this accurate but meager observation—they claim to address diversity but fail to address what makes differences different. Compromise Fallacies take us beyond black and white, but in the end only replace it with shades of gray.

Compromise Fallacies manifest most explicitly with Postmodern/Constructivist interpretations. But we also see them any time a person takes a polarity—content and process, masculine and feminine, or mind and body—and observes simply that both sides are true without also articulating just how they might both be true, and at least a bit about where that result takes us.

Polar fallacies of any of these three types represent shorthand concepts. As a start, no one type of fallacy is as distinct from the others as the labels might suggest. If you look closely, you will see, for example, that Unity Fallacies commonly carry a hidden Separation Fallacy, and that Separation Fallacies similarly often carry a hidden Unity Fallacy. A person who sees his own group as "chosen" and a conflicting group as "evil" succumbs to a Unity Fallacy with regard to his compatriots and a Separation Fallacy in relation to his adversaries.

There are also many versions of each type of fallacy. Some are common with certain personality styles and specific views of the future, some with others. For example, we can talk of multiple, very different kinds of Unity Fallacies. We encounter an intellectual sort of Unity Fallacy with academic and liberal thought that sides with the underprivileged and polarizes against conservatives and corporations. We confront a more ardent variety of Unity Fallacy with fundamentalist religious beliefs that ally with "family values" and polarize against intellectual elites. And we find Unity Fallacies of a more specifically spiritual sort with advocates of New Age or back-to-the-land philosophies.

It is also the case that certain kinds of thinking, depending on who is reaching the conclusions, can be used to argue for any one of these basic kinds of fallacies. Recognizing how this is so can help refine our understanding of how Cultural Maturity's changes alter understanding within particular spheres and also with regard to particular kinds of questions. For example, I've described how systems thinking can be used equally well to justify right-hand and left-hand conclusions. It can support an all-encompassing mechanistic picture or seem to reduce everything to an ultimate oneness. If we make systems thinking only about recognizing the fact that numerous apples-and-oranges variables commonly come into play, it can similarly become an argument for Compromise Fallacy.

In a related way, the postmodern thesis, depending on its advocate, can be used to argue for each kind of conclusion. Some postmodern theorists lean decidedly to the right in their positions (libertarian thought has postmodern roots), others lean more to the left (academic postmodernists can be almost Marxist in their sentiments), and it is possible to just as dogmatically believe that the task with everything is to split the difference.

Scientific concepts such as chaos theory that introduce uncertainty into an essentially mechanistic picture of reality can similarly be interpreted to support each of these ultimately unhelpful results. Such notions can be used to argue for a narrow scientism (to support the conclusion that even the most indeterminate of processes can be understood in ultimately right-hand terms), for spiritual conclusions (to argue for a universe in which mystery is part of everything), and for a postmodern kind of Compromise Fallacy (to support the claim that nothing can be known for sure).

The box-of-crayons image helps clarify just what is going on with polar fallacies and why even the most innocent-seeming versions leave us fundamentally short. The situation with extreme Unity Fallacies and Separation Fallacies is easiest to grasp. Either a more left-hand or a more right-hand "crayon" is calling the shots. In each case, the box's more systemic vantage and the larger part of systemic complexity that make up its contents, are absent. The situation with Compromise Fallacies requires a bit more careful reflection, but it is similarly straightforward. With Compromise Fallacies, the contribution of poles is more balanced, but because Integrative Meta-perspective is once again absent, rather than a new vibrancy of hues, we find only shades of gray.

CREATIVE SYSTEMS THEORY

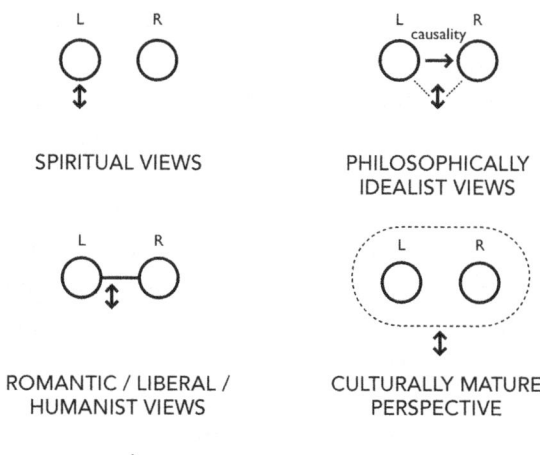

Fig. 7-3. Left-Leaning Views Contrasted with Culturally Mature Perspective

Often we need more nuanced distinctions to fully understand polar dynamics. The diagrams in Figure 7-3 contrast spiritual views with other more left-leaning views that I've made reference to in the book. With both romantic interpretation and related liberal and humanistic views, the person most identifies with left-hand aspects of experience while right-hand sensibilities may retain a significant presence. With philosophically idealist interpretations, again both hands have a role, but left-hand sensibility is assumed to drive more right-hand experience and thus ultimately define truth.[14] In each case, the lack of Integrative Meta-perspective—the absence of an ability to step back and draw consciously on the whole of our cognitive complexity—again provides the wheat-from-chaff distinction for making comparison with culturally mature understanding.[15]

---

14 Techno-utopian views can flip this relationship. Right-hand sensibilities are primary, but end up perceived as an almost spiritual kind of truth.

15 It helps to add related changes that come with Integrative Meta-perspective if we wish to fully grasp what is different in these examples. Several will become more clear with the next chapter's look at Parts Work. For example, polar aspects then remain wholly separate from one another (communication happens only with the person as a systemic whole), only the

The Creative Function provides a way to further expand such comparison. We can think of the Creative Function's picture of interplaying polar juxtapositions not just as a map of complexity, but also as a map of the various ways we protect ourselves from complexity's demands. Each point along the Function describes a particular, context-specific, creative juxtaposition. Whenever we fail to engage a polarity systemically—from Integrative Meta-perspective's more encompassing vantage—we effectively keep the full demands of the circumstances it pertains to at arm's length. In this way, the Creative Function offers an overarching framework for making detailed polar trap distinctions.

Recognizing polar traps most obviously helps us make better decisions and better appreciate when culturally mature perspective may be lacking. But learning to do so can also teach us a lot about ourselves. Identifying where we might be vulnerable to polar fallacies alerts us to broader tendencies in ourselves that may get in the way of what our times demand of us. We can learn a lot, too, by looking not just at personal vulnerabilities, but also at related tendencies in groups with which we may identify.

Temperament and Comparison

The Creative Systems Personality Typology, besides providing comparison of the more detailed patterning sort, also helps bring nuance to more big-picture comparison observations. For example, it provides added perspective that helps fill out the previous section's conceptual trap distinctions. Earlier I contrasted the kinds of Unity Fallacies that we find with thinkers of liberal persuasion, those common with fundamentalist religious thought, and ones we more frequently encounter with back-to-the-land or New Age advocates. These various types of Unity Fallacies have their origins respectively in more Late-Axis, more Middle-Axis, and more Early-Axis sensibilities.

We could delineate a parallel sequence of temperament-related Separation Fallacies and Compromise Fallacies. We could also go further and identify more Upper, Lower, Inner, and Outer manifestations of

---

person as a systemic whole has a relationship with the world, and causality is of the specifically creative sort that comes with Cultural Maturity's cognitive reordering.

each kind of fallacy. For example, the highly materialist Late/Upper/Outer Separation Fallacies that we might find with a corporate CEO are very different from the more fanciful, Early/Upper/Outer Separation Fallacies we might encounter with a person who delights in imagery of the more science fiction sort.

In Chapter Six, I made a couple of personality style observations with big-picture comparison implications. I noted how each temperament axis has particular strengths to contribute to culturally mature leadership. I also described how people with different temperaments tend to identify with specific kinds of religious and political beliefs. Since the religious and political beliefs I made reference to were each of a traditional, Modern Age sort, these observations could be thought of not just as ways to better appreciate conceptual diversity, but also as ways to help separate the wheat from the chaff as far as whether an idea succeeds at making the needed leap in understanding.

We can draw on Chapter Six's basic personality style descriptions to bring together this chapter's various comparison approaches. Below I've taken each primary personality style group and done three things. I've added some to previous observations about the particular gifts and curses that each temperament brings to the tasks of culturally mature leadership. I've described the scenarios for the future that each temperament is most likely to be attracted to. And I've reflected on the kinds of polar traps we are most likely to find with each personality pattern.

Earlies and culturally mature leadership: I've noted that high-Capacitance Earlies often contribute to addressing the future by being a source of new ideas. Earlies can also be particularly adept at looking toward the future more generally. Early-Axis is the personality style that by nature is most visionary and most interested in big-picture understanding. It is also the temperament most naturally comfortable with uncertainty and most open to the kind of fundamental change Cultural Maturity represents. Earlies also tend to be particularly adept at recognizing pattern and interrelationship.

But Earlies can also be vulnerable to losing their way when looking to the future. In particular, they can fall for naive wishful thinking and utopian conclusions. They can also be especially prone to cynicism and feelings of hopelessness. Of all groups, Earlies are the most likely to experience Transition in terms of a Crisis of Purpose.

Earlies can be attracted to any of the scenarios for the future I have described, but they will espouse versions that are specific to Early-Axis sensibility. Of all temperaments, Earlies are the least likely to ascribe to We've Arrived scenarios. The Early's delight in possibility and the unorthodox means that they tend not to find appeal in the status quo. And what attraction We've Arrived interpretations might hold comes up against the strong archetypally masculine bias of modern values and institutions.[16] Attraction to We've Gone Astray scenarios is fairly common with Early patterns, as we might predict with their vulnerability to cynicism.

We often find Early/Uppers in particular attracted to the more fanciful of Post-industrial/Information Age scenarios. Earlies can also be drawn to Postmodern/Constructivist conclusions, being both more comfortable than most temperaments with the positive contributions of postmodern interpretation (finding appeal in its challenging of cultural convention and its openness to multiple viewpoints) and particularly vulnerable to the seduction of existential noncommittalness. Of all the various temperament groups, Earlies are the most likely to be attracted to Transformational/New Paradigm scenarios, both versions that provide useful insight and interpretations that are at best diversions.

As far as polar traps, because Early-Axis temperaments are those most natively influenced by the archetypally feminine, Earlies can be especially vulnerable to Unity Fallacies. Particularly when sensibilities are more Inner, these tend to be of the more spiritual variety. More Lower sensibility may translate into a unitary identification with nature. With more Outer sensibilities we are most apt to see liberal/progressive Unity Fallacies, often of the extreme populist sort. We can also find Compromise Fallacies of the postmodern variety. And while Separation Fallacies have historically been rare with Earlies, in today's Digital Age those of the techno-utopian sort have become increasingly common.

Middles and culturally mature leadership: On the positive side, even when culturally mature perspective is limited, high-Capacitance Middles are some of the people most adept at social leadership. The

---

16 The identification that some Early/Upper/Outer scientists feel with a traditional scientific worldview is the one common exception.

Middle's ability to keep things together, along with their valuing of people and their respect for fairness, can provide great benefit. When these attributes combine with culturally mature understanding, the resulting contribution can be great.

There is also an interesting way in which Middles have a unique advantage when it comes to culturally mature contribution. The fact that they sit in the middle (between Early and Late) can make a balanced, if not necessarily integrative, view seem reasonable. Some of the people I know who are best at articulating culturally mature concepts in simple, obvious-seeming ways are Middles. Where Middles become capable of Integrative Meta-perspective, it is they who most quickly realize that the result is common sense.

At the same time, low-Capacitance Middles can feel particularly threatened by culturally mature ideas and be especially reactive in their responses to them. Because Middles have a high native need for control and order, the surrendering of familiar realities that Cultural Maturity requires does not tend to come easily for Middles. And the isometric organization of polarity within Middle-Axis dynamics (with right- and left-hand poles at near-equal potency) means that projective responses to being pushed beyond available Capacitance can be particularly intense in their expression. The fact that Middles tend to feel strong moral conviction and to manifest their beliefs in action amplifies both the richness of potential contribution and the risks when blindness and denial prevail.

As far as scenarios, people with Middle-Axis temperaments are the most likely to ascribe to We've Arrived beliefs. When such beliefs are held by high-Capacitance Middles, they tend, rather than being overly ideological, to reflect the Middle's basic preference to leave things that don't need to be changed unchanged and to focus attention on doing the work that needs to be done. Low-Capacitance Middles, on the other hand, can be ardent and extreme in their We've Arrived beliefs. Particularly in times of major social perturbation such as today, the Middle's inherent tendency toward conservatism can translate into a reactive identification with established social forms.

Middle/Upper/Outer We've Arrived beliefs tend to focus on archetypally masculine institutional structures—government, business, the military. With Middle/Upper/Inner We've Arrived interpretations, religious and/or educational institutions tend to get the greater emphasis. Where We've Arrived conclusions appeal to Middle/Lowers, they tend to center more around traditional notions of family, community, and morality. While there can also be identification with traditional institutions,[17] the resonance is less with institutions as structure than with the bonds of association and moral belief that institutions represent.

It is with low-Capacitance Middles that we tend to see the most extreme of We've Gone Astray interpretations, including end-time religious proclamations. Post-industrial/Information Age scenarios can also have strong attraction for Middles, in particular Middle/Upper/Outers. (Engineers tend to share this temperament.) Postmodern/Constructivist ideas tend to have much less appeal (given their emphasis on uncertainty), but some of the best of applied constructivist thinking is found in school settings, environments where Middle-Axis personalities and values predominate. Transformational/New Paradigm scenarios tend to have the least appeal for Middles. The strong archetypally feminine contribution in such views can make even the most well-thought-out Transformational/New Paradigm interpretations look suspicious from a Middle-Axis vantage.[18]

We can see adamant fallacies of both the Unity and Separation sort with Middles. Indeed, we can see them simultaneously—for example, a person expressing strongly felt Unity Fallacies with regard to their own kind, and equally strongly felt Separation Fallacies with regard to groups that they see as different. We also find Compromise Fallacies particularly with Middle/Inners, though appearing to be noncommittal then often has less to do with a lack of strong beliefs than a desire to seem fair and reasonable.

Lates and culturally mature leadership: High-Capacitance Lates tend to be particularly adept at putting ideas about the future into words and action. Where Lates are capable of Integrative Meta-perspective, we find some of the most articulate expression of ideas and some of the most facile translation of ideas into policy. Most books about the future

---

17 Religious institutions in particular appeal to Middle/Lower/Inners. Middle/Lower/Outers are more likely to profess strong nationalistic sentiments.

18 The establishment of Middle-Axis reality requires that the less-formed world of Early-Axis sensibility be kept well at arm's length.

are written by Lates, and the larger portion of academic futurists, particularly those who focus primary attention on the future of business, government, or technology, are Lates.

On the other hand, low-Capacitance Lates can be some of the people least able to recognize the limitations of Modern Age belief. Part of this blindness derives from how little dissonance may be felt between the convictions of people with Late-Axis temperaments and the normative assumptions of contemporary (Late-Axis) reality. But it is also a product of the way Late-Axis understanding tends to organize from the more surface layers of experience. Low-Capacitance intellectual views can lack the depth needed to grasp emerging complexities. And low-Capacitance social interactions can be strongly influenced by popular culture values.

Lates can identify with any of the five scenarios, but the Late's strong connection with the more creatively manifest aspects of formative process means that We've Arrived and Post-industrial/Information Age scenarios find the greatest number of adherents. Late-Axis We've Arrived views tend to focus on political and economic structures more than religious belief (the more archetypally masculine aspects of culture as structure). Post-industrial/Information Age scenarios that focus on science and technology are often accepted almost without question. It is common for Lates to simply assume that technology is culture's driver and that the future will be defined by the influence of new technological advances.

With Late/Upper/Outers, the temperament constellation most natively linked with financial, media, and global concerns, we find We've Arrived and Post-industrial/Information Age interpretations almost exclusively. With Late/Upper/Inners, the temperament most common in academic ranks, we find greater variety. We can see an ultimate sort of intellectual We've Arrived interpretation with logical positivist and extreme behaviorist worldviews (where Enlightenment belief finds culminating expression). We also find We've Arrived interpretations with a more liberal-humanist flavor (with modern forms of the arts and humanities getting closer to equal billing with harder concerns). Late/Upper/Inners can also be strongly attracted to Postmodern/Constructivist interpretation (both its most clear and useful expressions and its common reduction to an empty relativism). And with Late/Upper/Inners, we can sometimes see a version of We've Gone Astray cynicism (here a product of the way extreme rationality can result in an alienation from meaning).

Among Late/Lowers, we also find We've Arrived adherents. Those of Late/Lower/Outer tendency will focus most on the accomplishments of modern media and entertainment, and on the achievements of material culture. People with more Late/Lower/Inner tendencies can also be attracted to We've Arrived interpretations, but generally with greater emphasis on the artistic or on simple consumerism. In addition, we can find We've Gone Astray interpretations of the more philosophically romantic sort with Late/Lowers. On occasion, Transformational/New Paradigm beliefs can appear with Late/Lower/Inner dynamics. Indeed, it is here that we find some of the most extreme of New Age transformational interpretations.[19]

As far as polar fallacies, with Lates, Separation Fallacies are the most common, as we might expect given the Late's identification with more material aspects of experience. But Late/Upper/Inners, particularly of the academic sort, can also be attracted to Compromise Fallacies. And Unity Fallacies, most often of the liberal sort, are common with Late/Upper/Inners and with Late/Lowers.

Advocacy, Transitional Absurdity, and Apparent Paradox

A handful of topics that are not so obviously of a comparison sort provide distinctions that can have make-or-break significance. The first of three that we will examine turns to the often dramatic ways that the demands of leadership increase when the culturally mature leadership task includes not just right action, but the need to generate culturally mature understanding. A second topic brings us back to the concept of Transitional Absurdity for a more in-depth look. Finally, we will more closely examine apparent paradox and look at how it can help us distinguish the wheat from the chaff in our thinking.

---

19 Actress Shirley MacLaine, for example, a strong advocate of New Age belief, is a Late/Lower/Inner. I've noted the natural link between Early/Upper and Late/Lower dynamics (how Early/Uppers represent the most archetypally masculine pattern within the most archetypally feminine axis, while Late/Lowers represent the most archetypally feminine pattern within the most archetypally masculine axis).

The—Considerable—Demands of Culturally Mature Advocacy

An important basic comparison task confronts the culturally mature leader just in getting started.[20] He or she needs to discern the degree to which culturally mature perspective is needed. In many instances it isn't—there is work to be accomplished, and the leader's job is simply to articulate it clearly. At other times, needed leadership decisions may require culturally mature perspective, but it is not necessary that others fully understand how those decisions are reached. It may then be sufficient that the culturally mature leader stands ready to respond if decisions push others beyond what they can readily handle. But often broader understanding will be necessary—if formulating policy requires collaboration or if culturally mature policy decisions, when made, are to be accepted. And sometimes advocating for culturally mature understanding is what the culturally mature leadership task needs most fundamentally to be about.

Making these kinds of distinctions itself requires significant Capacitance. And when at least some degree of culturally mature understanding is needed, Capacitance requirements increase considerably. Where advocating for culturally mature understanding is what the culturally mature leadership task is ultimately about, the demands become considerably greater. The effective culturally mature leader must have a clear sense of these additional demands and just what they entail.

It is important to appreciate just what creates these additional demands. Most obviously the simple fact that the needed understanding is for most people unfamiliar increases demands. But that is only a start. As important is the fact that we are dealing not just with new ideas, but new kinds of ideas. The need for a leap in understanding applies even if what we are attempting to communicate requires only beginning steps over Cultural Maturity's threshold. I've described the double-bind quandary I encountered in first writing about culturally mature concepts—how making sense of culturally mature capacities itself requires culturally mature capacities. Much in this kind of circumstance comes with the territory any time we engage developmental processes—we can only understand what we are ready to understand. But a major

---

[20] Again here I refer to leadership in the broadest sense, not just positional leadership.

portion of what we encounter is a product of characteristics specific to Cultural Maturity's very particular developmental change point.

When we attempt to articulate culturally mature ideas, like it or not, we confront how deeply post-ideological perspective is new, and more than most people are ready for. We also confront the fact that even if an audience begins to be ready, communication can be more difficult than we might assume. The simple-answer conclusions of ideological belief are readily expressed—indeed, they readily translate into loud and lengthy diatribes. The Dilemma of Representation means that post-ideological understanding is less easily communicated.

The understanding challenge can be formidable even when only a few people need to grasp what is new and necessary, but it increases substantially with efforts to communicate with groups. While the best of thinking in most fields today takes on important questions and often makes a start at getting beyond now-outmoded Modern Age assumptions, culturally mature conception is as yet rare. For a group of any size to become established, a critical mass of agreement is needed. Thus we simply don't find groups today with any significant commitment to culturally mature understanding.

I've been particularly aware of this circumstance when I've been invited to speak at conferences. Most conferences attract people who share the same basic worldview. This may or may not be the case in an explicitly ideological sense, but people tend to be drawn together by shared assumptions and values. Culturally mature understanding will be the exception. And even if its beginnings are present, contributions made from a culturally mature vantage may simply not seem as dramatic and exciting to participants as contributions that express more ideological viewpoints. Where needed Capacitance is significantly lacking, the attention culturally mature advocacy does generate can easily be of the problematic sort—a reactive confusing of culturally mature perspective's more encompassing vantage with the polar opposite of whatever polar position defines the prevailing view. (If the conference's predominant inclination is politically conservative, I may be perceived as simply a liberal—or the situation can be reversed. If the underlying assumptions have a spiritual bias, I may be perceived as being overly rational or scientific—or, again, the situation's reverse.)

Advocating for culturally mature understanding confronts a related conundrum with any form of mass communication, whether written—with newspapers, magazines, or books—or with radio, television, or digital media that is intended for a broad audience. Such communication requires a critical mass of readers/viewers/listeners. That scale of audience is likely going to be generated either through a lowest-common-denominator, mass-consumer approach that threatens no one (with its appeal being that it requires little in the way of Capacitance) or through the attraction of groups of the ideologically like-minded. Online modalities make possible more individualized content and greater diversity of opinion, but their potential is as yet rarely realized. Too often we find only belief protected in communities of sameness and communication of the most superficial sort.[21]

Effective culturally mature leadership does not always require culturally mature understanding on the part of others. Indeed, in many instances, good decisions don't require anything beyond what good leadership has always been about. But the culturally mature leader needs to know when at least some degree of shared understanding is needed. And if culturally mature understanding is ultimately what the leadership task is about, he or she must be keenly aware of the very significant ways that demands increase. Certainly, such greater sophistication is needed when taking on the additional task of understanding today. How quickly that might change in years ahead, only time can tell.

Transitional Absurdity: Contemporary Craziness and Its Antidote (Or How the Ludicrous Can Coexist with Hope)

The concept of Transitional Absurdity deserves a deeper look. The culturally mature leader must be able to distinguish when Transitional

---

[21] I've come up against this conundrum throughout my life in my dealings with the book publishing world. Because large publishers are primarily interested in profit, quite reasonably they will not be interested in work that might have a limited audience. Smaller publishers sometimes apply other kinds of values, but most often they aim their books at audiences with a particular ideological bent. At this point, few publishers have interest in culturally mature content. And the challenge is ultimately deeper. We don't find sections in bookstores that focus even on the general topic of addressing the future.

Absurdities intrude on perception, and where they do, in just what ways. It is an important compare-and-contrast topic. Transitional Absurdities make us vulnerable to responding in ways that are at the least unhelpful.

Transitional Absurdities are most obviously problematical because they distort perception and result in poor and often dangerous choices. But they also present a more overarching kind of concern. I've proposed that the most fundamental crisis we face today is a Crisis of Purpose—in the end, a crisis of narrative. Transitional Absurdities leave us distanced from the ability to recognize the essential need for a new chapter in the human narrative, and further still from the ability to engage it.

I've previously touched on numerous issues where Transitional Absurdities come into play without necessarily labeling them as such, and I will address others in chapters to come. And we can use multiple themes that I have presented previously to shine light on why we might see Transitional Absurdities and some of their consequences. Here I'll pull some of these reflections together to help clarify the concept and make it most useful as a comparison tool.

The concept of Transitional Absurdity describes how a lot that we can find most disturbing—indeed ludicrous—in our time is predicted by how change in human systems works. Because the concept is easily misunderstood, I've not before written a great deal about it. It can be difficult to be sure that a particular phenomenon at a specific point in time is a product of these dynamics. And the concept can be used to justify ideology-based critiques of views that people may find "absurd" only because these views differ from their own. At the least, the concept of Transitional Absurdity can seem only to support cynicism and negativity—emotions that serve no good purpose.

But while the concept must be applied with care, I think of it as an essential tool in the culturally mature leader's tool bag. Understood with needed depth and subtlety, it helps make sense of much that might otherwise only confuse or disturb. In the end, it provides an antidote to exactly the dangers that can come with its misuse. The concept helps us get beyond ideological easy answers. And while cynicism could easily seem a warranted response, in fact the concept is consistent with hope. Indeed, it is difficult to justify being hopeful without such a concept.

CREATIVE SYSTEMS THEORY

I've described how Transitional Absurdities are products of three related mechanisms. Some Transitional Absurdities simply involve stopping short of what our times demand of us, either because we fail to recognize that anything new is required or because contemplating needed changes is more than we can tolerate. Other Transitional Absurdities reflect "overshooting the mark," avoiding what is being asked by extending old ways of thinking beyond their usefulness, often in extreme ways. And others still are products of overwhelm and regression in the face of new demands.

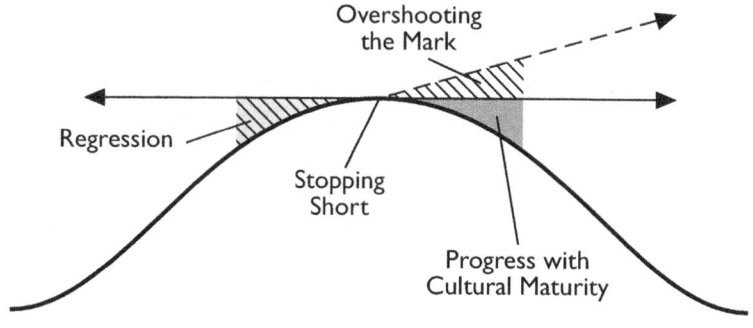

Fig. 7-4. Transitional Absurdity and the Dilemma of Trajectory[22]

Framing these three sorts of Transitional Absurdities in terms of the evolution of narrative provides a good way to begin to get at what each of them involves. I've described how we encounter a mix of overlapping cultural narratives today—heroic and romantic stories left over from Modern Age assumptions, postmodern belief, and the beginnings of culturally mature perspective. Our first kind of Transitional Absurdity—that which reflects stopping short—is a product of failing to see

---

[22] The Dilemma of Representation again intrudes with the concept of Transitional Absurdity. Here I have used a different, more shorthand way to represent the Creative Function—a sine wave. While simpler, it also introduces its own kind of possible confusion. The "progress with Cultural Maturity" segment might appear to be settling for a lack of progress, or even, because it includes Lower Pole sensibilities, diminished significance. In fact, it is the only direction in the diagram that represents real progress in the sense of increasing Capacitance.

beyond the heroic and romantic assumptions of times past. Our second kind of Transitional Absurdity—the overshooting-the-mark sort—involves attempts to apply the past's more familiar stories in exaggerated, and thus ultimately even more ideological, forms. And the last kind—that which comes with overwhelm and manifests in regression—is a negative reaction to the loss of past, more ideological truths and the need to confront easily disorienting new challenges. With each of these three basic kinds of Transitional Absurdity, the result is claims and actions that are at best unhelpful, at worst dangerously misleading.

Let's look briefly at examples. The most easily grasped of Transitional Absurdities involve keeping Cultural Maturity's demands at arm's length. When we lack the Capacitance needed to manifest the new capacities that a challenge requires, we may be unable—or at least unwilling—to confront what is being asked of us. Not only will our actions then prove ineffective, we will fail to appreciate the essential questions. We see this first kind of Transitional Absurdity today with climate change denial, our unwillingness to acknowledge health care limits, and with failure to appreciate the dangers inherent in extreme income inequality.

Many of the most consequential Transitional Absurdities reflect overshooting the mark in the transition from Modern Age realities into Cultural Maturity's needed next cultural chapter. Overshooting the mark is pretty much how things work at any major cultural change point—partly because we may fail to recognize that anything new is involved, partly as a result of fear, partly because systems are not homogeneous. When we overshoot the mark, mechanisms that have served us become amplified and distorted. I divide this second kind of Transitional Absurdity itself into three types: extreme right-hand "overshooting the mark" absurdities, "overshooting the mark" absurdities that exploit left-hand sensibilities, and postmodern "overshooting the mark" absurdities.

The most easily recognized "overshooting the mark" dynamics reflect right-hand sensibilities prevailing to the point of ludicrousness. I've described how cultural belief has evolved over the course of history from times in which archetypally feminine sensibilities prevailed—as with tribal realities—to today, when more archetypally masculine sensibilities largely hold sway. With some Transitional Absurdities this right-hand dominance is extended to a point that we fail to question quite insane behaviors and beliefs.

An important example has coursed through this book. I've described how future advancement requires that we leave behind making material achievement our bottom line and learn to measure both wealth and progress in ways that better reflect the diverse elements that contribute to meaningful lives. Recognizing the importance of rethinking our modern concept of progress starts with a key Transitional insight—materialism run amok ultimately makes us less, not more. At a personal level, we encounter Transitional Absurdity in the unending triviality of modern mass-consumer culture where what we buy, in effect, comes to define purpose. We confront a related more collective example in the common "growth is always good" assumptions of many modern economists.

Earlier in this chapter, I described a related way that Post-industrial/Information Age belief can translate into Transitional Absurdity. People can assume, without giving it great thought, that technologies yet on the horizon can solve all the world's problems. Post-industrial/Information Age Transitional Absurdities take their extreme today in techno-utopian beliefs that promise an almost spiritual kind of salvation. The result is titillating, simplistic-answer escape from the need to think in more encompassing, limits-acknowledging, and mature ways.

Another kind of overshooting-the-mark Transitional Absurdity involves the exploitation of values and aspects of experience that have come to have diminishing influence with Modern Age realities—such as the receptive, the world of children, the artistic, community, the life of the body, or the spiritual. Because Transition leaves us distanced from these essential aspects of who we are—and overshooting the mark leaves us distanced even further—their power becomes readily co-opted. Given that the sensibilities that give these aspects of experience significance have been largely "forgotten," this further dynamic may not be as readily recognized as those I've listed previously, but it is just as important.

The co-opting of today's last faint remnants of the receptive makes a good example. The word "receptive" captures the archetypally feminine at its most basic. Receptivity is about taking in. It is needed for any deep capacity to listen, for sensuality and pleasure, and if we are to effectively know what most moves us and thus understand meaning in our lives. Yet in spite of the fact that receptivity is so fundamental, when I use the word "receptive" today, very often people barely recognize what I am talking about. They assume that the opposite of active, rather than receptive, is simply passive. The receptive is, in fact, as fully dynamic, and fundamentally significant, as the active.

This situation leaves us easily exploited. In part this is because we are so distanced from the receptive that we can miss its significance. Equally it is because receptivity's rarity can amplify the felt importance even of imposters. I think of how often in modern times shopping serves as receptivity's most frequent expression. More recently we encounter this kind of confusion in how often people speak of today's world making us more "connected" when the opposite is frequently the case. Too easily, "likes" and "clicks" become defining measures of relationship and "selfies" our modern signifiers of identity. In the process, receptivity and the deep connection it gives us with others and with ourselves gets highjacked.

I will highlight a further example of such co-opting In Chapter Eleven when I use CST Patterning in Time notions to map the past and future of art. I will describe how the sensibilities that historically have produced great art take their most influential expression in our time with advertising. And I will propose that because advertising uses art's language of image and metaphor to get us to buy things—and most often does so in ways that involve deception—arguably the result is the antithesis of art's historical truth-telling function. This kind of Transitional Absurdity takes its most egregious form with advertising that is directed at children.

Another place we encounter this kind of exploitation of "forgotten" sensibilities is with how often, today, we co-opt body experience. I've described how body intelligence's primal potency has become largely a memory over the course of culture's evolution. With Transition's changes, we come to live almost entirely on the body's surface, a circumstance that can leave us both confused about our bodies and vulnerable to having whatever body connectedness remains exploited for economic gain. Such disconnect manifests in today's obsession with the most superficial aspects of physical appearance (witness our modern infatuation with plastic surgery) and with the use of sex to sell almost every kind of product. We have become so used to the trivialization and exploitation of the body that we fail to recognize that we are violating much in ourselves that is most precious. This observation provides useful further insight into the roots of addiction—whether the addicting substance is a physical drug, food, or the artificial stimulation of an electronic device. Too often, today, we lack the basic bodily feedback we need to distinguish real meaning from artificial substitutes.

I've made reference to postmodern overshooting-the-mark patterns indirectly at multiple times in the book. With them, the essential recognition that various people view the world in different ways gets replaced by belief that makes one choice as good as any other. We get randomness and ironic cleverness masquerading as meaning. At a personal level, such postmodern pseudo-significance leads to an increasingly prevalent moral aimlessness. At a cultural level, it results in "fake news," "alternative facts," and all manner of exploitation in the name of meaning. Truth becomes arbitrary, a function of little more than whim.

Our third kind of Transitional Absurdity is a product not so much of missing the big picture as of reacting in less than helpful ways to all that it asks. A common result its disorientation or regression. I've emphasized how, although any time of transition between developmental stages requires a lot of us, the specific transitional challenges presented by the Dilemma of Trajectory are disruptive in particularly fundamental ways. It is not unreasonable that people could become overwhelmed and respond regressively or with despondency and a loss of hope.

I think of current partisan insanity as regressive in this sense. More and more often today we find partisan gridlock, with neither side interested in any viewpoint other than their own. I've described how extreme polarization is a common response when systems are challenged to more than they can handle. The dangers of such extreme polarization go well beyond the inability to communicate. Polarization makes the needed new maturity of perspective nearly impossible. We've looked at how polarized conclusions, when viewed from a culturally mature perspective, reveal themselves to be complementary aspects of larger systemic realities. With regressive polarization, we not only lose what ability we may have had to hear opposing views, it becomes impossible to see the big picture. Politics comes to have less and less to do with governance. Indeed, such polarization puts the whole democratic experiment in jeopardy.

Another place we see regression is with the growing prevalence of authoritarian leadership on the planet. The election of authoritarian leaders is not necessarily a problem with pre-modern cultures. CST proposes that when the time is right, authoritarian structures are appropriate and ultimately most effective (at least if authoritarian leadership is of the more "benevolent" sort). But in recent decades we've seen the rise of authoritarian voices in countries where modern democratic structures have been well established. This is very much a problem—and specifically regressive. Why do we see it? Authoritarian leadership promises order and stability in a world in which changes such as today's postmodern weakening of social norms, globalization, and job loss through automation have for many people made life feel diminished and intolerably uncertain. Unfortunately, the ultimate result can only be further disorder and stability's opposite.

This third kind of dynamic likely also plays a significant role in today's increasing rates of suicide, depression, and anxiety. We can't know for sure just how directly such phenomena are products of Transition's mechanisms, but they are consistent with what those mechanisms predict. It should not surprise us that people who are not up to contemporary demands would respond with despondency. Where people's resources are limited and they see nothing to replace what new realities take away, a regressive loss of hope is a reasonable reaction.

I've emphasized that applying the concept of Transitional Absurdity effectively necessarily starts with a comparison task—making sure Transitional Absurdity is what we are dealing with. The concept can easily become a repository for any phenomenon that our particular worldview might find aversive. People can also use the concept to dismiss phenomena that are not appropriately seen in this way. But once we make the needed distinctions, the concept provides essential insight for going forward. And the insights don't stop with just giving us a better understanding ways our thinking can fail us. Some of these further insights have critical implications.

For example, the concept of Transitional Absurdity helps us make sense of why, in our time, we should see some of the disturbing results that I have described. The fact that these results are predicted at the least makes them more understandable. And of even greater significance, the concept of Transitional Absurdity helps us recognize how what we see may have ultimately positive implications. I've proposed that Transitional Absurdities reflect stage-specific dynamics within larger, ultimately creative mechanisms. In the end, they are wholly consistent with Cultural Maturity's realization—and thus with hope. Often the only alternative interpretation of crazinesses we see in the world if the concept of Transitional Absurdity is not correct is that we are reaching the end of humanity's grand experiment.

At a more practical level, the concept of Transitional Absurdity helps us by alerting us to the kinds of actions that can provide real benefit. This further contribution has both specific and big-picture aspects. The more specific aspect relates to how Cultural Maturity's changes bring with them new capacities that we can practice. Transitional Absurdities highlight the need for these new capacities—whether a new maturity in our relationship to limits, the ability to get beyond the either/or thinking of times past, or the application of more complete measures of advancement. The more big-picture aspect relates to the recognition that the antidote to each of the kinds of unpleasantness that I have described is, in the end, the same—Cultural Maturity and the more sophisticated ways of thinking and acting that it makes possible.

There is also a more everyday way in which recognizing the fact of Transitional Absurdity can assist us. It can help us avoid responding poorly to crazy circumstances. Transitional Absurdities can distract us, leaving us vulnerable to having our precious creative energies sidetracked. We can get caught up in the lunacy of political soap opera or become irate that some particular issue is met with denial. Such responses are understandable. And certainly it is important to speak out strongly when we encounter craziness. But responding reactively to how others might hide from the obvious is seldom, in the end, a good use of attention and resources. It rarely does any good. And it ignores the essential developmental recognition that, with time, most of today's idiocy will likely be viewed simply as history. Our task is to keep our eyes on what most matters and to support solutions when we find them. When we miss the larger picture, our reactions can end up feeding into—and prolonging—the absurdity. This maturity of response asks more of a person, but in the end it is what produces actions that make a difference.

The recognition that Transitional Absurdities carried very far into the future become not just absurd, but insane raises some obvious questions about what we should anticipate in the decades immediately ahead. Note that we see, simultaneously, two trajectories with markedly different implications. While the concept of Cultural Maturity points toward important new possibility, the fact of Transitional Absurdities suggests something quite different if such blindnesses continue on to any great degree—and it is likely that many of them will. We may well need to confront much that is quite insane in times ahead. Whatever proves to be the case, we can take comfort in the guidance implied by the concept of Transitional Absurdity. No matter how bumpy the road ahead, the task remains the same—and ultimately straightforward. We need to engage what we find with the perspective—indeed, the wisdom—that Cultural Maturity's more encompassing vantage provides.

Apparent Paradox

The apparent paradoxes that so often accompany culturally mature conclusions can also be applied as a compare-and-contrast tool. At the least they provide evidence that we are dealing with something fundamentally new. But they also provide support for the particular kind of newness. The fact that CST repeatedly reconciles paradoxes is one of the best indicators that not only does its thinking offer entry into a fresh territory of understanding, that new conceptual territory is of the specifically integrative sort that becomes possible with Cultural Maturity's cognitive reordering.

Chapter Two's examination of the workings of polarity provided an explanation for why we see this new relationship to paradox. Cultural Maturity's cognitive reordering "bridges" the polar opposites that produce the appearance of paradox. When we view such opposites through the polarizing lens of Modern Age thought, they seem irreconcilable. But step over Cultural Maturity's threshold and engage them with Integrative Meta-perspective's more systemic embrace, and the implied contradiction disappears. No fancy philosophical pyrotechnics are required. The result follows naturally.

To this point, I've given greatest attention to one particular such apparent paradox—the way culturally mature conclusions are both more complex and simpler than what they replace. How this could be the case should now be clear. Integrative Meta-perspective offers that we might better hold the whole of our own complexity. It also makes it possible to see beyond the distortions of projection and mythologizing and better appreciate complexities in the world. But at the same time, Integrative Meta-perspective helps us see complexities more systemically, more as integrated wholes. Understanding that is at once more multifaceted and simpler—at least in the sense of being more of an entirety—is a natural result.

Another place I've noted apparent paradox is with what happens when we engage limits maturely. Restricted to the heroic/romantic assumptions of Modern Age perspective, the fact of inviolable limits can seem only like loss. With maturity—in our personal lives and even more so with Cultural Maturity—we better see how limits are inherent in how living systems work. In the process, limits become essential teachers, helping us better appreciate how freedom and constraint are each intrinsic to life and meaning. With Cultural Maturity's cognitive changes, identifying inviolable limits becomes one of the best ways of recognizing where new ways of thinking could result in advancement.

A further apparent paradox, one I've implied with multiple concerns, is worth addressing in more detail: Any culturally mature concept increases our appreciation for both interconnectedness and for difference. We can think of the ability to think in ways that succeed at doing so as a further essential new capacity that comes with Cultural Maturity. We can also think of it as a litmus test for successful culturally mature understanding. We see this systemic result reflected in every CST concept. A creative frame by its nature takes us beyond the polarity of connectedness and difference.

Some examples from previous observations help fill out this key paradox. I've described how Integrative Meta-perspective takes us beyond thinking of morality only in terms of good versus evil. In doing so, it leaves behind absolute moral difference. But just as much, culturally mature perspective challenges a postmodern moral relativism in which one choice becomes as good as another (and real difference disappears). Culturally mature understanding helps us more deeply appreciate what moral discernment is about—including both its link to our individual sense of rightness and its role in aligning our lives with larger human meaning and connectedness. In the process, it makes possible moral choice that better reflects at once our uniqueness and the depth of our shared humanness. CST provides a set of tools for taking on this needed, more nuanced kind of moral responsibility and decision-making.

I've described something similar with reflections on love and gender. Culturally mature perspective takes us beyond the projections that in times past have had us treat men and women as distinct "opposite sexes" (wholly different). But as we've seen, such perspective does more than just replace a polarized picture with some unisex ideal (making us all the same). Rather, it helps each individual appreciate their unique experience of being an embodied—and gendered—being.

I touched on a Patterning in Time example of this apparent paradox in observing the way a culturally mature understanding of culture's evolution helps get us beyond the polarizations that in times past have justified bigotry and colonial oppression (historically, a picture of fundamental difference). It doesn't accomplish this by making everyone the same (making it all about connectedness). Rather it provides a deepened understanding of how cultural stages reflect real differences, and with this, how those differences in potential can be drawn on for positive ends (connectedness of the sort that actually matters).

We saw a related Patterning in Space example with our look at the Creative Systems Personality Typology. The typology helps us tease apart the roots of ideological differences. But it doesn't just replace ideological polarization with all-is-one acceptance. In fact, it highlights just how startlingly different we can be from one another. The greater interconnectedness comes with the recognition that those differences, at least in potential, work to make truly deep relationship more possible and existence more rich and creative.

A preview of coming attractions for Chapter Twelve's look at very big-picture questions hints at the possibility of reconciling a related, quite ultimate apparent paradox. In times past, we've tended to put the sacred and the secular—and the beliefs of science and religion—in wholly separate, indeed often opposite, categories. Integrative Meta-perspective suggests that this separate-worlds picture need not be an end point. And it gets there not by dismissing the "offending" viewpoint or by lumping viewpoints together—approaches we commonly see with notions that claim to end the science-versus-religion debate. Culturally mature perspective offers that we might understand the scientific and the spiritual as complementary aspects of a more encompassing picture. I will describe how it is an encompassing picture that brings together what we can think of as ultimately encompassing expressions of difference and interconnectedness. CST gives this picture detail. It also clarifies how this new picture inherently adds nuance and richness to our understanding of both science and religion.

Whether an idea effectively increases our appreciation for both commonality and difference provides one of the most reliable tests for a notion's success as culturally mature conception. Ideas that fall short will fail at one or the other of these tasks (and ultimately, in failing at one, will just as much fail with the other). The result is wholly different from what can sometimes be suggested with the word "paradox." Often the word is used to indicate postmodern irony. It can also be used to claim a disappearance of distinction, a dissolving of opposites into mystery or a comforting unity. Integrative Meta-perspective increases our appreciation of the significance of each pole in any polar relationship and brings new detail to understanding. And at the same time, it makes clear how, in the end, poles reflect aspects of larger systemic realities.

A New Common Sense

I've proposed that once we step over Cultural Maturity's threshold, needed new kinds of truth come to feel surprisingly straightforward—and, yes, even like common sense. While I've used the phrase "common sense" repeatedly in introducing Cultural Maturity's cognitive changes, it might not initially seem to have much to do with comparison. But once a person is familiar with how Integrative Meta-perspective alters experience, this recognition provides one of the most useful comparison tools. If an idea seems too esoteric, complicated, or dramatic, it is likely not what we are looking for.

I pointed toward this further critical comparison skill with earlier reflections about culturally mature leadership. I described how culturally mature leadership can feel in important ways more "ordinary" than what it replaces. I also emphasized that we need to be adept at distinguishing this exceptional kind of ordinariness from the more mundane variety. The importance of this additional kind of discernment applies with every kind of choice we might make.

Given some of the ways I've approached these reflections—such as talking about different kinds of systemic thinking, using abstract language like "crux" and "multiplicity," and drawing on the whole of human history—words like "straightforward" and "common sense" might not be a person's first associations. But the fact that we might experience the needed new kind of thinking in this way follows directly from observations to this point. I've described how the fact that we experience culturally mature understanding as common sense is a product of the developmental/evolutionary nature of the changes that produce it. At any developmental stage in our personal lives, time-appropriate realities feel obvious to us. And more specifically, it is a product of how Integrative Meta-perspective, by providing a completeness of understanding that has not before been an option, invites us to appreciate "just what is" with a generosity of embrace that we have not known before.

It turns out that we don't need to know anything about systems thinking, "crux" and "multiplicity" aspects of truth (culturally mature or otherwise), or the history of belief to begin making the sorts of discernments Integrative Meta-perspective makes possible. The changes that produce these new ways of thinking about truth come part and parcel with Cultural Maturity's larger changes. In the end, they are about nothing more than seeing in ways that are more accurate and complete.

One result of the common-sense nature of needed changes is that they can sneak up on us. It is very much the case that Integrative Meta-perspective requires not just greater awareness, but a whole new, more deeply discerning kind of awareness. But it is also true that Cultural Maturity's changes can happen without us being aware they are taking place. You would likely not have gotten this far in this book if you were not already making culturally mature discernments in many parts of your life. And likely you have not been doing so intentionally. For example, you may be carrying out daily life decisions with often only a glance to cultural convention. Successfully doing so requires getting more directly at what for you is true (a Whole-Person/Whole-System capacity). It also means being sensitive to context, both the particular contexts in which you are making choices and the context of your specific temperament (Patterning in Time and Patterning in Space kinds of discernments). Such more mature decision-making may be happening mostly at a level of personal maturity, but the context of our time and your interest in reading these words suggests that much too is taking place at the level of Cultural Maturity.

Given that these changes reflect innovation at the level of truth itself, this recognition might initially seem startling. Needed new understandings would certainly seem the appropriate work not just of a philosopher but, given the significance, depth, and newness of these changes, a philosopher of unusual acumen. But once we step over Cultural Maturity's threshold, these kinds of distinctions start becoming the kind that feel obviously important to make. They become what works. In noticing that they do, we may develop concepts about why they do. And in seeing other people make similar choices and hearing other people's ideas, we may refine those concepts. But if these are "ideas whose time has come," as I've suggested, it is not always important that we understand what we are doing, or why. These new kinds of distinctions become the obviously necessary tools if we are to successfully make our way.

A Comparison Exercise:

> How many steps into culturally mature territory do you feel you are capable of? (And what are the implications of this observation for choices you might make?) If historically you have been most likely to ascribe to one of the five futures scenarios I have described, which one would it be? (And what might be some of the consequences of your answer as far as where you have been able to be effective in your life and where your assumptions may at times have gotten in your way?) If you are most vulnerable to a particular kind of polar fallacy, just what type of fallacy is it? (And again, does your answer have implications as far as the kinds of decisions you have made and whether they have served you?) In addition, do your answers seem consistent with what a person might expect with your particular personality style? (And what can you predict about where your particular gifts and blindness might lie from this observation?) And finally, is it beginning to become understandable that the complexities and apparent paradoxes that come with Cultural Maturity's changes might ultimately feel obvious, like common sense?

CHAPTER EIGHT

Hands-On Methods

I've emphasized how much of a stretch it can be for people to fully grasp the kind of thinking that Creative Systems Theory represents. While it is true that once we step over Cultural Maturity's threshold the needed, more systemic kind of perspective that results can seem like "common sense," understanding can be difficult when a person is limited to how they have thought in times past. Culturally mature thought requires Integrative Meta-perspective, and Integrative Meta-perspective requires drawing, in a whole new sense, on the whole of who we are. I've described how just rational explanation by itself will rarely prove sufficient. And the Dilemma of Representation means that simple diagrams are similarly going to communicate at best by inference.

One consequence of this circumstance is that more "hands-on" methods are often going to provide the most effective learning approaches. Here I mean something different than just using experiential methods to augment learning—applying non-rational methods as decoration and illustration. I am also suggesting something specifically different than making truth about experience rather than thought—a common left-hand trap. I'm referring to the use of approaches that, by how they are structured, engage experience with Integrative Meta-perspective's more encompassing embrace.

With my efforts through the years, I've drawn on an array of such approaches. I will start here with an overview of the year-long Intensive that I led annually while directing the Institute for Creative Development. Each of the Intensive's ten weekend sessions, besides offering conceptual learning, applied particular kinds of hands-on methods. The ten sessions provide a good outline of the approaches that I have thus far found most useful. As a bonus, the way these various approaches relate one to another offers valuable further insight into both what makes culturally mature understanding new and the power of a creative frame.

I will then go into greater depth with a hands-on approach that I touched on briefly in Chapter One—what I call simply Parts Work. Parts Work provides the most direct way I know to generate culturally mature understanding. We will look more closely at just what Parts Work involves. We will also examine a handful of examples. And I will describe how an appreciation for the "cognitive rewiring" that results with Parts Work further supports both needed perspective and the fundamental newness of culturally mature systemic conception. I will also address some of the implications of Parts Work for the practice of psychotherapy and describe how its basic principles can be applied to work with larger systems.

Finally, we will turn to how the application of CST patterning concepts can work as a hands-on approach. I will guide readers in drawing on the various patterning notions this book has addressed to better understand the multiple systems that make up their lives. Applying CST notions provides not only a direct way to answer questions that may be important to us, but also a method for making the needed stretch in understanding.

The Intensive

When I look back today on the years that I led Institute Intensives, I find fresh appreciation for the uniqueness and sophistication of the Intensive's design. (I was often then not fully conscious of why I was structuring things just as I was.) Each of the ten weekends of the Intensive not only involved learning specific new ideas, it engaged participants in inhabiting culturally mature perspective's territory of experience. And each weekend did so in a different way. These ten weekend sessions provide a good summary of the best ways I currently know to directly engage culturally mature understanding and to begin to apply CST concepts.

Weekend #1: I'd take the early part of the first morning for introductions. I've described how I selected groups so that all the "crayons in the box" of temperament diversity were in the room. The introduction process itself thus could be thought of as a hands-on technique. I'd ask questions that began to reveal some of the depths of people's differences.

With the later part of the morning, we'd roll up our sleeves and get to work. I described some of the basic approaches that I drew on in Chapter Four's introduction to culturally mature skills and capacities. First, I'd have participants make a list of questions that they felt would be particularly important to address in times ahead. The questions could be most about people's individual lives—about love, parenting, or gender identity. They might be more about leadership, as many participants occupied formal positions of authority. Or they could involve more overarching societal concerns—such as the environment, poverty, terrorism, or the dangers presented by weapons of mass destruction. I'd conclude the morning by having people break up into small groups and share the questions that they had listed.

We'd start the afternoon again together in the large group. While people had been engaged in their small groups, I would have written brief descriptions of the various new skills and capacities that I've argued become possible with culturally mature understanding on a board at the front of the room. One by one, I would invite participants to share questions that seemed particularly significant. Where effectively addressing a question would require culturally mature perspective—which for most would be the case—I would make the provocative assertion that the question could not be answered if we limit ourselves to familiar assumptions. I would then introduce a new capacity that would be critical to addressing it—from thinking in ways that step beyond the polarity-based assumptions of times past, to appreciating the fact of ultimate limits, to learning to think more contextually (both in terms of truth's relativity in time and more here-and-now contextual relativities). I would describe how that new capacity was essential even if all we wanted to do was really understand what the question was asking. And I'd make a start at addressing each question.

Then, after taking on a handful of questions in this way, I would propose that in fact the great majority of important questions ahead for the species require such new capacities. And I would go further to argue that most of these questions would in some way require all of the new capacities that we had touched on. We would end the day examining more conceptually why this might be the case and looking at the implications for good decision-making in times ahead.

I'd start day two by again having people meet in smaller groups. I'd give each small group the task of engaging together in the same kind of teasing apart that I had modeled the day before. People were first to look at whether other questions on their lists similarly required thinking in new ways. They were then to work together to see if they could address these additional questions, drawing on the various culturally mature capacities we had examined.

In the afternoon, I would bring the large group back together for some deeper inquiry. I'd have people identify questions from their small group efforts where they had had a hard time making progress. I would then facilitate the group in taking on these particularly thorny concerns, in the process applying needed new skills and capacities in more nuanced ways. I'd end the day by asking people to reflect on how drawing on new capacities had altered the weekend's inquiry, both what it had added to the difficulty of discussions, and what outcomes it had made possible that had not been possible before.

Weekend #2: With the second weekend, we turned to intelligence's multiple aspects. I more formally introduced the concept of Integrative Meta-perspective. And I highlighted the essential recognition that culturally mature understanding requires drawing on the whole of our cognitive complexity. I then divided the weekend up into time for each of the major sensibilities/intelligences that CST identifies. With each intelligence, I applied approaches that brought it to the fore.

I'd start with the intelligence of the body. I've described how the whole notion that the body is intelligent can be difficult for people to grasp in our time—and particularly hard for people of certain temperaments. To begin engaging body intelligence, I would first have people stand up and move in different ways. I would then have them notice how their "felt sense" of things—the way they experienced the room, themselves, and the people around them—changed depending on the quality of the movement. I would also have people connect with experience from different parts of their bodies—their bellies, their hands, their heads, their genitals, their hearts—and examine how what felt most important to them changed depending on where in their bodies they were experiencing from. Next I would have people get in touch with a question that was important to them, this time a more personal question rather than the previous weekend's larger concerns. And I would guide people in seeing whether they could use their bodily knowing to help discern answers for the question. I would have people try out both different kinds of movements and the sensibilities of different body locales to see if useful information could be gleaned. I would also invite people to draw on multiple aspects of body intelligence simultaneously to see if this offered a more complete, more systemic way of holding experience. I would conclude by having people get together in small groups and share what they had learned.

With imaginal intelligence I made use of imagery/waking dream approaches. For example, after getting people into a relaxed state, I might have them imagine their lives as a journey—through a forest, across a desert, into outer space. I would then bring out large sheets of paper and have people draw what they had imagined—filling in added details that came to them as they did so (perhaps different kinds of terrain at different points on the journey or people that they encountered along the way). I would also invite people to again reflect on their daily-life question, this time looking to see whether anything in the journey imagery provided useful insights. Then, again in small groups, I would have each person act out their journey image, describing their experience as they moved and responding to questions from the other group members.

With emotional intelligence, I would start by having people reflect on various feelings/emotions that they had experienced at different important times in their lives. I would then invite people to write a few phrases that gave expression to each of those feelings/emotions—to in a sense be poets. I'd have people add these various feelings/emotions to their drawing, representing them as colors, shapes, or words. I would also have people look to see whether these different feeling/emotion constellations had useful things to say about the question they had been examining. Finally, again breaking into small groups, I would invite people to reflect on how this diversity of feeling perspectives could best be applied in making life choices.

For the rational, because few people question rationality's significance, I gave particular attention to how what can seem logical is more multifaceted than we tend to assume. I would start by having people return to their experiences with other intelligences—how different kinds of movement, different parts of the terrain in one's imaginal journey, or different emotional qualities evoked specific values and priorities. I would then ask if these values and priorities were also sometimes tied to particular "rational" conclusions. I would have people add words to their drawings that corresponded to various beliefs. I would also ask people to reflect on just how different those beliefs could be and on how they could directly contradict each other. And I would encourage people to imagine what it might mean to hold a larger picture, one that took them beyond these contradictions. Again people would share and explore in small groups.

At the end of the weekend, I would have people reflect back on their experiences with the various intelligences. I would also have people return to the more collective questions that they had listed on the first weekend. I would have people explore applying their various intelligences to these more overarching questions to see what surprising and useful information might result. We'd end by reflecting as a group on what people had found significant in the weekend's explorations.

Weekends #3 and #4: The next two weekends were dedicated to Parts Work. Parts Work engages each person's multiple aspects like characters in a play. First, I'd invite people to use the previous weekend's reflections to help them get in touch with different aspects of their makeup—characters in their particular inner story. I'd then demonstrate Parts Work and describe its basic principles. The remaining time was spent with participants facilitating each other in doing Parts Work, with me providing backup when needed. We will take a closer look at Parts Work shortly.

Weekend #5: This was the Patterning in Time weekend. I've described how simply grasping Patterning in Time concepts works as a hands-on method. To hold the whole of Patterning in Time's progression is ultimately to hold the whole of systemic organization. Participants came having done basic reading on the concept.

After first briefly introducing how Patterning in Time works, I'd proceed with the daylong "Evolutionary History of Music" presentation that I described in Chapter Three.[1] The presentation draws on

---

1 See www.Evolmusic.org.

multiple modes of expression—in particular music and movement—to illustrate the common underlying dynamics of human creative/developmental processes of all sorts.

With the second day of the weekend, I'd have participants apply Patterning in Time concepts to the multiple creative/developmental realities that interplay in their lives—specific creative or learning efforts, where they reside in their personal psychological development, the evolution of important relationships, the developmental stages of organizations they are a part of, and today's place in the evolution of culture. We ended the weekend by sharing in small groups and by practicing asking Patterning in Time questions in ways that would support systemic insights.

Weekend #6: With the next weekend, we turned our attention to Patterning in Space distinctions. As with Patterning in Time, we can think of a deep grasp of Patterning in Space concepts as a kind of hands-on exercise. I gave primary attention to personality style differences and the CSPT. Here we had the advantage of having the whole of Patterning in Space diversity there in the room to learn from. Again, people had done homework on the topic before arriving.

Over the weekend, I'd apply a handful of temperament-related approaches. Often I'd start by throwing a set of personality style cards we developed at the Institute out onto the floor. These cards included quotes and images that people of different temperaments might be drawn to. I'd ask people to choose a couple of cards with which they felt an affinity and also a couple of cards where they definitely did not. People then used the cards to further introduce themselves to the group. The group would use what they heard, combined with their experience of the person to that point, to guess the person's personality style within the CSPT framework.

We would also play a game I call "name that tune." Each participant would select someone from their lives that the group did not know. When it was a participant's turn, he or she would go out of the room and then come back in as that person. It was the group's job to ask the "mystery guest" questions and guess their temperament using the fewest number of questions. It was always great fun.

The last temperament approach produced some of the most surprising insights. I would break the larger group into three smaller groups by temperament axis—Earlies, Middles, and Lates. I would then give people in each temperament group a series of questions—such as the following: What do you most like to do for fun? How would you describe your political leanings? Do you think of yourself as a spiritual or religious person? And with regard to love, both how do you express love, and how do you know if someone loves you? I would have the three groups go off to different rooms and share answers to the various questions.

While the groups were away, I would set up a stage at one end of the large room. On the group's return, I would have each group in turn get up on the stage and share how they had answered the questions. The two groups that remained served as the audience. Their task was to ask questions that might clarify what they were hearing.

Frequently people's jaws would drop on recognizing how different the answers given by people from other groups could be. When people had been working in their small groups, often they had concluded that their particular group included great diversity. And it might, in part because of people's different backgrounds, but also because each group included people where Upper, Lower, Inner, and Outer aspects predominated. But when groups began to interview each other, they were quickly confronted by whole further levels of difference, differences so fundamental that often people could barely make sense of them.

The second love question—How do you know if someone loves you?—often provided particularly startling differences, and particularly striking insights. Answers could be almost opposite—for example, "the person calls me every day to tell me" and "the person is always protective of my alone time and privacy." Whether people were on the stage with their group or asking questions from the audience, they would find the experience fascinating, and also often unsettling.[2]

Weekend #7: The first day of the seventh weekend introduced Whole-Person/Whole-System Patterning Concepts and immersed participants in making these kinds of systemic discernments. We'd examine where each person experienced greatest Aliveness—in their personal lives, in groups they were a part of, and also in society as a whole.

---

[2] Chapter Ten offers a more detailed look at responses to the love question that ties particular temperaments to specific kinds of answers.

We'd also explore the concept of Capacitance and examine the kinds of Symptoms and conceptual traps to which the person and the various systems each person was a part of were most vulnerable.

The second day turned to application more broadly—now using all of the CST patterning concepts participants had learned about over the course of the Intensive. We'd examine more closely how various patterning notions related one to the other. And we'd apply them to each of the important systems in people's lives. Drawing on all the patterning concepts at once in this way would bring Integrative Meta-perspective and the use of a creative frame alive in particularly vivid ways. And small group sharing of people's reflections provided more opportunity to practice culturally mature facilitation.

Weekend #8: The next weekend again focused on application, but this time application to specific domains of culture. I'd have participants identify spheres where they had particular interest—education, love and family, government, science. Then, working in small interest-area groups, I'd have people apply what they had learned in the previous weeks of the Intensive to address key questions within that sphere.

This weekend always produced important additional learnings. Beyond specific insights, the observation that people could use the same change principles to address the future of diverse cultural domains increased people's appreciation for the systemic underpinnings of what we had been engaged in. And the recognition that we could think of cultural domains as the systemic crayons in the box of culture as a creative system helped further fill out the big-picture significance of our inquiry. (Chapter Eleven explores some of this kind of application.)

Weekends #9 and #10: With the last two weekends, I invited people to choose topics that they would like to explore in greater depth. Then, as a group we would design "hands-on" approaches that would let us do so. The concluding weekends took different directions with each year's group.

Parts Work

I've described Parts Work as the most direct means I know to generate culturally mature understanding. If a person is ready and Parts Work is done well, Integrative Meta-perspective is the inherent result. At the very least, this is the case at the level of personal maturity. With sufficient Capacitance, we also see culturally mature perspective and the appearance of culturally mature leadership abilities.

Our look at Parts Work here can only be an introduction. Any at all in-depth examination would require another book of this length. And even that would really not suffice. To appreciate all that Parts Work involves would require watching it being done—or better yet, taking part oneself. And that would need to be done over some significant time. When I work with individuals as a psychiatrist using Parts Work, it is usually in weekly sessions over a year or more.

But even this introduction should prove a powerful addition to this book's reflections. Parts Work, along with supporting Cultural Maturity's changes, provides a hands-on definition for culturally mature perspective and a simple way to make sense of its implications. In doing so, it also helps clarify the conceptual foundations of CST as a whole.

Parts Work's way of engaging our cognitive multiplicity might at first seem only metaphorical, but it becomes concrete and specific when viewed from a culturally mature vantage. Parts Work treats our various aspects—the crayons in our internal creative box—like characters in a play. Parts Work engages people in learning to appreciate and effectively draw on all of these various aspects/characters. In the process, people learn to hold and creatively manage the whole of who they are.

Parts Work can begin either with a person choosing a question or concern to explore, or just with them more generally talking about their life. The person, sitting in what will eventually be his or her Whole-Person chair (personally mature perspective chair—or perhaps, eventually, culturally mature perspective chair), is then guided in placing various parts around the room—perhaps a curious part, an angry part, a reasonable part, an intellectual part, a sexual part. Each part is given its own chair. Through engaging in conversation with the various parts, the person learns to consciously draw on and apply his or her larger—whole-box-of-crayons—complexity.

Three related cardinal rules guide the Parts Work process. Each ties directly to how our cognitive mechanisms become different with Integrative Meta-perspective. First, only the Whole-Person chair interacts with the world. This guarantees that interactions will be of a Whole-Person/Whole-System sort. Second, parts don't talk to the world, only to the Whole-Person chair. This contrasts with what we see with reactive personal responses and with more absolutist social assertions—where parts commonly do the talking. And third, parts don't talk with other parts.

If Parts Work is being done to address a marked Symptom or a strongly held ideological belief, it may take a person some time to get to the place where these rules are honored. But the rules define the process. Importantly, they are also directly modeled in the room in the therapist's relationship with the client. I take care to relate only to the person in the Whole-Person identity chair. If parts attempt to talk to me, I direct their attention back to where it belongs.

One result with Parts Work is the possibility of answers to questions that might have been the work's starting point. But ultimately more important is practice in holding experience more systemically. Through the dual process of simultaneously exercising authority from the Whole-Person chair and drawing deeply on the diverse viewpoints that parts represent, the person becomes increasingly facile at engaging experience in more conscious and complete ways. When this work is done at a personal level, the person learns both to take more conscious authority in their life and to draw more deeply on the diverse sensibilities that make them uniquely who they are. When the work happens at a more cultural level, Parts Work engages the person in drawing consciously and deeply on the diverse sensibilities and inclinations that make us who we are as humans.

Parts Work that is done over time tends to proceed through recognizable stages. Each stage reflects a kind of process that is key to Integrative Meta-perspective's changes. The first stage involves learning the difference between coming from the Whole-Person identity chair and coming from a part. The emphasis with this first kind of process is on separation and distinction. It involves recognizing how identifying with parts inherently produces distorted beliefs and polarized relationships. And it involves learning to say no when parts attempt to bleed in and take over.

With the next stage, the focus turns increasingly to the Whole-Person chair. I will often have the person make "leadership statements" to the parts, both to clarify who is in charge and to help the person become more adept at asking Questions of Referent and making Whole-Person choices. I also encourage the person to identify challenging life situations where they can practice making decisions from the Whole-Person chair's vantage.

The final stage involves a new and deeper kind of engagement with parts. Once people gain confidence in leading from the Whole-Person chair, they can turn their attention to drawing on different aspects as they can provide benefit. The results are frequently surprising. Often parts have contributions to make that the person had not anticipated. And the greatest surprise is frequently how richly potent and creative life can become when the person successfully draws on the full depth of their complexity.

Later in this chapter, I will describe how Parts Work provides a further useful image for depicting Integrative Meta-perspective's changes. We can think of Cultural Maturity's cognitive reordering as a kind of "rewiring." (See Figure 8-1 later in this chapter for a visual representation of this result.) For now, we can use the three cardinal rules to point toward how our cognitive "wiring" changes in doing Parts Work. Before doing the work, "wires" go from parts to the world. Afterward, we find only connections from the Whole-Person chair. In a similar way, before doing Parts Work, "wires" go back and forth between parts. Afterward, "wires" between parts, like those between parts and the world, are cut. Internal connections go only between parts and the Whole-Person identity chair.

As a therapist and also someone interested in change of a broader cultural sort, over the years I've come to draw more and more on the Parts Work approach. I don't know of other techniques that apply all of intelligence's multiple aspects so simply and unobtrusively. I also don't know of other ways of working that so directly support the various aspects of culturally mature understanding, and not just through what is said, but through every aspect of the approach, including the layout of the room. Of particular significance is how the fact that I as a therapist speak only to the Whole-Person chair (in keeping with the first cardinal rule) means that my relationship with the client directly models and affirms relationship of a Whole-Person sort.

Important recognitions that we've previously examined only conceptually are experienced directly when doing Parts Work. For example, Parts Work provides direct confirmation for my claim that ideological beliefs reflect identification with systemic aspects. In doing Parts Work, people find it increasingly obvious that parts by their nature hold simplistic and limited beliefs. People also see that allowing parts to talk to the world (in violation of the second cardinal rule) results in reactive and ideological assertions.[3] Parts Work also provides first-hand experience of culturally mature leadership, confirming in the process, for example, how such leadership is at once more powerful and more humble than what it replaces. Parts Work also offers immediate experience of the more complete kind of identity that CST describes with the Myth of the Individual.

Parts Work is not a "quick fix," even if the focus is primarily on concerns of a more personal sort. But engaged over time, more encompassing ways of thinking and acting follow naturally from the process. Ultimately Parts Work alters not just how a person engages specific issues, but also how he or she engages reality more broadly. The work becomes like lifting weights to build the "muscles" of culturally mature capacity. One of the litmus tests for success with this way of working is the appearance of culturally mature shifts with regard to questions that have not been directly addressed.

Later I will describe how this same general kind of approach can be applied to working with more than one person. I often use related methods when assisting groups where issues have become polarized, or with organizations where people wish to address many-sided questions that require careful, in-depth inquiry. When working in this way, I place individuals or small subgroups around the room to represent the various systemic aspects of the question at hand. Another group takes the Whole-Person chair role and attempts to articulate a larger systemic perspective.

Parts Work Examples

Four examples of Parts Work follow, each with a somewhat different emphasis. The first is a more filled-out version of an example I cited in *Cultural Maturity: A Guidebook for the Future*. It provides a good place

---

3 A subtle distinction underlies the second cardinal rule's dictate that parts don't talk to the world. Ultimately, the issue is not so much that problems arise when parts have relationships with the world, but that parts have never really been capable of having relationships with the world. Parts have only been capable of mythologized fantasies about the world. In another way, we recognize how Integrative Meta-perspective is simply about seeing life more accurately.

CREATIVE SYSTEMS THEORY

to start as it draws on only a couple of parts yet captures well the way Parts Work can readily shift between personal concerns and larger cultural issues. The example comes from individual therapy done with a fifty-five-year-old respected biologist and environmentalist. I will call him Bill.

Bill and environmental decision-making—

Bill's father had died. The immediate reason Bill had come to see me was the depression that followed this loss. But with time, along with addressing his grief, Bill recognized a further concern—what he described as a war within himself.

Bill's father had left him a beautiful piece of land that had been in the family for generations. Bill loved the place and planned to construct a cabin and move there when he retired. But new zoning regulations had made the land unbuildable. Suddenly, his plans were on hold. He felt deeply sad—and angry. The particular situation disturbed him, but even more disturbing to him ultimately was the way his response to it had left him torn from the comfortable moorings of a once-unquestioned set of beliefs. He was known for banging heads with property rights proponents and more often than not emerging victorious. Now, disparate internal voices were advocating not just different social policies, but two very different—and contradictory—views of the world. Bill found distress and confusion in this conflict and asked if we could somehow explore it.

I agreed. But I recognized that such work would present some difficulties. Bill was an exceptionally intelligent man with well-thought-out beliefs that were not easily questioned. We would have to do more than just talk if I was to be of help.

I began by having Bill imagine that the warring parts were like two actors on a stage. I asked him to describe everything he could about each character—what it wore, its age, the expression on its face. Then I had him invite them into the room. The environmentalist sat stage left, sensitive features, longish hair. The property rights advocate stood more distant, stage right, stockier in build, baseball cap tucked between his crossed arms. After a bit, he too sat down.

I instructed Bill to turn to the two figures and describe the issue he wanted to address. After a bit of initial self-consciousness, Bill proceeded to talk with them about the land, the new regulations, and the deep conflict he felt. Then I suggested that he go over to each chair and speak as that character—become it and give voice to what it felt about the questions at hand. I instructed him to return to his own chair when each character had said its piece and from there to respond to the chair that had spoken, and to follow up with any further questions he might have. I offered that he should let himself be surprised by what each character might say.

This back and forth went through multiple iterations, first Bill speaking, then, in turn, each of the parts. The character in the chair to the left spoke of the importance of protecting the environment in its natural state. The character on the right argued that government had no right to dictate what a person did with private property. Both expressed a longing to live in such a beautiful place. As the dialogue progressed, Bill's relationships with each of them deepened. He became increasingly able to find a place in himself where he could both respect what each character had to say and see limits to its helpfulness.

After some time, Bill again turned to me. He said he felt a bit disoriented, but that the conversation had helped. He commented that much of what the two characters said had indeed surprised him—and moved him. He found it particularly enlightening that each character seemed essentially well-intentioned. Before, he had framed the environmental/property rights conflict as a battle between good and ignorance (if not worse). We discussed how it was more accurately a battle between competing goods. Initially, it had been hard for him not to identify with the environmentalist, but, with time, he recognized that in fact each character had important things to say.

This brief piece of work hadn't given Bill a final answer for how to approach the property issue. But it had given him a more solid place to stand for making needed decisions. He had begun to see a more complete picture that offered at least the potential for more creative choices.

Later I asked Bill if the exercise might have broader implications for his professional efforts. We decided to continue with the hands-on approach. I tossed him particularly thorny questions that pitted environmental advocacy against property rights concerns. His task was to hold his Whole-Person chair and from there to use his two "consultants" to help him determine the most effective and fair approach. The result in each case was a deeper understanding of the dilemmas involved and, in several instances, novel solutions.

In fact, Parts Work almost always involves more parts than just two. And it often takes several months of work before a person can sit solidly in the Whole-Person—whole-box-of-crayons, Integrative Meta-perspective—chair. But the example illustrates a general type of method that is both straightforward and highly effective.

Rebecca and the making of major life choices—

The second example is similar in that it engages at both a personal and a collective level. But it is more complex in drawing on multiple parts. It also more explicitly applies CST patterning concepts. It comes from work with a thirty-two-year-old first-grade teacher who needed to decide whether she wanted to continue teaching. I will call her Rebecca.

Rebecca had been a teacher for eight years, working in a fairly traditional public school in one of the city's poorer neighborhoods. Students reflected a broad mix of ethnic backgrounds and countries of origin. English was often a second language. Rebecca has an Early-Axis personality style with a lot of Lower. In important ways this temperament made her a perfect fit for the job. The fact that she was an Early helped her connect with the Early-Axis developmental stage of the age group she worked with. And combined with her Lower Pole leanings, it helped her appreciate the challenges faced by people of diverse backgrounds.

But her temperament also meant that certain aspects of what she did were going to be more challenging for her than they might be for other teachers (most teachers are Middles). Teaching, particularly in complex environments, requires being skilled with making boundaries, something that tends not to come naturally for Earlies. And the school's reliance on traditional approaches meant that Rebecca was likely not going to feel as supported by the school culture as might be ideal.

Rebecca described herself on first coming to see me as feeling constantly anxious and sleeping poorly. She also often felt self-critical and inadequate as a teacher. She had pretty much decided that she was not cut out for teaching and was ready to quit. But in initially talking with Rebecca, it was clear to me that in fact she was a quite exceptional teacher. She had deep appreciation of and sensitivity to her students. And she obviously brought real creativity to the classroom. However, it was also clear that while as a person she had high Capacitance, circumstances were leaving her overwhelmed in a way that was ultimately neither healthy nor sustainable.

After taking a few sessions to become comfortable, I had Rebecca describe everything she could about the part of herself that was feeling anxious. That I spoke in this way at first took Rebecca aback. She had not thought of her anxiety as a part. But she was willing to play along and soon had brought the part into the room, placing it in a chair to her right. At the end of the session, Rebecca commented that while working this way felt a bit strange, just seeing the anxious part as separate from herself did seem to help her feel more relaxed.

In the next session, I had Rebecca more actively engage the anxious part and respond from its chair. It described itself as feeling unsafe and said that it wanted to run away. It also said it was angry at Rebecca for not protecting it, a comment that surprised and confused Rebecca. To help Rebecca gain perspective, I asked her if this part played any positive role in her teaching. She realized that it very much did. It was a sensitive part that she often drew on in relating to the kids. I then asked her an essential further question. I asked her whether it was often this part that was doing the relating. She realized that frequently this was the case.

Rebecca and I then talked more directly together. I observed that the same tendencies that gave the anxious/sensitive part sensitivity meant that it would have little grasp of the importance of boundaries, that the only way it had to protect itself was to flee. And then I described how the problem was really more fundamental. I described the three cardinal rules and how it was the Whole-Person chair's job not just to make choices, but also to do the relating—and how problems inevitably result when parts relate to the world. I also observed that a further essential part of the Whole-Person chair's task was to take charge in making boundaries. We agreed to talk in later sessions about how she could learn to make better boundaries as a teacher—and also in her life as a whole.

The next session brought attention to an additional part, and also to an important further kind of boundary. The anxious part described feeling criticized and demeaned. But when I asked Rebecca if the people around her were being critical, she said "no." In fact, they had been quite supportive. The criticism was coming from a critical part within herself.

I suggested that Rebecca also bring this critical part into the room. She placed it in a chair to her left. Again she described a certain relief in simply giving the part a chair—in this case because it helped her appreciate that rather than being an outside danger, it was something that she could, at least in potential, control.

Rebecca talked at length with the critical part. She was struck by how the part was ultimately not malicious—how it really just wanted her to do well. But she saw too how, more often than not, the result of its actions was harm. She found herself reflecting on how criticism she had gotten as a child in school had often left her feeling misunderstood. The claims of the critical part often mirrored that early criticism. And as she worked, Rebecca recognized another concern about the critical part that was ultimately just as important. It was talking not just to her, but also to the anxious part. The critical part was breaking the cardinal rule that parts don't talk to parts, and given that the anxious part had no way to protect itself, such "crosstalk" was going to be particularly problematical. Rebecca saw that leading from her Whole-Person chair would require her to make not just better boundaries in the world, but also better internal boundaries. She would need to stop the crosstalk, be sure that the critical part communicated only with her.

I suggested an exercise that might help Rebecca practice these needed new leadership skills. I would toss out specific classroom challenges and Rebecca would explore ways that she might now handle situations differently. She discovered to her fascination that both of her parts—once she had the right kind of relationships within them—could be of help. She saw that the sensitive part that before she had known most through feeling anxious helped her be empathetic toward students, appreciate their different needs, and also appreciate when she was starting to feel overwhelmed. She saw also that the more critical part that she had known mostly through unhelpful negativity could both help bring clarity to where boundaries in the world were needed and help her find the courage to make them.

While the exercise proved helpful, it also highlighted further work that would be essential. If Rebecca was to rethink how she taught, she would need to better understand what was important to her in teaching. She would need to more deeply understand her own values and explore the teaching approaches that might best serve them. Parts Work would again provide assistance, but she recognized that for this kind of questioning she would need the help of other aspects of herself. Over the ensuing weeks she brought in a playful/creative part, a strongly ethical part, a no-nonsense part, and a part that loved more big-picture understanding. After many useful "ahas," Rebecca was able to better describe the values and priorities that were most important to her as a teacher.

Eventually we returned to the exercise of trying on classroom challenges. Rebecca would imagine scenarios and use her parts to brainstorm how she would now manage them. This included working with students who had different kinds of needs. It also included classroom situations that might involve conflict or scary interactions. Rebecca was pleased to see that in most situations, as long as she kept her values in mind, she basically knew what to do. She also recognized that in situations where she didn't, some conferring with her parts often not only revealed workable strategies, it inspired her to try them. Rebecca was also encouraged by how much her sense of what was important to her further deepened in working with her parts. When she engaged questions from the whole of herself, she ended up thinking about learning and teaching—indeed, the whole purpose of education—in new, more creative ways. Some of this she found daunting. But she also found the beginnings of a new excitement in the teaching process.

I asked Rebecca if this new excitement was enough to have her again consider teaching. The recognition that she was still not sure alerted Rebecca to a further essential topic. She saw that to make her decision, she would need to reexamine her relationship to the school. Specifically, she saw that better boundaries there would also be important.

Some of these boundaries were pretty simple and easily done. For example, she had always before assumed she should share lunch each day with all the other teachers in the teachers' lunchroom. She realized that sometimes it would be better for her to be alone and have time to recharge herself. She also realized that frequent faculty meetings that often seemed to have little value could leave her drained. She decided she would talk to the principal about when attendance at meetings was important and when it could be optional. And Rebecca also saw something further that at once excited and disturbed her. She recognized that if she was going to stay on at the school, she would need to be outspoken in ways she had not been before. There were changes that the school needed to make if it were to be a quality learning environment. She would need to be ready to advocate for those changes if she was going to remain happy there for long.

Some sessions later, I again asked Rebecca how she was feeling about being a teacher. She responded that while in many ways the thought seemed even more overwhelming, it was also seeming more interesting. On hearing this, I asked Rebecca a further question that we had not touched on, but that I suspected would provide insight for the choices she would need to make. I asked her whether working at a different school, one that was more innovative and perhaps with a less challenging student population, might be a better fit.

She decided to try this additional question out with her parts. Again she found surprises. Their responses helped her recognize that much of what made teaching fulfilling for her was the diverse and challenging population. The parts' responses also helped her see that if she assumed the kind of leadership in herself we had been working on, she would likely be strong enough to handle what would be required.

Rebecca did decide to stay on. It was nearing summer break and the time away would give her a chance to get ready for the new year. Over that year we continued to work together and she continued to practice her new skills. Much did not become easier. Indeed, aspects of both teaching and being a part of the school environment became even more demanding. But she became increasingly effective in her teaching and found increasing fulfillment in her role as an educator.

Several years later we again crossed paths. I was just then starting an ongoing think tank on the future of education at the Institute. In time she would become a valued member.

Tim and today's Crisis of Purpose—

The third example highlights a kind of circumstance that I noted in first introducing the idea of a modern Crisis of Purpose in Chapter One. It also relates directly to reflections in Chapter Five about how the antidote to that crisis lies ultimately with addressing purpose directly—with asking the pertinent Questions of Referent. The example comes from work with a twenty-year-old who I will call Tim. Tim is a Middle with about equal balance between aspects. As I continue to work with Tim at the time of this writing, the description ends more with a question than with resolution.

On first meeting Tim, it was obvious to me that he was a bright person with a great deal of potential. But I also had major concerns about what might lie ahead for him. I mean this not just in the sense of whether his life would take a gratifying course, but also simply whether he would survive into adulthood. Addictive behavior consumed a major portion of his time—many hours a day playing video games, dependence on alcohol and marijuana, and off and on, the use of prescription painkillers. He was dangerously adrift.

With early sessions, I asked simple questions about Tim's daily life and what was important to him. Thankfully his Whole-Person chair was at least sometimes available to engage. And while his life lacked direction, he was capable of being reflective and often had strong opinions. We talked generally about interests and strengths. We also talked values. Because Tim had major questions about what he might want to do with his life, he found benefit in doing this basic work. But while these early sessions were useful and established trust, it was obvious that much that was going to be most important was being kept at arm's length. Finally, at one point Tim said, "We have to talk about the elephant in the room—how addicted I am to distraction."

Since Parts Work seemed like a natural match for what Tim was needing to do, I briefly introduced what it involved. I then invited Tim to give the part that was addicted to distraction a chair. I had him describe the part, observing everything he could about it. I then asked Tim how much of the time that part was in charge. He said probably 80 percent of his waking hours. This was a hard thing for him to admit.

Simply creating needed separation took multiple sessions. Initially, Tim found it hard to distinguish himself from the part. But through going back and forth between himself and the part's chair, gradually Tim made progress in knowing the difference. Tim also began to realize how important learning to be in charge from his chair was going to be if his life was going to work.

That was a start, but I knew from experience that the way Tim was thinking about addiction—simply that it was bad and that he has to do better—was not going to get him where he needed to go. I confronted Tim with a critical recognition. If he was going to be in charge, he would need to have something more powerful to offer than the addictive part could provide.

Engaging more actively in conversation with the distracted part began to point toward a path forward. When Tim asked the part why it took over, it answered that it felt hopeless—and not just about Tim's life. The part described how, when it looked at all that is going on in the world, it also often felt hopeless. The part proposed that, given what it saw, distraction was the safest and most rational choice.

The part's answer startled Tim, but Tim also appreciated that the part was being honest—and not unreasonable. I asked Tim if he in his Whole-Person chair also felt hopeless. He responded that he was not sure. I then asked Tim how he felt about the part's answer for this possible circumstance. I asked him if given the choice between distraction and looking squarely at the truth no matter how difficult the truth might be, he would also choose distraction.

There was a long pause. Tim got that somehow his answer would determine not just the course of therapy, but also of his life. Finally Tim responded. He said that he would choose the truth, even though it scared him to say so. I offered that from what I knew of him, I thought indeed that was the case. (This was how I honestly felt.) I also shared that I too had deep concerns about the future, probably as deep as his.

This exchange in an important sense brought us back to where our sessions together had begun. Our work together was ultimately not about stopping addiction. It was about finding a set of values and priorities important enough to Tim that distraction stopped being attractive. And it was about Tim finding the courage to incorruptibly follow those values and priorities in shaping his life. We agreed that therapy going forward would be about looking unswervingly at the truth. With this agreement, our work began in earnest.

Tim observed that when it came to values, he often felt confused. He felt strongly but was also often pulled back and forth between opposing conclusions. Identifying more parts would help shed light on these internal conflicts. It would also challenge Tim to get beyond them.

Tim was not lacking in strength as a person. But he did very much lack a picture of possibility that in any way stood up to scrutiny.

Tim had already recognized that the distraction part's view of the world didn't work as a final answer. So we tried to see if further parts might offer better direction. A next part was more a reflection of the models that Tim had grown up with. Tim's parents were both Lates. They had wanted him to go to business school or perhaps become a lawyer. In talking with that part, Tim realized that neither of these options would be a good fit. Each reflected values he could respect, but they didn't speak to what mattered most to him. He also saw that some of his vulnerability to distraction was a reaction to choices that would ultimately not give his life meaning.

Tim next turned to a part that spoke for a direction that many of his peers were taking. His best friend had become a software engineer. Tim liked that this direction seemed to point toward the future and would make use of his intellect. But in talking to the part, it became quickly clear that this direction, too, was for him not sufficiently compelling.

Tim's next thought was that he needed to do something with people, somehow work in the social services. He identified a liberal part that advocated for the disadvantaged. But conversations with this part proved in the end no more fruitful. While he shared many values with this part, when he looked deeply, he could not help feeling that its ideas were naive. He concluded that following that part's advice would not really lead to meaningful outcomes. Because of this, it would also not result in a life that could work for him.

At this point I confronted Tim. When people reject the advice of all of their parts, very often they are in fact in a part themselves. They are just avoiding commitment. I didn't think this was the case for Tim, but I wanted to be sure. And if this was the case, I wanted him to acknowledge it.

I described my concern and asked Tim what he thought. He responded that engaging these various parts had in fact made him more committed to making a contribution with his life. He also observed that parts he had identified had not been wholly unhelpful. Each had had something valuable to add to the conversation. There was a rigor in the part that advocated for more traditional roles that he had to admire. The character that had interest in a technology career brought a visionary quality that he liked. The part that emphasized more liberal values, while simplistic in its conclusions, was at least putting values forefront. And even the part that spoke for addiction had something to contribute. At least in feeling himself in contrast with it, he was reminded of the importance of courage and commitment even in the face of what might seem discouraging realities.

Our work today goes on. Tim continues to explore values and priorities and to try on directions that might be consistent with them. I've had him talk with people I know from different professions whose work I value. Tim's next steps are still not yet clear, but at this point I have no question that Tim will be someone who makes an important contribution with his life. Our conversations are direct and heartfelt. And Tim finds growing strength and confidence in drawing on his various parts. Addiction has stopped being a concern for the simple reason that Tim is finding real life too interesting and important. With each session, Tim has brought greater courage to looking at himself and the future. He is doing what our times are in some way asking of all of us.

Stephen and the immigration debate—

The next example ties directly to the task of addressing contemporary front-page-news issues more systemically. I've described how as a cultural psychiatrist I try to respond to issues that become polarized by engaging from a more systemic vantage. This example is adapted from my recent book, *Rethinking How We Think.* "Stephen" was in his mid-forties, sat on his town's city council, and was a respected member of his community.

I'd seen Stephen for several months when he came in for a session following the Thanksgiving holidays. He looked concerned. His family spanned the extremes politically, and the dinner table conversation had become quite heated.

Debate around the immigration question had left Stephen feeling particularly disturbed. Stephen's uncle was very conservative politically and left no doubt that he thought immigration should be severely restricted. Stephen's sister felt just as strongly that immigration benefited the country and that making citizenship possible for people from other countries, particularly where circumstances in their native countries were troubled, was the only moral thing to do. Stephen's uncle and sister had strongly bumped heads, with neither of them willing to back down.

As Stephen described the scene, I asked him what about the dinner table conversation had most bothered him. At first, he thought the answer to my question was obvious—no one would find that degree of conflict in a family a good thing. But with reflection, he saw that his reaction was also more personal. The immigration issue evoked a similar kind of conflict in himself. He could feel his stomach begin to hurt when he thought about it. Stephen realized that he didn't have good answers for the immigration question. Indeed, he really had little of great use to say about the topic. Particularly given his role on the city council, this was not a small matter. He would clearly need to spend more time with the question and discover better ways to think about it than he had found thus far.

After I described how Parts Work provides a simple way to address conflicted issues, Stephen agreed to give it a try. The first part Stephen identified was very much like his uncle—indeed, so much so that Stephen felt a bit embarrassed to own it as a part. It wore a cowboy hat and bordered on being overtly racist. Stephen gave it a chair off to his right.

At least initially, Stephen felt more comfortable with the second part that he identified. It was a college professor and held views more like those of his sister. But as Stephen got more in touch with this second part, he found himself also questioning its conclusions. The professor's views seemed too pat, even arrogant.

In preparation for engaging the parts, Stephen and I talked further about the Parts Work approach. I shared the cardinal rules. I also described how it appeared that parts in him had been talking to other parts. I suggested that the pain that Stephen felt in his stomach was likely a symptom of this internal tension. We talked about how Stephen's first task would be to cut the "wire" between the parts so they would be talking directly to him. His second task would be to talk with each part to find out what it had to contribute, to discern what was helpful and not helpful in what each had to offer.

Stephen went back and forth multiple times, talking first with one part and then the other. Doing so at least helped him begin to appreciate that the immigration question was legitimately complex. Stephen saw that the values expressed by each part were in their own ways valid. Each reflected a kind of good. His cowboy part talked about pride of place and the importance of protecting community and heritage. It also talked about wanting to be sure there would be good jobs for people's children. It sounded scared, and also angry that what many people had worked hard for might be taken away. The professor part, too, voiced values that Stephen could get behind. It spoke about how the U.S. was a country of immigrants and how it was our differences that made us strong. It proposed that immigration was good for the economy, not the reverse. And it made the same moral argument that Stephen's sister had voiced, that taking people in when they are in need is the compassionate thing to do.

But as Stephen spoke with the parts, it also became clear to him that each part in its own way also missed the mark. Each left out important pieces of the puzzle and often ended up reaching conclusions that were problematic—and sometimes simply wrong. For example, at one point the more conservative part argued that immigration puts us in danger because immigrants are so often criminals—an observation that Stephen knew was not supported by the evidence. With similar conviction, the more liberal part at times talked as if having totally open borders was the answer—a conclusion that Stephen knew came no closer to the truth and that was in its own way just as dangerous.

At one point, I asked Stephen if his Parts Work conversations were proving helpful. His first response was to express disappointment that not much had changed. He felt no closer to having an answer for the immigration question—indeed, in some ways, he felt a lot further from an answer. At least his parts had been sure of their convictions. Conversing with them had left him with an impossibly complex picture of potential benefits and potential harms.

But I disagreed. I offered that while Stephen had yet to derive much that could help at the level of policy, I saw important change. I asked him if it wasn't the case that he was seeing things more clearly, better taking everything that needed to be considered into account. He agreed that he was. I also asked him how his stomach was doing. To his surprise, he found that it felt considerably better.

As we talked further, I shared an experience that had helped me more usefully frame the immigration debate. A colleague in Europe had contacted me angrily after reading an article I had written on immigration policy. A dramatic influx of immigrants into his town had totally overwhelmed social services and, in his view, had left little of the town's tradition and history intact. He had come to regret his past more liberal feelings about immigration. While I had felt moved by what my colleague said, I recognized how different the circumstances were in the state of Washington where I live. Here, the consequences of immigration have been almost entirely positive. We would not have either an apple industry or a high-tech industry—industries central to the state's economy and identity—without the contributions of immigrants. My colleague and I found ourselves deeply struck by how dramatically different the immigration question became depending on the context.

After describing this experience to Stephen, I also shared an image that had helped me think about the immigration question more contextually. The image is that of a cell's outer membrane. A solid outer membrane is critical to a cell. Without it, life would be impossible. But it is just as critical to the cell's well-being that the membrane be permeable, that it be able to let in essential nutrients. The cell's task is to discern the relationship of solidity and permeability that is just right at particular times and places.[4]

Stephen found the image and the more systemic understanding it pointed toward useful. Certainly it helped him better appreciate how there was no one-size-fits-all answer with immigration. But it also helped him better understand that it was possible to arrive at "good enough" answers for particular contexts. Stephen saw that his task, if he was to provide leadership with the town council, would be to help its members discern the right balance—the right degree and kind of permeability—for the town's specific circumstances.

I suggested that Stephen again turn to his parts and articulate his new approach—make an internal "leadership statement." He clarified how he saw his task as making this more nuanced kind of discernment. He also shared with his parts that he felt each of them had important input to contribute for this thinking, how each could be a valuable consultant.

---

4 Notice how this image helps tie social/political belief together with polarity at its most fundamental. I've described how polarity at its most basic juxtaposes difference/distinction and oneness/connectedness. With the immigration question, conservative belief tends to identify more with boundary and difference ("build the wall"), liberal belief with connectedness and boundary permeability.

Stephen then had an additional recognition that would prove just as important. He saw that he would need more than just these two parts if he was to make decisions most effectively. He needed to have parts that voiced everything that went into creating healthy and vibrant communities. The work Stephen did over the ensuing months helped him both find greater equanimity in himself and be more effective and comfortable in his leadership role with the city council.

At the end of Chapter Ten's application of CST concepts to questions of gender and love, I will include a couple of additional Parts Work examples adapted from my book *On the Evolution of Intimacy*.

Cognitive Rewiring

Earlier I observed that we can understand the result with Parts Work as a kind of "cognitive rewiring." A deeper look at just how this is the case both helps clarify what Parts Work accomplishes and further supports my claim that the result is something fundamentally new. A related but more limited kind of "rewiring" takes place with maturity in individual development. With Cultural Maturity, it manifests in a way that redefines our relationship to experience as a whole.

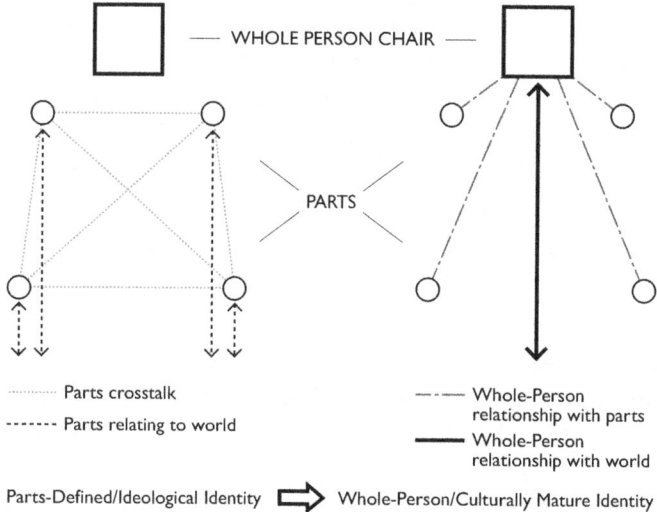

Fig. 8-1. Parts Work and Cultural Maturity's Cognitive Rewiring

I've noted how we can think of what becomes different in terms of Parts Work's cardinal rules. Prior to Cultural Maturity's cognitive changes, "wires" often run from parts to the world. "Wires" also run between parts. With Integrative Meta-perspective, all connection with the world happens from the Whole-Person chair. "Wires" between parts and the world are cut. And "wires" that have gone between parts are similarly cut. The only internal connections are between specific parts and the Whole-Person chair.

Appreciating that Parts Work produces this specific sort of cognitive rewiring helps us in multiple ways. Most immediately, it provides a further way to think about Integrative Meta-perspective, one that for many people is more readily grasped than the depiction of cognitive reorganization that I introduced in Chapter Two (see Figure 2-1). It also offers additional information not captured by the box-of crayons image. Culturally mature perspective comes to be about sitting solidly in that Whole-Person chair with this now more conscious, and explicitly creative relationship with parts.

Parts Work and this rewiring representation can also help fill out more particular conceptual insights. For example, I've observed how Parts Work supports CST's framing of ideology and its implications. Ideological beliefs are products of parts talking with each other and also with the world. They share that in some way they fail at Parts Work's cardinal rules.

We can also use Parts Work and this rewiring depiction to help us make sense of some of the more easily confusing aspects of culturally mature understanding. For example, they help clarify how it is that culturally mature perspective often results in apparent paradox. I've given particular attention to how culturally mature perspective makes understanding both more complex and simpler than what it replaces. Cultural Maturity's cognitive rewiring produces a result that is more complex in the sense that it requires greater Capacitance and also in the way that it more explicitly draws on a diverse array of creative elements. But in the sense that internal and external conflicting tendencies give way to the Whole-Person chair's single, encompassing locus of determination, it is also simpler.

One of the most important conceptual applications of Parts Work and this rewiring picture is the way it provides a more concrete way to think about culturally mature leadership. Culturally mature leadership becomes leadership that takes full responsibility from that Whole-Person chair. It is leadership that cuts the "wires" between parts and the world and also cuts the wires that before have linked parts with parts—leadership that engages life directly. This observation is pertinent to leadership of every sort, from making culturally mature choices in our personal lives, to engaging in relationships from a more Whole-Person/Whole-System place, to leading organizations and nations. All the various needed new leadership skills and capacities I've described follow naturally from what happens when we sit solidly in the Whole-Person chair. In doing Parts Work, we experience this result firsthand.

Parts Work and this rewiring picture also directly support a creative framing of truth. Sitting solidly in the Whole-Person chair doesn't give us last-word understanding, but it does have us better ask the right questions—questions that have the potential to lead to useful answers. The outcome of doing so is very specifically the new, more life-acknowledging and life-creating kind of discernments needed to effectively address today's most important questions.

This creative result helps reconcile an important leadership-related apparent paradox. We reasonably ask whether what we then see describes greater control or less control. Again we find both to be the case. We glimpsed how this might be so with Chapter Five's examination of the more "exploratory" kind of determination we find on the other side of Cultural Maturity's threshold. The Whole-Person chair's single point of determination in one sense very much means greater control—certainly it makes us more explicitly responsible and in charge. But "in charge" comes to have new meaning. Rather than greater control in the conventional sense, what we see is something ultimately much more significant: greater creative effectiveness and power.

An inherent consequence is important both to appreciating this more creative kind of determination and to perceiving it as something we might want. Having the Whole-Person chair in charge does not diminish the significance of parts as would be the result with control in the more traditional sense. The Whole-Person chair's new solidity and authority supports each part being most fully potent. Previously, the fact that parts taking over could have dangerous consequences kept parts from fully manifesting their significance. With Integrative Meta-perspective firmly established, such danger disappears. Cultural Maturity's cognitive reordering creates the ability to at once better manage the whole of our complexity and to draw most powerfully on that complexity. Returning to our box-of-crayons image, we become able not just to hold the whole box, but also to draw on the contributions of each of the crayons in ways that deeply tap each hue's particular vibrancy.

If we wish, we can also use Parts Work and the wiring diagram to be more specific with regard to the workings of ideology. In Chapter Seven, I used the idea of polar fallacies to tease apart some of the most common kinds of ideological worldviews. Parts Work and the wiring diagram provide a way to come at making these kinds of compare-and-contrast observations that provides additional nuance. We come back to the recognition that ideological beliefs all in some way fail at Parts Work's cardinal rules.

The more extreme of Separation Fallacies, for example, reflect what happens when a right-hand—more rational, scientific, or economically materialist—part directs the show and relates directly with the world. With the more extreme of Unity Fallacies, a left-hand—more spiritual or emotional—part prevails and again interacts directly with the world. With Compromise Fallacies, two parts talk with each other (rather than with the Whole-Person chair) and in various ways split the difference in their conclusions. Just how they split the difference will determine the kind of belief system that results. For example, with liberal/humanist belief, the conversation emphasizes more left-hand values (we often see a blurring of compromise and left-leaning conclusions with such belief). With postmodern belief of the different-strokes-for-different-folks sort, the conversation is going to be more balanced. And we commonly see a more right-hand bias along this same continuum with more libertarian conservative beliefs. With philosophically idealist belief, left-hand parts again talk with right-hand parts, but the left-hand part has a special status—it is assumed to be the ultimately causal force. Depending on the particular kind of philosophically idealist belief, the "voice" that speaks to the world may talk from a variety of points on the left/right continuum. I've described how various philosophically idealist views may frame the future in more spiritual or more political terms (and political conclusions can themselves span the left/right spectrum[5]).

---

5 The ideas of both Marx and Hitler were ultimately of this sort.

With Chapter Seven's descriptions, I summarized how culturally mature understanding differed from more ideological worldviews in terms of the way Integrative Meta-perspective lets us step back from and more consciously draw on the whole of our cognitive complexity. We can use the language of Parts Work and the wiring diagram to make the same kind of distinction. With none of these more ideological "wiring patterns" does the Whole-Person chair hold the needed defining authority, nor are multiplicity's aspects drawn on in ways that can give their diverse creative contributions full expression.

An important observation implied in some way in almost all of these descriptions is worth highlighting. It concerns the important recognition that prior to the full realization of Integrative Meta-perspective, parts rarely work in isolation. The influence of one part may be most obvious, but most often, parts work in collaboration with an opposite part.

This is easiest to recognize at a personal level. Dynamics that underlie procrastination provide a simple example. When we procrastinate, we tend to be most aware of the part that is digging in its heels. But it wouldn't be digging in its heels if there were not an opposite more controlling/authoritarian part that it was acting in reaction to. Where Parts Work involves helping a person deal with a pattern of procrastination, work with both parts is always necessary.

We can easily miss this more multifaceted picture with cultural level concerns for a simple reason. Historically we've tended to view cultural dynamics through the lens of projection. But most often more complex relationships have worked beneath the surface. For example, while it works adequately as a shorthand to think of liberal ideology as identifying more with the archetypally feminine and conservative views more with the archetypally masculine, the roots of such views are always more interesting than just opposing parts. More accurately, liberal views reflect a masculine/feminine polarity that leans more toward the archetypally feminine and conservative views a masculine/feminine polarity that leans more toward the archetypally masculine. If both poles were not involved in each case, we would not find liberals effectively competing on the political stage (well, not always that effectively), and conservatives often identifying as much with religious as political beliefs.

We can use this more nuanced picture to help us better appreciate the particular ideological beliefs of previous historical times. Each of history's previously defining cultural narratives can be understood in terms of parts-talking-to-parts "crosstalk" between the defining parts of that cultural stage. The result is the Patterning in Time progression that I described in Chapter Three. Direct conversation between parts at a cultural level gave us the easy complementarities of thought found in Early-Axis cultural realities (think of the yin and yang of Taoist thought or the intertwined serpents of the Greek caduceus), the warring absolutes of Middle-Axis belief (as with how medieval realities set good clearly against evil, and feudal lords solidly separate from peasantry), and the more cleanly cleaved distinctions of Late-Axis truth (as we see with our Modern Age juxtaposing of heroic and romantic narratives, and the separate-worlds assumptions of Cartesian dualism). CST describes how each of these parts-talking-to-parts realities in its time served us. Each helped drive the formative dynamics that ordered that period in history as a creative process. But CST also makes clear that parts talking to parts at a cultural level is incompatible with Integrative Meta-perspective and can ultimately only get in the way of going forward.

Addressing a potential confusion that can accompany this chapter's Parts Work reflections brings us back to an essential systemic observation that I touched on briefly with our look at Whole-Person/Whole-System truth in Chapter Five. We reasonably ask whether it is best to picture culturally mature truth as something that we find "at the center," like the arrangement of chairs in Parts Work might suggest, or whether we more accurately think of culturally mature truth as something that surrounds experience's complexity, as with how I've described the crayon's encompassing box. The answer is that both interpretations are again correct. More precisely, a culturally mature systemic picture requires that we hold both realities at once—pick either interpretation alone and we fall for predictable traps. Once more, we confront the Dilemma of Representation. This further apparent paradox provides additional support for the claim that we are dealing with understanding of a new sort.

Parts Work and the History of Psychology

Given its relationship to culturally mature understanding, we might expect Parts Work to make an important contribution to the future of psychology and psychiatry. In important ways it does. But as with culturally mature contributions in other spheres, it is also the case that Parts Work challenges familiar approaches and asks practitioners to think in ways that often run counter to favorite, more ideological beliefs. For the most part, psychology and psychiatry don't yet see the need for a tool like Parts Work. Viewing Parts Work through the lens of psychology's history helps point toward what would be needed for the kind of approach it represents to be widely utilized. It also helps clarify just what is new in the approach's contribution.

We appropriately think of modern psychology's beginnings as anticipating the eventual importance of culturally mature thought. I've described how the idea at the start of the last century that much in human functioning takes place beneath conscious awareness challenged Modern Age beliefs about the nature of intelligence. And while early thinking in modern psychology and psychiatry assumed that the task was simply to make the unconscious conscious, ideas that saw psychological functioning as having parts—most famously Freud's division of the psyche into id, ego, and superego—at least pointed toward more complex ways of thinking about who we are and how we understand. Most of the early theorists had some related framework for thinking about major parts. Carl Jung, for example, spoke of anima, animus, self, and shadow.

But right off we recognize key ways in which culturally mature methods such as Parts Work are different. First is how the task with Parts Work is no longer just to make the unconscious conscious. Parts Work does involve greater awareness and responsibility for one's choices. But where it takes us is wholly different from some final realization of the Modern Age ideal of bringing everything into the light of pure reason. The task with Parts Work is to more consciously hold the whole of who we are as thinking, feeling, imagining, sensing beings. The fact that much in who we are lies necessarily—and appropriately—always beyond conscious awareness is a key recognition with Integrative Metaperspective. This first difference supports both the significance of Parts Work as an approach and the claim that CST's ideas more generally reflect a leap in understanding.

A further difference with Parts Work might initially seem more just a matter of technique, but ultimately it has a more fundamental kind of significance. Parts Work steps beyond framing our human multiplicity in one-size-fits-all terms. Concepts like id, ego, and superego reflect common patterns. But what we find in doing Parts Work is always much more individual and nuanced. Each person's parts are different and the particular ways in which internal relationships and realities change over the course of psychotherapeutic work are unique to each person. Engaging a person's multiplicity doesn't depend on overlaying a conceptual framework. It follows directly from the Parts Work approach.

An additional key difference relates to what the practitioner assumes produces change. People who apply more humanistic approaches tend to assume that just giving a client the opportunity to express emotions will produce the desired outcome. Sometimes it does, but especially if one's interest lies with change of a culturally mature sort, this will rarely be enough. With analytic approaches, the methodology often focuses more on the therapist analyzing and interpreting the client's experience. The assumption is that this will result in the client then becoming more conscious—and symptoms resolving. Again, while we sometimes see useful change, the approach is limited.

The very particular way in which the relationship between the client and the therapist is structured in doing Parts Work helps clarify how the methodology is different in Parts Work and why we might expect to see a different kind of result. I've described how Whole-Person relationship is modeled in the therapeutic relationship. The therapist talks only to the Whole-Person chair, never to parts. Both more humanistic and more analytic psychotherapeutic approaches are based on very different ideas about the therapeutic relationship.

Humanistic approaches tend to assume that the therapist's job is to listen and perhaps reflect back what they hear. All that sounds good, but note that this way of thinking about the therapist's task implies that from the beginning the therapist is likely talking to parts. Indeed, in getting the person to explore their feelings—and perhaps earlier life events tied to those feelings—the therapist is very likely encouraging the person to speak even more deeply from parts. In contrast, with Parts Work the therapist doesn't talk to the part having those feelings. Rather, the therapist gets the person to engage the part—with that part now in a separate chair. The therapist's relationship with the person is of a Whole-Person sort from the start, and the therapist continues to model Whole-Person relationship throughout the course of the work.

We find a related difference with analytic approaches. I've spoken of how the analytic method is based on interpretation and analysis. In particular, it is based on interpretation of events that happen in the therapeutic relationship—to use analytic language, on the analysis of transference. With transference, it is assumed that the therapist is being experienced symbolically, most often as a projected parental figure. The therapist uses interpretation of this projection to help the person better understand early life experiences. With Parts Work, the therapist views transference as a signal that an additional part—that expressed in the projection—needs to be brought into the room. While the therapist in Parts Work sometimes makes interpretive observations, ultimately he or she is there to help the person hold experience in such a way that the person can engage their own truth in the most complete ways.

With both more humanistic and more analytic approaches, more often than not the therapist ends up talking to parts. And unless the therapist is very skilled, the result can be even more problematical—a therapist/client relationship in which parts in the therapist are talking to parts in the client. At the worst, real progress is undermined. At best, we are left with very weak levers for change. In the most sophisticated of hands we might see culturally mature insights, but there is very little in either kind of process that actively supports them.

Other approaches developed in the middle part of the last century share with Parts Work the fact that they draw on parts unique to the person and work activity in the sense of placing parts around the room and directly engaging them. I think in particular of Fritz Perls' gestalt therapy, Roberto Assagioli's psychosynthesis, and the psychodrama methods of Jacob Moreno. But these methods similarly differ from Parts Work in that with each the therapist is free to talk to parts. Again, while interacting with parts can yield legitimate psychotherapeutic results, ultimately it undermines the possibility that the approach will result in Cultural Maturity's deeper and more encompassing changes.

Something else we see with Parts Work is worth noting because it ties directly to CST's creative framing of cognition—and human understanding as a whole. It concerns how parts evolve over the course of doing Parts Work. Early on in the Parts Work process, it is largely the person's relationship with parts that changes, not the parts themselves. The person comes to see parts as separate and becomes better able to make use of parts when they are helpful and ignore them when they are not. A person may try to change a part, but efforts to do so will most often prove futile. Parts tend to interpret the attention as evidence that they are being of benefit.

But parts do change with Parts Work, just in ways that are less a product of intent and more a product of the Parts Work process and the creative nature of cognitive functioning. Parts ultimately want to be helpful. If a person repeatedly tells a part that something it is communicating is not helpful and stops listening to it, the part will begin looking to see if it can find a way to actually contribute. A key result may at first seem paradoxical, but ultimately it makes sense. Given that the parts that a person initially identifies as problems are likely to be some of a person's strongest parts (otherwise they would not be able to cause so much trouble), once the person sits solidly in the Whole-Person chair, the ways those parts change tend to make them particularly valued resources.

Importantly, it is not possible to wholly predict just how a part will change and how it will ultimately contribute. I find this creative unpredictability to be one of the most intriguing and enjoyable aspects of doing Parts Work. You'd think that with my years of experience, I could guess pretty accurately how parts would change. But I am continually surprised. In retrospect I can usually recognize that the way a part changes fits with the person's personality. I can also most often appreciate how changes reflect what is becoming timely and uniquely true for the person. But these are creative changes. In the end, what takes place is always different—and more interesting—than either I or the client might have anticipated.

Related Approaches with Groups—and Broader Applications

I've mentioned that I often use the same general kind of approach that I apply with Parts Work with groups. I am particularly likely to do so with groups that are experiencing internal conflicts or where a group is dealing with controversial issues. I then start by having individuals or small subgroups represent various competing voices. A second group assumes the equivalent of the Whole-Person chair role.

People in this second group have a sequence of tasks. First they are to engage the advocate groups in conversation to clarify the divergent positions. They then converse among themselves and seek to find larger systemic perspectives. And finally, they attempt to articulate conclusions and describe how these conclusions could be translated into right and timely action.

I'll share a brief example. I worked a few years back with a health care organization that wanted to bring greater maturity—and mutual respect—to the abortion debate. The topic had become a hot-button issue and contentious feelings were getting in the way of people working together effectively.

I began by separating out two small groups, one to advocate for a pro-life position, the other for pro-choice policies. (To make things more interesting, I switched the groups so that people in each group had to advocate for a position opposite to what they actually believed. I then had people who actually held the assigned positions be consultants to help the advocates effectively make their arguments.) The rest of the participants sat in a circle a distance back from the advocate groups.

To start the process, the advocate groups spoke in turn (with the consultants coaching so the advocates didn't miss important points). The main arguments were those we commonly hear. The pro-life group argued that abortion was murder. The pro-choice group countered that the decision should be in the hands of the woman (or the woman and her doctor).

Next the people in the outer circle were invited to ask curiosity questions. Their task initially was simply to clarify positions (the process allows no debate at this point). They then took on the further task of attempting to engage the issue of abortion as systemically as they were then able. And eventually they did their best to articulate their conclusions.

The efforts of the people in the outer circle did not produce final answers, but they did gradually move the question from one of right and wrong to one of competing goods. Several contributions proved particularly useful in this regard.

A man who leaned more pro-choice offered that he found it impossible to escape that abortion was in fact killing—at least the ending of a potential life. He confronted his pro-choice colleagues that denying this reality was only hiding from the real question.

A woman who leaned more pro-life first apologized that while what she had to offer had helped her, others might find it too philosophical. She described how she had found herself questioning whether death was the right way to think about the opposite of life. She proposed that maybe instead of being pro-life in a literal sense, people needed to think instead in terms of what was most supportive of life, this in the sense of what will support life being alive and vital. Several of her colleagues countered that such semantics accomplished nothing—that death could not be consistent with life—but the observation did get some in the group thinking in more encompassing ways.

The conversation continued on for about an hour. Rarely was there full agreement, but the stated goal—of generating greater mutual respect—was achieved. Gradually people were able to get to the place where productive conversation at least became possible.

Parts Work techniques in potential have broad application. While they are rightly thought of as psychological methodologies, because of the particular ways they are structured and the Whole-Person relationship the facilitator maintains with the individual or group doing the work, Parts Work approaches can ultimately be used any place where engendering culturally mature capacities is an appropriate objective. I think most immediately of educational settings. While today most educational institutions would not be comfortable utilizing such approaches, it could be powerful if they did. Such methods would be most obviously a good fit with interdisciplinary learning. They also might be particularly appropriate where education's task involves not just factual learning, but values-related inquiry. Given culturally mature perspective's argument that all questions today have become questions of value, arguably Parts Work approaches have a place with education of every sort—certainly leadership-related education, but also religious education, art education, business education, or the education of scientists.

Hands-On Approaches in Organizational Settings

I've frequently drawn on insights that come from the various kinds of hands-on approaches we've looked at with this chapter in working with organizations. Most often in these settings I've applied such approaches more informally. I think immediately of work I did some years back with our local public television station. The station wanted my help with regard to how it was functioning as an organization. It also wanted assistance with determining the direction that public media should take if it were to make the greatest cultural contribution. I suggested putting together an ongoing "internal think tank" to address these questions.

I started by selecting participants according to the same general criteria I described with the Intensive. I looked for high Capacitance. I also wanted maximum creative diversity. For the latter, I chose representation from each major part of the station (which, because various aspects of an organization often draw on people with specific temperaments, also meant some diversity of personality style) and also selected for diversity of background, gender, and more directly for personality style diversity. We met once a month for over three years. The group's assigned task was to identify the questions that were most important with regard to both of the think tank's objectives and to take them on. My job was to actively facilitate in a way that would produce culturally mature engagement. The approach proved powerful.

While I didn't overtly draw on hands-on techniques or apply culturally mature patterning notions, each was implied in what we did. At the heart of the think tank process was keeping the ultimate Question of Referent always at the forefront—our job was to address the concerns that could most enhance the station's contribution. I drew directly on the group's Patterning in Space diversity. The way I led the group meant that people actively applied culturally mature skills and capacities. And often I made observations that in some way gave voice to more detailed patterning distinctions.

Our work together did not alter the organizational structure or basic organizational functions in any obvious way. (Sometimes culturally mature organizational change significantly alters the structure of an organization, but often it doesn't need to.) We simply added—with the ongoing "think tank" group—a new organizational element. It could be thought of as a place for doing ongoing Parts Work with the organization as a system.

Two things were key to that element's creative influence. First, the organization's positional decision-makers, the CEO and the COO, were active participants. The decision-making hierarchy was not changed, but those making final decisions had ongoing creative input from the larger group, and formal leadership was held accountable just by the fact of continued involvement in the group. Also, participants were instructed to find ways to engage people in their departments in a related inquiry process—at the very least to ask people to assist in identifying questions that could be brought to the larger think tank group. The result supported the station as a whole becoming an increasingly conscious, continually evolving, creative system.

Application as a Hands-On Tool— Putting CST Patterning Concepts Together

Application of CST patterning concepts provides one of the best hands-on tools for enhancing culturally mature understanding. I've emphasized how practicing new skills and capacities that come with Integrative Meta-perspective supports the realization of Integrative Meta-perspective. And I've suggested that the same is ultimately true for applying any kind of CST patterning concept. The last few weekends of the Intensive often engaged participants in this kind of application. We'd work at applying CST patterning concepts to all parts of our lives, now all at once. It is beyond the scope of this book to apply such "CST analysis" in great detail, but a quick look at the kinds of distinctions that tend to prove most helpful at different systemic scales helps fill out previous reflections.

For this inquiry, the important recognition is that whatever kind of system we wish to examine—and whatever level of detail is pertinent—in some way each of CST's basic kinds of patterning distinctions provides important information. And there is more. Because all CST patterning concepts are based on the recognition that human systems are creatively ordered and share a common language, this kind of analysis often makes it possible to address highly complex phenomena in surprisingly compact ways. For the same reason, the use of a creative frame means that such analysis is inherently dynamic in a way that honors our living, human natures.

Below I've outlined the general kinds of discernments that might be most important when applying Creative Systems patterning concepts to the creative life of an individual, a relationship, an organization, and a nation-state. I encourage you to use these brief descriptions as an exercise. Try applying the discernments I describe to the important systems in your life:

Application at the Level of the Individual: When the system in question is an individual (in this case, yourself), the obvious place to start is with Aliveness, with asking the pertinent Questions of Referent and discerning where the most creative answers lie. Capacitance and temperament discernments also obviously provide essential information. And we can't leave out stage in personal development. Internal Patterning in Space complexity (parts, if you were doing Parts Work) and Symptom patterns that may arise if you are stressed are also clearly pertinent.

Also important to consider are all manner of patterning observations related to larger systems—for example, the Patterning in Space function of your profession (being a teacher, a salesperson, or a lawyer requires drawing on different sensibilities). And more contextual developmental observations may also be relevant—for example, the creative stage and emerging critical questions that define your larger cultural context.

Application at the Level of Relationship: To the above considerations about yourself, we necessarily here add Aliveness and Capacitance observations as they pertain to the individual identities of other people. We also necessarily add how the temperaments of people we relate to may be similar and different from our own. We may also want to consider the developmental stage of a relationship (inspiration stage, perspiration stage, and finishing and polishing tasks make very different demands that affect people of different temperaments in different ways), and the creative edge of the relationship as a process, where potential for new Aliveness in the relationship most resides.

In addition, cultural Patterning in Time context will be a major variable when it comes to relationship options. This is the case at any cultural time (for example, with love, it was just as true when intimate bonds were determined by matchmakers), but in our time, with the new potential for Whole-Person relationship, it takes on particular importance.

Application at the Level of Organizations: A full analysis of the health and functioning of an organization draws on all of Creative Systems Theory's patterning tools. Whole-System organizational concerns start with where the growing edge of the organization's contribution lies—where new organizational Aliveness/creative substance is most likely to be found. They also include the Capacitance of the organization as a whole and the Capacitance demands of the particular challenges the organization faces. We also want to be sensitive to ways in which the system as a whole, as well as specific individuals within it, are likely to respond when stressed beyond available Capacitance.

With regard to Patterning in Time, particular attention needs to be given to the developmental stage of the organization and the creative stage at which key projects reside. Cultural-scale Patterning in Time variables may become specifically important if an organization functions internationally, or if culturally mature leadership and organizational functioning are considerations (as they more and more must be for any organization that wants to be vital in our time and attract the best people).

Patterning in Space organizational concerns include the organization's creative role (Early-Axis, Middle-Axis, and Late-Axis organizations require different kinds of organizational cultures and different approaches to leadership and management). They also include the temperaments of key people, how those temperaments match or don't match the expectations and demands of particular organizational functions, and the potential synergies and conflicts that temperament differences in particular relationships might be expected to produce.

Application at the Level of Nations and the Planet: Cultural-scale Patterning in Time observations here provide the most important distinctions. They alert us both to our own defining tasks and also to what relationships with other people on the planet who may reside at different developmental stages may require of us. Patterning in Space observations that have to do with the functions of specific aspects of culture—government, business, science, religions—can help support culturally mature changes within various spheres. And Capacitance discernments also have an essential place—from understanding the Capacitance demands of particular cultural challenges to the ultimate question of whether we as a species can make manifest sufficient Capacitance to effectively confront (bring sufficient wisdom to) the challenges before us.

Making the multifaceted discernments these various patterning observations suggest might at first seem a rather daunting task. But all these factors are systemically pertinent—leave any of them out and we risk making poor decisions. And because each kind of discrimination reflects a related architecture—or at least draws on a parallel formative perspective—with practice, such analysis can feel straightforward—and fun.

CHAPTER NINE

Applying Creative Systems Theory Patterning Concepts #1: Front-Page News Concerns

The next four chapters turn to application. We will look at how Creative Systems Theory patterning concepts help us address all manner of concerns—the most immediate of current issues, specific broader cultural questions, the defining challenges of various cultural spheres, and the most encompassing and ultimate of human quandaries. The success of CST patterning concepts in doing so helps illustrate their practical usefulness. It also supports the accuracy of these notions and helps clear up confusions that might remain.

The topics this chapter touches on are the most immediately visible—front-page news questions. Reflections in previous chapters addressed content that could easily be included here. In Chapter One, I noted how chosen-people/evil-other dynamics put us at risk of nuclear annihilation. In Chapter Four, I confronted the question of what is ultimately needed if we are to effectively address the health care delivery crisis and used the answer to illustrate the importance of a new maturity in relationship to death. The Parts Work example in Chapter Eight that addressed the immigration debate included reflections that I've often written about more formally. And Chapter Eight's group Parts Work example engaged the question of abortion.

Here I've included ten pieces adapted from articles that I originally wrote for the Cultural Maturity blog and that were also later published in other settings. Topics include lessons to be learned from the 2020 coronavirus pandemic (a series of four short articles); climate change and what it asks of us; making sense of today's extreme polarization and partisanship (a more extended piece); addressing gun violence; understanding freedom systemically; avoiding cynicism in the face of easily disturbing circumstances; and how device addiction, particularly when combined with advances in machine learning, presents one of our time's greatest concerns. Because the original articles were written for audiences that did not have detailed knowledge of CST, they tend to focus primarily on the needed new skills and capacities that come with culturally mature understanding. But more specific CST patterning notions will almost always at least be implied. And sometimes patterning concepts will have a central place.

These pieces will often include content that I've presented in other ways in other places in this book or that overlaps with other articles. As I did with articles in Chapter Four, for the most part I will leave such content intact. Including pieces in their entirety provides perspective for understanding how over the years I've communicated difficult concepts. I've spoken of how culturally mature advocacy presents major challenges—because culturally mature perspective is new, certainly, but also because culturally mature understanding confronts us with the Dilemma of Representation. For many people, the insights these pieces provide for the tasks of teaching and articulation will be at least as important as the specific ideas, if not more. Also, with these overlaps intact, the articles serve as a way to bring important concepts presented over the course of the book together.

Lessons from the Coronavirus Pandemic

[Because I completed this book during the 2020 coronavirus pandemic, a series of pandemic-related articles makes an apt place to begin. I wrote these four pieces over the first couple of months of the pandemic to help people grasp what they would likely be confronting, prepare for the tasks ahead, and meet circumstances in the most healthy ways.]

Lessons from the Pandemic #1:
Key Insights

As a cultural psychiatrist, I endeavor to bring big-picture perspective to our time's important questions. In particular, I try to highlight how our times are requiring more "grown-up" human skills and capacities—what I call a new Cultural Maturity—and how this relates to the challenges we face. An obvious question for today as we begin to confront the coronavirus pandemic is just what we can learn from it. Most important immediately is the advice of public health experts and epidemiologists. But in the long term, there is a lot that ties quite directly to the task of thinking and acting in newly mature ways. Here are the four such insights I find most key:

Foresight is critical to our future well-being—and is a capacity we are only beginning to fully appreciate. People have spoken as if the pandemic were a surprise. But in fact, the only surprise is that it did not happen sooner. Epidemiologists have been warning us for decades that it was only a matter of time before we confronted something like what we are seeing. With SARS, MERS, H1N1, and Ebola, in each case we dodged a bullet.

How could we have failed to heed the obvious warnings? In fact, thinking with the needed depth about the future is something we are only beginning to become capable of. Note that we have all had classes on history, but very few people have had classes on what may lie ahead. The needed responsibility for our future well-being could not be more important. But it asks of us a level of human maturity that we barely understand, much less manifest.

We need to be comfortable making decisions in the context of real uncertainty. The coronavirus was a "novel" virus. Initially we knew almost nothing we needed to know to manage it effectively, and what we did know was always a moving target. Even well into the pandemic, there were often more questions than answers. Each step along the way, we had to do our best to assess risk and plan in the context of dynamic circumstances and real uncertainty.

This is not something we tend to be comfortable doing and something we have rarely done effectively in times past. We like to know for sure. And in times past, culture has shielded us from having to confront such uncertainty too often, providing us with ready ways to keep it at bay—God-given rules of right and wrong and the simple-answer solutions of ideology (whatever the persuasion). Increasingly today, we confront challenges where hiding from uncertainty could well be our undoing.

The kind of sophistication needed to effectively tolerate uncertainty and think in terms of assessment of risk is new. It requires a level of maturity we are only now becoming capable of. But it will be increasingly essential. I argued twenty years ago, for example, that the climate change debate was essentially over, but not because the science had provided the needed evidence (science can't provide once-and-for-all answers to such questions). Rather the debate is over because climate change is a question of risk assessment. Like it or not, the most important questions in life involve significant uncertainty. They are "creative" in this sense, not about final answers, but about effectively assessing risk (and possibility). But it asks a lot to hold questions this way. We are just beginning to become capable of the maturity of perspective needed to do so.

Our times challenge us to define human advancement in more mature and complete ways. When self-described futurists talk about the future, you are likely to hear about traveling to Mars or self-driving cars. And the average person is likely to think about progress primarily in terms of new inventions and material growth. The coronavirus pandemic makes one of the central messages of the concept of Cultural Maturity hard to escape. Wealth and progress today need new, more complete definitions.

Needed foresight would have produced some very different priorities. Certainly hospitals and health care systems more generally would have been better prepared, and mechanisms needed to support them more in place. And governmental agencies tasked with keeping an eye on potential pathogens and with emergency preparedness would have been better funded. But more than this, our priorities more generally need to reflect what is required for societies to be robust and vital. The list can seem rather mundane, but it addresses what is needed for a healthy future. A few things it might include: more attention to essential infrastructure like roads and bridges, establishment of widely available mental health resources, a better way of addressing poverty and homelessness, and a greater emphasis on renewable resources and the well-being of the environment. And those things are just a start.

Defining progress in terms of the requirements of healthy and resilient societies and of an environmentally sustainable planet can at first seem less "sexy" than our more familiar onward-and-upward imagery. But what I describe is not about settling for something less interesting. It is about finding the place in ourselves where we experience larger well-being as the goal that is ultimately most life-affirming, and thus most ultimately "sexy."

There is much we can learn from confronting death. The coronavirus pandemic has required a more intimate relationship with death than many people have before experienced. If we have not found ourselves personally standing face to face with mortality, certainly we know someone who has. This is legitimately frightening. But it is also the case that death is one of life's most profound teachers. And arguably it is a teacher of exactly what we are most needing in our times to learn.

I've written extensively about the importance of realizing a new maturity in our relationship with death. The topic has implications not just for our personal lives, but for the choices we make as a species. The need to confront death as directly as the coronavirus pandemic demands can help support the needed new maturity in our relationship with death more generally. And that in turn can help support the greater human maturity that we need to bring today to concerns of every sort.

Both personally and collectively, today, we confront what I've called a Crisis of Purpose. Too often people feel rudderless, without a deep sense of meaning and direction in their lives. I've described how we find the necessary antidote in asking about what matters in deeper and more complete ways. I also describe how confronting death can help us do so. I put it this way in my most recent book, *Rethinking How We Think*:

"Coming face to face with mortality in our individual lives teaches us about what most matters to us as individuals—death is a personal life's most pointed teacher of meaning, and ultimately of wisdom. As we learn to engage death collectively with a new maturity, it is reasonable to think that this engagement should help us in a similar way to more deeply confront what ultimately matters to us more broadly—as humans.

"Death confronts us with the fact that life as we know it ends. But it also confronts us with what is an even more final and easily disturbing limit. Death confronts us with limits to what is possible to control, and perhaps ultimately to understand. The humility required to accept this limit should play an essential role in helping us generate the wisdom that effective future decision-making in all parts of our personal and collective lives will increasingly require."

Confronting the pandemic and its consequences is at times simply wrenching. The best we can do is deal with the pain and disorientation as we are able. But there are also ways in which what we are experiencing provides an important "teachable moment." All of these lessons pertain at every scale of life, from the most personal, to the health of neighborhoods and communities, to the global connections that will be needed if we are to act together effectively. That is another lesson. In a way that has not before been the case, the future is making it inescapable that we are all in this together.

Lessons from the Pandemic #2:
Political and Social Polarization—
A Real Danger We Can Do Something About

Last night I awoke disturbed by images of a situation that could put us at even greater risk with the challenges we now face. I saw that unless we choose not to let it happen, the increased polarization we've witnessed in recent years could make the already dire consequences of the coronavirus pandemic significantly worse.

I've written extensively about how we humans have tended to view issues in polarized terms even where concerns really don't have sides. I've also described how continuing this tendency threatens to be our undoing. The pandemic confronts us in a particularly stark way with how political and social polarization today puts us at risk. That is the bad news. The good news is that this is a risk we can do something about.

About a month ago, one of my clients asked if I expected to see partisan reactiveness in response to the coronavirus pandemic. I responded that in the short term I was not too worried. We humans are often at our best when faced with emergencies. But I also shared that I was quite concerned about what we might see if the possibility of infection extended out over a significant time, which as a physician I think is highly likely. We could imagine we have won the battle as we begin to successfully "flatten the curve," but in fact the larger part of the work remains to be done and the greatest challenges, at least psychologically, likely still lie ahead. Not falling for old ways of thinking and reacting that could significantly amplify dangers will be key to making it through successfully.

The images that woke me up brought that added danger into high relief. We are beginning to see a fissure with how those on the political left are putting greatest emphasis on public health and preventing infection while those on the political right are tending more to emphasize jobs and the economy. Both are appropriate concerns. But if this fissure becomes more pronounced, the polarizing that could result might easily be experienced not just in terms of conflicting ideologies, but in terms of differing interpretations that could each be seen as having life-and-death implications.

People on the Left could experience the words and actions of those on the Right as putting their lives at risk in a very immediate and personal sense (a person not adhering to social distancing is legitimately seen not just as a threat, but as fundamentally irresponsible and a potential cause of death). And people on the Right might experience the words and actions of those on the Left as putting their lives at risk in the very real sense of livelihood. Emotionally the reaction could be just as strong, and just as immediate and personal (to have social distancing result in the loss of a business that has taken a person's life to build could be felt not just like a death, but as a wholly unnecessary death, and thus in an important sense like murder).

The challenge with the pandemic would be demanding enough even with the best of leadership (which we currently lack at least at a national level) and the best of science (which is now coming on board). The months (and perhaps years) ahead will require highly sophisticated, level-headed thinking able to address complex realities and adjust quickly to changing circumstances. If we let our fears complicate the situation by creating meaningless animosities and false narratives, our chances of getting through all of this in an at all healthy fashion are dramatically reduced.

To be clear in what I am suggesting, the task is not just to somehow split the difference. While the needs expressed by each polar position are valid and important, the best strategies involve putting the strongest initial emphasis on health. This might seem like siding with the Left, but ultimately it is not. If we don't start there, businesses will collapse however well we handle the economic side of the equation. Over time, the voices of the Left and Right more explicitly each have significance. As we attempt to reestablish robust and equitable societies, both health and economic concerns are each critically important to consider—indeed, they can't be separated.

The need for this kind of one-hand-then-the-other, but ultimately two-handed response is not unique to a pandemic—the best policies with polarized and polarizing issues often depend on timing. Climate change requires first taking the issue seriously and recognizing that prompt action is essential—which might again look like siding with the Left. But later the values of the Right and the Left have equally essential roles as conversations turn to how our long-term choices can best result in a resilient and sustainable world. The appropriate order can go either way. With the 2008 financial collapse, most immediately we needed to be sure banks did not fail—if they did, there would be total chaos. But very quickly, it was the financial needs of average citizens that as much or more required our attention.

Not everyone needs such nuanced conceptual framing. My point here is simply that this time around we don't have the luxury of business-as-usual partisan pettiness. At the very least we could end up being hateful and cruel toward one another exactly when perspective and compassion is most needed. At worst we could make choices that would result in many more deaths than would otherwise to be necessary.

So what is the task if we feel ourselves polarizing as we face the fears and difficult uncertainties of the pandemic? It is the same for individuals and for policy makers: First, stop—then step back and take time to consider a larger picture. We are all in this together. And everyone's well-being has multiple aspects that in the end need to be considered.

As we look to the future, the pandemic can serve as a powerful teacher to help us leave behind ways of thinking that in all parts of our lives have ceased to serve us. If we can manage the needed greater maturity now, we may well look back on the coronavirus pandemic of 2020 as a critical time in which we took important steps toward the kind of greater human maturity that questions of all sorts will increasingly require going forward.

Lessons from the Pandemic #3:
The Next Two or Three Months

As a psychiatrist, I've noted a pattern over the last couple of weeks with clients (and also friends). While everyone seemed to be doing remarkably well over the early weeks of the pandemic, now I am beginning to see despondency and depression. This should not be a surprise. We humans tend to respond with strength in the face of emergencies. We tend to do less well when challenges become more drawn out, as is the case today. We face ongoing anxiety and uncertainty, and depending on our circumstances, either burnout from being on the front lines or boredom and loneliness from self-isolation. Either situation is a ready formula for depression.

I've included here some reflections from my role as futurist and cultural psychiatrist that might prove helpful in getting through this next phase in a healthy way. They don't provide an antidote to depression, but they do offer perspective for what is being asked of us.

The short version: We will do best if we can acknowledge that our current situation will likely go on for quite a while. It will be a marathon, not a sprint. We also need to accept that significant uncertainty will remain a part of it. Many of the most important answers can only come over time. And we need to avoid falling for easy-answer responses that in the long run will only make matters worse. Like it or not, the months ahead will require immense patience and a degree of maturity and level-headedness that we may not be used to.

We will find our capacity for maturity and level-headedness particularly tested as we begin to open our doors and return to some semblance of normality. There is no simple formula for how to do it. And certainly there is no ultimately safe way to do so. Inevitably we will all feel pain as people continue to die from the virus and businesses fail to make what will often be very difficult, perhaps impossible, transitions. The key to meeting the challenge will be bringing mature perspective to what is being asked.

Even with the best of testing and contact tracking, it will likely be a bit like playing Whac-A-Mole as we get containment in some places only to see new outbreaks in others. Different places in the world will come at it differently and at different paces. We need to be able to engage it as an experiment, realizing that there is no way to know ahead of time just what will work best. We aren't accustomed to this kind of experimental, risk assessment–based approach. But that is what is needed. We need to take our best shot at guessing what might work, then be as intelligent as we can in evaluating the evidence and making further decisions accordingly.

A key in all of this will be avoiding responses that only increase our likeliness of feeling overwhelmed while providing no real information or benefit. It is our tendency when things get to be too much to polarize and run to favorite simple-answer beliefs. This kind of response, while it has often served us in times past (by reducing our experience of uncertainty and complexity), will work less and less often going forward. Without question, this is the case with the pandemic and what it will ask of us in the months ahead. If we are not to fall into depression, we must avoid reactive responses in ourselves. We must also avoid having our attention distracted by the reactive responses of others and by actions that exploit our uncertainties.

In particular, we need to shield ourselves from such responses in the political sphere and in the media. Early on, political figures—with a few marked exceptions—also did pretty well, as the population did. For similar reasons, leaders tend to respond admirably in the face of crisis. But I could imagine this being less the case in the months ahead. Polarized responses stand ready on both the Right and the Left. On the Right, people will be vulnerable to pushing too quickly into getting businesses up and running—with major new outbreaks a potential result. On the Left, people will be vulnerable to making the desire to keep everyone safe from disease its own kind of ideological purity—again only putting people further at risk in the process. Avoiding either kind of polarized response will be essential to good policy. It will also be essential because we have enough to deal with, with the virus and all it asks of us. Having to deal with partisan polarizing becomes a distraction that we really can't afford.

How the media responds, and how we respond to it, will also be important. The media similarly did pretty well early on. It was clearly an emergency, and there was plenty of real information that people needed. Over the months ahead, the amount of news that will really be news—anything that is new and actually informs us—is likely to be pretty small. There will be important information to keep up on: what we are learning about virulence and immunity; progress that is being made with testing, treatments, and vaccines; how the "experiments" with different approaches to reopening are proceeding. But beyond these things, there will likely not be a lot to report. The media tend not to be at their best when what is called for is patience and perspective. When they run out of good front-page news content, they start looking for drama. Similarly, we really don't have the luxury of letting our already taxed emotional bandwidth be highjacked by clickbait and drama.

For our mental health, we need to keep in mind that we are in this for the long haul. We also need to accept that much will remain uncertain for many months into the future. And, yes, like it or not, it will be Whac-A-Mole, with many more variables than we can count and all of it a moving target. Our task will be to keep the "moles" as small and infrequent as possible so that our health care systems don't get overwhelmed and so that we have time to develop treatments and vaccines. But that doesn't mean that outbreaks will not appear—indeed, if we are doing the experiments in the ways that will save the most lives in the long term, they certainly will. Our task is to learn as much as we can from when they do. It is also to not tolerate behaviors that only make overwhelming circumstance more difficult. We must stay vigilant in calling out claims that might appear to protect us from real uncertainties and shun distractions that become attractive because they shield us from our fears.

This degree of maturity and level-headedness asks a lot of us. But if we can bring it to bear, what is needed going forward, while unquestionably a challenge, becomes pretty straightforward. We should be able as individuals to avoid overwhelm and despair. And together, we should find the resilience needed ultimately to thrive. We should also learn a lot in the process, and a lot that will serve us going forward. It is a kind of maturity that we as a species will likely need with growing frequency in the decades and centuries ahead.

Lessons from the Pandemic #4:
Finding Simplicity in a Time of New Complexities

This is the fourth in a series of articles I have written in my cultural psychiatrist's role since the start of the pandemic. It is a bit more demanding than those previous, but important. The pandemic today confronts everyone with new complexities. Certainly this is the case if we are on the front lines battling a virus that easily overwhelms resources and too often acts in ways that we cannot fully understand. But we also face both practical and emotional complexities if we are now living our days in social isolation. And those who are doing so cooped up with partners and children can find themselves confronting relational complexities that they before could not have imagined.

A major contributor to making what we encounter feel complex and overwhelming is how often circumstances are confronting us with real limits. In the simple fact of the virus, we are all having to face limits to what we can control and to what we can know about what the future holds. If we are on the front lines, we are having to face limits to our skills and knowledge, and also limits to what we can yet understand about the virus. In social isolation, we confront limits in the loss of options that before we may have taken for granted. And parents at home with children are discovering limits to their ability to make everything right in relationships and new appreciation for the heroic work that teachers do with our children.

I've noted that the fact of real limits works to increase our experience of complexity and overwhelm. But there is also a way in which being conscious of real limits and intentional in our relationship with them can have an opposite effect. It can make life decidedly simpler. In the process, it can also make life more meaningful. This observation might seem contradictory, but when put into practice, it can come to feel like common sense.

There is a limits-related formula for approaching life that I draw on extensively myself and sometimes share with clients confronting particularly challenging situations. I tend not to write about it because it can seem too stark and perhaps too philosophical. It can also sound too uncompromising, a bit too much like "tough love." But it is powerful in its ability to make life simpler whatever the circumstances. And while it can feel abrupt on first encounter, ultimately it results in the ability to relate to both others and to oneself in the ways that are ultimately most loving.

The formula goes like this: 1) Observe what the real limitations are in your life situation, 2) Determine as best you can what the options and potential learnings are within those limits, and 3) Commit yourself to making the most powerful, creative, and purposeful choices given these circumstances.

I've been reminded with the pandemic of the writings of fellow psychiatrist Viktor Frankl. Frankl spent the Second World War in a series of German concentration camps. With inhuman treatment and no escape, he decided that he would not let the situation defeat him. He looked at the very real constraints of his situation and asked himself how he might live that would be most significant, given these limitations. He asked what ways of engaging the situation could for him most create meaning. One result of this choice was a rich body of psychological thinking that would be a profound gift to others for years to come. We are not today prisoners, but at least metaphorically, the limits can feel similar.

This is a general approach that works whatever the circumstances. Notice that the limits we find at various times and places can be very different. For example, the real limits a thirty-three-year-old faces have little to do with those faced by that same person as a three-year-old or at eighty-three. Notice, too, how deeply the approach changes our felt relationship to life. Most people expend a lot of time and energy struggling with limits. They focus on hopes and feel fear that these hopes may not be realized. And they bemoan constraints that could possibly restrict them. Fighting against limits can sometimes be the right approach, but it stops serving us if the limits are real.

The formula I have described keeps things simple by eliminating the use of attention and emotional energy in ways that don't provide real benefit. This doesn't mean that grieving the loss of certain freedoms or possibilities is not an important thing to do—particularly in these times when those losses might be considerable. But when experience is held from this more mature perspective, doing so doesn't remain important for long. Soon we get on with asking what is possible given the circumstances that exist and opening ourselves to the surprises that can come from using our resources in the most creative and purpose-focused ways. Often we will then find what might seem a paradoxical result. The formula in a sense offers that limits might be transcended. But this is not because limits somehow go away (though if we have misperceived them, they might). Rather, it is because we come to understand the significance of limits in more useful and wise ways.

I've written extensively about how our times are challenging us to realize a new maturity in relationship to limits. In the old story, our task when we encountered limits was to heroically defeat them. Today, in all parts of our lives, we are confronting situations where not only is this not an option, attempting to do so only leads to further complexity. The need to acknowledge environmental limits, such as with climate change and the extinction of species, provides the most obvious example. We are being challenged to more directly acknowledge limits and to engage limits in more creative and wise ways. I did most of my writing about limits before the pandemic, but certainly this recognition applies. Indeed, we could use the pandemic to make important strides in learning this new skill. The fact of real limits confronts us with the recognition that limits can be one of our greatest teachers, and not just with regard to what is possible, but also of new, more mature ways of thinking and acting that will become ever more important in times ahead.

Culturally Mature Perspective and the Climate Change Debate: How Asking the Wrong Question Results in Actions That Are, in Effect, Suicidal

[I've written about climate change extensively over the years. I wrote this piece in 2018 as fresh attention was beginning to be brought to the issue. I've described how, when issues become reflexively polarized, the important question has likely yet to be acknowledged. Climate change presents a striking example. I've also emphasized how closely the ability to acknowledge real limits is tied to addressing challenges ahead. In climate change, we confront a particularly critical limits-related challenge.]

Given the level of denial that persists and today's extreme political polarization, the topic of climate change deserves an update. In part I return to the topic simply to put an exclamation point on the craziness—indeed, suicidal craziness—of such denial. But that conclusion doesn't really need my help. More specifically I revisit the topic to reemphasize the close relationship that the climate change question has to Cultural Maturity's larger challenge.

Climate change presents one of a handful of essential issues where at least some degree of culturally mature perspective is needed if we are to find workable solutions. And like it or not, it is one of the issues that over time may prove to have most teach us about the need for Cultural Maturity's "growing up." Climate change gives us no choice but to confront the necessity of bringing greater maturity, nuance, and responsibility to our human choices.

Culturally mature perspective's contribution starts by alerting us to the fact that we are failing to ask the right question. It then makes clear that when we succeed at doing so, the climate change "debate" is really over. Whether we should take climate change seriously appropriately hinges not on whether we can be certain about the science—which we can never be, absolutely, just by the nature of science—but on basic systemic risk assessment. By that measure there is really no debate to have.

In my recent book *Cultural Maturity: A Guidebook for the Future*, I use the metaphor of playing Russian roulette to clarify how systemic risk assessment essentially ends the conversation: "We witness an example of misconceiving systemic risk today with climate change. A person makes the accurate, limits-related observation that we can't know with absolute certainty that global climate change is real and then uses it to justify not responding to the threat. I often ask people who resort to such logic what they think the odds are that human-caused warming of the planet is happening and could have dangerous consequences. I make them commit to a number. I then ask them how they would feel about their children playing Russian roulette. Few people are willing to claim that the odds of global warming being real and significant are less than Russian roulette's one in six. And the few who might maintain this claim have a hard time escaping the recognition that their conclusion has more to do with ideology than carefully considered evaluation."

In fact, the science suggests we are playing with at least five bullets in the gun's cylinder. And even if it were just one, that would be far from a sane circumstance. Indeed, it is not being overly dramatic—simply observing what most anyone would consider obvious were the gun held by an individual rather than a species—to say it is suicidal. The origin of this suicidal circumstance is not any desire to do harm, but simply a lack of needed perspective. But this fact makes the reality no less real or consequential.

Culturally mature perspective presents a "good-news/bad-news" picture when it comes to climate change. On the "good-news" side, it makes the answer to the basic question straightforward. It reveals the climate change picture to be more complex than we tend to recognize, but at once it makes the fact that we must act, and sooner rather than later, obvious.

On the "bad-news" side, culturally mature perspective alerts us to how effectively addressing climate change will ask of us something deeper than just being smarter or more informed. We can make a start by just opening our eyes to the obvious. But acting proactively with the needed nuance and complexity will ultimately require new steps in how we understand—and in an important sense in who we are. The fact that we are just beginning to realize Cultural Maturity's changes adds significantly to the challenge.

Needed New Capacities

The simplest way to see Cultural Maturity's relationship to what is being asked of us turns to the fact that effectively addressing climate change will require human capacities that are as yet rare. The concept of Cultural Maturity describes how questions of all sorts today are requiring capacities new to us as a species. Four apply with particular directness to the climate change challenge: the need for a new, more mature relationship to limits; the need for greater comfort with uncertainty; the need for a new depth of human responsibility; and the need for a new ability to hold and grapple with complexity.

The need for a more mature relationship with limits is the most obvious with the tasks of climate change. Our old cultural story was heroic. When we encountered limits, our task was to conquer them. With Cultural Maturity's "growing up" we better accept that limits are often inviolable. Effectively addressing climate change starts with acknowledging both real planetary limits and necessary limits to what we can do. It also requires us to accept limits to technology as a solution for our problems. Technological advances will play an important role in needed changes—in particular, advances that support more sustainable energy production and more efficient energy utilization—but in the end we will succeed at addressing climate change only to the degree to which we accept that limits are real.

We recognize the importance of greater comfort with uncertainty with my assertion that the climate change question is ultimately about risk assessment. Our tendency in policy debates is to think in terms of warring certainties. With climate change, we juxtapose "climate change is not proven and thus not to be taken seriously" with "climate change is proven and thus unquestionable." Neither claim holds up—and each ultimately misses the real question. Culturally mature perspective highlights how ideological views, views that have their origins in limited aspects of larger complexities, inherently make claims for final truth—that is a major part of their appeal.

Effectively addressing climate change will require that we take our best shot at making wise choices in the face of inescapable uncertainty. Effectively addressing climate change also necessarily entails a new level of human responsibility. It requires the acceptance of responsibility for the well-being of humanity—and life—as a whole. And the fact that this is responsibility not just for dealing with current circumstances, but for bringing foresight to our choices—being responsible well into the future—suggests an even more profound kind of acceptance that the buck stops with us.

And finally, effectively addressing climate change requires that we get our minds around a degree of complexity that before would have overwhelmed us. This is not just technical complexity; it is also moral complexity. It requires confronting what it may and may not make sense to do—ultimately a question of value. It also requires addressing the very different effects our decisions may have on different people and different species. We will need to make a lot of hard choices, and very often those choices will require taking into account a complex array of often conflicting variables. Many of the most difficult choices will come with the task of mitigating damage that has become inevitable even if we now commit ourselves aggressively to reducing greenhouse gases.

Political Blindnesses

I hinted at a further way in which the climate change question relates to Cultural Maturity in emphasizing the importance of getting beyond ideological certainties. The political right and the political left each commonly stop short in their thinking. As with all critical issues before us, conventional conservative and liberal worldviews each lack the needed systemic sophistication.

The Right stops short in ways that are most obviously limited and ultimately ideological. Their response to the evidence for climate change and its human origins is, if not outright denial, that we can't know for sure. That is correct. But this is a correctness based on missing—if not simply choosing to ignore—the real question.

The Left tends to respond by arguing the opposite—that the evidence is sound. They are close to being right in this case—the larger portion of climate scientists agree that climate change is real, that the major part of such change is human-caused, and that the consequences could be extreme. But the way the Left gets caught up in the proof/no proof debate has them also missing the real question. And often their simplistic reactions leave them, in their own ways, in denial about all that is being required of us.

For example, the common assumption that simply replacing fossil fuel use with energy sources like solar, wind, and hydroelectric will take care of things easily blinds people to the magnitude of the challenge.

Liberals tend to have a hard time considering that less ideal options may need to play a significant role. (I have not reached a conclusion about whether nuclear power needs to represent a major part of the solution, at least in the short term. But when liberals dismiss this possibility out of hand, they are obviously reacting more from ideology than reasoned reflection.) Liberals are also commonly in denial about the severity of economic consequences that could result from poorly thought-out and poorly timed policies (and perhaps even the best of policies). They also tend to lack appreciation for the very different ways those consequences could play out in different cultural contexts and the need to be sensitive to these differences.

Climate Change as Teacher
I've noted that there is a further critical relationship between climate change and Cultural Maturity beyond culturally mature perspective's direct pertinence to addressing the issue. The climate change challenge may serve as an essential teacher for bringing culturally mature perspective to less clear-cut concerns and for the more general cultural "growing up" our times demand of us. Addressing climate change will in no way be easy. I've suggested that doing so effectively will require essential steps forward not just in how we think, but in who we are. But what climate change ultimately asks of us—a carbon-neutral future—is not that hard to grasp. The goal—if not exactly how to get there and the ultimate implications—is straightforward.

This tends not to be the case with many of the most important Cultural Maturity–related challenges we will face over the next hundred years—for example, the need to engage a next chapter in how we conceive of morality, economics, or love and the family. With each of these concerns, I can comfortably articulate why changes are needed and what first steps into culturally mature territory might require. But when it comes to describing what ultimately is being asked of us, there is a lot we are only beginning to know. The fact that the ultimate task with climate change can be simply articulated combined with the potentially calamitous consequences of denial means that the climate change challenge can readily serve to help catalyze the broader cognitive changes needed to address other, less obvious, but also critical, concerns.

We see this most immediately in how climate change helps us appreciate the new capacities I've described. Each of these capacities—a new more mature relationship to limits, being more comfortable in the face of uncertainty, assuming greater responsibility, and learning to better hold contradiction and complexity—necessarily stretch us. But each also applies throughout our personal and collective lives.

It is interesting to entertain how being forced to address climate change's potentially cataclysmic consequences could also help stimulate changes in institutions. The concept of Cultural Maturity challenges the common assumption that Modern Age institutions represent ideals and end points. The fact that climate change is not just a scientific question, but a question of just how much risk we are willing to accept, makes it an appropriate concern of multiple institutional spheres. Here I will touch briefly on three: education, government, and religion. With each, the challenge of addressing climate change could serve as an important catalyst for needed evolutionary changes.

In *Cultural Maturity: A Guidebook for the Future*, I describe dramatic changes that should reshape higher education in times ahead. Spiraling costs and the growing contribution of online learning will drive some of these changes. But I propose that the more important contributor will be the way assumptions common to Modern Age education get in the way of its ability to provide leadership when it comes to the most important tasks before us as a species.

The board of Amherst College recently committed the school to being a model of sustainable environmental practices—including divesting from corporations that are major greenhouse gas producers (not unlike divestiture in times past from companies that profited from apartheid). So far, few other schools have been willing to take such steps—including institutions like Harvard that we tend to look to for example. It is interesting to reflect on why the moral example we see with Amherst has not been the norm, given that the kind of risk assessment I have described is not that conceptually difficult and something we would expect higher education to be good at. In my writing, I've described how a new level of moral leadership will be key if higher education is to effectively prepare our young people for the future and continue to be relevant. Amherst should be applauded not just for intelligent policy, but for modeling culturally mature decision-making for its students and for society as a whole.

The concept of Cultural Maturity also points toward the need for major changes in how we think about government and governance. Thus far, governments have contributed much less than we might hope when it comes to addressing the climate change crisis. A person could say this is just how it is with governments. But protecting us from harm is one of government's most explicit mandates. Government should not only provide needed leadership in decision-making, but lead the way in alerting us to dangers and what addressing those dangers may require. The question of what would need to change for government to take on the required responsibility and provide the needed foresight offers a good lens for examining governance and government as whole.

Climate change presents a related challenge to religion. Historically, religion has claimed to be where we appropriately turn with questions of a moral nature—and it has, at least adequately for its times, carried out this function. I've suggested that once we are past the particulars, climate change is less a scientific concern than a moral one. It has to do with making hard choices that are ultimately questions of value. I don't see religion today doing any better than education or government when it comes to providing needed leadership—indeed, it has often served as a major voice for denial. Religion that can serve us going forward must be able to guide us toward the moral courage needed with questions like climate change. It is fascinating to contemplate what would be required of religion for it to provide this kind of leadership.

The most important way that the climate change challenge may help further the needed cultural "growing up" relates to the overarching question of narrative, of an effective guiding story for our time. I've argued that the ultimate crisis of our time is a crisis of purpose—a crisis of cultural story. Climate change is requiring us to rethink wealth and progress—indeed, to reexamine what constitutes human meaning. It asks us, "What does it mean to be a mature adult living at a moment in history when the evidence for potential climate change disaster became inescapable?" "And what will we say to succeeding generations of children and grandchildren the world over if we fail to take needed action?" It is very possible that in time we will look back on climate change as human history's most significant teacher of mature systemic perspective—and with this, ultimately, of wisdom.

What Lies Ahead

The recognition that effectively addressing climate change will require culturally mature capacities can leave a person wondering whether hope is warranted. The problem by itself seems overwhelming enough without the need for changes in ourselves. Add the bizarre current reality of climate change denial at the highest levels of government in the U.S. and it can be hard to feel optimistic. But it is important to appreciate that we also see positive signs.

We can take some solace in the fact that other countries are stepping in to provide leadership. (The majority of the world has signed on to the Paris agreements.) We also see state and local governments increasingly making their voices heard. (I think in particular of California and its willingness to enforce stringent emissions standards.) And increasingly, businesses are stepping up. In part this is because the economics are increasingly on the side of more renewable energy sources and because the need for more sustainable technologies provides a huge business opportunity. But often, too, it is because they are recognizing the larger moral responsibility that we all necessarily hold in our time.

There is also the fact of Cultural Maturity itself. The same changes I have described as altering assumptions in realms as different as love, leadership, and the most fundamental levels of science should make bringing greater maturity to the climate change question increasingly seem "common sense."

In the years ahead, our evolving relationship to the climate change question should prove a good barometer for measuring our more general progress with Cultural Maturity's needed "growing up" as a species. Will the suicidal nature of ignoring real limits take many more decades to become broadly accepted? Will denial perhaps fade quickly as the need for greater maturity in how we understand and act becomes obvious? Whichever proves the case, climate change's consequences, even if we act wisely, will extend well into the future. Like it or not, climate change will serve as a reminder and teacher for generations—and possibly centuries—to come.

Perspective for a Time of Deep Discord: Why We See Things So Differently (and Why Just Trying to Talk About It Is So Often Not Helpful)

[I wrote the following piece in 2017 to address increasingly extreme social/political polarization. It addresses both why we see what we do and what

effective decision-making going forward will require of us. This is a more detailed article than most in this chapter. In the extended version I have included here, it brings together a number of specific CST notions addressed earlier in this book—including the concept of gender archetype, the mechanisms of polarity, the application of a creative frame, CSPT temperament distinctions, Parts Work, polar fallacies, and Integrative Meta-perspective.]

In these times of extreme social/political polarization it can be unsettling—indeed, frightening—just how differently people with conflicting views can see things. We can legitimately wonder if the discord we encounter today will in time put the whole democratic experiment in peril.

If we are to move forward, we need to better understand why we tend to think in polarized terms in the first place. We also need to better grasp why in our time polarization can be so extreme and communication so difficult. And if possible, we need an answer to how we might move beyond today's often seemingly intractable differences.

Why Do We See Things So Differently?

A simple but radical recognition helps get us started. We tend to assume that conflicting beliefs reflect simple differences of opinion. But the evidence suggests something deeper. At the least we confront differences in values. And I would suggest that differences have even deeper origins. What we see reflects differences not just in what we think, but how we think.

We get a hint of more fundamental influences with the simple observation that elections tend to be closer than we would predict if people voted only on the basis of the quality of candidates or the particulars of policy. With high frequency a few percentage points determine outcomes. More than we would expect, the voting public segregates into groups of roughly equal size.

Looking at the level of metaphor brings further insight. In his 1996 book *Moral Politics*, linguist George Lakoff proposes that conservative voters tend to be attracted to "strict father" images and values while liberals are more drawn to language that suggests a "nurturant parent."[1] I've noted MSNBC commentator Chris Matthews' use of the terms "daddy party" and "mommy party" to describe modern Republicans and Democrats.

---

1 George Lakoff, *Moral Politics*, 1996, University of Chicago Press.

This interpretation is obviously simplistic in that it lumps together all manner of differing views. But it gets at something important. Psychology speaks of sensibilities that are more "archetypally masculine" and more "archetypally feminine." Alternatively, we could speak metaphorically of harder and softer tendencies. On the Right we find greater identification with competition, with unfettered individual rights, with hard-and-fast moral codes, with clear national boundaries, with gun rights, and with military might—each leanings of a "harder" sort. On the Left we find greater identification with cooperation, with concern for the less advantaged, with acceptance of differences in moral assumptions, with more open borders, with gun control, and with diplomacy as the preferred first response in the face of conflict—each reflective of "softer" leanings.

This recognition of an underlying polar architecture is significant theoretically in that it suggests that there is something basic in how understanding works that has us divide things in two and do so in a very particular way. More practically it helps us begin to understand political alliances that otherwise make little sense—politics does indeed make strange bedfellows. It also makes the fact that people often support policies that would seem not to be to their self-interest (at least their economic interest) less puzzling.

A closer look at some of the very different groups that commonly identify with being conservative or liberal helps fill out these more practical implications. "Harder" and "softer" inclinations can take a lot of different forms and can be held by people who in more obvious ways could not be more different.

Groups that commonly identify with the political right (along with the particular "harder" inclinations they tend to subscribe to)

- Big business and the wealthy [identification with competition and material values]
- The religious right [identification with absolute moral distinctions (as with opposition to abortion and gay rights)]
- White rural and working-class populations [identification with hard work (and pulling oneself up by one's bootstraps), the nation-state (in a my-country-right-or-wrong sense), and racial and ethnic differences]

- The military [identification with national boundaries and with military action as a response to threat]
- Reagan-style Republicans [identification with local control and a mistrust of government as a vehicle for social good]
- Libertarians [identification with individual autonomy and freedom from collective influence]

Groups that commonly identify with the political left (along with the particular "softer" inclinations they tend to subscribe to):
- Social justice advocates [identification with the disadvantaged—the poor, racial minorities, women, and those of differing sexuality]
- Advocates of liberal/socialist economic policy [identification with the sharing of resources and bottom-up approaches to decision-making]
- Environmentalists [identification with the well-being of "mother" nature]
- Philosophical globalists (as contrasted with purely economic globalists) [identification at least in part as global citizens—and within one's own country, with diversity as a good and with liberal immigration policies]
- Academics and intellectuals [identification with diplomatic rather than military responses to conflict, moral pluralism, and government as a compassionate parent who protects and cares for all]
- Media and Hollywood types [identification with creative freedoms and diversity of expression]

Given the dramatically different ways these basic polar identifications can manifest, strange-bedfellow alliances and policies that might seem not in a group's immediate self-interest should not surprise us.

How Creative Systems Theory Helps Fill Out What We See

CST helps us answer three key questions implied in what I have described. First, why do we find polar identification in the first place? Second, why does polarity predictably express this curious kind of symmetry—setting archetypally masculine versus archetypally feminine, harder versus softer? And third, how do we best understand the multiple, often dramatically different kinds of identification within each side of this polar picture?

We can miss that the first question should be a question at all. Polarity seems to be just how things are—as the saying goes, "there are two sides to every question." But very few questions, in fact, have only two sides. More often multiple factors interplay, and those factors affect different groups in a variety of different ways. There is no obvious reason why polarity is what we should see.

CST proposes that the reason we think in polar terms is that doing so is inherent in how human intelligence works. Polar thinking is not limited to social/political differences. We find it with understanding of every sort—matter juxtaposes with energy, subjective with objective, humankind with nature. Robert Frost observed that, "It almost scares a man the way things come in pairs."

CST offers an explanation for why this might be so, although full understanding requires some familiarity with the theory. CST describes how human intelligence is structured to support our toolmaking, meaning-making—we could say simply "creative"—natures. It also describes how polarity plays an essential role with human developmental processes—of all sorts. Such creative/formative processes begin in an unbroken whole, bud off new form, then progress as an evolving sequence of polar relationships.

CST also directly addresses the second question. It describes how the right-versus-left polar architecture I've described is predicted by polarity's role in formative process. That evolving sequence of polar relationships juxtaposes what remains of formative process's original whole with increasingly manifest forms. We experience the time-specific "original whole" aspects as having archetypally feminine qualities. And we experience the time-specific "manifest form" aspects as having more archetypally masculine qualities.

A more basic way of thinking about political alliances helps make the connection to this underlying mechanism. CST delineates how, beneath the surface of more obvious opposites, polarity at its most basic juxtaposes unity/connectedness on one hand with difference/distinction on the other. The wealthy, those most concerned with individual freedom, farmers and coal miners, those who are most strongly religious, each, though in relationship to very different concerns, identify with difference (at least difference with others—they can feel particularly strong bonds with their own kinds). Those who advocate for the disadvantaged, people who identify with leveling the economic playing field, nature lovers, postmodern academics, those who think of themselves as "global citizens," and individuals of more creative inclination each in their own ways identify with dissolving differences (whether the boundaries that establish differences are those that separate people from one another, people from nature, or traditional ideas about right and wrong).

Note an important implication of CST's explanation for why polarity manifests as it does. It suggests that polarity itself is not a problem. Polar opposites work together to support and drive our audaciously innovative natures. CST proposes that the basic relationship between polar opposites is "procreative." We find evidence for this creative conclusion in the political domain. Historian Arthur Schlesinger described American history as progressing through alternating periods in which more private interest–oriented and more public purpose–oriented sentiments most prevailed. Over the history of modern democratic government, we've seen a back and forth between more right-hand and more left-hand advocacies.

With regard to the third question—how we best understand the multiple, often dramatically different kinds of identification within each side of this polar picture—CST also offers beginning insight. The details of the Creative Systems Personality Typology, CST's framework for making sense of temperament differences, are again beyond the scope of this short article, but the general picture it offers provides important perspective.

The Typology describes how we can understand beliefs and values that come with each of the more conservative and liberal postures noted earlier as predicted expressions of particular personality constellations. It goes on to delineate how we can understand the sixteen basic constellations it describes in terms of specific balances of archetypally masculine and archetypally feminine tendencies. The fact of "strange-bedfellow" alliances follows. We find personality styles that manifest biases toward the harder or softer side of things scattered all over the temperament map. (Some examples for those familiar with the CSPT: We most commonly find archetypally masculine bias of a business/wealth-focused sort with Late/Upper/Outers and Middle/Upper/Outers, of a more fundamentalist or blue-collar sort with Middle/Lower/Outers, and of a more individualist/libertarian sort with Early/Uppers, particularly Early/Upper/Outers. Beyond the general archetypally masculine bias, these people could not be more different. Similarly, we most commonly find archetypally feminine biases of a postmodern/academic/intellectual sort with Late/Upper/Inners, identification with the less advantaged with Lower/Inners of any sort, and strongest environmentalist identification with Earlies. Beyond the general archetypally feminine bias, again these people could not be more different.)

These temperament-related observations suggest a recognition key to larger understanding. They offer that there may be method in the madness with the depth of our human differences. I've observed that polarity has an important creative purpose. If personality style differences are products of the parts of who we are as systems that as individuals we most live in, then there may also be a good creative reason for the very different ways we see our worlds.

This recognition in turn hints at something further that I will elaborate on shortly. It suggests that getting beyond today's seemingly intractable polarization might be an option. Right now, such differences can seem beyond us to bridge. But if they ultimately serve us, there is no reason to assume they cannot do so again. CST goes further to propose that Cultural Maturity's changes, by making it possible to more consciously engage and make use of the diverse aspects of our complex natures, should result in these differences serving us in even more powerful ways in the future. It also argues that this result will be essential to our future well-being as a species.

A Collision of Different Worlds

For these claims to fully make sense—and before that, for what we encounter today to fully make sense—we need to appreciate just how deep the differences in how we see things go (even in times when differences are not the same kind of obstacle they can be today). Given the multiple dynamics involved, it should not at all be surprising that just trying to talk about differences of opinion is rarely as helpful as we might hope.

In fact, we often interpret things in radically different ways even when no real difference exists. Conclusions can become distorted as a simple consequence of being on opposite sides of a debate. When the fans of two rival football teams argue a controversial call, to a remarkable degree what they "see" is not the same (even with video replay).

In the football example, we at least agree on the basic rules of the game. If we add actual differences in belief, difficulty is compounded. And if, in addition, conflicting positions have to do with underlying differences in how we organize experience—as with right-versus-left alliances and personality style differences—in an even more real and basic sense we can live in different worlds.

A further, easily startling dynamic that accompanies this deeper kind of difference complicates things even more. We can encounter conclusions that are in effect just made up—self-serving "fake news." This is not intentional deception. Rather, again, it is a product of how our cognitive mechanisms work.

I'm reminded of classic "split-brain" research done over fifty years ago (research done with people who had the fibers that connect the two sides of the brain—the corpus callosum—cut as a treatment for severe epileptic seizures). Researchers found a most provocative result when they gave instructions to only one hemisphere—such as to move in a particular way. When the other hemisphere was asked why the person had moved, rather than saying it didn't know, it would make up an explanation, often an elaborate one.

We now know that popular beliefs about "right-brain" and "left-brain" differences are highly simplistic. And the "wiring" gaps with differences in personality style are not so absolute. But to a remarkable degree, not only do people with different cognitive styles live in different worlds, they are all too happy to fill in the blanks where holes exist in the worldview that comes with their particular kind of cognitive organization.

The psychotherapeutic approach I call Parts Work" provides further support for this "separate worlds" picture and how it can result in distorted conclusions. With Parts Work a person addresses the multiple aspects of his or her psyche as if they are characters in a play. Often a person's parts reflect not just different opinions, but wholly different and nearly opposite realities. And like what we see with differences in personality style, individual parts will commonly fill in gaps in the "completeness" of their story. We might think that we would see this degree of separate functioning only in someone with "multiple personalities." But, in fact, this is how things work in all of us. Sometimes parts most reflect personal tendencies—an angry part, a sensitive part, an intellectual part. But parts also commonly reflect more general/societal tendencies. Then you may get a more conservative part or a more liberal part, a more religious part or a more scientific part.

A central "rule" in Parts Work sheds further light on the roots of intractable conflict. It also highlights the necessary role culturally mature perspective plays in moving forward. That rule: Parts don't get to talk to the world or to each other, only to the person doing the work. When a person gets caught up in polarized debate, a part within that person is locking horns with an opposite part in the other person. Inevitably the argument goes nowhere—for the simple reason that it was never about policy. Rather, it was about which of two mutually exclusive patterns of cognitive organization, each a legitimate aspect of a larger reality, will prevail.

The Current Situation

I've described how human systems grow and evolve through a back-and-forth between more right-hand and more left-hand creative tendencies. If this is the case, how do we make sense of the modern social/political condition? With the extreme partisan gridlock we find today, back-and-forth is no longer generating creative results.

There are multiple possible explanations. What we see could be a momentary blip—something we will soon get beyond. It is also possible that the reason is more dire, that we are witnessing governmental and societal collapse. But there are also big-picture explanations that are more ultimately consistent with hope. Each is in keeping with the broader concept of Cultural Maturity.

One explanation turns to the weakening of bonds that before have served as the basis for cooperation and compromise. In his book *Democracy: A Case Study*,[2] David Moss observed that, "In the end, it's what we have in common that makes productive conflict possible." I've described how traditional cultural absolutes are today losing their past influence. In times past, such once-and-for-all beliefs gave us our

---

2 David A. Moss. *Democracy: A Case Study*, Belknap Press, 2017.

shared rules to live by and a common sense of social identity. I've also described how we are beginning to step beyond our past need to divide humanity into "chosen people" and "evil others." Shared animosities have before served to cement national bonds (as the saying goes, "the enemy of my enemy is my friend'). Both of these changes are ultimately positive, predicted aspects of Cultural Maturity's needed cultural "growing up." But each also makes it more difficult to appreciate how differences may serve us.

Other Cultural Maturity–related factors again require reference to previous articles. I've introduced a couple of CST concepts—the Dilemma of Trajectory and Transitional Absurdity—that have particular pertinence to today's realities. CST views the time we live in as an in-between period linking Modern Age sensibilities and the possibility of Cultural Maturity's more encompassing ways of understanding. I've described how this often-awkward time of transition can leave us feeling estranged from essential aspects of who we are. One of these aspects we might call our "connection to connectedness." Its weakening is most readily felt in how disconnected we can be today from both nature and from our own bodies. But we also predictably see it in a loss of felt connection to our shared humanness and with this to our sense of common good. I think of this dynamic as playing a key role in what I have previously called humanity's modern Crisis of Purpose. The concept of Transitional Absurdity adds the fact that attempting to apply Modern Age realities when they no longer serve us can result in some quite crazy-seeming dynamics—including extreme polarization. What we see with these additional mechanisms is appropriately unsettling. But it is also the case that each is predicted by the concept of Cultural Maturity. Because of this, it is not inconsistent with an ultimately positive future.

One additional explanation for why the old polar back-and-forth has stopped serving us has particular pertinence to future possibilities. It may no longer be working for a more specifically creative reason. CST proposes that modern democratic government is not the ideal and end point that we tend to assume it to be, that more mature stages in how we think about governance predictably lie ahead. It also describes how a next chapter in government depends on the ability to think in the more encompassing and complete ways that come with Cultural

Maturity. If this picture is accurate, then what we see today would be expected as part of a time of transition. If accurate, it also provides further evidence as far as where the needed antidote to gridlock and intractable animosities necessarily lie.

What Do We Do?

What is the appropriate response to today's extreme social/political polarization? Especially if one's particular "side" is not doing well, it might seem that the task is to figure out how to make its argument more convincing. But if culturally mature policy is our goal, sides are not what our task is about. While blocking efforts by the other side might provide short-term benefit, as a long-term strategy it only hastens nonfunctionality.

Efforts toward compromise might seem a more mature response, but even they ultimately fall short. In the end, splitting the difference fails us just as fundamentally as siding with one pole or the other. In my book *Necessary Wisdom: Meeting the Challenge of a New Cultural Maturity*, I ended each issue-specific chapter with a list of what CST calls Separation Fallacies (more right-hand fallacies), Unity Fallacies (more left-hand fallacies), and Compromise Fallacies. With today's challenges, falling off the right- or left-hand side of the road or walking down the white line in the middle each leaves us equally short of where we need to go.

CST proposes that in the end, not only is the task not compromise, it isn't even mutual understanding—though that can be a start. Rather, it is the cognitive reordering that produces culturally mature thought—what CST calls Integrative Meta-perspective. Integrative Meta-perspective allows us to at once step back from and more deeply engage the rich complexities that make us who we are. We find what our times ask of us in the more encompassing and systemic kind of understanding that results.

I've proposed that the depths of our differences ultimately serve us. And I've gone further to claim that in the future they may do so in even more powerful ways. With Cultural Maturity's cognitive changes, for the first time we are able to step back and recognize how polarity reflects underlying complementarity—the juxtaposition of mutually important creative aspects. With the multiplicity of viewpoints that

I've described with personality differences and with Parts Work, we see something similar. Culturally mature perspective lets us hold a larger systemic picture—with regard to particular issues, and ultimately with regard to reality as a whole. In the future, this ability will be more and more critical. Once we are over Cultural Maturity's threshold, increasingly it becomes common sense.

The reflections in this article shed important further light on what I have proposed is the best argument for the concept of Cultural Maturity. I've written extensively about how the most critical challenges of our time require mature systemic perspective if we are just to understand the questions, and more so if we are to find useful answers. Many of these challenges—for example, nuclear proliferation, climate change, the growing gap between the world's haves and have-nots, and the need to define progress in more sustainable ways—could be our undoing if we fail to bring the necessary greater maturity of perspective to bear. Our inability to get beyond today's seemingly intractable difference in the end presents no less a threat. It could put the possibility of effective governance increasingly out of reach. And it would be doing so at a time when wise decision-making could not be more critical.

We face the possibility that not just our future well-being, but perhaps our survival depends on a deeper and more creative understanding of our human differences. The concept of Cultural Maturity suggests that while such understanding might seem beyond us, there is legitimate reason for hope. Importantly, the new, more conscious relationship to differences that culturally mature perspective provides is not something we need to invent. The potential for the needed cognitive reordering is developmentally built into who we are. Hope for the future thus requires only the courage to take needed next steps. Arguably, our only hope lies in this willingness to expand who we are and how we see our worlds.

The Crisis of Gun Violence: Mature, Big-Picture Perspective

[The topic of guns and gun violence is a critical concern that becomes front-page news with each mass shooting, but that always simmers beneath the surface. It is a concern about which opinion becomes immediately polarized. I wrote the following piece in 2014 in an attempt to offer more encompassing perspective.]

The kind of big-picture/long-term vantage provided by culturally mature perspective stretches usual understanding in a couple of key ways. First, it commonly requires that we take into account multiple, interwoven causal factors. Second, it alerts us to the fact that effectively addressing many of those factors necessarily involves thinking and acting in ways that before now would not have made sense to us.

Today's crisis of gun violence in the United States makes a good example. Most attempts to address the issue reduce to ideological debate. Liberals argue that gun control measures will make us safer. Conservatives argue that such measures will make us less safe, often shifting the focus to mental health concerns. Pieces of the truth lie in each claim, but each position is limited by simplistic assumptions. And other critical aspects of the gun violence question are rarely part of the conversation.

Numerous factors play a role in the modern problem of gun violence, with many of the most important requiring that we stretch how we usually think. Given this complexity, a brief listing of factors can provide but a start toward the needed more complete understanding—but here is my list. Only the first two factors below are directly addressable through policies. At the same time, all must play a role if we wish to reach a mature, systemic understanding of this essential issue.

Limiting access to guns certainly has a place in curbing gun violence. Statistics show that gun violence is less common in countries where guns are less readily available. But limiting access to guns, alone, is less of a solution than people like to think. Gun advocates are correct in their assertion that people who are determined to get guns will find ways to do so.

As a psychiatrist, I agree that increased **availability of mental health services** can make a significant difference—both better treatment for those whose mental states might lead them to commit violent acts and better systems for identifying such individuals. But many people who perpetrate gun violence do not have obvious psychiatric diagnoses. And while those who resist gun control measures can be quick to shift attention to the mental health of perpetrators, often these same people are the first to resist increased spending for mental health services.

The remaining factors all in some way concern the degree to which people experience meaning and possibility in their lives. When people do not, they become more vulnerable to perpetrating violent acts. As a start, *poverty, bigotry, cultural background or simply temperament* can deprive people of meaningful options. In the long term, improving economic opportunity, reducing bullying, and increasing multicultural awareness should all have important roles in lessening gun violence.

The role of *violence in media and popular culture* is frequently acknowledged, but the mechanism of its effect tends not to be fully appreciated. Certainly violence is dramatically more pervasive in the media than it is in daily life. "If it bleeds it leads" too often determines what is on the evening news, and it is rare to see television programming after 9:00 pm that doesn't include at least one shooting. And violence is central to the easily addictive attraction of video games. Research supports that this constant barrage of violent imagery by itself contributes to the problem. But there is also a more troubling mechanism at work beyond just familiarity. At a deep neurological level, people come to associate the jolt of excitement that accompanies witnessing violent acts with significance. Given violent imagery's defining importance in the media, we should not be surprised when someone who feels a lack of purpose in his or her life responds violently.

Fully grasping the last two factors more explicitly requires culturally mature perspective. First is the need for a *new maturity in our relationship with death*. I've spoken of the need for a new maturity in our relationship with death most frequently in relationship to health care. But it is ultimately just as pertinent to how we relate to violence in the media. The fact that we keep death at arm's length is directly tied to the sense of false significance we feel when viewing violent imagery. Nothing is more precious than life, but given that all of our lives end eventually, it is also true that few things are more ordinary than death. A more culturally mature relationship with death should help us better recognize violent imagery in the media for what it tends to be—artificial stimulation used to manipulate emotions (and sell more products).

The last factor is likely the most important, ultimately, but it also most specifically requires an understanding of the broader cultural change processes that the concept of Cultural Maturity describes. Again it concerns people's experience of significance, but here at the most encompassing of scales. The concept of Cultural Maturity proposes that underlying all more specific crises in our time is a more basic *Crisis of Purpose*. As culture functions less as a symbolic parent, traditions and cultural dictates stop providing the same ready sense of meaning. Today we reside in an awkward "in-between-stories" place in these changes and often feel adrift. Ultimately, the most important factor in reducing gun violence may be the recognition of a new, more mature cultural narrative able to provide a renewed sense of individual meaning and shared purpose.

Given the complexity of this picture, a person attempting to make sense of gun violence could easily feel overwhelmed, or even dispirited. But we have to accept that the challenge confronts us this deeply if we are to really make progress in addressing it. Like it or not, easy-answer solutions of any sort are going to leave us short.

The "good news" about applying culturally mature perspective to public policy is that it helps us understand with the systemic sophistication needed to act wisely. The "bad news" is that it doesn't let us off easily. It alerts us to how single-cause/single-cure thinking most often has its roots in ideology, and it makes clear that with most policy questions, multiple evolving, systemically related causal variables come into play. It also confronts us with the recognition that effectively addressing key variables may require that we think in new—often fundamentally new—ways. The result asks more of us, but it offers the possibility of getting us where we need to go.

Toward a Mature Understanding of Freedom:
Reflections Following the Fortieth Anniversary of the Fall of Saigon

[I wrote this article in 2015. I could have included this article's topic in Chapter Twelve where I delve into how CST helps us address ultimate human questions. Freedom is an ultimate concern both sociologically and philosophically. And as with the other topics I will address there, our thinking has traditionally been limited. But because this article has its inspiration in a front-page-news topic and has such immediate application, I will include it here.]

"Freedom" can be an inspiring word. But it is also a word we must use with great caution—especially when "freedom" is used as a rallying cry. Just where freedom is best thought to lie is more often than not legitimately debated. The observation that "one man's terrorist is another man's freedom fighter" holds more truth than we like to admit. And while almost all revolutionary movements identify with freedom, successful revolutions often do little more than replace old repressive regimes with regimes that are equally repressive (or at best they result in incremental change). At its ideological worst, the word "freedom" becomes little more than a linguistic justification for seeing one's own kind as "chosen" and some other group as worthy of dismissal and antipathy.

Even when the word "freedom" is not applied in such blatantly ideological and self-serving ways, it tends to be a partial notion that easily gets in the way of good decision-making. It can do this in a couple of further ways. The word's use can blind us to the fact that cultural systems evolve and that people at different stages in culture's evolution can see the world in very different ways. It can also shield us from the fact of real limits. A defining characteristic of culturally mature understanding is that it acknowledges limits—limits and freedom become aspects of a single larger picture. Because of the importance of understanding freedom in more mature and creative ways, Creative Systems Theory speaks specifically of a Myth of Freedom.

I was reminded of the essential task of rethinking freedom with the recent fortieth anniversary of the fall of Saigon. Each of these ways in which the word "freedom" can get in the way of mature systemic perspective was reflected in how the word was used during the Vietnam War. Certainly it served as a polar rallying cry. The Cold War ideological thinking that provided the war's context and ultimate justification set an idealized picture of the West as the "free world" in opposition to a representation of communism that demonized it as freedom's antithesis. If Vietnam fell, it would be but one domino in evil communism's destruction of freedom throughout the whole of Asia.

If I understand Vietnamese history correctly, the larger portion of the Vietnamese people experienced the situation quite differently. While Ho Chi Minh (the North Vietnamese leader) was accurately described as a communist, more than this he was a nationalist. The essential recognition for understanding the Vietnam War is that it was this identity as a nationalist that produced his great attraction for the Vietnamese people. Vietnam has never trusted its overbearing communist neighbors to the north, neither before nor since. Rather, the issue was 100 years of French colonial rule, and since 1945, American support for that rule. The South Vietnamese government was identified—not inappropriately—with those years of foreign domination. The North Vietnamese also identified their cause with "freedom."

Given their history, they had as good a claim—and arguably a better one—to the word than did South Vietnam and the United States.

The second way the word "freedom" in its common usage can get in the way—how it can blind us to the fact that cultural systems evolve—also played a role in the Vietnam War. A person could justifiably object to the argument that I just presented by pointing to the very real differences between the governmental systems advocated by the two sides in this conflict. Communism reflects centralized control. Democracy (though not necessarily as then practiced in South Vietnam) is about more popular determination—and thus greater freedom.

This is an accurate and important observation. But if we are to use the word "freedom" at all usefully, we must recognize that it describes a development difference, not one of right versus wrong. This distinction is critical. Clearly we would be missing the point if, on comparing two individuals, we used the accurate observation that a young adult is more developed in his perceptions than an adolescent to argue that young adults represent good and adolescents represent evil. The distinction becomes even more significant with the recognition that while we commonly regard modern representative democracy as an ideal and end point, there is every reason to conclude that it is neither. The concept of Cultural Maturity includes the recognition that further important chapters in the evolution of government and governance lie ahead.

If we are to understand freedom in a way that can serve us going forward, we also need the second additional observation noted earlier—that freedom as we customarily think of it leaves out the fact of real limits. The recognition that limits are intrinsic to how things work represents one of culturally mature perspective's pivotal insights. When that insight is missing, our thinking inevitably becomes narrow and ideological. We can come at this further observation in a handful of ways that each shed a somewhat different kind of light.

The first turns to cultural narrative, to the stories we tell about how things work. The kinds of stories we are most familiar with all in some way support myths of limitlessness. In doing so, they imply ultimate freedom as a reward. Certainly this has been true of our most recent cultural narratives, the heroic and romantic stories that ordered Modern Age belief and more recent postmodern narratives. Heroic narratives imply that if we can overcome some obstacle, all will become possible. Romantic narratives proclaim that connectedness with some other (usually another person, but it could also be nature or some spiritual ideal) produces complete and final fulfillment. And while postmodern narrative might seem to discard such fanciful conclusions, the anything-goes claims that lie at the heart of such beliefs in the end represent an even more ultimate argument for limitlessness.

The box-of-crayons image I use to depict culturally mature systemic understanding in another way highlights such partiality. With it, we can think of ideology as what results whenever we make a single crayon (or several in combination) final truth. Single-crayon views of any sort—political, religious, scientific—similarly hide myths of limitlessness. They imply that we only need to give that crayon ultimate say and anything we might wish becomes possible. Whole-box-of-crayons systemic perspective makes us confront the fact that claims of limitlessness—and final freedom—are in the end self-serving and illusionary. Ironically, because single-crayon claims of ultimate freedom protect us from recognizing underlying dogmatism, in an important sense they represent freedom's opposite. They undermine any kind of freedom that can ultimately serve us.

Creative Systems Theory provides a further, more explicitly conceptual challenge to conventional notions of freedom. It draws on how human cognitive processes—and human reality more generally—ultimately work. Creative Systems Theory proposes that intelligence is structured to support our toolmaking, meaning-making—creative—natures. It also describes how creative processes evolve as a generative interplay of polar relationships. We can usefully think of the most fundamental polar relationship in a variety of ways—oneness and separateness, mystery and manifestation, the spiritual as opposed to the material. We can also think of it as freedom set opposite to limitation. Any human creative act—and certainly any act of choosing that is at all responsible—is ultimately a conversation between freedom and limitation. In another way we see how "freedom" as we commonly use the term is not some ideal and end point, but rather just one aspect of what it means as humans to be whole and ultimately vital. (Creative Systems Theory goes further. It proposes that the fact that we have life, indeed that anything exists, is ultimately a product of this kind of generative conversation within existence as a whole.)

If the concept of "freedom" as we commonly think of it so readily gets in the way of today's needed maturity of perspective, just what should we do with the word? Often it is best just to find other language. We can also apply the word in ways that put it in appropriate historical perspective or explicitly expand the word's usual definition. What is most important, ultimately, is simply that we appreciate the larger implications of however it is that the word is used.

Beyond the Cynicism Trap: A Friend Confronts the Very Real Possibility of Human Extinction

[*As we look to the future, we face the very real danger that the Capacitance required to engage questions effectively will leave us overwhelmed and thus ineffective. Cynicism represents a particularly common response to such circumstances. I wrote the following article after a conversation with a valued friend and colleague who can be vulnerable to this trap.*]

Culturally mature perspective challenges us to ask big questions and also makes it more possible to do so. This greater sophistication comes from how such perspective helps us frame questions in larger, more systemic ways. But tolerating the answers such perspective suggests can ask a lot of us. The work of a valued friend and colleague provides a great illustration, one that helps us in a couple of important ways. It highlights how difficult it can be to get essential "big-picture" questions acknowledged. It also demonstrates how much of a stretch making full sense of possible answers can be even for someone experienced at doing so … and committed to doing so.

My friend is a respected biologist and educator. Early on he studied with systems pioneer Gregory Bateson, so he is no stranger to asking systemically complex questions. Today, an important part of his work focuses on a particularly provocative example. Biologists commonly ask about the "carrying capacities" of environments and how this quantity relates to the health of specific organisms. They want to know how large a population can thrive sustainably in a specific place. My friend and a close colleague have taken the audacious step of asking this question about the human species—about us. They did the same kind of analysis biologists commonly do, but made our planet as a whole the environmental system and the organism in question you and me. And they crunched the numbers.

It is important to appreciate the radical nature of their inquiry. Whether we might destroy ourselves simply from our numbers is in fact a reasonable—indeed very practical—question. But it is a more encompassing kind of question than even the most forward-thinking of biologists commonly consider. And certainly it is not a particularly comfortable question to entertain.

There is also the historically questionable way my friend and his colleague framed the question, how they had treated humans as simply another kind of organism. Certainly doing so breaks religious taboos. Most religions see humans as God's special creation, fundamentally distinct from the creaturely. But just as much it breaks scientific taboos—or at least scientific orthodoxy. Scientists have traditionally gone out of their way to keep the methodologies they use to study the purely biological and those they use to study human beings distinct.

The question my friend and his colleague were asking also runs afoul of common Age of Technology beliefs. Modern technological-gospel thinking assumes that we can invent our way out of any trouble we might get ourselves into. Simply acknowledging the question requires that we also acknowledge how this assumption has no reasonable basis in fact.

The results of their study were striking—and of no small significance. Their computations suggested that we had already exceeded our carrying capacity—indeed, dramatically so. Given that we have not yet reached the point at which the global population curve might naturally level off, this is not good news.

Not surprisingly, given the study's unorthodox methodology, trying to get the results published proved more difficult than my friend and his colleague had hoped. They approached multiple publications, and tried articulating the results in different ways that might work best for different journals. For a long time, they had no success. With persistence, their article was published in a respected scientific journal.

It is important to note an insight that came while working on the paper, one that expanded the question they were asking. This insight helped them with describing their results most usefully. But it was equally significant that it had implications for how my friend would engage this work going forward—and approach his life contribution more generally.

My friend and I often hike together. While doing so, we listen to—and often challenge—each other's thinking. I remember once asking my friend if, in taking on the historical blindnesses that come with placing the human and the simply biological in wholly separate worlds, he wasn't falling for an opposite kind of trap—lumping these two kinds of creation together in a way that might be ignoring important differences. The question had importance both for how the research should be interpreted, and to my friend more personally. We are all vulnerable to particular ways of limiting ourselves. My friend can be vulnerable to becoming cynical. It would be all too easy for him to conclude from the data that we are beyond hope.

CST proposes that while most basically we are creatures, at the same time we are a particularly creative kind of creature. We are conscious toolmakers and also makers of meaning, able both to create with a unique prodigiousness and to step back and reflect on the significance of what we create. This way of thinking about what makes us particular suggests that thinking of the biological and the human as wholly separate and thinking of their worlds as one and the same, each, in their own ways, miss the mark.[3]

This expanded picture alerts us to the importance of adding a further question to the systemic analysis: How much might our creative, toolmaking prowess offset what might seem end-of-story implications? Certainly it is a practical addition. It helps us focus our attention on what can possibly be done and set necessary priorities going forward. Advances of times past—from the advent of agriculture to modern sewage systems— while they haven't done anything to alter ultimate limits, have served to increase the number of people environments can tolerate.

With regard to the article, this acknowledgement that human creativity, applied wisely, could play a constructive role in times ahead helped my friend and his colleague most effectively articulate the significance of their results. It further supported the importance of reflecting deeply on unsupported beliefs that got us here—in particular, that our species does not need to follow the systemic rules of the planet. And, at the same time, it highlighted the recognition that, with appropriate care, it is possible to innovate in ways that provide benefit.

---

3   The article "The Big Band Theory: Creative Systems Theory Takes on Existence as a Whole" included in Chapter Twelve expands on this observation.

Expanding the question in this way also had more personal implications for my friend. I remember asking him if it turned out that there was only a small chance that human action could save us from extinction—say 2 to 5 percent—would that be enough to motivate him to continue bringing his best to his important efforts. He responded that it would be. While framing the "carrying capacity" question as large as a culturally mature perspective suggests is necessary made the results of his work inescapably stark, it also provided an antidote to cynicism.

With regard to human extinction, a culturally mature perspective asks, first, that we be humble to the fact that this outcome could very well be our fate, and sooner rather than later. Climate change (and the major social upheaval that could very well accompany it), nuclear proliferation (and the possibility of weapons of mass destruction being used not just by nation-states, but also by terrorist groups), increasing population pressures and the environmental degradation that would predictably come with it, and events that are not our fault such as the possibility of an asteroid collision, could all be our undoing. Our time on the planet has been very short compared to that of the dinosaurs. I'm not sure wagering that we will outlive their years as the dominant species would be a good bet.

That said, a culturally mature perspective just as much emphasizes the importance of not letting such recognitions undermine our creativity and our will to survive and thrive through a true desire to live sustainably. To do so would be to fail to fully take in the facts. Positive options exist—even if they can't guarantee that we will dodge extinction. New technologies have the potential to help us live in more efficient ways (though we must be very sure that in fact they do—our ability to deceive ourselves is immense). And if the concept of Cultural Maturity is accurate, even more important when it comes to survival is the possibility of bringing greater foresight and moral responsibility to the choices we make in all parts of our lives.

Culturally mature perspective also more directly challenges cynicism. It is a challenge that we all confront in some way. For myself, the difficulty of getting the importance of culturally mature capacities heard and understood can at times leave me frustrated and tired. Add to this the amount of Transitional Absurdity today's world requires us to endure and I too can fall victim to cynicism.

Culturally mature perspective does not at all advocate for always being positive—it is very much about seeing clearly and confronting hard truths. But one of those hard truths is that cynicism serves nothing. Indeed, in the end, it is a copout. It lets us feel right and at the same time avoid committing ourselves to any useful action. CST delineates how cynicism leaves us blind to larger systemic realities and is just as limited and limiting as other self-serving and more obviously ideological kinds of belief. In moments when cynicism tempts us, it is essential to recognize that it has no useful purpose. Whether the question at hand is more personal or more collective, we need to ally ourselves with the most creative and life-affirming outcome possible. Often today that means responding with a maturity of insight and responsibility new to us as a species. The stretch doing so requires can feel like too much. But taking on this task is what will ultimately determine our sense of purpose in our time. With regard to our human future, it will play a central role in determining not just how rewarding that future will be, but also how far out our time on the planet will extend.

Device Addiction and Machine Learning— A Mix That Could Well Be the End of Us

[*I wrote this article in 2018 in response to a kind of concern that will very much need our attention going forward. The piece includes observations about a couple of technologies that at their best benefit us—often greatly—and that at their worst can put us in significant danger. I've previously tied device addiction to our modern Crisis of Purpose. When device addiction is combined with machine learning, the result is a troubling mix that could even be our undoing as a species.*]

The aspect of today's broader addiction epidemic that I find most troubling when I look to the long term is not addicting drugs or obesity, but addiction to our electronic devices. These dangers are amplified dramatically when we add the mechanisms of machine learning. Cultural Maturity's cognitive changes are directly pertinent to this circumstance. Today's Crisis of Purpose both increases the risks and provides insight into what will be needed to escape major harm. And a further kind of insight that requires Integrative Meta-perspective will be key if we are to address dangers at all proactively—understanding the fundamental differences between human intelligence and "artificial intelligence"

(AI).[4] Each of these recognitions relates directly to the more encompassing task of effectively managing emerging technologies.

First, device addiction. While our electronic devices can do so many things that we find useful—and are often just plain fun—if we are to use them wisely, we need to examine not just what they can do, but our relationship to them. With growing frequency today that relationship is not a healthy one. Numerous writers have described concerns, for example, with how screen time can get in the way of developing real relationship skills and result in increased rates of depression. But the greatest danger is more basic. Too often our devices addictively hijack our attention—and our lives.

To grasp how this might be so, it helps to better understand the mechanisms of addiction. Addiction works by providing artificial substitutes for real fulfillment. In an experiment often described in psychology classes to teach about addiction, wires are run from excitement centers in a rat's brain to a depressible pedal in its cage. After the rat discovers the pedal, it pushes it with ever greater frequency, in the end abandoning other activities including eating, and dies. Device-related addictive mechanisms are most obvious with video games, where shootings and explosions create readily repeatable jolts of excitement. But addictive dynamics present arguably even greater dangers with more everyday electronic devices such as cell phones—in part just because cell phones and the like have become aspects of most everyone's lives, in part because of the immense commercial rewards that come with their ability to manipulate our choices.

Several times a week I walk around a lake near my home in Seattle. (It is in one of the city's most popular parks.) Over a third of the people walking around the lake do so while staring at their cell phones. Often this is the case even for couples. Not only are they missing the beauty of the lake, they are substituting the stimulation of their devices for real relationship, a phenomenon we see with growing frequency more generally with social media. I've found myself seriously wondering if this is what science fiction writers have been anticipating with images of a zombie apocalypse.

---

4 Because of this fundamental difference, I rarely use the term artificial intelligence, preferring instead to speak of "machine learning," as I will most often in this article.

People's attachment to their devices is not simply a product of the device's usefulness. It is a dirty little secret of the tech world (fortunately becoming less of a secret) that programmers consciously design their software to be addictive. They build in dynamics that make visiting a favorite site like playing a slot machine. The result is biochemical responses that have us feel anxiety if we are away from our devices for long. The fact that most of the content on our cell phones is advertising-driven means that we should find addictive mechanisms becoming only more sophisticated in times ahead.

Device addiction takes on particular significance with Transitional changes and today's Crisis of Purpose. As a start, these phenomena make us more vulnerable to addiction. As traditional cultural beliefs stop providing needed guidance and social connections, artificial substitutes for significance become increasingly attractive. And the Dilemma of Trajectory and the common intrusion of Transitional Absurdities can leave us feeling even further distanced from anything that matters.

Transitional dynamics also mean that we pay a particularly high price—and not just personally, but as a species—when we confuse addictive pseudo-significance with meaning. I've described how the antidote to our modern Crisis of Purpose lies ultimately in a fresh engagement with culture's Question of Referent. We need to be asking what most matters to us collectively with new depth and courage. Being distracted and addicted makes success with this critical task essentially impossible. In this context, the selling of addictive substitutes for meaning could not pose a greater risk or be more ultimately immoral—in the sense of diminishing who we are and undermining future possibility.

As yet, few people sufficiently recognize either the depths of the dangers that device addiction presents or how impervious device addiction can be to solutions. I often work in therapy with young people. It is rare that they don't come in addicted to their electronic devices. Young men tend most often to be addicted to video games. With young women it is more often the pseudo-relationship of social media that provides the hook.

The risks that accompany device addiction increase dramatically when we add the mechanisms of machine learning. As with our electronic devices, machine learning reflects a kind of technological advance that in potential provides great benefit. Indeed, machine learning will almost certainly be the source of some of the digital revolution's most important contributions going forward. But for machine learning to benefit us in the long run, we similarly need to appreciate ways it can result in harm.

A defining characteristic of machine learning algorithms is key both to its positive applications and to potential dangers. If a person gives them a goal, they will pursue that goal unquestioningly and unceasingly. Assign to such an algorithm the task of maximizing traffic to a website, for example, and it will do so irrespective of what it may take to accomplish this end. This fact has an easily missed but deadly consequence. Because addictive dynamics provide the most reliable way to get such attention, there is no need to design digital systems to be addictive. Over time, the inevitable result is ever more powerful digital designer drugs.[5] Dangers are further amplified by the fact that human operators commonly don't have access to the underlying machine learning processes (and commonly could not understand them if they did—the processes are just too multifaceted).

I think of three scenarios in which machine learning could have truly cataclysmic consequences. In the first, some kind of bad actor on the world stage wages an AI-based attack on a perceived enemy. The goal could be the destruction of physical infrastructure such as electrical grids and water supplies, disruption of communications networks, or, as we have seen attempted in very rudimentary form with Russian interference in elections, a fundamental undermining of social and governmental structures. We legitimately include this kind of application when we think of "weapons of mass destruction." In time, it may prove the most problematical example of such weaponry.

The second scenario is what people in the technology world most often point toward when they warn that AI could have cataclysmic results. Systems applying machine learning could eventually outcompete us. It is easy to make the goal of a machine learning algorithm simply to have the mechanism propagate itself. Since such algorithms can be

---

5 Another inevitable result is "fake news." It turns out that the polarized emotionality of fake news makes it more effective for getting attention than the real thing.

single-minded in their competitiveness in ways that we humans will never be, and would never want to be,[6] the likelihood is high that they would prevail.

But I think the greatest danger lies ultimately with addictive dynamics and the way machine learning could make those dynamics so overwhelmingly powerful that we would have no real defense. Put in systems terms, the result could be a runaway feedback loop that we have no way to understand, much less control. As the consumption of artificial stimulation increasingly replaced meaningful activity in our lives, we would become less and less able to discern the choices that would most ultimately benefit us. This is a scary picture, and not just a possible picture. Increasingly we see its beginnings in our daily lives. A good argument can be made that it is inevitable.

Is there anything we can do to counter this great potential danger? An approach I use with any addiction, but also in particular with device addition, helps point toward what ultimately will be necessary. It turns addiction's own mechanisms—the substitution of artificial fulfillment for the real thing—against it. I will commonly start by asking the person questions about what they most like to do, simple questions that help reveal what uniquely matters to the person. We talk together about the importance of honoring and protecting the things that for them most create meaning. I then confront the person with how the addiction, in providing an artificial substitute for fulfillment, is undermining and doing damage to real fulfillment. I help the person practice living their life in ways that say yes to the real thing and no to the imposters. The therapy process becomes an exercise in making life-affirming choices.

Related intervention at a broader cultural level immediately confronts obstacles. It will require not just that people appreciate the extent of the danger, but also that they are sufficiently connected to what matters in their lives that they can effectively discern when a particular activity serves them and when it does not. As I've suggested, this is a depth of connection that is too often lacking with Transitional dynamics and our modern Crisis of Purpose. But the basic principles of what

---

6 In spite of how we often frame human nature in simplistic Darwinian fight-for-survival competitive terms, humans—thankfully—are more complex than just this.

needs to happen are very similar. And Cultural Maturity's changes make it possible for us to do what we need to do.

One particular recognition needs to be central if we are to avoid the kind of runaway mechanisms that could result in the combination of addictive dynamics and machine learning being the end of us. It concerns the nature of human intelligence. We need to better appreciate just how machine learning and human intelligence are different. In fact, machine learning and human intelligence work in ways that are hardly related at all, an observation that for someone like myself who works every day with intelligence's multilayered complexities is so obvious it hardly needs stating.

One difference is particularly pertinent to the dynamics of addiction and where needed solutions lie. I've described how machine learning is single-minded in pursuing its goal. There is an important sense in which human intelligence is not just more complex in all it considers, it is by its nature purposeful. This recognition is somehow always central in my work as a therapist. There is no need for me to work specifically to help a person live a more meaningful life. Indeed, if I believe this is my task, I risk undermining the desired outcome (it is too easy to end up imposing one's own notions of purpose). Instead, as I just described with the example of addressing addiction, all I need do is ask the person in different ways what most matters to them. Challenge the person to shape their life in ways that honor their answers, and purposeful choices will be the result. Put in CST terms, human intelligence is inherently creative. It seeks out the solutions that are most affirming of life. More than this, it seeks out the options that will be most consistent with generativity, with the possibility of newly vital expressions of life.

Another way to describe this same conclusion has particular relevance to the challenges presented by device addiction. There is an important sense in which human intelligence is ultimately moral. This claim may seem radical given how frequently we are not at all moral in our everyday dealings. And given how often history confronts us with acts for which we should not at all be proud, the claim might seem preposterous. But most often in our daily lives we act with basic kindness. And history's big picture finds humanity bringing ever greater complexity to its moral discernments.

This last observation has pertinence for these reflections both because it further highlights the inherently purposeful/moral nature of human intelligence and because it invites the intriguing question of whether new moral capacities might become possible in the future. In earliest societies, much that we would today consider totally unacceptable was common—for example, human sacrifice, slavery, and even cannibalism. The rise of civilizations saw more formal attention given to philosophical questions, but as we witnessed with the early Greeks and Egyptians, at least slavery continued as a common practice. The appearance of monotheism brought with it greater emphasis on moral concerns, but the resulting moral absolutism often left us still far from what we would find acceptable in our time. The Middle Ages gave us the Magna Carta, but it also brought the barbarism of the Crusades and the Spanish Inquisition, with thousands of people executed simply for their beliefs. In our Modern Age, we've witnessed important additional steps with, for example, the Bill of Rights and its stated freedoms not just for religion but for speech more generally. And with the last century, we've seen essential further advances—for example, with the civil rights and women's movements, and more recently with advocacy for the rights of people with differing sexual orientations.

None of this is to suggest that today we are always moral in our actions. Commonly we are far from it. My point is simply that there is clearly something in what it means to be human that is allied not just with advantage, but with a larger good. And it is embedded deeply enough that we can think of the human narrative as a whole as a story of evolving moral capacity. Human intelligence by its nature engages us in questions of value and purpose. We are imperfect beings, but we are also in the end moral beings. In contrast, machine learning is a tool, and while it is one with great potential for good, there is nothing in it that makes it inherently good, and much that makes it vulnerable to being a force for the opposite.

We need to address a question embedded in this distinction if we are to use machine learning in ways that ultimately serve us: Just what is it that makes human intelligence purposeful, and moral? CST proposes that the key lies in human intelligence's multiplicity. Human intelligence, with its multiple aspects, is not just more complex than can be modeled with a computer; it reflects a wholly different *kind* of complexity. I've described how the way human intelligence is structured makes it inherently "creative."

By virtue of our multiple intelligences, we are not just inventive, but also inherently purposeful—and moral—in our actions.

For the sake of simplicity, we can think of the mechanisms of machine learning as roughly parallel to those of one specific aspect of human intelligence—the rational. In fact, machine learning, even at its best, mimics rational processing only imprecisely. If we look closely at rationality, we see that it functions in ways that are more subtle and layered than we tend to assume. But the analogy works adequately as a point of departure for grasping the basic strengths and limitations of machine learning.

The idea that we might have machines that can carry out many of the more rational/mechanistic tasks of cognition—and much more rapidly and complexly than we can—is a great thing. But as I've made clear in describing intelligence's multiplicity, rationality alone is not sufficient if we are to effectively engage the future's important challenges. Certain purely technical challenges can be addressed in this way, but not concerns that in any way include values, human relationships, or creativity of any deep sort—as most any questions that really matter to us eventually do. The common belief that machine learning could eventually address all of our concerns is not based on evidence. Rather, it is a product of the defining role that rational intelligence has played in Modern Age understanding. Extended into the future, such belief becomes a particularly dangerous expression of Transitional Absurdity.

These reflections on how machine learning and human intelligence are different have both good-news and bad-news implications. On the good-news side, they mean that the more complex and sophisticated kind of thinking needed to make the required discernments is not only possible, as potential it is built into who we are. Integrative Meta-perspective again provides a solution. On the bad-news side, they mean that appreciating what is needed if we are to make good choices becomes very difficult without at least the beginnings of culturally mature skills and capacities. Today we readily idealize and mythologize the technological—in effect, we make it our god. With machine learning, we can get things turned around completely. Caught in techno-utopian bliss, we can make it what we celebrate. And when we add addictive dynamics, the needed way forward becomes ever more difficult to recognize.

The power of machine learning to amplify addictive dynamics represents only one example of how mythologizing invention can put us at risk, but it puts potential consequences in particularly high relief. If you came upon a person who, being especially fond of his hammer, put it on an altar and burned incense in its honor, you might find him weird, but let it pass. If, however, the hammer the person worshipped was capable of rising up on its own, hitting the person on the head and killing him—and perhaps killing everyone else in the process—then you would appropriately consider the person insane. That is the reality that we face today with machine learning. Machine learning can serve us richly as we go forward. But it can do so only if we are clear in our understanding of what it is and what it is not.

The key to avoiding calamity lies with how Integrative Meta-perspective helps us better appreciate how our tools, however amazing they may be, are only tools. This acknowledgment is essential if we are to use our tools in ways that will ultimately serve us. It is a fact that becomes obvious—common sense—once we are over Cultural Maturity's threshold. With Cultural Maturity's cognitive changes, we no longer confuse ourselves with our tools. And certainly we stop mythologizing our tools, treating them as gods.

Effectively managing machine learning and its effects will require drawing on the purposeful/moral nature of human intelligence and doing so with whole new levels of sophistication. Every step of the way, we have to ask whether particular applications benefit us in the sense of being ultimately life-affirming. We also have to be exquisitely sensitive to possible unintended consequences. (It is unintended consequences, rather than malevolence, that are most likely to be our undoing.) Moving forward effectively will require not just applying a moral lens, but bringing to bear an encompassing maturity of moral decision-making that before now would have been beyond us to grasp. Integrative Meta-perspective offers that we tool makers might learn to use our tools in ways that are not just clever, but ultimately wise.

CHAPTER TEN

Applying Creative Systems Theory Patterning Concepts #2: Broader Questions (Love, Gender, and Relationships Between the Sexes)

Some of the most powerful applications of Creative Systems Theory involve in-depth inquiry into broader questions. Here we've also made a start. For example, we've inquired into what makes an act moral, looked at changes reordering leadership, examined how love is asking new things of us, and probed the workings of human intelligence. This chapter's reflections continue the kind of inquiry into changes reshaping love that I began in Chapter Four and adds the essential topics of gender and relationships between the sexes. I brought these topics together in my 2019 book *On the Evolution of Intimacy: A Brief Exploration into the Past, Present, and Future of Gender and Love*.

The book had its origins in efforts to write a front-page news issue piece as I listened to conversations growing out of the #MeToo movement and the like.[1] I was pleased that important and timely issues were being engaged, issues that had often been topics of focus at the Institute decades before. But it was also clear to me that much of significance was being left out of the conversations, and that the price to pay for addressing these topics simplistically could, at least in the short term, be significant. I saw that today's new gender-related conversations could have two very different outcomes. They could bring a

---

1 For those who are reading this book well after its initial date of publication, the #MeToo movement was an effort in the spring of 2018 to bring new attention to male abuse of power and sexual misconduct. It began with the highlighting of exploitative behavior in Hollywood.

new depth of engagement between men and women and an important kind of reconciliation of the historical battle of the sexes. But just as easily they could result in an exacerbation of the historical battle of the sexes with even greater polarization, as we witness today with so many social issues.

I didn't get too far into my effort before it became obvious that more than a short article was needed. Getting at all that was important to consider would at the least require a parallel examination of changes reshaping love, and also changes reshaping identity more generally. It would also require not just reflection on current gender-related issues, but the application of a long-term historical lens. *On the Evolution of Intimacy* was the result. I began the book with these words:

> Nothing more defines the worlds of gender and love today than change. Indeed, because these changes are so striking—and so far-reaching and fundamental in their implications—I often use them as examples of broader changes reordering culture. This short book turns specifically to how changes in the worlds of gender and love are altering the human experience.

Here I will draw directly on material from *On the Evolution of Intimacy* with additions where context or filling out is needed. These can only be selected snapshots, as my approach even with the intimacy book involved covering complex topics quickly. I will also make selections of material keeping in mind this book's larger purpose. *On the Evolution of Intimacy* is most explicitly about more deeply understanding love and gender and making good choices in times ahead. But beneath the surface, the book's contribution lies as much with the evidence it provides for the importance of the concept of Cultural Maturity and the accuracy of the ideas of Creative Systems Theory.

The concept of Cultural Maturity's role in *On the Evolution of Intimacy* is most explicit. This book examines how, while aspects of the changes reordering love and gender today reflect Modern Age tasks, much that is most important is a product specifically of Cultural Maturity–related changes and challenges. It also proposes that the determining factor as far as whether today's love- and gender-related conversations will bring better communication or an exacerbation of the historical battle of the sexes will be people's ability to engage those conversations with some degree of culturally mature perspective.

CST's contribution in *On the Evolution of Intimacy* has multiple levels. The book looks at how Whole-Person relationship and Whole-Person identity—notions that follow from CST's framing of the evolution of culture—alter the truths we apply in making choices. And it draws extensively on how CST uses the concept of gender archetype to get beyond the polarized assumptions of times past. In addition, it delineates how Patterning in Time notions help us understand the very different ways we've perceived love and gender through history. The book also makes use of hands-on CST approaches such as Parts Work and expands on more specific CST topics such personality style differences and the dynamics of violence.

With this chapter, I've often quoted directly from the book.[2] As with previous instances where I have drawn specifically on other writing, I've tended to leave material that might overlap intact. I've done this when such repetition may provide useful insight for the task of communicating ideas that may be several decades ahead of most people's thinking.[3]

Setting the Stage

As I did with this book's initial stage-setting reflections, I began *On the Evolution of Intimacy* by laying out a series of claims and promises. As these short paragraphs provide a good summary of the territory the book traverses, I present them verbatim:

> I will describe how the way we think about and experience love has evolved, and continues to evolve. I will propose that our

---

[2] I have indicated where I have done so by indenting paragraphs.

[3] While *On the Evolution of Intimacy*'s general observations are pertinent to people of all sexual orientations and people with nonbinary gender identification (and I often make references more specifically to how these circumstances alter realities), I chose to give primary attention in the book to heterosexual relationships. I made this choice because the book otherwise would not have been a "brief exploration" and also out of acknowledgement of limits to my experience and expertise. I make a similar choice here.

times are challenging us to engage a major new chapter in that evolution, one as significant as that which brought us Romeo and Juliet–style romantic love three hundred years ago.

I will also describe how the way we think about identity is, similarly, not static, but has evolved, and continues to evolve. Of particular significance for this inquiry, this includes gender identity. We will see how changes happening today are as fundamental in their significance as those that brought us the Modern Age concept of the individual.

Over the course of the book, we will see how both love and identity today are requiring skills and capacities new to us as a species. We will examine how this is similarly the case whether our concern is authentic equality between the sexes, effectively honoring gender diversity, or learning to love in ways that can work going forward. Much of my reason for writing this book is a desire to help people understand and develop those needed new skills and capacities.

We will delve into how today's new picture of gender identity confronts us with a recognition that at first can seem paradoxical. On one hand, men and women become more similar than we have assumed in times past. We will see how our historical view of men and women as, if not opposites, at least fundamental in their differences, has been more a product of how our thinking processes have worked in times past than of what is actually the case (with different perceptions of such differences particular to different times in culture). And at the same time, today's new picture of gender helps us better appreciate real difference. I will argue that confusing equality with equivalence—simply making men and women the same—gets us no closer to the truth than the polarized perceptions of times past and in the end undermines engaging either identity or love with the necessary sophistication.

I will propose that the tasks ahead will challenge men and women equally. Those challenges relate both to how men and women see themselves and how each views the other. For example, I will describe how historical perspective often brings into question popularly accepted conclusions about the roots of conflict between the sexes. I will also describe how both men and women in our time tend to be disconnected from aspects of our human complexity needed for really deep human connecting. I will propose that the changes this book is about require a newly possible depth of engagement with that complexity—and that they follow naturally from it.

Following these preview-of-coming-attractions reflections, I briefly introduced the concept of Cultural Maturity and Creative Systems Theory's basic approach. And I put the book's task in context and established appropriate expectations:

> This book is not for everyone—at least not everyone right now. Depending on your life experience, it may be decades before the emerging realities examined here manifest in a major way in your life. That said, I will argue that the demands and possibilities this book is about will be pertinent to everyone eventually.

The Roots of Gender Identity

The book's first chapter reflects on the changes reordering love that I described here in Chapter Four and ties them to the concept of Cultural Maturity. I observe that Modern Age romantic love is not the ideal and end point we've assumed it to be and propose that in fact it has involved something very different from what we have before thought it to be about. I describe how romantic love, instead of being based on individual choice in any Whole-Person sense, has been based on projection. The book then examines the possibility of stepping beyond such two-halves-make-a-whole relating—and with Cultural Maturity's changes, the option of a more complete kind of love.

The book then turns more specifically to the topic of gender. I address how our understanding of gender has also evolved over the course of history. And I make the provocative assertion that, in a way similar to what I have described for love, in times past we have fundamentally misconstrued what gender is about. Historically, our ideas have again been based on projection. I propose that it is these projective dynamics that have had us think in terms of opposite sexes when in fact our similarities are much greater than our differences.

To make these claims more understandable, I offer some overarching reflection. First I introduce the concept of gender archetype. I note that while the notion is new to many people, it is key to understanding gender in any deep way. I describe how men and women each draw on both archetypally masculine and archetypally feminine qualities. And I observe that it is gender archetypes that historically we have projected. I propose that the reason men and women have before seen each other as opposite is that we have been perceiving one another as the embodiments of these qualities that are, in fact, opposite.

The book then draws on CST's Patterning in Time concepts for more detailed historical perspective. I propose that we can make sense of why polarized interpretations of gender have taken the various forms that they have through history by combining the concept of gender archetype with an appreciation of how cultural systems evolve. I observe that gender archetypes manifest in specific ways with each cultural stage. And I describe how our ideas about gender have been products of projections made from this evolving symbolic landscape. Depending on when we have done the projecting, our beliefs have reflected how gender archetypes have manifested at that particular point in culture's story.

The book then turns to the obvious question once we recognize that the polarized perceptions of times past have distorted our understanding of gender: Just what are we left with when we step beyond the mythologized projections of times past? And more specifically, just how are we then in fact different, if we are at all? I acknowledge the fact of biological differences, and how, by virtue of particular biology-specific activities we engage in, such as bearing children, we may have different life experiences. But the question as I frame it has to do with what we think of as psychological differences. Are men and women different in terms of values, attitudes, beliefs, and emotional responses?

The question of gender differences is legitimately controversial given that it has been used as a basis for unequal treatment and even harm. But I caution that we can just as much stop short by denying differences. I expand on the kind of observation that I noted here in Chapter Six with our look at temperament differences and gender. I propose that while men and women are much less natively different in this sense than we tend to assume—indeed we find as much or more variation within sexes as differences between them—we do see differences. I observe that once we leave behind polarized expectations, we find the kind of general 60/40 balance relative to gender that I described previously.

Further essential questions addressed in *On the Evolution of Intimacy* turn to what this more complete picture of love and gender asks of us. I describe new skills and capacities that good choices in all parts of our lives will increasingly require. I also look closely at new learnings specific to the future of love and relations between the sexes, both new learnings needed by everyone and learnings more specific to men and to women. I emphasize that love and gender can continue to reward us going forward only to the degree to which we take on these essential learning tasks.

Applying CST to the kinds of concerns *On the Evolution of Intimacy* addresses puts in high relief the inherent trickiness that I have described with other questions when it comes to communicating ideas that have their basis in culturally mature perspective. Talking about love, sex, and gender under any circumstances can make people uncomfortable. But in our time, these topics are particularly prone to creating controversy. Conclusions in the book often step beyond political correctnesses—of all sorts, both those of the Right and of the Left.

Challenges to the more traditional-value beliefs of the Right are most obvious. Today's new picture requires leaving behind historical assumptions about love, marriage, and gender. These are beliefs that people of the Right in particular may often before have considered not just absolute, but sacred. Those on the Right are also likely to object to the applications of evolutionary ideas and feel aversion to views that give the archetypally feminine this depth of significance.

Challenges to the Left are just as fundamental, and given that today's popular conversations tend most often to view needed changes through the lens of postmodern or liberal ideology, arguably the more important to recognize. Several topics I have noted are essentially taboo in many contemporary settings where gender questions are given attention. For example, discussion of gender differences is often quickly dismissed—or worse[4]—

---

4 Contemporary academic thought, with its postmodern leanings, can claim that psychological differences, if they exist at all, are products only of conditioning, of the different ways boys and girls are raised. Indeed, it is possible

where liberal ideology prevails. The book's observation that along with new learnings for men being critical (which the Left emphasizes), new learnings for women are similarly fundamental would in many settings not be well received. (The book includes a whole chapter with separate sections on "learnings for men" and "learnings for women.") And places where the book brings into question common conclusions about conflict between the sexes could be particularly controversial. *On the Evolution of Intimacy* describes how circumstances that get framed in terms of oppression can sometimes be better understood in terms of culture's evolving story. (An evolutionary picture includes oppression when it is the appropriate interpretation, but it also finds that when events are placed in a larger context, often other ways of thinking more usefully describe what we see.)

Obviously I am not someone who is shy about speaking the truth as I see it. But it is also the case that if I am invited to be on a panel that addresses gender- or sexuality-related questions today, I am careful first to be sure that there is in fact interest in a culturally mature exchange.

The ideas I present in *On the Evolution of Intimacy* present a more complex and nuanced picture than we commonly encounter. But I find thinking with this level of complexity essential if we are to successfully engage pertinent questions. Again, if we take needed steps far enough, we often find essential complexities revealing a world that is also in important ways simpler.

The Concept of Gender Archetype

Since the concept of gender archetype is so central to *On the Evolution of Intimacy*'s inquiry, I take time in the book to examine it in particular depth. I introduced the concept early on in this book and have drawn on it in some way with most every chapter since. But the more filled-out descriptions that I offer in the intimacy book make a valuable addition to this book's reflections.

Even people who are familiar with the notion of gender archetype rarely recognize the full depth of its importance. Certainly observations that draw on an understanding of gender archetype have been critical to this book's

---

in academia today to lose one's job simply for suggesting the existence of differences of a more fundamental sort. In contrast, few people who spend much time around young children find the conclusion that conditioning provides a complete explanation persuasive.

CREATIVE SYSTEMS THEORY

insights. Indeed, nothing in this inquiry makes real sense without gender archetype-related changes working beneath the surface. In introducing the Creative Function in Chapter Three, I observed that the evolving ways that the archetypally masculine and archetypally feminine have related throughout history help us make sense of how we have thought about almost every aspect of our lives. I've also described how appreciating the creative underpinnings of this kind of big-picture pattern helps us understand what most fundamentally makes us human. In some way, the concept of gender archetype is implied in every kind of CST patterning notion.

The concept of gender archetype has particular pertinence for the task of thinking of questions of love and gender with needed subtlety. Gender archetype is what with love and gender in times past we have projected. It is also what now we need to re-own if needed new steps in how we relate to others and to ourselves are to be realized.

The descriptions that follow are themselves adapted from even earlier writing, from observations made in my first book, *The Creative Imperative*. In part I reached this far back because *The Creative Imperative* is the place in my work where I've described the archetypally masculine and archetypally feminine in greatest detail. But there is also a reason that I noted in this book's beginning. In crafting *The Creative Imperative*, I attempted to draw with equal measure on the more rational aspects of intelligence that best give voice to the archetypally masculine and the less visible, more imaginal and emotional aspects of intelligence that better voice the archetypally feminine (and that we are less used to associating with observations of a theoretical sort). The book can be thought of as equal parts prose and poetry.

As I did with *The Creative Imperative*, in *On the Evolution of Intimacy*, I addressed these tendencies by drawing on the whole of intelligence's multiplicity. I also provided a further level of differentiation that I've only suggested here, how we can think of the archetypally masculine and the archetypally feminine as each having both horizontal and vertical aspects. Because of the nuance these descriptions from *On the Evolution of Intimacy* bring to concepts important to thinking throughout this book, the paragraphs that follow present the text largely unaltered.[5]

---

5 A recognition embedded in these descriptions is essential if their implications are to fully make sense. I've observed how, in our time, we find it much easier

The Horizontal—Archetypally Masculine Manifestations

Horizontal aspects come most alive in relationships with others. The archetypally masculine manifests here in expressive dynamics—in the thrust of a sword, in a well-chosen word, in a song sung powerfully. When we use words like "assertive" or "penetrating" we are referring to this aspect of the archetypally masculine.

A few quotes that give this aspect voice:

Three kinds of souls, three prayers: I am a bow in your hands Lord,
Draw me lest I rot.
Do not overdraw me, Lord. I shall break.
Overdraw me, Lord, and who cares if I break.
　　　　　　　　　—Nikos Kazantzakis (Report to Greco)

But such is the irresistible nature of truth, that all it asks, and all it wants, is the liberty of appearing.
　　　　　　　　　—Thomas Paine

When I am a man then I shall be a hunter.
When I am a man then I shall be a harpooner.
When I am a man then I shall be a canoe-builder.
When I am a man then I shall be a carpenter.
When I am a man then I shall be an artisan.
Oh father! ya hahaha.
　　　　　　　　　—A Kwakiutl song

---

to understand archetypally masculine qualities than we do qualities of a more archetypally feminine sort. For example, focusing on the horizontal, I've described how we commonly confuse the receptive with simply being passive. This applies as well to vertical aspects. Similarly, while we don't have any problem with understanding the role of standing tall in authority, my reference to what I call "the ground of being" as an equally important aspect of the vertical even with explanation might still seem obscure and even a bit mysterious. I've noted how we find just the opposite if we go back far enough in history. With culture's beginnings, the archetypally feminine played the more defining role. While still by its nature it was less explicit, it got very much the greater attention.

Who are we as the expressive? Much of it is quite "straightforward." Our concern is with acting and doing. Myth offers us some good beginning images. The expressive embodies symbolically as the hero, and specifically as the hero's more active aspect. This active aspect can be personified in an infinity of forms—the poet, the warrior, the inventor, the magician. But the essential quality is quite specific: the capacity to penetrate reality.

Our colloquial language is rich with figures of speech that depict the expressive. Some simply describe movement outward, or how movement outward engages another's reality. We speak of "getting through to someone," of "making a point" or "an impression," of "getting something across," or "speaking out." Others emphasize the finality intrinsic to expression: We "put our cards on the table." Many such figures of speech give voice to the inherent vulnerability of expression. We speak of "going out on a limb," or of "putting ourselves on the line."

It is important to appreciate that the forms expression takes need not be obvious. Many of the most important are highly nuanced. A favorite quote from Cooper Edens's children's book *Remember the Night Rainbow* counsels us that "If your heart catches in your throat ... ask a bird how she sings." It is equally important to appreciate the sense in which expression is more than just a matter of choice. The Gnostic Gospels remind us that "If you bring forth what is within you, what you bring forth will save you. If you do not bring forth what is within you, what you do not bring forth will destroy you." (Gospel of Thomas. Saying 70)

The Horizontal—Archetypally Feminine Manifestation

Horizontally, the archetypally feminine manifests in receptive dynamics: in acts not just of listening but of hearing, in being aroused or moved, in aesthetic perception. When we see someone "taking in" experience or offering "invitation" we are witnessing the receptive. This complementary aspect of the horizontal similarly often comes most alive in relationships with others.

A few quotes that give this aspect voice:

The sound of the gates opening wakes the beautiful woman asleep.
—Kabir (trans. Robert Bly)

Learning to draw is really a matter of learning to see—to see correctly—and that means a good deal more than merely looking with the eye.
—Kimon Nicolaides

... and then I asked him with my eyes to ask again yes
and then he asked me would I yes ...
and first I put my arms around him yes
and I drew him down to me so he could feel my breasts all
  perfume yes
and his heart going like mad
and yes I said yes I will yes.

—James Joyce

Since it is not possible to define the receptive by "making a point," I will begin with a couple of images. The first comes from the legend of King Arthur. With his sword broken in battle, Arthur is led by Merlin to the shore of a small body of water. In it lives the beautiful Lady of the Lake. From her Arthur receives the mighty sword Excalibur with which he will found the great Round Table, and its scabbard. The sword is broad and sharp, embellished in gold. Engraved on one side are the words "take me," on the other "cast me away."

Standing before him, Merlin asks Arthur which he likes better, the sword or the scabbard. The sword is Arthur's quick choice. To this Merlin responds, "In that you are unwise. Excalibur is a good sword, the best in the world. But the scabbard is worth far more. For however sorely you are beset in battle, you will not lose a drop of blood a long as you have the scabbard with you ...."

The second image is from the beloved European folktale, "Beauty and the Beast." We engage the story as Beauty, having run many hours through the entangled forest, finds the Beast outside his castle, his breath gone, the spell having done its evil work. Through her tears, moved by the love that has grown within, she embraces his terrible image. At that moment, the interminable spell that has imprisoned the prince is broken ....

Because this aspect of our power is so elusive to usual thought, we most often refer to it by saying what it is not, or by alluding to it indirectly. Frequently we use sensory metaphors, though the five senses may not literally be central. We may say we "got a taste" of or "drank in" an experience, that we "saw" what someone was saying, or that we were "touched" or "moved" by the depth of a person's response. Frequently our words reflect the surrender of control intrinsic to the receptive moment. We speak of being "amazed" (from the same root as "maze") or being "taken" by an experience. Our words may reflect the letting down of boundaries, a recognition that we had let ourselves be "open," or that another person has "gotten through to us." Or they may describe our bodily experience when we do, such as feelings of warmth and responsiveness, or of being "turned on...."

What is it we derive from the receptive? If the purpose of the expressive is to actively have an effect, how might we best describe the "purpose" of the receptive? Perhaps the simplest way to say it is that our receptivity is the way we derive our human sustenance. We are fed by each aspect of real contact that we allow. When our "diet" is appropriate and sufficient, our life feels "full"; when it is not, we hunger.

To receive is always a vulnerable thing. We are inviting another to enter a room in our psychic house, knowing that with this visit the room will never again be quite the same. And there is no guarantee that what is offered by the visitor will be positive. It could be that this visitor comes on false pretenses, intending only to rob or violate. As with expression, receptivity is always in the end a leap into the unknown. Ultimately, we can never know the effect of an experience until we have risked its transforming touch. Yet how fully alive we are is precisely a function of how deeply we can trust in, and engage, that risk.

It is important to appreciate how deeply this aspect of who we are can confuse and elude us. By its nature it is invisible—often we know it is there only by what becomes visible in its presence. In addition, as I've suggested, the receptive can be particularly hard to make sense of in our time. Equally important is the recognition that the receptive is just as much a reflection of power as the expressive. Indeed, in many circumstances it is where the greater power lies. The Chinese sage Lao Tzu reminds us that "The softest thing in the universe overcomes the hardest thing in the universe." And again there is an important sense in which the receptive is more than just a matter of choice. I like these words from economist John Stuart Mill: "We must neglect nothing that could give the truth a chance to reach us."

The Vertical—Archetypally Masculine Manifestations

To fully grasp the archetypally masculine and the archetypally feminine, we also need to include their more vertical manifestations. In the vertical, the archetypally masculine manifests in the dynamics of ascent: Think of the crown on the head of a king or queen, the crafting of an abstract idea, the construction of a great building, or a rocket headed into space. When we stand and take ownership in our lives, we are giving emphasis to the ascendent aspect of experience. Ascent is about the power of above as opposed to the power of below.

A few quotes that give this aspect voice:

In each of us there is a king; speak to him and he will come forth.
—A Norse saying

[A new theory] is rather like climbing a mountain, gaining new and wider views, discovering unexpected connections between our starting point and its rich environment.
—Albert Einstein

Form acts the father:
tells you what you may and
may not do.

—Theodore Roethke

What is it that each new ascendent impulse offers that was not there before? I think of three primary things. First, ascent gives us perspective. With it, we rise above, find a place that allows us to see the forest where before we could see only trees. Second, it gives new form and substance to our reality. To ascend is at once to climb a mountain, and to be creating that mountain. Each new act of standing tall offers a leap in monumentality and complexity. And third, it offers us authority and autonomy. To grow up is to define our natures as distinct.

Our cultural images for ascent and the ascendent trace a proud and dramatic lineage: the primitive's great bird of the spirit: the Greek sun god Helios or Apollo, driving each day across the heavens in a chariot with four great horses; Odin, wise and omnipotent, sitting in his throne in the upper branches of Yggdrasil (an eagle beside him, a crown on his head); the mountain as home of the divine—Qaf, Olympus, Sinai; the word as God; the uplifting spire of a European cathedral, Middle Eastern mosque, or Buddhist stupa; the firmament of heaven; the lifted transept of the Latin cross; the nation as flag; Washington, Napoleon, Churchill; Newton's laws of motion; the Bill of Rights; the Empire State Building; the first human walking on the surface of the moon.

Some further recognitions about ascent are important to appreciate. Again, there is how it is essential, not simply a matter of choice. A traditional song of the Bahamas announces: "Oh children, no grave could've keep that body down. Ain't no grave gonna keep that body down. When the trumpet sound ...." There is also how it is inseparable from responsibility. I think of these words of Martin Buber: "He has stepped out of the glowing darkness of chaos into the cool light of creation. But he does not possess it yet: he must first draw it truly out, he must make it into a reality for himself, he must find his own world by seeing, hearing, touching, and shaping it." It is also important to appreciate the close relationship between ascent and awareness. From William Blake: "Awake! awake, O sleeper of the land of shadows, wake."

The Vertical—Archetypally Feminine Manifestations

As with the receptive in the horizontal, the archetypally feminine aspect of the vertical confronts us with dimensions of our human power that are less recognized in our time—indeed easily missed entirely. But they are essential. In the ground of being, we find nurturance and also the germinal beginnings of things. In addition we find what, in our learning to stand tall, gives us something to stand upon.

Vertical aspects of the archetypally feminine manifest in our connectedness with nature, in religious imagery such as that of the Madonna holding the Christ child, and in the body's contribution both as the starting point of life's erotic impulses and the foundation of our being. CST describes how the way we experience the ground of our being, as with each polar tendency, is not a single thing, but an evolving dynamic that takes us through a sequence of markedly different experiential realities.

A few quotes that give this aspect voice:

The land is a mother that never dies.
—Maori saying

All matter is created out of some imperceptible substratum .. nothingness, unimaginable, and undetectable. But it is a particular form of nothingness out of which all matter is created.
— Physicist Paul Dirac

The spirit of the valley ... is called the mysterious female,
The gate of the mysterious female
   is called the root of heaven and earth,

Dimly visible, it seems as if it were scarcely there,
Yet use will never drain it.

— Lao Tzu

In the "ground" of our being, we find the power of mystery. Through our relationship with it, we experience the fact of our generativity and the "foundation" of our existence. When this relationship is right and timely, it imbues life with such qualities as belonging, playfulness, rootedness, passion, and compassion.

In the earliest stages in any creative process, this "nothing" that is at once something is reality's predominant force. Here we encounter a secret shared by the very old and the very young. It is the place into which we die and from which we are born. It is from here that we know the eternal magic of things. In ancient Celtic myth it is the Tír na nÓg, the place that existed before the beginning of time. Winter rituals often pay homage to its irrational latencies.

The lower pole of the vertical is also where we find the erotic. This is so equally in men and in women. It is also where we find deep connection in nature. The erotic and the wild are key to who we are. And at the same time, encountering them may not be comfortable. They are always as much about destruction as creation.

A key Patterning in Time recognition is important to making sense of cultural dynamics where the lower pole feminine plays a significant role. Over the course of any creative process, we gradually push away from the archetypally feminine in this sense of ground (and from the archetypally feminine in general). Indeed, at times, we push away quite forcefully. This is equally so if our creative concern is a simple creative act like writing a book, individual development over the course of a lifetime, or the evolution of culture. This recognition provides explanation for how difficult it can be to make sense of the archetypally feminine in our time. It also helps us better understand some of the particular ways that men and women have viewed each other at specific times in culture's story.

These reflections on the specifics of gender archetype point toward some general recognitions important to questions of love and gender. A first is most obvious yet in our time often missed. Each archetypal tendency represents a particular kind of power. Appreciating that the archetypally feminine is not just power, but a critical kind of power, today is essential. It is important to thinking that affirms gender equality. It is also critical to effectively engaging Whole-Person identity, whether in a man or a woman.

A further question follows from this recognition: Which kind of power is most important? The most immediate answer is that each is essential. CST goes further to clarify how neither could exist without the existence of the other. But we can also answer the question more contextually. Then the answer depends on where and when you look.

For example, the archetypally masculine tends to have greater influence with more in-the-world concerns such as in the traditional workplace (this for both men and women). The archetypally feminine tends to have greater influence in the home and with family (irrespective of who "wears the pants".) In relationships, it may appear that the masculine has the greater say (as with the assumption that a man will initiate), but in most instances in fact here too the feminine prevails (relationship is most about connectedness). It turns out that the kind of power that has the greatest influence is also going to be different depending on the stage in the evolution of culture and on an individual's personality style.

Skills, Capacities, and Perspectives

Before we turn to how the Creative Function can help us understand the evolution of gender and relationships between the sexes, let's reflect a little further on just what today's new love and gender realities ask of us. The new skills and capacities that I introduced earlier in this book have direct applicability to this chapter's concerns. Indeed, in these pages I've often turned to love and gender for examples. In *On the Evolution of Intimacy*, I describe an array of challenges and learnings that come with today's new picture of love and gender. Some reflect needed new skills and capacities that I've described here in relation to Cultural Maturity's changes more generally. Some are more specific to the tasks of relationship and gender identity. A few that I highlight in the book include:

CREATIVE SYSTEMS THEORY

A New Acceptance of Uncertainty, Responsibility, and Complexity

I've observed how Cultural Maturity's changes make being with another person and being ourselves each more expressly creative—more available to multiplicity and possibility and more complete in all that they draw on in our generative natures. In love we realize whole new freedoms, both in the forms intimacy can take and in ongoing choices we make in crafting relationship. As gendered beings we witness the acceptance of greater options—from nonbinary notions of gender to ways of thinking about identity that turn traditional gender expectations on their heads.

But precisely because of these creative possibilities, love and identity also become more demanding in what they ask of us. The now familiar importance of accepting greater uncertainty, responsibility, and complexity is an inescapable part of that more challenging picture. Without the reliable guideposts of times past, nothing is quite so certain. We also become newly responsible for our choices—and this specifically in the responsibility-twice-over sense that I introduced in Chapter Five. When we leave behind traditional cultural guideposts, we become responsible not just for making good choices, but for determining just what makes a choice good. And both because there is a greater multiplicity of options and because we must draw on more of our own multiplicity in making choices, it all becomes more complex.

The Need to Acknowledge Real Limits

I've emphasized the essential role that a new maturity in our relationship with limits plays with Cultural Maturity's changes. We find some of the best examples with changes that today reshape love and identity. A kind of limit inherent in Whole-Person relating that I noted in Chapter Four's look at love can be particularly unsettling—limits to what we can be for another person (and them for us). I've described how the romantic ideal seeks someone who can be our completion. While Whole-Person love affirms that there are rich and amazing things we can be for one another, it also makes clear that being another's completion is not one of them.

It is not easy to accept that there are limits to what we can be for one another. It can leave a person feeling uncomfortably, even desperately alone. In *On the Evolution of Intimacy*, I describe some ways that culturally mature understanding can begin to lessen this discomfort.

Appreciating how little two-halves-make-a-whole relationship is actually about knowing the other person provides a start. There is also the recognition that bonds of a more Whole-Person sort are deeper and more resilient (and thus more secure) than what they replace. We can also see, simply, that we have no choice. Increasingly we recognize that when we need something to be different from what is true, we only create pain.

The fact of real limits confronts us just as fundamentally with the tasks of identity, including gender identity. Whole-Person identity requires being as clear-eyed as we can be not just about what is possible, but also about limits to what may be possible. We also confront the Myth of the Individual. Like it or not, we no longer have the option of defining our individuality in terms of one half of two-halves-make-a-whole realities. While we may not at first celebrate this fact, in the end it offers that identity might manifest with a kind of completeness that has not before been an option.

The concept of Cultural Maturity suggests that love and identity that can work going forward are really not possible without a new, more mature acceptance of real limits. When we step back sufficiently, we recognize that this is about nothing more than just seeing the facts more accurately—which is ultimately a good thing.

Understanding a More Demanding Kind of Commitment

A third kind of new learning takes us beyond the new skills and capacities that I listed earlier in this book, but it follows from them. We find the need for a new, more demanding kind of commitment. Again this task applies across the board, equally to commitment in relationship and the kind of commitment to oneself needed to shape one's life in ultimately rewarding ways.

It would be easy to think that stepping beyond the clear cultural dictates of times past would make commitment less of a concern. But instead, commitment's demands increase. At the least, the fact that commitment now can take a greater multiplicity of forms implies the need for greater discernment. But we also confront the importance of a deeper and more demanding kind of commitment both to oneself and to another person in relationship. Our commitment to ourselves is to do everything we can to be sure that we make our life choices from the whole of who we are (in Parts Work terms, from the Whole-Person chair). When we fail at this task, we fail ourselves, fundamentally. Commitment with love is ultimately the same. We must commit to making every effort to engage the other person from that Whole-Person place. Our task if we fail is to apologize and also to take responsibility for doing a better job of doing so going forward.

This further kind of commitment ups the demands considerably. But, again, the rewards are similarly great. One reward is commitment we can better count on. Another is the ability to bring greater nuance to our discernments. We become able to make better choices in love, in life.

Beyond "Until Death Do Us Part"

A further additional new learning more specifically concerns relationship. It pertains both to limits and to commitment—and in particular to appropriate expectations. Traditional wedding vows include a promise to love "until death do us part." But like it or not, love relationships today are often not forever. That they aren't can sometimes be a product of our failings. But it is also something we might predict as we leave behind making another person our completion.

We reasonably ask how we might leave behind the "until death do us part" aspect of the romantic dream without hope being replaced with cynicism. The simple recognition that love stories, like all good stories, appropriately have beginnings, middles, and ends provides a start. Sometimes the end of the story may come with one person's death at the end of a well-lived life. But even with the best of efforts, right endings can also happen sooner. Another way to view things is to think of love as a creative process. Love stays alive as long as it remains creative. At a certain point, even with the deepest of commitment, it may, appropriately, stop being so.

The recognition that getting beyond this aspect of the romantic narrative supports mature love provides a more concrete kind of assistance. At the least, leaving this old way of thinking behind us can make us kinder toward one another. In Chapter Four, I noted how vicious people can be when a relationship comes to an end. I observed that we can think of this response as evidence for the fact that traditional romantic bonds have been based on projection. (In order to extract the projected part, the person who we before mythologized and made special must now be demonized.) I also mentioned that the more common response with Whole-Person love is very different. We may feel pain at the loss, but we will also tend to find gratitude for the time we have shared.

A further—and often unexpected—benefit of this more mature holding of love as narrative is that relationships that end in one form often come to endure in another. One of my closest friends is a woman I was lovers with for over a decade many years ago. At one point she shared that trying to be friends, colleagues, and lovers had come to feel like too much for her. We agreed that it would be best if we stopped being lovers. That would not have been my first choice, but I trusted her judgement. Looking back, I think she was right. The more important point is that our friendship endured. And over time it has continued to deepen. I don't think this continued evolution could have happened if we had not each been coming from a generally Whole-Person place in our relationship.

Culturally mature perspective suggests that this requirement that we let go of the "until death do us part" of the traditional narrative is ultimately a good thing. In fact, it may be key to having relationships that endure.

Learning to Make Clear Yeses and Nos

I give particular attention in *On the Evolution of Intimacy* to one specific needed new skill. I propose that all the various relationship and identity lessons that accompany Cultural Maturity in the end come down to being clearer with our yeses and nos. In times past, traditional roles and relationship assumptions have delineated the most important yeses and nos for us. Today, as traditional guideposts abandon us, life's yeses and nos increasingly become our responsibility to determine, and also to voice.

Certainly this is the case with relationship. If you ask people what ability is most important to good relationship, most will answer something like "clear communication." But we can be more specific, and we need to be if our concern is relationship in today's new relationship landscape. Success at love more and more requires being skilled at discerning and articulating our yeses and nos.

Past assumptions about how dating appropriately proceeds highlight some of the particular ways in which things are changing in this regard for men and for women. Traditionally, men were supposed to do the pursuing, and women were supposed to, at least a bit, play hard to get. In this picture, it is assumed that men will persist even if at first the message they get is "no."[6] Today, if we are not careful, these assumptions get us into trouble. Leaving them behind presents important lessons for both men and women. Men need to do a better job of hearing and respecting a woman's nos. And for this to work, women need to be much clearer in making their nos. They also need to be willing to be more direct if in fact "yes" is what they wish to communicate.[7]

Ultimately the same task defines the foundational challenge with identity. Engaging identity in a Whole-Person sense is in the end about nothing more than making increasingly refined, ongoing yes and no choices. We venture forth and each step along the way note what works for us and what does not. Life engages us in a constant process of discerning what choices are most life-affirming, and accepting or rejecting options accordingly.

Giving Up Gender-Related Myths

On the Evolution of Intimacy touches on an array of past gender-related myths. These range from "men are strong and women are fragile" (it depends on the individual and what one means by strength) to "men are violent and women are peacekeepers" (again it depends on the individual and what one means by violence).

One gender-related myth I address in the book is worth some elaboration because it is particularly pertinent to reflections here: "Men are more rational and women are more emotional." I describe how, as a very broad generality, men do tend to be somewhat quicker to draw on

---

6 I remember being confused as a boy that when I honored what seemed like a no from a girl instead of persisting, often the girl would then think of me as less interesting.

7 Notice how this emphasis on clear yeses and nos in another way brings us back to the two halves of polarity at its most fundamental. Nos are about difference, and yeses are about connectedness. Culturally mature relationship requires that we learn to honor each more consciously and act on each more explicitly.

rational intelligence as their primary mode for processing information. And women tend to draw a bit more immediately on the emotional. But once again we are dealing with a 60/40 balance, not qualitative differences. And differences within each sex are larger than average differences between sexes.

A further essential distinction becomes obvious with the appreciation for intelligence's multiplicity that comes with culturally mature perspective. The fact that men on average might be quicker to draw on the rational in no way suggests that they are somehow more intelligent. That people could reach this conclusion reflects how we have tended in recent times to equate rational intelligence with intelligence as a whole. In fact, not only does drawing first on the rational not necessarily make one smarter, it can have the opposite result. It can make a person vulnerable to confusing rationality with truth.

It is important to note that this distinction goes both ways. Because women on average tend to be a bit quicker to draw on emotional processing, people can assume that women are therefore more "emotionally intelligent." Women can be. But they can also fall for their own version of the same kind of trap. Reaching first to emotional processing can leave women vulnerable to confusing emotionalizing—emotional reactiveness[8]—with accurate perception.

When it comes to culturally mature intelligence—the capacity for Integrative Meta-perspective, the ability to make nuanced culturally mature discernments, and the acceptance of ultimate responsibility for one's choices—neither men nor women have any advantage. Men and women may on average go about getting there in slightly different ways, but as far as the needed complexity of perspective, neither gender has a leg up.

Giving Up Power

One of Cultural Maturity's most fascinating and consequential gender-related demands is the way it requires both men and women to give up familiar kinds of power. Successful relationship has always required that men and women surrender aspects of their gender-based power. Part of love is the tacit agreement by each party to not do harm that each is perfectly capable of perpetrating. With Cultural Maturity

---

8 In Parts Works terms, engaging from an emotional part.

and the possibility of more Whole-Person identity, this requirement expands. It comes to include not just personal power, but power in more specifically cultural manifestations. It also includes kinds of power closely tied to success with love's old definition. Again, doing so presents new challenges. But it also again produces essential rewards.

Because male power is easier to describe, the tasks for men are also easier to describe, but they nonetheless take us into fundamentally new territory. A first has always been necessary—men have to choose to not use what is generally greater physical strength. This is obviously the case with physical harm. But just as much it pertains to using the potential for such harm to intimidate or create an unequal power relationship.

In our time, men also need to give up kinds of power that follow from ways power relationships between genders have evolved through history, ways that no longer serve us. That includes the assumption up until recently that the "man of the family" appropriately had the last word, and going back in history, that being a husband implicitly or explicitly implied ownership. It also includes giving up past advantages in the workplace that have had less to do with the ability to do the job than with the fact of gender. And it means giving up any beliefs men might have that they have a right to venture uninvited into the physical or emotional life of a woman.

A final way men need to give up power can at first take people by surprise. A man interested in Whole-Person relationship will avoid acting in ways that intentionally trigger projections. This means giving up a kind of power that before could be thought of as a man's primary initial task with romantic love. In a Whole-Person reality, it is to the great benefit of everyone if men are understood and appreciated for their authentic power. But the culturally mature man knows that mythologized significance, however titillating it can seem at least initially, in the end only gets in the way of appreciating the real thing. He can enjoy romantic projections as a kind of shared play, but beyond this he learns to sidestep them.

Importantly, it is just as much the case that women need to give up power. Certainly in these times when the archetypally masculine rules, women can abuse power in this more traditional meaning of the word as readily as men when they get it. But my reference here is to the parallel need to give up key aspects of archetypally feminine power.

Notice that making sense of this importance requires the recognition that women, just by being women, in fact wield immense power when relating to men. The larger portion of this power is emotional. On many levels, men have traditionally felt a strong need to have women in their lives. And some is more specifically sexual. Most men are hardwired to feel considerable attraction to the female body. In each case this is real power and not to be taken lightly. The culturally mature woman knows such power is never to be misused.

The complement to the last kind of power I mentioned for men can be particularly hard for women to surrender. Women have to give up using their feminine cues to evoke projections on the part of men. The culturally mature woman rightfully enjoys the delight she can create with her feminine attractiveness. But she also realizes that she does as much harm ultimately to herself as she does to the man if she creates an impression that misrepresents who she in fact is. Women, like men, need to step back from the need for romantic projections. They too can enjoy such projections as a kind of mutually consenting play if they wish, but they must also learn to set such attraction to projection aside when it begins to get in the way of the real thing.

Gender and the Creative Evolution of Culture

Bringing CST's big-picture historical lens to this chapter's reflections provides essential additional insight. *On the Evolution of Intimacy* draws on the Creative Function in a way that gives particular attention to how archetypally masculine and archetypally feminine aspects interplay over the course of culture's story. I propose that the evolution of gender archetype provides perspective for an understanding identity, gender, and love that would be very hard to achieve in other ways.

For our purposes here, developmental/evolutionary perspective has a couple of key applications. The first relates to my observation that historically, our perceptions of gender differences have been based on the projection of gender archetypes. An understanding of how gender archetypes have creatively evolved over the course of history (and thus just what at any particular time we are likely to have projected) provides essential perspective for making sense of gender assumptions of times past.

In *On the Evolution of Intimacy*, I note three themes running through time that are directly pertinent to this kind of understanding. Each should now be familiar. First is how the balance between archetypally feminine and archetypally masculine follows the predictable sequence that I've described for any formative process. The archetypally feminine plays the larger role early on, with the archetypally masculine gradually assuming the greater influence with creation's more manifest stages. Second is how the manner in which poles relate evolves in characteristic ways with essential implications for how we experience each pole. Third is how integrative dynamics help us see a larger picture and appreciate how the relationship between the archetypally feminine and archetypally masculine through history, in spite of its often dramatic and conflicted twists and turns, has been complementary—in the end a (creative) conspiracy.

The second application comes back to my observation that circumstances that are commonly framed in terms of oppression can often be better understood in terms of culture's evolving story. Thinking in terms of the evolution of archetype affirms that inequalities and often significant harm have indeed occurred, but it also challenges us to get beyond thinking only in terms of victimization. For example, this progression illustrates how "perspiration" stage mechanisms naturally involve a pushing away of the archetypally feminine—a dynamic that can easily be misinterpreted. The way the archetypally feminine's role naturally becomes more decorative with culture's "finishing and polishing" stage can similarly cause confusion. Thinking in terms of the evolution of archetype also provides perspective for better making sense of commonly misunderstood more overarching notions such as the role and consequences of "patriarchy." I will later come back to each of these kinds of implication.

Again these observations present only an outline. In addition, in laying out this progression in *On the Evolution of Intimacy*, to keep things simple, I limited observations to the evolution of vertical polar relationships. Arguably, because the projections that have most produced polarized concepts of gender through history have been of the more explicitly relational sort, it would have been best to focus on horizontal polarities. But bringing the needed nuance to language is significantly more difficult with the evolution of horizontal polarity (and difficult enough with vertical polarity). Given that the book's interest lay with general principles more than detail, I chose the simpler route of limiting descriptions to the vertical.

Pre-Axis:

> We've seen how any formative process begins before the appearance of creation as form—in original wholeness. Put in the language of gender archetype, creation begins in the deepest reaches of the archetypally feminine. With Pre-Axis in culture, the relationship to the archetypally feminine is total. I've described how it manifests at once as connectedness with the earth, with the tribe, with the body, and with time. Deific symbols take the form either of images that personify human experience in the "mother" language of nature (deer, bear, or raven; the breath of the wind; the spirit of the forest), or representations of the great goddess, abundant of hip and breast.[9] The tribe more than its individual members is primary. And in a very important sense, reality is bodily reality—it is not possible to be part of a tribe without knowing its songs and dances. Time, as the seasons, exists as an ever repeating present.
>
> As with all past cultural periods, in Pre-Axis times there tends to be clear gender roles. But it is also the case that just where influence lies can be less clear than we might assume. When I visited Swaziland some decades back, people were quick to tell me with pride that their king had over a hundred wives. My understanding of the significance of this statement changed dramatically when I was later told that the most important of those wives were chosen not by the king, but by his mother.

Early-Axis:

> We've seen how Early-Axis brings first separation. Before, the archetypally feminine was everything—we were it and immersed in

---

9 The most famous is the "Venus of Willendorf" from about 30,000 BCE found in Willendorf, Austria.

it. Now there is it and something else. It is with Early-Axis that truth first becomes explicitly polar. Newly created form comes to sit in juxtaposition to the primordial ground of its origins.

What happens over the course of Early-Axis is particularly important to understanding the evolving relationship between the archetypally feminine and the archetypally masculine. We see a gradual progression from clear archetypally feminine preeminence to realities in which the archetypally masculine comes to play an increasing role. Because of the particular significance of this progression for this book's reflections, we should look at it more closely. Classical Greece offers that we might view this progression through the lens of myth.

I think of classical Greek civilization spanning the full length of culture's Early-Axis period. Over its course, the gods became increasingly ascendent. They also more frequently became human, and male. During earliest times, the primary deity appears to have been the earth goddess Gaia. The pantheons of gods had not yet taken up residence atop Olympus. Homer speaks of Gaia as the "universal mother, firmly founded, the oldest of divinities." During the middle years of Greek flowering, the pantheon settled in its familiar lofty abode. With that ascent, male figures increasingly assumed positions of greater influence, though the realms below generally maintained female representation. Later the female mythic keepers of the underworld were replaced by male overlords—Poseidon for the sea, Hades for the earthly underworld, Dionysus for the wisdom of the body and intuition. By the later years of Greece's eminence, the transposition had become virtually complete. Zeus resided as supreme patriarch, his ascendency only slightly tempered by the persuasions of his wife Hera, the most powerful remaining female figure on Olympus.[10]

---

10 Upper Pole characteristics came to take especially strong expression for their time in classical Greece. Because of this, ancient Greece makes a particularly good place to see this emerging significance of the archetypally masculine. By the time of Plato and Aristotle, we see further evolution in this direction as more philosophical sensibilities began to eclipse the mythic.

But while the archetypally masculine assumes greater influence over the course of Early-Axis in culture—and can most immediately capture our attention—throughout this stage, the archetypally feminine remains the stronger force. Mystery is always present and most often prevails. In fact, because we now juxtapose the light and the dark, mystery's dark power can be felt in ways that are even more pronounced. In the vertical, mystery now has a specific orientation. It is something which, when we are identifying with the conscious Upper Pole of experience, we specifically stand upon and exist in relationship to. It speaks as the underworld of existence.

We see this change with new ways the archetypally feminine finds depiction. In Pre-Axis, the feminine's primary manifestation was the primordial mother, the mother as source. Now we begin to find additional forms whose chthonic potency can evoke very different feelings. One example is the "death mother" or "terrible mother." We know her in Hindu myth as Kali.[11] Say the Vedas, "All this, whatever exists, is made to share in the sacrifice." Skulls around her neck, corpses beneath her feet, Kali is fire, dancing that life can be renewed. While the death mother can manifest with an audacity unsettling to modern sensibilities, she has an acknowledged, even venerated place in Early-Axis cultures. Then she is seen not as negative, but as simply part of the primal potency of existence. A faint memory of her can be heard in Shakespeare's reminder that "Nature's bequest gives nothing but doth lend." Even near the culmination of Early-Axis, the underworld of experience is still seen in predominantly positive terms. For example, while the Greek Hades, like the Celtic Tír na nÓg and the Scandinavian Hel, was dark and unfathomable, it was still thought of as inhabited by largely generative forces.

While again with Early-Axis we tend to see clear gender roles, it is then that we are most likely to see the roles of woman now

---

11 In the rituals of Bali, she is the ferocious and all-powerful Rangda, battling illusion and bringing what is not timely to its demise. In ancient Mexico, the death mother, her body clothed in snakes, was called Coatlicue.

taking preeminence. It is with the rise of agriculture that we most often encounter civilizations that are explicitly matriarchal.

Middle-Axis:

I've observed how creation's perspiration stage takes first possibility and gives it solid form. The work progresses by virtue of commitment, as an expression of heart and guts. With the changes of Middle-Axis, culture's Upper Pole gives expression to a now more structured kind of authority. In figures such as kings, emperors, and dictators, we see culture's new powers of dominion, the capacity to take control over the politically chaotic and disparate. In the image of the church, and figures such as the Pope, we see symbolized the parallel imperative to keep dominion over the personal below. The teachings of religion are increasingly moral, set in the language of good-versus-evil and written in scriptures and canons of holy law.

In Chapter Three I observed how the relationship of Upper Pole and Lower Pole changes in marked ways as we move through Middle-Axis. Again, because of the particular importance of these changes for this chapter's reflections, I will give them special attention. Key to Middle-Axis dynamics is a distancing from the archetypally feminine. Greek philosopher Ostanes describes the progression this way: "Nature rejoices in nature. Nature subdues nature. Nature rules over nature." A traditional Hebrew saying observes that "In the mother's body man knows the universe. In life he forgets it."

With Middle-Axis, for the first time, the influence of poles approaches equally. In addition, poles are no longer experienced as complementary—magic and mystery. The relationship now manifests as a kind of isometric tension—a struggle between at once conspiring and opposing forces. Ascent now requires an active pushing away of the below. Without this pushing away, the newly created form risks falling back into the immense power of mystery and formlessness.

Feminine symbolism helps flesh out this more complex picture. We find images that represent some of the aspects of the feminine that we most cherish. We could call the most acknowledged of the more positive aspects of the feminine at this stage the nurturant or good mother. She is the mother that cradles, the part of us that is supportive and unconditionally caring. Religion represents her with images like the Madonna. She finds more everyday expression in depictions of the peasant farm woman, children all about, loaves of warm bread just from the oven. When someone says, "Now that is a kid only a mother could love," this mother is the part of us that can see the child as nothing but beautiful.

But we also encounter symbols that evoke markedly negative feelings. Middle-Axis reality relegates certain faces of the Lower Pole feminine that were seen to have generative roles in previous stages—such as the chthonic mothers of death and passion—increasingly to the demonic. We juxtapose an all-loving god of light above with forces of darkness—even evil—below. Darkness and the unformed are more and more often equated with sin.

While our relationship with the archetypally feminine at this stage can feel ambivalent, it is important to emphasize that such ambivalence reflects not some lack of significance, but the fact that the feminine's power remains great. We feel ambivalence at this stage because we at once value the feminine deeply and in some way know that if we value it too deeply all that has been gained could be lost.

This recognition is key if we are to interpret Middle-Axis cultural phenomena at all usefully. For example, people in the modern West can assume that wearing of the hijab or the burka in certain Middle Eastern societies reflects a dismissing of the feminine. While it does reflect a need to distance from the feminine, the significance of such attire is almost the opposite of dismissing. Set in the context of Middle-Axis times, its wearing reflects an acknowledgment of the feminine's continuing power. As the Middle East becomes more modern, it is appropriate that such attire be questioned. But more traditionally, the protection such attire has provided has been important to the safety of both men and women.[12]

Late-Axis:

I've described how Late-Axis gives new form its finishing touches. Attention shifts increasingly to refinement and detail. With this, poles become even more separate. Truth now has two nearly distinct faces—objective and subjective, material and spiritual. And masculine and feminine become more cleanly cleaved in their perceived relationship. At the same time, the tension between poles found with Middle-Axis subsides significantly. As I've observed, this is less due to resolution than the fact that the distance between poles has increased sufficiently that they come close to inhabiting separate worlds. And with the Upper Pole now clearly dominant, there is less to struggle about.

We recognize this new relationship between poles in how we came to think about awareness and thought with Modern Age understanding. People then assumed that conscious awareness had prevailed and that it was only a matter of time until we vanquished darkness—now thought of as ignorance—once and for all. Separation is sufficiently complete that fears of re-engulfment need no longer be major preoccupations. The aspects of the primordial feminine that remain are relegated to specifically separate realms: feelings to the subjective, the imaginal to the arts. These qualities are valued—sometimes even elevated—but they are also clearly secondary, regarded more as decoration than as substance.

---

[12] The recognition that the pushing away of the feminine that comes with Middle-Axis has a creative purpose is not to deny the fact of real and significant harm. The burning of witches in the late Middle Ages provides the most dramatic example. While we tend to associate witch hunts with 17th century Salem, many hundreds of thousands of people perceived to be witches were killed in Europe from the 13th century on.

Particularly given how often today we hear critiques of patriarchy, it is important to appreciate that this Late-Axis cultural period has in fact been a time of major accomplishment. Governmental forms became representative with determination by rule of law, religion came to reflect a newly direct relationship with the divine, and economic competition combined with dramatic new scientific discoveries gave us the Industrial Age. We encounter such accomplishment's polar counterbalance in the romantic ideal. In the world of love, we saw the medieval practice of having marriages determined by families replaced by Romeo-and-Juliet style images of romantic love. The Romantic Age also gave us a fresh emphasis on nature and the artistic.

For much of the Modern Age, gender roles became even more separate, with men clearly in charge and women often treated (as with the archetypally feminine wherever it manifests) more as adornment. But over time, the same push toward individual freedoms that gave us the Bill of Rights gradually translated into fuller autonomy and greater equality for women.

Current Times:

After this journey through history, *On the Evolution of Intimacy* turns to current circumstances. The points it makes are now familiar. It looks at how the cultural structures and beliefs of Late-Axis culture are neither ideals nor end points. It also observes how postmodern perspective necessarily stops short of the kind of understanding needed for times ahead. And it gives particular attention to what I've here called the Dilemma of Trajectory, how continuing on as we have would eventually leave us severed from aspects of ourselves critical to our humanness.

What we are potentially severed from has particular pertinence for this chapter's reflections on gender. Put in the language of gender archetype, we would lose any connection with the archetypally feminine. That means ultimately losing touch with the feeling parts of us that provide the roots of relationship, with more imaginative aspects that give us art and music, with nature, with the spiritual, and with bodily experience. The book goes on to tie these losses to our modern Crisis of Purpose and to describe how Cultural Maturity's changes reconcile this impossible predicament.

CREATIVE SYSTEMS THEORY

These evolutionary reflections conclude with a couple of consequences of Cultural Maturity's changes that are key to the book's inquiry. First is how today we see the possibility of stepping beyond the two-halves-make-a-whole connections of times past and learning to love more as whole people. Second is the possibility of identity that is more systemically conceived and experienced, what I have called Whole-Person identity. I also emphasize that while these changes represent a dramatic step forward, they are predicted by where the progression I have described inherently takes us.

Developmental Insights

The following observations that I make reference to in the book highlight insights that draw on and extend this developmental/evolutionary picture:

In another way we see how the feminine is very much a kind of power.

While in Late-Axis times we've tended to look on the archetypally feminine as secondary at best, this evolutionary progression makes clear that not only is the feminine equal in its significance to the masculine, at certain times in any developmental process—and specifically in the developmental story of culture—it represents the much greater power. ("Power" as I use the term here refers not so much to positional power, which tends to reflect more the archetypally masculine even when it manifests in a woman, but rather the kinds of values and sensibilities that prevail.)[13]

When we fail to appreciate archetypally feminine power, we are left not just insufficiently appreciative of women, but also vulnerable to misinterpreting events. I've made reference to how the wearing of the hijab or the burka in traditional Middle Eastern societies reflects not a dismissing of the feminine as people in the West can assume, but an acknowledgment of feminine power—indeed, a depth of such power that is but a faint memory in modern times.

---

13 I've noted how this recognition is as important—and as easily foreign—for women as it is for men. While one part of the task for women in our time is getting more in touch with the archetypally masculine, just as important is a deeper engagement with the archetypally feminine. With Transition, women as frequently as men find themselves disconnected from the receptive and the ground of their being.

Developmental/evolutionary perspective helps us distinguish various factors that go into what we see today.

We see how today's gender- and love-related changes reflect the developmental challenges of multiple overlapping cultural stages. Much that we encounter is best thought of as an extension of the Modern Age project. For example, equal rights, by itself, does not require Cultural Maturity. Rather, it reflects a culminating Late-Axis task, the same affirming of the individual that brought us the Bill of Rights and drives us today to address the importance of equal opportunity for people of different ethnicities and classes.

Whole-Person identity and Whole-Person relationship, on the other hand, require further changes, ones that become possible, and really only become understandable as options, with the beginnings of Cultural Maturity. Thinking of these changes in a couple of steps lets us make some further, more nuanced contextual distinctions. Transitional dynamics produce the first step and important achievements such as the recognition of a greater multiplicity of options. But with this first step we remain yet short and find ourselves vulnerable to common postmodern misperceptions. For example, we can think of the unisex ideal—a view of gender that is best understood as how we experience identity when our connection with bodily experience is at its minimum—as a Transitional belief. With the second step, we engage Cultural Maturity's cognitive reordering and the realization of a new, deeper, and more conscious relationship to our natures as embodied beings. One result is the possibility of Whole-Person identity and Whole-Person relationship. With regard to gender, we find it newly possible to appreciate at once just how much we are ultimately the same, and how deeply we can be different.

Big-picture evolutionary perspective also helps us grasp just why we have before thought about gender as we have.

These reflections add in essential ways to my previous assertion that history's polarized picture of gender differences is a product of the projection of gender archetype. The evolution of gender archetype fills out this conclusion by bringing detail to our understanding of just what we have projected. We see how the gradual evolution from archetypally feminine to archetypally masculine preeminence over the course of history combined with the different ways the relationship between gender archetypes has manifested at different times—from perceived complementarity, to isometric tension, to greater acceptance of the feminine but in a more decorative role—has directly influenced both the qualities we have associated with being men and women and how we have perceived relationships between the sexes.

A major implication of this evolutionary picture is that it challenges us to rethink assumptions that frame circumstances only in terms of blame and victimization.

I've promised to return to the recognition that evolutionary thinking helps us get beyond making oppression our default explanation. We've seen here how all sorts of phenomena begin to make better sense when viewed from an evolutionary vantage—from how women are often kept out of view and severely punished for what might seem minor transgressions in Middle-Axis cultures to how women are often treated more as adornments for men than individuals in Late-Axis times. It is important to acknowledge that much in history has been unfair, painful, and often brutal. But it is also true that thinking of such harm only in terms of malevolence can miss much of what is actually going on. We are to blame if we don't effectively confront the challenges that define the tasks of our time. But when we think more systemically, the recognition that history's deep patterns are ultimately expressions of being human can change perceptions dramatically.

Holding the big picture this generously is difficult for most people, and there will be people who will find it objectionable that I might. But stepping back in this way frees us from traps that get in our way in efforts to move forward. One such trap is the tendency to end up thinking only in victim terms. People who identify as victims tend to project aspects of themselves onto the world and see others only as oppressors. In doing so, they give away their own real power.[14]

---

14 This kind of trap brings us back to the topic of limits. In the face of real limits, people can end up defining themselves as victims, and often angry victims. The "offending" limit may be to how quickly some change can happen or simply how complex realities often in fact are. When appropriate, anger can serve to drive change. And often real victimization has taken place. But even when harm has occurred, identifying as the angry victim is a specific kind of response with ultimately unhelpful consequences. In Parts Work terms, the person has ended up coming from a chair. Certainly then culturally mature engagement becomes impossible. But effecting any meaningful kind of change also becomes very difficult. At the extreme, as

There are also more general traps. I've made reference to how today we often hear critiques of "patriarchy." Particularly people of a more liberal bent may view patriarchy as inherently oppressive and the problem to be solved. Developmental/evolutionary perspective describes how the archetypally masculine's ever greater influence through history, whether manifest in values and priorities or the undue influence of men, has been a natural creative product of civilization's rise. This is not at all to suggest that moving beyond patriarchy in this sense is not an important thing to do. Cultural Maturity's integrative mechanisms engage us in just this task. But if we miss the larger picture, we ultimately undermine our efforts. When people reduce the cultural task to "fighting patriarchy," in the end they entrench themselves even more deeply in the narrative they claim to be moving beyond.

Developmental/evolutionary perspective helps us tie processes that today are reordering gender, identity, and love to broader cultural changes.

It helps when thinking about the evolution of love and gender to view them within change's larger context. The evolution of the body as experience makes a good example. What I've described suggests that we can understand all the changes that come with culturally mature relationship and identity in terms of a new, more conscious and integrated engagement with the body as experience.[15] Making connection to a related kind of change that similarly follows from Cultural Maturity's cognitive reordering invites us to expand this picture further. The same developmental dynamics that have distanced us from the archetypally feminine and from bodily experience have also distanced us from nature. A future that is at all healthy and sustainable will require a similar, more integrative relationship with the natural world. This more encompassing picture helps affirm the claim that these are changes that are predicted and whose time has come.

---

psychologists recognize, people who view themselves as victims are some of the most vulnerable to themselves becoming victimizers.

15 For this statement to fully make sense, we need to appreciate how being embodied in this conscious and integrated sense is new, as wholly different from times past when body intelligence stood forefront as more recent times when we've often forgotten we had bodies at all.

Further Historical Perspective

In *On the Evolution of Intimacy*, I give primary attention to the evolution of gender archetype rather than the more common practice of basing conclusions on behavioral observations such as family and kinship structures, specific gender role expectations, and sexual practices. I chose this approach because it has the most to teach us if our interest is the future. But I also note that the more familiar kinds of observations provide pertinent information. They also tie in useful way to these more gender archetype–related patterns. A couple of very broad-brushstroke observations that I describe in the book are worth including here in this regard.

The first concerns how people through time have viewed sexuality. With Pre-Axial cultures, consistent with the deep engagement with bodily reality that comes with this stage, we tend to find the greatest comfort with sexuality and greatest openness to diversity in sexuality's expression. Some examples: The Bugis, an ethnic group in Indonesia, long ago recognized five genders, each with its own attractions. The Waorani, an Amazonian tribe, believe that both men and women should sleep with as many lovers as possible. And the Etoro of Papua New Guinea believe that all men should have a male lover.[16] With Early-Axis cultures, consistent with how in this stage we see only the beginnings of separation from the body, while we find sexual practices more specifically prescribed, we don't yet see the explicit distancing from the sexual we encounter later on. For example, we often find the sexual and the spiritual celebrated together—as with the erotic imagery commonly found with Eastern temple artistry or ancient Greece's idealization of the human body. The ancient Greeks also not only accepted, but idealized, certain homoerotic relationships. With Middle-Axis and the rise of monotheism, we encounter the most rigorous prohibitions. We find this both with the strict practices of the European Middle Ages and in contemporary cultures where Middle-Axis dynamics prevail such as in the Middle East. Over the course of Late-Axis culture, we see a gradual relaxing of prohibitions. The new comfort with the body we find in Renaissance art anticipated this further change. The Victorian

---

16 From Janice Zarro Brodman, *Sex Rules! Astonishing Sexual Practices and Gender Roles From Around the World*, Mango Media, 2017.

era appropriately gets associated with being strait-laced, but throughout Late-Axis culture, at least conversation about the sexual became increasingly acceptable.

Another kind of big-picture generality has direct pertinence to this book's reflections on love and identity. It concerns the systemic whole that functionally defines identity. I've described how, in modern times, while we've tended to associate identity with the individual, more accurately the determining unit has been the couple (or the nuclear family). The systemic whole that has functionally defined identity has also evolved over cultural time. Earlier, it was the extended family and village that defined identity. And in our distant past, it was the tribe. This additional kind of developmental recognition has fascinating implications when it comes to how we think about how our choices get made. It also provides larger perspective for understanding the Myth of the Individual and what it suggests about identity going forward.

Personality Style Reflections

A handful of observations in *On the Evolution of Intimacy* concern the relationship of gender and personality style difference. They are worth including here as they add important detail to previous reflections in this book.

A first kind of observation has major significance for current gender-related debates. I've noted that from a culturally mature vantage we see as much or more variation within the sexes as between them. An appreciation for the contrasting ways people with different personality styles embody gender archetypes adds detail to this observation. It turns out that when we see variation from the 60/40 balance that I described earlier, it can generally be predicted by personality style. And within that variation, it is not uncommon to find what we might assume turned on its head. Depending on temperament, the balance between more archetypally masculine and more archetypally feminine characteristics in a man may be more archetypally feminine than in the average woman, and that in a woman more archetypally masculine than in the average man.

Generally speaking, the progression from Early-Axis to Late-Axis takes us from temperaments where the archetypally feminine plays the larger role to temperaments where the archetypally masculine predominates.

An Early/Inner man (perhaps someone who is a visual artist) or even more an Early/Lower/Inner man (maybe a teacher of young children) will embody the archetypally feminine more deeply than the larger portion of Late-Axis women. And a Late/Outer woman (perhaps a television news anchor) or even more a Late/Upper/Outer woman (maybe a Wall Street broker) is going to embody more of the archetypally masculine than the much larger portion of Early-Axis men.

Temperament observations that I included in *On the Evolution of Intimacy* also help fill out earlier reflections in this book about temperament and love. In describing how I use temperament differences as a hands-on learning tool in Chapter Eight, I noted that the question, "How do you know if someone loves you?" tends to offer particular surprises. Besides highlighting the depth of the differences we find with various personality styles, the dramatically contrasting answers people give also confirms how much of a stretch it can be when we choose to be with someone from a different temperament world.

Here I reversed the usual order for descriptions because answers given by Late-Axis types most immediately make sense—for the understandable reason that the answers given by Lates tend to parallel popular media expectations (most people in the media are Lates). Lates know their partner loves them when they hear words of endearment, when they receive gifts like flowers or jewelry, and when their partner makes an effort to "look good." Middles tend to give quite different answers, though because Middles, too, are affected by media expectations, it can take some reflection for them to recognize what it is that they really find most important. Middles tend to value gestures that communicate constancy and evoke a sense of home and family. They want to know that the other person is solidly there for them. That may be simply remembering a birthday. Or it may not be a gesture at all, nor anything that requires words. It may be simply the fact of being there, of being always present in a way a person can count on. Answers commonly given by Earlies can seem almost the opposite of love to Lates and Middles. Earlies often express that they most know another person loves them when their private time is honored and respected. This perhaps mysterious-seeming answer begins to make sense with an understanding of what such honoring signals to the Early. It communicates respect for the creativity that happens in that private time, and with this, that what most matters to the Early is safe in the other's presence. Earlies also often answer that shared laughter is what most deeply tells them they are cared about.

A further personality style–related topic brings us back to the subject of Violence that I introduced in Chapter Five. I observed there that we can think of Violence, as Creative Systems Theory uses the term, as having archetypally masculine and archetypally feminine forms and proposed that expanding our conception of violence in this way adds essential nuance to understanding. I've made clear that men and women are each capable of each of these ways of doing harm. *On the Evolution of Intimacy* uses the CSPT to fill out earlier reflections. There I kept to the briefest of observations, and for the sake of simplicity, again limited them to dynamics that manifest more vertically.

With Late-Axis, Upper Pole violence (the vertical expression of archetypally masculine violence), simple competitiveness becomes viciousness. With Middle-Axis, Upper Pole violence, order is used to diminish rather than empower. With Early-Axis, Upper Pole violence, the capacity to inspire becomes instead a kind of seductive charisma. We see a complementary progression for Lower Pole violence (the vertical expression of archetypally feminine violence). Late-Axis, Lower Pole violence manifests as sexual or emotional manipulation. Middle-Axis, Lower Pole violence more specifically undermines and obstructs (like its complement, it is about control, but here control from below). Early-Axis, Lower Pole violence does harm by merging or suffocating.

Again, I emphasize that these are broad generalities. But even these simple observations can help us protect ourselves from harm and also better avoid inflicting harm. They would help us at any time, but as relationships of all sorts—not just love relationships, but friendships and also business relationships—more and more often bring together people with a diversity of personality styles, such insights take on even greater importance.

Needed Mutual Understanding

I noted in introducing this chapter that *On the Evolution of Intimacy* was inspired by current gender- and sexuality-related conversations. In the book, I describe how culturally mature perspective not only applauds the larger portion of current changes, it predicts their importance in our time. But I also observe that current efforts can stop short, and propose that in just how they do, they can get in the way of exactly the changes they hope to engender. Some warnings adapted from the text:

> I see the larger portion of what we encounter today with the "#MeToo" movement and related efforts continuing one of the most important social change directions of the last century. And without question I support clearer prohibitions with regard to sexual exploitation and abuse and support anything that might enhance clearer communication between the sexes. But I have also found aspects of the current debate worrisome.
>
> In particular I've been concerned to see people's readiness to lump together behaviors and circumstance that should not at all be painted with the same brush. The most obvious lumping together has happened between kinds of implied misconduct in the workplace. Publicized examples have ranged from rape and extreme abuse of power, to lewd and clearly inappropriate behavior, to instances where, if there was any transgression at all, it was minor and by all evidence unintentional. And situations that had nothing to do with workplace power discrepancies, but rather with social relationships and dating, also quickly ended up being tossed into the same pot.
>
> That accusations are coming to light and that violating behaviors that should have been called out years ago are getting the attention they deserve is essential—I am not in any way proposing that we should return to a time when women hesitated to speak up for fear of not being taken seriously. But I do suggest that we need to learn to think with greater complexity about violation and do everything possible to get the evidence required to make needed distinctions.
>
> Obviously the task is tricky. Making needed discernments requires thinking with greater detail about things we may not want to think that much about. And the old "he said/she said" dilemma can be hard to escape. But this is the only solution. Simple-minded thinking in the end only undermines the support women need and deserve in these times.

Throughout the book, I note complexities that need to be acknowledged if we are to engage the gender/sexuality/abuse conversation with the needed humility and sophistication—if we are to step past both the liberal political correctness implied by much of current advocacy and polarized reactions to such advocacy. These include how changing social norms can lead to miscommunication, how gender-related expectations of times past were often incompatible with making clear yeses and nos, how inappropriate behavior can differ in its psychological mechanisms (from willfully abusive, to simply unthinking, to psychopathology), how big-picture historical perspective challenges us to rethink popular assumptions about causality and blame, and how violence is more multifaceted in its manifestations than we tend to assume.

I acknowledge that including all of these factors in our considerations requires thinking with greater nuance than most people are ready for. But I emphasize that at least making the effort is necessary if potentially important steps forward in our time are to ultimately benefit us. I also observe that we can be encouraged by the fact that Cultural Maturity's changes support the ability to engage conversations about gender and sexuality with the needed sophistication.

Parts Work

Near the end of the book, I introduce how Parts Work provides a way to develop the kind of mature perspective the book has been about. I present an abbreviated version of the description of Parts Work that I presented in this book in Chapter Eight and offer some examples that touch on relationship and gender questions.

I observe in getting started that Parts Work, besides helping us learn to hold reality in the needed more complete ways, also provides quite precise definitions for Whole-Person identity and relationship. I describe how our ideas about identity in times past have been based on identification with parts and relationships between parts—for instance, a strong part as opposed to a weak part. In contrast, Whole-Person identity is based on holding and taking responsibility in the whole of one's multifaceted complexity. And I describe how the defining change with Whole-Person relationship is analogous. In two-halves-make-a-whole love, complementary archetype-infused parts in each person are projected onto the other person and relationship happens through connection between symbolic parts. Whole-Person love is about relating and living from the whole of who we are, in ways that consciously draw on the whole of our complex natures.

The following is a Parts Work example from therapy work just completed at the time of this writing:

May and the Power of Yes and No—

My work in therapy with May began at a very personal level, but it eventually turned to questions related to changes reshaping how we think about love and gender. On first meeting, May recounted how love relationships in her life had rarely gone well. She had had one marriage that ended in divorce and a series of intimacies that she felt she had ultimately undermined. She also described how she felt it was time to face what she was pretty sure was the source of the difficulty. She had been repeatedly molested as a young girl by a cousin and had never spoken to anyone about it.

As we delved into the history of May's relationships, a common pattern emerged. First, she would be strongly attracted to a man and quickly end up in bed with him. Often these were men who were not good for her and not good to her. Then, after a few months, even if the relationship seemed relatively healthy, she would pick a fight and leave.

In doing Parts Work, the first part May identified was the one that got her so quickly into relationships. It was a young girl who dressed and acted seductively. May talked with this young girl part over several weeks, gradually getting to know her and gaining her trust. May was not sure how she felt about her.

In time, May asked the young girl part what she remembered about the molestation. A couple of things surprised May in hearing the response. First was how the young girl part experienced that it had been her (rather than May) who had been molested. The young girl part was also pretty sure that the molestation had been her fault. At first, she had felt confused and frightened by the older cousin's behavior. But she also described feeling complimented by his attention. She described feeling that she could not really say no.

May also identified a second part. It had a sword and shield and was dressed for battle. May described feeling that this part had come to the young girl part's rescue. It is this part that had finally said no to the cousin and eventually talked to May's parents about her cousin's behavior. May initially expressed more clearly positive feelings toward this part, but as she got to know it, the picture that emerged also became more complex. Certainly she appreciated that this part had stepped in. But in talking with it in more depth, she realized that it was also this part that was now keeping her from getting close even when she met a man who might be good for her.

Over time, May and I spoke together about what needed to happen. She rightly observed that she needed to assure the young girl that the molestation had not been her fault. But I offered that something else was needed before she could really do this—May first needed to forgive herself. I described how, just by the way psychological development works, May in her Whole-Person chair would not have been there to protect and intercede at that young age. Once May had forgiven herself, it would be possible for her to tell the parts that she was sorry that she had not been able to be there for them. She could also commit to them that she would always be there for them in the future.

We also talked about how May would need to be clear with each part that her relationship with it would be changing, fundamentally. No longer would it be acceptable for either of them to take over. And it would certainly not be okay for either part to act on her behalf in the world. The parts could talk with her and share with her what they found important. But it would always need to be her in her Whole-Person chair who had the last word.

May and I also discussed how she would need to stop communication that had been happening between the parts. It took time for May to fully grasp why this would be important. But eventually she recognized that she could understand the constant internal drama and ambivalence that had characterized intimate connectings in her life to that point in terms of crosstalk between these conflicting parts.

Eventually, May had more specific conversations with each part. In talking with the little girl, along with assuring her that she was not to blame for what had happened, May was also able to clarify that the fact that she liked closeness was ultimately a good thing. But May also made clear to the little girl that going forward it would need to be her in her Whole-Person chair, not the little girl, who decided when closeness in the world was appropriate. May was also able to clarify something further for the little girl that would ultimately be key. She described how while relating to a man could not provide completion for the little girl, there was a kind of closeness that would be essential for her well-being: her relationship with May in the Whole-Person chair.

In talking with the warrior part, May affirmed that she was grateful that it had provided protection in the past. But she also made clear that protecting was now her task. The warrior part could tap her on the shoulder if it felt things might not be safe. But from now on, it would be May's job in her Whole-Person chair to determine when things were safe and to decide appropriate action if they were not.

In time, our conversation turned to the future and the question of just what relating to a man from her chair might look like. The first thing that May saw was that doing so would require more patience than before she had brought to relationships—that it would necessarily involve knowing both herself and the man she was with more deeply than with intimacy as she had known it. She also saw that love of this sort was probably going to have less drama. We talked about how she might need to grieve some of the reliable intensities of times past if she was to find love that could work for her going forward.

These observations eventually opened up a deeper conversation about how love in our time is changing. I was surprised at just how far this further conversation was able to go. It started with looking at some of the practical skills required to make Whole-Person relationships work. I offered that in an important sense they all came down to making clear yeses and nos. The nos started within herself. She needed to make clear nos to each of her parts in the sense of being sure that she was always in charge. But she also needed to be sure she was comfortable saying her nos emphatically in the world when that was required.

As far as yeses, May saw that she needed to draw on what each part could contribute. And May made a further yes-related observation that began to take the conversation to a different level. She asked whether, if what we were talking about was really going to work, she wouldn't also need to be more overt in expressing her "yeses" to the man. I offered that I thought this observation was very insightful. With these reflections, May had taken important steps toward grasping what love, and relationships between the sexes more generally, might look like in a culturally mature reality.

Eventually, May again turned to more personal questions, now about the kinds of choices she wanted to make going forward. As she worked, she found the two parts that she had previously identified evolving, becoming increasingly voices in herself she could rely on in making decisions. Using that language of yeses and nos, the little girl part gradually matured into an advocate for not being afraid of saying yes when that was what was true. The warrior part came to look less fierce, but at the same time became an even more uncompromising advocate for making healthy choices. Over time, May also added further parts that could help her live the most caring and effective life.

An Awkward In-Between Time

I conclude *On the Evolution of Intimacy* by acknowledging that none of the changes I've described are easy and that with all of them we are at best taking baby steps. I observe that simply being willing to question past concepts of love and past gender stereotypes can be a stretch for many people. And I emphasize that the deeper task the book had examined—fundamentally rethinking both love and identity—can be hard simply to make sense of. While we witness a start in how we are beginning to recognize the importance of more options in the forms that love and identity can take, engaging a wholly new chapter in the story of love and identity is necessarily a challenge to grasp, and even more of a challenge to fully take on in our lives.

But in bringing the book to a close, I also emphasize that the rewards for even just baby steps are immense. We begin to recognize the possibility of more fulfilling intimate connections, and deeper and more solid identities as men and as women. We also begin to discover the paradoxical fact that engaging love and identity in needed new ways, while more demanding than what we have known, is also in important ways simpler. I come back to what is now a familiar refrain in this book, how we can think of it all as part of a needed new common sense. In a whole new way, we are being challenged to live and love from the whole of who we are—as fully embodied beings.

CHAPTER ELEVEN

Applying Creative Systems Theory Patterning Concepts #3: Academic Disciplines and Cultural Domains

We can also use Creative Systems Theory's developmental/evolutionary picture to rethink the assumptions of entire spheres of understanding. These can be spheres in the sense of academic disciplines—history, sociology, anthropology, or physics. They can also be spheres in the sense of domains of activity and cultural function—government, religion, medicine, education, the media, science, art, or business. In each case, CST offers more systemic perspective for understanding both specifics within particular spheres and how various spheres interrelate.

We will start here with some brief academic discipline–related observations, giving particular attention to the social sciences and humanities. CST is pertinent in some way to every discipline, but because the social sciences and humanities are most expressly about ourselves, it is there that its contribution is most immediate. There is an important sense in which CST rewrites them. We will take a quick look at how this is so.

We will then turn to broader cultural domains. I will briefly address some of the expected consequences of Cultural Maturity's changes for the future for five of the domains I've noted: education, government, the media, medicine, and business together with economics. Previous reflections have at least touched on implications for each of these spheres. I've proposed that education's bottom-line purpose going forward must be to provide not just literacy and basic knowledge, but to support the capacities needed to create a culturally mature world. We've looked at how changes in how we think about leadership and identity will be critical to the future of government. I've touched on how modern media's common "if it bleeds, it leads" approach ultimately fails us. I've described how medicine in times ahead will require a new maturity in our relationship to death. And I've observed how rethinking wealth and progress gives business and economics pursuits inescapable moral/ethical implications.

Here we will go a bit deeper with regard to each domain. I will put current changes in broader historical perspective. I will also tie changes to key themes in these pages—such as the need to get beyond parental assumptions, the importance of leaving behind heroic and romantic narratives, how questions of all sorts require new skills and capacities, and the way needed understandings must be systemic (and systemic in the more dynamic and complete sense needed to effectively represent human systems).

I will then delve with special depth into a realm of inquiry and innovation that we could either associate with an academic discipline or think of as a cultural domain—the arts, and here in particular art's history and future. Artistic expression might seem a curious topic to choose for more extended reflection. But for a very important reason, it could not be more appropriate. I've proposed that the ultimate purpose of art is to give expression to just-emerging capacities in the "psyche of culture" (or framed in a different way, in the evolution of culture as a system). Art presages changes to be found later in both more formal academic disciplines and more applied domains of culture.

I have left two domains for the next chapter. Chapter Twelve's look at "ultimate" questions includes an article that takes a similarly extended look at science and religion. Titled "Science and Religion—Toward a Larger Picture (and How Creative Systems Theory Gets Us Very Close)," it applies CST patterning concepts to the history and future of these two domains that we are most apt to associate with final truth.

This chapter's reflections take on added pertinence with today's crisis of confidence in leadership and institutions. In some way that crisis manifests in all of these spheres.

Academic Disciplines

My proposal that CST in effect rewrites the social sciences and humanities might seem extreme. But, at the least, CST provides larger perspective for understanding what the social sciences and the humanities accomplish. It also brings nuance and detail to conclusions not possible when we limit understanding to Modern Age assumptions.

CST has most obvious implications for the social sciences, and within them for psychology. I've described how Integrative Meta-perspective—and in more detailed ways CST—brings more systemic perspective to our understanding of many of the most pivotal concerns of psychology—such as intelligence, identity, conscious awareness, meaning, human capacity, and violence. We've seen too how Patterning in Time concepts reshape our thinking about developmental processes, providing explanation both for why individual development proceeds as it does and, at a cultural scale, for many of today's most essential psychological challenges, from the need to rethink love and gender to today's Crisis of Purpose.

I've also made observations more specific to the work of the psychotherapist. I've noted how Integrative Meta-perspective reframes the psychotherapeutic relationship and challenges the therapist to revisit the basic purpose of the psychotherapeutic endeavor. And with Parts Work and the like, I've introduced new kinds of psychotherapeutic approaches that directly support culturally mature awareness. We've also examined how the Creative Systems Personality Typology helps us more deeply and accurately understand personality differences (and looked briefly at how the Typology can also help us with gender and cultural background–related distinctions).

CST also presents a direct challenge to much in psychological research. What happens when we add new insights with regard to human diversity makes particularly good illustration. Because the much larger part of research to this point has been based on the assumption that we can think of "normal" as some average, the simple recognition of how dramatically people can be different from one another as a function of temperament brings a major portion of traditional psychological research into question.

With social sciences such as sociology and anthropology that deal with more collective human experience, Patterning in Time concepts in particular highlight CST's contribution. They help us more deeply grasp how what we understand collectively is specifically a product of when we understand. And of special importance for today's rethinking task, they help clarify the limitations of Modern Age belief and traditional academic assumptions. Patterning in Time notions also clarify the importance of abandoning the belief that social systems in the future will work according to the same principles that they have in times past. The contextual implications of Patterning in Space distinctions—in particular, how deeply the recognition that what we see depends on who is doing the seeing—also have major consequences for social sciences that deal with more collective experience.

In the end, CST's implications for the humanities are just as transforming. Of particular importance is the perspective it provides for rethinking history. We've seen how CST's developmental/evolutionary frame not only puts the facts of history in perspective, it helps us better understand our human story as a story—a chronicling of how, over time, we have experienced purpose and possibility. The theory also helps us step back and better understand the nature of understanding and its evolution. Here, I've used it to map philosophical thought from ancient times to today's challenge to think with a newly systemic kind of completeness.

Of all spheres of understanding, it is the social sciences and humanities that have been most influenced by the postmodern contribution. Most of the references to postmodern thought in this book have been drawn from these spheres. With each of these references, we've seen the same juxtaposition of important insights and the major limitations that come with postmodern understanding more generally. The postmodern contribution has radically challenged Modern Age assumptions. And at the same time, with each sphere we have touched on, it has proven to be severely limited in its ability to provide a useful way forward.

With both the hard sciences and the arts, CST's implications tend to be less direct, but the fact that CST addresses how we understand along with specifics means that its contribution remains significant. At the least, the theory helps us put understanding in these domains in historical perspective. It also helps us appreciate the larger systemic relationship of the hard sciences, the social sciences, the humanities, and the arts, a kind of recognition that provides valuable guidance with more interdisciplinary inquiry.

We can map that relationship in terms of ultimate creative polarity. The hard sciences (and to a somewhat more tempered degree, the social sciences) engage experience from a more right-hand creative perspective (and with the aspects of intelligence that most effectively address it) and give their attention to the particular parts of experience where doing so gives us useful information. The arts (and to a somewhat more tempered degree, the humanities) engage experience from a more left-hand creative perspective (and with the aspects of intelligence that most effectively address it—keeping in mind that in academia the rational still gets its special status) and give their attention to the particular parts of experience where doing so provides benefit.

Domains of Culture

I use the term "domains" when referring not just to spheres of inquiry as with academic disciplines, but to realms of activity in culture as a system. My work has frequently given specific attention to this systemic scale. In my writings, I've gone into considerable detail examining the past, present, and future of particular domains. In consulting with organizations, bringing larger systemic perspective to the cultural domain that an organization occupies has often provided important insight. And I often make use of domain-specific reflections in my teaching. (I've mentioned how the yearlong Intensives included using what people had learned to address the future of domains where they had particular interest.)

Applying CST ideas helps bring essential perspective to needed changes within specific domains in multiple ways. Of particular importance, the theory's evolutionary vantage helps us get beyond thinking of any domain's needed changes in terms of fixing broken systems. It brings attention to how we can understand the most important of future domain-specific changes in terms of developmental challenges. In addition, the way Integrative Meta-perspective and each of the new skills and capacities that follow from it apply to the needed new realities of each domain helps bring into focus challenges that should present themselves in times ahead. And CST patterning concepts bring attention to distinctions that before now we might not have recognized were important—or recognized at all.

Applying CST to particular domains also supports making needed connections. It helps us appreciate how changes that may initially seem to have little to do with one another, both within domains and in far-flung spheres, often relate in essential ways. It also helps us recognize how the new challenges presented by these various domains in the end come together as aspects of a single, more encompassing challenge—engaging understanding from a more dynamic and complete, all-the-crayons-in-the-box, systemic vantage. This sort of application also helps refine our appreciation of ways that thinking can stop short. It brings attention to how the various kinds of conceptual traps we have examined play out with particular domains (and in the process, helps solidify our grasp of ideological fallacies more generally). It also provides further insight by highlighting specific Transitional Absurdities and how they make the need for next steps in understanding inescapably important.

A couple of ways in which cultural domains become more systemic when we step over Cultural Maturity's threshold that we also see with academic disciplines are worth noting. First is how domains stop being distinct categories of activities and become instead contrasting, but ultimately interrelated, crayons in culture's systemic box—aspects of here-and-now systemic "multiplicity." With academic disciplines, I described how we can map them from right to left as Patterning in Space locales. We can do something similar with domains, with business and economics on the far right and religion on the far left. As is ultimately also the case with academic disciplines, this is not a wholly linear progression. Particularly with midrange domains such as education, government, and medicine, the balance of right-hand and left-hand qualities can be pretty similar. I've often in the past used the image of a chocolate chip cookie as an alternative way to depict systemic interrelationships between cultural domains (with the chips representing domains and the dough representing connecting links). Given that a systemic mapping does extend out somewhat at the extremes, perhaps it would be better to think of a "chocolate chip football." This recognition of systemic relationships helps us better appreciate the function of each domain—answer its Question of Referent. It also helps better understand how various cultural spheres might best function together.

The second systemic insight notes that each domain/crayon itself becomes newly systemic, a specific expression of our particularly vibrant kind of living complexity. In working with groups, I've often made use of a simple hands-on exercise that draws on this second kind of systemic realization. I have people list the polarities that have traditionally defined understanding and action within their domain. People then represent these polarities together like spokes of a wagon wheel. Finally, they explore what it might mean to "bridge" each of these polarities and what might happen if each polarity began to be held more systemically.

Fig. 11-1. Juxtaposing Domain-Specific Polarities

As always when using the idea of bridging, we must be careful to distinguish the result from adding or averaging. But approached systemically, the wagon-wheel representation helps us in essential ways. Of particular importance, by highlighting the recognition that systemic changes rarely happen in isolation, it serves to counter the common trap of making one kind of needed change (even if maturely conceived) "the" solution. When working with a group interested in delving deeply within a particular domain, I may follow this mapping exercise by having people choose one polarity that they find particularly significant and address it using the kind of group Parts Work approach I described in Chapter Eight.

Looking in detail at future challenges within particular cultural domains is outside my intent with this book, and as often as not, beyond my expertise. But a few more specific observations help fill out previous reflections. Below I've taken five "midrange" cultural domains—education, government, the media, medicine, and economics along with business. For each, I've first framed its task systemically—identified its Question of Referent—and provided some historical perspective. I've then presented four "snapshot" reflections that link changes and challenges we see today in each domain with what the concept of Cultural Maturity predicts and the kinds of distinctions that become possible with CST patterning concepts. For the most part these will be big-picture, long-term reflections, but where front-page-news issues highlight essential challenges, I will now and then excerpt from a pertinent article or blog post. Additional detail with regard to each domain can be found in *Cultural Maturity: A Guidebook for the Future* and in the "library" section of the Cultural Maturity Blog.

Education

Because education has essential implications for every other domain, bringing culturally mature perspective to understanding education's place in culture's story—and in particular, its future place—has special significance. Appropriately, we start with education's Question of Referent. With Chapter Five's examination of Whole-Person/Whole-System Patterning concepts, I described how there is a sense in which education's purpose has always been the same: to teach the skills and sensibilities needed to live aware and productive lives. But I also emphasized that what an aware and productive life requires has evolved, how with each stage in culture what such a life entails—and thus what effective education entails—becomes different. Today, this has become the case in particularly consequential ways. Education's referent going forward must be to foster the capacities needed to live in—and create—a culturally mature world.

Historical/Developmental Perspective

We can use developmental/evolutionary perspective to put education's new defining task in context. Each chapter in culture's story has conceived of both the content of education and how education should occur in different ways. Education's cultural beginnings emphasized the body-centered learnings of nature and tribal ritual. Imagine a father, spear raised in his hand, hunting a lizard, his son behind him mimicking his movements (with no words spoken). From civilization's early rise to the Middle Ages, education for the great majority of people remained everyday and practical, but for the limited number of elites who had access, it became more structured. Medieval monastic education provided training of a moral and philosophical sort. And the rise of guild systems that brought together artisans and merchants provided training in essential crafts. More specifically academic education, with its emphasis on accumulation of factual information and verbal/rational understanding is more recent. And widely available, "universal" education has been more recent still. I've described how modern Western education derived its power through providing the literacy needed for democratic governance and the skills required for an industrial age.

We can think of culturally mature education as a next essential step in this progression. Its role as we look to the future could not be more important. Educators must inspire the courage and commitment needed if we are to take on the critical challenges ahead, including the challenge of Cultural Maturity. And they must teach the skills and capacities required to engage essential questions of all sorts more maturely and systemically. In short, education must work to make us all culturally mature leaders, in all the various aspects of our lives.

Four Change Snapshots

Changes in the Content of Education: It is beyond our scope to conjecture in any detail about the future content of education, but there are a few general things we can say. We should note first that culturally mature education appropriately includes some very traditional educational curriculum. Learning that focuses on established knowledge in diverse fields—history, science, literature, mathematics, and more—should have no less a place in times ahead. Future curriculum must also address essential abilities such as the skills needed to maneuver in a digital age that, while new, may often be largely technical in nature.

But there are also needed new learnings more particular to Cultural Maturity's changes. Many follow directly from previous reflections in this book. If nothing else, the concept of Cultural Maturity argues for bringing the future more fully into education. Until now, education has emphasized what is and what has been. The present and the past should continue to be just as important with culturally mature curriculum, but arguably what most defines culturally mature education is the greater awareness and responsibility it brings to future concerns. Some of the best education I've observed uses grappling with particularly thorny future challenges as the starting point for more specific kinds of learning.

Many of the most defining content-related changes follow from the pivotal recognition that the larger portion of challenges before us require systemic solutions. Along with how content within specific disciplines needs to be more systemically conceived, education that can support a culturally mature future must often be highly interdisciplinary. Not long ago, education that spanned disciplines was thought of as lacking rigor. Today we are beginning to appreciate how education that does not span disciplines tends to be irrelevant.

If Cultural Maturity's argument holds, we should also find each of the needed new capacities I've addressed increasingly informing the content of education. Just a few illustrations of a great many more we could note: Learning to recognize how simple-answer ideological beliefs necessarily leave us short will be essential if education is to help us learn to make effective choices. Emphasizing the deep importance of limits will be critical to education that reflects not just knowledge, but mature—wise— understanding. And attention to the significance of context and contingency will provide a necessary foundation for more specific learnings.

Certainly something like the concept of Cultural Maturity—whatever language and characteristics we use to describe needed changes— must in some way infuse curriculum. Culturally mature education must be able not just to bring perspective to the larger human story, but also to help us understand the particular significance of our current time in that story. It must help us appreciate what being newly conscious in writing culture's story involves and what making culturally mature choices in all parts of our lives requires. The best of education will inspire because it effectively shines light on the profound importance of the times in which we live, both the major new risks we face today and the immense promise that successfully addressing today's challenges holds for the future.

Changes in the Processes of Education: Much that will be most important for culturally mature education will have to do with education as process as much as the content of education. We should see changes both in what we do with what we learn and how we go about learning. We should find education focusing increasingly not just on the accumulation of information, but also on discerning where meaning lies, on applying information in ways that support collaboration, and on learning to use information wisely. We should also find the growing application of more experiential and exploratory approaches.

Multiple factors should play into this shift. I've noted the contribution of "constructivist" ideas in education in this regard, how they give particular attention to how through our choices we shape experience.

While such thinking gets us only part of the way, it has had an important role in bringing emphasis to the process aspects of needed changes. The digital revolution is also playing a role. With the best of content increasingly available to almost anyone, we can turn our attention to more process aspects of learning. But ultimately, this shift should be driven by a growing need (and growing capacity) to engage information creatively—essential to a world in which change is ever-present and in which solutions must be not just multidisciplinary and systemic, but also dynamic in their conception.

A couple of essential "bridgings" contribute to this more dynamic picture. One links the academic and the psychological. Modern Age education, with its focus on "objective" learning, kept the personal safely at arm's length. Education for the future must include not just personal reflection, but the willingness to grow personally, and in deep ways. The other key bridging links with the ethical/moral realm. I've emphasized the essential sense in which all of the most important questions ahead for the species are in the end moral questions. Modern public education, as part of maintaining clear separation between church and state, has also separated the moral and the academic. Placing moral/ethical questions forefront—and doing so in a way that engages them from a culturally mature perspective—will be increasingly essential to future education being relevant.[1]

Some of the most important process-related changes in education follow from the need to better include not just our rationality, but the whole of intelligence, both in what we learn and in how we learn. Multidisciplinary learning of the depth we have interest in is impossible without it, as is addressing any question that requires culturally mature systemic perspective. I've described how appreciating that intelligence has multiple aspects brings into question many of the most basic assumptions of modern academic education. Along with challenging how we think about what makes the answer to any question right, it also brings into question traditional learning approaches and encourages the application of more dynamic and exploratory educational methods.

---

1 With faith-based education, the connection we find with earlier times tends to remain, but rarely there do we find moral questions engaged from a culturally mature perspective.

Changes in the Structures of Education: We will likely also witness significant changes in the basic structures in which education takes place in years ahead. We should see such changes both in higher education and in education for younger students, but for different reasons.

With higher education, the need for structural changes will come in part from changes I've just described. The lecture halls of times past tend not to be a good fit with highly interdisciplinary learning and with education that emphasizes process as much as content—education that is often more hands-on and two-way. But structural changes in higher education will also be driven by broader social and technological changes, in particular spiraling costs and the digital revolution. These factors could combine to propel us toward a higher education picture in which large residential campuses with ivy-covered edifices are no longer the primary locales where higher education takes place. Certainly we should see a more multifaceted picture with diverse options available to different people depending on their needs.

It has been observed for some time that online education may eventually replace major parts of higher education as we have known it. Partly this result will come from discovering ways that online resources can improve the quality of education. But as much it will come from the recognition that there is no reason that higher education needs to be as expensive (and thus often out of reach) as it is today. The 2020 coronavirus pandemic is providing an involuntary experiment in the roles at-a-distance resources can play and how to use them most effectively. There is a very good chance that higher education will never be the same.

While I don't think of online education as "the answer" in the sense sometimes suggested today, it likely will be an important part of the answer. Even with fairly traditional content, 400 students and a professor in a university classroom is rarely a good use of resources. (The most common critique of online education is that it lacks personal contact. In fact, personal contact of any significant sort was lost years ago.) In my experience, approaches that in some way combine online content with opportunities for face-to-face exchange provide the best results for most purposes—for example, combining the best instructors in the world teaching electronically with the use of small groups that meet together for more personal and in-depth inquiry.

Note an essential consequence of these observations. Local resources—such as community colleges—could well do as good a job (or even a better job) of providing the more in-person part of education. There is much to be gained from having education embedded in the particulars of specific communities. And there is a further easily-missed benefit that could come with getting a major part of learning out of large formal institutions. The skills needed to lecture and provide content tend to be very different from those required to effectively facilitate the more process aspects of education. Having the best of formal instruction happening at a distance—even globally—with the more process aspects of education happening more locally could help us draw on the people who are the best fit for the tasks all the way around.

A related kind of structural change could ultimately be just as transforming. Along with large universities less and less being where learning takes place, they may also stop being the primary places where we certify learning. When education and credentialing become separate processes, learning can be acquired in varied ways without penalty. This change supports not just more options, but society deriving the greatest benefit from learning. When employers draw on more multifaceted measures than simply degrees, the result ultimately is a more diverse and dynamic—and in potential more educated—workforce.

Neither of these more structural changes for higher education is wholly dependent on Cultural Maturity's changes. But they are consistent with them and would help support needed broader changes in education. And making them manifest becomes much easier with the greater creative flexibility and tolerance for complexity that comes with Integrative Meta-perspective.

Changes of a more structural sort when it comes to education for life's earlier years could be just as dramatic. They start with an almost opposite recognition as far as cost. Education that can effectively prepare young people for the future will require significant economic investment. Countries with the best educational systems give teachers high status and spend generously on education. And additional ingredients important to the culturally mature education of young people do not come cheaply—for example, making education more dynamic and exploratory; engaging learning at the level of purpose; and being more deeply responsive to human differences.

We also need to appreciate that while digital technologies have a role with education for young people, the younger the student, the more it is the case that face-to-face engagement—and high-quality face-to-face engagement—becomes essential to the learning process. Culturally mature education for young people will require making education a very high societal priority—a significantly higher priority than we do currently, at least in the United States.

We legitimately ask how we can afford this greater attention to education's early years. The better question is how we could ignore its inescapable necessity. I find it striking how blind we can be to the gap that exists between the idealized way we often speak about children and our behavior when it comes to creating environments that really serve them. CST suggests that the explanation for this gap comes back to our relationship to the sensibilities that define childhood. I've described how Transitional dynamics inherently distance us from childhood experience and what makes it particular and significant. If this is an accurate way of understanding what we see, then there is also good news as far as costs and priorities. We should expect Cultural Maturity's cognitive changes to help us better appreciate both the qualities that make childhood unique, and the unique contributions that young people bring to our lives. The needed priorities should follow.

Diversity and the Future of Education: Better appreciating individual differences—of all sorts—will be key to the future of education. Educators need to be cognizant of just how different various people's worlds of experience can be depending on their ethnicity, gender, or socioeconomic background. And education represents the sphere where the particular significance of appreciating personality style diversity comes into highest relief. Education has made a start with regard to the latter sort of diversity by acknowledging that we don't all learn in the same ways. But education has a very long way to go in recognizing how deeply we can be different at the level of temperament. Greater sensitivity to differences of all these sorts will be important both to better supporting each student's unique contribution and to more deeply appreciating how differences can add to who we are together.

Cultural Maturity's new picture challenges beliefs that get in the way of appreciating such diversity, ones that with Transitional times have become commonplace in educational circles. I think in particular

CREATIVE SYSTEMS THEORY

of the assumption that the use of universal standards with frequent testing to demonstrate proficiency will produce the highest quality education. Regular testing has a place as a safety net for students and for identifying failing schools. But testing should be applied in moderation. Overreliance on testing too easily results in one-size-fits-all education that ignores diversity of experience and undermines the depth and creativity of learning needed for the future. Education that successfully supports taking responsibility for the truths we apply and thinking in more complete ways must give top priority to each learner's passion for life. It must also be responsive to the very different ways a passion for life may manifest in different situations and with different students.

Further Thoughts

Given that culturally mature education's concern is mature understanding, a person might reasonably ask whether formal culturally mature curriculum might not best be left for graduate-level classes (or even restricted to continuing education). In fact, culturally mature curriculum should begin on day one (remember the critical distinction between personal maturity and Cultural Maturity). Some of the people who have worked closest with me in developing CST's ideas—and in particular in the development of the Creative Systems Personality Typology—are teachers of young children. They emphasize that the earlier we start, the better.

The following is excerpted from *Cultural Maturity: A Guidebook for the Future*. It references making culturally mature "crux" and "multiplicity" discernments, a task we might rightly think would require significant life experience. I propose that learning to make such discernments appropriately serves as the core of education at any age:

> To teach crux distinction skills, a preschool teacher might ask: "Sarah, which of those stories did you like best? And can you tell us anything about why you liked it?" And contrary to what we might think, we can begin just as early to teach about systemic multiplicity, about context and human difference. That same teacher might ask Ayesha and Evan and Miguel "and which story did each of you like best?" She might then comment on how interesting it is that different people like different stories

and wonder aloud just why that might be. Later, when looking together at the tadpoles in the tank in the room she might turn to Evan, a somewhat quirky kid who is often made fun of and tends to get left out of classroom conversations, and say: "Evan, you liked the story with the funny creatures in it. I bet you know a lot about tadpoles. Can you tell us about them?" Complement that with chances for others to similarly highlight their gifts—and with conversation that reflects on just how these diverse gifts are different, and also how different gifts can work together—and we are well on our way toward a curriculum that not only teaches about Cultural Maturity's needed larger holding of systemic complexity, but embodies it.

Government and Governance

I find few questions more intriguing than the future of government and governance. With Chapter Four's reflections on leadership, I proposed that modern institutional democracy is likely not the final accomplishment that we tend to assume it to be. We are only just beginning to glimpse what a next chapter in the story of government beyond today's Late-Axis forms might look like. And shortly, I'll reflect on how current social/political circumstances may be putting even familiar forms at risk. CST at the least helps us recognize the limitations inherent in the governmental approaches that we have known. It also helps us appreciate basic aspects of what future approaches must be able to accomplish.

We need to start by stepping back and thinking about government less in terms of structures and more in terms of governance, the functions that government serves. Governance is concerned with how collectively we make choices, and with government in particular, with how we make choices that have to do with more right-hand societal concerns such as economies, armies, and infrastructure.[2] Its Question of Referent asks about the kinds of values, discernments, and institutional approaches that we need at particular times and places if we are to effectively make such choices. Today its asks what it means to govern within a culturally mature reality.

---

2 Education, art, and religion each also involve collective choice, but collective choice where more left-hand elements play roles that are at least as large.

Historical/Developmental Perspective

Governance's evolutionary story, how it has gone through identifiable stages, should now be familiar. I've described a progression from tribal rule, to the times of god-kings, to the authority of emperors and the kings of medieval times (who were not quite divine, but also not just mortal), to the emergence of democratic principles and governmental structures. I've also pointed toward how more fine-grained discernments can help us appreciate intermediary structures. For example, we can think of recent authoritarian governmental forms, from right-wing dictatorships to modern communist authoritarian regimes, as reflections of the Middle-Axis, Age of Empire substage within Late-Axis dynamics.

In previous chapters, I've touched on multiple ways in which democratic governance as we have known it appears to stop short of what future governance will require. I've described how Late-Axis forms remain mythologized and parental. I've also observed how the back and forth between polar advocacies that in times past has effectively produced governmental change ceases to do so when the task is culturally mature decision-making. In addition, I've delineated how new capacities needed today with leadership of all kinds will be critical to the effective future functioning of government.

An observation I highlighted in Chapter Five serves in a particularly striking way to argue not just for refinements to what we have known, but a wholly new chapter in government's evolutionary story: What we have witnessed thus far in the governmental sphere is not yet in fact "government by the people." I've described how the Myth of the Individual applies directly to government and has profound implications for governance's future. And I've proposed that realizing something more akin to authentic government by the people—government by individuals in the Whole-Person sense—represents one of Cultural Maturity's most essential tasks.

If the concept of Cultural Maturity is accurate, changes in how we think about governance will be key to a healthy, and perhaps even survivable, human future. Certainly governmental leadership that is more culturally mature will be essential. It will be the job of political leaders going forward to place before us culturally mature images of possibility, take tough stands in the face of very real limits, and provide initiative in the crafting of institutional structures that are more creative, consciously systemic, and accountable. The role of culturally mature followership will be just as critical (and arguably more so). It will be the job of culturally mature citizens to elect leaders with needed new capabilities. It will also be their task to take on the essential responsibilities that come with governance of a more participatory—more fully and explicitly creative—sort.

Four Change Snapshots

Leaving Behind the Mythologizing of Government and Leadership: In first introducing the concept of Cultural Maturity, I spoke of the central importance of getting beyond thinking of authority in parental terms. With regard to governance, this change manifests most immediately with the importance of leaving behind our past need to mythologize government and artificially elevate its edifices—in particular, the governments of nation-states. Getting beyond the mythologizing of government will be necessary to the making of good governmental decisions going forward (a perceived exalted status inherently distorts perceptions). It will also be key to people assuming a more fully empowered relationship to government—to a needed greater ownership of authority in government's functioning.

Just as fundamentally, this change reorders our relationship to governmental leadership. I've emphasized the fact that culturally mature leadership of any sort is at once more humble and more significant than what it replaces. Certainly this is the case with political leadership. When we step over Cultural Maturity's threshold, we come to better appreciate political leaders as simply people with hard jobs (and with Transitional times, perhaps nearly impossible jobs). I've noted that leaving behind the mythologizing of leadership can produce mixed feelings. We may want leaders to get off their pedestals and then not be happy when they do. But with the political sphere, as with leadership more generally, we really have no choice—if we are to get the kind of political leadership we need (and be the kind of citizens in relationship to it that will be necessary).

Stepping Beyond Us-Versus-Them Thinking: I gave particular attention to this essential change in first introducing needed new capacities in Chapter One. The importance of getting past our historical need for "evil others" and the concomitant need to view our own kind as "chosen people" manifests most dramatically in how governments on the world stage need to relate to one another more maturely. With the increasing availability of weapons of mass destruction, this new capacity becomes critical to any kind of world we would want to live in.

Just as important, ultimately, will be bringing more systemic sophistication to the internal functioning of government. I've observed how the way governmental decision-making before has functioned—through back-and-forth "crosstalk" between right-hand and left-hand ideological parts—is not compatible with what is needed going forward. And I've emphasized the particular importance of getting past the extreme partisan bickering that has more and more come to characterize political discourse. Success in this regard has thus far been limited, but people increasingly recognize that the degree of petty partisanship we see today cannot continue. I've described it as a key example of Transitional Absurdity. Integrative Meta-perspective helps us appreciate how ideological positions, even when tempered with compromise, cannot get us where we need to go. We've looked at how even just asking the right questions requires us to think about challenges of all sorts more systemically.

A More Dynamic and Multicentric Picture of Governance: We should also see changes in times ahead with regard to the boundaries that define governmental influence—both where those boundaries reside and how we interpret their significance. As a start, we should find the nation-state less often serving alone as our primary definer of collective identity. Culturally mature perspective's multifaceted systemic picture predicts what might seem contradictory trends—both of which we are witnessing. First we should see increased identification at larger, more regional and even global scales. Even if we don't specifically identify as global citizens, the growing number of issues that will need to be addressed at a global scale means new, more broadly based approaches to decision-making will be essential. And at the same time, we should witness renewed appreciation for local traditions and bonds. Combine these two trends with how often entities—from nongovernmental organizations and multinational corporations to terrorist groups—today define themselves in ways that cut across traditional boundaries, and the need to think about governance in more multicentric ways becomes inescapable. When I think far out into the future of governance on the planet, the image that comes to me is a set of nesting bowls, or more precisely, a set of intersecting and overlapping nesting bowls. Different spheres of determination and identification, from the most local to the most global, become most important depending on the kinds of concerns we need to address.

Such a more complexly systemic picture asks a lot of us. Certainly it requires getting beyond the absolutist national allegiances of times past. But beyond this, it also requires a newly sophisticated understanding of interrelationship. A couple of earlier topics provide assistance. We can think of what is needed in terms of the creative management of semi-permeable interfaces that I described with Chapter Eight's immigration example.[3] We can also think of it in terms of Chapter Ten's description of how human relationships of all sorts will depend on the conscious making of an ongoing array of increasingly nuanced, creative, yes-and-no determinations.

Detethering Government and Money: Rethinking money's hold on the workings of government will be key to any effective next chapter in the evolution of government. The task links directly to the challenge of realizing more authentic "government by the people." What we see today with modern democracies is much closer to "one dollar, one vote" than "one person, one vote." A recent study from Princeton and Northwestern Universities made news by reaching the conclusion that the U.S. is really less a democracy than an oligarchy.[4]

The observation that large corporations and wealthy individuals wield political influence far beyond that of people with lesser means should not be a surprise. But recognizing the degree of discrepancy helps clarify how what we see can only be destabilizing in the long term. I've suggested that we appropriately think of it as Transitional Absurdity. The way culturally mature perspective brings with it a redefining of wealth and progress should produce major changes in how we think about the influences of money in government.

---

3 Where I made analogy with the workings of cell membranes.

4 See "Testing Theories of American Politics: Elites, Interest Groups, and Average Citizens" by Martin Gilens (Princeton University) and Benjamin I. Page (Northwestern University).

Further Thoughts

All of this leaves us with an essential question: Will a needed next stage in the evolution of governance require radically new governmental forms? It is hard to know for sure. Effective government going forward will certainly require a deep rethinking of how our forms work and that we draw on more systemic ways of understanding them. It will also require getting beyond current government-related Transitional Absurdities such as the partisan shrillness that can make arriving at effective policy nearly impossible, and the extreme hold that money has on governmental functioning. But it is quite possible that all of the changes I have mentioned could happen through the modification of forms we already know.

Lately I've found myself reflecting on one very different kind of structure that in various forms could have an important role with a next chapter in the story of governance. Something like it may become not just essential, but almost inevitable if we are to successfully make our way. The image's inspiration comes from think tank groups I've led through the years.

This new kind of structure would be a deliberative body that brings the best of thinkers together and gives them the tasks of identifying essential future questions and engaging those questions from a culturally mature vantage. If there is one critical thing missing with today's crisis of confidence in leadership, it is a body that we can regard as a "trusted agent." This new kind of structure could function as, in effect, a fourth branch of government (in the U.S.—or whatever would be the equivalent in other countries), though to work it would not need to have formal authority. In fact, it would work best if it did not.

The idea has inherent complexities that might seem to immediately derail it, most immediately questions about just how membership in this group would be determined and how the group would relate to the other three governmental branches. But if its authority came wholly from the power of its contribution—the degree that it effectively functioned as that trusted agent—these concerns disappear. Note, too, that making its role advisory means that there is no reason we should be restricted to only one such group (or limit such groups to particular spheres). It also means that we don't need to wait for such deliberative bodies to be established by legislation.

Everything we need exists right now. And with today's Crisis of Purpose, their significance could be recognized more quickly than we might imagine.

Arguably, it is not just possible that what I'm describing might have a role in the future of governance, if the concept of Cultural Maturity accurately captures the future tasks of government, then something at least related to it is predicted and will be necessary to moving forward. In its many forms, this kind of culturally mature deliberative body could come to seem only common sense. In another way, we see how needed new steps are at once more profound than what we have known, and at the same time more ordinary.

I've promised to return to how current circumstances may be putting even Modern Age governmental achievements in peril. I wrote the following article in June of 2020 during the last six months of Donald Trump's presidency while populist marches were filling the streets of my city of Seattle. It brings attention to how Transitional Absurdities from all sides today put us at risk:

A Very Disturbing and Dangerous, Situation—
Political Polarization and Populism Run Amok

> I was awakened in the middle of the night this week with a disturbing recognition. We are seeing the rise of a regressive left-wing populism that is not that different from the right-wing populism that put our current president in power. This reality troubles me in relation to humanity's general well-being. None of the really important questions of our time can be addressed from the positions of either extreme. And certainly the last thing we need is more polarized drama and distraction in times that are demanding enough. It also troubles me in a more personal sense.
>
> My life's work has involved training leaders in the more mature and systemic kind of thinking needed to address most any of the most important questions ahead for the species. In the present context, when it might seem that my contribution could not be more important, I find myself at an impasse. I can't come close to saying what ultimately needs to be said about most any issue today

without violating political correctnesses of either the Right or the Left, and commonly both at once. And these are not quibbles about details. In making the most obvious elephant-in-the-room assertions, I am challenging beliefs that each side regards not just as true, absolutely, but sacred.

On waking, I found myself asking a question that I never thought I would consider, and that would not occur to me in a waking state. In Seattle, where I live, there is a person on the city council who identifies as a socialist and consistently says things that are quite beyond comprehension, and as inflammatory as anything our current president would say. I consider Donald Trump to be not just the worst U.S. president in history, but someone who presents particular dangers for our time. I found myself asking that if our city council person were to run against him, who I would vote for. In fact, that situation would never present itself and I wouldn't vote for either if it did. But it leaves the question of who would be the most dangerous. Trump's dangers have less to do with ideology than his basic mental health. The councilwoman is an absolutist, unswerving, simple-answer ideologue.[5]

To be clear, I am not just complaining about extremism, which has always been a problem. Middle-of-the-road thinking gets us no closer. As a start, I'm talking about leaders claiming to present "big" ideas when in fact they are failing to ask the hard questions. And of particular concern, I'm talking about how large a percentage of people on both the Right and Left are today finding comfort in becoming hoards of the like-minded—all too ready to collude in ignoring the complexities of what our times ask of us. And also of great concern, I don't see the media (either the media

---

5 Left/populist Unity Fallacies are nothing new. And we have plenty of examples of the dangers that can come with more extreme versions. Chairman Mao's Cultural Revolution in China and the more violent excesses of the French Revolution (think Robespierre and the guillotine) provide only a few of the more familiar illustrations. I would not expect such extreme consequences in our time. But appreciating where such ideology can lead helps put it in perspective.

of the Right or the media of the Left) at all ready to challenge this shared simple-mindedness. Too often, the media considers the soap opera that results when Right and Left clash almost the definition of news. Such drama reliably attracts ears and eyeballs, but in fact it only distracts from the questions that today desperately need our attention (and that if given needed attention, would actually be news).

I've written extensively about how our future well-being will require sophistication of understanding that before now would not have been an option. Instead we are seeing regressive thinking across the board. Given the magnitude of the challenges we face, if we are not willing to open our eyes, we could find ourselves increasingly in peril.

There is a good reason why I might wake up feeling disturbed. Sometimes issues that come with middle-of-the-night awakenings temper considerably with the light of day. I am now awake, and I feel even more concerned.

An observation implied in this piece puts an exclamation point on the particular significance of rethinking governance in our time. It is not just that we are seeing increasing conflict between the positions of the Right and the Left; we hear assertions from both the Right and the Left that are really quite nonsensical—indeed rather crazy. In having conversations with the best of thinkers, more and more often I encounter outright bewilderment at what we are witnessing and the use of words like "lunacy" in their desperate attempts to make sense of it. And I find the people who have the maturity to engage questions with the needed complexity all too often walking on eggshells in a desperate attempt to avoid the endless ideological land mines.

It is impossible to know whether this circumstance will be short-lived or more prolonged. It is likely best thought of as an extreme example of Transitional Absurdity. But it cannot continue for long. And the fact that it puts the democratic experiment at risk may be the smaller part of it. It would be reasonable to conclude that if even familiar governmental forms are in peril, we really can't waste time dreaming about next chapters in the evolution of governance. But if what I have described is accurate, it may be the case that we have gone past the point where the governmental forms that we have known historically can save us. If this is true, we have no choice but to directly take on the absurdities of social/political polarization and move forward.

The Media

Here I will give greatest attention to the news media, then conclude with reflections more pertinent to popular media. The news media's systemic function is to help us be informed. At its best, in its role as the "Fourth Estate," it has served as that trusted agent. The news media's Question of Referent asks about what we need to know to be effective citizens. Media more broadly carries on our human storytelling tradition, mirroring back to us our cares, pains, and desires.

The media today—of all kinds—tends to fall well short of needed next steps. For the most part, this reflects simply how rarely we as yet see well-developed culturally mature capacities more generally. But shortly I will touch on how, particularly with the news media, we also see more regressive dynamics similar to what I've just described with governance. Today people consistently rate the news media even lower than politicians when it comes to trust.

In times ahead, the news media—both traditional and in all its new, increasingly decentralized forms—will be critical to effectively embracing Cultural Maturity's challenge. The news media must support the articulation of essential new questions, provide the informational resources a culturally mature populace requires, and engage essential issues with commitment to bringing needed systemic completeness to understanding. Popular media channels also have essential roles. They must stand opposed to the artificial-stimulation-as-substance diversions that today too often pass as entertainment and put forward images that can model and inspire culturally mature lives.

News Media and Historical/Developmental Perspective

The news media's story through history by itself adds in only limited ways to previous observations. We could examine how different intelligences have predominated both with how we have communicated and with what we have found important to communicate at different times in culture, but that is now a familiar topic. And while I could describe how means of communication have evolved—from drumbeats, to wandering minstrels making their rounds between medieval villages, to the advent of movable type, to the digital revolution—this is largely a technical history. Historical perspective's most important contribution may simply be to affirm the importance of the news media's role—how it has functioned to provide us with key information that we have needed to live safe and productive lives. Ultimately, it is also to affirm the importance of carrying out this function in further, more sophisticated ways going forward.

Four Change Snapshots

Getting Beyond the Sensationalizing of Content and Redefining What We Call News: The most obvious way that the news media today falls short is with how often sensationalized content—content that appeals to the most adolescent of impulses—tends to prevail. There is nothing new in this phenomenon. We can think of it as a remainder from now timeworn heroic/romantic proclivities. Such content reliably attracts eyeballs, but in the context of today's needs, it is barely news at all.

Decades back, in preparation for a speech at a media literacy conference, I taped a week of television news from each of Seattle's local commercial stations. We might expect local news to be some of the most reliable, but in fact historically it has often been the worst offender in this regard. Two-thirds of the content—setting aside sports and weather—was either the latest killings, crimes, and natural disasters, or tabloid sensationalism—at that time, O.J. Simpson, Tonya Harding, and the like. What most struck me in gathering this material was how little of what I witnessed was actually news—in the sense of anything new, anything that could add to what people know. And I'm referring here not just to the obviously tabloid content. We can predict pretty accurately how many killings and crimes are likely to happen in a year. Parading the latest examples before us each evening (often from locales far distant) really isn't news—except in the unlikely chance that we know the people involved.[6]

---

6 Changes in those statistics could be news. And creative ideas about how statistics might be affected would certainly be news.

Particularly at the national level, the news media has often done better. Indeed, at times, as with the iconic reporting of Edward R. Murrow or Walter Cronkite, it has fulfilled important aspects of that trusted agent role. But even at its best, the news media has tended to give priority to controversy and conflict. Subtly, or not so subtly, it has fallen for the "if it bleeds, it leads" trap. The bloodshed may be on a battlefield, but just as often it is the metaphorical bloodshed of ideologies warring over whatever has become the latest hot-news controversy.

How have we done with the advent of digital media? Digital media arrived with great promise. Suddenly an array of new voices could be heard, voices from all over the world. And as news moved out of the constraints of linear time, there was hope that we might see more long-form, in-depth reporting. But thus far that potential has rarely been realized. It is important to understand that there is nothing in a more diversified media environment that by itself protects us from the sensationalizing of content and the confusion of empty stimulation with news—indeed, these dangers increase. Frequently, today, we see an amplification of the tendency of media to create gated communities of the like-minded. And, all too often, we find content that is more "clickbait" than substance.

Culturally mature journalism starts with rethinking what we call news. It shuns sensationalism and by its quality and integrity takes away sensationalism's appeal. It helps us not just to accept that the important questions are difficult, but also to appreciate that the greatest fulfillment and meaning lies in confronting such difficulty. And it takes us beyond ideological easy answers and ready polemics and models the courage, magnitude, and creativity of perspective our future requires.

Beyond Balanced Reporting: It is important in evaluating whether news media succeeds at being culturally mature that we not confuse "balanced reporting" with culturally mature systemic perspective. Even with the best of news media today, commentary too often translates into a voice from the Left uttering predictable responses followed by a representative from the Right voicing equally tired conclusions. I've emphasized the fundamental difference between compromise and culturally mature understanding. If Left, Right, and somewhere in between are our only options, then not only will the media fail to provide useful commentary, it will fail to ask the important questions. Culturally mature journalism confronts political correctnesses of all sorts, including the political correctness of including "both sides," and challenges people to engage questions with the depth and nuance that concerns of all sorts increasingly require.

Expert Opinion Versus Populist Media: One of the dangers that accompanies today's increasingly diverse and decentralized digital media environment follows from one of its greatest strengths—how it can take the last word when it comes to news out of the hands of established experts. The good news in this new picture is that we experience greater diversity of opinion, and with greater frequency opinion that takes on established truths. The bad news is that it can be difficult to tease apart what has substance from what does not. If we are not confronted with outright fake news, we are at least diminished by an anything-goes atmosphere in which any depth of inquiry is abandoned.

I see an important opportunity in this changing media landscape, one that comes back to the kind of observation I made in the previous section on governance about the possibility of new kinds of deliberative bodies. New types of media can help us develop resources to triage and filter information. Our trusted agents no longer need to be established figures—such as Walter Cronkite in his time—with the resources of major networks behind them. And new media modalities invite the development of media resources that specifically highlight information able to help us create a culturally mature world. This is a possibility that we have yet to significantly realize. It is essential that we successfully do so.

Diversity and the Media: I include one last snapshot because it specifically incorporates CST patterning notions. The media has made strides in recent decades in incorporating greater diversity in programming. Women increasingly play major roles not just on the screen, but also in making the decisions that determine programming. And something similar is happening with people of diverse racial and ethnic backgrounds. On all these fronts there is more work to do. But it is important to acknowledge progress.

An area where we have seen less progress is with incorporating people of diverse personality styles. With visual media, recognizable figures are most commonly Lates. There are understandable reasons. Lates project in ways that tend to make them look best on screen (and tend to be more classically attractive to begin with). They also tend to sound the most articulate. Personality style diversity might seem like a minor concern compared to diversity issues related to gender and race. But it has its own kind of significance beyond just fairness and the benefit of people seeing others like themselves depicted. Particularly with news media, the fact that visible figures tend to be Lates contributes to news too often lacking needed depth. (I've described how Lates, of all temperaments, tend most to engage experience from its more surface layers.) Including greater temperament diversity could further support bringing whole-box-of-crayons sensibility to engaging important questions.

Further Thoughts

I promised to return to regressive dynamics that we encounter with news media today. Lately, I've found myself reflecting back on the ongoing think tank on the future of public media that I did in the first decade of the century with Seattle's public television station (which I described in Chapter Eight). These memories put an exclamation point on how what we are seeing today warrants deep concern. The think tank involved directly engaging the question of what culturally mature programming might look like. Aspects of that vision have sometimes been realized, particularly with public media. But as often more recently we have seen backsliding and polarization similar to what I have described for the political sphere. Increasingly, even basic balanced reporting is hard to find. We encounter media designed for the social/political Right or media designed for the social/political Left, with little else. This is the case whether we look to TV, radio, print, or online modalities—and whether public or private. An essential result is that people are losing trust not just in opinion, but whether there is any place to go simply to find the facts. As with what I described for extreme political polarization, it is difficult to know whether this is a short-lived phenomenon, or something of deeper consequence. But, again, this is a reality that we can't let continue for long.

Let's turn now to popular media. Changes in popular media similarly involve both new dangers and new possibilities. The business of popular media is the telling of stories. Old stories necessarily leave us short. I've described how Modern Age storytelling has tended to apply either heroic (about winning, usually against the odds) or romantic

(Romeo and Juliet) narratives. Each of these familiar kinds of narrative has derived much of its attractiveness from idealization, projection, and dreams of limitlessness. But we also have the option of telling new kinds of stories.

The growing influence of postmodern narrative in contemporary popular media has begun to take us beyond the past's heroic and romantic alternatives. But I've emphasized how postmodern narrative, too, ultimately stops short. Too easily it translates into a difference-for-its-own-sake, ironic glibness that produces at best cleverness, at worst distraction from exactly the questions our stories need to engage. Such offerings are often not of great concern—being more silly in their consequences than significant—but they can also present real dangers. I've described how interactive digital media can draw on psychological mechanisms that differ little from those of addicting drugs. In doing so, they contribute to one of our time's most destructive forms of Transitional Absurdity.

I often challenge friends and colleagues in the entertainment world to expand their thinking to include culturally mature narrative and to reflect on how such new storytelling can be translated into effective expression. We see bits of culturally mature narrative in the best of contemporary popular media—stories of people, often in very different ways, seeking personal meaning in a world where traditional guideposts are not as helpful as in times past; of relationships in which people not only step outside the bounds of expectations, but attempt to engage one another in more complete (Whole-Person) ways; of people looking toward the future in a manner that steps beyond outdated idealized imagery (and equally its dystopian twin) and provides authentic hope and creative inspiration for going forward. It is true that culturally mature narrative can initially seem less sexy than what it replaces. But, as I've suggested, for the simple reason that culturally mature possibility describes what is becoming creatively right and true in our times, more and more often we should find storytelling that draws on culturally mature themes the most ultimately compelling.

I'm a strong advocate for media literacy classes in the schools. Good media literacy classes continue to be rare, and I think it is important that media literacy insights inform education at all levels. I have particular interest in how media literacy becomes critical in our digitally interconnected world. The emphasis with media literacy curriculum has changed in recent years in ways that have sometimes caused conflict between media literacy advocates. Not long ago, the primary focus was learning to "deconstruct" media so that students could better recognize biases and not be exploited by the media—particularly by television with its too often numbing effects, and, within media of all sorts, by advertising's distorting influence. The emphasis was largely protective. Newer media literacy advocates tend to be more positive and proactive, giving greatest attention to how digital media offers the possibility of endless media options and of students creating their own content.

Today, particularly given the easily confusing, in-between place in which we reside with the promise of the digital revolution—where what we encounter is so often empty stimulation more than substance—a next step has become essential. I sometimes suggest a simple exercise for teachers to do with students that captures what is needed, and in a way that draws on the best of the two media literacy traditions. The teacher challenges each student to put together an online site that provides links to information (and entertainment) that the student finds personally most useful and important (most life-affirming)—to, in effect, practice assuming that trusted agent role. Students then engage in discussions about why they chose to include what they did, and also about what they found to be missing that should somehow be included. This simple exercise not only captures what needs to be at the heart of good media education, it begins to get at the timely task for all of us if digital technologies—and the media more generally—are to serve us in a culturally mature world.

Medicine (and Health Care More Generally)

My own background means that here and in other places I've often given particular attention to health care–related changes and challenges. In particular, I've written about how health care professionals need to ask deeply what it means to offer quality, universally available care in the face of inescapable economic limits. I've also emphasized the importance of thinking more expansively and creatively about what the enhancing of health ultimately entails.

The basic answer to health care's Question of Referent is straightforward: Health care is about keeping people healthy. But it is also true that how we have thought about health and healing has not always been the same. Culturally mature perspective highlights the need for a more systemically conceived answer, and also the importance of engaging the particulars of health care more systemically.

Historical/Developmental Perspective

In Chapter Three, I observed that we can identify general patterns in how each cultural stage has viewed the human body and, with this, how healing is understood. For the task of addressing health care's future, the changes of recent centuries help us appreciate both the strengths of what we have known and also what a more systemic picture can contribute going forward. I've described how the body of medieval times was the body of visceral humors and observed that healing then took place through their manipulation. I've also described how, in keeping with Modern Age, machine-model thinking, the body of modern medicine became the body of anatomy and physiology. In our time, we've come increasingly to view health care as the fixing of broken anatomy and physiology.

As important for addressing health care's future are historical observations that relate to how we have viewed medicine's role in culture. Particularly over the last century, we have witnessed a significant change in the status afforded the practice of medicine. It was not long ago that surgery was commonly done by barbers. We have come increasingly not just to better respect medicine, but also to mythologize it. In part, this elevated status has been a product of major successes. Especially important were successes that followed from the germ theory of medicine—first, the transforming application of sterile technique, and later, the discovery of antibiotics. And more recent successes such as the growing prevalence of organ transplantation and new insights coming from the biotechnology revolution have also contributed. But this newly elevated status has also reflected underlying cultural changes—in particular, how in modern times we've come to mythologize any activity that we associate with science. As medicine has more and more been thought of as a scientific pursuit, we've gradually come to describe its cultural role in grand heroic terms. Health care has come to be about defeating death and disease—and, as I've observed, often at essentially any cost.

Four Change Snapshots

Confronting Economic Limits: In Chapter Four's article on a needed new maturity in our relationship with death, I described how modern health care's heroic mythology must inevitably confront real economic limits. I noted that there is a good reason why this confrontation might prove particularly challenging, how it eventually brings us face to face with life's final limit, the fact of our mortality. But we can't let that stop us. It is important to appreciate how confronting economic limits leads to addressing concerns that go well beyond just the cost of care. Addressing economic limits in health care should contribute to increasingly mature and empowering insights regarding what it takes to be healthy, what it means to heal, and, more broadly, the requirements of a healthy society.

Earlier, I described an exercise I've done with leaders at the Institute that involves giving groups a budget along with a handful of patient biographies. I noted that the wrenching choices required reflected the inescapable task we face as societies if we are not in total denial (and which we face indirectly even if we are in denial). After the exercise was complete, the conversation would inevitably turn to larger health care concerns. Questions would come to the fore that expanded the health care picture dramatically; some obvious, others that require more of a stretch. For example, participants might ask, "Wouldn't it make sense to spend more of our money on prevention?" And then, "If prenatal care is valuable prevention, what about good nutrition?" And we can go on. "If good nutrition is important, what about cleaning up toxic chemicals in the environment?" And if that too is part of health care's larger picture, what about the effects of poverty, and lack of housing—and today's larger Crisis of Purpose? All that may take the systemic analysis too far, at least farther than we can now readily put into practice. But we can't escape that acknowledging economic limits leads to rethinking health care as a whole—fundamentally.

When we acknowledge economic limits, one recognition in particular stands out. Major discrepancies in health care availability in the end sicken us all. We recognize that societies must somehow ensure that people have access to care. That doesn't necessarily mean "making health care a right" in the sense of government assuming the costs as is sometimes proposed by the progressive Left. (I've emphasized that this is not a Left versus Right issue—a variety of approaches could be used to achieve equitable access to care.) But it does mean that everyone must have affordable, quality care available to them. And it means reining in the excesses of anyone who profits inordinately from their role in health care (hospitals, drug companies, insurance companies).

Rethinking Health Care Relationships: In Chapter Four, I used the doctor/patient interaction to illustrate both the importance of rethinking past authority relationships and how legitimately challenging doing so can be. My story of observing surgery as a student highlighted the necessity for humility in this rethinking task. But I went on to emphasize how this evolution would be essential not just for care that was appropriately compassionate, but also simply for effective treatment.

In fact, the practitioner/patient relationship is one of the places where the value of more Whole-Person leadership is most being recognized. We increasingly appreciate the importance of doctors listening deeply to their patients as well as writing orders. And patients are coming both to take greater responsibility for their care and to be better informed so that they can do so effectively. Closely tied to this shift toward greater patient responsibility is ever greater emphasis on prevention. This includes preventive screening, but also, and at least as important, making good lifestyle choices—eating healthy foods, getting adequate sleep and exercise.

Moving Beyond "Broken Machine" Health Care Models: Some of the most interesting changes we see today involve leaving behind familiar mechanistic ways of thinking about health and healing. That includes the simple recognition that the body we are treating is somebody. We are better appreciating the role that psychological influences such as stress can play in personal well-being. We are also better recognizing how both a healthy physical environment and a healthy social environment are key to health. In the future we should find ourselves better realizing that often the "patient" that needs treating is the context in which someone lives—even perhaps society as a whole.

Thinking that views the body more systemically is as yet unusual, but we are seeing beginnings here too. Discoveries derived from attempts to tease out the complex workings of the immune system (many spurred by the AIDS epidemic) come immediately to mind, along with new insights from efforts to understand the genetic underpinning of disease. Medicine is being forced to think about bodily processes in more dynamic ways. I suspect some of medicine's most important advances in the long term will be ones that challenge Modern Age thinking's clear separation of mind and body and revisit the question of what it means to have a body.

We can think of the need to give ethical questions new priority as a further part of this more systemic picture. The moral/ethical implications of technological advances that will likely play an even more transforming role in medicine's future in particular stand out. Some of those implications will follow from the specific nature of the innovations—as with treatments that work at the level of genetics. Other implications are again economic. So often, today, we celebrate each new, more expensive medical advance without raising the question of whether the advance is something that we can ultimately afford. (I consider this contradiction a prime example of Transitional Absurdity.) I've described how all questions become moral/ethical questions in a culturally mature reality. This is certainly the case for the most important future questions in medicine.

That needed new maturity in our relationship with death can also be thought of as part of this more systemic orientation. Again, we have a long way to go. But I've noted how health care professionals today are gradually becoming more comfortable speaking about death with their patients. I've also observed how hospice care has become an increasingly respected aspect of health care's contribution.

Individualized Treatment and Human Diversity: Medicine is at least making a start at better appreciating the importance of human differences. For example, we are beginning to structure research so that it helps tease apart the often very different ways that men and women or people of different ethnicities may respond to the same treatment. Greater attention to genetic differences and temperament diversity in times ahead should bring greater refinement in making these kinds of distinctions.

Further Thoughts

The 2020 pandemic has placed essential aspects of what health care will require of us going forward in high relief. And often needed steps have highlighted the importance of culturally mature capacities in addressing future health care challenges. Articles that I included in Chapter Nine that I wrote at the beginning of the pandemic emphasized the need for better foresight, risk assessment, and planning for the unexpected; investment in public health and the long-term resilience of heath care systems; acknowledgment of economic and racial disparities in access to care; the confronting of real limits (including death); avoiding ideological traps in the face of potentially overwhelming circumstances; and giving new attention to what long-term cultural well-being (health in the largest sense) will ultimately require of us.

Economics and Business

The Question of Referent for economics and business is again straightforward. The economic sphere provides a simple, shorthand way of measuring value that allows for ready exchange. But this simple function also necessarily engages us in some of our time's most essential rethinking. Consistent with other spheres, we have come to define value in the most abstract, right-hand terms. Economics as we traditionally think of it is almost solely about material accumulation. But defining value in this way is serving us less and less well. I've described how one of the most essential results of Cultural Maturity's cognitive changes is that they make it possible to think about wealth and progress more systemically. Cultural Maturity's changes also make it obvious that any kind of world we would want to live in requires that we do so.

Cultural Maturity's call for new responsibility applies in particularly consequential ways to the economic and business spheres. In the context of today's rapidly changing social and technological realities, economists, bankers, and business professionals must work to establish sustainable economic practices that succeed for all the world's people—and for the planet as a whole. The most forward-thinking among them will provide leadership with that most pivotal task of rethinking profit and progress.

Historical/Developmental Perspective

While material wealth has always had importance, consistent with its ultimate right-hand contribution, in very early times its significance remained secondary to more basic determiners of value such as connection with nature and tribe, spiritual truths, and the bonds of

CREATIVE SYSTEMS THEORY

blood and family. Native American potlatches involved the exchange of wealth, but their primary purpose was the solidifying of tribal bonds. Over time, we saw growing separation of the monetary from the social, but the process has been gradual. Trading in the Middle Ages prospered, but it was also often thought of as morally suspect, and wealth was commonly associated with avarice. Medieval belief made greed one of the seven deadly sins. With the more commerce-based world of the Modern Age, material wealth came increasingly to be accepted as an encompassing measure for value and an appropriate determiner for our actions.

Today, we see a continuation of this trajectory. Money in our time represents much more than just a medium of exchange. It has become the aspect of experience that we most mythologize—in effect, our determining ideology. It has also come increasingly to define identity—our measure of "net worth." As we approach Transition, this equating of material wealth with value often reaches a startling extreme. This particularly defining Transitional dynamic—like any dynamic carried beyond its timeliness—increasingly puts us in danger. It has become a major contributor to today's Crisis of Purpose. And it can't continue even to serve us economically. It plays a major role in modern economic instabilities, producing inevitable house-of-cards dynamics.

The emerging picture of business and economics must include moving beyond such assumptions. We are at least seeing its beginnings.

Four Change Snapshots

Leadership in Leadership's Changes: Some of the most innovative thinking about leadership in recent years has come from the business world. That we find such innovation springing from business—where values tend not to be the initial concern—might seem a surprise. But it very much makes sense. Globalization and technological advancement have had particularly immediate effects on business, requiring it to deal with ever more rapid change and an increasingly networked world. More than any other sphere, business quickly pays the price if leadership is not up to the task. In times ahead, we should expect to see leadership innovation continuing if for no other reason than that businesses want to attract the best of workers. Increasingly, the best of workers will be those with culturally mature capacities. To appeal to such workers, business leadership and business structures must better reflect, and more directly draw on, culturally mature beliefs and values.

Greater Acceptance of Moral Accountability: I've emphasized how all important questions have become moral/ethical questions. The world of business and economics is a realm where this evolution in how we think about value has some of the most important and easily surprising consequences. With Cultural Maturity's changes, we should better appreciate how business decisions, far from being value-free, have pivotal moral/ethical implications.

At a macroeconomic level, we should find ourselves endeavoring to replace wholly monetary measures such as GDP with referents that better take into account all that contributes to well-being—not just material growth, but also the health of our families and communities, the continued vitality of natural environments, and psychological and spiritual well-being. At a business level, we should find businesses taking more direct responsibility in the health of the communities they serve. We should also find business leaders more willing to speak out on larger social issues and more often modeling social leadership through innovative business practices. Customers and employees will demand it.

As part of this needed greater accountability, economists and business leaders should also become more attentive to limits—for example, to the danger of business institutions becoming too big to fail. When we begin to think of profit not just in terms of short-term gain, but in terms of ultimate benefit, greater maturity in the face of limits becomes clearly important—and not just socially, but also economically. An obvious illustration: While addressing climate change may involve significant short-term costs, if we are at all attentive to the long term, it becomes clear that climate change denial would prove ultimately much more costly.

The Role of Diversity in Healthy Businesses and Sustainable Economies: On many different levels, thinking more systemically about human differences should play a significant role in the future of business and economics. The importance of greater inclusion and fairness is most recognized with gender and ethnic diversity. We are better appreciating how we can't have healthy and vital workplaces without equal opportunity and an ethic of equal pay for equal work.

The importance of attention to personality style diversity is not so obvious, but CST suggests that the gifts of a broad diversity of temperaments are needed if organizations are to be most dynamic and creative. I've described how, in consulting with businesses, I've often brought together think tank groups that draw on all the different parts of the organization, and, with this, the particular personality styles most common to them. This diversity contributes greatly to the needed creativity of exchange.

At the largest of scales, the most important diversity recognitions concern economic advantage. I've described how today's growing discrepancy between rich and poor presents one of our times' most glaring—and ultimately dangerous—Transitional Absurdities. Inequality itself is not the problem—within limits, it spurs individual initiative and wealth creation. But extreme inequality threatens institutions and results in ultimately unstable economies. It is quite possible that the harshest lessons about economic limits in times ahead will come from ignoring the instabilities that such discrepancies inevitably create.

More Systemically-Conceived Economic Models: Culturally mature perspective makes it clear that free market purism ultimately can't work, that it leads to benefit primarily for the rich and a lack of attention to shared assets such as infrastructure, health care, and the environment. But just as much, it brings attention to how centralized control and ill-conceived regulation can undermine economic vitality in ways that are damaging all the way around. Cultural Maturity's cognitive changes should help us better appreciate the complementary roles that freedom and limitation each necessarily play in fair and sustainable economic policies, and through this, help us develop more systemically conceived, and ultimately creative, economic models and policy approaches.

We are left with the same kind of question that I previously posited for government. Will major changes of a structural sort be required in the economic sphere? In a similar way, I think we just can't know. Future economic structures will need to be both more fully global in their scope and more flexible in their ability to address more local needs.[7]

---

7 I've observed how nation-state boundaries will likely play a less defining role in the future. If what I have described is accurate, we will need more

They will also clearly need to better support long-term benefit along with short-term profit. We may very well also see innovations such as new kinds of currencies or new, more cooperative business approaches. But it is too early to know whether basic economic mechanisms will need to be radically different from what we see today. What we can know is that culturally mature values and ways of thinking must better determine our actions. New structures, if they are needed, will follow from these more basic changes.

Further Thoughts

An article I wrote in the middle of the 2008-2009 "great recession" brings front-page-news immediacy to the importance of confronting basic assumptions in the economic sphere. It also helps further tie what I have described to the larger task of rethinking human advancement:

Money as Ideology: Bringing Culturally Mature
Perspective to the 2008-2009 Financial Collapse

> What caused the recent financial collapse? Simple greed and incompetence? The unfortunate "perfect storm" confluence of economic cycles, globalization, and other hard-to-predict factors? Yes, yes, and yes. But something deeper was also at work. Understanding this more fundamental ingredient in what we saw will be key to a healthy and sustainable economic future.
>
> I suspect that the more basic contributor was ideological. "Ideology" as I use the word here refers not to liberal or conservative economic theories, but rather to commonly held but ultimately limited and limiting beliefs. We appropriately ask how the best of economic and political minds—and all of us—could have been blind to what was in hindsight a situation that was as unstable as

---

generally accepted economic rules and expectations for global commerce along with new ways of establishing more local and regional economic relationships. Our future economic structures must support both greater big-picture uniformity and greater differentiation and decentralization.

a house of cards. Neither self-interest nor simple ignorance ultimately explains why events unfolded as they did.

Just what did the experts miss? Certainly they missed how deregulation had created perverse incentives that changed how bankers behaved. Had experts viewed the industry even with the most rudimentary of systemic thinking, they would have been alerted to the potential for destabilization and crisis. Back when banks were self-contained entities, bankers were conservative folk. But when regulations changed so that mortgage banks could sell loans to investors, the incentive situation changed too. The financial meltdown was commonly attributed to bankers taking unwise risks. But in most cases, the loans really weren't risks—for the bankers. Because bankers resold the loans relatively quickly, they would profit whether the loan ultimately failed or not. With the financial collapse, individual mortgage holders and investors suffered miserably. Bankers, for the most part, escaped unscathed. Some profited enormously.

But the blindness ultimately reached further. Economists—and most everyone else—were in denial about the fact that housing prices could go down as well as up (an occurrence that any look at history suggests not only happens, but is inevitable given enough time). All it would have taken to produce the cascade of events that we observed was for housing prices to go down 10 percent. Prices eventually went down nationally an average of over 30 percent.

How could people be so blind—including very smart people? In 2004, then chairman of the U.S. Federal Reserve Alan Greenspan proclaimed, "Not only have individuals become less vulnerable to shocks from underlying risk factors, but also the financial system as a whole has become more resilient"[8]—specifically in reference to highly interlinked financial instruments such as derivatives that played a central role in the eventual meltdown. (Some

---

8 From a speech given to the American Bankers Association on October 5, 2004.

people did anticipate the problem. Warren Buffet warned that derivatives were "financial weapons of mass destruction carrying dangers, that while latent, are potentially lethal."[9]) It is forgivable that economic experts did not accurately forecast just when an economic downturn might occur. But that the greater portion of economic minds did not recognize fundamental instabilities—which were in hindsight glaring—suggests a more deeply rooted kind of blindness than just selfishness or stupidity.

That deeper blindness is a product of our time. Today we mythologize money, make it our "bottom line," and in the end, our god. Culturally mature perspective does not condemn this. Rather, it sees our worship of money as a predicted culminating expression of our most recent stage in culture's story. We may criticize as naive the "masters of the universe" belief that unfettered free markets can be self-regulating. But this kind of thinking is what we get if we extend to its logical extreme the materialist/individualist worldview that has produced much that today we most prize in our modern lives.

At the same time, culturally mature perspective also makes clear that such belief cannot continue to serve us. At the very least, the belief that such a worldview is sufficient makes us vulnerable to dismissing—or not even seeing—potential risks. But, in fact, it does even more. It leaves us short of the maturity of perspective we need not just for stable economies, but for a future that can work at all. I quote Thomas Friedman from an article of his in the *New York Times*: "Let's step out of the usual boundaries of analysis of our current economic crisis and ask a radical question—What if the crisis of 2008 represents something much more fundamental than a deep recession? What if it is telling us that the whole growth model created over the last 50 years is simply unsustainable economically and ecologically and that 2008 was when we hit the wall—when Mother Nature and the market both said no more."[10]

---

9 From the Annual Letter to Shareholders of Berkshire Hathaway in 2002.

10 Thomas Friedman, *New York Times*, February 2009.

Today we confront limits not just to the effectiveness of past economic policies, but also to how we have until now thought about wealth and advancement more generally. This more encompassing factor may or may not have been a major ingredient in this particular downturn. But if the concept of Cultural Maturity is correct, it will be a factor eventually.

We've come in our time to measure social and individual well-being almost wholly in economic terms—such as individual "net worth" and rising GDP (a wholly monetary measure). But today we find a new willingness to question this limits-denying picture on both fronts. We are recognizing how a solely material yardstick is inadequate for measuring the health of societies or even the stability of economies. More personally, empty materialism is a major contributor to the loss of hope and purpose so common in our time. For a healthy and vital future, we will need more encompassing and complete ways to think about and measure what matters.

The advances of the Modern Age have been wondrous. And Modern Age advances would not have been possible without today's more individualist and materialist view of the world and the values that accompanied it. But for the future we can't stop there. This is not to call for some opposite "small is beautiful" advocacy. It is to call loudly for rethinking collective and personal wealth in ways that more fully take into account all that creates human meaning, and, more specifically, all that human meaning asks of us in our particular time.

The Arts

I will go into particular depth with regard to one sphere of human manifestation—the arts. This might seem surprising given that the arts in our time often seem not to have great significance. I've chosen the arts for this more extended treatment for a number of reasons. First there is the observation noted at the beginning of this chapter that one function of art has been to give voice to the newly possible. We should expect the arts to provide particular insight about the future. In addition, there is how the workings of more left-hand realms such as art have always been elusive to grasp—and how with Transition they become decidedly more so. Some added attention helps us more deeply appreciate the implications. And finally because thinking more creatively is so central to CST's picture of understanding, there is an important new way in which we all, in the broadest sense, need to become artists.

These observations are adapted from *Cultural Maturity: A Guidebook for the Future*. With them, in particular, I go into greater depth than I have with previous domains in terms of the relationship of art's story to culture's larger evolutionary picture. Along with further filling out previous Patterning in Time reflections, these observations shed important light on some of this evolutionary picture's more easily confusing dynamics, ones essential to deeply understanding current circumstances.

> Art's Question of Referent asks just what makes something art, and more, what makes a piece good or even great art. Framed more systemically, it asks about how art serves us and what is going on when it serves us most powerfully. Art's significance has been a question of eternal debate, and final definition inevitably escapes us. But culturally mature perspective makes art's function newly amenable to scrutiny.

> Art would still be of value if its purpose were simply to create things of beauty. But culturally mature perspective suggests that its significance is deeper—and in ways with particular pertinence to culture's emerging tasks. Art's deeper contribution follows from the fact that art takes expression from the most germinal of intelligences—the body, the imaginal, and the more internal aspects of the emotional. That deeper contribution has a couple of parts. First, art functions as an "advocate" for, and reminder of, the more germinal realms and values tapped by the artistic endeavor. It provides us with a collective ongoing link with left-hand sensibilities. The second kind of contribution is less obvious, but it has particular importance for this inquiry. Art fulfills a visionary function. It connects us with new possibilities. Rainer Maria Rilke counseled the artist: "Fear not the strangeness you feel. The future must enter you long before it happens."

We find the most familiar example of this visionary function in how the art of the Renaissance anticipated advances in science and government that we did not see until centuries later. This visionary function is a product not of exceptional capacity on the part of artists (though exceptional art requires exceptional capacities), but rather of the creatively germinal intelligences that predominate in the artistic personality. When we call something art, we claim that in some way it gives voice to truths just peeking over the horizon. Good or great art is art that serves this anticipatory function in especially powerful ways—in the psyche of the individual, but also, and particularly, for the "psyche of culture."

Art's developmental/evolutionary story confronts us immediately with an apparent contradiction that we find with all more left-hand contributions. A person could argue equally well that early forms or modern forms are most significant—early forms on the basis of the preeminence of the underlying sensibilities, and modern forms on the basis of the stage in cultural development. It is hard to disagree with the assertion that the artistic had its most dominant significance in times well past. The central role that dance has played in tribal societies, and that mythic imagery played in the daily lives of people in ancient Egypt or classical Greece, reveals a decidedly more defining presence for the artistic than we find in today's world. But, at the same time, it is also clear that Modern Age forms reflected an aesthetic "sophistication" we had not seen previously.

This apparent contradiction follows quite "logically" from how the relationship between left-hand and right-hand sensibilities evolves over cultural time. I've described how history to this point follows a progression from more left-hand dominance toward realities in which right-hand values and ways of understanding increasingly prevail. Domains where left-hand sensibilities are strongest have greatest influence early on. But, as with all spheres, such left-hand domains manifest with particular refinement in culture's "finishing and polishing" stages.

A more detailed examination of why we see this apparent contradiction adds further nuance to our now-familiar developmental/evolutionary progression. And art's origins in sensibilities of a more left-hand sort means that a closer look at the story of art through history provides important further insights for understanding Integrative Meta-perspective's specifically systemic changes.

I've described how, early in culture's evolution, the sensibilities that underlie artistic expression are primary. In tribal realities, it is difficult to separate art and cultural identity—particularly art that takes expression in movement and sound. To not know the dances and songs—the most direct voices of bodily reality—is unthinkable. Artist Barnett Newman proposed that "man's origin was that of the artist." Arguably, the birth of art—in cave paintings and the like—is synonymous with the birth of reflective consciousness.

Somewhat later, with the rise of early civilizations—and imaginal intelligence now primary—we see art at once becoming a bit more distinct and reaching its greatest visual preeminence. We can't picture classical Greece, the ancient cultures of Mesoamerica, or the artistry of classical China or Japan without also imagining sculpture that many would say has not been equaled, and deeply compelling written and painted images—of gods and goddesses, harvests and rituals, heroic deeds. Art in these early times is not quite truth, but it is venerated as a direct route to truth.

With each succeeding stage, while art has arguably gained in its refinement, it has also stepped further from center stage. In medieval times, art still commands great appreciation—what could be more inspiring than the aesthetic intricacy and monumental power of a Romanesque or Gothic cathedral? But at the same time, art's influence in the Middle Ages becomes secondary. The institutional church and the crown now hold sway. Art exists to proclaim their wonder and dominion.

With the Modern Age—and archetypally masculine preeminence—we see a dramatic further refinement of aesthetic and some of history's most significant artistic accomplishments. The Renaissance (Late-Axis Europe's Early-Axis substage) witnessed an artistic exuberance not seen since classical times. But art also moved to a still more secondary role. It became something separate, something to give pleasure, to decorate—a treasured but ultimately subordinate function to those of commerce, science, government, and culture's other harder endeavors.

With the Modern Age, we also see right-hand sensibilities influencing artistic expression in a variety of more specific ways—to art's benefit or diminishment, depending on one's view. Art became increasingly an activity of experts. (All children make art—in childhood, the more germinal aspects of intelligences are primary, irrespective of cultural stage. But in modern times, growing up has meant setting such activities aside, unless a person makes the dubious choice of becoming an artistic professional.) Also, art became much more the expression of the individual as opposed to an expression of collective (animistic or divine) forces. For the first time, we find the larger portion of visual art signed and musical composition (at least with music of a more Upper Pole sort, rather than from folk/traditional origins) attributed to particular composers. We also saw more specific changes that directly impacted the art itself. For example, we witnessed the advent of three-point perspective, and with it visual art reflecting a more material and objective vantage (more similar to that of a photograph).

As we venture into Transitional times and face the challenges of Cultural Maturity, expression in the arts can seem schizophrenic. At times, art's recent contributions have very much reflected art's past visionary function. But just as often, art has come to seem irrelevant, even absurd. As with other spheres at Transitional times, we commonly encounter overlapping realities.

A lot in the art of the last century gave articulate expression to essential aspects of Cultural Maturity's new challenge. I think of how the cubist works of Pablo Picasso and Georges Braque emphasized multiple perspectives. The writings of Samuel Beckett,

James Joyce, D.H. Lawrence, and others introduced a newly participatory aesthetic (where what we see is explicitly as much about ourselves as what we might be looking at). We see truth's new dynamism reflected in Salvador Dali's melting watches and the impermanence of much performance art. And we recognize a beginning of the kind of reengagement with early-stage sensibilities that comes with Cultural Maturity in the inspiration that Wassily Kandinsky, Aaron Copland, Stephen Reich, and others found in the artistic expression of earlier times in culture.

But it is also the case that art has come to have diminishing significance for most people over the last century. Few people can name major figures in the visual arts of the last thirty years. And much of twentieth century visual art that people recognize may seem baffling, if not ludicrous. (Campbell's soup cans and toilets as art?) The arts that do have effect on people's lives today tend to be either classical forms that appeal to a limited audience or expression (mostly musical) that is highly commercialized, often more a product of mass culture (who will be the next teenage pop diva?) than anything that serves art's underlying cultural function.

Even with its diminished significance, however, art's cutting edge has often continued to reflect art's primordial task. Part of that task in our time has been to chronicle its own demise—or, more accurately from the perspective of Cultural Maturity, the predicted effect that Transitional dynamics will have on artistic sensibility (and left-hand understanding as a whole). Twentieth century artists challenged art itself—both what makes something art and art's role in culture—certainly art with a capital A. We hear Dadaism's proclamation: "Art is dead—long live art." Pop art's claim to status as high art left us to ponder whether everything is art, or perhaps nothing.

CST proposes that the reason such art has left most people baffled is only in part that good art always does. Some of what more is involved relates to what we find at Transition with any domain. Art becomes increasingly existential/postmodern—its strength is that it effectively challenges what before has been mythologized, its weakness that it is yet unable to really replace what has been taken away. But as much or more of the reason reflects Transition's odd requirement of art that it take expression from a reality in which the more archetypally feminine sensibilities that have been art's primary source have become nearly absent. We can understand the triviality of much of art today as an expression of Transitional Absurdity.

What lies ahead for art? A person might appropriately ask whether art as experience will ever again claim the potency of times past. Cultural Maturity proposes its now familiar answer to such questions—it will and it won't. If the creative dissolving of past amnesias predicted for other more left-hand cultural functions—community, spirituality, our human connection with our bodies and nature, or the experiential world of children—similarly re-enlivens artistic sensibility, art should gain new attention and respect. We should find a reconnecting with the germinal dimensions that give rise to art. But the integrative dynamics that produce culturally mature perspective always also exact a (major) price. They challenge notions that make any one part of the whole distinct or supreme. For art, we would expect that to translate into a surrendering of special status, the death of art with a capital A.

If Cultural Maturity's predictions are accurate, we may well connect with art more deeply in the future—art in all its guises, from the most formal to the most personal or alternative. But at once such connecting should be of a more humble, less mythologized sort. Art in a culturally mature reality becomes an increasingly human enterprise, newly cherished, but at the same time no longer elevated and separate. As part of these changes, we should see the boundaries that separate the artist and the non-artist becoming more permeable. The professional artist should still be highly valued. But, too, we should come to view the artistic—or more precisely, the germinally creative—as something each person appropriately claims (and, as with a muscle group, learns to exercise). We see at once "bridgings" of art and the everyday, and the artist and the non-artist.

We should also see other more aesthetic bridgings. As we have witnessed with performance art over the last half century, art will likely continue its forays across the boundaries of traditional disciplines—linking visual art with theater with music with the written word. We should also encounter further creative links between the artistic work of different cultures—of both the same and different cultural stages. (Digital media should dramatically accelerate both of these integrative processes.) And certainly we will see deeper links between the artistic and the technological as we are already beginning to witness with current explorations in new media.

Temperament-related Patterning in Space observations highlight a further kind of bridging. With increasing frequency, we should find people of artistic temperament contributing outside the formal bounds of art. In times ahead, every profession should have a growing need for people who are good at the new—both comfortable with change and facile with the imaginative capacities needed to envision the possible. If business wants to be more entrepreneurial, it needs more people who are natively skilled at imagining the yet unimagined. And a few more imaginative types might greatly help the CIA stay ahead of the ingenuity of terrorists.

One arts-related Transitional Absurdity has particular relevance to this inquiry. We reasonably ask what art's dominant form is today. The answer: If we define "art" in terms of the sensibilities expression draws on, and define "dominant" in terms of dollars spent, then, hands down, today's dominant art form is advertising.[11]

This answer—at once obvious and unsettling—presents an essential quandary. If art's purpose is to presage, to aesthetically

---

11 Advertising's power derives from its use of the trusted and largely invisible grammar of art—metaphor, image, movement, sound, and feeling. This power can be amplified today by how distanced the average person has become from these languages (and thus both unconscious of their workings and often hungry for their sustenance).

lead, then advertising's ultimate effect is precisely the opposite of art, at least as defined by art's historical mandate. Advertising promotes extreme material values that can no longer serve us. And its purpose, rather than to provide insight and guidance, is to mislead, making it hardly a solution to today's Crisis of Purpose.[12] Advertising's hold on the modern psyche represents a particularly consequential Transitional Absurdity. We know we are being misled, but this does not seem to diminish advertising's effect.[13]

This contradictory picture confronts us with an important follow-up leadership question: What, if we value art—and our well-being more generally—do we best do with advertising's lock on the artistic? The question is particularly relevant to this inquiry, as addressing it at all deeply requires that we venture into the territory of every other domain—besides art, certainly economics and business (advertising is a business pursuit); government (there are public policy implications); education and the media (there could not be a more important media education topic); and both science (we need to ask about the cognitive effects of advertising) and religion (is this not one of the pivotal moral issues of our time?).

---

[12] Classes on advertising teach that one should never say anything logical in an ad—for the simple reason that doing so would encourage people to think and question (and then likely not buy the product). Instead, advertising juxtaposes images of what a person is supposed to buy with images of fulfillment: "Salems are springtime fresh" (this from when tobacco companies were well aware of smoking's health effects); "Coke is it" (as obesity becomes more and more an epidemic). In the end, advertising is a form of lying. Ultimately, advertising promotes our time's most dangerous lie: that consumption in itself brings fulfillment.

[13] This kind of Transitional Absurdity takes a particularly insidious form with advertising directed at children. According to CBS News, in 1983 companies spent $100 million marketing to kids. Today that figure is closer to $17 billion. Somehow we find it acceptable to make the leap from the fact that spending billions on marketing to children is highly profitable to assuming that doing so is moral. It would be better to think of it as a form of culturally sanctioned child abuse.

A person might appropriately argue that the correct answer to the follow-up "what do we do" question should be to do nothing. If the purpose of art is to mirror what most defines culture, then advertising, given these highly material times, is just art doing its job. But if art's purpose is not just to mirror, but to presage, then advertising fundamentally fails at art's task. And it ultimately fails us in a deeper way. I've proposed that what ultimately makes an act moral is the degree to which it supports and furthers life. Art in its dominant guise today not only fails as art, it fails the test of morality.

I've mentioned that I am a strong advocate for media literacy curriculum in schools. The importance of having a more conscious relationship to advertising's influence is a major reason why. Advertising's capacity to inform remains an essential element in the workings of a free market and will continue to be in the future. But becoming more conscious of advertising's effects—and, when necessary, reining in its excesses—will be essential to a psychologically and spiritually healthy future.[14] If, with Cultural Maturity's changes, we can become more conscious of and facile with the languages of aesthetic expression, we should become more capable of such creative management (with regard to both advertising and societal forces more generally).

---

14 Previously I wrote about how device addiction, particularly when combined with the mechanisms of machine learning, could well be the end of us. The fact that the business model behind the workings of our devices is advertising-driven is much of what creates this potentially cataclysmic situation.

CHAPTER TWELVE

Applying Creative Systems Theory Patterning Concepts #4: Ultimate Human Quandaries (New Insights for Timeless Questions)

A particularly striking consequence of Creative Systems Theory's application of a creative frame is that it lets us address questions that in times past have either left us baffled or produced limited, ultimately unhelpful answers. This includes really quite ultimate questions, overarching eternal concerns that we might easily think are beyond the province of mere mortals. My book *Quick and Dirty Answers to the Biggest of Questions* engages this particular implication of CST. Taking time with a few such questions contributes to this inquiry if for no other reason than that the concerns we will look at are themselves fascinating. But doing so also contributes by providing further evidence for both the newness of the kind of thinking CST represents and the significance of that newness.

We've already made a start. With most every chapter, we've touched on topics that at least in limited ways address ultimate concerns. Chapter Three used philosophy's history to address how our conceptions of truth have changed, and by implication, what it is that ultimately makes a conclusion true. With Chapter Three, we also looked at both the nature of time and the question of what, in the end, it means to have a body. Chapter Five provided more encompassing ways to think about human purpose, and with the Myth of the Individual, challenged us to fundamentally rethink the nature of identity. Chapter Six invited us to think in more foundational ways about the nature of human differences. And Chapter Nine probed the meaning of freedom.

This chapter includes three articles that address particularly ultimate concerns. The first takes on the debate between free will and determinism. The second pushes beyond the historically conflicting explanations of science and religion. And the last turns to a particularly ultimate ultimate question: How do we best understand existence as a whole?

How is it that CST is able to help us with such quandaries? That it can is a specific consequence of Cultural Maturity's cognitive reordering and the leap in understanding it produces. In the end, none of the questions we will look at are that complicated. But answering any of them—indeed, just asking them in ultimately useful ways—requires systemic understanding, and systemic understanding of the more dynamic and complete sort that becomes possible only with Integrative Meta-perspective.

The topics I have chosen each in different ways help bring together and fill out previous observations. As with articles I've included in earlier application chapters, I've often chosen to leave passages that repeat ideas that I have previously introduced intact. Again, I do this in part because I consider insights these pieces might provide for the task of teaching and communicating to be as important as the specific content. But I've also done so to support this chapter working as a vehicle for further clarifying how the ideas of CST function as a coherent whole.

Come On Stephen Hawking: The Quandary of Free Will in an Apparently Deterministic Universe

[The following piece is adapted from an article I wrote after watching physicist Stephen Hawking's public television series Genesis. The series took on a variety of intriguing questions, from the possibility of time travel to how as humans we got here. For this chapter's purposes I've excerpted the part of the article where I responded to how Hawking addresses the apparent contradiction between free will and determinism. It provides further support for CST's reframing of the nature and role of conscious awareness that I presented in Chapter Two.]

Physicist Stephen Hawking introduced his recent series on public television with the claim that he will show how ordinary people, just by looking closely, can make sense of ultimate questions. I applaud the effort. Much in the series provided useful information. And I have immense respect for Hawking's contributions to physics. But I have frequently been disappointed. Often, I have found myself responding "Come on, Stephen. You can do better than that."

The series stops short in a couple of ways. First, it is in fact less about how ordinary people can address ultimate questions than about how contemporary physics answers such questions. His participants are led by the hand to reach predetermined conclusions—a common failing with science education.

And there is a second, more fundamental and consequential shortcoming. As often as not, his demonstrations and explanations fail to prove what they claim to illustrate. Frequently, what Hawking's assertions most make clear is that physics to this point, even at its best, is unable to help us with really ultimate concerns. This additional shortcoming is what makes the series pertinent for these reflections.

Here I will specifically address the topic of the second program: the dilemma of "free will." We can miss how deeply the question of free will challenges usual understanding. You would not be reading this article, and I would not have written it, if we did not believe in free will in some form. Yet basic cause and effect, at least as classical science conceives of it, describes a deterministic world. Free will and determinism each seem self-evident. But as we conventionally think of them, they present mutually exclusive realities.

Throughout these reflections, I will expand on a key recognition that ties them together. When Hawking's explanations stop short, they tend to do so for the same basic reason. They reflect machine model thinking. Appreciating what is missing offers valuable insight into how contemporary understanding, even at its best, often stops short. It also sheds valuable light on what a needed next chapter in human understanding asks of us and makes possible.

Free Will and Determinism

Whether our experience of free will can be reconciled with science's picture of a deterministic world presents one of modern understanding's great quandaries. With the second program in Genesis, Hawking claims to have successfully addressed it. But I found his explanation unsatisfying. At best it was unnecessarily complicated. More, I am quite sure it was simply wrong.

Hawking introduced his examination of free will and determinism with the familiar tale of Newton's apple. He notes that Newton's laws of motion give us a deterministic—mechanistic cause-and-effect—universe. He cites Laplace's often-quoted claim that if we knew the position and velocity of every object in the universe, we could predict the whole of future events. He then correctly observes that if Newton's picture is right and complete, free will is necessarily an illusion.

Hawking then describes an experiment from cognitive science that he claims demonstrates this illusion at work. In the experiment, subjects are first wired up to an EEG machine (which measures brain waves). Then a large red button is placed before each subject. The subjects are instructed to hit the button whenever they choose. The results contradict what we might expect. The EEG readings demonstrate that we see evidence of "choice" (in the form of observable brain wave activity) well before the subjects hit the button (consciously make the choice).

I included the word "claims" in the previous paragraph because of how Hawking interprets the results of this experiment. Hawking proposes that the body is "a complex machine" that works according to the deterministic laws of a Newtonian world. From this, he concludes that because the subject's actions were seen first in their bodies (in the EEG recordings), what they experienced as "choice" was in fact predetermined and thus not free will at all. Later I will describe how his conclusions are based on limited—and increasingly outdated—understandings of both the body and the nature of conscious awareness.

Having boxed himself into a corner if he is going to do anything more than side with determinism, Hawking then gives himself some wiggle room. It is good that he does, as it is hard to imagine Hawking making the effort to develop this series—and certainly to live the courageous and creative life that he has—if he did not believe at some level that his choices could alter outcomes.

Hawking describes how modern advances add an important further layer of complexity to classical physics' deterministic picture. Quantum mechanics—which functions at the level of the very small—requires that we include uncertainty in our understanding of the physical universe. (Those who have taken a physics class will remember Schrödinger's cat.) Hawking proposes that we best think of existence as having two layers that work according to wholly different sets of rules: a subatomic world ordered by "random" processes, and our more everyday world that follows the deterministic rules of simple cause and effect.

Because this way of thinking introduces uncertainty into the equation, it at least opens the door to the possibility that we might bridge the before irreconcilable assumptions of free will and determinism. But this two-world explanation only opens the door a crack. And Hawking's next demonstration illustrates that for him it does so in only a trivial way.

The demonstration uses a two-part apparatus to illustrate how Hawking sees the relationship between these two kinds of determination. The lower part of the apparatus contains a radioactive element—a substance that decays according to the indeterminate mechanisms of quantum mechanics. On top is a catapult that launches a projectile on a pre-established (Newtonian) path once its mechanism is triggered. Subatomic particles released from the lower compartment do the triggering. Hawking proposes that this two-step mechanism accurately describes how things in the real world work. Quantum mechanical randomness gets things started. After this, events follow the laws of classical determinism.

The demonstration is fine to a point, but it stops short if our interest is free will. Two recognitions are key to understanding just how. First, as long as we remain in a mechanistic reality, the apparent paradox of free will and determinism is really not addressed. And second, "random" processes, like deterministic process, are fully consistent with a mechanistic worldview. Certainly they tell us nothing about will in any directed sense. Thus while Hawking's apparatus may defy prediction, it again offers little that helps us with the free will/determinism quandary. Hawking's description leaves us with an "explanation" that, while superficially accurate, explains very little.

Hawking concludes by proposing an additional mechanism that he claims puts the free will/determinism question once and for all to rest. It draws on the idea from contemporary physics that there is not just one universe, but an infinite number of parallel universes. Hawking takes this "multiverse" hypothesis as fact. He argues that "Parallel universes are more than a theory. I believe they are inevitable." And he puts it forward as an ultimate explanation for free will. In his words, "Everything does happen, just in another universe."

Again we find an "explanation" that, even if it holds up, fails to address the free will versus determinism paradox in any convincing way. While the notion of an infinite number of universes may prove accurate, in fact there are very good reasons to question it.[1] And even if it does prove accurate, it stops short as explanation. At the least, drawing on the multiverse hypothesis makes for an inordinately complicated way to answer the free will/determinism question. Culturally mature perspective suggests we can address it in ways that are straightforward—even simple.

Free Will, Conscious Awareness, and the Life of the Body

We can begin to grasp the possibility of simpler explanation by returning to the important recognition that Hawking illustrated with his EEG demonstration—how the conscious experience of choice can be a secondary phenomenon. Hawking interprets the outcome of his demonstration to mean choice is a product of deterministic, mechanical processes. In his words: "Brain is made of matter, which must follow the laws of nature. There is no ghost in the machine."

Culturally mature perspective concurs that there is no "ghost" (a reference to some separate subjective counterpart to the body's objective workings[2]). But in agreeing with this assertion, it is not taking sides in the objective versus subjective debate (nor the related science versus religion debate). Similarly, it does not take sides in the free will versus determinism debate. Rather, it argues for the importance of thinking in ways that are more encompassing—more systemic.

I've suggested that Hawking's interpretation of his EEG demonstration reflects limited understandings of both how the body functions and the nature of conscious awareness. The questions raised by a related "thought experiment" help illustrate. Imagine a gifted running back in football making his way down the field, rapidly cutting this way and that. We are confronted with the simple fact that the running back's cuts take place more quickly, and in ways that are more nuanced, than could ever

---

1 Footnote #14 later in this chapter addresses why we legitimately question the "multiverse" hypothesis.

2 As we see, for example, with vitalism.

happen by consciously choosing them one at a time. The conscious aspects of awareness simply aren't built to function that rapidly.

Does this mean, then, that the running back is not choosing? And, more specifically, does it mean that because his body moves before he "chooses" that what we witness is nothing more than mechanical reflex following the rules of a deterministic world? Even if we include Hawking's addition of quantum mechanical randomness, we are left with a less than convincing picture. Are the outcomes of games then predetermined—or, alternatively, perhaps random? Either way, we are left wondering why we would attend a football game—and perhaps feeling a bit duped. I think in fact it is the explanation that is ultimately silly. Clearly in the running back's movements we witness something that is not just vital, but profoundly so.

Culturally mature perspective provides a more conceptually demanding—but also ultimately simpler—interpretation. It starts with the recognition that more sophisticated ways of thinking about the body and about conscious awareness are not just possible, but predicted. I've described how Cultural Maturity's changes involve not just changes in what we think, but fundamental changes in how we think—specific cognitive changes. Integrative Meta-perspective lets us both more fully step back from, and more deeply engage, the whole of our cognitive complexity. We become able to more consciously engage all of intelligence's multiple aspects and do so in more integrated ways.

As far as the body, Integrative Meta-perspective offers an expressly more systemic picture of what it means to be embodied. We come to see the body not as a separate machine, but as an integral part of who we are as dynamic, living—and specifically human—beings. We appreciate how body sensibilities represent one part of intelligence's larger complexity. Is it not obvious that what we so delight in in the running back's movements is "intelligent"?

Culturally mature perspective also alters how we think about conscious awareness. Traditionally we have thought of conscious awareness as who we are. It was captain of the cellular ship. This kind of identification reached an extreme with Modern Age belief. Objective became wholly separate from subjective and gradually assumed the mantle of final truth. With this, individual identity became associated almost wholly with conscious awareness. We are conscious awareness; we have a body.

How deeply this outmoded picture of conscious awareness now fails us has been one of the key contributions of modern psychology and psychiatry. In his classic book, Man and His Symbols, psychiatrist Carl Jung challenged our Modern Age interpretation back in the middle of the last century with these words: "Where there is a will there is a way is the superstition of modern man." He went on to observe that "what we commonly call 'self-knowledge' is a very limited knowledge."[3]

Integrative Meta-perspective makes clear that thinking of free will as free and willful in the unfettered sense implied by our Modern Age picture leaves us short. Indeed, in the end, this now outdated way of thinking translates into but another kind of determinism. It is just that with this kind of determinism it is we who get to do the determining. Cultural Maturity's cognitive reordering presents a more challenging, but also more complete picture. Conscious awareness comes to have a new, at once more humble and ultimately profound role. Rather than determining our actions, it serves as a facilitator and catalyst for intelligence's richly dynamic workings.

Culturally mature perspective's more sophisticated vantage alerts us to the fact that the way we have viewed the free will versus determinism debate in modern times has been a product of a developmentally appropriate, but systemically incomplete view of the world. In the end, it has been based on a falsely framed dichotomy, a juxtaposing of alternative determinisms, neither of which ultimately holds up. Each determinism has served in similar ways to protect us—as polar explanations of every sort do—from life's ultimately rich, but also easily overwhelming uncertainties and complexities. And as with other polarized explanations, today each equally leaves us short.

A Creative Frame

While a basic understanding of Integrative Meta-perspective takes us a long way toward reconciling the apparent contradiction of free will and determinism, CST's more specific formulations take needed insights important steps further. They help us more deeply grasp both why we have seen things as we have and how new ways of understanding may be possible. They also let us think in ways that are more detailed and nuanced.

---

3 Carl Jung, *Man and His Symbols*, Dell, 1968.

CST proposes that what makes us particular, if not unique, as creatures is the audacity of our toolmaking, meaning-making—we could say simply "creative"—capacities. The theory goes on to describe how human intelligence is structured specifically to support and drive these capacities. Conceptually, CST replaces Newton's notion that the universe is a "great machine" with the idea that reality—certainly the reality of human experience—organizes creatively. This more explicitly creative picture provides big-picture perspective for rethinking the free will versus determinism debate. As with all culturally mature interpretations, the implied results are at once more humble and more profound than what we have known.

As far as free will, conscious awareness remains just as amazing—in its creative possibilities in many ways more so—but it is also no longer free and willful in the same unrestrained sense it has been our preference to assume. Certainly freedom in a creative reality does not translate into being able to do whatever we might choose. In a creatively engaged life, both limits and uncertainty play necessary roles. Choice is also always contingent, at least in relationship to its creative time and place. Our freedoms are always exercised within systemic contexts.

What becomes free will's function in this creative picture? At the same time free will becomes not so unfettered, it becomes even more radically significant. Free will serves as an essential catalyst, spark, and point of self-reflection in the creative mechanisms that ultimately make us who we are.

We see related changes on the determinism side of the equation. Traditional determinisms of all sorts stop being cut and dried in the ways we have thought them to be. Causal relationships tend to involve a multiplicity of systemically related factors, frequently more factors than we can begin to keep track of. And more often than not we encounter factors that function beyond our ability to fully anticipate or control. Of particular importance, one of those factors that always intercedes is ourselves. We can't escape—as physics has well demonstrated—that the state of the observer affects the act of observing. Thus limits and uncertainty, again, play necessary roles in what we witness.

Viewed through a creative lens, free will becomes not as free, nor as much ours to direct, as those of an individualistic bent might prefer. And neither is determination as determined as advocates of either a more scientific determinism or the determinisms of religious faith might wish. This more complex picture makes outcomes less readily determined, but the particular way that it does makes the result ultimately more significant. The complexity that we encounter is the generative sort that makes existence vital, and life an option. Such complexity is ordered, deeply, but this is not the order of one thing guaranteeing another. At its best, it is the order of creative possibility. In human life, this creative picture takes particularly explicit expression.

Science and Religion—Toward a Larger Picture (and How Creative Systems Theory Gets Us Very Close)

[*This piece is adapted from an article I wrote following the release of* Quick and Dirty Answers to the Biggest of Questions. *It is pertinent not just to debates about truth, but also to ideological conflicts in the social sphere. In the way it draws together the basic observations that underlie CST, it provides important further support for the theory. If the reader finds the article's perspective helpful, it becomes hard to deny the importance of the ideas that generate it.*]

The conflicting views of science and religion present a particularly intriguing "ultimate question" example. Here most crudely the question asks, Which interpretation is right? The better question might be, How do science and religion relate to one another—if they do at all?

In modern times, starting with Descartes, we've tended to place the material and the spiritual in wholly separate worlds. This is not an entirely unhelpful solution. It has shielded us from perceived contradictions so basic that they have resulted historically in people being burned at the stake. But this is not a solution that can satisfy for long. Descriptions that depend on two mutually exclusive explanations can't ultimately be sufficient.

In *Quick and Dirty Answers to the Biggest of Questions*, I briefly introduced how CST reconciles the conflicting perspectives of science and religion. I described how, when we step back sufficiently, "not only do the material and spiritual relate as aspects of something larger, the specific way they relate reflects dynamics at the heart of what makes us human." I went on to propose that "in spite of how often through history the relationship between science and religion has appeared adversarial, science and religion have all along been engaged in an essential kind of conspiracy."

This article expands on these conclusions and does so with some detail. It fills out the basic observations that produce them. It helps make the different ways we have thought about science and religion through history more understandable. It examines how CST calls into question traditional assumptions of both science and religion. And it offers a glimpse of what may lie ahead.

The "Procreative" Structure of Human Cognition

CST proposes that our ideas about science and religion at any point in time (like our ideas about most anything at a point in time) are as much products of how we understand as what is "out there" to understand. From CST's overarching vantage, science and religion are best thought of not as conflicting truths, but as "ways of knowing," each of which through history has contributed in important ways.

To appreciate this perspective, it helps first to examine how CST expands our understanding of cognition. CST proposes that what makes us unusual if not unique as creatures is the complexity of our toolmaking— "creative"—capacities. It goes on to describe how human cognition is structured specifically to support these capacities.

To get to this conclusion and give it detail I most often draw on one of two kinds of observations—the role of polarity in how we think, and the workings of intelligence's multiple aspects. In different ways each observation highlights the underlying "creative" mechanism of human understanding. Each also provides key insights for addressing the science/religion question.

Let's look first at the role of polarity. Throughout history we humans have thought in polar terms. We've juxtaposed masculine with feminine, humankind with nature, mind with body, and more. We've tended also to put sacred and secular in separate worlds. We've done this as if perceived polarities were opposites without giving much thought to whether they actually are.

CST offers a more encompassing picture. It describes how polarized, separate-worlds thinking is a product of how human understanding up until now has appropriately and predictably worked. It delineates how we can understand past perceived either/ors to be complementary aspects of larger systemic realities. And it highlights how the ability to get our minds around past polar assumptions is a key characteristic of the new more systemic kinds of thought on which our future depends.

Culturally mature understanding is a product not just of new ideas, but of specific cognitive changes that lets us at once step back from, and more deeply engage, cognition's complex workings—what CST calls Integrative Meta-perspective. One consequence of this more sophisticated vantage is that we are able to get beyond the sort of thinking that in times past has set one polar conclusion in opposition to another.

A provocative polarity-related observation is key to addressing how the thinking of science and religion could come together in a larger picture. Underlying any particular polar juxtaposition we find a single more fundamental polarity: difference/multiplicity on one hand juxtaposed with connectedness/oneness on the other. We tend to think of oneness not as half of a polarity but as reconciling/healing polar differences. But in fact when we identify with oneness we are quite specifically taking sides.

Other ways of talking about polarity support this observation. With any polar juxtaposition we find an underlying symmetry. In some way polarities contrast a "harder" quality with something "softer" and more permeable.

Drawing on more psychological language, we can think of polarities as juxtaposing more right-hand, archetypally masculine characteristics with qualities of a more left-hand, archetypally feminine sort. Framed creatively, the two sides of polarity are not just different, they work together to support and drive new insights and change. The gender-infused language I just used hints at this larger relationship. Polarity's more archetypally masculine and archetypally feminine right and left hands, while they may sometimes appear at odds (and at times necessarily function as if they are), juxtapose in ways that are, in the end, "procreative."

CST's conclusion with regard to science and religion at its simplest can be described in terms of this basic right-hand/left-hand creative relationship. Framed creatively, science and religion are reflections of these complementary "harder" and "softer" polar proclivities expressed as extremes and at the largest of systemic scales. They are what we see when we view the world through the lenses of these contrasting/complementing aspects of cognition's creative workings. Science is about collective right-hand, archetypally masculine experience—the "difference/multiplicity" half of ultimate polarity—in its purest manifestation. Religion is about collective left-hand, archetypally feminine sensibility—ultimate polarity's complementary "connectedness/oneness" dimension—similarly cleansed of contamination by the right.

A closer look at the contrasting contributions of science and religion supports this interpretation. Science is about distinction—this as opposed to that. Biology delineates the creaturely into taxonomies of genus and species, chemistry gives us the periodic table and the interplay of atoms and molecules, and classical physics describes objects of differing mass and the this-versus-that laws of material cause and effect.

Spiritual/religious experience, in contrast, highlights oneness. We can think of religious belief through history in terms of four connectedness-related themes: how things arose from the undivided ("in the beginning"), community (congregation and communion), right thought and behavior (shared moral assumptions), and how experiences interrelate (and, in the end, how it all interrelates). In Latin, *re-ligare*, the root of the word "religion," means "to connect." William James put it this way: "In mystic states we both become one with the Absolute and we become aware of our oneness."

Framed in terms of polarity, science and religion reflect how the world looks when viewed through the lens of creative polarity at its most fundamental. Integrative Meta-perspective offers that we might see a larger picture. It also offers that we might entertain more dynamic and complete understandings of each.

Intelligence's new picture adds further substance and nuance to this creative picture. Key to culturally mature perspective's more dynamic and encompassing picture is the recognition that intelligence is multiple. We are not just rational beings. More emotional, imaginal, and body-derived aspects of intelligence play essential roles in making us who we are.

Descartes's Modern Age picture not only placed polarities in separate worlds, it also placed intelligences in separate categories. Rationality came to stand distinct, idealized as the basis of final, "objective" understanding. The remaining aspects of intelligence were then lumped together in a secondary world of "subjective" experience. While this act cleaved us from ourselves, in its time it served an essential purpose. It took us beyond the strangling constraints of medieval mysticism. But as with what I observed earlier for polarity, such separate-worlds thinking can't work as an ultimate solution.

Cultural Maturity's cognitive reordering again offers a more encompassing vantage. Integrative Meta-perspective lets us get our minds around intelligence's multiplicity. The implications are intriguing, and also critical and timely. Essential challenges ahead for the species will demand that we be not just intelligent, but also wise. To be wise in the sense needed requires the ability to draw consciously, and in a newly possible, more integrated fashion, on the whole of our cognitive complexity. We also find that applying a more complete picture of intelligence alters the conclusions we reach in particular realms of understanding—including those of science and religion.

Understanding how all of this might be so brings us back to CST's claim that human cognition is structured to support our creative capacities. Different aspects of intelligence manifest in critical and predictable ways over the course of any human formative process. This includes the evolution of culture. CST brings detailed understanding to how our multiple intelligences have worked together to drive the evolution of human values and human understanding. It also highlights how human understanding in times ahead must draw on a more complete, more fully systemic picture of intelligence.

We can tie intelligence's new picture directly to the contributions of science and religion. Historically, the most creatively manifest aspect of intelligence—the rational—has given us the more material and mechanistic sensibilities that inform the worlds of science and engineering. Science is not just rational in some "coldly objective" sense. Every good scientist appreciates the "spirit of science" and the awe and wonder of the world it reveals. But at least within classical science, the world is assumed to be rationally understandable. In contrast, spiritual/religious experience draws on the more creatively germinal aspects of intelligence—in particular, animistic sensibilities, the more magical/intuitive sensitivities of the imaginal, and emotional intelligence. CST delineates how we can understand specific beliefs in terms of the various ways in which these more germinal sensibilities manifest in different times and places. Integrative Meta-perspective, in offering that we might more consciously engage the whole of intelligence's generative multiplicity, reveals the possibility of a more encompassing, and ultimately creative picture for science and religion.

Science, Religion, and the Evolution of Narrative

Along with providing insight into how the beliefs of science and religion might ultimately relate, a creative frame also helps put their relationship in larger historical perspective. A first way it does turns to the stories we tell, to the nature and purpose of human narrative. A second way involves insights that bring detail to how beliefs have evolved through time. It also has essential implications for how belief might continue to evolve in the future.

The topic of narrative highlights how we can think of science and religion as history's two great "creation story" storytelling traditions. All cultures have their tales about how existence originally came into being. And most too include ways of accounting for key events that followed—such as the amazing and mysterious emergence of the world's creatures and also of ourselves, this creature who not only creates, but is conscious in doing so. We can think of all of history's great encompassing stories as versions of this story—told in ways appropriate to their time, place, and perspective. Past stories have taken the forms they have in part because of each time's practical circumstances (for example, the invention of the telescope resulted in a dramatic challenge to past belief), but even more they have taken the forms that they have because of the internal vantages from which they have been told. Our early animistic and much later Enlightenment interpretations were different not just because of what we knew, but because of how we knew.

A creative interpretation of the science/religion debate proposes that these two narrative traditions have also taken the forms they have because of the developmentally specific sensibilities that at different times have ordered our worldviews. Science has observed creation's story from a more right-hand vantage, from the perspective of the more difference-emphasizing aspects of intelligence. Religious/spiritual traditions simultaneously observed creation's story from a complementary more left-hand creative vantage and from the perspective of the more connectedness-affirming aspects of intelligence.

Applying a creative frame to the task of more detailed discernment helps us make sense of the various, often very different ways we have conceived of science and religion through time. Just how it does provides important support for the accuracy of a creative interpretation. It also provides essential perspective for addressing what may lie ahead. CST's approach starts with the recognition that human developmental processes of all sorts organize creatively—and not just personal change processes, but also societal change. We can use this progression to map the stories of science and religion through time. CST describes how the kinds of stories scientific and spiritual belief have drawn on (from animistic to the humanistic and rationalistic), the kinds of imagery they have referenced (from the creaturely, to the magical and mythic, to a world pictured as separate and objective), and the general kinds of behaviors that they imply are societally appropriate and morally acceptable can each be understood to follow predictably from how more right-hand and more left-hand sensibilities manifest with each of culture's creative stages.

We see this creatively ordered progression in science's evolution from the nature-centered beliefs of tribal times, to more philosophically idealist sorts of understanding (as with Aristotle's notion of an "unmoved mover"), to views in the Middle Ages that postulated mystically infused forces (as with alchemy), to the scientific method and its formalization with Modern Age understanding. Similarly we see it with religion's evolution from animism, to polytheism, to absolutist monotheism, to the more liberal monotheism of the Reformation.[4]

Along with helping us make sense of how (and why) the particular beliefs of science and religion have evolved as they have, CST's developmental formulations also help us understand how their relationship has evolved through time. Here two further observations become important. The first concerns which "creative hand" at a particular time has the most prominent influence. A consistent trend runs through history's evolutionary story. Culture's larger creative narrative has progressed

---

4 This chronicling of religious forms refers to the West. The more reflective sensibilities of the East have often resulted in stages manifesting in ways that can feel more philosophical or even psychological. I place the nature-centered contemplations of Taoism early on in this progression, and the more mythic beliefs of Hinduism and Buddhism's more specifically meditative worldview, somewhat later. Beliefs emphasizing strong social authority, such as Confucianism, happened developmentally in parallel with early monotheism in the West. More modern sensibilities have only come with the last century in the East.

from a time of archetypally feminine dominance in our tribal beginnings toward today when archetypally masculine proclivities hold the much larger sway. As we would predict from this progression, we see a parallel evolution over time from realities defined almost wholly in spiritual terms with animistic beliefs, toward what we find in our time, a world in which many people hold strong religious beliefs, but in which more material values (scientific, but even more than this, economic) ultimately have greater influence.

The second observation concerns the different ways that the relationship between science's more archetypally masculine and religion's more archetypally feminine worlds have been experienced. The sequence of juxtapositions we discover is just what we would expect to find if the relationship between science and religion is ultimately creative. In early societies, material and spiritual sensibilities tended to be spoken of almost as one. Later, as in much of the European Middle Ages, material and spiritual inclinations more often took expression in ways that were explicitly at odds. Later still, as with Cartesian dualism, science and religion more comfortably coexisted, but accomplished the feat by, in effect, ignoring each other's presence. Creative polarities go through just this sequence of relationships with any kind of human formative process.

Critical to this evolutionary picture—and to the observations in this article being possible—what a creative interpretation predicts does not stop there. Cultural Maturity's changes produce a necessary next step in this evolving story, and with it a whole new kind of narrative. Integrative Meta-perspective lets us step back and celebrate a now more dynamic and encompassing story, one in which science and religion, however irreconcilable their conclusions have often seemed, have all along been working together to support and drive culture's creative manifestation.

For this result to fully make sense, we need to appreciate just how fundamentally Cultural Maturity's cognitive changes alter understanding. The simple image of a box of crayons helps get at what is new and its radical implications. The crayons represent different aspects of understanding (this could be polar aspects, contrasting intelligences, or equally well domains of understanding, such as science and religion). The box represents Integrative Meta-perspective—the ability to stand back and get our minds around systemic complexity.

Historically, scientists have tended to make science the last word—act as if it were the encompassing box. Those of more religious bent have tended to do the same for the spiritual. What we see with culturally mature perspective is wholly different. The truths of science and of religion in each case become crayons. With science our interest lies with crayons that represent experience at its most bold and explicit. With religion we find crayons that help us depict and connect with the inner "essences" of things, the easily hidden inklings that give rise to spiritual experience. Rather than the encompassing box, instead each represents an aspect of truth's larger creative picture.

A couple of essential consequences follow from this whole-box-of-crayons picture. The first comes back to the relationship of these two realms of experience. We might assume that in going forward we would simply stop thinking of them as separate—and in a basic sense that is true. But what we find is very different from either some simple merging together or compromise, some meeting halfway. Our box-of-crayons image helps clarify this important distinction. If compromise was the task, the resolution of opposing hues would give us only muddy brown. In contrast, culturally mature perspective gives us the ability to hold the whole box with its vibrant multiplicity of hues—and an essential new chapter in our evolution as creative beings.

The second consequence concerns how new formulations in science and religion each themselves becomes newly systemic, in the sense of at least acknowledging the validity of both more left-hand and more right-hand aspects of understanding. With Cultural Maturity's cognitive changes, both science and religion should manifest in ways that are more dynamic and embracing than we have known before. While in each case this will require a stretch, it will be necessary if science and religion in times ahead are to reflect human understanding at its most complete. It will also be necessary if science and religion are to effectively contribute to the maturity of perspective that will be essential if, as a species, we are to make wise decisions going forward.

Culturally Mature Perspective's Challenge to Science

A person could imagine that because this new picture requires us to step beyond thinking of either science or religion as final truths, it would leave our experience of these historically exalted realms diminished. In fact, it does almost the opposite. In times ahead, we should find ourselves better able to see science and religion as aspects of a larger story. We should also find ourselves more cognizant of the unique contributions that each has made to that story. And we should find ourselves able to think about both science and religion with a sophistication and nuance that has not been an option in times past.

That said, Integrative Meta-perspective doesn't let either science or religion off easily. Appreciating the challenge it presents to each of them provides intriguing hints about where our understanding might go in the future. Thinking very far beyond our present view is difficult no matter how culturally mature our vantage, but examining how the traditional beliefs of both science and religion are necessarily challenged helps get us started in the most useful directions.

Beginning with science, we appropriately first ask just what defines science and its contribution—address what CST would call science's Question of Referent. Modern science combines a particular kind of methodology with specific assumptions about the nature of truth. The scientific method involves experimentation and the generation of repeatable, measurable evidence. And scientific thinking is rational, having its origins in logical inquiry and the application of mathematical principles.

Culturally mature perspective confronts classical science in two key ways. First, it challenges the common conclusion that science can explain anything if pursued far enough. Given the larger context of Modern Age belief, it is not unreasonable that many people have assumed that with time science's approach could be applied to understanding as a whole. Cultural Maturity brings the notion that science's method works for everything immediately into question. Seen from a culturally mature perspective, science becomes a kind of tool that is great for some tasks and of limited help for others.

This recognition has particular pertinence for our time. The contributions of science today could not be more amazing. But we need only think about how little scientific observation as we have known it can tell us about many of the most important things in our lives—love, meaning, creativity, and much more (including, ultimately, the fact of life itself)—to recognize inherent limits to the approach. CST's recognition that intelligence is multiple and that rationality represents only one aspect of our full cognitive complexity makes such limitations explicit. That everything is rationally intelligible becomes at best a "faith claim," and in the end a faith claim that does not well hold up. Like it or not, an approach can't be thought of as complete and all-encompassing if it draws on only limited aspects of who we are. And certainly it will stop short if challenges require that we think more systemically, as is so often the case with tasks we face today. The better observation is that science's method is great for those aspects of reality that are in fact materially measurable and rationally intelligible. Put another way, science is great in most instances for teasing apart the difference/multiplicity aspects of experience. For this, we rightly celebrate its considerable power.

The second way that Cultural Maturity confronts classical science is by bringing into question its mechanistic and objectivist foundations. Integrative Meta-perspective makes clear that not only does mechanistic thinking fail when it comes to explaining everything, it ultimately stops short, too, when it comes to the difference/multiplicity side of things that has traditionally been science's purview. (Note the phrase "in most instances" in the preceding paragraph.) CST argues for the importance of a more explicitly systemic science, and systemic not just in the sense of better including all the mechanistically related pieces (like a car is a system), but systemic in the creative sense that acknowledges deep connectedness as much as it does difference and distinction.

The modern scientific world has made the materially understandable primary. And in the minds of many thinkers, it has made the mechanistic and objective all there is. Beliefs that reduce to a narrow "scientism"—that make it all about physical interaction—have recently often been celebrated. Where this is the case, the implications for the science/religion debate are clear and final. Popular advocates of such beliefs (Richard Dawkins being the most widely known[5]) tend to reach explicitly atheistic conclusions.

But the best theorists in even the hardest of the sciences today view such conclusions as simplistic and out of date. Over the last century a recognition of systemic interconnections has more and more come to shape the cutting edge of scientific understanding, from the linking of

---

5   Richard Dawkins, *The God Delusion*, Transworld Publishers, 2006.

matter and energy in physics, to ecological perspectives in biology, to psychology's bringing together of conscious and unconscious.

It is worth noting that the absolute cleaving of science and religion is historically quite new (and the absolute dismissing of religion much more so). Aristotle's "unmoved mover" was in effect a soul guiding the world of things. And Isaac Newton was a deeply religious man (as were most all scientists of his time). This observation is not at all to suggest that the task is somehow to go back to the thinking of times past. If what we need is the more fully systemic kind of understanding suggested by the concept of Cultural Maturity, none of these previous views can be sufficient for the tasks ahead. I offer the observation simply to highlight how the more extreme views often found today are specific to our time and not universal.

With science's emerging picture, connectedness—and connectedness of a deep sort (not just that of mechanical interrelationships)—is specifically affirmed. But rather than some separate dualistic force, connectedness now becomes an inherent property of existence at all levels. It becomes intrinsic to a more vital and dynamic picture of what it means to be alive, of what it means to be human, and ultimately of existence as a whole. We are just beginning to appreciate what all this might mean. But it promises an increasingly provocative and vital kind of science in times to come.[6]

Culturally Mature Perspective's Challenge to Religion

Spirituality/religion and its ways of knowing present us with two different sorts of questions. The first is most familiar: Does God—or however we think of ultimate spiritual/religious authority—exist? Later I will come back to how Cultural Maturity's challenge to understand authority in ways that leave behind the parental imagery of times past might alter how we conceive of such authority. But culturally mature perspective is limited in what more it can say with regard to this kind of question.

Or at least it is limited if we restrict ourselves to how we have traditionally framed the question. CST helps us go a bit further. It suggests that the standard "Is God real" question is really the wrong question.

---

6 The next article in this chapter expands on this more encompassing picture.

A person reading about how CST frames spirituality and religion could conclude that I am making an argument for atheism. But in fact I find atheism as a concept rather silly. This is not because CST answers the God question, but rather because the question as framed can only end up in endless circular debate.

In the end, atheism as an argument fails to be useful because it leaves the evolutionary dimension out of understanding. If I argued, indeed became obsessed with arguing, that the ancient Greeks were wrong for believing there were gods atop Olympus, or that tribal societies have been wrong for having animistic deities, you would appropriately conclude that I had missed the point. While these kinds of beliefs tend not to work today, in their time they gave expression to an important kind of need, and more deeply, an essential aspect of human sensibility. While the common claim of the atheist that the more modern idea of a monotheistic God with a capital "G" has resulted in harm as well as benefit is accurate, CST proposes that the larger portion of that harm, while it may have been done in the name of religion, has been a product of our past need for worlds of us-versus-them, rather than religion *per se*. And while the atheist's observation that religion makes little sense rationally and can lead to some assertions that are really quite absurd similarly has merit, in the end it fails to get at what is important. Religion through time has given expression to essential aspects of being human, aspects that are just as important in our time, and arguably now more important than ever. CST proposes that religion as we have known it in modern times is best thought of not in terms of the rightness or wrongness of its assertions, but as one chapter in an evolving story.[7]

The second sort of question that spiritual/religious experience and its ways of knowing present concerns the nature of that story, how it has contributed through history and how that contribution may now be changing. As with science, we want to answer religion's Question of Referent. And we want to understand more about how it can be addressed. With this second sort of question, CST and the concept of

---

7 The argument for atheism certainly sells books, but I suspect the explanation has less to do with the power of the idea than that the absoluteness of atheism's conclusions means that it is essentially a form of fundamentalism—and one all too ready to do battle with polar opposite beliefs.

Cultural Maturity have a great deal to tell us, and this article has taken a start at answering it.

It is important to appreciate that the simple notion that there is a Question of Referent to ask about by itself challenges traditional assumptions. Conventionally, religious truth is God's word (or the word of Allah, the utterance of a polytheistic pantheon, the inclinations of a collection of animistic forces, or whatever) and that is that. No larger perspective is needed—or desired. Here I've framed religious experience's ultimate purpose creatively. CST proposes that we can think of our diverse interpretations of the spiritual dimension as time- and space-specific expressions of the far extreme of archetypally feminine, left-hand sensibility as it manifests at a cultural scale.

We must be careful with such reframing not to just psychologize the sacred, a negation of the spiritual of which the social sciences have often rightfully been accused. The spiritual as understood in CST's interpretation represents more than just projection from within ourselves (though the images we attach to our beliefs may be just that). Rather, it marks our felt connection with every aspect of creative context—the personal, interpersonal, and cultural, certainly, and, at least metaphorically, also the biological, and the cosmos as a whole.

To fully make sense of how a creative interpretation provides perspective not just for understanding religion's role and appreciating its past, but also for making sense of current circumstances and conjecturing about religion's future, we need to appreciate a quandary that the historical picture I've documented in this book presents for the spiritual dimension. I've described how the influence of right-hand sensibilities has increased over the course of history while that of left-hand sensibilities has gradually decreased. CST predicts that, in our time, the influence of ways of thinking that draw at all deeply on the archetypally feminine would be largely eclipsed. CST calls this the Dilemma of Trajectory. The Dilemma of Trajectory presents religion with a circumstance shared with other more left-hand social functions such as art. It might seem to suggest that spiritual/religious experience has run its course.

Certainly if this direction were to continue unmodified, it would not bode well for things spiritual. We would appropriately pronounce God dead. Respected thinkers through the last century and earlier have argued just that, and not just thinkers from science, but also those of a more philosophical sort. Friedrich Nietzsche proposed that, "A casual stroll through the lunatic asylum shows that faith does not prove anything."[8] Noting religion's role in world conflict, Bertrand Russell argued good riddance to any notion of divine causation: "[If life has] deliberate purpose, the purpose must have been that of a fiend. For my part, I find accident a less painful and more plausible hypothesis."[9]

Integrative Meta-perspective suggests a different result going forward. It makes clear that the underlying sensibilities of religious/spiritual experience are inherent in who we are—they can't really be lost. Truth's left hand is necessary for anything creative. It also suggests that the contribution of spirituality's root experience should in fact grow in times ahead. With mature systemic understanding, the difference and connectedness aspects of truth are recognized as making equally important contributions.

This way of thinking about the fate of left-hand sensibility in times to come has critical implications not just for how we think about religion's future, but also for our future human well-being. I've described spiritual/religious experience in terms of four connectedness-related themes. Without them manifesting in some form in times to come, the likelihood that the species will make wise choices going forward becomes very small. We will need to expand how we hold these themes—for example, our connections in community must manifest as a new and deeper appreciation not just for people similar to ourselves, but also for our shared humanity—but we need what each theme points toward if our future is to be healthy, and perhaps simply survivable.

For people who identify strongly with religious belief, this picture presents reason to celebrate. If the concept of Cultural Maturity accurately describes today's fundamental challenge, in the future the sacred should manifest with even greater significance than in times past. But the concept of Cultural Maturity does not at all let religion off unscathed. The price for this renewal is high—extremely so. The doorway

---

8 Friedrich Nietzsche, *The Antichrist*, Alfred A. Knopf, 1924.

9 Bertrand Russell, *Why I Am Not a Christian*, George Allan & Unwin, 1927. Note that this kind of conclusion is what one would predict with the dynamics of Transition.

CREATIVE SYSTEMS THEORY

to this deepened spirituality can open only to the degree to which we are willing to reexamine much in the very foundations of belief.

Certainly the concept of Cultural Maturity brings into question culturally specific notions of the sacred. It argues that life in the future will be most unhappy if we cannot transcend differences of belief. This is especially the case where beliefs make one religion true and all others false (as through history they always have). Such beliefs are not compatible with life in a globally interconnected world.

Religion also comes up against Cultural Maturity's challenge to truth's past parental/mythologized status. Inherently that challenge includes spiritual truth. Whether manifest in the more maternal imagery of animism and mysticism or in the sterner and more philosophical images of patriarchal religious structures, the incarnate forms of sacred authority have served as mythic protectors, shielding us like children from the all-too-easily-overwhelming complexities and ambiguities of mortal life. Cultural Maturity's changes call into question the value of this kind of protection. Integrative Meta-perspective repeats the Reformation's call for responsibility in a further, quite ultimate way.

There is also an arguably more fundamental kind of dislocation, one that for many people is ultimately even more disturbing. I pointed toward it earlier in drawing on the box-of-crayons metaphor. Culturally mature systemic perspective challenges the notion that spirituality lies at truth's center (as it does for scientific truth and the truths of any other approach to knowing—but for many people that it might for religion can feel particularly disorienting). Drawing on the box-of-crayons metaphor, the kind of experience that through history we've described in spiritual/religious language becomes one crayon in the systemic box—very much an essential crayon, but only one of many we must draw on. Integrative Meta-Perspective views spiritual experience as an important aspect of truth, but only that, an aspect. If we make the spiritual some last word today, it not only fails as truth we can rely on, ultimately it fails as spiritual truth—which to be the real thing must honor the particular truth challenges of its time.[10]

---

10 Parts Work provides a more hands-on way to represent (and reach) this conclusion, both for religion and for science. A simple, though easily at first startling, recognition becomes pivotal if a person doing Parts Work

For our time, CST predicts something very similar to what we witness today—an often conflicting mixture of doubt, dogmatism, and fresh, if often misguided, curiosity. Rarely is the result wholly satisfying. Many people find themselves deeply questioning religion, at least as conventionally conceived. Some of their concerns are fairly immediate—for example, the sexual and financial transgressions of church leadership that grace the pages of our morning newspapers—but their doubts can also be more basic. Other people find reassurance in a regressive return to absolutist beliefs. The fact that past beliefs are being questioned can be interpreted as evidence that we need to adhere to them ever more strongly. And others still turn to what they believe to be new kinds of beliefs that in fact are rarely new at all.

Culturally mature perspective can't tell us just what spirituality in times ahead will look like. It does propose that each of these responses leaves us ultimately short of where we need to go. What it does say is that whatever we find, it should require that we think about the role of connectedness in ways that are fundamentally new—more complex

---

wishes to engage issues that relate specifically to religion or science. Within our systemic complexity, religious and scientific belief each represent parts. Neither the truths of religion nor those of science appropriately occupy the Whole-Person chair. The chairs that advocate for more spiritual and material sensibilities each have much to contribute to the Whole-Person/Whole-System chair's reflections. But they are at best consultants. A person doing Parts Work quickly appreciates that when they miss this essential fact, ultimately unhelpful—indeed dangerous—conclusions result.

Parts Work's third cardinal rule—that parts don't get to talk to parts—provides further valuable insight when it comes to the contributions of religion and science. In addition to learning that neither the religion chair nor the science chair gets to sit in the Whole-Person/Whole-System chair, the person also learns to recognize how "crosstalk" between the religion and science chairs similarly gets one in trouble. This kind of internal debate had a function in times past. Indeed, we can understand each of history's previous views of how the spiritual and the material relate in terms of it. Such direct conversation between parts gave us the easy complementarities of more magical thought (as with yin and yang in classical Chinese belief), the warring absolutes of medieval dogmatisms, and the separated-worlds assumptions of Cartesian dualism. But CST argues that it only makes us less going forward.

and more complete. Culturally mature perspective's more whole-box-of-crayons picture challenges us to understand the sacred in ways that are more fully systemic, and systemic in ways not conceivable from within the worldviews of times past.

Actually, we can say a bit more about what getting there asks of us— which is a good thing given that the previous paragraph might suggest something terribly complicated. As tends to be the case with Cultural Maturity's cognitive changes, we can think of the task as at once more radical and more straightforward and ordinary than what we have known. Framing the task in terms of the receptive makes at least a good place to start. We need to engage experience as receptively and deeply as possible in all parts of our lives—in our relationships with friends, when in nature, in self-reflection, in how we relate to our own bodies, in how we engage the larger world around us. Receptivity opens us to all of experience, but in particular it provides a direct doorway to the experience of connectedness. (Prayer and meditation still work too. Think of them as timeless ways to engage deeply and receptively.) This simple task is of no small significance given the Dilemma of Trajectory. So much of life today is lived on the surface—from consumerism, to pop culture, to social media. To become a spiritual person in any deep sense in our time becomes a radical act. If the concept of Cultural Maturity is correct, it also inherently takes us into new territories of experience.

In Summary

Given the multiple ways this article has come at the science/religion question, a brief summary is warranted. In modern times we've tended to think of science and religion as separate, competing realities. We've also elevated and mythologized the conclusions of science and religion—made them ultimate truths. Culturally mature perspective suggests a more encompassing and less idealized picture that challenges past assumptions of both science and religion and invites us to understand each of them in more dynamic and complete ways. CST goes on to add detail to this more encompassing picture. The theory proposes that beliefs of a material and spiritual sort are inherent products of human cognition's creative workings. From CST's overarching vantage, the conclusions of science and religion through time become contrasting ways the world has looked when viewed through the lenses of polarity at its most fundamental and intelligence's multiple aspects. The theory invites us to appreciate how science and religion have all along been essential parts of a larger story, one that is more encompassing, and also more deeply reflective of understanding's—and life's—rich vitality and complexity.

The "Big Band Theory":
Creative Systems Theory Takes on Existence as a Whole

[This last piece is also adapted from an article I wrote following the release of Quick and Dirty Answers to the Biggest of Questions. *It addresses arguably the most ultimate of ultimate questions: Existence as a whole and our place in the larger scheme of things. It expands on the previous article's emerging picture of science (and also, in a sense, of religion). It also draws on reflections from Chapter One on the nature of systems and how CST adds to systems understanding. While it extends beyond the formal thinking of CST, it provides an addition to this chapter's big-picture reflections that at least provokes further thought.]*

How do we best think about the whole shebang, existence in its entirety? Here CST might not immediately seem terribly pertinent. Its contribution lies with the human dimension, with who we are and how we understand. But in fact just that is what makes it relevant. Understanding our conclusions about existence as a whole necessarily starts with understanding the cognitive lenses through which we make sense of it.

We can't in the end know for sure what is "out there." Indeed, as philosophers are quick to tell us, we can't even be sure that there is an "out there" to know. But there is a lot we can say about understanding and understanding's evolution. CST addresses why through history we have thought not just about ourselves, but also about the physical and the biological, in the specific ways that we have. And of particular importance for these reflections, it proposes that there is a lot we can say about how understanding today is changing.

Why did Descartes see a clockworks universe? And why, before that, did people in the Middle Ages see a universe ordered by religious/moral principles? What they understood reflected how they understood. And today that evolution continues. Descartes's clockworks picture of the universe is more and more often proving insufficient. CST helps us make sense of why, what may lie ahead, and also why the world as we are beginning to see it has the characteristics that it does.

CST proposes that we can understand changes over the last century in how we conceive of existence as a whole in terms of the cognitive reordering that today accompanies Cultural Maturity's new chapter in culture's story. Integrative Meta-perspective, in bringing a more encompassing and complete vantage to understanding, replaces Age of Reason formulations in which truth reduced to rationality and simple cause-and-effect relationships with ways of thinking that are more systemic and also more dynamic. It reveals a world that is more complexly interwoven and often contradictory-seeming than what we have known. It is also a world in which change, and often change of a generative/evolutionary sort, becomes inherent to how things work, and in which uncertainty plays a key role.

We could say it is a world that is more "creative," but when we apply the word "creative" to existence as a whole we need to take particular care. We've tended historically to make existence a mirror of how we have thought—as we witnessed with the Age of Reason's rationalistic lens. If we are not careful, we can fall prey to a related trap and make the whole of existence creative in the same sense we are as humans. Fortunately culturally mature perspective and a creative frame can provide help here too. Integrative Meta-perspective's overarching vantage helps us better distinguish ourselves from what we wish to understand. It also helps us appreciate not just the rich interconnections and often provocative generativities of existence as a whole, but also essential differences in ways that various aspects of existence may be "creative."

Just for fun, we could call the encompassing picture that results the "Big Band Theory" of existence. I don't consider it a part of Creative Systems Theory, rather more a thought experiment that follows from CST's conclusions. It invites us to reflect on what existence as a whole might look like when viewed through a creative lens.

Polarity, Integrative Meta-perspective, and a Creative Frame

I've emphasized how a defining characteristic of needed new ways of understanding is that they leave behind the polarized assumptions of times past. A couple overarching polarity-related observations help with this big-picture reframing task. The first relates to how it has been our tendency in times past to divide not just particular beliefs, but also existence as a whole, into polar worlds. We've done this in different ways depending on when in history we look. We've also done it in different ways depending on whether our basic inclinations tend more toward the material/scientific or spiritual/religious side of things. In modern times, science has tended to divide existence into animate and inanimate, lumping ourselves together with the creaturely and setting this in contrast to a "dead" world of rocks and rivers. Religion has tended more to place the human species separate, make us in some way "chosen" with dominion over the rest of creation. With Cultural Maturity's cognitive changes, we would expect that we might begin to think about existence in its entirety more as a whole—more systemically. It is something we are beginning to see.

The second overarching polarity-related observation concerns change and just how it happens. Every cultural period has had its creation stories, explanations for how what we see around us came to exist. For the Dogan tribe of Mali it is the tale of how Amma broke the Egg of the World. In the creation story of the ancient Mayans as told in the *Popol Vuh*, multiple deities came together to bring existence into being. Christianity has its Hebrew Genesis. Modern science has its Big Bang. In addition, every cultural period has had its explanations for why things work as they do day to day—both why things change and why too they are as stable as they often are—from the whims of gods to Descartes's image of a clockworks universe.

Past explanations with regard to change have also been polar. They've posited some separate driving impetus, be it in earliest times an animistic force, or with modern, more mechanistic thinking, an action with its equal and opposite reaction. Ideas about change too are changing. Increasingly we find thinking that makes change and stability together aspects of larger ways of understanding. Dualistic formulations—both of the extreme type that posits a separate animating force and of the more mundane sort that juxtaposes separate causes and effects—are giving way to more encompassing and dynamic ways of thinking. And often dynamic refers not just to having more moving parts, but to being somehow generative. Change and the coherence through which we identify something as having existence become parts of a single larger, "self-organizing" picture.

CREATIVE SYSTEMS THEORY

These two overarching, polarity-related observations taken together help bring a more systemically conceived picture into focus. Wherever we look, when we leave behind past dualistic assumptions and polar projections, we find ourselves thinking in terms of complex interconnections, dynamic change processes, and the necessary role of uncertainty. As part of this expansion of perspective, we better appreciate existence as a whole as interrelated. We also begin to better appreciate the unique ways that various layers/levels [11] of existence give this more "creative" picture expression.

It suffices for our purposes to keep things simple and talk in terms of the three levels that everyday thought suggests: there is inanimate creation; there is life; and there is this odd addition, conscious life (including ourselves and to lesser degrees other higher life forms). Seen through the lens of culturally mature perspective, these layers/levels become fundamentally linked—aspects of an encompassing whole—and also unique manifestations of existence's generativity.

Limited to how we commonly think, we could find this at once more coherent and more multi-layered outcome confusing. More conventionally, ideas that highlight connectedness and ideas that delineate difference work as opposites. But this kind of result is almost the rule with culturally mature conception. I find a simple and familiar image useful: Neapolitan ice cream. Rather than wholly different categories, we get a reality in which each layer/level is at once the same stuff (like ice cream) and wholly different. Actually, what we see somewhat stretches the metaphor. The various layers/levels are not just different in kind (as with flavors), they reflect distinct levels of organization. The systems concept of "emergent properties" helps us complete the needed stretch. Emergent properties are characteristics unique to a set of systemic relationships. In the new picture, each level is defined/separated/joined by an emergent property—in this case existence (in contrast to non-existence), life, and the capacity for conscious reflection.

---

11 I use this combination term because each word captures part of what we see and has its particular historical reference. Religion has tended to see the relationship of parts in this sense as hierarchical—thus "levels." Science, having emphasized a lack of hierarchy, would be more comfortable with a word like "layers."

CST's creative frame helps make this basic description more specific. Instead of ice cream, with CST the "same stuff" becomes creation. And what differentiates these various emergent realities is the amount of creative information each inherently embodies. Each new layer/level is distinguished by a "creative multiplier" (or several creative multipliers working together) that radically increases the rate at which creative reorganization can take place. In the case of life, this creative multiplier is natural selection and the learning/adapting capacities that come with life's workings. In the case of ourselves, the multiplier is the option of fresh creation happening with every new "aha" that arises with conscious awareness and our unique toolmaking, idea-making, meaning-making prowess. The innovations that separate the various layers/levels of existence qualitatively increase the amount of creation/formativeness each succeeding layer/level is capable of embodying/manifesting. In this way, the application of a creative frame helps us both appreciate interconnectedness and grasp just how layers/levels are different one from the other.

A Layered Multiplicity

Let's look more closely at the various layers/levels in this new picture. With each over the last century, we've seen at least the beginnings of more "creative" interpretation. We find interconnectedness more deeply appreciated, change manifesting as an intrinsic attribute of that systemic level's functioning, uncertainty playing a newly integral role, and the acknowledgment of dynamics that can seem contradictory limited to usual ways of thinking. Many of these observations will be familiar from previous reflections in this book.

The physical:

It is with the hard sciences that people are most likely to appreciate that we've been witnessing something new, and new in this creative sense. Albert Einstein's 1905 elucidation of special relativity provocatively linked the before separate worlds of time and space, and was followed in 1915 with general relativity's more systemic approach to understanding gravity, a phenomenon that always before had been thought of as separate and mysterious. Both special relativity and general relativity leave mechanistic/deterministic thinking intact, but Einstein's physics colleagues, and ultimately the general public, also rightly came to view these contributions as revolutionary. The early thinking of quantum mechanics, the work of Niels Bohr and colleagues,[12] presented a more direct challenge, throwing understanding into a world that directly confronted deterministic assumptions. Waves and particles, energy and matter suddenly became less "things" than alternative ways of thinking. In quantum mechanics, the answer to the question of which is most real depends on when and how you look.

Contributions at the biggest of cosmic scales would prove similarly radical. Edwin Hubble's demonstration that the universe is expanding required that science abandon its previous picture of a stable, eternally constant universe. The Big Bang Theory—the idea that the universe in fact had a beginning, and a dramatic one—followed from these essential observations. In the new picture, creation, rather than being either created by a separate entity or something that had always existed, became integral in the larger story of existence.

A further contribution from cosmology has more recently provided some of the most intriguing inquiry—and important unanswered questions—in the physical sciences. The recognition that past calculations can't account for much of the universe's makeup have led to the search for the missing "dark matter" and "dark energy." One aspect of this search—the phenomenon of black holes—has resulted in particularly dramatic discoveries and presents questions especially pertinent to a creative picture. Certainly black holes involve destruction, but in ways we are only beginning to understand, they may also be generative. It has recently been demonstrated that supermassive black holes reside at the center of virtually every large galaxy, and there is conjecture that very small black holes may exist all around us. Might it be that not just the universe's beginnings, but also its ongoing existence, could appropriately be thought of as "creative?" The image is at least metaphorically provocative.

I should add one more often-cited contribution from physics: the phenomenon known as "entanglement." It turns out that subatomic particles that are linked by virtue of being complementary can remain

---

12 Including Einstein, Werner Heisenberg, Max Planck, Wolfgang Pauli, Erwin Schrödinger, Louis de Broglie, and Paul Dirac.

linked even when separated by significant distances. The connection is not causal in a traditional sense. And it is immediate—not limited by the speed of light. While entanglement was originally assumed to require proximity, recent experiments done between an orbiting satellite and the earth suggest that distance is not an obstacle. Entangled links are fragile and easily disrupted, but the phenomenon of entanglement has rich potential applications in both communication and computing. It also raises fascinating questions about the nature of connectedness in the universe and just how connected things may be.

Life:

Arguably biology's newly "creative" picture began even earlier—with Charles Darwin's 1859 publication of *On the Origin of Species* and Gregor Mendel's 1866 publication of his work with pea plants that demonstrated the actions of "invisible factors" that we now call genes. Evolutionary biology presents a picture of life in which creation, rather than something that happens to life, is understood as following in an ongoing way from the nature of life.

Ecological thought, first formally introduced with explorations of food webs and food cycles in the 1920s, added important further pieces to biology's new, more systemic picture. Today it is so familiar to us that we can miss its radical significance. Both interconnectedness and change are intrinsic to ecological thought. Increasingly it has become second nature for biologists to think in terms of communities and ecosystems and the interplaying life cycles of organisms and populations.

Neither of these contributions in biology—at least in their early forms—fundamentally challenged mechanistic assumptions (the best of thinking today in both evolutionary and systems biology begins to do so). But new attention brought by biologists to an age-old question confronted the classical picture directly. That question: What is life? A person might think that the answer would be obvious for a biologist, but in fact biology has never been able to address the life question in any ultimately satisfying manner.

With Chapter One in this book, I observed how the life question has been answered historically in two main ways and noted early attempts to get beyond them. Most recently scientists have tended to think of life as just a very complex machine. Looking back, we are more likely

CREATIVE SYSTEMS THEORY

to find dualistic explanations that locate life's source in some separate animating force—from Aristotle's "unmoved mover;" to, in medieval times, a separate soul that directs action; to, with nineteenth century vitalism, a separate animating energy.

With the middle of the last century, early systems thinkers challenged both views and argued that we needed to understand living systems as integrated wholes. I've described how biologist Ludwig von Bertalanffy presented the first formal explication of this kind of perspective with his 1940 book *General Systems Theory*. His thinking emphasized the fact that living systems are open systems, systems that maintain themselves in highly dynamic states far from equilibrium. I also noted how cybernetics, the invention of Norbert Weiner and his circle of colleagues, gave particular attention to feedback loops and self-regulation. And I highlighted the particular pertinence of the work of cognitive theorists such as Gregory Bateson, who argued that if we understood understanding deeply, we will have understood life.

Recent contributions from biology have added a further important cognition-related insight. More traditionally, cognitive mechanisms have been framed in command-and-control terms. Brains ran bodies; DNA ran cells. In the new picture, determination becomes a complex product of the system as a whole. We see, for example, how the cell membranes of eukaryote cells (cells that don't yet have nuclei, and thus DNA) make an array of highly nuanced yes-and-no "decisions" with regard to what they let in and what they do not. More generally, we are better recognizing how cells with nuclei along with the many cells, tissues, and organs of more complex organisms often engage their worlds through complexly networked and often highly decentralized informational processes.

Biology's version of today's more systemically interconnected, often mysterious and contradictory, uncertainty-permeated picture has deepened and filled out considerably in recent decades. Increasingly we are recognizing how creatures of all sorts are more complex, and complexly intelligent, than we have before assumed. We are also better appreciating how evolution is as much about cooperation as competition, and not just cooperation with one's own kind, but also between species (think of the increasingly recognized role of bacteria in our gut—they keep us healthy and we in turn keep them nourished and alive). Of particular significance, the question of what it means to think about living systems in living terms is being recognized more and more by biologists as not just legitimate, but pivotal to effective understanding.

Human Life:
We've seen how CST's reframing of understanding in the human sphere starts with an explicitly creative assertion, that what makes us unusual as creatures is the audacity of our creative proclivities. The theory describes how human intelligence is structured specifically to support and drive creative/formative process. And it delineates how we can understand all manner of phenomena—such as the human experience of meaning, the ways human developmental processes progress, and how it is that different people think and act as differently as they do—in terms of patterns that follow from the ultimately creative nature of human intelligence.

I've noted how we find precursors to this kind of understanding in the best of early thinking in psychiatry, psychology, and sociology, beginning with the simple yet historically radical recognition that much that is most important in being human functions outside of conscious awareness. I've also described how we can understand much of the history of twentieth century psychiatry and psychology as an inquiry into various ways of knowing and how they work together to make us who we are. I've also observed how the middle part of the century saw efforts to bring formal systems thinking into psychology.

Such efforts today are further supported by advances in cognitive science that have accompanied technical innovations such as advanced imaging techniques. One increasingly recognized conclusion is particularly pertinent to this more systemically complex, self-organizing picture. It appears that conscious awareness, rather than being located in some particular part of the brain, is more accurately an emergent capacity of our neurology as a whole.

Where It All Takes Us and Important Distinctions
The short version: Cultural Maturity's cognitive reordering suggests a picture of existence as a whole that is both more systemically interconnected and more clearly differentiated than how we have thought of things in times past. The worlds of the physical, the biological, and

of more conscious creatures such as ourselves come to reflect emergent systemic levels within a more encompassing systemic picture. In this more complex and uncertainty-permeated interpretation, existence as a whole—at least as we can know it—becomes in an important new sense "creative." And what makes layers/levels different can similarly be thought of in creative terms. Succeeding layers are distinguished by "creative multipliers," innovations that produce quantum leaps in the rate at which creative reorganization can take place.

We need to distinguish this kind of picture from ideas that at first might seem related. I think of two basic sorts of big-picture interpretation that might seem similar but which in fact differ fundamentally. CST argues that neither kind of interpretation ultimately helps us when it comes to the kind of understanding needed for the future.

The first is most common with those of more scientific or rational bent and is often found with Post-Industrial/Information Age interpretations. Here the kind of picture that I have described gets confused with ideas that extend Descartes's clockworks world to an ultimate extreme. Reference is often made to innovations that might appear to make the needed leap in understanding. One example is the modern "mathematics of complexity" with its ability to model phenomena that before have defied analysis, such as cloud patterns, the flow of rivers, and even the shapes of leaves. I suspect that a major reason people have found these new kinds of mathematical formulations compelling is that while being ultimately mechanistic, they often incorporate uncertainty. They also produce results that remind us aesthetically of a creative picture.[13] I suspect it is also likely that we would not have made these discoveries without the beginnings of

---

13 The mathematics of complexity can be used to argue for almost opposite kinds of misperception. Chaos theory, the most familiar example, demonstrates how simple equations can generate not only highly complex results, but results that defy prediction. Because these equations produce nondeterministic results yet have their roots in mechanistic formulations, they have proven attractive to those who remain committed to an ultimately mechanistic world view. But as I noted in Chapter Seven, the fact that they highlight uncertainty means that they can also be attractive to people who ascribe to Transformational/New Paradigm conclusions.

Cultural Maturity's cognitive changes. But that is very different from concluding that we can reduce a creative picture to mathematics.[14]

The second kind of trap is most common with people of more humanistic, liberal, or spiritual inclination. It has a couple of different forms. The first, often encountered in conjunction with environmental concerns, confuses a creative picture with the conclusion that existence as a whole is somehow "alive." It involves projecting the attributes of one creative layer/level—the animate—onto existence's entirety. There is nothing new about doing so. It is common in pantheistic thought from tribal times to Spinoza. Today we see more limited versions of this trap with views that make the whole of the earth as a system "alive." More accurately, the earth is a complex, self-maintaining/self-organizing system, that includes life as one part of that complexity.

The second form confuses a creative picture with the conclusion common with New Age thought that the universe as a whole is somehow "conscious." Here we project a uniquely human characteristic onto existence as a whole. Again, such thinking is not at all new. We find versions with any cultural time or locale where more spiritual/mythical beliefs prevail. CST affirms that existence is more interconnected than we have thought. But this is not at all the same as concluding that it is conscious.

It is important to reemphasize in putting forward this creative interpretation that CST does not claim to tell us what is actually "out there." Its contribution lies with understanding the implications of

---

14 The debate over whether mechanistic explanation is sufficient continues today even at the cutting edge of scientific inquiry. For example, the common belief in contemporary physics that there are an infinite number of universes, each with its own reality, has its roots in formulations that adhere to the mechanistic conclusions of classical thought. This is part of what makes such belief attractive to many people. But as seen from the perspective of CST, it is also a legitimate reason to question it. There is also a more contextual reason to have doubts. A picture that reduces to endless options with no one option inherently better than the others looks suspiciously like postmodern ideology and related notions that come with Transitional dynamics. "Multiverse" theory may very well prove to be accurate. But it will be fascinating to see how we look back on this currently popular way of thinking fifty years from now.

how human cognitive processes work. Personally, I'm willing to go a little further. In contrast to many theorists with more postmodern inclinations, I am comfortable making the leap that there is in fact something "out there" to understand—if for no other reason than that intelligence would have little reason to be if there weren't. I am also comfortable with the conclusion that ideas that reflect culturally mature perspective take us a bit closer to what actually is. In part this is because each step in understanding's evolution appears to have done so. It is also because of how Integrative Meta-perspective produces understanding that is inherently more encompassing than what we have known in times past. We might expect it to be not just more complete, but also more ultimately in keeping with what is the case.

Our Place in the Scheme of Things

A creative frame invites conjecture with regard to a related but more specific eternal quandary: our place in the larger scheme of things. We can put this question in science-versus-religion terms. From a scientific viewpoint, we can appropriately ask—as many great thinkers have asked—"Are we but a speck in an essentially purposeless universe, an odd momentary impulse of no real ultimate significance?" Or do we better think of ourselves as God's special children, as most religions through time have in some way seen us? A creative perspective offers a third option—neither quite so random nor quite so grand, but arguably more intriguing.

Reframed, the question becomes, What is our place and significance in creation?—as creation becomes what "the scheme of things" is ultimately about. A creative interpretation emphasizes that not all creation is the same and proposes that the answer to our question lies in just how this is so. Interpretations of times past have tended either to idealize the human—make us separate and special—or simply lump us together with life more generally. I've described how a creative interpretation offers that it may all be more like Neapolitan ice cream.

Our place in the larger scheme of things? At the least we represent a fascinating bit of creative innovation (with the jury far from in on just how ultimately successful). If we want to feel a bit more special, we could claim ours to be a particularly significant sort of creative innovation. We are the only creature, at least on our particular earth, that is not just consciously aware, but aware of itself as part of something that has evolved and continues to evolve. In an interesting sense, through us, creation, not just as fact but as process, has become conscious of itself.

In a way, this interpretation makes our human achievement even more remarkable. But it also makes it more tenuous, more explicitly "experimental." It is quite possible that exactly that which makes us special—our great creative prowess—will be our undoing. Our time on the planet has been extremely short (compared to, say, the dinosaurs—for us 300,000 years with civilization a product of only the most recent 20,000, compared to 180 million years for the dinosaurs). And with growing frequency, modern invention, and human choice more generally, has dangerously two-edged potential consequences.

In our time, the human creative "experiment" continues, and in ways that have major implications for its ultimate success. CST describes the possibility—and necessity—of a more aware and more deeply engaged relationship with our creative, toolmaking, meaning-making natures. Homo sapiens sapiens—"man the wise"—is perhaps coming to better deserve his audaciously proclaimed status (proclaimed twice over for emphasis). If the theory is accurate, certainly our continued creative well-being, and perhaps our survival, depends on it.

AFTERWORD

Contribution, Evidence, and the Legitimacy of Hope

In the book's preface, I listed some of what Creative Systems Theory purports to accomplish. I proposed that while some of these claims might seem audacious, by the end of the book each will have been substantiated. A quick return to this list provides a useful summary of CST's contributions. And by inviting the reader to reflect on whether claims have been fulfilled, doing so offers a test for CST's conclusions.

- *CST helps us make sense of the easily confusing and overwhelming times in which we live.* We've seen how the CST concept of Cultural Maturity addresses what makes our times unique and also just what today's challenges ask of us. Along with articulating a new kind of guiding story, the concept of Cultural Maturity shines a light on the new sorts of values, ways of relating, and approaches to understanding that will be needed if we are to successfully progress as a species.
- *CST clarifies how the future will require not just that we think new things, but that we learn to think in fundamentally new ways.* We've examined how Cultural Maturity is a product of specific cognitive changes. And we've seen how Integrative Meta-perspective, the new kind of vantage that follows from these changes, makes it possible to understand in ways that are fundamentally more dynamic and systemic. CST's specific strategy—the application of a creative frame—offers that we might think in ways that directly reflect the fact that we are alive, and alive in the particular way that makes us human.
- *CST helps us get beyond the simple-answer, ideological conclusions of times past.* We've examined how Integrative Meta-perspective directly challenges any belief that takes one part of a larger systemic complexity and

makes it the whole of truth—whether political, religious, philosophical, or scientific. Integrative Meta-perspective also helps make visible the more demanding questions that ideological beliefs protect us from.

- *CST helps deepen our understanding of human intelligence.* We've looked at how intelligence has multiple aspects—along with our rationality, more emotional, imaginal, and bodily dimensions. And we've seen how these various aspects work together to support and drive our remarkable creative/inventive capacities. We've also examined how the whole of CST can be understood to follow from these basic intelligence-related observations.

- *The theory provides a more dynamic and integrated picture of human developmental processes of all sorts.* We've explored how specific creative efforts, individual psychological development, the growth of relationships, and the evolution of social systems at the largest of scales can each be understood to organize creatively.

- *CST helps us better understand history—and not just the facts of history, but the evolution of beliefs, institutional forms, and our felt experience of meaning.* I've described how the recognition that cultural evolution organizes creatively allows us both to map the human story's past and begin to anticipate what may lie ahead. And we've seen how the picture of history that results helps us appreciate the human narrative as a story of purpose and possibility.

- *CST helps us recognize how capacities new to us as a species will be increasingly necessary in times ahead.* We've examined how related new skills and capacities will be needed to address questions of all sorts. We've also seen how these needed new skills and capacities follow naturally from Cultural Maturity's cognitive reordering. And I've described how each can be thought of as a "creative" capacity, part of what becomes possible when we are able to consciously hold the whole of intelligence's generative complexity.

- *CST helps us bring big-picture perspective to a wide array of truth-related questions where the thinking of times past becomes inadequate today.* We've seen, for example, how it helps us address moral quandaries more systemically, rethink human identity in ways that take us beyond the Modern Age concept of the individual, and understand relationships of all sorts in more complete—dynamic and systemic—ways.

- *CST helps us appreciate how understanding always happens in a context.* We've seen how CST Patterning in Time concepts address temporal context—how what happens at one time may have wholly different significance than what happens at another. We've also looked at how Whole-Person/Whole-System Patterning Concepts help us appreciate the way truth in our time requires that we both engage experience with the whole of our internal complexity and understand in terms of all the larger complexities of which we are a part. And we've examined how Patterning in Space concepts help us better understand here-and-now contextual distinctions, such as those that manifest as ideological differences or differences that are products of temperament/personality style.
- *CST helps us separate the wheat from the chaff in our thinking.* I've described how the results with Integrative Meta-perspective differ fundamentally from other ways of thinking about the future. I've also introduced specific kinds of conceptual traps that can get in the way of the needed maturity of understanding. In addition, I've teased apart how CST is different from more familiar kinds of systemic understanding—and not just in the specifics of its conclusions, but also in the kind of idea that it represents.
- *CST also helps address many eternal quandaries, ultimate questions that have always before left us baffled.* Throughout the book, I've touched on how CST reframes and addresses eternal concerns from what ultimately makes something true, to the nature and purpose of conscious awareness, to how science and religion might in the end relate.
- *CST provides not just ideas, but also methodologies.* We've seen how practicing culturally mature skills and capacities and applying them to essential challenges helps build the needed new conceptual muscles. And I've described specific "hands on" methods such as Parts Work that actively support culturally mature understanding.

The Evidence

The most important evidence for CST's conclusions is their utility. If the notions we have looked at successfully answer important questions, and particularly if these questions are ones we otherwise struggle to effectively address, then we have important evidence. But we can also be more specific. I've touched on further evidence, both for the concept of Cultural Maturity and for CST's specific approach to culturally mature conception throughout the book.

I ended Chapter Four by summarizing more particular evidence for the concept of Cultural Maturity. Each of these multiple pieces of evidence is indirect in the sense that it is either evidence by analogy or evidence that follows from observed consequences, but each provides pertinent support for the concept of Cultural Maturity's accuracy and timeliness. We've seen how the concept follows from how developmental processes of all sorts in human systems work, and in particular from the kind of cognitive reordering that underlies the defining changes in the mature stages of any such process. We've seen too how new skills and capacities needed in all parts of our lives can be understood to follow naturally from this new kind of cognitive organization. I've also described how Cultural Maturity's changes make understandable, and also directly address, what I've proposed is the ultimately most defining challenge of our time, today's Crisis of Purpose.

More specific evidence for the power of a creative frame and the accuracy of CST patterning concepts is of multiple sorts. There is how all of the developmental dynamics we have looked at follow a general sequence predicted by the workings of creative/formative process. There is also how the fact of polarity—and how polar relationships change—can be explained by the recognition that creative/formative processes manifest as an evolving interplay of generatively related polar relationships. In addition, there is how intelligence's multiple aspects can be understood to work together to support and drive formative processes of all sorts. The fact that CST patterning notions allow us not just to describe change and interrelationship in human systems, but also to predict outcomes and consequences provides an important further layer of evidence.

What about evidence of a more traditionally experimental sort? Here the nature of the ideas results in certain limitations. Concepts that draw on multiple intelligences and that always in some way include the archetypally feminine as well as the archetypally masculine present inherent challenges to formal experimental methodologies. Experimental work we've done at the Institute with the personality typology illustrates the challenge. We've constructed tests designed to determine a person's personality style (a necessary prerequisite to doing comparative studies), but at least thus far these tests have tended to fail with some of the trickier personality distinctions that I have described. The fact that a person can be trained to make these distinctions points toward a key part of the difficulty. When what we want to measure is an attribute of a living system, often the only instrument that can measure it with the needed nuance is another living system.

That said, there are many kinds of studies that could both help confirm CST observations and add further valuable understanding. Studies that draw on modern imaging techniques such as fMRI could be particularly powerful. A kind of experiment I would love to see: I've proposed that CST is unique in suggesting parallels between Patterning in Time and Patterning in Space observations. If those parallels could be demonstrated neurologically the result would be a particularly provocative kind of evidence.

The Legitimacy of Hope

We are left with the question I am most often asked in presenting ideas such as these that have obvious implication for the tasks ahead: Am I optimistic about the future? As this book's reflections should make clear, I am neither an optimist nor a pessimist. I've described how the tasks ahead present immense challenges and how I see us often doing less well than we might hope at responding to this challenge. But at the same time, the fact that the potential for what a positive future requires is developmentally built into who we are gives good reason for hope. I've suggested that if this were not the case, optimism would be hard to justify.

It is important to acknowledge that plenty of things could go wrong even in the face of the very real potential that the concept of Cultural Maturity describes—possibility is not destiny. I've observed that periods of regression are common in the workings of creative change and described how the dynamics of Transition can produce particular instabilities and absurdities. I've also noted how Transitional changes combined with more specific stressors such as globalization, climate change, terrorism, and the growing gap between the lives of the world's haves and have nots could push the species over its available Capacitance with dire results. And we face the possibility of events such as the use of weapons of mass destruction by a rogue state or terrorist group that could trigger a cascade of destruction.

I've also emphasized that even if we avoid calamitous circumstances, what the concept of Cultural Maturity suggests asks a lot of us, perhaps more than we are capable of. I've described how having a critical mass of people able to provide culturally mature leadership may be decades away.

What we can know in the face of these realities is that bringing what foresight we can to bear as we look to the future will be critical. The contributions made by the concept of Cultural Maturity and the ideas of CST are limited in the sense that notions of a conceptual sort necessarily are, but they have major significance for this task. We've seen how the concept of Cultural Maturity provides guidance that is in the end "common sense." And CST as a whole offers a conceptual tool bag that can help us make the needed sophistication of choices going forward.

The foundational insight of CST offers its own particular kind of hope. We've seen how all of CST's ideas follow directly from the notion that human intelligence is structured to support creative possibility. If this observation is accurate, CST has essential implications not just for our understanding of who we are and what we can say about the world around us, but also for the possibility that we might engage the future in ultimately creative—and wise—ways.

APPENDIX

A Glossary of Selected Creative Systems Terms

A Creative Frame—
Creative Systems Theory proposes that what most defines us as humans is our toolmaking, meaning-making—"creative"—natures. It goes on to describe how human intelligence is structured to support creative change and how human systems of all sorts are organized in ultimately creative ways. (The term "creative" here refers to the scientific as much as the artistic, to completions as much as beginnings—in short, to formative process wherever we find it.) The use of a creative frame applies most directly to human systems. CST uses a creative frame to develop a detailed "pattern language" for making highly detailed human systems–related distinctions.

Fundamental Organizing Concept—
The Fundamental Organizing Concept is the notion that at a particular time in culture is seen as ultimately defining reality. From our beginnings, when reality was understood in terms of animistic forces (or later, the will of pantheons of gods) it has been thought to reflect ultimate truth. With culture's Modern Age, the Fundamental Organizing Concept became the Cartesian notion that we could understand existence as a "great machine." In our time, we better recognize that final truth as we perceive it, rather than being separate and objective, is a product of how at a particular point in time we are capable of understanding. CST invites us to entertain the idea that reality as a whole—including biological and physical systems—in being self-organizing and generative, is in the largest sense "creative."

Cultural Maturity—
CST delineates how Modern Age institutions and ways of thinking are not the ideals and end points we commonly assume them to be—indeed, how they can't be if our future is to be bright. The theory describes how human developmental processes of all sorts—from individual growth, to change processes in relationships, to the evolution of culture—progress in related, creatively ordered ways. It goes on to propose that we can understand the times in which we live in terms of a series of creatively predicted, "developmental" tasks and changes. It calls today's new creative challenge Cultural Maturity.

The concept of Cultural Maturity makes analogy with the particular kind of maturity that produces passage into a lifetime's second half. Cultural Maturity challenges us to step beyond the absolutist, one-size-fits-all beliefs that come with relating to culture as a symbolic parent. And it makes it possible to think in more dynamic and complete ways. CST observes that parallel "developmental" changes mark the first sub-stages of the second half of any human formative process.

Integrative Meta-Perspective—
CST describes how culturally mature understanding is a product of specific cognitive changes that produce a new kind of conceptual vantage. Integrative Meta-perspective reflects a dual process—at once more fully stepping back from, and more deeply engaging, the whole of our human complexity. Of particular importance, that dual process involves more fully stepping back from and more deeply engaging the multiple aspects of intelligence. With Modern Age understanding, we stepped back and looked out—as if from a balcony—over a new, rationally understandable world. With Integrative Meta-perspective, we more fully step back from the rational as well as other aspects of intelligence. We also more deeply engage our complex cognitive natures. In doing so, Integrative Meta-perspective makes it possible to see ourselves, and everything around us, in more fully systemic ways.

Intelligence (as described by Creative Systems Theory)—
CST describes how the diverse aspects of intelligence are creatively related and work together to support and drive the mechanism of human formative process. The theory delineates four primary kinds

of intelligence. Each kind of intelligence is present in some form throughout any formative process, but each finds strongest expression in a particular creative stage.

The first, *Somatic/Kinesthetic Intelligence*, is body intelligence. It finds strongest expression in creation's "incubation" stage. *Symbolic/Imaginal Intelligence* is the intelligence of myth, dream, and imagination. It finds strongest expression in creation's "inspiration" stage. *Emotional/Moral Intelligence* is affective intelligence. It finds strongest expression in creation's "perspiration" stage. *Rational/Material Intelligence* is intellectual intelligence. It finds strongest expression in creation's "finishing and polishing" stage.

CST describes how intelligence manifests in different ways at different times and places. It also delineates how the ways in which we make sense of our worlds follow from how this is so. CST proposes that making sense of today's essential questions requires at least a beginning ability to more consciously apply the whole of intelligence.

Whole-Person/Whole-System Perspective—
The theory describes how we can understand human experience at every scale—from the personal, to relationships, to the familial, to the cultural, to the global—as systemic. It also describes how we can understand the various ingredients that make up any of these spheres—from elements within our psychological makeups to domains in culture as a system—as contrasting generative aspects within that particular systemic whole.

Beyond emphasizing the importance of thinking in systemic terms, CST also clarifies how the kind of systems thinking required by the challenges we face is necessarily of a new sort. It describes how the sort of systems thinking used by good engineers necessarily fails us if we wish to effectively describe living systems, and certainly if we wish to describe human systems. (And ultimately it stops just as short for addressing physical systems.) A creative frame offers a way to understand systems that directly reflects our living, human natures.

CST describes how ideas that fall short of the needed systemic sophistication leave us trapped in ideology—if not the us-versus-them ideologies of now-outmoded advocacies, at least the more overarching ideological simplifications that come with Modern Age heroic/romantic belief.

It delineates how we can understand modern-day, limiting assumptions of all sorts—from those that produce common traps in how we conceive of love to those that accompany how we think about government and economics—in terms of the importance of learning to think and act in more systemically complete ways.

The Dilemma of Differentiation—
The Dilemma of Differentiation alerts us to a dual quandary. It highlights the difficulty of making distinctions without reducing how we understand to the mechanistic—putting everything into "this-versus-that" categories. And at the same time it cautions that avoiding distinctions—making everything about connectedness (in the hope of escaping the trap of mechanistic thinking)—gets us no closer to where we need to go. Creative Systems concepts get beyond the Dilemma of Differentiation by defining difference (and connectedness) in creative terms.

Culturally Mature Truth—
CST challenges us to step beyond the absolutist beliefs of times past and understand truths of all sorts in ways that are more dynamic, contextual, and systemic. It also highlights new kinds of truth concepts and emphasizes their importance for effectively addressing the questions before us.

CST identifies two basic kinds of new-truth notions. *Concepts of Creative Differentiation* help us better understand generative processes and relationships within and between systems. Of these, *Patterning in Time* concepts address temporal relationships. *Patterning in Space* concepts address here-and-now creative relationships. *Whole-System Patterning Concepts* are Whole-Person/Whole-System measures. They are of three types: *Questions of Referent* (along with their systemic answers), *Capacitance* (generic capacity), and *Creative Symptoms* (protective responses that occur when situations threaten to overwhelm Capacitance).

All Creative Systems patterning concepts in some way put understanding in a larger context. They address what is creatively "right and timely." They help us discern what, at any particular time and place, best supports generativity and larger well-being. Truth in this

CREATIVE SYSTEMS THEORY

sense (you can think of it as a system's growth-producing and life-sustaining "creative edge") represents a fine balance. When systems retreat from their creative edges, they become stagnant. But if they push too far beyond them, they risk being overwhelmed, immobilized, or even destroyed.

Patterning in Time—
Patterning in Time concepts describe how change in human systems is creatively ordered and conforms to predictable patterns. CST delineates how a parallel sequence of creative ordering principles and sensibilities manifests over the course of human formative process of all sorts—from invention, to individual development, to the growth of a relationship, to organizational change, to the evolution of culture. Patterning in Time concepts can be used to tease apart highly complex processes and make highly nuanced discriminations. Being creatively framed, they allow detailed delineation while increasing our appreciation for the dynamic, life-imbued (and human life-imbued) nature of what we observe.

Creative Differentiation—
Creative Differentiation refers to the creative dynamics that characterize the first half of any human formative process. Here the newly created content buds off from its creative context, grows, and evolves. With each succeeding stage, new content becomes more defined and more separated from the context from which it arose.

Creative Integration—
Creative Integration refers to the creative dynamics that characterize the second half of any human formative process. The newly created content reconnects with its original context, in the process seasoning, maturing, and contributing to a now expanded context.

Transition—
Transition is the midpoint of any formative process—where processes of Creative Differentiation and Creative Integration meet. With culture as a creative process, this is where we find Cultural Maturity's "threshold."

The Creative Function—
The Creative Function is a visual depiction of formative process in human systems as conceived by CST. The Creative Function represents formative process as an evolving progression of creatively related polar relationships. It includes Creative Differentiation, Transition, and Creative Integration.

Creative "Bridging" and "Third Space" Perspective—
One way of understanding culturally mature perspective is that it systemically "bridges"—draws a circle around—concepts that we've traditionally described in polar terms (such as political left versus political right, freedom versus constraint, science versus faith, humankind versus nature, or matter versus energy). Bridging is not about adding or averaging, but rather about realizing a wholly different, more "third space" kind of perspective. The concept of "bridging" comes together with the idea of a creative frame in the recognition that polarities have a predictable symmetry—they juxtapose a "harder," more right-hand, more archetypically masculine element with a "softer," more left-hand, more archetypally feminine ingredient. The result with bridging is systemic in a specifically "procreative" sense. Bridging can be seen with the mature stages in any formative process. The kind of bridging we find with culturally mature thought is a product of how today's time in cultural change reflects creative integration at an ultimately defining scale, at the level of culture and understanding as a whole.

"Whole-Box-of-Crayons" Perspective—
A simple box of crayons provides a more detailed and nuanced way to represent culturally mature systemic understanding. Integrative Metaperspective involves stepping back so we can hold the whole systemic "box"—getting our minds around all the pertinent systemic elements. At the same time, it involves more deeply engaging the various systemic elements—all the "crayons" with their particular hues—so that we can apply them in the most ultimately creative ways.

Patterning in Space—
Patterning in Space concepts describe creative differentiation within and between human systems at any one point in time. They can be

CREATIVE SYSTEMS THEORY

used to help us better understand contrasting aspects of the individual psyche, personality differences between individuals, the functions of different parts of an organization, or how various domains in culture—such as government, business, art, science, education, or health care—function and interrelate. As with Patterning in Time notions, Patterning in Space concepts help us delineate highly complex processes while deepening our appreciation for their creative dynamism.

The Question of Referent ("Aliveness")—
Questions of Referent are the basic measures we use for making decisions. The concept can be applied to truth whenever or wherever we find it, but it is particularly pertinent to discerning what is true in a culturally mature reality (when culturally defined measures stop being enough). Decision-making then requires both a more conscious relationship to the referents we use and the application of more fully integrative/systemic measures. In our time, we need to draw on more wholly systemic referents if we wish to address wealth beyond material accumulation, learning beyond the mere acquisition of facts and skills, or health beyond the simple absence of disease.

The concept of Aliveness provides a shorthand language for needed systemic responses to Questions of Referent. Truth in the sense of Aliveness is only in part tied to particular actions or beliefs. Every thought, feeling, image, and sensation that exists can, in some context, reflect what is most life-affirming. Aliveness refers to what in any moment makes us (creatively) more.

Capacitance—
Capacitance measures a system's overall capacity—think of a balloon, that if stretched too far, could break. Capacitance replaces more specific notions of potential such as skill, IQ, or health. We can talk about a system's average Capacitance. We can also talk of the Capacitance available to a system at a particular moment. Creative Capacitance is the one thing that increases consistently over the course of any human formative process. Cultural Maturity, like all developmental dynamics, is a Capacitance-dependent notion. Without sufficient Capacitance, culturally mature perspective is largely impossible. And at a certain Capacitance, culturally mature conclusions become increasingly self-evident.

Creative Symptoms—
Creative Symptoms are unconscious protective mechanisms. They reflect a way that human systems respond when challenges exceed their available Capacitance (and when systems are not able to grow in response or to more consciously protect themselves). Creative Symptoms function by getting the system out of the line of fire—by moving it above the creative challenge (by intellectualizing, for example), below it (perhaps by the system becoming depressed), inside of it (the system might unconsciously withdraw), or outside of it (by the system becoming preoccupied with something safer, for example). The concept applies to human systems at all scales.

Whole-Person/Whole-System Relationship—
In contrast to "two-halves-make-a whole" relationships in which bonding happens through the mutual projection of systemic parts (a projected gender ideal, an evil other), with culturally mature relationships each participant maintains its systemic completeness. The term Whole-Person/Whole-System relationship pertains to human relationship wherever we find it—between intimates, between parents and children, between leaders and follows, between organizations, or between one country and another.

Culturally Mature Leadership—
Culturally Mature Leadership is Whole-Person/Whole-System leadership. It is the kind of leadership we find when we leave behind parental notions of authority. Culturally mature leaders (and in ideal situations, also those being led) make their choices from the whole of themselves as systems. In doing so, they step beyond both polarized identifications within systems they lead (for example, between management and labor in a business) and also between systems (for example, with ally-versus-enemy beliefs in relationships between countries). The culturally mature leader may be a strong advocate—indeed, the ability to advocate strongly increases with culturally mature capacity—but that advocacy is expressed from a mature systemic perspective.

Whole-Person Identity (and the Myth of the Individual)—
With Integrative Meta-perspective, identity comes to reflect who we are as systemic wholes. Whole-Person identity is a necessary corollary of

Whole-Person/Whole-System relationship. Note that this recognition directly challenges how we have thought of individuality in modern times. The kind of individuality we have previously identified with—what we see idealized with romantic love and traditional heroic leadership—in fact reflects but half of what identity becomes when understood systemically.

Meta-determinacy—
Meta-determinacy refers to the recognition that understanding causality in creative systems requires us to step beyond the polarity of certainty versus uncertainty. Creative outcomes are not predetermined—nothing more marks creative processes than the fact that we cannot know ahead of time exactly what they will produce. But they are also not simply uncertain. Creative processes are highly patterned, and the results they produce are always in some way linked to their creative contexts.

Creative "Reengagement"—
Reengagement describes a dynamic intrinsic to Creative Integration. Creative Differentiation involves necessary amnesias for developmental realities that we have progressed beyond (so that we will not fall back into the familiar). With Creative Integration we see a reconnecting with these forgotten underlying sensibilities (a mechanism critical to Integrative Meta-perspective's more complete and dynamic picture). Reengagement is not about going back. What we "reengage" is forgotten sensibilities as we experience them in the present.

The Dilemma of Trajectory—
Over the course of Creative Differentiation, archetypally feminine values and sensibilities diminish in influence, while archetypally masculine values and sensibilities become increasingly dominant. At Transition, the archetypally feminine in essence ceases to exist. With this circumstance, it is not possible to continue "progressing" in the same way we have known. Creative Integration resolves the Dilemma of Trajectory.

The Dilemma of Representation—
The Dilemma of Representation describes how usual approaches to both language and pictorial depiction necessarily fails us when it

comes to representing Creative Systems concepts (and culturally mature conclusions more generally). This result, rather than a reflection of anything mysterious, is a product of culturally mature perspective's systemic complexity and completeness.

Polar Fallacies—
The concept of polar fallacies describes basic ways that we can fall short of culturally mature understanding. Creative Systems Theory describes three basic kinds of polar fallacies distinguished by the polar tendency with which they most identify. Unity Fallacies identify with the archetypally feminine. Separation Fallacies identify with the archetypally masculine. And Compromise Fallacies split the difference.

Pre-Axis—
The Pre-Axis stage is creation's "incubation" stage. Somatic/Kinesthetic Intelligence predominates. (With Patterning in Space, Pre-Axis refers to the systemic elements that most embody Pre-Axis sensibilities as they manifest at a particular point in time.)

Early-Axis—
The Early-Axis stage is creation's "inspiration" stage. Symbolic/Imaginal Intelligence predominates. (With Patterning in Space, Early-Axis refers to the systemic elements that most embody Early-Axis sensibilities as they manifest at a particular point in time.)

Middle-Axis—
The Middle-Axis stage is creation's "perspiration" stage. Emotional/Moral Intelligence predominates. (With Patterning in Space, Middle-Axis refers to the systemic elements that most embody Middle-Axis sensibilities as they manifest at a particular point in time.)

Late-Axis—
The Late-Axis stage is creation's "finishing and polishing" stage. Rational/Material Intelligence predominates. (With Patterning in Space, Late-Axis refers to the systemic elements that most embody Late-Axis sensibilities as they manifest at a particular point in time.)

CREATIVE SYSTEMS THEORY

Transitional Absurdities—
Transitional Absurdities are the nonsensical ways that reality can appear with Transition's near absence of creatively germinal (archetypally feminine) values and sensibilities. Some examples: How readily we ignore damage done to the environment, the extreme material values of modern times, how disconnected we can be from our bodies, and how often today extreme social/political polarization obscures the important questions.

Cross-Polar Dynamics—
The term "cross-polar" refers to dynamics in which a system identifies with the pole opposite to that which it most inhabits. For example, we often see cross-polar dynamics with both liberal/humanist and postmodern belief. With liberal/humanist belief, we can find a strongly intellectual and idealized (Upper Pole) identification with the underprivileged (Lower Pole). With postmodern writings, we can see lengthy, hyper-rational (Upper Pole) arguments for the inadequacy of the rational and for the impossibility of ultimately knowing anything (Lower Pole).

Archetypally Masculine and Archetypally Feminine Violence—
Creative Systems Theory defines violence as any action that results in damage to Capacitance. Archetypally masculine violence damages Capacitance through direct insult. It may take the form of physical assault, harshly condemning words, or the simple impeding of possibility. Archetypally feminine violence works more covertly. It may take the form of undermining, passive aggression, emotional entanglement, or manipulative seduction. Depending on the context, either kind of violence can prove the more damaging.

Parts Work—
CST includes hands-on techniques that support culturally mature systemic understanding. The most powerful it calls simply Parts Work. In doing Parts Work, people engage the various aspects of their cognitive complexity like characters in a play.

Creative Systems Analysis—
Any system, or set of related systems, can be examined using a multi-layered application of Creative Systems patterning concepts. Because

Creative Systems notions are based on underlying organizing principles, such analysis can help us get at what is most fundamentally important in any situation. Also, because all Creative Systems concepts are based on a single notion—that human systems are creatively ordered—such analysis often makes it possible to address highly complex phenomena in surprisingly simple ways. And the use of a creative frame means that such analysis is inherently dynamic in a way that honors our living, human natures.

WORDS OF THANKS

The people who have contributed in important ways through the years to the development of Creative Systems Theory are far too numerous to list here. To them I offer a shared thanks. For this particular volume, I wish to express particular gratitude to Larry Hobbs, Dan Senour, and Lyn Dillman for their support in the conversations that led to its writing. I also wish to thank Kathy Krause for her skilled and committed editing and Teresa Piddington for caring editorial assistance, Les Campbell for his beautiful work designing the book's interior, and Mohammad Abdus Sattar for his sensitive design of the book's cover.

INDEX

A

abortion 37, 176, 178, 397, 404, 426
advertising 225, 350, 533, 552–554
advocacy 241, 297–298, 342–344, 405, 498, 608
Afghanistan 130
Age of Reason 4, 57, 67–68, 89, 119, 136–137, 195, 203, 583
Aliveness 213–214, 219–222, 225–227, 233, 235–236, 239–241, 245, 251–252, 259, 261, 278–279, 285, 291, 305, 367, 401–402, 607
amnesia 95–97, 100, 105, 132, 137, 139, 223, 551, 609
analytic approaches 394–395
archetypally feminine 24, 28, 82–83, 85, 97, 125, 137, 141–142, 151, 154, 216, 253–254, 275, 281, 297–299, 302, 325, 327, 332, 338, 340, 342, 348, 391, 426–427, 429–430, 460–461, 463–465, 468, 470–472, 479, 481–482, 484–486, 488–490, 492, 494, 496, 551, 566, 571, 577, 598, 606, 609–611
archetypally masculine 24, 82–83, 85, 97, 125, 141–142, 151, 216, 253, 254, 297–299, 302, 332, 338–339, 341, 342, 348, 391, 426–427, 429, 460, 463–464, 468, 472, 479–481, 483, 489–490, 492, 494, 496, 548, 566, 571, 598, 606, 609–611
architecture 29, 99, 154–156, 426, 428
Aristotle 19, 141–142, 145, 483, 570, 575, 589
art xii, 14, 16, 45, 74, 86, 112, 149, 174, 222, 262–263, 274–275, 282, 288, 350, 398, 488, 493, 504, 545–552, 554
Assagioli, Roberto 395

B

Bateson, Gregory 20, 442, 589
Beckett, Samuel 549
Bertalanffy, Ludwig von 19, 589
Big Band Theory 444, 582, 583

Big Bang Theory 27, 587
black holes 587
Blake, William 470
body intelligence 5, 62, 64, 73–74, 76, 96, 106–108, 112, 154, 157, 160, 272, 302, 311, 350, 363–364, 492, 603
Bohr, Niels 16, 60, 587
boundaries 117, 178, 247, 250, 255, 257–258, 306, 375–378, 426–427, 429, 467, 521, 541, 544, 551, 552
box of crayons 25, 57, 243, 571, 606
Braque, Georges 16, 549
"bridging" 78–81, 85, 138, 171, 265, 330, 509, 513, 551–552, 606
Buber, Martin 469
Buffet, Warren 544
business 75, 118, 149–150, 174, 179, 191, 260, 262, 271, 280, 283, 289, 339, 341, 403, 410, 426, 429, 496, 503–504, 508–509, 531, 538, 539, 540–542, 552–554, 607–608

C

Campbell, Joseph 5, 60, 71, 220
Capacitance 128, 213–214, 232–235, 237–238, 240–241, 245–246, 249–252, 259, 270–272, 278, 295–296, 303, 337–341, 343–345, 347–348, 368–369, 376, 388, 399, 401–403, 442, 599, 604, 607, 608, 611
chaos theory 326, 334, 591
climate change xx, 11, 36–38, 104, 127, 169, 174, 230, 348, 404, 407, 410, 416–424, 435, 445, 540, 599
cognitive reordering xiv, xvi, 31, 51–52, 54, 56–58, 78, 80, 85, 91, 98, 123, 128, 138, 147, 164–165, 167, 170, 172, 177, 182, 186, 189, 203, 214–215, 264, 299, 309, 336, 354, 371, 390, 434–435, 490, 492, 556, 562, 568, 583, 590, 596, 598
commitment 65, 72, 94, 153–154, 229, 278, 284, 344, 382–383, 474–475, 485, 511, 527

complexity xiii–xv, xvii, 6, 15, 27,
    29–30, 35, 49, 52, 54–55, 57,
    59–60, 69, 93, 100–102, 123, 136–
    137, 139, 144, 158, 169, 171–172,
    179–180, 188, 193–195, 200, 206,
    208, 210–211, 219, 222–223, 225,
    235, 238, 243, 248, 251, 265,
    269–271, 298–299, 311, 320, 322,
    326, 334–336, 354, 363, 369, 371,
    390–392, 401, 413, 415–416,
    418–420, 422, 436, 438, 451–452,
    462, 469, 473, 478, 497–499, 508,
    515, 518, 526, 558, 561, 564–565,
    568, 571, 574, 580, 582, 591–592,
    595–597, 602, 610–611
Compromise Fallacies 24, 48, 215,
    332–334, 336, 338, 340, 342, 390,
    434, 610
Concepts of Creative Differentiation
    45, 211–215, 246, 250–251, 268,
    604
containers 107, 154, 255–257, 259
context xviii, 40, 46, 62, 66, 79, 85,
    90–91, 105–107, 110, 112, 123,
    127, 136–137, 150–151, 172, 181,
    194, 210, 222, 232, 244, 246, 253,
    255–256, 258, 266–267, 274, 298,
    315, 358, 386, 401, 406, 421, 462,
    486, 492, 510, 512, 517, 536, 563,
    577, 597, 604–605, 607, 609, 611
Copland, Aaron 550
coronavirus 404–409, 411, 514
Creative Function 51, 86–89, 119,
    126, 139–140, 145, 159, 160–161,
    233, 241, 261–263, 336, 347, 463,
    472, 480, 606
Creative Imperative, The 6–7, 44, 69,
    133, 154, 160–162, 463
Creative Integration 65–66, 122–123,
    605–606, 609
creative periodicities 87, 105
Creative Systems Personality Typology
    (CPST) 2, 8, 70, 182, 261–262,
    264, 269–271, 294, 300, 306, 312,
    336, 356, 429, 505, 517
Crisis of Purpose 7, 9, 42, 121, 162,
    205, 208, 219, 226, 337, 346, 379,
    408, 423, 433, 437, 446, 448, 450,
    488, 505, 524, 535, 539, 553, 598
crux 46–47, 215–217, 219, 243, 245,
    265, 309, 312, 357, 517
*Cultural Maturity: A Guidebook for the
    Future* 9, 17, 35, 38–39, 92, 191,
    313, 372, 418, 422, 510, 517, 546
Cultural Maturity (basic concept) xi–
    xiii, xvi, xix, xxi, 7–8, 10, 13–14,
    30–31, 35, 38, 40, 44, 48, 50–51, 54–
    59, 67–68, 77–81, 84–86, 91, 96, 98,
    104–105, 118–119, 125, 127–128,
    138, 143–144, 146–147, 149–150,
    153, 162–168, 170, 172–173, 175–
    183, 185–186, 189–191, 193–198,
    203, 205, 207–209, 214–216,
    219–220, 224–225, 227, 231–232,
    234, 239–241, 264, 266–268, 270,
    295, 299, 302, 309–313, 318–319,
    321–322, 325, 327–330, 332–333,
    336–337, 339, 343, 347–348, 353–
    355, 357–360, 369, 371, 387–389,
    395, 405, 407, 417–418, 420–424,
    430, 432–434, 437, 440, 445–446,
    451, 454, 456, 459, 472–474, 478,
    488, 490, 492, 498, 503, 508–509,
    511–512, 515–520, 524, 527, 538,
    540–541, 545–546, 549–551, 554,
    556, 561–562, 568, 571–575, 577–
    579, 581, 584, 590, 592, 595–596,
    598–599, 600, 602, 605, 607
cynicism 316–317, 337–338, 346, 405,
    442, 445, 475

D

Dali, Salvador 16, 276, 550
Darwin, Charles 26, 588
Dawkins, Richard 574
death xiv, 148, 162, 166, 170, 174,
    180, 192, 197–198, 200–204, 206,
    397, 404, 408, 410–411, 437, 484,
    486, 504, 534–535, 537–538

depression 43, 248, 278, 285, 305, 352, 373, 411–413, 447
Descartes, René xv, 14, 19, 68, 72, 80, 134, 143, 145, 215, 564, 567, 582, 584, 591
determinism 38, 556–560, 562–564
device addiction 43, 226, 405, 446–448, 451, 554
Diamond, Jared 131
Differentiation Phase 62, 84, 87
Dilemma of Differentiation 23–24, 30, 47, 88–89, 207, 214, 221, 311–312, 604
Dilemma of Representation 49, 51, 88, 221, 233, 312, 344, 347, 360, 392, 405, 609
Dilemma of Trajectory 42, 47, 97–98, 105, 125–127, 143, 164, 207, 240–241, 311, 315, 330, 347, 351, 433, 448, 488, 577, 581, 609
discord 115, 424
dualism 143–145, 392, 571, 580

E

Early-Axis 88–89, 109–112, 130, 134–135, 141–142, 145, 148, 152–155, 160, 261–262, 273–278, 281, 284, 292–294, 298, 300, 336–338, 340, 375, 392, 402, 482, 484, 493–494, 496, 549, 610
economics xx, 118, 142–143, 421, 424, 503–504, 508–509, 538–540, 553, 604
education xx, 15, 28, 46, 61, 72, 103, 134–139, 218–219, 223–224, 240, 262, 270–271, 286, 304, 324, 340, 368, 378–379, 398, 422–423, 503, 508–518, 532–533, 553, 557, 607
Egypt 5, 67, 111, 142, 155, 452, 547
Einstein, Albert 16, 27, 468, 586–587
emergent properties 585
emotional intelligence 65, 71–72, 75, 112–113, 364, 568
entanglement 253, 257, 326, 587–588, 611

evidence 125, 207–208, 308, 310, 354, 597–599
Evolutionary History of Music 139, 365
existentialism 13, 135, 321–322
extinction 39, 416, 442, 445

F

fake news 225, 351, 431, 449, 530
"finishing and polishing" phase 62, 65, 73–74, 87, 116, 119, 263, 286, 401, 481, 547, 603, 610
Fitzgerald, F. Scott 78
foresight 39, 173–174, 210, 235, 406–407, 420, 423, 445, 538, 600
Frankl, Viktor 415
freedom xiii, 118–119, 168, 183, 206, 323, 355, 405, 416, 427–428, 438–441, 452, 488, 541, 555, 563, 606
free will 38, 556–560, 562–563
Freud, Sigmund 21, 297, 393
Friedman, Thomas 544
front-page news 404, 413, 435, 455
Fundamental Organizing Concept xii, 601

G

Gardner, Howard 61
Garfias, Robert 138
Gebser, Jean 141, 325
gender xviii, xx, 9, 11, 24, 37, 82, 159, 162, 176, 180, 183, 256, 267–268, 301, 302, 312, 356, 362, 387, 399, 425, 455–463, 472–474, 477–478, 480–481, 484, 488, 490, 492–494, 497–499, 502, 505, 516, 531, 540, 566, 608
gender archetypes 302, 460, 480, 491, 494
government xx, 15, 28–29, 36, 38, 46, 48, 83, 103, 118, 140, 162, 196, 240, 242, 258, 262, 271, 339, 341, 368, 374, 403, 422–424, 427, 429, 433–434, 488, 503, 508–509,

518–524, 526–527, 535, 541, 547, 549, 553, 604, 607
Greece 5, 67, 111, 142, 155, 483, 493, 547, 548
Greenspan, Alan 543
ground 464, 470, 471, 483, 489
gun violence xx, 174, 253, 405, 435, 437–438

H
hands-on approaches 361, 374, 398
Hawking, Stephen 274, 556–561
health care 11, 36–37, 41, 170, 192, 198–200, 207, 218, 240, 348, 404, 407, 414, 437, 533–537, 541, 607
Hegel, Georg 100, 143, 145, 325
Heisenberg, Werner 16, 587
heroic xviii, 12, 14, 40–42, 77, 191–192, 198, 200, 218, 241, 243–244, 310, 321, 347–348, 355, 392, 419, 440, 504, 528, 531–532, 534–535, 548, 603, 609
hope 103, 105, 346, 352–353, 416, 424, 432, 435, 475, 532, 545, 595, 599–600
Hubble, Edwin 27, 587
Hugo, Victor xiii
humanistic approaches 394

I
ideology xii, xvi, 13, 49, 77, 172–173, 194, 205, 213, 242, 244–245, 296, 302, 311, 321, 324, 327–328, 346, 388, 390–391, 406, 418, 421, 438, 441, 461, 525, 539, 542, 592, 603
imaginal intelligence 49, 64, 67, 69–70, 110–111, 364, 548, 603, 610
immigration 174, 178, 383–386, 404, 427
"incubation" phase 3, 64, 67, 89, 106, 108, 603, 610
Industrial Age 41, 102, 126, 137, 153, 318, 488, 511
"inspiration" phase 3, 64, 71, 74–75, 87, 89, 109, 273, 401, 603, 610

"integration" phase 62, 87, 89, 124
Integrative Meta-perspective xiv, xvi–xvii, xix, 9, 32, 35, 38, 40–41, 43–44, 46, 51–52, 54–59, 61, 76–78, 80–81, 85, 91, 95, 97–98, 100, 125, 137, 144, 147, 151, 161, 165, 167–171, 173–174, 206, 208–209, 212, 214, 216, 221, 243, 244, 252, 254, 260, 267, 269–270, 302, 309–312, 320, 330, 334–336, 339–340, 354–358, 360, 363, 368–372, 375, 388–389, 391–393, 400, 425, 434, 446, 453–454, 478, 505, 507, 515, 521, 548, 556, 561–562, 566–568, 571, 573–574, 578, 579, 583, 593, 595–597, 602, 606, 608–609
intimacy 9, 89, 110, 121, 181, 189, 299, 302, 387, 456–457, 461–463, 472–474, 476–477, 480–481, 488, 493–496, 501–502
Iraq 130

J
James, William 244, 567
Joyce, James 466, 550
Jung, Carl 21, 27, 254, 270, 274, 297, 325, 393, 562

K
Kandinsky, Wassily 222, 550
Keats, John 140

L
Lakoff, George 425
Lao Tzu 468, 471
Lawrence, D.H. 550
leadership xviii, 7–9, 11, 41, 77, 81, 127, 131–133, 164, 166, 168, 170, 174, 189–197, 205, 207, 212, 234, 238, 242, 246, 262–263, 282–284, 295–296, 310, 325, 331, 337–338, 340, 342–343, 345, 352, 357, 362, 369–370, 372, 377, 379, 386–387, 389, 398–399, 402, 410, 422–424, 455, 503–504, 518–520, 523, 536, 538–540, 553, 580, 600, 608–609

CREATIVE SYSTEMS THEORY

limits xviii, 33, 38–40, 65, 125, 140, 165, 169–170, 186, 194, 198, 200, 205, 210, 213, 232–233, 235, 237–238, 240, 246, 250, 254, 312, 321, 348–349, 353, 355, 362, 374, 408, 415–419, 422, 424, 439–440, 444, 457, 473–475, 491, 512, 519, 533, 535, 538, 540–541, 545, 563
love xviii, xx, 16, 24, 69, 77, 81, 87, 89, 113, 115, 117–121, 124, 162, 166, 170, 174, 180, 182–189, 193, 197, 207, 212, 217, 223–224, 228–229, 230–231, 242, 299–300, 302, 331, 356, 362, 367–368, 387, 401, 421, 424, 456–459, 461, 463, 472–476, 478–479, 486, 488–490, 492, 494–496, 498, 502, 505, 573, 604, 609
Lower Pole 85, 88, 90, 91, 116, 263, 281, 283, 302, 347, 375, 471, 485, 486, 496, 611

M

machine learning 22, 320, 405, 446–449, 451–453, 554
Maslow, Abraham 21
mathematics of complexity 326, 591
Maturana, Humberto 20
mechanistic xiv–xv, 15–16, 20–21, 23–24, 49, 129, 153, 221, 310, 313, 319, 325, 334, 453, 536, 558–559, 568, 574, 584, 586, 588, 591–592, 604
media 185, 204, 261, 289, 324, 341–342, 399, 413, 437, 447, 495, 503–504, 509, 525–533, 552–554, 581
Mendel, Gregor 27, 588
meta-determinant 232
Middle Ages 5, 12, 14, 40, 56, 67, 72, 80, 89, 114–115, 134, 142, 183, 452, 487, 493, 510, 539, 548, 570, 571, 582
Middle-Axis 87, 89–90, 112–116, 130, 134–135, 141–142, 145, 148, 151–153, 155, 158, 160, 261–263, 280–282, 284–285, 292, 294, 303, 336, 339–340, 392, 402, 485–486, 491, 493, 496, 519, 610
Middle East 114, 469, 486, 489, 493
midlife 88–89, 120
Modern Age xi–xii, xv, xviii, 5, 7, 12, 15, 17, 22, 31, 36, 38, 40, 41–42, 51–52, 54, 56, 58, 61, 69, 72–73, 75, 77, 80, 102, 118–119, 129, 137, 142–143, 149, 151, 156, 158, 168, 183, 186, 190, 198, 200, 203, 242, 310, 315, 322, 337, 341, 344, 347–349, 354–355, 392–393, 422, 433, 440, 452–453, 456, 458–459, 487–488, 490, 505–506, 513, 524, 531, 534, 537, 539, 545, 547–549, 561–562, 567, 570, 573, 596, 601–603
money 289, 522–523, 539, 542, 544
morality xv, xx, 38, 47, 166, 174–176, 178, 181–182, 252, 331, 340, 355, 421, 554
Moreno, Jacob 395
Muir, John 150
multiple intelligences 4, 30, 56, 58, 61–63, 66, 68, 75, 123, 265, 304, 311, 453, 568, 598
multiplicity 6, 29, 45, 47, 49, 56–57, 61–64, 68, 76, 101, 208, 215–216, 245–246, 248, 251, 260, 264–268, 306, 309, 312, 320, 357–358, 369, 391, 393, 434, 452, 563, 566, 568
Myth of Freedom 439
Myth of the Individual xviii, 119, 186, 197, 217, 241–242, 313, 372, 474, 494, 519, 555, 608

N

Naisbitt, John 318
narrative 1, 8, 11–14, 17, 40–42, 164, 240, 309–311, 314, 322, 346–347, 392, 410, 423, 438, 440–441, 475–476, 492, 504, 532, 569–571, 596

Neapolitan ice cream model 585, 593
Necessary Wisdom: Meeting the Challenge of a New Cultural Maturity 8, 78, 81, 331, 434
New Age belief 31, 128, 134, 137, 145, 311, 325, 328, 332, 333, 336, 342, 592
Newman, Barnett 548
Nietzsche, Friedrich 578
nuclear war 404, 435

O

Obama, Barack 133, 295
objectivity 14, 16, 51, 57–58, 76, 143–144, 155, 203, 290, 315
oneness 13, 24, 49, 78, 82–83, 86, 313, 330, 332, 334, 386, 441, 566–567
Ostanes 485
Outer Aspect 90, 243, 264, 276, 282, 286, 302, 367

P

paradox 35, 46, 52–53, 76, 80–81, 104, 147, 182, 205, 225, 310, 342, 354–357, 359, 388–389, 392, 559–560
Parts Work 51, 81, 249–250, 335, 361, 365, 368–373, 375, 378, 380, 384, 387–394, 396, 398–399, 401, 404, 425, 431–432, 435, 457, 475, 491, 498–499, 505, 509, 579–580, 597, 611
patriarchy 481, 488, 492
Patterning in Space xv, xx, 24, 45, 47, 68, 87, 91, 150–151, 161, 250, 260–265, 268–269, 283, 294, 296, 301, 303, 311–312, 356, 358, 366, 399, 401–402, 506, 508, 552, 597, 599, 604, 606–607, 610
Patterning in Time xv, 24, 29, 45–46, 54–55, 68, 77, 87, 90–91, 95, 99–100, 105, 116, 128–130, 133, 136–139, 145–147, 150–151, 154, 159, 161–162, 164, 209, 211, 214, 246, 250, 255, 260–261, 264–265, 267–271, 283, 294, 302, 309, 350, 356, 358, 365–366, 392, 401–402, 457, 460, 471, 505–506, 546, 597, 599, 604–605, 607
Perls, Fritz 395
"perspiration" phase 3, 65, 67, 74–75, 87, 89, 112, 114–115, 142, 263, 280, 401, 481, 485, 603, 610
philosophical idealism 31, 100, 325, 327
philosophy x, 45, 99, 111–112, 139–146, 262, 555
Picasso, Pablo 16, 222, 274, 549
Plato 23, 31, 141–142, 145, 215, 483
polarity 24, 30, 33, 38, 46, 55, 76–78, 80–82, 84–86, 88, 90–91, 106, 110, 112–114, 118, 125, 145, 159–161, 170–171, 204, 248–249, 251, 253–254, 311, 330, 332–333, 336, 339, 354–355, 362, 386, 391, 425, 427–428, 430, 434, 477, 481, 506, 509, 565–567, 582–584, 598, 609
populism 524
Post-industrial/Industrial Age scenarios 145, 313–314, 317–321, 338, 340–341, 349, 591
Postmodern/Constructivist scenarios 144–145, 313–315, 321–324, 330, 333–334, 338, 340–341, 348
pragmatism 244, 246, 322
Pre-Axis 87, 89–90, 106–107, 141, 145, 148, 151–152, 154, 158, 160, 482, 484, 610
Prigogine, Ilya 27
pseudo-significance 225–226, 318, 351, 448

Q

Question of Referent 44, 212–213, 219, 223, 245, 399, 448, 508–510, 518, 527, 533, 538, 546, 573, 576–577, 607
Quick and Dirty Answers to the Biggest Questions: Creative Systems Theory Explains What It Is All About (Really) 9, 555, 564, 582

R

rational intelligence 16, 58, 65, 67, 73, 112, 119, 453, 478
Reengagement 96–97, 162, 223, 550, 609
Reformation 570, 579
Reich, Stephen 550
Reich, Wilhelm 21
religion 13, 24–25, 38, 45–46, 71, 118, 135, 138, 140, 143, 146, 162, 179, 201, 203–204, 240, 262, 288, 296, 315, 331, 356–357, 403, 422–423, 443, 452, 503–504, 508, 556, 560, 564–582, 584–585, 593, 597
Renaissance 14, 67, 134, 152, 493, 547, 549
responsibility 72, 94–95, 131, 153, 168, 172, 174, 177, 182, 192, 194, 210, 211, 227–231, 235, 312, 322, 355, 389, 393, 406, 417, 419, 422–424, 445–446, 469, 473, 475–476, 478, 498, 511, 517, 536, 538, 540, 579
rhythms 67, 113, 255, 257–258
Rilke, Rainier Maria 64, 274, 546
romantic xviii, 12–14, 23, 40–42, 61, 77, 80, 115, 118–119, 136, 141, 143, 170, 183–186, 188, 197, 242–244, 283, 287, 290, 300, 310–311, 316, 321, 325–327, 332, 335, 342, 347–348, 355, 392, 440, 458–459, 473, 475–476, 479–480, 488, 504, 528, 531–532, 603, 609
Romantic Era 119, 153, 488
Rorty, Richard 245, 324
Russell, Bertrand 287, 578

S

scenarios for the future 102, 127, 309, 313, 337, 338
Schlesinger, Arthur 134, 429
science xii, 2, 9, 15–17, 21–24, 27–28, 38, 44, 46, 60, 71, 75, 84, 119, 141, 143, 145–146, 149, 162, 179, 202–203, 228, 240, 262, 274, 287, 326, 331, 341, 356–357, 368, 403, 407, 410, 417–418, 424, 503–506, 511, 534, 547, 549, 553, 556–558, 560, 564–578, 580–582, 584–587, 590, 593, 597, 606–607
second-half-of-life maturity 86, 126
Senge, Peter 325
Separation Fallacies 24, 31, 48, 332–334, 336–338, 340, 342, 390, 434, 610
simplicity xiii, 52, 188, 223, 257, 414
steps into culturally mature territory xxi, 308, 328–330, 359, 421
Stone Age 108, 154
substages 132–133, 136, 305–306, 602

T

"third space" perspective 81, 606
"three-plus" representation 49, 78, 88
time 46, 80, 99, 147–150, 482, 555–556, 577, 586
Toffler, Alvin 318
Transformational/New Paradigm scenarios 104, 145, 313–314, 324–328, 330, 338, 340, 342, 591
Transition 58, 88–89, 105, 119–122, 124, 126–127, 135–136, 140, 144–145, 155–157, 310, 322, 324, 337, 349, 350, 352, 448, 450, 489–490, 516, 520, 539, 546, 549, 550–551, 578, 592, 599, 605–606, 609
Transitional Absurdities 47, 97, 105, 122, 125, 127–128, 144, 157, 226, 310, 321, 324, 342, 345–348, 350–354, 433, 445, 448, 453, 508, 521–524, 526, 532, 537, 541, 551–553, 611

U

uncertainty xiii, xvii, 16, 35, 120–121, 169, 173, 179, 186, 192, 194, 210, 227, 230, 235, 236, 238, 251, 326, 334, 337, 340, 406–407, 411, 413, 419, 420, 473, 558–559, 563, 583, 585–586, 589, 591, 609

Unity Fallacies 24, 31, 48, 215,
  332–334, 336, 338, 340, 342, 390,
  434, 525, 610
Upper Pole 85, 90, 109, 116, 263, 285,
  288, 298, 302, 483–485, 487, 496,
  549, 611

V

violence xx, 47, 174, 196, 214,
  252–254, 405, 435, 437–438, 457,
  477, 496, 498, 505, 611
vitalism 19, 31, 560, 589

W

Weiner, Norbert 19, 20, 589
West, Bing 130
We've Arrived scenarios 313–316,
  330, 338–342
We've Gone Astray scenarios 313–
  314, 316–317, 326, 330, 338, 340,
  342
Wheatley, Margaret 325
Whitehead, Alfred North 29
Whole-Person/Whole-System
  relationship xv, xix, 44–47, 68,
  171, 193–194, 210–215, 217, 219,
  223, 225–226, 232–233, 239, 242,
  244–246, 259, 264, 329, 358, 367,
  369, 389, 392, 510, 580, 597,
  603–604, 608, 609
Wilde, Oscar 136, 290
Wilford, John Noble 92

Y

Y2K 326

ICD Press is the publishing arm of the Institute for Creative Development. Information about the Institute and other Institute publications can be found on the Institute website (www.CreativeSystems.org) or on Charles Johnston's Author Page (www.CharlesJohnstonmd.com).

The Institute for Creative Development (ICD) Press
4324 Meridian Ave. N.
Seattle WA 98103
206-526-8562

Made in the USA
Monee, IL
26 April 2026

48984658R20354